Jack Mandelbaum and Steven Haley
Inclusive Capitalism

Jack Mandelbaum and Steven Haley

Inclusive Capitalism

A Rational Foundation for the World Economy

Volume 1

DE GRUYTER

ISBN 978-3-11-223547-8
ISBN 978-3-11-223548-5 (PDF)
ISBN 978-3-11-223549-2 (EPUB)
DOI https://doi.org/10.1515/9783112235485

Library of Congress Control Number: 2026941407

Bibliographic information published by the Deutsche Nationalbibliothek
The Deutsche Nationalbibliothek lists this publication in the Deutsche Nationalbibliografie; detailed bibliographic data are available on the internet at http://dnb.dnb.de.

De Gruyter and Walter de Gruyter GmbH are part of De Gruyter Brill.
www.degruyterbrill.com

Questions about General Product Safety Regulation:
productsafety@degruyterbrill.com

Cover illustration: Rosmarie Wirz / Moment / Getty Images; Fit Ztudio / shutterstock; Alexander Supertramp/ shutterstock; CeltStudio / shutterstock; Antoni M Lubek / shutterstock; salimin / shutterstock; boldg / Adobe Photo Stock; Photocomposition: Lara Taber
Printing: CPI books GmbH, Leck

FSC www.fsc.org MIX Papier | Fördert gute Waldnutzung FSC® C083411

Advance Praise for *Inclusive Capitalism, A Rational Foundation for the World Economy*, Volume 1

"Mandelbaum and Haley use the context of history to teach, to illustrate and to argue that there is great opportunity and an urgent need to reevaluate the incentives and institutions that enable capitalism to drive extraordinary innovation and growth. This work must reestablish the primacy of the moral center of the economy including societal wellbeing, full participation, universal access to all benefits and genuine equity. Over the course of my 45-year career in medicine, capitalism has fueled breathtaking advances in prevention, in diagnostics and in treatments. However, access and the effects of largely economic and social non-medical factors, are so severely skewed that zip code is among the strongest predictors of life expectancy. The authors' penetrating insights, their optimism and their humility make a compelling case for joining them in building the scaffolding to address these structural issues."

--Gary L. Gottlieb, MD, MBA
Professor of Psychiatry
Harvard Medical School; Former CEO
Partners HealthCare System (now Mass General Brigham)

"I came to this expecting another argument about what's wrong with capitalism. What I got was something truly insightful and more honest: a case that the failures are built into the incentives, not the people – and that design, not ideology, is where the fix lives. Mandelbaum and Haley take Smith seriously enough to want to complete him, and they've earned the right to try. Both authors have been immersed in the realities for years. Readers won't be disappointed and will walk away with fresh, thoughtful, constructive opinions."

--Andy Boynton
John and Linda Powers Family Dean
Carroll School of Management
Boston College

"In my work in integrative health and healing, I have watched our system reward managing disease over preventing it, and seen the human cost of incentives quietly working against the people they should serve. Mandelbaum and Haley name this precisely: the problem is not intent, it is structure. They show that capitalism's most troubling outcomes are not accidents or moral failures but the predictable result of an incomplete architecture. Their framework places human dignity, access, and wellbe-

 | https://doi.org/10.1515/9783112235485-202

ing at the center of how markets can work, without sacrificing innovation. This is the rare book that both diagnoses the problem and charts a path forward – toward an economy that lets far more people, and the planet, be well."

--**Shay Beider, M.P.H.**
Founder & CEO
Integrative Touch

"Few would argue against the remarkable achievements of capitalism. It has lifted billions from poverty, fueled innovation, and created unprecedented economic opportunity. What makes *Inclusive Capitalism* particularly valuable is that it approaches the future not by rejecting these strengths, but by asking whether the system can be thoughtfully refined to address some of its unintended consequences. The ideas presented are ambitious, intellectually rigorous, and deserve careful consideration by business leaders, policymakers, and anyone interested in the long-term evolution of our economic system."

--**Ben Matheson**
Founder and CEO
Furst Holdings
Former Executive, Microsoft,
VMware, AWS, Oracle, and Visa

Contents

Preface

Capitalism in the United States in the 2020s has generated extraordinary prosperity, yet that prosperity is increasingly experienced as uneven and exclusionary. In an economy defined by extraordinary technological advancement and productive capacity, affordability has become a persistent concern across housing, healthcare, and education. High-skill, technology-driven roles have expanded rapidly, while pathways to stable, middle-income employment have narrowed. At the same time, the pervasive influence of financial markets has imposed relentless short-term pressures on firms, often prioritizing quarterly performance over long-term investment and resilience. For many individuals, the system does not consistently translate effort into stability, upward mobility, or a sense of economic dignity.

This book proceeds from a simple premise: a more effective version of capitalism is possible—one that preserves its extraordinary capacity to drive innovation and growth while expanding participation, supporting human dignity, and improving societal well-being. The Inclusive Capitalism project is proposed as a path toward that objective.

This volume establishes the foundation for that effort. It examines the historical evolution of capitalism in a deliberately objective and apolitical manner, identifying what should be preserved and where structural change is required. The central argument that emerges is that many persistent challenges arise not from intent, but from the design of underlying incentive systems—suggesting that improvement is ultimately a matter of institutional design and systems engineering.

This preface provides context on the origins of the project and its intellectual grounding. The core argument begins in the Introduction, "Completing the Smithian Project."

Project Origins

The intellectual origins of Inclusive Capitalism emerged largely from Jack's longstanding interest in economic systems. The Inclusive Capitalism framework was strengthened through Steven's decades of executive experience designing and managing incentive systems across global technology enterprises.

For Jack, the starting point to Inclusive Capitalism was an early exposure to economics. While the mathematical structure of economic models was intellectually compelling, he sensed a persistent disconnect between their formalism and the realities of everyday decision-making—an intuition that the models did not fully capture the complexity of the systems they sought to describe. That unease persisted through his professional career and through graduate study, where large-scale econometric models, for all their ambition, often seemed too abstract to provide convincing explanations for the behavior of complex economic systems. Many of the mechanisms shaping modern economic life—tax systems, cost accounting frameworks, and corporate

 | https://doi.org/10.1515/9783112235485-204

incentives—appeared counterintuitive when viewed through a formal lens, reinforcing a broader suspicion that the architecture of capitalism contained unresolved tensions.

The rise and fall of Digital Equipment Corporation intensified Jack's beliefs about economic systems in general and the impact of incentives on outcomes specifically. DEC was one of the most innovative technology companies in the world. Despite extraordinary talent and technological achievement, the organization made a series of decisions that ultimately undermined it and led to its collapse. This raised the question of how could a system populated by intelligent and well-intentioned individuals produce outcomes that none of them desired?

Over time, a series of discussions with economists—including conversations with leadership in the economics department at the Massachusetts Institute of Technology—helped shift these concerns from intuition to inquiry, and eventually toward the outline of a more systematic approach. The central challenge became not simply identifying what was not working but determining whether a more coherent alternative could be designed.

More recently, Jack's experience building market models for technology companies, particularly those operating within open-source ecosystems, crystallized many of the unresolved tensions within capitalism. Open-source software can be distributed globally at near-zero marginal cost, yet it must still be monetized through mechanisms that reintroduce scarcity. This raised a fundamental question: why should technologies capable of creating abundance become economically valuable primarily through scarcity? Once again, the answer appeared to lie in the incentive structure itself.

For Steven, four decades of leadership across the computer, networking, and software industries—including commercial operations spanning the United States and dozens of countries—provided a practical education in how incentives shape behavior at every level of an organization. His career included leadership roles at companies such as Stratacom (acquired by Cisco), Cisco Systems, and Juniper Networks, among others, giving him direct experience of how even the most capable and well-intentioned organizations often produce outcomes dictated less by individual intent than by the incentive structures embedded within the systems they inhabit.

Throughout his career, Steven designed and managed incentive systems at the individual, divisional, corporate, and partnership levels. One lesson emerged repeatedly: people and organizations respond predictably to what is measured and rewarded. In practice, the overwhelming majority of those measures are financial, creating a powerful alignment between compensation and economic performance. Yet Steven observed that success as measured by conventional financial metrics does not necessarily correspond to contributions to societal well-being, particularly when reward systems encourage scarcity, enclosure, or the concentration of economic advantage. While he fully embraces the competitive and innovation-driven nature of capitalism, he also came to recognize persistent tensions between what organizations are rewarded to do and what society ultimately needs them to achieve. Over time, this led him to explore broader measures of performance and to conclude that many of capitalism's most significant challenges cannot be addressed through incremental adjustments alone but may require a more coherent redesign of the underlying incentive architecture.

In parallel, Steven has decades of collaboration in the healthcare sector — in neuroscience research and clinical initiatives, an experience that deepened his understanding of how incentive structures shape outcomes in complex institutional settings beyond the purely commercial. The U.S. healthcare system provided a particularly revealing example. Its funding structure blends public, institutional, corporate, and philanthropic capital, each operating under distinct incentive structures and often pursuing different objectives. The resulting tensions reinforced a broader conclusion: outcomes in complex systems are shaped less by the intentions of participants than by the incentives governing their behavior.

Observing these patterns across both of our careers led to a shared conclusion and a shared passion for the Inclusive Capitalism project: when intelligent and generally well-intentioned individuals, responding rationally to the incentives they face, consistently produce outcomes that are misaligned with long-term societal well-being, the problem lies in the design of the system itself. The search for a more coherent institutional framework—one capable of preserving capitalism's innovative capacity while aligning incentives more closely with long-term societal well-being became the motivation for this book and the foundation of the framework we call Inclusive Capitalism.

Intellectual Foundations of "Inclusive Capitalism"

Our engagement with the economics literature led us to a body of work that would prove particularly influential, including Why Nations Fail by Daron Acemoglu and James A. Robinson. Their distinction between inclusive and extractive institutions provides a clear and historically grounded framework for understanding why some economies generate broadly shared prosperity while others do not.

The significance of this work lies not in identifying a new concern, but in giving structure to a set of observations that had accumulated across our combined experience—in economic models, in corporate decision-making, in the evolution of global markets, and in the institutional dynamics of healthcare and research. The recurring patterns we had each observed can be understood, at least in part, as consequences of institutional design.

The term Inclusive Capitalism, used to describe this broader initiative, builds on that insight. It extends the logic of inclusive institutions into the economic architecture itself—examining how incentive structures, measurement systems, and organizational design shape participation and long-term outcomes. In this sense, the concept is not primarily normative or programmatic, but structural: it focuses on how the rules and mechanisms of the system influence behavior over time.

Position in Economic Thought

This book is written within the intellectual tradition that began with Adam Smith. Smith's vision of a decentralized market system—guided by competition, informed by local knowledge, and grounded in a moral framework that recognized both self-interest and social responsibility—remains one of the most powerful institutional designs developed for organizing economic activity.

This work proceeds from the view that the core moral and productive logic of that system remains fundamentally sound. Market exchange, competition, and decentralized decision-making have demonstrated an extraordinary capacity to generate innovation, prosperity, and rising standards of living.

At the same time, the evolution of capitalism suggests that the institutional architecture surrounding this system has remained incomplete. Over time, persistent patterns have emerged that are not easily explained by intent or ideology alone but instead point toward structural features of the system itself.

This book therefore approaches capitalism not as an ideological object, but as an evolving institutional system. It examines how economic doctrines, legislative frameworks, and cultural norms have shaped outcomes across different periods, with the aim of identifying both what should be preserved and where refinement may be required. The analysis that follows is guided by a simple premise: when rational actors, responding to the incentives they face, repeatedly produce outcomes that combine significant benefits with persistent unintended consequences, the problem may lie not with the individuals, but with the design of the system itself.

Structure of the Two-Book Project

The scope of this work ultimately extended beyond what could be addressed within a single volume. For that reason, the project is presented in two parts. This volume examines the historical development of capitalism and establishes the analytical basis for understanding its strengths and limitations. A second volume builds on that foundation by exploring how the system's design might evolve.

Acknowledgments and Collaboration

We have each been fortunate to benefit from mentors, colleagues, and communities whose guidance shaped both our professional work and this book.

Jack is grateful to Dr. Paul E. Green, who shaped his approach to analytics and the management sciences; Dr. Paul Berger, who helped establish the methodological foundation of Management Insight; and Dr. John R. Hauser, whose mentorship in both analytics and practice has been invaluable over many decades. He is grateful to his team at Management Insight, whose excellence and independence made this work possible, and especially to Lisa Stone, Chief Operating Officer, whose leadership over the past decade created the space for its completion. He also thanks his clients across the technology sector, whose engagement with complex problems provided a continuous real-world test of these ideas. He is especially grateful to his family for their patience and support—at least some of the time—and thanks his daughter Karen for her thoughtful early reviews, and his spouse Bernice and son Will for their careful reading of key sections. He is particularly indebted to Bernice for a question that proved both direct and necessary: what, precisely, was he going to do about it?

Steven is grateful to the technology leaders including Scott Kriens and John Chambers, entrepreneurs, and research collaborators, particularly Dr. Gary Gottlieb. Many have helped test, refine and influence his perspectives across four decades of global practice— and in long-running medical research partnerships. He thanks Kathy Haley for her patience and steadfast support throughout this project.

We are deeply grateful to our publishing partner at De Gruyter, Jaya Dalal, who recognized the potential of this work and guided it through the publication process with care and conviction.

Invitation to Dialogue

The initial two volumes of the Inclusive Capitalism project are intended to establish a conceptual foundation and develop a preliminary architectural framework. They do not represent a finished system, but rather the launch of an initiative requiring further development, refinement, and critical evaluation.

Subsequent work will seek to extend this framework into specific domains, translating general principles into more detailed institutional and policy considerations. It is likely that these efforts will begin with sectors such as healthcare and technology, where the interaction between innovation, incentives, and societal outcomes is particularly pronounced—domains in which both authors bring direct and sustained experience.

We recognize that the design of economic systems is inherently collaborative and benefits from diverse perspectives across disciplines and experience. Progress in this area will depend not only on theoretical development but also on practical insight, empirical testing, and constructive critique. We therefore welcome thoughtful engagement from those interested in contributing to the continued development of this framework.

Jack Mandelbaum
Steven Haley

Introduction: Completing the Smithian Project

Capitalism is the most effective economic system ever developed for mobilizing human ingenuity, coordinating decentralized decision-making, and converting innovation into widespread prosperity.[1] Its achievements are neither accidental nor overstated in the historical record.[2] Capitalism's achievements are the predictable result of institutional environments that repeatedly convert technological possibility into sustained prosperity.[3] Yet the most consequential challenges now associated with capitalism do not arise from moral deficiency, policy error, or leadership failure. They arise from architecture—more precisely, from the absence of a fully specified economic architecture. The system's objectives, incentives, and institutional structures were never fully specified in the context of the moral vision for capitalism[4]—particularly for operation at modern scale, under conditions of global integration and accelerating technological abundance.[5] This book advances the claim that what is often described as capitalism's "failures," which we have reframed as "unintended consequences," are better understood as symptoms of an incomplete economic systems architecture—and that articulating and completing that architecture is both possible and necessary.[6] This is the central premise of Inclusive Capitalism, and it is the foundation on which the analysis proceeds.

This claim matters because it reframes the problem in a way that most contemporary debates do not. Public discourse around capitalism's shortcomings tends to polarize quickly. On one side, critics attribute dysfunction to greed, ethical decay, or insufficient regulation. On the other, defenders emphasize capitalism's historical success and argue that its excesses are episodic, self-correcting, or the unavoidable price of freedom and growth. Both positions miss the deeper issue. The outcomes now provoking concern are not moral deviations or policy accidents; they are enduring tendencies of a system whose objectives, incentives, and institutional structures were never fully specified or bounded, even at its inception, in a manner that aligns with the moral intentions of the founder.[7] Capitalism continues to perform extraordinarily well at mobilizing effort and innovation, but it has always operated with architectural incompleteness—an incompleteness whose consequences intensify as scale, complexity, and technological abundance expand.

This book therefore does not approach capitalism as an external critic, nor as a reformist patching a fundamentally sound machine.[8] It approaches capitalism as an engineer would approach a powerful system that was never fully architected—one whose core principles proved extraordinarily generative but whose objectives, incentives, and institutional boundaries were left incomplete from the outset. The task is not condemnation or nostalgia but diagnosis and completion. Inclusive Capitalism is an internal reconstruction of capitalism, grounded in its original intent and animated by its enduring strengths, while supplying the architectural clarity required for the scale and complexity the system has since attained.

 | https://doi.org/10.1515/9783112235485-001

That intent is most clearly articulated in the work of Adam Smith.[9] Smith did not envisage capitalism as a complete economic system, nor did he offer a blueprint for unrestrained extraction or morally neutral markets. He articulated a vision—moral, institutional, and behavioral—of how decentralized exchange could expand abundance, widen participation, and align individual ambition with social benefit under conditions of scarcity, limited information, and human fallibility.[10] In Smith's framework, markets were instruments of coordination, not ends in themselves; competition and fair play were essential disciplines, not optional virtues. Monopoly power, rent-seeking, and exclusion were not tolerated outcomes but distortions to be resisted.[11] Smith's contribution was not a theory of greed but a principled account of how incentives and institutions might harness human motivation toward broadly shared prosperity.

What history demonstrates, however, is that while Smith's principles proved extraordinarily powerful, they were never instantiated as a complete economic architecture. Capitalism evolved pragmatically rather than deliberately. Institutions accumulated. Incentives hardened. Scale increased. Technology advanced. Yet the system's organizing objective—maximizing output and efficiency under scarcity—remained largely unchanged even as the operating environment transformed beyond recognition.[12] The result is a system that still generates extraordinary productivity but does so while systematically producing instability, exclusion, artificial scarcity, short-termism, and an erosion of dignity at a scale that now threatens its own legitimacy.[13]

Capitalism, by any empirical measure, remains the most successful economic system ever created. It has mobilized human ingenuity, coordinated decentralized decision-making, accelerated innovation, and lifted billions out of material deprivation. To dismiss these achievements would be neither serious nor necessary to the argument that follows. The question this book asks is not whether capitalism works. It clearly does. The question is whether capitalism, as currently architected, can endure the realities of modern scale, technological abundance, and global interdependence without fracturing under the weight of its own unintended consequences.

Those consequences are not peripheral. They are structural. Increasingly, vast institutional effort is devoted not to advancing prosperity but to mitigating the side effects of the system's own operation. Regulation proliferates to counteract concentration and instability. Redistribution expands to address exclusion after it has occurred. Crisis management becomes permanent rather than episodic. Political polarization intensifies as legitimacy erodes. These responses are not evidence of ideological overreach; they are evidence of architectural deficiency.[14] When a system requires continuous intervention to prevent its own outputs from undermining its foundations, the problem is not at the margins. It is at the core.

This book argues that the core problem lies in incentives and institutions optimized for an objective function that no longer reflects economic reality. Capitalism continues to reward behavior appropriate to an era of pervasive scarcity, even as technology renders non-scarcity feasible across expanding domains.[15] It continues to concentrate power and privilege exclusion because scale amplifies advantage under existing rules. It continues to discount the future because short-term financial metrics dominate the scoreboard.[16] These outcomes are not aberrations. They are the predictable results of rational actors responding to the system as it currently operates.

The implication is both sobering and hopeful. If capitalism's failures are systemic, then they cannot be solved through moral exhortation or incremental policy adjustment alone. But if they are systemic, they are also amenable to systemic redesign. Capitalism does not need to be abandoned, suppressed, or replaced by alternative systems that history has repeatedly shown to sacrifice dynamism, innovation, and freedom.[17] It requires completion—by specifying the architecture that Smith could not have designed but that modern conditions now demand.

This is where Inclusive Capitalism departs from existing economic literature. It is not a policy platform, a regulatory agenda, or a hybrid ideological compromise. It is a proposal for a full economic architecture—explicit, incentive-aligned, and grounded in systems engineering rather than doctrine.[18] The ambition of this work is not to argue for better intentions but to design a system in which rational behavior by self-interested actors reliably produces outcomes compatible with societal well-being.

That ambition reflects both humility and resolve: humility, because economies are complex adaptive systems that resist centralized control and ideological certainty; resolve, because the tools required for deliberate design—measurement, feedback, modularity, and enforcement—now exist in ways they did not for Smith or his successors.[19] The choice confronting capitalism today is therefore not between preservation and replacement. It is between reactive decline and deliberate design.

Inclusive Capitalism argues for the latter.

Adam Smith Revisited: Intent vs. Instantiation

Any serious attempt to evolve capitalism must begin by reclaiming Adam Smith from the caricature that has come to dominate popular and even academic discourse.[20] Smith was not a doctrinaire advocate of unbounded markets, nor a proto-libertarian indifferent to social outcomes. He was a moral philosopher first, an institutional thinker second, and only then an economist. To read him otherwise is to misunderstand both his intent and his contribution.[21]

Smith's project was never the glorification of self-interest in isolation. It was the reconciliation of individual ambition with social order. *The Wealth of Nations* (1776) cannot be separated from *The Theory of Moral Sentiments* (1759). Together, they form a coherent vision of an economic system grounded in human psychology, moral judgment, and social legitimacy.[22] Markets, in Smith's view, were not self-justifying mechanisms; they were instruments whose legitimacy depended on whether they advanced the material and moral conditions of society as a whole.

Central to Smith's framework was the idea of moral sentiments—the capacity for sympathy, fairness, and mutual recognition that enables complex social cooperation. He understood that economic actors do not operate as abstract utility maximizers but as social beings embedded in norms, expectations, and reputational constraints.[23] The invisible hand he envisioned was never a license for predation; it was a description of how decentralized coordination could emerge when behavior was bounded by moral restraint, competition, and fair play.

Equally important was Smith's explicit opposition to monopoly and rent-seeking. Few passages in economic literature are as unambiguous as Smith's denunciations of concentrated market power, collusion among merchants, and the manipulation of markets to extract unearned advantage.[24] He viewed monopoly not merely as an economic inefficiency but as a moral failure—an affront to fairness and a threat to legitimacy. Markets, for Smith, only functioned properly when participation was broad, entry was feasible, and rewards flowed from contribution rather than position.

Smith was therefore not an advocate of laissez-faire in the modern sense. He supported public investment in infrastructure, education, and institutions where private incentives alone were insufficient. He recognized that markets required governance—not micromanagement but a framework of rules that preserved competition, limited abuse, and maintained public trust.[25] His was a system grounded in institutions, norms, and governance, not ideological minimalism.

The difficulty is not that contemporary capitalism has "betrayed" Smith. It is that capitalism has expanded far beyond the economic conditions for which Smith's principles were articulated. Smith wrote for an economy characterized by relatively small firms, limited technological leverage, localized markets, and slow-moving capital. He could not have anticipated multinational enterprises with revenues exceeding those of nation-states, financial systems operating at digital speed, or technologies capable of collapsing marginal costs toward zero.[26] Nor did he attempt to specify institutional or incentive structures suited to an economy in which scale, data, and automation fundamentally reshape the relationships among production, labor, and distribution.

This architectural under-specification matters. Smith provided principles, not a full system design. He articulated the moral and competitive conditions under which markets could serve society, but he did not—and could not—engineer the mechanisms required to preserve those conditions at global scale. As capitalism expanded in scope, speed, and complexity, its foundational principles remained rhetorically intact while its institutional supports lagged behind.[27] The result has not been the abandonment of Smithian ideals, but their gradual erosion through structural drift.

This architectural under-specification was not revealed only by modern scale. Even in capitalism's earliest industrial phase, structural tensions appeared almost immediately. The factory system generated extraordinary productivity gains, yet it also produced conditions—child labor, extreme hours, unsafe workplaces—that required the English Factory Acts and subsequent oversight to restrain.[28] The problem was not the absence of ambition or enterprise; it was that competitive pressures rewarded cost minimization without internalizing social cost. In other words, the incentives were misaligned from the outset. What later became global-scale distortions were present in embryonic form at capitalism's birth, suggesting that the issue was architectural rather than episodic.

Inclusive Capitalism is therefore presented explicitly as a continuation and completion of the Smithian project, not a departure from it. It does not graft socialism onto markets, replace competition with technocracy, or subordinate enterprise to central planning. It preserves what Smith understood best: decentralized decision-making, ambition, competition, and the productive power of markets.[29] What it adds is the architectural rigor required to sustain those principles under modern conditions.

Where Smith relied on proximity, social norms, and limited scale to enforce moral behavior, Inclusive Capitalism relies on incentive design and institutional structure. Where Smith assumed competition would discipline power, Inclusive Capitalism designs for diffusion when scale would otherwise entrench dominance.[30] Where Smith treated systemic consent as an emergent consequence of fair participation, Inclusive Capitalism treats systemic consent as an explicit, measured, and rewarded objective of system performance.

This reframing is essential. The question before us is not whether to preserve Smithian capitalism or replace it. It is whether we are willing to do the harder work Smith himself could not: translating enduring moral and economic principles into a modern, explicit, and resilient architecture capable of operating at planetary scale. Inclusive Capitalism takes up that task—not as a critique of Smith but as an act of fidelity to his deepest intentions.

Why This Book, Why Now – A Crisis of Legitimacy

The case for Inclusive Capitalism is not driven by ideology or dissatisfaction with markets. It is driven by accumulating empirical signals that the system's legitimacy is under strain. Across advanced economies, capitalism continues to generate extraordinary wealth and innovation, yet it increasingly does so without producing the broad participation, stability, and dignity that once sustained public trust.[31] Prosperity has decoupled from inclusion. Innovation has decoupled from diffusion. Scale has decoupled from legitimacy. Efficiency has decoupled from lived security.

These are not abstract concerns. They are observable system-level patterns. Median wages lag productivity. Access to essentials becomes more fragile even as technology advances. Large enterprises grow more powerful while public confidence in economic institutions declines. Political systems polarize not because citizens misunderstand capitalism's achievements but because too many experience those achievements as distant, uneven, or contingent.[32] A system can perform exceptionally on aggregate metrics and still lose the consent of those who live within it.

Social anger, in this context, is not an ideological phenomenon; it is data. When an economic system repeatedly socializes losses while privatizing gains, when households absorb volatility while institutions retain optionality, legitimacy erodes regardless of headline growth.[33] This erosion does not require moral outrage to be dangerous. It only requires persistence. Once a critical mass of participants no longer believes the system operates in their interest—or can be reformed from within—pressure builds for reactive, destabilizing change.

Nowhere is this incentive pathology more visible than in healthcare. Industry professionals have openly acknowledged dynamics such as "Cancer is good for our business" and "A cancer patient is a six-year annuity." These statements are not presented here for shock value, nor as moral indictments of individuals. They are diagnostic. They reveal a system in which rational actors, operating under existing incentives, are rewarded more for managing chronic disease than for eliminating it.[34] The problem is not intent. It is structure.

This pattern is not unique to healthcare. It appears wherever long-term societal outcomes conflict with short-term monetization: in housing, education, financial markets, and digital infrastructure. When incentives reward persistence of the problem rather than its resolution, outcomes follow predictably. Over time, the public learns this—even if it cannot always articulate it formally—and trust deteriorates.[35]

The urgency of this book lies precisely here. Capitalism does not face a crisis of productivity or creativity. It faces a crisis of legitimacy rooted in misaligned incentives operating at modern scale. If that misalignment remains unaddressed, correction will come not through careful redesign but through political backlash, institutional overreach, or systemic fracture.[36] Inclusive Capitalism is written on the premise that deliberate, internal evolution is preferable to reactive disruption—and that the window for such evolution, while still open, is narrowing.

Methodology: The Analytical Framework on Which Inclusive Capitalism Resides

Inclusive Capitalism proceeds from a simple methodological premise: complex economic systems must be evaluated as systems.[37] They must be analyzed not by intentions, slogans, or isolated policies but by their objectives, incentives, institutional structures, and the behaviors those structures reliably produce at scale.[38]

This book therefore adopts a systems-level analytical framework that integrates four complementary lenses.

First, it employs historical analysis across major capitalist epochs. Capitalism is not treated as a static doctrine but as an evolving system whose behavior has changed as scale, technology, finance, and institutions have changed.[39] By examining successive periods—from early industrial capitalism through the postwar settlement and into the contemporary, financialized economy—the analysis identifies which outcomes were contingent on context and which emerged repeatedly as scale increased.[40] History is used here not to romanticize or condemn but to observe patterns that recur under similar structural conditions.

Second, the book relies on empirical outcome evaluation, rather than theoretical purity. Growth rates, productivity, wages, access to essentials, volatility, concentration, innovation diffusion, and social mobility are treated as observable outputs of the system, not as incidental side effects.[41] Where outcomes diverge persistently from stated goals—such as broad prosperity, opportunity, or stability—the analysis treats that divergence as evidence of structural misalignment rather than as proof of bad actors or insufficient effort.[42]

Third, the analysis treats industrial leadership behavior as the unit of action. Economies do not act; people operating within institutions do. In modern capitalism, the most consequential decisions are made by a relatively small number of leaders who allocate capital, set strategy, design products, manage labor, and shape innovation pathways at scale.[43] This book assumes that these leaders are not irrational, malicious, or uniquely virtuous. It assumes they are rational, achievement-driven, and responsive to the incentives and constraints they face.[44] Their behavior is therefore a diagnostic signal of system design. When similar strategies emerge across sectors, epochs, and geographies, the cause is rarely individual pathology; it is incentive alignment.[45]

Fourth, the analysis locates institutions and incentives as the causal layer. Policies, regulations, and cultural norms matter, but they are downstream. What ultimately governs behavior is what the system measures, rewards, penalizes, and permits.[46] This book therefore evaluates capitalism by asking a disciplined question: What does the system systematically select for? Not in theory but in practice. Not episodically but persistently. And not at small scale but at the scale that now defines the global economy.[47]

Several methodological commitments follow directly from this framework.

The book does not assume irrational actors. It does not moralize outcomes. It does not rely on idealized behavior, altruism, or civic virtue as prerequisites for success. It does not treat capitalism's shortcomings as deviations from an otherwise self-correcting equilibrium. Instead, it assumes rational behavior under constrained choice and asks whether the system's design does indeed channel that rationality toward outcomes society actually wants.[48]

Conversely, the book does assume that incentives matter more than intentions, that institutional structures shape behavior more reliably than norms, and that systems should be judged by what they produce rather than what they promise.[49] Where a system repeatedly generates exclusion, volatility, or artificial scarcity, the analysis treats those outcomes as design signals—not as accidents.[50]

This methodological stance distinguishes Inclusive Capitalism from earlier economic frameworks. Where Marx offered an ideology rooted in historical determinism, this book offers no theory of inevitable collapse.[51] Where Keynes offered policy regimes designed to stabilize demand, this book does not propose macro-management as a primary solution.[52] Where neoliberalism offered doctrine centered on market primacy, this book does not treat markets as self-justifying abstractions.[53]

Inclusive Capitalism offers architecture.[54]

It asks how objectives should be specified, how incentives should be aligned, how institutions should be structured, and how feedback should operate in a system that must function at unprecedented scale under conditions of technological abundance.[55] It treats capitalism not as an article of faith or a set of policy preferences but as an engineered system—one that can be evaluated, redesigned, tested, and improved.[56]

This analytical framework governs the entire project. Book One applies it diagnostically, to understand how capitalism's current lack of architecture produces its unintended consequences.[57] Book Two applies it constructively, to specify an alternative architecture capable of preserving capitalism's strengths while aligning its outputs with societal well-being.[58]

The Diagnostic Work of Book One: The Inclusive Capitalism Foundation

Book One performs the diagnostic work on which the remainder of this project rests. Its purpose is not to argue against capitalism, nor to propose premature solutions, but to establish—empirically and systematically—what modern capitalism reliably produces, why it produces those outcomes, and why marginal reform has repeatedly failed to correct them.[59]

The analysis begins from a simple but underappreciated premise: economic systems must be evaluated by their systematic outputs, not by their stated intentions or isolated successes.[60] When capitalism is examined through this lens, a consistent pattern emerges across time, geography, and policy regimes. At modern scale, Smithian capitalism generates a set of outcomes that are neither anomalous nor accidental but structurally predictable.[61]

Book One identifies six unintended consequences that have accompanied capitalism since its earliest institutionalization. These consequences have emerged wherever capitalist incentives have operated without sufficiently aligned institutional constraints over the past two and a half centuries. They appeared in embryonic form from the system's beginnings—most visibly in early industrial England, where they provoked the Factory Acts and other corrective legislation—and they have recurred with increasing force as capitalism expanded in scale, complexity, and technological reach.[62] They are not presented as ideological critiques or episodic failures but as structural tendencies rooted in incentive and institutional design. Each consequence is examined in depth, with attention to how it first manifested, how it intensifies under scale and financialization, how it reinforces the others, and why it persists even as leadership, regulation, and rhetoric change.[63]

Book One demonstrates that these consequences recur across historical epochs. From the late mercantile period through the Gilded Age, the postwar settlement, and the contemporary neoliberal era, similar pathologies appear whenever scale outpaces institutional adaptation.[64] This recurrence is critical. It shows that the problem is not tied to a particular political ideology, regulatory posture, or moral climate but to deeper architectural features of the system itself.[65]

The analysis shows that these outcomes persist under widely different policy regimes. Heavily regulated systems, lightly regulated systems, social-democratic hybrids, and market-centric regimes all display versions of the same failures once incentives and scale interact in comparable ways. This finding explains why alternating cycles of deregulation and reregulation—what the book describes as ping-pong economics—have failed to produce durable resolution.[66]

The unifying conclusion is that these failures endure because incentives remain misaligned. Industrial leaders, investors, and institutions respond rationally to what the system rewards. When success is defined narrowly—around short-term financial performance, extraction, and enclosure—outcomes follow predictably, regardless of intent or ethical posture.[67]

The most consequential insight of Book One is that scarcity is no longer merely a condition of economic life—it has increasingly become a business model.[68]

Under conditions of technological abundance, falling marginal costs, and rapidly expanding productive capacity, the economically efficient outcome in many sectors should be diffusion. Yet contemporary capitalism frequently suppresses diffusion in order to preserve pricing power, defend margins, or entrench advantage. Scarcity is no longer always natural; it is often strategically maintained.[69]

This shift explains a wide range of modern phenomena: affordability crises amid abundance, innovation without broad access, rising exclusion despite productivity gains, and public anger that appears disconnected from aggregate economic performance.[70] The system is not malfunctioning; it is operating consistently with its inherited objectives and incentives—optimizing for scarcity preservation where abundance is feasible because that is what the structure rewards.[71]

By the conclusion of Book One, three things are made explicit.

First, what must be preserved is established. Capitalism's core strengths—decentralized decision-making, competition, entrepreneurial risk-taking, scale, and the rule of law—remain unmatched. Any attempt to suppress these mechanisms undermines both prosperity and freedom.[72]

Second, what must change is established. Objectives optimized for output and extraction under scarcity conditions no longer produce legitimacy, stability, or inclusion at modern scale. Incentives and institutions designed for an earlier era now generate outcomes that threaten capitalism's own durability.[73]

Third, why marginal reform cannot work is established. Regulatory overlays, redistributive corrections, and episodic interventions treat symptoms after harm has occurred. They do not alter the incentive logic that regenerates the same failures. Without architectural change, reform becomes permanent triage.[74]

This book develops its argument as a single, accumulating case. It recognizes capitalism's extraordinary productive achievements while showing why reactive regulation and redistribution have repeatedly failed to resolve its deeper pathologies. It demonstrates that the same unintended consequences recur across eras and national contexts, and that they arise not from moral failure or doctrinal error but from the interaction of incentives, scale, and underspecified institutional architecture. On that basis, the book clarifies what must be preserved, and explains why modern technological capabilities now make deliberate, system-level redesign both feasible and necessary.[75]

The final chapter of Book One—the chapter that immediately precedes Book Two—serves as the hinge. It aligns diagnosis with vision, identifies the architectural pillars required to resolve the failures identified, and prepares the reader for the constructive work ahead.[76]

Book One, in short, answers the question: What is happening, and why does it keep happening? Book Two takes up the only remaining question: What must be built instead?

What Must Be Preserved

Any serious effort to evolve capitalism must begin with clarity about what cannot be sacrificed. Capitalism's extraordinary achievements were not accidental, and they were not produced by generic economic activity.[77] They emerged from a specific configuration of institutions, incentives, and freedoms that unlocked human ambition at scale.[78] Inclusive Capitalism therefore begins not with constraint but with preservation. Before redesigning incentives or refactoring institutions, it is essential to reaffirm the core mechanisms that made capitalism the most productive economic system in history.

First and foremost, market signals must remain central. Markets are not merely allocation devices; they are information-processing systems.[79] They aggregate dispersed knowledge, translate preferences into action, and coordinate complex activity without command or coercion. No alternative mechanism has demonstrated comparable capacity to adapt dynamically to changing conditions or to harness localized knowledge embedded in millions of independent decisions.[80] Inclusive Capitalism does not seek to override markets or substitute bureaucratic judgment for market signals. On the contrary, it seeks to improve markets by ensuring that the signals they transmit more accurately reflect real value rather than narrow proxies such as short-term financial extraction.[81] Better objectives produce better outcomes. Markets remain the engine; the redesign focuses on what they are incentivized to optimize.[82]

Closely related is the preservation of competition. Competition is not an ideological preference; it is a discovery process. It reveals what works, disciplines incumbents, and prevents the ossification of power.[83] Across the history of economic thought, there is near-universal agreement on this point.[84] Where capitalism has repeatedly faltered is not in the presence of competition but in its erosion—often as an unintended consequence of scale, network effects, and financial incentives that reward enclosure.[85] Inclusive Capitalism does not dilute competition in the name of stability or fairness. It strengthens it by addressing the structural conditions under which concentration becomes rational and persistent.[86] Competition must remain fierce, continuous, and outcome-determining.

Private property is likewise non-negotiable. Property rights are foundational to investment, innovation, and long-horizon risk-taking. They enable individuals and firms to commit capital, effort, and imagination to uncertain futures.[87] Inclusive Capitalism does not weaken property rights, collectivize assets, or blur ownership. What it addresses is not ownership itself but the incentive regimes attached to ownership at scale—particularly where property rights are used to entrench scarcity in domains where technology makes abundance feasible.[88] Preserving private property while refining the obligations that accompany its large-scale exercise is a strengthening move, not a dilution.

At the heart of capitalism lies entrepreneurial ambition, and this too must be preserved in full force. Capitalism's greatest strength is not efficiency alone; it is aspiration. Entrepreneurs take risks that no planner would authorize.[89] They pursue uncertain paths, absorb failure, and generate breakthroughs that redefine what is possible. Attempts to suppress ambition in the name of stability or equality have consistently produced stagnation, risk aversion, and bureaucratic inertia.[90] Inclusive Capitalism is explicitly pro-ambition. What changes is not the intensity of competition but the definition of winning. Success remains asymmetric. Rewards remain large. Failure remains real. But the most rewarded forms of success increasingly align with outcomes that compound over time rather than extract in the short run.[91]

Scale and innovation velocity must also be preserved. Modern civilization depends on large, complex enterprises to deliver infrastructure, logistics, energy systems, pharmaceuticals, digital platforms, and global coordination.[92] Proposals that treat scale itself as pathological misunderstand both history and reality.[93] The problem is not size; it is purpose. Under misaligned incentives, scale becomes a mechanism for entrenchment.[94] Under well-aligned incentives, it becomes a diffusion engine.[95] Inclusive Capitalism preserves the advantages of scale—efficiency, reach, and speed—while redesigning the institutional context so that scale expands access and resilience rather than concentrating power and fragility.

Equally important is decentralized decision-making, which remains one of capitalism's most decisive advantages over every alternative economic system yet attempted.[96] Capitalism's strength lies not in centralized intelligence or superior intentions but in its rejection of centralized control: Decisions are made close to the point of information, experimentation is distributed across millions of actors, and failure is localized rather than systemic.[97] Inclusive Capitalism does not replace markets with planning or technocracy. On the contrary, it strengthens decentralization by improving the incentive environment within which decentralized actors operate—much as modern computing systems scale by refining protocols and feedback rather than centralizing computation.[98] The objective is not to direct behavior, but to ensure that the most socially valuable actions are also the most rational ones for independent, competitive actors.[99]

It is essential to state clearly what Inclusive Capitalism does not do. It does not suppress ambition or cap success. It does not replace markets with bureaucracy or competition with coordination. It does not centralize economic planning or assume benevolent administrators. It does not dilute property rights, flatten incentives, or moralize performance. These moves have been tried, repeatedly, and they have failed.[100]

Instead, it proceeds from a simpler and more demanding premise: that capitalism's core mechanisms have always worked extraordinarily well at mobilizing effort and innovation but that they have never operated without producing predictable distortions in the absence of countervailing structure—distortions that intensify as scale, complexity, and technological leverage increase.[101] Preserving markets, competition, property, ambition, scale, and decentralization is not in tension with this goal. It is the precondition for completing capitalism in a way that aligns private success with societal durability.[102]

This preservation is not nostalgic. It is pragmatic. The question is not whether capitalism's core should survive but whether it can be made stable, legitimate, and adaptive under conditions far beyond those for which its founding principles were articulated.[103] Inclusive Capitalism answers in the affirmative—by preserving what works, and by completing what was never fully specified.

The Inclusive Capitalism Vision

Book One does not propose policy, prescribe mechanisms, or specify institutional blueprints. Its task is more foundational. It defines the vision that any viable evolution of capitalism must satisfy if the system is to preserve its strengths while addressing its unintended consequences. That vision is not aspirational rhetoric. It is a set of explicit design goals derived from empirical observation of how capitalism behaves in practice, how incentives shape leadership decisions, and how institutions perform under scale.[104]

The starting point of the vision is preservation, not replacement. Capitalism's core mechanisms—markets, competition, private property, entrepreneurial ambition, decentralized decision-making, scale, and innovation velocity—are not incidental features. They are the sources of the system's unmatched capacity to mobilize human ingenuity and convert discovery into prosperity. Inclusive Capitalism therefore does not seek to weaken or constrain these mechanisms. It seeks to complete the system in a way that allows them to operate without reliably producing exclusion, instability, artificial scarcity, and erosion of legitimacy.[105]

From that foundation, Book One articulates four interlocking design goals that together define the Inclusive Capitalist vision.

First, incentives must be aligned rather than contradictory. Under contemporary capitalism, private success and public durability often diverge. Leaders are rewarded for behaviors—scarcity preservation, short-term extraction, enclosure, and rent-seeking—that are rational under existing scoreboards but corrosive at the system level.[106] The Inclusive Capitalist vision replaces this contradiction with alignment: private success is increasingly achieved through outcomes that expand societal well-being, diffusion, resilience, access, and long-term value creation.[107] This is not an appeal to virtue. It is a reorientation of what the system rewards.[108]

Second, institutions must be rechartered to reflect the roles they already play. Large enterprises today are not merely private profit-seeking entities; they are de facto administrators of labor markets, innovation pathways, essential services, and access to opportunity.[109] Treating them as if they operate in a small-firm, nineteenth-century context creates persistent mismatch between power and obligation.[110] The vision articulated in Book One is not one of nationalization or bureaucratic control but of institutional charters that explicitly internalize societal responsibilities proportional to institutional scale and impact.[111]

Third, money and capital must be refactored to reflect economic heterogeneity. A single, economy-wide monetary logic has proven incapable of stabilizing a system composed of radically different sectors—where some sectors are driven by near-zero marginal costs and rapid innovation, others are constrained by physical capacity and essential human needs.[112] The Inclusive Capitalist vision recognizes that stabilizing essentials while preserving innovation elsewhere requires differentiated monetary and capital structures, designed to reward capacity, access, and resilience rather than speculative positioning.[113]

Fourth, innovation itself must become more inclusive. Capitalism's future depends not only on the pace of discovery but on the breadth of participation and the speed of diffusion.[114] Book One advances a vision in which innovation is no longer narrowly gated by capital access, network position, or enclosure strategies but is instead accelerated by openness, interoperability, and widespread recombination.[115] The objective is not to suppress competition but to move competition toward expanding the frontier of shared capability rather than defending artificial scarcity.[116]

Taken together, these design goals define what an Inclusive Capitalist economy is intended to do. They describe a system in which markets remain decentralized and fiercely competitive but in which the rational path to success increasingly runs through contribution rather than extraction; in which leaders gain power by building durable value rather than fragile advantage; in which workers experience opportunity without bearing disproportionate systemic risk; and in which dignity is embedded as a system property rather than treated as a discretionary outcome.[117]

Book One therefore completes its work by making the vision explicit. It clarifies what must be preserved, what must change, and what the system must optimize for if capitalism is to remain both dynamic and legitimate under modern conditions.[118] It does not yet specify how this vision is instantiated. That task belongs to Book Two.

Book Two translates this vision into architecture. It specifies the objective functions, sector-level formulations, institutional charters, incentive mechanisms, monetary structures, governance systems, enforcement logic, and transition pathways required to make Inclusive Capitalism operational.[119] Where Book One defines the destination, Book Two designs the machinery.

This separation is deliberate. Vision without architecture degenerates into rhetoric. Architecture without vision degenerates into ad hoc reform.[120] Inclusive Capitalism insists on both—beginning with a disciplined statement of purpose and proceeding to a system design capable of realizing it.[121]

Why The Vision Matters

The contribution of Inclusive Capitalism is not a new critique of markets, nor a new moral appeal to leaders, nor a new policy agenda layered atop existing institutions. It is an attempt to do something that economic thought has largely avoided: to specify an explicit, incentive-aligned economic architecture capable of operating at modern scale, under modern technology, and with human behavior as it actually is.[122]

Economic theory has produced powerful insights into prices, incentives, institutions, and growth.[123] Political economy has documented capitalism's cycles, inequalities, and crises.[124] Policy frameworks have oscillated between intervention and retrenchment.[125] What has been missing is a comprehensive systems design—one that treats capitalism not as an abstract equilibrium, nor as a collection of policy levers, but as a large-scale, incentive-driven system whose behavior is determined by its objective function, institutional structure, and feedback mechanisms.[126]

This work is novel because it operates at that level. It does not ask how to redistribute outcomes after the fact, nor how to regulate away symptoms once harm has occurred.[127] It asks how the system itself can be specified so that rational, achievement-driven actors reliably produce outcomes compatible with societal durability.[128] That requires architecture, not exhortation.[129]

Inclusive Capitalism is now feasible because earlier eras lacked the enabling conditions to make such an architecture possible. For most of capitalism's history, scarcity was dominant, measurement was coarse, and enforcement was slow.[130] GDP became the primary scoreboard not because it captured human well-being but because it was one of the few metrics that could be calculated consistently enough, even if far from perfectly, to guide markets and policy.[131] Incentives were therefore necessarily blunt, and governance operated through lagging correction rather than real-time alignment.[132]

Technology changes that constraint. Near-zero marginal costs in expanding domains make abundance feasible rather than theoretical.[133] Digital infrastructure makes outcome measurement, verification, and audit possible at scales earlier systems could not support.[134] Modular architectures make it possible to govern heterogeneous sectors without imposing one-size-fits-all control.[135] These capabilities do not determine outcomes—but they expand the feasible design space.[136]

That distinction is essential. Technology is not the solution to capitalism's contradictions. It is the enabler that makes a better solution possible.[137] Without explicit architecture, technology accelerates extraction as readily as it accelerates diffusion.[138] Artificial intelligence, automation, and data-intensive systems will intensify whatever incentive structures they are embedded within.[139] Alignment is therefore not a technological problem. It is a design problem.[140]

What Inclusive Capitalism offers is a framework for addressing that problem directly. It treats incentives as the primary causal layer, institutions as the mechanism of persistence, and outcomes as the test of legitimacy.[141] It specifies a vision that can be translated into objective functions, sector-level equations, governance rules, and enforcement mechanisms—explicit enough to be tested, revised, and iteratively improved.[142]

Why this matters is straightforward. Capitalism remains the most powerful engine of prosperity ever created, but its legitimacy now depends on whether it can align private success with public durability under conditions of scale, speed, and abundance.[143] If that alignment remains accidental, reactive, or moralized, instability and backlash will continue regardless of aggregate growth.[144] If it is made structural, capitalism can evolve without abandoning the mechanisms that made it successful in the first place.[145]

This book argues that such an evolution is now possible—not because human nature has changed but because the tools required to design an aligned system finally exist. Whether they are used deliberately, or left to intensify existing contradictions, is no longer a technical question. It is an architectural one.

A Call to Action!

This book does not claim to deliver a final answer. It claims to begin a necessary process.[146] If the diagnosis is correct—if capitalism's unintended consequences arise from incomplete incentive and institutional specification rather than from moral failure or ideological error—then the work ahead cannot be completed by any single author, discipline, or constituency.[147] Designing a durable economic architecture for a technologically abundant, globally interconnected world requires broad participation:

economists, industrial leaders, technologists, policymakers, institutional designers, and citizens with lived experience of the system's failures and strengths.[148]

Book One has articulated a vision grounded in capitalism's enduring principles and informed by empirical evidence of how the system behaves at scale. Book Two proposes an initial architecture—explicit, testable, and deliberately open to refinement. But architecture improves only through use, critique, and iteration. The objective of Inclusive Capitalism is therefore not closure, but engagement: to catalyze a serious, multidisciplinary effort to specify, test, and evolve an economic system capable of preserving capitalism's dynamism while restoring its legitimacy and durability.[149]

Readers who agree with the vision are invited not merely to endorse it but to help build it. Contributions may take many forms: alternative formulations of societal well-being metrics; refinements to incentive mechanisms; proposals for institutional charters or governance models; critiques of feasibility; pilot designs; or forums for structured debate and empirical testing. Progress will depend on disagreement as much as consensus, provided it is grounded in evidence and oriented toward construction rather than critique alone.

Capitalism has always evolved through practice as much as theory. The next stage will be no different. The purpose of this work is to start that evolution deliberately—to move from reactive correction to intentional design. The task now belongs to the community willing to take it forward.

Notes

1 Deaton, Angus. *The Great Escape: Health, Wealth, and the Origins of Inequality*. Princeton, NJ: Princeton University Press, 2013, 1–44; Milanović, Branko. *Capitalism, Alone: The Future of the System That Rules the World*. Cambridge, MA: Harvard University Press, 2019, 1–52.
2 Ibid.
3 North, Douglass C. *Institutions, Institutional Change and Economic Performance*. Cambridge: Cambridge University Press, 1990, 3–14; Simon, Herbert A. *The Sciences of the Artificial*. 3rd ed. Cambridge, MA: MIT Press, 1996, 5–23.
4 Adam Smith, *The Theory of Moral Sentiments*, ed. D. D. Raphael and A. L. Macfie (Indianapolis: Liberty Fund, 1982), Part I, Section I.
5 Ibid.
6 Simon, Herbert A. *The Sciences of the Artificial*. 3rd ed. Cambridge, MA: MIT Press, 1996, 5–23, 129–160.
7 Ibid.
8 W. Brian Arthur, *Complexity and the Economy* (Oxford: Oxford University Press, 2015), 1–26, 43–79; F. A. Hayek, *Law, Legislation and Liberty*, vol. 1 (Chicago: University of Chicago Press, 1973), 8–35; Donella H. Meadows, *Thinking in Systems* (White River Junction, VT: Chelsea Green, 2008), 1–34, 145–170.
9 Adam Smith, *The Theory of Moral Sentiments*, Part I, Section I.
10 Adam Smith, *The Wealth of Nations*, Book I, ch. 8; Book IV, chs. 2–3.
11 Adam Smith, *The Wealth of Nations*, ed. Edwin Cannan (Chicago: University of Chicago Press, 1976), Book I, chap. 10, Book IV, chap. 2; Milton Friedman, *Capitalism and Freedom* (Chicago: University of Chicago Press, 1962), 28–36, 119–126.

12 E. P. Thompson, *The Making of the English Working Class* (New York: Vintage, 1966), chs. 9–10.
13 Karl Polanyi, *The Great Transformation* (Boston: Beacon Press, 1944), chs. 6–7.
14 Douglass C. North, *Institutions, Institutional Change and Economic Performance* (Cambridge: Cambridge University Press, 1990), 3–35, 73–104; Daron Acemoglu and James A. Robinson, *Why Nations Fail* (New York: Crown, 2012), 68–109, 398–426; George J. Stigler, "The Theory of Economic Regulation," *University of Chicago Press* journal *Bell Journal of Economics and Management Science* 2, no. 1 (1971): 3–21.
15 Friedrich A. Hayek, *The Use of Knowledge in Society*, American Economic Review 35, no. 4 (1945).
16 Hyman P. Minsky, *Stabilizing an Unstable Economy* (New Haven: Yale University Press, 2008), 1–35, 195–229; William Lazonick, *Profit Without Prosperity* (Cambridge, MA: Harvard Business Review Press, 2014), 1–44; Greta R. Krippner, *Capitalizing on Crisis* (Cambridge, MA: Harvard University Press, 2011), 27–66, 141–178.
17 Ludwig von Mises, Socialism: *An Economic and Sociological Analysis* (Indianapolis: Liberty Fund, 1981), chs. 1–3.
18 Amartya Sen, *Development as Freedom* (New York: Knopf, 1999), chs. 1–2.
19 Martin Wolf, *The Crisis of Democratic Capitalism* (New York: Penguin Press, 2023), chs. 3–4.
20 Adam Smith, *The Theory of Moral Sentiments*, Part I, Section I.
21 Ian Simpson Ross, *Adam Smith: An Enlightened Life* (New Haven: Yale University Press, 2010), 134–168, 275–310, 327–339.
22 Adam Smith, *The Wealth of Nations*, Book I, ch. 8; Book IV, chs. 2–3.
23 Adam Smith, *The Theory of Moral Sentiments*, Part I, Section I.
24 Adam Smith, *The Wealth of Nations*, Book I, ch. 8; Book IV, chs. 2–3.
25 Robert Heilbroner, *The Worldly Philosophers*, 7th ed., chs. 2–3.
26 Varian, "Market Structure in the Network Age," 137–150; Baldwin, *The Great Convergence*, 1–45; Brynjolfsson and McAfee, *The Second Machine Age*, 47–78.
27 Karl Polanyi, *The Great Transformation*, chs. 6–7.
28 Hobsbawm, Eric. *Industry and Empire: The Birth of the Industrial Revolution*. New York: The New Press, 1999; Nardinelli, Clark. *Child Labor and the Industrial Revolution*. Bloomington: Indiana University Press, 1990; Ashton, T. S. *The Industrial Revolution, 1760–1830*. Oxford: Oxford University Press, 1948; Marx, Karl. *Capital: A Critique of Political Economy, Volume I*. 1867. Trans. Ben Fowkes. London: Penguin Classics, 1976, chs. 10, 15.
29 Friedrich A. Hayek, *The Use of Knowledge in Society*, American Economic Review 35, no. 4 (1945).
30 Douglass C. North, *Institutions, Institutional Change and Economic Performance* (Cambridge: Cambridge University Press, 1990), chs. 1–2.
31 Piketty, Thomas. *Capital and Ideology*. Cambridge, MA: Harvard University Press, 2020, 1–44; OECD. *Under Pressure: The Squeezed Middle Class*. Paris: OECD Publishing, 2019.
32 Thomas Piketty, *Capital in the Twenty-First Century*, trans. Arthur Goldhammer (Cambridge, MA: Harvard University Press, 2014), 1–39, 237–280, 571–685; Joseph E. Stiglitz, *The Price of Inequality* (New York: W. W. Norton, 2012), 1–44, 81–123, 243–289; Bureau of Labor Statistics, "Labor Productivity and Compensation," Washington, DC.
33 Occupy Wall Street, *Declaration of the Occupation of New York City*, September 29, 2011.
34 Mariana Mazzucato, *The Value of Everything* (New York: PublicAffairs, 2018), chs. 2–3.
35 Thomas Philippon, *The Great Reversal* (Cambridge, MA: Harvard University Press, 2019), chs. 1–2.
36 Martin Wolf, *The Crisis of Democratic Capitalism*, chs. 3–4.
37 W. Edwards Deming, *Out of the Crisis* (Cambridge, MA: MIT Press, 1986), chs. 1–3.
38 Peter M. Senge, *The Fifth Discipline* (New York: Doubleday, 1990), chs. 1–2.
39 Adam Smith, *An Inquiry into the Nature and Causes of the Wealth of Nations*, ed. R. H. Campbell and A. S. Skinner (Indianapolis: Liberty Fund, 1981), Vol. I, Book I, chs. 1–3; Book IV, ch. 2.
40 Karl Polanyi, *The Great Transformation*, chs. 6–7.

41 U.S. Bureau of Economic Analysis, *Real GDP per Capita, 1975–2018.*
42 U.S. Bureau of Labor Statistics, *Median Usual Weekly Earnings of Wage and Salary Workers.*
43 Alfred D. Chandler Jr., *The Visible Hand* (Cambridge, MA: Harvard University Press, 1977), 1–25, 281–324; Herbert A. Simon, *Administrative Behavior* (New York: Free Press, 1997), 87–118, 241–260; Oliver E. Williamson, *The Economic Institutions of Capitalism* (New York: Free Press, 1985), 15–45, 61–90.
44 Milton Friedman, *The Methodology of Positive Economics*, in Essays in Positive Economics (Chicago: University of Chicago Press, 1953).
45 Douglass C. North, *Institutions, Institutional Change and Economic Performance*, chs. 1–2.
46 Ibid.
47 W. Edwards Deming, *Out of the Crisis*, chs. 1–3.
48 Milton Friedman, *The Methodology of Positive Economics*, in Essays in Positive Economics (Chicago: University of Chicago Press, 1953).
49 Douglass C. North, *Institutions, Institutional Change and Economic Performance*, chs. 1–2.
50 Mariana Mazzucato, *The Value of Everything*, chs. 2–3.
51 János Kornai, *The Socialist System*, chs. 10–12.
52 Keynes, John Maynard. *The General Theory of Employment, Interest, and Money*. London: Macmillan, 1936, chs. 1–3, 24.
53 Friedrich A. Hayek, *The Use of Knowledge in Society*, American Economic Review 35, no. 4 (1945).
54 Peter M. Senge, *The Fifth Discipline*, chs. 1–2.
55 Ibid.
56 W. Edwards Deming, *Out of the Crisis*, chs. 1–3.
57 Karl Polanyi, *The Great Transformation*, chs. 6–7.
58 Peter M. Senge, *The Fifth Discipline*, chs. 1–2.
59 Acemoglu, Daron, and James A. Robinson. *Why Nations Fail: The Origins of Power, Prosperity, and Poverty*. New York: Crown Business, 2012, 73–100; Rodrik, Dani. *The Globalization Paradox: Democracy and the Future of the World Economy*. New York: W. W. Norton, 2011, 184–210.
60 Milton Friedman, *The Methodology of Positive Economics*, in Essays in Positive Economics (Chicago: University of Chicago Press, 1953).
61 Douglass C. North, *Institutions, Institutional Change and Economic Performance*, chs. 1–2.
62 E. P. Thompson, *The Making of the English Working Class*, chs. 9–10.
63 Karl Polanyi, *The Great Transformation*, chs. 6–7.
64 Joseph A. Schumpeter, *Capitalism, Socialism, and Democracy*, 3rd ed. (New York: Harper & Brothers, 1950), chs. 7–8.
65 János Kornai, *The Socialist System*, chs. 10–12.
66 Friedrich A. Hayek, *The Use of Knowledge in Society*, American Economic Review 35, no. 4 (1945).
67 Milton Friedman, *The Methodology of Positive Economics*, in Essays in Positive Economics (Chicago: University of Chicago Press, 1953).
68 Jeremy Rifkin, *The Zero Marginal Cost Society* (New York: Palgrave Macmillan, 2014), 1–28, 89–123, 257–289; Carl Shapiro and Hal R. Varian, *Information Rules* (Boston: Harvard Business School Press, 1999), 3–27, 173–215; Shoshana Zuboff, *The Age of Surveillance Capitalism* (New York: PublicAffairs, 2019), 8–27, 94–131, 375–411.
69 Thomas Philippon, *The Great Reversal*, chs. 1–2.
70 Thomas Piketty, *Capital in the Twenty-First Century*, trans. Arthur Goldhammer (Cambridge, MA: Harvard University Press, 2014), Introduction and Part I.
71 Mariana Mazzucato, *The Value of Everything*, chs. 2–3.
72 Adam Smith, *An Inquiry into the Nature and Causes of the Wealth of Nations*, ed. R. H. Campbell and A. S. Skinner, Vol. I, Book I, chs. 1–3; Book IV, ch. 2.
73 Raghuram G. Rajan, *The Third Pillar: How Markets and the State Leave the Community Behind* (New York: Penguin Press, 2019), chs. 1–3.

74 Martin Wolf, *The Crisis of Democratic Capitalism*, chs. 3–4.
75 Erik Brynjolfsson and Andrew McAfee, *The Second Machine Age* (New York: W. W. Norton, 2014), chs. 1–2.
76 W. Edwards Deming, *Out of the Crisis*, chs. 1–3.
77 Joseph A. Schumpeter, *Capitalism, Socialism, and Democracy*, 3rd ed. (New York: Harper & Brothers, 1950), chs. 7–8.
78 Adam Smith, *An Inquiry into the Nature and Causes of the Wealth of Nations*, ed. R. H. Campbell and A. S. Skinner, Vol. I, Book I, chs. 1–3; Book IV, ch. 2.
79 Friedrich A. Hayek, *The Use of Knowledge in Society*, American Economic Review 35, no. 4 (1945).
80 Ludwig von Mises, Socialism: *An Economic and Sociological Analysis*, chs. 1–3.
81 Mariana Mazzucato, *The Value of Everything*, chs. 2–3.
82 Douglass C. North, *Institutions, Institutional Change and Economic Performance*, chs. 1–2.
83 Joseph A. Schumpeter, *Capitalism, Socialism, and Democracy*, 3rd ed. (New York: Harper & Brothers, 1950), chs. 7–8.
84 Amartya Sen, *Development as Freedom*, chs. 1–2.
85 Thomas Philippon, *The Great Reversal*, chs. 1–2.
86 Jean-Charles Rochet and Jean Tirole, "Platform Competition in Two-Sided Markets," *Journal of the European Economic Association* 1, no. 4 (2003): 990–1029; Carl Shapiro and Hal R. Varian, *Information Rules* (Boston: Harvard Business School Press, 1999), 173–215; Geoffrey G. Parker, Marshall W. Van Alstyne, and Sangeet Paul Choudary, *Platform Revolution* (New York: W. W. Norton, 2016), 17–52.
87 Martin Wolf, *The Crisis of Democratic Capitalism*, chs. 3–4.
88 Mariana Mazzucato, *The Value of Everything*, chs. 2–3.
89 Martin Wolf, *The Crisis of Democratic Capitalism*, chs. 3–4.
90 János Kornai, *The Socialist System*, chs. 10–12.
91 Mariana Mazzucato, *The Value of Everything*, chs. 2–3.
92 Erik Brynjolfsson and Andrew McAfee, *The Second Machine Age* (New York: W. W. Norton, 2014), chs. 1–2.
93 Ray Dalio, *Principles for Dealing with the Changing World Order*, chs. 1–3.
94 Thomas Philippon, *The Great Reversal*, chs. 1–2.
95 Linus Torvalds, *The Linux Kernel and the GPL*, GNU General Public License v2 (1991).
96 Friedrich A. Hayek, *The Use of Knowledge in Society*, American Economic Review 35, no. 4 (1945).
97 Ibid.
98 W. Edwards Deming, *Out of the Crisis*, chs. 1–3.
99 Peter M. Senge, *The Fifth Discipline*, chs. 1–2.
100 Ludwig von Mises, Socialism: *An Economic and Sociological Analysis*, chs. 1–3.
101 Karl Polanyi, *The Great Transformation*, chs. 6–7.
102 Douglass C. North, *Institutions, Institutional Change and Economic Performance*, chs. 1–2.
103 Ray Dalio, *Principles for Dealing with the Changing World Order*, chs. 1–3.
104 Douglass C. North, *Institutions, Institutional Change and Economic Performance*, chs. 1–2.
105 Mariana Mazzucato, *The Value of Everything*, chs. 2–3.
106 Ibid.
107 Ray Dalio, *Principles for Dealing with the Changing World Order*, chs. 1–3.
108 Milton Friedman, *The Methodology of Positive Economics*, in Essays in Positive Economics (Chicago: University of Chicago Press, 1953).
109 Douglass C. North, *Institutions, Institutional Change and Economic Performance*, chs. 1–2.
110 Raghuram G. Rajan, *The Third Pillar: How Markets and the State Leave the Community Behind* (New York: Penguin Press, 2019), chs. 1–3.
111 Douglass C. North, *Institutions, Institutional Change and Economic Performance*, chs. 1–2.

112 Erik Brynjolfsson and Andrew McAfee, *The Second Machine Age* (New York: W. W. Norton, 2014), chs. 1–2.

113 Minsky, Hyman P. *Stabilizing an Unstable Economy.* New Haven, CT: Yale University Press, 1986, 1–28, 285–308; Borio, Claudio. "The Financial Cycle and Macroeconomics: What Have We Learnt?" *Journal of Banking & Finance* 45 (2014): 182–198.

114 Linus Torvalds, *The Linux Kernel and the GPL*, GNU General Public License v2 (1991).

115 Ibid.

116 Thomas Philippon, *The Great Reversal*, chs. 1–2.

117 W. Edwards Deming, *Out of the Crisis*, chs. 1–3.

118 Ray Dalio, *Principles for Dealing with the Changing World Order*, chs. 1–3.

119 Peter M. Senge, *The Fifth Discipline*, chs. 1–2.

120 W. Edwards Deming, *Out of the Crisis*, chs. 1–3.

121 Peter M. Senge, *The Fifth Discipline*, chs. 1–2.

122 Douglass C. North, *Institutions, Institutional Change and Economic Performance*, chs. 1–2.

123 Alfred Marshall, *Principles of Economics* (London: Macmillan, 1890), bk. V; Paul A. Samuelson and William D. Nordhaus, *Economics* (New York: McGraw-Hill, 19th ed., 2010), 25–55, 157–198; Douglass C. North, *Institutions, Institutional Change and Economic Performance* (Cambridge: Cambridge University Press, 1990), 3–35; Robert M. Solow, "A Contribution to the Theory of Economic Growth," *Quarterly Journal of Economics* 70, no. 1 (1956): 65–94.

124 Thomas Piketty, *Capital in the Twenty-First Century*, trans. Arthur Goldhammer, Introduction and Part I.

125 Martin Wolf, *The Crisis of Democratic Capitalism*, chs. 3–4.

126 W. Edwards Deming, *Out of the Crisis*, chs. 1–3.

127 Ibid.

128 Milton Friedman, *The Methodology of Positive Economics*, in Essays in Positive Economics (Chicago: University of Chicago Press, 1953).

129 Douglass C. North, *Institutions, Institutional Change and Economic Performance*, chs. 1–2.

130 Robert M. Solow, *Technical Change and the Aggregate Production Function*, Review of Economics and Statistics 39, no. 3 (1957).

131 OECD, *Report by the Commission on the Measurement of Economic Performance and Social Progress* (Paris, 2009).

132 W. Edwards Deming, *Out of the Crisis*, chs. 1–3.

133 Erik Brynjolfsson and Andrew McAfee, *The Second Machine Age* (New York: W. W. Norton, 2014), chs. 1–2.

134 OECD, *Report by the Commission on the Measurement of Economic Performance and Social Progress* (Paris, 2009).

135 Peter M. Senge, *The Fifth Discipline*, chs. 1–2.

136 W. Edwards Deming, *Out of the Crisis*, chs. 1–3.

137 Erik Brynjolfsson and Andrew McAfee, *The Second Machine Age* (New York: W. W. Norton, 2014), chs. 1–2.

138 Mariana Mazzucato, *The Value of Everything*, chs. 2–3.

139 Erik Brynjolfsson and Andrew McAfee, *The Second Machine Age* (New York: W. W. Norton, 2014), chs. 1–2.

140 Douglass C. North, *Institutions, Institutional Change and Economic Performance*, chs. 1–2.

141 Ibid.

142 Peter M. Senge, *The Fifth Discipline*, chs. 1–2.

143 Raghuram G. Rajan, *The Third Pillar: How Markets and the State Leave the Community Behind* (New York: Penguin Press, 2019), chs. 1–3.

144 Martin Wolf, *The Crisis of Democratic Capitalism*, chs. 3–4.

145 Adam Smith, *An Inquiry into the Nature and Causes of the Wealth of Nations*, ed. R. H. Campbell and A. S. Skinner, Vol. I, Book I, chs. 1–3; Book IV, ch. 2.
146 W. Edwards Deming, *Out of the Crisis*, chs. 1–3.
147 Douglass C. North, *Institutions, Institutional Change and Economic Performance*, chs. 1–2.
148 Peter M. Senge, *The Fifth Discipline*, chs. 1–2.
149 Martin Wolf, *The Crisis of Democratic Capitalism*, chs. 3–4.

1 Feudalism and Landed Power: An Economy of Scarcity

This book begins with feudalism because it represents the first large-scale economic system in the Western world in which incentive design, leadership structure, and societal outcomes were tightly coupled—and deeply misaligned.[1] Feudalism offers a baseline case for understanding how economic systems shape behavior long before formal economic doctrines emerged. It reveals, in its most elemental form, how concentrated power, inherited authority, and weak accountability produce stagnation, exclusion, and manufactured scarcity rather than growth. Long before capitalism, feudalism profoundly demonstrates that when leadership incentives are disconnected from societal well-being, economic systems reliably underperform their potential.[2]

Feudalism also offers the earliest expression of two themes that recur throughout this book: manufactured scarcity and the security–freedom tradeoff.[3] In a world of chronic insecurity, protection became the primary economic good, exchanged for labor, loyalty, and access to land—much as economic insecurity today can foster support for populist leaders and political extremism.[4] This tradeoff sharply constrained mobility, suppressed innovation, and normalized inequality as an accepted feature of social order. Scarcity was not a natural condition but an institutional outcome, reinforced by rigid hierarchies, restricted access to productive assets, and incentives that rewarded extraction over improvement. The result was a system that delivered stability for elites at the expense of freedom and broad-based prosperity.[5]

By examining feudalism first, the book establishes a diagnostic lens that applies across all subsequent economic epochs. Each system that follows—mercantilism, early capitalism, industrial capitalism, and modern neoliberal capitalism—can be evaluated by the same criteria: how leadership incentives are structured, how scarcity is produced or alleviated, how freedom and security are balanced, and how innovation is enabled or suppressed. Feudalism is not merely a historical precursor to capitalism; it is the archetype against which all later economic systems can be measured. Understanding its failures is essential to understanding why Inclusive Capitalism must be designed—not assumed—to align power, productivity, and societal well-being.[6]

With this diagnostic framework in mind, we begin by examining feudalism as the first major economic architecture to emerge in the Western world after the collapse of Roman authority.[7] It was not a market economy but a hierarchical structure of land, power, and obligation. Emerging gradually between the ninth and fifteenth centuries, feudalism filled the vacuum left by fragmented imperial institutions, as military insecurity and the absence of centralized law made local authority the primary means of survival.[8] Land became the central unit of economic value, and those who controlled it functioned as the industrial leadership of their time. The lord—not the

 | https://doi.org/10.1515/9783112235485-002

merchant or entrepreneur—was the dominant economic actor, and the manor served as the basic productive unit.[9]

Feudalism may be defined as a decentralized system in which land is exchanged for military or agricultural service, producing a stratified hierarchy of obligations: king to nobles, nobles to vassals, vassals to knights, and the peasantry at the bottom.[10] Political authority, legal rights, and economic privilege were inseparable; the right to rule was the right to extract surplus. Innovation was rare, mobility limited, and economic outcomes determined largely by one's inherited position.[11]

The chapter's structure reflects the analytical approach used throughout the book: we begin by defining the system, followed by explaining its emergence, examining the doctrines and norms that sustained it, analyzing the incentives and resultant behaviors of those in power, assessing the lived experience of the population, identifying strengths and failures, and end by tracing the forces that led to its decline. Each chapter distills lessons for Inclusive Capitalism.

Significantly, feudalism vividly demonstrates how concentrated and inherited power generates scarcity rather than growth. When leadership is accountable only to itself, innovation decays and general economic freedom and mobility collapses. The emergence of more open systems of exchange was not accidental but the product of new incentives, new technologies, and the revival of economic freedom—one of the central themes of this book.[12]

Defining Feudalism

Feudalism does not lend itself to precise boundaries or rigid chronology. Historians situate it broadly between the ninth and fifteenth centuries, but its contours varied by region and evolved over time. It was a constellation of practices responding to disorder and insecurity. Tribal and military elites—the Visigoths, Vandals, Franks, Ostrogoths—filled the vacuum left by Rome's collapse. Trade contracted, urban life diminished, and Europe reverted to predominantly rural, self-sufficient production. Technological progress slowed, with exceptions such as the heavy plow and the three-field system.[13]

In this context, feudalism emerged as a social, political, and economic order structured around protection and obligation rather than market exchange.[14] Kings or high nobles granted fiefs to lords and vassals in return for service, creating localized centers of authority. Manors—largely self-contained agricultural estates—served as the core productive units, worked by peasants or serfs who received subsistence rights in exchange for their labor, rents, and loyalty. Economic relationships were governed by personal bonds enforced through custom, power, and coercion rather than impersonal price signals. As Susan Reynolds observes, feudal tenure functioned as a "network of reciprocal obligation, sustained by power and tradition."[15]

Agrarian production generated surplus that flowed upward through these obligations, tightly linking social position and economic outcome to one's place in the system. Marc Bloch captured this structure succinctly when he described feudal society as one in which individuals were "bound to another by the ties of service and loyalty," an economy defined less by exchange than by enduring personal dependence.[16]

External threats strengthened the system. Raids by Vikings, Magyars, and others made centralized defense impractical. Local lords could mobilize rapid protection. Norman Cantor observes that decentralization "allowed for local defense networks to form," making the feudal hierarchy as protective as it was coercive.[17]

The Church reinforced the system by distributing land, legitimizing hierarchy, and embedding feudal relations in religious doctrine. As F. L. Ganshof notes, ecclesiastical authorities "strengthened its legal and social foundations."[18]

Feudalism thus created order but not mobility; stability but not growth. It ensured survival at the price of stasis. Its logic reveals an enduring pattern: when leadership is unaccountable, surplus accrues upward, innovation slows, and societies organize around scarcity.[19] Many contemporary institutions still exhibit these traits. Inclusive Capitalism seeks to reverse them by dispersing surplus, accelerating innovation, and structuring society around abundance.

Emergence of Feudalism

Beginning the study of capitalism with feudalism is not antiquarianism. It is an analytical necessity. Economic history asks and then explores how societies allocate scarce resources and structure authority. Feudalism shows how societies respond when security is scarce, institutions are weak, and power concentrates. It also marks the earliest emergence of private property and contractual exchange—precursors to capitalism.[20]

Feudalism did not emerge suddenly. It arose from the political and economic fragmentation following Rome's decline. The deposition of Romulus Augustulus in 476 symbolized this collapse, but the process had long been underway.[21] Roman taxation disintegrated, trade deteriorated, and cities shrank. The military structure decayed, leaving populations vulnerable to raids and famine. Historians attribute Rome's unraveling to fiscal strain, political corruption, overextension, and repeated incursions.[22]

The fall of Rome is often cited as a warning: when fiscal demands exceed productive capacity and institutions cannot mediate conflict, economic systems regress. Contemporary analysts, including Ray Dalio, have noted parallels in today's political economies, where rising debt, polarization, and global overextension mirror earlier cycles.[23] Although not strict analogies, they highlight how institutional fragility can precipitate economic contraction.

The post-Roman world was a mosaic of tribal polities. Land replaced coinage as the primary store of value. Wealth was measured by the capacity to command agricultural labor and provide military protection. A decentralized system arose: fiefs granted for loyalty; manors as productive centers; serfs exchanging autonomy for subsistence.[24] As Bloch emphasized, ties of service and loyalty structured every dimension of life.[25]

Persistent violence reinforced the system. Between the eighth and tenth centuries, Viking, Magyar, and Saracen raids made rapid local defense essential. Centralized armies could not protect dispersed settlements; local lords could. Cantor's observation that "local defense networks" defined feudal power captures the system's essence: coercion and protection intertwined.[26]

Other factors reinforced feudalism: agrarian dominance, land-based hierarchies, and the Church's institutional power. Ganshof notes that ecclesiastical authorities institutionalized feudalism through land grants and spiritual sanction.[27]

Feudalism, therefore, was not just political; it was a complete socio-economic order linking land, labor, law, and protection. Innovation was rare, growth minimal, and hierarchy durable. Yet the system endured because it met the deepest need of its age: security.[28]

The willingness to trade autonomy for security remains a constant in human societies. From anti-terror surveillance to pandemic lockdowns, populations often accept reduced societal freedoms and personal liberty when fear rises. The pattern is ancient and persistent: security purchased through subordination.[29]

This insight forms a core lesson for Inclusive Capitalism: institutional design must align incentives with autonomy, opportunity, and accountability. Without such alignment, systems naturally drift toward hierarchy and scarcity. Inclusive Capitalism begins from the opposite premise—i) building structures that protect security without suppressing freedom and ii) that expand opportunity rather than constrain it.

Feudal Economic, Legal, and Technological Landscape

To understand feudalism, it is essential to recall that it predates the intellectual vocabulary of modern economics. The term "economics" itself did not enter common usage until the eighteenth century, and the medieval world possessed neither monetary theory nor fiscal policy, neither left nor right, neither capitalism nor socialism. There were no competing schools of thought, no formal frameworks for efficient allocation, and no institutional checks on power beyond custom and force. What existed instead was a society organized around survival. When food security is precarious, when violence is endemic, and when the state is weak, economic behavior reflects basic human instincts more than abstract theory. Feudalism therefore reveals leadership behavior in its most threadbare form—a critical lens for understanding how systems function when they lack mechanisms to align power with societal well-being.[30]

This point matters because Inclusive Capitalism is ultimately an argument about designing institutions that shape incentives. Markets do not succeed because individuals are virtuous but because institutions constrain and channel behavior. In feudal Europe, there were no such guardrails. The lords who controlled land held legislative, judicial, and economic authority simultaneously. They set the rules, extracted surplus, enforced punishment, and owned the means of production. As a result, the incentives upon which the leadership acted were often misaligned with the welfare of the broader population. Stability mattered, but innovation did not; security mattered, but mobility did not; hierarchy mattered, but human potential did not. Feudalism therefore makes crystal clear what happens when leadership is accountable only to itself.[31]

Yet, this system also established the early building blocks of modern capitalism. Land functioned as capital, and the right to control and alienate land gradually evolved into the legal concept of private property. Over time, as land became transferable, inheritable, and exchangeable, it laid the groundwork for market-based allocation. Both Adam Smith and Karl Marx recognized this lineage. Smith viewed the right of laborer and producer as the foundation of all other forms of property, writing in 1776 that "the property which every man has in his own labor . . . is the most sacred and inviolable."[32] For Smith, this right established the dignity of work and the legitimacy of exchange. Marx, from a different perspective, argued that "the dissolution of the feudal system of land tenure" was a necessary precondition for capitalism.[33] Despite profound disagreement on capitalism's merits, both Smith and Marx centered on its origins in the breakdown of feudal structures.

This historical perspective matters for the argument of this book. Smith's bottom-up model—the invisible hand—was not a naïve claim that selfishness is virtuous, nor an endorsement of unrestrained greed. Rather, it was Smith's observation that in a competitive market, individuals pursuing their own improvement and personal gain, without centralized coordination, can unintentionally contribute more effectively to the public good than any system of top-down planning. The invisible hand describes an emergent ordering process: prices, competition, and decentralized decision-making transmit information and align effort in ways no planner could replicate.[34]

Crucially, Smith understood this mechanism to operate only within a broader moral and institutional framework. The invisible hand was never meant to function in isolation from justice, norms, and public purpose. It assumed restraints on monopoly power, protection of labor, and a society in which sympathy and civic virtue tempered self-interest. When later interpretations stripped the invisible hand of these preconditions, it was transformed from a conditional insight into an absolute doctrine—one that mistook efficiency alone for the common good.[35]

This distinction is foundational to Inclusive Capitalism. The objective is not to reject Smith's invisible hand but to complete it: to design incentives and institutions such that decentralized self-interest once again aggregates toward societal well-being rather than away from it. What failed historically was not the principle of emergent coordination but the assumption that it would remain aligned with human dignity and the common good without deliberate system design.[36]

Feudalism therefore serves as more than a remote historical curiosity. It is a baseline—a world in which leadership incentives were unrestrained, institutions were weak, and survival eclipsed opportunity. By examining how that system functioned, and why it eventually exhausted its usefulness, we can isolate the variables that determine whether economic systems generate widespread prosperity or entrenched hierarchy. Inclusive Capitalism aims to build where feudalism failed: aligning leadership with societal well-being through institutional design, incentive structure, and measurable outcomes.[37]

Incentives and Behaviors of Feudal Industrial Leaders

The structure of feudalism created a distinctive incentive environment for its leadership class. Lords derived their authority and wealth almost entirely from land. Land was the one asset that conferred economic surplus, political jurisdiction, and military command. As François Guizot observed, "feudalism made the land the measure and the master of all things," capturing the extent to which property defined status, privilege, and obligation.[38] Currency existed, but its circulation was limited; precious metals were stores of value, not engines of growth. The real foundation of wealth was agricultural output, and the real indicator of power was the number of dependents, vassals, and serfs whose labor one could mobilize.[39]

In this environment, the incentives facing the lord were fundamentally conservative. With land fixed and productivity growth limited, the most reliable way to preserve status and power was to maintain the existing hierarchy rather than to expand output or opportunity. Innovation was therefore rare and often actively discouraged, as it threatened established customs and the prevailing distribution of surplus. In this sense, feudalism represents an early and explicit form of manufactured scarcity. Across all economic systems, scarcity and abundance—whether natural or intentionally produced—function as core variables shaping inclusiveness and societal well-being.[40]

The lord delegated day-to-day administration of the manor to vassals and stewards, who managed agricultural production, enforced labor obligations, and organized military contingents. Leadership thus centered on control and oversight rather than enterprise or experimentation. As Georges Duby observes, much of the lord's time was devoted to "administering justice and ensuring that vassals fulfilled their obligations," tasks oriented toward preserving authority rather than expanding opportunity.[41]

The incentive structure of the system explains this orientation. Because wealth flowed upward, and because power was inherited, the lord's rational strategy was to safeguard what he possessed, not to transform the conditions under which production occurred. Risk-taking or investment in new technologies entailed asymmetric risks, since gains might accrue to the peasantry or to competing nobles rather than to the lord, whose position depended on preserving existing arrangements. The manorial system thus rewarded vigilance, defense, and social control more than economic progress, which threatened the stability of the feudal system itself. The serf's lack of economic mobility reinforced this equilibrium: bound to the land, lacking legal autonomy, and obligated to provide labor services, the peasantry had little capacity to generate or demand change.[42]

These leadership incentives drove a process in which the wealth of the crops planted and harvested by the serfs across the length and breadth of the lord's land paid for the construction and maintenance of the lord's fine "keep"—most often a fortified castle. The trade of these commodities, once transported to town or city, in turn provided the currency, gold, or silver that were used to buy fine linens and clothes for the lord's household, a tutor for his children, wine for his supper, and soldiers not just for the protection of his serfs but for control of the serfs when necessary.[43]

The lived reality of the elite was, by modern standards, remarkably modest. Nobles unquestionably enjoyed far greater comfort than the peasantry, yet even the aristocracy of the High Middle Ages faced short life expectancy, rudimentary medicine, and harsh living conditions. Castles were cold, damp, and poorly lit; disease and injury were commonplace; material security remained fragile. While the relative gap between nobles and peasants was vast, the absolute standard of living for both groups was low when compared to even the lower deciles of modern industrial societies. This paradox underscores a central insight: systems that prioritize relative hierarchy can preserve status without meaningfully improving human welfare.[44]

Dani Rodrik's classroom thought experiment—where most would prefer to be in the top percentile of a poor society rather than among the lower deciles of a wealthy one—reveals a powerful human tendency to value relative position even when absolute well-being is diminished. That instinct helps explain why hierarchical systems such as feudalism exhibit such remarkable persistence. When status is derived from rank rather than from expanding the total productive pie, elites can rationally prefer stasis to transformation. The feudal order maximized relative advantage, not absolute progress, and therefore lacked internal pressure to improve living standards broadly. Innovation was not merely unnecessary; it was destabilizing.[45]

This helps clarify why feudal leadership behaved as it did. If a lord's status and security had depended on measurable improvements in collective outcomes—higher yields, healthier populations, technological adoption, or expanded learning—rather than on the extraction of a fixed surplus, incentives would have favored experimentation and investment. Under such conditions, irrigation, crop rotation, mechanical tools, or freer labor arrangements might have emerged earlier and more widely. Their absence was not a failure of imagination or morality on the part of individual lords but a structural consequence of a system that rewarded relative dominance over absolute advancement. Feudalism thus illustrates a core deficiency that Inclusive

Capitalism seeks to address: when leadership incentives are tied to position rather than progress, societies can remain stable for centuries while remaining poor. The incentives structure defined by Inclusive Capitalism must be powerful enough to overcome the propensity for relative rather than absolute standard of living.[46]

Feudal leadership also faced constant insecurity. Because political authority rested on personal loyalty rather than law, the maintenance of power required continuous surveillance of rivals and subordinates. Vassals who failed to provide military service, peasants who resisted corvée obligations (free persons fulfilling obligations through their labor), or nobles who asserted independence jeopardized the lord's position. Much of the leadership's time and energy was therefore directed toward self-preservation. Internal conflict, feuds, and local warfare were common, diverting resources from productive uses and constraining the emergence of stable markets or long-distance trade.[47]

Ultimately, the system proved unsustainable. Its rigid hierarchies inhibited innovation, its narrow incentive structure limited economic development, and its dependence on personal loyalty created chronic political instability. As commercial towns emerged, as monetary exchange expanded, and as agricultural productivity slowly increased, the logic of feudal leadership became misaligned with the evolving economy. The decline of feudalism was therefore not only the decline of a social order but the decline of a leadership class whose incentives were tied to stasis rather than improvement.[48]

The contrast with Inclusive Capitalism is instructive. When leadership incentives are aligned with measurable social well-being—instead of extraction, hierarchy, or short-term control—systems evolve. Feudalism provides the clearest historical demonstration of what happens when they are not.[49]

Lived Experience of the Population

If leadership incentives in the feudal world were oriented toward preservation and control, the lived experience of the majority reflected the consequences of that structure. For the serf—the backbone of the agrarian economy—life was bounded by obligation, immobility, and vulnerability. Most peasants were born into a condition they did not choose and could not escape. Their horizon was the manor: a cluster of thatched huts, a small plot of subsistence land, and the lord's demesne (the land retained by the lord for personal use), which they were required to cultivate. Barbara Hanawalt's research on rural life emphasizes that peasants "worked from sunrise to sunset, enduring heavy physical labor, and yet lived in conditions that left them vulnerable to hunger and illness."[50]

The serf grew up knowing no other lifestyle and no other world than those that defined life on the manor. The serfs had to watch, day in and day out, their father's and mother's daily scrape and acquiescence to the lord's authority. Although living in sight of the lord's riches and luxury, he or she had learned early on to accept as normal—and inevitable—the bare walls of the spartan, thatched-roof serf huts of just one room, the frugal allotments of food and clothing, and the daily grind of hard labor while seeing little in return. He or she had also come to accept the general inescapability of this situation, and to understand the generational predestination that had landed him or her in this situation.[51]

The serf's obligations were numerous. He owed labor services on the lord's fields, rents in kind, fees for using the mill and oven, and taxes assessed by both secular and ecclesiastical authorities. He lived within sight of the manor house—the material symbol of hierarchy—and performed work that sustained a system from which he received little more than subsistence. Social mobility was minimal. The structure of feudal incentive made improvement improbable, and innovation undesirable. The stagnation of the peasantry was a structural feature of the system, not merely a consequence of individual hardship.[52]

The options available to serfs for improving their condition were narrow and often perilous. A skilled individual—a blacksmith or miller, for example—might occasionally accumulate enough resources to purchase manumission for himself and his family. A lord might grant freedom in exchange for extraordinary service. Such cases were exceptional and depended on personal favor rather than any established institutional pathways. The most common route to freedom was illicit: flight. Medieval law often granted liberty to fugitives who could evade recapture for "a year and a day," and towns provided anonymity for the fortunate few who could manage it.[53] But the risk was extreme. Capture meant punishment, and failure often brought retribution upon families left behind.

Literacy offered another narrow escape, typically through entry into monastic life. Some men who gained basic reading skills could become monks, scribes, or lower clergy, thereby accessing a more educated and materially stable world. On the opposite extreme, a few peasants sought escape as mercenaries or brigands. Given the crushing poverty of serfdom, it is striking how few chose outlawry; but the risks—violent death, mutilation, execution—were high, and social networks rooted people to their manors. Peasant revolts did occur, yet they were rare, fragmented, and swiftly suppressed. Feudalism relied on this equilibrium of dependency, fear, and limited alternatives.[54]

For the leadership class, this underlying resentment created a persistent sense of insecurity. Lords understood that their authority rested on a combination of tradition, coercion, and the absence of alternatives for the peasantry. They spent substantial time adjudicating disputes, enforcing obligations, policing borders, and managing the behavior of vassals. Their fears were not unfounded: famine, plague, mismanagement, or external attack could trigger unrest, flight, or violence. The very structure of the system—one that suppressed opportunity for the many while concentrating power in the hands of a few—generated the conditions for cyclical instability. The lord's vigilance, his need to "watch his back," was therefore a rational response to the incentives embedded in feudal order.[55]

Towns and urbanization offered the first structural alternative to this stasis. By the High Middle Ages, growing market towns hosted artisans, merchants, and guilds whose regulated crafts created opportunities unavailable on the manor. Guilds, though often restrictive, introduced early forms of self-governing economic institutions. Adam Smith criticized them for suppressing competition and "conspiring against the public,"[56] but they also signaled a shift toward contractual rather than hereditary economic relationships. Town charters granted residents limited autonomy from feudal obligations, enabling the first stirrings of civil society and commercial discipline.[57]

The Church, meanwhile, shaped both the moral and institutional world of peasants. It controlled vast tracts of land, collected tithes (theoretically one-tenth of agricultural output or income, though applied unevenly in practice), offered alms, and provided the only widespread system of education. Crucially, it articulated the ideological justification for the feudal hierarchy. Jacques Le Goff notes that the Church played a dual role: it "legitimized the power of kings and lords while also serving as the moral conscience of medieval Europe."[58] By teaching that social rank was divinely ordained, it reinforced the system even as it mitigated its harshest consequences through charity and pastoral care.

Feudal life thus reveals the deep connection between leadership incentives and societal outcomes. Because leaders were rewarded for extraction rather than improvement, the serf's world stagnated. Because mobility threatened the stability of the hierarchy, innovation was discouraged. Because fear was an organizing principle, coercion was normalized. These conditions produced resentment but offered no structured outlet for reform.[59]

A system organized around Inclusive Capitalism principles could have altered this dynamic. If leadership had been incentivized to improve measurable social well-being—productivity, health, education, resilience—rather than preserve inherited advantage, the rational strategy would have been to invest in the peasantry rather than control it. Technological adoption, agricultural innovation, and even basic literacy could have increased output, reduced risk, and expanded opportunity in ways that benefited both leaders and workers. Instead of fearing the population, leaders would have depended on its prosperity. The absence of such mechanisms in the medieval world explains not only the stagnation of feudal society but the fragility of its ruling class.[60]

What Worked Under Feudalism and What Failed

Evaluating feudalism requires holding two ideas at once. By modern standards it was a highly inefficient, unjust, and stagnant system. Yet, relative to the chaos that preceded it, feudalism provided a workable—if deeply imperfect—solution to the problem of survival in an age of disorder. Georges Duby described feudalism as "the best solution that could be devised to face an age of disorder," emphasizing that its virtues were relative rather than absolute.[61]

Its first strength lay in security. In a world of Viking raids, Magyar incursions, and the collapse of Roman military infrastructure, local lords could mobilize armed men far more rapidly than any distant king. Vassals and knights formed the backbone of these forces. The feudal hierarchy, however coercive, imposed a recognizable order where previously there had been fragmentation. It provided a chain of command, an understood set of obligations, and a reasonably predictable framework for defense.

Its second strength lay in basic subsistence. Feudalism created a pattern of local, largely self-sufficient agricultural economies. Manorial estates produced much of what they consumed. In an environment where long-distance trade routes were dangerous and unreliable, this reduced vulnerability to external shocks. Peasants, in return for their labor, received access to plots of land and the protection of the lord's fortifications. As Marc Bloch observed, feudal justice and manorial courts, however partial, resolved disputes rapidly enough to allow the agricultural cycle to continue, preserving a minimal social equilibrium.[62]

Third, feudalism offered a rudimentary form of governance. Manorial courts, seigneurial jurisdictions, and ecclesiastical structures functioned as basic institutions for dispute resolution and rule enforcement. These institutions were deeply unequal, but they were not wholly arbitrary. Customary law, communal expectations, and the moral authority of the Church placed at least some constraints on the most extreme abuses. In this sense, feudalism served as a bridge between the institutional vacuum of the early medieval centuries and the more complex legal and economic orders that would follow. Fernand Braudel's characterization of feudalism as "a necessary interlude, an imperfect bridge between antiquity and the modern world" captures this transitional role.[63]

In summary, feudalism met the most fundamental demand of the average person in its time: physical and economic security. It did not, however, address what modern democracies consider essential—freedom, mobility, and the systematic improvement of living standards.

Measured against other epochs—the Roman imperial economy, the commercial expansion of the Renaissance, the industrial era—feudalism compares poorly. Its rigid social hierarchy severely limited opportunity and depressed incentives for innovation. Serfs, while not chattel slaves, had few legal rights and almost no realistic avenues for upward mobility. Their obligations to the lord—labor services, dues in kind, and various fees—left little time or surplus for investment, experimentation, or education. Marc Bloch described this as "an onerous system in which peasants were overburdened by their obligations, creating a cycle of dependence and exploitation that left little room for improvement."[64]

Economically, the system was oriented toward subsistence rather than growth. The manorial estate, designed to be self-sufficient, discouraged specialization and long-distance exchange. Thomas Sowell emphasized that trade allows societies to overcome the limitations of geography by exchanging local surpluses for external goods and ideas.[65] By contrast, the feudal economy limited such exchanges. As Duby notes, a structure "based primarily on local subsistence farming" was ill-suited to the expansion of commerce and the development of diversified industries.[66] Norman Cantor similarly characterizes feudal society as fundamentally conservative, privileging the stability of the known over the risks inherent in innovation.[67]

There were exceptions. The adoption of the heavy plow and the three-field system increased yields and brought new lands under cultivation. Marc Bloch rightly points out that these innovations, though slow to spread, improved the efficiency of the manorial economy and reduced the risk of crop failure.[68] But such advances were incremental and sporadic. They did not alter the underlying incentive structure of the system.

The social consequences were profound. A large majority of the population remained trapped in poverty and dependence across generations. Because the leadership class was rewarded for extraction rather than improvement, there was little reason to invest in the capabilities of the population. Education for peasants was minimal; health conditions remained poor; and demographic shocks—famine, plague, war—could erase decades of fragile gains. Compared to the Roman world's trade networks, urban infrastructure, and broader access to manufactured goods, feudal Europe represented a significant regression in economic complexity and living standards. Only when compared to the anarchic conditions of the immediate post-Roman period does feudalism appear as an improvement, and even then only modestly.

This historical record underscores a central lesson: time does not guarantee progress. Economic systems can stagnate or regress when institutional structures suppress mobility, innovation, and exchange. Feudalism illustrates how hierarchy, lack of scale, and neglect of trade combine to inhibit development.

Although many elements of an inclusive capitalism—particularly its emphasis on non-scarcity in domains such as software or digital media—cannot meaningfully be projected onto the medieval world, its core principle of aligning leadership incentives with societal well-being can. The crucial question is how feudal society might have evolved if its leadership class had been rewarded not for preserving hierarchy and extracting surplus but for improving measurable outcomes for their dependents.

Consider, as a thought experiment, an "inclusive-capitalist lord"—a counterfactual figure whose position depended on the prosperity and resilience of his manor rather than the mere maintenance of inherited privilege. In such a system, the lord's status and security would rise with increases in agricultural productivity, reductions in famine and mortality, improvements in basic education, and the gradual creation of local surplus that could be traded beyond the manor. Investment in innovation would become rational rather than threatening.

Even within the technological constraints of the medieval period, such a shift in incentives could have produced meaningful differences. A lord whose authority depended on the well-being of his population might have encouraged the adoption of new agricultural techniques more rapidly and widely, reduced the most onerous labor dues to enable peasants to cultivate their own plots more productively, supported local craftsmanship and trade so that proto-industrial activities could emerge alongside agriculture, and invested in basic religious or practical literacy, recognizing its long-term benefits for administration and productivity.

These measures would not have converted a feudal manor into a modern market economy, nor would they have produced anything resembling contemporary levels of prosperity. But they could have accelerated the transition away from pure subsistence, reduced the volatility of crises, and created more space for human agency. Most importantly for this book's argument, they illustrate that leadership behavior responds to incentives. When leaders are rewarded for narrow, short-term extraction, systems stagnate. When they are rewarded for broad, long-term improvement, systems evolve.

This counterfactual clarifies the central claim of Inclusive Capitalism. Economic systems are not neutral; they are architectures of incentives. In highly centralized systems—whether medieval lordships or contemporary corporations—the incentives of leadership disproportionately determine outcomes. Feudalism organized those incentives around preservation of hierarchy. Inclusive Capitalism seeks to organize them around measurable societal well-being. The failure of feudalism, in this light, was not simply that it was unequal but that it lacked mechanisms to direct leadership power toward the common good.

We return to this theme in the modern context. Just as feudal lords were rewarded for preserving status through extraction rather than expanding opportunity, contemporary corporate leaders are frequently rewarded for extractive short-term financial performance rather than long-term social value. The mechanisms differ, but the incentive logic rhymes. Feudal extraction of surplus from dependent labor finds its modern analogue in platform rent capture, where digital intermediaries appropriate value generated by users, developers, or complementors without proportionate reinvestment in their long-term prosperity. Corvée labor, compulsory and inescapable, is echoed in forms of locked-in digital dependence, where firms and workers become structurally reliant on proprietary platforms, data ecosystems, or algorithmic management systems they cannot meaningfully exit. Manorial immobility, which bound populations to land and lord, reappears today in interoperability barriers that constrain mobility across markets, tools, and networks, reinforcing hierarchy without overt coercion. Inclusive Capitalism proposes that if we wish to change outcomes, we must change the incentives that govern leadership behavior. The feudal epoch thus serves as an early and stark—if dramatic—demonstration of what happens when incentive structures reward control and extraction rather than expansion of opportunity and societal well-being.

Forces That Shaped the Decline and Collapse of Feudalism

Feudalism did not collapse suddenly; it unraveled gradually between the fourteenth and eighteenth centuries under the cumulative weight of demographic shocks, commercial expansion, military transformation, and political centralization. Each of these forces weakened the institutional pillars that had sustained the manorial order for centuries. By the early modern period, the logic of feudalism no longer aligned with the emerging economic and political realities of Europe.

The most dramatic catalyst was demographic. The Black Death (bubonic plague between 1347–1351) is estimated to have decimated between one-third and one-half of Europe's population. Marc Bloch noted that "the sudden demographic collapse caused by the plague upset the traditional balance of feudal obligations, as the scarcity of labor empowered peasants to negotiate better terms or abandon their obligations altogether."[69] With labor now scarce rather than abundant, peasants demanded higher wages, freer tenures, or the right to migrate. Many moved to towns, where alternative livelihoods became increasingly accessible. Lords, unable to maintain their estates under the old model of labor service, shifted toward leasing land to tenant farmers who paid monetary rents. This single development destabilized the core mechanism of feudal extraction: corvée labor.

Economic change reinforced this shift. As towns grew, regional trade revived, and markets expanded during the eleventh through thirteenth centuries, peasants and artisans found avenues for economic mobility unavailable within the confines of the manor. Georges Duby observed that "the commercial revival and the growth of towns offered a real alternative to the manorial economy," drawing labor and talent away from the countryside.[70] Money—rather than land—became increasingly central to economic exchange, allowing rents, taxes, and obligations to be denominated in currency rather than labor. Tenant farming, guild-regulated crafts, and early forms of wage labor gradually eroded the manorial system's autarkic foundations.

The military dimension was equally significant. The feudal order had been built around mounted knights and fortified castles. But the spread of gunpowder, artillery, and professional infantry between the fourteenth and sixteenth centuries rendered these military assets less effective. Norman Cantor explains that "the introduction of gunpowder and new military technologies rendered the heavily armored knight and castle fortresses redundant, leading to the rise of standing armies and centralized control over warfare."[71] With monarchs increasingly reliant on paid soldiers rather than vassals, the military justification for feudal obligation faded.

Parallel to these military changes, political authority consolidated. Centralized monarchies in England, France, and Spain expanded their administrative reach, asserting royal jurisdiction in matters of taxation, justice, and military organization. F. L. Ganshof notes that "the rise of strong centralized monarchies directly challenged the decentralized power structure of feudalism," replacing personal bonds with institutional governance.[72] Legal reforms, including England's Magna Carta (1215), curtailed arbitrary feudal authority and established the principle that rulers themselves were bound by law. The growth of royal courts, standardized procedures, and written law gradually weakened the seigneurial courts that had long adjudicated local disputes.

Social pressures further strained the system. Peasant unrest—including the English Peasants' Revolt of 1381—revealed tensions inherent in a rigid hierarchy. Although such uprisings were swiftly suppressed, Barbara Hanawalt observes that they "demonstrated the growing unwillingness of peasants to accept the harsh restrictions of feudalism."[73] While revolt did not overthrow the system, it signaled that the equilibrium of fear, obligation, and custom had begun to erode.

Taken together, these developments undermined feudalism's fundamental logic. Its virtues—protection, subsistence, local stability—were no longer unique. Centralized states now provided security; towns and markets offered economic alternatives; monetary exchange displaced in-kind obligations; military innovation rendered the knight obsolete; and legal reforms weakened hereditary jurisdiction. The system's liabilities—rigidity, lack of mobility, stagnation—became increasingly untenable in a world where opportunity was expanding elsewhere.

Just as the late medieval world confronted structural pressures that rendered its institutions obsolete, the contemporary American economy faces destabilizing forces driven by rapid technological and demographic change. The diffusion of cloud computing has reduced the marginal cost of computation, accelerating the scale at which firms can grow; social media has altered political communication and social cohesion, amplifying polarization and eroding trust in institutions; and artificial intelligence is beginning to automate increasingly complex forms of judgment and coordination. At the same time, the United States confronts profound demographic shifts: declining birth rates, rising life expectancy, and immigration patterns that introduce both economic vitality and political contention. These forces, taken together, echo the disruptive demographic effects of the feudal epoch—not in mortality but in their ability to reshape labor markets, unsettle long-standing social compacts, and strain institutional capacity.

As in earlier periods of transition, multiple paths are imagined and indeed possible that could include: the entrenchment of dominant digital hierarchies that trigger regulatory fragmentation as states and firms improvise response; a collapse of American capitalism as we know it in the same sense that feudalism became obsolete; or on a more positive path, the emergence of new institutional architectures capable of aligning technological and demographic realities with broad social benefit. Inclusive Capitalism is developed in this book as the most rational alternative—an incentive-aligned framework designed to ensure that the gains from digital production and demographic renewal translate into measurable improvements in societal well-being rather than the reinforcement of structural advantage. The analogy with feudal decline underscores that when profound technological and demographic forces outpace existing institutions, systemic redesign becomes not merely desirable but necessary.

The decline of feudalism was accompanied by gradual improvements in freedom, mobility, and economic choice. These gains were uneven and often fragile, but they marked the beginnings of an economic order no longer organized around scarcity and inherited rank. As constraints loosened, specialization increased, trade expanded, and rudimentary markets for labor and goods emerged. The result was not an immediate transformation but the slow dissolution of a structure that had dominated for centuries.

Feudalism's collapse illustrates a broader argument central to this book: economic systems endure only as long as their institutional incentives align with societal needs. When a system suppresses opportunity, innovation, and mobility, it becomes vulnerable to both internal and external forces of change. The end of feudalism, like the later crises of other economic systems, demonstrates that institutional design—and the incentives it creates for leadership and population—is the ultimate determinant of a system's viability.

Conclusions and Implications for Inclusive Capitalism

Viewed from the standpoint of societal well-being, feudalism delivered only the most basic threshold of material security.[74] It protected rural populations against raiders, preserved subsistence food production, and offered a predictable—if harsh—structure of obligations. But it failed almost entirely to promote innovation, mobility, or improvements in living standards.[75] The overwhelming majority of the population lived and died within a narrow band of opportunity, performing repetitive labor without the realistic prospect of advancement.[76] This stagnation was not incidental; it was structural.[77] The manorial economy, based on subsistence rather than exchange, generated neither the surplus nor the incentives required for sustained progress.[78] Only when political, commercial, and demographic forces loosened the strictures of feudal hierarchy did opportunities for expanded choice and modest economic improvement begin to emerge.[79]

The central lesson of feudalism, and one that echoes across centuries, is the power of incentives in shaping leadership behavior. Lords behaved as the system rewarded them to behave. Their wealth, authority, and security depended on maintaining extraction, suppressing mobility, and preserving inherited hierarchy. Behaviors we now characterize as exploitative or ethically indefensible—corvée labor, jurisdictional coercion, arbitrary taxation—were rational responses to the incentives embedded in the institutional order.[80] Incentives, not morality, governed outcomes. The system's design encouraged stasis, not improvement; extraction, not innovation.[81]

These incentives were not merely powerful—they were self-reinforcing. The leadership class faced profound risks in altering the status quo: greater peasant freedom could threaten rents; technological change could undermine authority; market exchange could reduce dependence on the manor. The rational strategy for a feudal lord was therefore to maintain scarcity wherever possible, whether by limiting peasant autonomy, restricting trade, or discouraging new techniques.[82] Scarcity, in this sense, was manufactured. The result was a society where the majority remained under-motivated and under-incentivized, leading to a near-complete absence of innovation across many generations.[83]

This structural logic did not disappear with feudalism. Variants of the same incentive patterns persisted throughout the evolution of capitalism.[84] As we take you on this exploration of capitalism's evolution in subsequent chapters we reveal persistent structural patterns of leadership incentives that repeatedly favored accumulation, protection of advantage, and the deliberate creation of scarcity in various forms from mercantilist monopolies to the chartered companies of the early modern period, from the trusts of the Gilded Age to today's platform giants.[85] In each epoch, the scale and technology differed, but the underlying behavioral drivers were consistent: when institutional frameworks reward concentration and extraction, leaders will rationally pursue those ends.[86]

Because no society can sustain the long-term consequences of unchecked extraction, countervailing systems emerged. Regulation and oversight is sought and set as policy to constrain undesirable behavior—sometimes effectively, often belatedly.[87] Alternative political-economic systems, most notably socialism and communism, arose in part as reactions to the excesses associated with capitalist leadership incentives and societal consequences. Their historical record demonstrates both the aspirational power of egalitarian ideals and the risks of replacing one concentrated hierarchy with yet another. The oscillation between laissez-faire capitalism and regulatory or collectivist responses has produced the enduring left–right divide that characterizes modern politics.[88] That divide persists because the underlying issue—misaligned incentives at the top of the economic hierarchy—remains unresolved.

A further lesson emerges from how societies respond to instability: periods of uncertainty often produce a retreat toward local institutions and familiar forms of authority.[89] In the feudal age, insecurity led communities to rely on manorial structures and localized protection rather than distant central powers. The instinct persists in the modern world. Economic dislocation, technological disruption, and geopolitical anxiety have fueled renewed skepticism toward global institutions and international exchange, encouraging inward-looking policies such as tariffs, supply-chain retrenchment, and the elevation of local identities over broader civic or national frameworks.[90] While such responses can offer psychological reassurance and short-term stability, they rarely sustain long-term prosperity.[91] Inclusive Capitalism therefore must incorporate institutions capable of operating at scale—particularly in domains such as technology, standards, and global coordination—while maintaining the legitimacy and trust that local institutions often command.[92] The challenge is not to reject scale but to design it in a way that aligns with societal well-being rather than competing with it.

A final lesson follows from the long arc of feudalism's rise and decline: economic and legislative frameworks are not fixed, objective structures; they are but contingent responses to underlying material, demographic, and geopolitical conditions. Feudalism endured only so long as the demographic, technological, and military realities of its age supported its logic.[93] When those realities changed, its institutional structure proved brittle. A well-designed economic system must therefore do more than align incentives at a moment in time; it must be capable of adapting to structural shifts in population, technology, resource availability, and global interdependence.

Observing today's digital and financial economy reveals familiar structural patterns, as it increasingly reproduces several features that are distinctly feudal in character.[94] Leadership incentives remain tied overwhelmingly to quarterly earnings and share price, encouraging behaviors that rationally prioritize short-term financial gain over long-term societal well-being.[95] Scarcity is again manufactured—not through corvée labor but through proprietary standards, barriers to interoperability, pricing strategies in pharmaceuticals, and intellectual property regimes that restrict diffusion of innovations with near-zero marginal cost.[96] As in the feudal world, these patterns eventually generate disengagement, loss of trust, and periodic popular backlash.[97]

Inclusive Capitalism begins from the recognition that these incentive structures cannot be reformed at the margins. They must be redesigned.[98] An economic architecture that aligns leadership rewards with measurable societal well-being is not merely ethically appealing; it is pragmatically necessary for creating a stable and prosperous society.[99]

That is the goal of this book and the companion volume. Book One examines how leadership incentives shaped each major epoch of economic history, revealing recurring patterns of behavior and institutional failure.[100] Book Two proposes the specific mechanisms—governance, metrics, incentive structures, charter redesign, and currency refactoring—through which Inclusive Capitalism can realign leadership behavior with societal well-being.[101]

In the next chapter, we turn to mercantilism. Mercantilism inherits feudal extraction logic but replaces landed hierarchy with state-sanctioned monopoly. In this sense, mercantilism does not resolve feudal incentive failure—it repackages it at state scale.[102]

Notes

1 Bloch, Marc. *Feudal Society*, Translated by L. A. Manyon. 2 vols. Chicago: University of Chicago Press, 1961. 18–25.

2 Tawney, R. H. *Religion and the Rise of Capitalism*. New York: Harcourt, Brace & World, 1926. 15–18.

3 Bloch, Marc. *Feudal Society*, 34–36.

4 Bloch, Marc. *Feudal Society*, 52.

5 Cantor, Norman F. *The Civilization of the Middle Ages*. New York: Harper Perennial, 1993. 142–145.

6 Ganshof, François Louis. *Feudalism*. Translated by Philip Grierson. Toronto: University of Toronto Press, 1964. 27–33.
7 Dalio, Ray. *Principles for Dealing with the Changing World Order: Why Nations Succeed and Fail*. New York: Avid Reader Press, 2021. 49–78.
8 Greenspan, *The Map and the Territory*, 115–118.
9 Bloch, Marc. Feudal Society, 18–25.
10 Tawney, R. H. *Religion and the Rise of Capitalism*, 15–18.
11 Ganshof, François Louis. *Feudalism*, 27–33.
12 White, Lynn, Jr. *Medieval Technology and Social Change*. Oxford: Oxford University Press, 1962. 41–52.
13 Ibid.
14 Ganshof, François Louis. *Feudalism*, 27–33.
15 Reynolds, Susan. *Fiefs and Vassals: The Medieval Evidence Reinterpreted*. Oxford: Oxford University Press, 1994. 112–118.
16 Bloch, Marc. Feudal Society, 57.
17 Cantor, *The Civilization of the Middle Ages*, 139–142.
18 Ganshof, François Louis. *Feudalism*, 34–39.
19 Bloch, Marc. *Feudal Society*, 18–25.
20 Guizot, François. *The History of Civilization in Europe*. Translated by William Hazlitt. London: Penguin Classics, 1997. 54.
21 Bloch, Marc. Feudal Society, 18–25.
22 Tawney, R. H. *Religion and the Rise of Capitalism*, 15–18.
23 Dalio, Ray. *Principles for Dealing with the Changing World Order*, 49–78.
24 Bloch, Marc. *Feudal Society*, 34–36.
25 Bloch, 52.
26 Cantor, Norman F. *The Civilization of the Middle Ages*, 142–145.
27 Ganshof, François Louis. *Feudalism*, 27–33.
28 Duby, Georges. *Early Growth of the European Economy: Warriors and Peasants from the Seventh to the Twelfth Century*. Ithaca, NY: Cornell University Press, 1974. 38.
29 Braudel, Fernand. *A History of Civilizations*. New York: Penguin Books, 1995. 178.
30 Le Goff, Jacques. *Medieval Civilization, 400–1500*. Oxford: Blackwell, 1988. 102–109.
31 Bloch, Marc. *Feudal Society*, 18–25.
32 Smith, Adam. *An Inquiry into the Nature and Causes of the Wealth of Nations*. Indianapolis: Liberty Fund, 1981. *The Wealth of Nations*, 78.
33 Marx, Karl. *Capital: A Critique of Political Economy*. Vol. 1. New York: Penguin Classics, 1990. 876–880.
34 Smith, Adam. *The Wealth of Nations*, 78.
35 Smith, 135–136.
36 Bloch, Marc. *Feudal Society*, 246–250.
37 Bloch, Marc. *Feudal Society*, 18–25.
38 Guizot, François. *History of Civilization in Europe*, 54.
39 Duby, Georges. *Early Growth of the European Economy*, 38.
40 Bloch, Marc. *Feudal Society*, 246–250.
41 Duby, Georges. *Rural Economy and Country Life in the Medieval West*. Columbia: University of South Carolina Press, 1968. 87–91.
42 Hanawalt, Barbara A. *The Ties That Bound: Peasant Families in Medieval England*. New York: Oxford University Press, 1986. 44–47.
43 Le Goff, Jacques. *Medieval Civilization*, 102–109.
44 Cantor, Norman F. *The Civilization of the Middle Ages*, 199–203.

45 Rodrik, Dani. *Economics Rules: The Rights and Wrongs of the Dismal Science.* New York: W. W. Norton & Company, 2015. 12–14.
46 Duby, Georges. *Early Growth of the European Economy,* 41–43.
47 Hyams, Paul R. *Rancor and Reconciliation in Medieval England.* Ithaca, NY: Cornell University Press, 2003. 201–206.
48 Bloch, Marc. *Feudal Society,* 77–80.
49 Bloch, 246–250.
50 Hanawalt, Barbara A. *The Ties That Bound,* 44–47.
51 Hanawalt, Barbara A. *The Ties That Bound,* 213–218.
52 Bloch, Marc. *Feudal Society,* 232–235.
53 Hyams, Paul R. *Rancor and Reconciliation,* 201–206.
54 Bloch, *Feudal Society,* 246–250.
55 Duby, Georges. *Rural Economy and Country Life,* 87–91.
56 Smith, Adam. *The Wealth of Nations,* 135–136.
57 Le Goff, Jacques. *Medieval Civilization,* 102–109.
58 Ibid.
59 Cantor, Norman F. *The Civilization of the Middle Ages,* 278–281.
60 Duby, Georges. *Early Growth of the European Economy,* 41–43.
61 Duby, Georges. *Early Growth of the European Economy,* 38.
62 Bloch, Marc. *Feudal Society,* 246–250.
63 Braudel, Fernand. *A History of Civilizations,* 178.
64 Bloch, Marc. Feudal Society, 255.
65 Sowell, Thomas. *Wealth, Poverty and Politics: An International Perspective.* New York: Basic Books, 2015. 44–46.
66 Duby, Georges. *Early Growth of the European Economy,* 41–43.
67 Cantor, Norman F. *The Civilization of the Middle Ages,* 199–203.
68 Bloch, Marc. *Feudal Society,* 232–235.
69 Bloch, Marc. *Feudal Society,* 77–80.
70 Duby, Georges. *Rural Economy and Country Life,* 112–116.
71 Cantor, Norman F. *The Civilization of the Middle Ages,* 278–281.
72 Ganshof, François Louis. *Feudalism,* 61–65.
73 Hanawalt, Barbara A. *The Ties That Bound,* 213–218.
74 Bloch, Marc. *Feudal Society,* 18–25.
75 Bloch, Marc. *Feudal Society,* 34–36.
76 Hanawalt, Barbara A. *The Ties That Bound,* 44–47.
77 Ganshof, François Louis. *Feudalism,* 27–33.
78 Duby, Georges. *Rural Economy and Country Life,* 87–91.
79 Duby, Georges. *Early Growth of the European Economy,* 38.
80 Duby, Georges. *Rural Economy and Country Life,* 87–91.
81 Ganshof, François Louis. *Feudalism,* 27–33.
82 Bloch, Marc. *Feudal Society,* 255.
83 Duby, Georges. *Early Growth of the European Economy,* 41–43.
84 Dalio, Ray. *Principles for Dealing with the Changing World Order,* 49–78.
85 Sowell, Thomas. *Wealth, Poverty and Politics,* 44–46.
86 Bloch, Marc. *Feudal Society,* 246–250.
87 Rodrik, Dani. *The Tyranny of Partisanship.* Project Syndicate, January 2017. 2–3.
88 Rodrik, Dani. *Economics Rules,* 12–14.
89 Guizot, François. *History of Civilization in Europe,* 54.
90 Rodrik, Dani. *The Tyranny of Partisanship.* 2–3.

91 Sowell, Thomas. *Wealth, Poverty and Politics*, 44–46.
92 Dalio, Ray. *Principles for Dealing with the Changing World Order*, 49–78.
93 Bloch, Marc. *Feudal Society*, 232–235.
94 Sowell, Thomas. *Wealth, Poverty and Politics*, 44–46.
95 Bloch, Marc. *Feudal Society*, 246–250.
96 White, *Medieval Technology and Social Change*, 41–52.
97 Rodrik, Dani. *Economics Rules*, 12–14.
98 Bloch, Marc. *Feudal Society*, 246–250.
99 Smith, Adam. *The Wealth of Nations*, 78.
100 Dalio, Ray. *Principles for Dealing with the Changing World Order*, 49–78.
101 Rodrik, Dani. *Economics Rules*, 12–14.
102 Guizot, François. *History of Civilization in Europe*, 54.

2 Mercantilism: The Cornerstone of Capitalism

This chapter examines mercantilism as a critical transitional architecture in the evolution of modern economic systems.[1] Mercantilism matters not merely as a historical episode but because it serves three distinct conceptual roles in the analytical framework of this book:

1. It represents the earliest large-scale attempt to deliberately design an economy at the level of the state, aligning commerce, power, and national strategy through centralized incentives.[2]
2. It stands as the immediate predecessor—and intellectual foil—to Smithian capitalism, shaping the conditions against which Adam Smith formulated his critique of trade, monopoly, and state privilege.[3]
3. Mercantilism marks the origin point of several incentive pathologies that persist today in modified form: monopoly protection, extraction over value creation, and the strategic manufacture of scarcity.[4]

Understanding mercantilism is therefore essential not only to understanding capitalism's emergence but to diagnosing why certain failures recur as economies scale and why incentive design, rather than ideology, determines long-term outcomes.[5]

Mercantilism represents the second great pre-capitalist system through which we can observe economic behavior before economics existed as a formal discipline.[6] As with feudalism, its value to our analysis lies in its pre-theoretical character. Mercantilism did not arise from abstract models, economic axioms, or ideological commitments—there was no capitalism, socialism, communism, "left," "right," or "market theory" in any recognizable modern form. Rather, mercantilism emerged organically from the practical concerns of early modern states: how to secure power, accumulate wealth, manage trade, finance war, and govern increasingly complex societies.[7] It was an empirical system without a formal science, shaped by monarchs, merchants, and military necessity rather than by economists.[8] This makes mercantilism uniquely instructive for understanding how economic structures evolve under pressure and how incentives—long before Smith or Marx—shape national behavior.[9]

Where feudalism was local, defensive, and agrarian, mercantilism was global, expansionist, and state-directed.[10] It marked a profound shift from decentralized subsistence economies to that of centralized national economies capable of fielding armies, projecting power overseas, and organizing trade on a scale previously unimaginable. Monarchs sought not security through local bonds but supremacy through wealth accumulation, naval dominance, and colonial expansion. This transition—from protecting the manor to conquering the world—fundamentally reshaped the nature of economic organization. The early modern world became a competitive system of states, each vying for limited resources in what they saw as a zero-sum struggle for survival.[11]

 | https://doi.org/10.1515/9783112235485-003

Mercantilism can be best understood as the cornerstone upon which capitalism was built. Adam Smith did not develop *The Wealth of Nations* in a vacuum; he wrote in direct reaction to the distortions, inefficiencies, and moral hazards that mercantilist policies produced at scale.[12] Smithian capitalism emerged as a critique of mercantilist monopolies, of trade restrictions, of state favoritism, of zero-sum assumptions, and of the concentration of economic power in royal charters and privileged firms.[13] The very architecture of capitalism—competition, free trade, decentralized market signals, and the invisible hand—was constructed as an intellectual and practical antidote to mercantilism's excesses.[14] To understand capitalism's design, we must begin with the system it was designed to replace. Similarly, to design Inclusive Capitalism, we must begin with the systems it is designed to refine.

Before analyzing the capitalist predecessor system, mercantilism, it is important to note that economic systems, as they have unfolded across history, are far less the product of deliberate design than of reaction—each new system emerging as a corrective to the failures of the one that came before it.[15] Feudalism arose from the collapse of imperial order; mercantilism emerged as a response to feudal fragmentation; capitalism was constructed explicitly to remedy the distortions of mercantilist monopoly; socialism took shape as a critique of capitalism's inequities; and for more than a century, capitalism and socialism have continued to oscillate in what might fairly be called "pingpongonomics"—each side reacting to the excesses of the other without resolving the structural flaws at the core. Inclusive Capitalism departs from this reactive lineage. Rather than serving as a counterpunch to any single system, it steps back from the entire historical arc, evaluates what worked and what failed across all prior models, and proposes a forward-looking, normative framework—one in which the aggregate math of societal well-being, incentives, scale, and long-term stability finally aligns.[16]

Mercantilism is not merely a historical curiosity. Its core tendencies—centralization of power, reliance on scale, state-directed industrial policy, suspicion of foreign competitors, and the fusion of economic and military strategy—remain deeply embedded in the economic practices of the twenty-first century.[17] Tariffs, industrial subsidies, strategic resource controls, and great-power competition all reflect what might be called mercantilist persistence.[18] Even the modern digital economy—dominated by global platforms, protected markets, and strategic control of data—has mercantilist undertones. By studying mercantilism, we are not just looking backward; we are diagnosing living patterns that still shape today's world economy.[19]

Distinctly, this chapter examines mercantilism both as a historical system and as a transitional phase defining capitalism's emergence. We analyze how the consolidation of state power, the rise of global trade, and the pressures of interstate conflict produced new incentive structures that prized accumulation, conquest, and control.[20] We assess how monarchs engineered national policies to maximize wealth, how chartered corporations like the British and Dutch East India Companies institutionalized monopoly power, and how these structures influenced the development of markets, labor, and technology.[21] As in the feudalism chapter, we trace how industrial leadership behavior aligned—or failed to align—with societal well-being, and how the incentives of the era produced both innovation and exclusion.[22]

Finally, we draw from mercantilism lessons that carry forward into our analysis of capitalism's evolution and its contemporary unintended consequences. Mercantilism teaches that scale without moral guardrails concentrates power; that state-favored institutions tend toward extractive rent-seeking; that economic systems built on scarcity logic perpetuate zero-sum thinking; and that incentive structures—more than ideology—shape outcomes.[23] By grounding our analysis in mercantilism, we establish the bridge from pre-capitalist systems to the world that Adam Smith sought to reform—and to the world that Inclusive Capitalism seeks to repair.[24]

Mercantilism Defined

Mercantilism addressed the fundamental questions of production, distribution, and wealth by focusing on state power, trade, and the accumulation of national resources.[25] From the sixteenth to the eighteenth centuries, it shaped the social, legal, commercial, and military institutions of Europe. Mercantilists viewed wealth—especially gold and silver—as limited and largely fixed. In this worldview, economic success could only be achieved at another nation's expense. As Eli Heckscher summarized, "the fundamental principle of mercantilism is that wealth is indeed finite; thus, for one nation to become wealthy, others must become poorer."[26] This zero-sum logic led states to prioritize controlled trade, a favorable balance of exports over imports, and the stockpiling of precious metals as the basis of security and strength.[27]

Although mercantilism and modern capitalism are often portrayed as opposites—one rooted in state control, the other in market freedom—they share a deeper structural assumption that has proved remarkably durable: the belief that economic gain is fundamentally constrained by scarcity.[28] Mercantilism treated wealth as fixed, a zero-sum contest over limited stores of gold and silver. Capitalism rejected the bullion model but quietly inherited the same foundational logic in the form of manufactured scarcity—artificial limits on knowledge, technology, and access that sustain profits by restricting abundance.[29] Fast-forward from the mercantilist era to the present, and the parallel is not rhetorical but structural. In industries where marginal costs approach zero—software, digital media, and increasingly biotechnology—firms often pursue strategies that deliberately preserve scarcity through control of platforms, data, standards, or distribution.[30] This behavior reflects an inherited mercantilist logic: value is protected not by expanding production or access but by restricting entry and mobility. The result is a systematic misalignment of incentives, in which economic energy is diverted away from innovation and toward gatekeeping, rent capture, and the defense of position rather than the creation of new societal value.

Inclusive Capitalism breaks from this lineage by proposing institutions, metrics, and incentive structures designed to reward the proliferation rather than the restriction of near-zero-cost goods and services.[31] By shifting from fixed-sum logic to abundance logic in large segments of the economy, Inclusive Capitalism seeks to convert one of capitalism's deepest inherited constraints into a generative force for societal well-being.[32]

Societal well-being was certainly not an agenda item in the mercantilist epoch. Thomas Mun, director of the British East India Company, articulated the mercantilist logic in *The Treasure of Foreign Trade* (1623), arguing that a nation must "sell more to strangers yearly than we consume of theirs in value."[33] Joshua Child, writing in *A Discourse of Trade* (1668), similarly advocated for tariffs to protect domestic industries.[34] Although Adam Smith and the classical economists later rejected these doctrines in favor of free trade, mercantilist-style tariffs continue in modern policy debates, including the United States' early twenty-first-century trade practices.[35] The logic is not identical, but the resonance is clear: states still turn to trade barriers, industrial policy, and strategic subsidies when global competition intensifies.[36]

The mercantilist era also linked economic strategy directly to national defense.[37] A strong navy, fortified trade routes, and colonial extraction were considered essential to maintaining national wealth. England's Navigation Acts (1651–1849) required colonial goods to be shipped on English vessels, limited exports to England, and required goods bound for the colonies to pass through English ports.[38] In France, Jean-Baptiste Colbert's economic program under Louis XIV used high tariffs, strategic subsidies, and colonial expansion to promote national self-sufficiency and strengthen the monarchy's fiscal foundation.[39]

Mercantilism further relied on exclusive trade monopolies and state-chartered enterprises.[40] Companies such as the British East India Company (1600) and the Dutch East India Company (1602) were granted sweeping privileges, including monopolies over vast regions, the right to raise armies, and authority to make treaties.[41] These entities were not merely commercial firms; they were extensions of state power. Spain's extraction of gold and silver from the Americas stands as another vivid example of how mercantilist aims drove imperial expansion.[42] As Heckscher observed, "the search for gold and silver led to the conquest of vast territories, and the colonial system developed as a logical extension of mercantilist theory" (1935).[43]

In this framework, economic leadership became inseparable from state ambition. Wealth accumulation served war-making capacity. Trade served national survival. Colonies served metropolitan industry.[44] Mercantilism thus offered both a coherent economic worldview and a powerful set of incentives that shaped the emergence of capitalism and continue to reappear, in altered form, wherever economic power is exercised through gatekeeping, protection, and the preservation of advantage rather than through open competition and innovation.[45]

Emergence of Mercantilism

Like feudalism and other early economic forms, mercantilism did not appear suddenly or with a clear boundary. It emerged gradually out of longstanding debates on trade, justice, property, and governance. Long before economics became a formal discipline in the eighteenth century, societies had already grappled with core economic questions. Hammurabi's Code (c. 1754 BCE) established rules for trade, contracts, wages, and debt.[46] The Instruction of Amenemope (c. 1100 BCE) reflected early moral reasoning about wealth and responsibility. Kautilya's *Arthashastra* (c. 600–400 BCE) provided an extensive analysis of taxation, agricultural management, labor, and the state's economic role.[47] Confucius emphasized moral governance and productivity; Plato explored the ideal organization of labor; Aristotle distinguished between natural and unnatural forms of wealth, anticipating debates revived by Marx two millennia later.[48] Roman legal texts codified trade, property, and contract law. While not "economics" in the modern sense, these works formed an intellectual substrate that later thinkers would build upon.[49]

By the late medieval period, the local, defensive, and highly fragmented world of feudalism no longer aligned with Europe's geopolitical and technological realities. The shift to mercantilism was driven in large part by the rise of strong centralized monarchies in England, France, and Spain. As Charles Wilson wrote, "the rise of strong, centralized monarchies . . . facilitated the conditions necessary for mercantilism to flourish."[50] These emerging states needed revenue and administrative capacity to consolidate domestic authority and project power abroad. The local, manorial economies of feudalism could not supply the scale required for interstate warfare, imperial competition, or the maintenance of national institutions.[51]

Interstate conflict—in the Anglo-Dutch wars, the Franco-Spanish rivalry, and numerous other contests—transformed the nature of economic necessity. Wealth accumulation became closely associated with military power, a relationship that endures in modern systems where economic resources continue to shape coercive and strategic capacity. Paul Kennedy later described mercantilism as "a strategy to enhance a state's wealth and military might, ensuring its survival in an intensely competitive international system."[52] This environment also produced an intense desire for national self-sufficiency. Colbert captured this ethos: "Manufacturing and exporting goods within the kingdom is the best way to keep the gold within."[53] Producing domestically and exporting aggressively were interpreted as acts of national preservation.[54]

The broader geopolitical context accelerated this transition. The discovery of the Americas and new sea routes to Asia unlocked global markets and triggered early globalization. Historian Jacob Viner observed that "the emergence of mercantilism coincided with the age of discovery," and that European states quickly adapted their institutions to exploit new opportunities in trade, extraction, and territorial control.[55] Colonies became sources of raw materials and captive markets for manufactured goods; navies became indispensable tools of commerce; and wealth accumulation became an imperial imperative.[56]

Technological and organizational factors reinforced the shift. Where feudalism operated through personal loyalty and local obligation, mercantilism required centralized bureaucracies, long-distance logistics, standardized currencies, and large-scale enterprises.[57] State-chartered trading companies provided early templates for modern multinational corporations. Their leadership, driven by incentives that combined profit, privilege, and geopolitical ambition, foreshadowed many of the patterns later seen in industrial capitalism, the Gilded Age, and the technology giants of the twenty-first century.[58]

Scale—political, economic, and administrative—was both the defining advantage and the defining danger of mercantilist systems. Scale enabled innovation, resource accumulation, and structural efficiency. But it also fostered exclusion, exploitation, and concentrated power.[59] As we will explore throughout this book, the tension between the benefits of scale and its social costs remains unresolved, even today. The leadership of the Dutch East India Company, the industrialists of the nineteenth century, and many contemporary corporate leaders all operate within incentive structures shaped by scale. These structures can spur growth, but they can also produce significant societal harm when not properly aligned.[60]

In this sense, mercantilism represents a critical turning point. It moved Europe from a world of local subsistence and defensive organization into an era of global competition, centralized authority, and economic institutions capable of mobilizing vast resources.[61] At the same time, it introduced new forms of inequality, exclusion, and extraction that would later provoke both the rise of classical capitalism and the critiques of socialism.[62] Understanding its emergence is therefore essential to understanding the roots of modern economic behavior and the need for a normative, incentive aligned system such as Inclusive Capitalism.

Mercantilist Incentives and Industrial Leader Behavior

Leadership under mercantilism operated within an incentive structure fundamentally different from feudalism, yet deeply familiar to modern readers. Where feudal lords inherited authority and extracted value through position, mercantilist merchants earned authority through participation in a rapidly expanding market system. The transition from serfdom to commerce created, for the first time in centuries, genuine—though uneven—paths for upward mobility.[63] It was good to be a merchant in 1600, and the structures that made it good back then continue to shape leadership behavior today.[64]

At its core, mercantilism rewarded initiative, capital formation, risk-taking, and the cultivation of networks. But it did so within a system defined by state privilege, controlled access, and zero-sum competition for fixed pools of wealth.[65] This mixture of opportunity and exclusivity produced a leadership class whose incentives bear striking resemblance to today's industrial leaders: pursue scale, protect advantage, manage risk aggressively, and align with the state when necessary to secure privileged access.[66]

The first route into the merchant class was birthright. Merchant families—like the Medici in Florence—passed down capital, relationships, and commercial knowledge across generations.[67] Their heirs enjoyed structural advantages resembling those of today's dynastic business families. Opportunity existed, but its distribution was neither equal nor fair, and that tension has persisted across all eras of capitalism.[68]

A second path to merchant leadership ran through access to capital. Overseas trade required ships, crews, insurance, inventories, and the capacity to absorb loss—constraints that sharply limited participation. In this respect, early commercial capitalism closely resembles modern technology entrepreneurship, where entry depends on access to hardware, software, regulatory clearance, and scale. Investors, wealthy families, and early joint-stock companies functioned as the venture capital ecosystem of the era, determining which ventures could be launched and which ideas could be realized.[69] The logic was identical to that of contemporary startup economies: those who controlled capital controlled opportunity.[70]

Over time, this dynamic enabled the emergence of durable financial dynasties whose influence extended across generations. Families such as the Rothschilds did not merely accumulate wealth; they built informational networks, credit systems, and political relationships that allowed capital to move faster and more reliably than states themselves. Their longevity illustrates a core continuity in economic systems: when access to capital compounds across generations, leadership becomes path-dependent, and opportunity concentrates unless counterbalanced by institutional design.[71]

A third path ran through skills and apprenticeship. Young men—far more rarely women—entered guilds or apprenticed under established traders to learn bookkeeping, negotiation, accounting, logistics, and languages.[72] This was the mercantilist equivalent of the MBA. Merchants who mastered these skills could navigate complex trade networks, arbitrage regional prices, and manage information flows across continents.[73]

A fourth and decisive route involved networks—social, religious, political, and ethnic. Sephardic Jews leveraged Diaspora networks; Armenians built linguistic bridges; Jesuit ties facilitated Catholic commercial reach.[74] Connections to the state were especially valuable. Trading licenses, monopolies, and chartered companies were granted at royal discretion. Those who aligned with the crown gained access unavailable to ordinary merchants.[75]

Together, these pathways created a leadership class centered on access, networks, scale, and political alignment. These incentives—not unlike those shaping tech founders, financial executives, and multinational CEOs—encouraged behaviors rational for merchants but often could be destabilizing for society.[76] The merchant pursued scale because scale amplified returns; exclusivity because exclusivity suppressed competition; and state favor because it secured monopoly rents.[77]

The rewards for successful merchants were substantial. Wealth from long-distance trade elevated merchants into the rising bourgeoisie. They entered governance, funded civic institutions, and sometimes ascended into nobility.[78] Their lives were cosmopolitan—managing warehouses, negotiating contracts, traveling across continents, and maintaining relationships among bankers, captains, and diplomats.[79]

Yet the risks were equally formidable. Ships sank; pirates raided; prices collapsed; monopolies excluded smaller entrants; state policies shifted; wars disrupted supply lines.[80] Merchants relied on insurance, diversification, partnerships, and hedging strategies resembling modern financial engineering.[81] They also faced profound ethical dilemmas—particularly those engaged in the slave trade, colonial extraction, and exploitation of indigenous labor.[82]

The parallels to modern capitalism are direct. The biotech founder whose decade of research collapses faces the same existential shock as the merchant whose ship goes down in a storm.[83] The semiconductor firm confronting IP theft faces a threat as severe as piracy at sea. The startup competing against entrenched incumbents confronts barriers reminiscent of mercantilist-era monopolies.[84]

Changing this long arc of leadership behavior is one of the greatest challenges for Inclusive Capitalism. The incentives shaping seventeenth-century merchants—and capitalist leaders across later centuries—are foundational behavioral patterns built into systems of scarcity and positional advantage. To replace them with incentives that reward contribution, collaboration, broad opportunity, and long-term societal well-being requires altering perceived self-interest at the top.

The essential purpose of this book series is to make that case.

The day-to-day experience of the merchant involved operational oversight, financial management, political navigation, and interpersonal diplomacy.[85] Merchants supervised warehouses, negotiated with suppliers, arranged shipments, and inspected cargo.[86] Bookkeeping consumed large parts of the day—tracking inventories, managing accounts, forecasting profits, and complying with expanding domestic and international regulations.[87]

Merchants lived itinerant lives, traveling between Amsterdam, London, Lisbon, Antwerp, and Venice. Social capital—cultivated through correspondence, dinners, religious ties, marriages, or diplomacy—was essential for accessing markets, securing protection, and obtaining credit.[88] Political engagement was purposeful and central in life. States shaped trade through tariffs, monopolies, naval protection, and colonial charters.[89] Merchants petitioned courts, navigated bureaucracies, and sought exemptions or guild positions. Lobbying existed long before the word did.[90]

The mercantilist world was volatile. Wars, blockades, diplomatic disputes, shifting royal succession, and commodity discoveries constantly reshaped trade patterns.[91] Prices could collapse overnight; cargoes spoiled; ships were lost. Merchants became early masters of risk assessment, risk management, and mitigation through contingency planning.[92] These pressures entrenched leadership tendencies—information asymmetry, secrecy, scarcity management, and competitive defense—still visible in modern capitalism.[93] Founders and CEOs today face different technologies but the same structural incentives.

The mercantilist era established three essential building blocks of capitalist leadership: market orientation, scale, and incentives. Merchants served markets, not lords; aligned production to demand; and operated under incentives rewarding efficiency, initiative, and innovation.[94]

Inclusive Capitalism seeks to retain these virtues while redesigning the incentive architecture so that access, opportunity, and rewards do not depend disproportionately on birthright, capital endowment, privileged networks, or political capture.[95] Mercantilism reveals the origins of capitalism's dynamism and its inequities. To preserve the former, its dynamism, while resolving the latter, its inequities, requires acknowledging mercantilism's central lesson: incentives shape behavior and institutions shape incentives.[96] These incentive structures did not disappear; they mutated. Capitalism inherits mercantilist incentive logic minus formal state charters but plus market legitimization.

Lived Experience of the Population in the Mercantilist Epoch

For all its dynamism and upward mobility for a select few, mercantilism rested on a foundation of profound inequality and widespread human suffering.[97] It is easy, from a distance, to focus on the spectacular gains: global trade routes, early industrial specialization, soaring wealth for merchants and monarchs. But beneath these visible successes lay a rigid and extractive system that imposed structurally debilitating costs on those whose labor and land financed the empire-building ambitions of European states.[98]

For the vast majority of people within Europe, life under mercantilism bore an uncomfortable resemblance to life under feudalism. Agricultural production was subordinated not to local needs but to the strategic ambitions of the crown and the profit motives of the merchant elite. Farms were increasingly converted into monocultures dedicated to export crops, depriving local communities of the balanced food production they needed to survive. Peasants were pushed into debt, dispossession, or dependence as state policies prioritized gold inflows over human sustenance. Colbert's France provides an archetype: the king's coffers filled as rural peasants sank deeper into poverty. "The sweat of a French peasant helped to enrich the king," one historian noted, "but left the peasant and his family in rags."[99] It is difficult to argue that the average peasant in a mercantilist economy was markedly better off than a serf in the feudal world he had ostensibly left behind.[100]

If life for Europe's working poor was harsh, life in Europe's colonies was catastrophic. Mercantilism transformed entire continents into extraction zones. As Robert

DuPlessis observed, "Colonial peasants and laborers were reduced to the role of producers of raw materials, their lives dictated by the demands of far-off markets they would never benefit from."[101] Sugar, tobacco, cotton, gold, and silver flowed into Europe—while hunger, disease, and forced labor were left behind. Colonial economies were constrained and more often explicitly prevented from industrializing or diversifying, locking them into a perpetual dependence engineered for the sole benefit of the colonizing power. Charles Wilson captured this systemic cruelty starkly: "Under mercantilism, the colonies existed solely to serve the mother country's interests."[102]

Nowhere was the brutality of mercantilist extraction more visible than in the transatlantic slave trade. The mercantilist obsession with high-value commodities—sugar for one—created a demand for labor so immense that it spawned one of the largest forced migrations in human history. Millions of Africans were forcibly taken – essentially kidnapped, shipped across the Atlantic in horrific conditions, and coerced into labor regimes whose brutality defies modern comprehension. Eric Williams famously argued that "the rise of mercantilism and the transatlantic trade in slaves were symbiotic,"[103] with European wealth accumulating as African lives were destroyed. The sugar fortunes of London and Amsterdam were built on blood.[104]

Even within Europe's cities, mercantilism imposed heavy costs. While some artisans found modest opportunities in state-subsidized industries, many more found their livelihoods suffocated by rigid guild structures, state monopolies, and protectionist policies. Innovation was constrained by government fiat. Skilled workers who attempted to break into regulated industries often faced insurmountable barriers. Fernand Braudel's judgment is succinct: "The guild system preserved tradition—but stifled progress."[105]

Government control permeated daily life. Tariffs and monopolies dictated which goods could be bought or sold and at what prices. Smuggling became a necessity for survival among poorer populations. Ordinary consumers routinely paid inflated prices as monarchs protected favored industries and wealthy trading firms. As Jacob Viner argued, "The pursuit of national wealth led to high tariffs, raising prices for ordinary consumers."[106] State intervention was omnipresent—yet its benefits flowed overwhelmingly upward.

When judged across all social strata, mercantilism created a bifurcated society: a smallish circle of monarchs, merchants, and military officers accrued extraordinary wealth, power, and global reach; everyone else—peasants, laborers, slaves, colonized peoples—paid the price. Far from being a system of shared prosperity, mercantilism institutionalized exploitation on a global scale. It replaced the feudal manor with the global empire, the serf with the colonial subject, the lord with the merchant-adventurer backed by the state. The result was progress but progress purchased at staggering human cost.[107]

Evaluation of Mercantilism – What Worked, What Did Not

With this glimpse into daily life under mercantilism, we can now turn to a macro-level analysis—examining what functioned effectively, what failed, and why the system ultimately declined, even as several of its defining characteristics persist in modified form today. Relative to feudalism and earlier forms of economic organization, mercantilism represents an unmistakable inflection point in human progress. It created national economies where fragmented local markets once stood; it enabled the first sustained period of global trade; and it placed Europe on a trajectory toward industrial capitalism.[108] Unless one argues that stagnation at a lower baseline is preferable, the gains under mercantilism were extraordinary.

Yet as the logic of Inclusive Capitalism urges, we must also ask the counterfactual question: Could these gains have been achieved in a more inclusive, sustainable, and less destructive manner? To answer that question, we must examine the strengths and weaknesses of mercantilism with clear eyes—and connect them to their modern manifestations.

Mercantilism contributed powerfully to the economic stability and geopolitical influence of the major European powers. By prioritizing the accumulation of precious metals, maintaining strict oversight of trade, and pursuing national self-sufficiency, mercantilist states established predictable economic frameworks that reduced uncertainty and enabled long-term planning.[109] Bullionism—the belief that wealth resided in gold and silver—allowed governments to fund wars, infrastructure, and colonial administration without relying excessively on debt. Spain's immense silver inflows from the Americas financed an empire; England's growing reserves underpinned the rise of London as a financial center.[110] Even today, the United States leverages the privileged status of the dollar, both as the primary currency for global trade pricing and as the world's leading reserve currency, to support foreign policy objectives and domestic consumption, though increasingly through debt rather than direct mercantilist accumulation.[111]

Mercantilism also strengthened domestic industries by shielding them from foreign competition. State subsidies, tariffs, and monopolies fostered the growth of nascent manufacturing sectors—textiles, shipbuilding, armaments—that would later form the backbone of industrial capitalism.[112] As with modern debates around industrial policy, these protections delivered both real benefits and real distortions. The Navigation Acts in England ensured that profits flowed back to English shipbuilders and merchants.[113] China's contemporary use of state-owned enterprises (SOEs) similarly blends geopolitical strategy with economic planning, echoing mercantilist practice.[114] Just as the Dutch East India Company and the British East India Company were arms of state strategy, China's COSCO, Sinopec, and State Grid operate today as economic extensions of national ambition.[115] These forms of state-guided capitalism demonstrate that mercantilism is not a historical artifact; its logic remains potent. And as

Inclusive Capitalism emphasizes, the challenge is not to reject what worked but to capture these benefits without the accompanying harms.

Mercantilism enabled colonial expansion on an unprecedented scale. Colonies served as both repositories of raw materials—sugar, cotton, tobacco, minerals—and as captive markets for metropolitan manufacturers. This arrangement generated immense profits. As historian Robert DuPlessis argued, "Colonies were essential cogs in the mercantilist machine."[116] The geopolitical advantages were equally powerful: control of overseas territories provided leverage in war, diplomacy, and global trade.[117]

These benefits mirror modern practices. China's multi-continental Belt and Road Initiative (BRI) functions as a contemporary analog of mercantilist expansion. Through port construction, oil concessions, infrastructure loans, and strategic investments, Chinese SOEs secure influence, access to resources, and geopolitical advantage in ways that parallel European colonial strategies—even if the mechanisms differ in form rather than substance.[118]

Responses to international challenges, such as the neo-mercantilist challenge from China, is beyond the initial scope of Inclusive Capitalism in this, our initial, two book series. That stated, history suggests that the United States cannot out-mercantilist a rising mercantilist power without reproducing the very pathologies it seeks to resist.[119] The more promising strategy is to change the game. Rather than competing over who can impose the tighter web of dependency, the U.S. can lead in building institutions that reward abundance—of energy, information, and capability—over scarcity.[120] Economic innovation—rather than counter-mercantilist imitation—is the United States' most effective response to China's neo-mercantilism.

Mercantilism also promoted national unity by aligning economic activity with state power. Merchants and monarchs shared an overarching mission: enrich the nation and thereby secure its place in a competitive world. This fusion of economic and political identity remains visible today in nationalist economic narratives—from "America First" to China's "dual circulation strategy."[121]

If mercantilism worked so well for national elites and state power, why did it collapse? The answer lies in its core structural flaws—flaws that modern capitalism continues to inherit and embrace. Mercantilism's reliance on monopolies and protected industries produced significant inefficiencies.[122] Barriers to entry prevented competition; guilds blocked new ideas; state privilege insulated firms from market discipline. As Adam Smith observed, mercantilism "diverted a nation's efforts toward sterile accumulation rather than productive activity."[123]

Protectionism enriched producers at the expense of consumers. Domestic goods were often inferior, yet consumers had no access to alternatives due to tariffs and quotas. Smith's criticism that "the interest of the consumer is almost constantly sacrificed to that of the producer"[124] remains relevant today in debates over tariffs, pharmaceutical pricing, broadband monopolies, and platform lock-in.

A central structural flaw of mercantilism lay in its doctrine of bullionism. By treating the accumulation of gold and silver as the primary measure of national success, mercantilist states adopted a top-level metric that was mathematically and economically constrained.[125] Precious metals exist in finite supply, and tying economic vitality to their accumulation imposed a hard ceiling on monetary expansion, credit formation, and real economic growth.[126] Mercantilism did not collapse simply because it was exploitative or coercive but because its optimization target was flawed. An economy cannot sustain expanding production, specialization, and innovation when its primary unit of account and store of value is rigidly scarce.[127] Modern capitalism faces a structurally analogous risk—not because money is finite but because growth is increasingly measured through metrics that tolerate extreme capital concentration while assuming endlessly expanding effective demand.[128]

Mercantilist gains were profoundly uneven. Benefits accrued to monarchs, merchants, and chartered companies. Peasants, artisans, urban workers, and colonized peoples bore the costs—often violently.[129] A theme that becomes increasingly clear in the mercantilist epoch—and that still resonates today—is that whenever economic power concentrates, oversight becomes both a necessity and inevitable. Mercantilism unintentionally created the conditions for early economic regulation, because concentrated privileges produced widespread abuses that only the state itself could correct.[130] Modern capitalism mirrors these dynamics. Whenever platforms, tech giants, pharmaceutical firms, or financial institutions accumulate outsized power, oversight emerges as a political necessity. Regulation is not an ideological choice—it is a structural response to concentrated economic authority.[131]

Mercantilism's strengths—scale, organization, national purpose, investment in strategic capacity—are real and worth preserving. Its weaknesses—zero-sum logic, exclusion, inefficiency, exploitation—are profound and cannot be revived. Inclusive Capitalism seeks what no historical system has achieved: to retain the strengths of mercantilist and capitalist dynamism while eliminating the structural deficiencies embedded in their scarcity-driven incentive architectures.[132] As we will see, abundance-based incentives along with contemporary technologies shift the likelihood of achieving this objective from near impossible in the past to now inevitable. Our goal is to accelerate this process.

The Decline of Mercantilism

Mercantilism began to lose its grip on European political and economic life in the late eighteenth century. Its erosion was not the result of a single event but of converging pressures—technological, ideological, political, and geopolitical—that slowly made the doctrine untenable. Although mercantilist logics endure in modern policy debates, the system as a governing framework became increasingly unsustainable. Understanding why it collapsed is essential, not only for interpreting the rise of capitalism but for recognizing warning signs within contemporary capitalism itself.[133]

The Industrial Revolution delivered the first decisive blow. The rigid, state-managed, zero-sum framework of mercantilism simply could not accommodate the productivity leaps unleashed by mechanization. A textile mill in Manchester, England, could produce more cloth in a week than an entire region had produced in a year. Such scale required larger markets, more flexible supply chains, and a legal environment that rewarded innovation rather than protecting charters and monopolies.[134]

Mercantilist mechanisms—tariffs, quotas, guild restrictions, and politically granted monopolies—were built for a world of scarce production and slow change. Industrial capitalism was built for a world where supply could expand explosively. As economist Robert E. Lucas observed, "The industrial revolution fundamentally altered the conditions of production, rendering the state-centered, protectionist policies of mercantilism increasingly obsolete."[135] Wealth generation now flowed from productivity, not from hoarding bullion or micromanaging trade.

In this sense the decline of mercantilism mirrors a challenge visible in capitalism today: a system designed for one era of production struggles when technology fundamentally alters the scale, speed, and nature of economic output. Just as seventeenth-century institutions could not keep pace with steam, twenty-first-century institutions now struggle to keep pace with digital and agentic AI technologies.[136]

The second major destabilizer was ideological. The emergence of economics as a formal discipline allowed mercantilism, for the first time, to be analyzed—and dismantled—systematically. Adam Smith's *Wealth of Nations* (1776) delivered a frontal intellectual assault on its premises. Smith rejected the notion that wealth was finite. He argued instead that wealth is continually created through productive labor, specialization, and voluntary exchange. For Smith, mercantilism's obsession with accumulating precious metals was not only mistaken but profoundly counterproductive. He wrote, "The natural effort of every individual to better his own condition . . . is so powerful a principle that it is capable of carrying on the society to wealth and prosperity."[137]

Smith and his classical successors—David Ricardo, Jean-Baptiste Say, and later John Stuart Mill—attacked every foundation of mercantilism: its zero-sum worldview, its suspicion of competition, its reliance on state privilege, and its conflation of national power with hoarded treasure. Ricardo's theory of comparative advantage, in particular, was a conceptual bombshell. It showed that two nations could both gain from trade even if one was more efficient in every sector—an idea fundamentally incompatible with mercantilist fear of imports.[138] The intellectual shift away from mercantilism helped delegitimize a system that was already straining under technological disruption.

The third force behind mercantilism's decline was political. As industrial and commercial wealth increased, political power began to shift. The emerging middle class—factory owners, merchants, financiers—wanted freer markets, lower tariffs, and access to global consumers. Mercantilist monopolies, once seen as instruments of national glory, were now viewed as barriers to economic opportunity. The Reform

Act of 1832 in Britain, which extended voting rights to the commercial classes, signaled a realignment of power away from aristocratic landholders and toward industrial capitalism.[139] As historian Robert Heilbroner observed, "Political and economic reforms of the early 19th century signaled the end of mercantilism and the rise of Liberal Capitalism."[140]

This dynamic has striking parallels today: as new economic elites emerge around technology, data, and finance, political pressures mount to dismantle (or reinforce) regulatory structures that no longer map cleanly to the sources of economic value. Economic evolution strains against political institutions built for an earlier era.[141]

The fourth pressure came from global trade dynamics. As European empires expanded, it became increasingly difficult—and increasingly costly—to enforce the tight trade restrictions mercantilism required. Smuggling exploded. Colonial resistance intensified. The American Revolution was partly a repudiation of mercantilist constraints such as the Navigation Acts. When Britain lost the colonies, it lost not only territory but the viability of its most rigid mercantilist instruments. As historian Robert DuPlessis noted, "The American Revolution exposed the limits of mercantilism's colonial monopoly system."[142]

The repeal of the Corn Laws in 1846 symbolized the final ideological victory of free trade over mercantilism. The Corn Laws—tariffs and import restrictions on grain designed to protect British landowners by keeping food prices artificially high—had long transferred wealth from industrial workers and consumers to agricultural elites while raising the cost base of the emerging industrial economy. Their repeal was therefore not merely a policy adjustment but a formal renunciation of a centuries-old doctrine grounded in protectionism, scarcity preservation, and rent extraction. By the mid-nineteenth century, Britain's industrial expansion had outgrown the mercantilist framework. As the historian Charles Wilson observed, the abolition of the Corn Laws marked a watershed moment, signaling Britain's full embrace of free trade principles that would dominate the next century.[143]

Finally, mercantilism contained mathematical and structural flaws that made its collapse inevitable. A system that equates wealth with bullion is ultimately bounded by the finite supply of precious metals. A system that treats trade as zero-sum invites perpetual conflict. A system that depends on state-granted monopolies will eventually face administrative complexity, corruption, waste, and declining returns.[144]

Capitalism emerged not simply because it was superior but because mercantilism became too inefficient, too brittle, and too misaligned with the technological and social realities of the time. It was a system that could not scale with innovation—and once innovation accelerated, the system could no longer govern it.[145]

This decline carries a warning for modern capitalism. Today's economy increasingly exhibits scale-driven concentration of power, mounting political backlash, technological disruption that outpaces institutional frameworks, and the re-emergence of mercantilist logic in global trade.[146] If mercantilism collapsed under the weight of its own contradictions, the question becomes: What contradictions are accumulating within capitalism today? This question frames the central analytical inquiry of Inclusive Capitalism. Chapter 10 identifies six such contradictions, each arising as an unintended consequence of Smithian capitalism's incentive structure.

Conclusions and Insights for Inclusive Capitalism

Mercantilism offers a rich set of lessons for the design of Inclusive Capitalism—not only because the period introduced the economic logic we still live with but because it reveals the deeper behavioral, institutional, and structural forces that shape economic systems regardless of era or ideology.[147] Three insights are paramount.

First, it is all in the incentives. Mercantilism demonstrates with unusual clarity that when economic and political systems reward extraction, exclusivity, and short-term accumulation, leadership behavior will reliably converge on those outcomes—even when the human costs are extreme.[148] Merchants and state officials did not participate in the slave trade, colonial exploitation, or monopoly abuse primarily because they were uniquely immoral, though moral failures were certainly present. They did so because the structure of mercantilist incentives made such behavior rational, competitive, and often necessary for survival within the system.[149] Control over trade routes, exclusive charters, coerced labor, and artificial scarcity translated directly into power, wealth, and state favor, while restraint carried real competitive penalties.[150]

This is the deeper lesson. Under conditions of existential competition, human behavior becomes less a question of virtue than of design. Systems that reward brutality will select for brutal outcomes; systems that reward extraction will produce extractive leaders. This does not excuse the suffering inflicted under mercantilism but it explains its persistence and scale.[151] Inclusive Capitalism is built on this insight. If we want leaders to behave differently, we must change what success is measured by and rewarded for. Moral exhortation cannot counteract structural incentives; history shows it cannot even slow them.[152] When incentives are aligned with societal well-being, innovation, and broad-based prosperity, progress compounds. When they are not, even intelligent, capable, and well-intentioned leaders can generate destructive outcomes at scale.

Second, the counterfactual of a more inclusive mercantilist system was not historically likely—even if it appears conceptually attractive in hindsight. It is tempting to imagine that mercantilism could have been organized to produce greater prosperity with far less human suffering. In principle, this intuition is not wrong. In practice, however, the preconditions for such a system did not exist. Scarcity defined nearly every dimension of life: energy was limited to muscle, wind, and wood; food production was fragile; capital was scarce and illiquid; information traveled slowly; and labor mobility was severely constrained.[153] Under these conditions, sustained abundance was technologically impossible, and economic coordination required centralized control rather than distributed decision-making.

Equally important, the institutional and human foundations of inclusivity were absent. Populations were largely illiterate, politically disenfranchised, and embedded in rigid social hierarchies. Legal systems were underdeveloped, property rights unevenly enforced, and mechanisms for accountability weak or nonexistent. Attempting to impose broad participation or democratic economic governance in such an environment would likely have produced instability rather than progress—much as the abrupt transplantation of democratic institutions into societies lacking institutional capacity often yields disorder rather than development.[154] The lesson is not that inclusion is undesirable but that it becomes viable only when technological capacity, institutional maturity, and incentive design evolve together.

Modern conditions, however, are fundamentally different. Digital technologies, AI, globalized knowledge networks, and near-zero marginal cost production in large sectors of the economy make broad-based prosperity and inclusive governance not only possible but economically advantageous.[155] The counterfactual that could not exist under mercantilism can exist today—if we are willing to redesign the system accordingly. Inclusive Capitalism is therefore not an ahistorical fantasy; it is the primary economic framework designed for a technologically abundant world.

Third, mercantilism reveals the origins of regulation—and why regulation alone cannot solve capitalism's modern problems. Regulation emerged in the mercantilist era as a reaction to predatory or destabilizing behavior: price-fixing, monopoly abuse, exploitation of labor, and geopolitical overreach.[156] But regulation was always a second-best solution. It attempted to counteract the very incentives the state had set in motion. The result was a perpetual tension: rules were imposed to constrain behavior that the system itself encouraged. This pattern persists today. Modern capitalism often relies on regulatory "patches" to control externalities—environmental, financial, social—that arise directly from the primacy of profit-maximizing incentives.[157]

Seen through the diagnostic lens developed in Book One, mercantilism can be understood as the first large-scale instantiation of several structural failures that later reappear within capitalism at greater scale. Chartered monopolies such as the British and Dutch East India Companies functioned as early versions of what this book later terms the black hole effect: institutions whose privileged access to capital, state protection, and scale enabled them to absorb disproportionate economic surplus while contributing little to broad-based societal advancement. Bullionism, in turn, represents an early example of a flawed top-level optimization metric—one that rewarded accumulation over productivity and treated scarcity as a feature to be preserved rather than a constraint to be overcome. Together, these incentives produced predictable outcomes: concentration of wealth and power, exclusionary opportunity structures in which access depended on birth, capital, or political favor, and an efficiency-first logic that subordinated human dignity to extraction and control. The fact that these same patterns—monopoly power, capital centralization, gatekeeping, and scale-driven coercive influence—recur in modern capitalism is not coincidental. Mercantilism did not merely precede capitalism; it established incentive architectures that were never fully dismantled, only refined and amplified as economic systems grew larger and more complex.

Inclusive Capitalism takes a different approach. Rather than layering oversight atop flawed incentives, it proposes institutional design in which the incentive structure itself is aligned with societal well-being, reducing the need for regulatory antagonism. Regulation will always play a role, but a system that constantly pits regulators against industrial leaders is inherently unstable, costly, and politically corrosive. Durable reform requires incentives that encourage leaders to internalize long-term societal benefits as part of their own self-interest. And this, critically, requires buy-in from industrial leadership—because no economic transformation in history has succeeded without the participation of those who control capital, technology, and organizational capacity.[158]

Taken together, these insights reveal why mercantilism produced both extraordinary progress and extraordinary harm. It launched global trade, created financial infrastructure, accelerated industrial development, and fostered a merchant class whose dynamism helped break the stagnant hierarchy of Feudalism. But progress was captured by a narrow elite, and the system's extractive design produced predictable outcomes: exploitation of the third estate,[159] economic nationalism, severe inequality, colonial brutality,[160] and eventually political backlash that fractured societies and reshaped the world order.

Mercantilism thus teaches two simultaneous truths. Progress was possible under a deeply flawed system, and far greater progress would have been possible under a better-designed one. That better design could not have been implemented then. It can be implemented now.

Inclusive Capitalism embraces the mechanisms that worked—innovation, scale, industrial organization, and market dynamism—while correcting the failures at their structural root. It does so not by moralizing, nor by regulating away natural incentives, but by engineering incentives that make long-term prosperity, fairness, and societal well-being the rational strategy for firms and their leaders.

With these lessons in mind, we now turn to early-stage capitalism, where innovation accelerates, inequality sharpens, and the design flaws of the traditional economic playbook become far more visible—beginning the long arc that Inclusive Capitalism seeks to finally bend toward sustainable, widespread prosperity.

Notes

1 Eli F. Heckscher, *Mercantilism*, trans. Mendel Shapiro (London: Allen & Unwin, 1935), 1–22.
2 Ibid.
3 Adam Smith, *An Inquiry into the Nature and Causes of the Wealth of Nations*, ed. Edwin Cannan (Chicago: University of Chicago Press, 1976), IV.ii.1–10.
4 Jacob Viner, "Mercantilist Thought," in *Studies in the Theory of International Trade* (New York: Harper & Brothers, 1937), 67–91.
5 Robert DuPlessis, *Transitions to Capitalism in Early Modern Europe* (Cambridge: Cambridge University Press, 1997), 45–62.
6 Eli F. Heckscher, *Mercantilism*, 1–22.
7 Charles Wilson, *England's Apprenticeship: 1603–1763* (London: Longmans, 1957), 113–130.
8 Robert Heilbroner, *The Worldly Philosophers*, 7th ed. (New York: Simon & Schuster, 1999), 38–53.
9 Fernand Braudel, *Civilization and Capitalism, Vol. II: The Wheels of Commerce* (Berkeley: University of California Press, 1982), 203–221.
10 Paul Kennedy, *The Rise and Fall of the Great Powers* (New York: Random House, 1987), 62–85.
11 Jacob Viner, "Power Versus Plenty as Objectives of Foreign Policy," *World Politics* 1, no. 1 (1948): 1–29.
12 Adam Smith, *An Inquiry into the Nature and Causes of the Wealth of Nations*, 1–10.
13 Adam Smith, Wealth of Nations, IV.iii–IV.iv.
14 David Ricardo, Principles of Political Economy and Taxation (London: John Murray, 1817), 128–147.
15 Robert Heilbroner, The Worldly Philosophers, 54–69.
16 Aristotle, *Politics*, trans. C. D. C. Reeve (Indianapolis: Hackett, 1998), I.8–10.
17 Paul Kennedy, *The Rise and Fall of the Great Powers*, 412–434.
18 Jacob Viner, "Power Versus Plenty," 21–29.
19 Fernand Braudel, *The Wheels of Commerce*, 437–455.
20 Paul Kennedy, *The Rise and Fall of the Great Powers*, 62–85.
21 Charles Wilson, *The Dutch East India Company* (London: Weidenfeld & Nicolson, 1967), 57–78.
22 Robert DuPlessis, *Transitions to Capitalism*, 123–138.
23 Jacob Viner, "Mercantilist Thought," in *Studies in the Theory of International Trade*, 67–91.
24 Fernand Braudel, *The Wheels of Commerce*, 437–455.
25 Eli F. Heckscher, *Mercantilism*, 1–22.
26 Ibid.
27 Thomas Mun, *England's Treasure by Forraign Trade* (London, 1623), 10–17.
28 Ibid.
29 Ibid.
30 Josiah Child, *A Discourse of Trade* (London, 1668), 3–11.
31 Jean-Baptiste Colbert, *Œuvres de Colbert*, ed. Pierre Clément (Paris: Imprimerie Impériale, 1861), 221–239.
32 Jacob Viner, "Power Versus Plenty as Objectives of Foreign Policy," *World Politics* 1, no. 1 (1948): 1–29.
33 Thomas Mun, *England's Treasure by Forraign Trade*, 10–17.
34 Josiah Child, *A Discourse of Trade*, 3–11.
35 Ibid.
36 Charles Wilson, *England's Apprenticeship: 1603–1763*, 113–130.
37 Paul Kennedy, *The Rise and Fall of the Great Powers*, 62–85.
38 Navigation Acts (1651–1849), in *Statutes of the Realm*, Vols. V–X (London: Record Commission).
39 Jean-Baptiste Colbert, *Œuvres de Colbert*, ed. Pierre Clément, 221–239.
40 Adam Smith, *An Inquiry into the Nature and Causes of the Wealth of Nations*, 1–10.

41 Charles Wilson, *The Dutch East India Company*, 57–78.
42 Fernand Braudel, *The Mediterranean and the Mediterranean World in the Age of Philip II* (Berkeley: University of California Press, 1972), 412–439.
43 Eli F. Heckscher, *Mercantilism*, 1–22.
44 Fernand Braudel, *The Mediterranean and the Mediterranean World in the Age of Philip II*, 412–439.
45 Jacob Viner, "Mercantilist Thought," in *Studies in the Theory of International Trade*, 67–91.
46 *The Instruction of Amenemope*, trans. Miriam Lichtheim, in *Ancient Egyptian Literature*, Vol. II (Berkeley: University of California Press, 1976), 146–163.
47 Kautilya, *Arthashastra*, trans. L. N. Rangarajan (New Delhi: Penguin Classics, 1992), 115–132.
48 Aristotle, *Politics*, trans. C. D. C. Reeve (Indianapolis: Hackett, 1998), I.8–10.
49 Roman *Corpus Juris Civilis*, ed. Paul Krueger (Berlin: Weidmann, 1877), "Digest," 14–22.
50 Charles Wilson, *England's Apprenticeship: 1603–1763*, 113–130.
51 Robert DuPlessis, *Transitions to Capitalism in Early Modern Europe*, 45–62.
52 Paul Kennedy, *The Rise and Fall of the Great Powers*, 62–85.
53 Jean-Baptiste Colbert, *Œuvres de Colbert*, ed. Pierre Clément, 221–239.
54 Jacob Viner, "Power Versus Plenty as Objectives of Foreign Policy," *World Politics* 1, no. 1 (1948): 1–29.
55 Ibid.
56 Fernand Braudel, *The Mediterranean and the Mediterranean World in the Age of Philip II*, 412–439.
57 Fernand Braudel, *Civilization and Capitalism*, Vol. II: *The Wheels of Commerce*, 203–221.
58 Charles Wilson, *The Dutch East India Company*, 57–78.
59 Jacob Viner, "Mercantilist Thought," in *Studies in the Theory of International Trade*, 67–91.
60 Fernand Braudel, *The Wheels of Commerce*, 437–455.
61 Fernand Braudel, *Civilization and Capitalism*, Vol. II: *The Wheels of Commerce*, 203–221.
62 Eric Williams, *Capitalism and Slavery*, 49–74.
63 Navigation Acts (1651–1849), in *Statutes of the Realm*, Vols. V–X (London: Record Commission.
64 Fernand Braudel, *Civilization and Capitalism*, Vol. II: *The Wheels of Commerce*, 203–221.
65 Eli F. Heckscher, *Mercantilism*, 1–22.
66 Paul Kennedy, *The Rise and Fall of the Great Powers*, 62–85.
67 Fernand Braudel, *Civilization and Capitalism*, Vol. II: *The Wheels of Commerce*, 203–221.
68 Fernand Braudel, *The Structures of Everyday Life* (Berkeley: University of California Press, 1981), 233–249.
69 Charles Wilson, *The Dutch East India Company*, 57–78.
70 Dutch East India Company (VOC) Charter (1602), in *Resolutiën der Heeren Zeventienen* (The Hague: Rijksarchief, 1905), 33–49.
71 Fernand Braudel, *The Wheels of Commerce*, 437–455.
72 Fernand Braudel, *The Structures of Everyday Life* (Berkeley: University of California Press, 1981), 233–249.
73 Fernand Braudel, *Civilization and Capitalism*, Vol. II: *The Wheels of Commerce*, 203–221.
74 Ibid.
75 Charles Wilson, *The Dutch East India Company*, 57–78.
76 Jacob Viner, "Mercantilist Thought," in *Studies in the Theory of International Trade*, 67–91.
77 Charles Wilson, *The Dutch East India Company*, 57–78.
78 Fernand Braudel, *Civilization and Capitalism*, Vol. II: *The Wheels of Commerce*, 203–221.
79 Fernand Braudel, *Civilization and Capitalism*, Vol. II: *The Wheels of Commerce*, 203–221.
80 Fernand Braudel, *The Mediterranean and the Mediterranean World in the Age of Philip II*, 412–439.
81 Jacob Viner, "Mercantilist Thought," in *Studies in the Theory of International Trade*, 67–91.
82 Eric Williams, *Capitalism and Slavery*, 49–74.
83 Paul Kennedy, *The Rise and Fall of the Great Powers*, 62–85.

84 Fernand Braudel, *The Structures of Everyday Life* (Berkeley: University of California Press, 1981), 233–249.
85 Ibid.
86 Charles Wilson, *The Dutch East India Company*, 57–78.
87 Navigation Acts (1651–1849), in *Statutes of the Realm*, Vols. V–X.
88 Fernand Braudel, *Civilization and Capitalism*, Vol. II: *The Wheels of Commerce*, 203–221.
89 Paul Kennedy, *The Rise and Fall of the Great Powers*, 62–85.
90 Robert Heilbroner, *The Worldly Philosophers*, 7th ed., 38–53.
91 Jacob Viner, "Power Versus Plenty as Objectives of Foreign Policy," *World Politics* 1, no. 1 (1948): 1–29.
92 Jacob Viner, "Mercantilist Thought," in *Studies in the Theory of International Trade*, 67–91.
93 Robert E. Lucas, "On the Mechanics of Economic Development," *Journal of Monetary Economics* 22, no. 1 (1988): 3–42.
94 Jacob Viner, "Mercantilist Thought," in *Studies in the Theory of International Trade*, 67–91.
95 Robert Heilbroner, *The Worldly Philosophers*, 7th ed., 38–53.
96 Eli F. Heckscher, *Mercantilism*, 1–22.
97 Ibid.
98 Eric Williams, *Capitalism and Slavery* (Chapel Hill: University of North Carolina Press, 1944), 29–47.
99 Jean-Baptiste Colbert, *Œuvres de Colbert*, ed. Pierre Clément, 221–239.
100 Robert DuPlessis, *Transitions to Capitalism in Early Modern Europe*, 45–62.
101 Robert DuPlessis, *Transgressions: Slavery, Dependency, and Abolition in the Atlantic World* (New York: Routledge, 1997), 101–118.
102 Charles Wilson, *The Dutch East India Company*, 57–78.
103 Eric Williams, *Capitalism and Slavery* (Chapel Hill: University of North Carolina Press, 1944), 29–47.
104 Eric Williams, *Capitalism and Slavery*, 49–74.
105 Fernand Braudel, *The Structures of Everyday Life* (Berkeley: University of California Press, 1981), 233–249.
106 Jacob Viner, "Power Versus Plenty as Objectives of Foreign Policy," *World Politics* 1, no. 1 (1948): 1–29.
107 Fernand Braudel, *The Wheels of Commerce*, 437–455.
108 Eli F. Heckscher, *Mercantilism*, 1–22.
109 Thomas Mun, *England's Treasure by Forraign Trade*, 10–17.
110 Jean-Baptiste Colbert, *Œuvres de Colbert*, ed. Pierre Clément, 221–239.
111 Josiah Child, *A Discourse of Trade*, 3–11.
112 Jacob Viner, "Power Versus Plenty as Objectives of Foreign Policy," *World Politics* 1, no. 1 (1948): 1–29.
113 Navigation Acts (1651–1849), in *Statutes of the Realm*, Vols. V–X.
114 Paul Kennedy, *The Rise and Fall of the Great Powers*, 412–434.
115 Jacob Viner, "Power Versus Plenty," 21–29.
116 Robert DuPlessis, *Transgressions: Slavery, Dependency, and Abolition in the Atlantic World* (New York: Routledge, 1997), 101–118.
117 Fernand Braudel, *The Mediterranean and the Mediterranean World in the Age of Philip II*, 412–439.
118 Jacob Viner, "Power Versus Plenty," 21–29.
119 Ibid.
120 Fernand Braudel, *The Wheels of Commerce*, 437–455.
121 Paul Kennedy, *The Rise and Fall of the Great Powers*, 412–434.
122 Heckscher, Eli F. *Mercantilism*. Vol. 2. London: George Allen & Unwin, 1935, 1–44, 203–246.
123 Adam Smith, Wealth of Nations, IV.iii–IV.iv.

124 Adam Smith, *An Inquiry into the Nature and Causes of the Wealth of Nations*, 1–10.
125 Eli F. Heckscher, *Mercantilism*, 1–22.
126 Jacob Viner, "Mercantilist Thought," in *Studies in the Theory of International Trade*, 67–91.
127 David Ricardo, Principles of Political Economy and Taxation, 128–147.
128 Robert E. Lucas, "On the Mechanics of Economic Development," 29–41.
129 Eric Williams, *Capitalism and Slavery* (Chapel Hill: University of North Carolina Press, 1944), 29–47.
130 Jacob Viner, "Power Versus Plenty as Objectives of Foreign Policy," *World Politics* 1, no. 1 (1948): 1–29.
131 Robert Heilbroner, The Worldly Philosophers, 54–69.
132 Fernand Braudel, *The Wheels of Commerce*, 437–455.
133 Robert Heilbroner, The Worldly Philosophers, 54–69.
134 Robert E. Lucas, "On the Mechanics of Economic Development," 29–41.
135 Robert E. Lucas, "On the Mechanics of Economic Development," *Journal of Monetary Economics* 22, no. 1 (1988): 3–42.
136 Robert E. Lucas, "On the Mechanics of Economic Development," 29–41.
137 Adam Smith, *An Inquiry into the Nature and Causes of the Wealth of Nations*, 1–10.
138 David Ricardo, Principles of Political Economy and Taxation, 128–147.
139 Charles Wilson, England's Apprenticeship, 304–319.
140 Robert Heilbroner, The Worldly Philosophers, 54–69.
141 Paul Kennedy, *The Rise and Fall of the Great Powers*, 412–434.
142 Robert DuPlessis, *Transgressions: Slavery, Dependency, and Abolition in the Atlantic World* (New York: Routledge, 1997), 101–118.
143 Charles Wilson, *England's Apprenticeship: 1603–1763*, 113–130.
144 Eli F. Heckscher, *Mercantilism*, 1–22.
145 Robert DuPlessis, *Transitions to Capitalism in Early Modern Europe*, 45–62.
146 Jacob Viner, "Power Versus Plenty," 21–29.
147 Fernand Braudel, *The Wheels of Commerce*, 437–455.
148 Eli F. Heckscher, *Mercantilism*, 1–22.
149 Eric Williams, *Capitalism and Slavery* (Chapel Hill: University of North Carolina Press, 1944), 29–47.
150 Charles Wilson, *The Dutch East India Company*, 57–78.
151 Jacob Viner, "Power Versus Plenty as Objectives of Foreign Policy," *World Politics* 1, no. 1 (1948): 1–29.
152 Eli F. Heckscher, *Mercantilism*, 1–22.
153 Fernand Braudel, *The Structures of Everyday Life* (Berkeley: University of California Press, 1981), 233–249.
154 Robert DuPlessis, *Transitions to Capitalism*, 161–175.
155 Robert E. Lucas, "On the Mechanics of Economic Development," 29–41.
156 Navigation Acts (1651–1849), in *Statutes of the Realm*, Vols. V–X.
157 Paul Kennedy, *The Rise and Fall of the Great Powers*, 412–434.
158 Robert Heilbroner, *The Worldly Philosophers*, 7th ed., 38–53.
159 Fernand Braudel, *The Structures of Everyday Life* (Berkeley: University of California Press, 1981), 233–249.
160 Robert DuPlessis, *Transgressions: Slavery, Dependency, and Abolition in the Atlantic World* (New York: Routledge, 1997), 101–118.

3 Early Capitalism: An Emergent Market-Driven Economy

One of the most striking parallels between past and present is that economic revolutions rarely appear as revolutions at the time. They more often appear as gradual shifts – that, ultimately, play out to be transformative to the economic landscape. When Bill Gates and Paul Allen saw the potential of the Intel 8008 microprocessor and left the safety of convention to found Microsoft in 1975, they were responding instinctively to technological possibility.[1] Two hundred years earlier, in the late eighteenth century, a similar cascade of technological breakthroughs set ambitious innovators in motion. The Spinning Jenny, the water frame, the Watt steam engine, the power loom, improved iron smelting, and later the cotton gin collectively created an unprecedented acceleration in productive capacity which, ultimately, all proved to be transformative to economic landscapes.[2] Inventors such as Richard Arkwright, James Watt, Matthew Boulton, Josiah Wedgwood, Eli Whitney, and John Wilkinson transformed production from decentralized craft to centralized industry.[3]

This wave of innovation did more than increase output. It exposed the structural weaknesses of the mercantilist order. A system built on guild restrictions, state-chartered monopolies, colonial extraction, and zero-sum competition could not accommodate factories capable of producing more in a day than entire towns once produced in a month.[4] Early-stage capitalism emerged not as an ideological movement but as a workable response to the change already unfolding on the ground. Technology shifted the feasible set of economic arrangements, and society followed.[5]

Early-stage capitalism represents the first major pivot toward a market-driven economy in the modern sense: decentralized, dynamic, innovation-responsive, and rooted in private initiative rather than state design. It was not designed as a coherent system; it evolved organically in response to mercantilism's existential failures and the new possibilities created by technological progress. The division of labor, centralized production, and large-scale markets created a new economic environment in which state-directed trade and rigid privileges became liabilities.[6] Inclusive Capitalism, as this book will argue, must likewise emerge from real technological and institutional conditions—not from abstract theory alone.

The analogy to the present day is unavoidable. The speed and scale of twenty-first-century innovation have created a widening mismatch between technological capability and institutional design. Global cloud infrastructure, non-scarce digital goods, AI-driven productivity, programmable money, decentralized coordination, and bio-digital manufacturing are straining economic frameworks built for scarcity—much as steam power and mechanized production once overwhelmed mercantilist institutions.[7] Just as pre-industrial institutions could not anticipate mass production or steam power, our current system has not evolved to handle algorithmic productivity,

 | https://doi.org/10.1515/9783112235485-004

zero-marginal-cost information goods, or financial instruments scaling faster than human governance.

Inclusive Capitalism is not meant to be a narrowly focused attempt to "improve" capitalism at the margin. It is broader; the intent is to provide a present-day response to similar structural forces—technological leaps, demographic transitions, global integration, and institutional mismatch—that gave rise to early-stage capitalism itself. The question is what system best fits the technological and social possibilities of the twenty-first century, just as Adam Smith asked what system best fit the eighteenth century.

A central hypothesis advanced in this chapter—and substantiated throughout Book One—is that capitalism's divergence from the intentions of its original visionaries reflects a failure of system design rather than a failure of human character. In particular, the early capitalist framework lacked a coherent incentive and institutional architecture capable of scaling with technological progress. This was not due to negligence but constraint: the technological landscape was primitive, economic and managerial doctrine was nascent, and empirical data were largely unavailable. As a result, capitalism evolved without an explicit core design capable of aligning individual success with societal well-being at scale. The recurring pattern that follows—periods of extraordinary growth accompanied by outcomes severe enough to demand external correction—points to a structural conclusion: when an economic system repeatedly requires intervention to remain tolerable, the fault lies in its incentive architecture, not in the intentions or morality of those operating within it.

This period also marks the emergence of economics as a more formalized intellectual field, though still grounded in moral philosophy rather than empirical science. Adam Smith's *Wealth of Nations* (1776) provided the first comprehensive articulation of market dynamics rooted in decentralized self-interest rather than state directive.[8] Thinkers like John Locke, Jean-Baptiste Say, David Ricardo, Thomas Malthus, Robert Owen, Pierre-Joseph Proudhon, and John Stuart Mill extended debates about wealth creation, labor, and distribution.[9] Yet this "science" of economics was built largely on observation, ideology, and logical inference rather than data or controlled experimentation—what we would today call a pseudo-science.

Still, as Keynes observed, "Economics is not an exact science, but it is essential for understanding human society."[10] And that is precisely what Smith and his contemporaries achieved: they provided a conceptual framework capable of explaining—and accelerating—the new market dynamics emerging around them. Their ideas became the intellectual foundation for early-stage capitalism, just as the present volume seeks to provide the intellectual foundation for Inclusive Capitalism.

This chapter analyzes early-stage capitalism using the same analytical framework applied to feudalism and mercantilism—focusing on industrial leadership behavior, its societal and workforce impacts, the prevailing intellectual doctrines, and the legislative and institutional structures that directed the system's evolution. The analysis reveals both the extraordinary dynamism and the extraordinary human costs of the early capitalist transformation—costs that continue to reverberate through the global economy today.[11]

Capitalism Definition and Emergence

Early-stage capitalism is best understood not as a system designed in advance but as the first large-scale, market-driven alternative to the rigid, state-directed mercantilism that dominated Europe through the eighteenth century. Although Adam Smith provided the intellectual scaffolding for understanding markets, he never used the term "capitalism" in *The Wealth of Nations*.[12] The term originated later, first among French socialists such as Louis Blanc—who used *capitalisme* to describe a system in which capital was concentrated in the hands of a few—and later through Karl Marx's analysis of the "capitalist mode of production."[13] The English term emerged in the mid-nineteenth century as a translation of *capitalisme*, gradually acquiring its modern meaning as the dominant economic system of industrializing nations.[14]

Because capitalism evolved rather than being invented, there is no definitive boundary separating what it is from what it is not. Modern scholars (for example, Hall and Soskice's *Varieties of Capitalism*)[15] highlight two broad types—liberal market economies like the United States and the United Kingdom, and coordinated market economies such as Germany and Japan—but actual practice blends elements of both. Even in its earliest form, capitalism was neither uniform nor doctrinally pristine.

What did emerge consistently in the late eighteenth century were several defining features. Smith's liberal capitalism emphasized private property, markets organized around voluntary exchange, limited government intervention, and incentives that aligned individual initiative with social benefit through what he famously described as the "invisible hand." Markets, in this view, were the principal mechanism for coordinating human activity and allocating resources efficiently. Government existed primarily to protect property rights, enforce contracts, and ensure the basic functioning of competition.[16]

Inclusive Capitalism preserves Smith's defining features—private property, market coordination, limited but essential government, and incentive systems that reward initiative and value creation—while redesigning how they operate in a radically different technological context. In contrast to the manufactured goods of Smith's era, many of today's most economically significant products and services—software, digital media, and networked services—are non-rival and near-zero marginal cost.[17] Their natural logic is abundance, not scarcity. Recognizing and designing around this shift is central to moving beyond the capitalism Smith envisioned—still the dominant doctrine in the United States today—toward an economic system capable of delivering broad, durable societal well-being in an economy increasingly shaped by non-scarce goods and services.

Early-stage capitalism emerged gradually as mercantilism became increasingly misaligned with technological, political, and commercial realities. The flaws of mercantilism—high tariffs, rigid state-sanctioned monopolies, and the hoarding of gold and silver—became increasingly apparent by the seventeenth and eighteenth centuries.[18] These policies restricted competition, suppressed innovation, and locked productive potential behind layers of regulation. As trade expanded and domestic markets grew more complex, mercantilist institutions proved too blunt and inflexible to sustain economic dynamism.

Technological change accelerated the breakdown of the old order. The early Industrial Revolution—steam engines, mechanized looms, coke-fired iron production, and the factory system—made it possible to produce goods at scales unimaginable under mercantilism.[19] Production moved from guild-controlled workshops to centralized factories, most visibly in textile centers in the United Kingdom such as Manchester and Birmingham. These new industrial enterprises required open markets, free entry, labor mobility, reliable capital, and the ability to scale without state-imposed constraints. In effect, technology made capitalism not only possible but necessary.[20]

Financial innovation reinforced this shift. The rise of private banks, joint-stock companies, and increasingly sophisticated stock exchanges enabled investment to flow into new ventures without dependence on monarchs or mercantilist charters. The Amsterdam Stock Exchange (1602) and the Bank of Amsterdam (1609) pioneered financial structures that later supported industrial expansion across Britain and the Continent.[21] Capital could now be raised privately and deployed flexibly—something mercantilism's bullion-centric worldview had never envisioned.

Political transformations completed the transition. Enlightenment thinkers such as John Locke and Adam Smith articulated the philosophical and economic foundations for individual rights and market coordination.[22] The American and French Revolutions weakened the political power of monarchs and landed aristocracies, shifting influence toward industrialists, merchants, and the rising middle class. The rejection of British mercantilist restrictions during the American Revolution marked an explicit ideological and practical shift toward market-driven economic organization.

By the mid-nineteenth century, early-stage capitalism had replaced mercantilism as the dominant framework in industrializing nations. The repeal of the British Corn Laws in 1846 symbolized the culmination of this transition: a decisive move away from protectionist, state-centered economic management toward free trade, competitive markets, and private enterprise.[23]

As we turn to the doctrinal foundations of capitalism, it is essential to keep this historical context in view. Capitalism did not emerge because Smith or Ricardo won an intellectual argument—it emerged because technological and political forces made the old system untenable.[24] The same dynamic is at work today. The transition toward Inclusive Capitalism will not be driven by theory alone but by the mismatch between modern technological potential and the limitations of our current institutional design!

Capitalist Economic Doctrine, Early-Stage Legislation, and Cultural Norms

To design a better economic system, we must begin at the core. The central thesis of this book is not that capitalism requires cosmetic repairs at the margins but that several of its foundational assumptions must be re-engineered. Doing so requires a clear understanding of how those foundations were originally constructed. The period from the late eighteenth to the mid-nineteenth century is when capitalism's core architecture took shape; the two and a half centuries since have largely consisted of adaptations, reactions, and incremental patches layered atop that original design.

The unintended consequences of capitalism we now confront—extreme concentration of wealth, exclusionary opportunity structures, recurrent financial crises, and the need for ever-expanding regulatory oversight—did not appear all at once. They emerged gradually as Smith's framework interacted with real institutions, real politics, and real human behavior. What began as a "system of natural liberty" evolved, through legislative choices and cultural norms, into something more brittle and more unequal than its architects intended.[25]

For that reason, it is necessary to examine the technical foundations of early capitalism: the economic doctrines, legislative choices, and cultural practices that translated Smith's ideas into an operating system. This was the period in which the rules of the game were set—by Ricardo and Babbage as much as by Smith; by factory acts and the Corn Laws as much as by treatises; and by the habits and expectations of early industrial leaders as much as by formal theory. If the objective is to propose core-level redesign rather than yet another round of peripheral reform, then the operating model itself must be understood in detail. What follows is therefore not doctrine for its own sake but groundwork for redesign.

Adam Smith and the Architecture of Early-Stage Capitalism

Before turning to the broader doctrinal, legal, and cultural landscape of early-stage capitalism, it is necessary to anchor the discussion in its foundational vision. Adam Smith's *An Inquiry into the Nature and Causes of the Wealth of Nations* (1776) remains the clearest articulation of the system that would come to dominate industrial society.[26] Smith did not design capitalism as a finished blueprint; rather, he articulated a set of principles—markets, property, competition, specialization, limited government, trade, and capital—that proved scalable, portable, and durable across contexts. Smith is treated here not as doctrine to be defended but as an initial operating model whose assumptions were stress-tested by scale and technology.

These principles demonstrated extraordinary power. Yet they were formulated in a world of small firms, limited financial abstraction, and material scarcity. As capitalism expanded technologically, geographically, and institutionally, several of Smith's assumptions strained or broke, producing unintended consequences that he anticipated in part but could not resolve in full. Inclusive Capitalism does not reject Smith's framework; it treats it as an early operating model—one whose strengths must be preserved and whose limits must now be addressed under conditions of scale and technological capability that Smith could not have foreseen.[27]

Smith's vision was not merely technical. He believed that both markets and government should ultimately serve ordinary people and remain accountable to them. In his view, capitalism was a mechanism to reduce poverty and broaden prosperity, not to entrench privilege. Although he did not use the term "capitalism," he described a "system of natural liberty" in which free markets, competition, and limited state intervention could generate widespread prosperity.[28] Widespread was not rhetorical; it was a substantive criterion of success. A system that concentrates its gains narrowly fails its purpose. Inclusive Capitalism extends this principle of service and accountability beyond markets and government to the most consequential institutions of modern capitalism—large private-sector enterprises themselves.

To understand both the power and the limits of Smith's framework, it is useful to distill *The Wealth of Nations* into seven building blocks that have defined capitalism as it evolved:

1. Free markets and self-regulating economies benefit society.
2. Private property incentivizes productivity and investment.
3. Competition encourages efficiency, innovation, and fair prices.
4. Division of labor drives economic growth and industrialization.
5. Limited government provides security, justice, and infrastructure.
6. Free trade expands wealth by reducing tariffs and protectionism.
7. Capital investment enables long-term economic expansion.

Smith repeatedly warned against monopoly, collusion, and state favoritism. Yet the system that developed in his name often amplified precisely these pathologies as scale increased.[29] What follows is a focused evaluation of these seven building blocks—not to rehearse doctrine but to test how each behaved as capitalism industrialized, scaled, and concentrated. This evaluation provides the foundation for diagnosing capitalism's unintended consequences and identifying which elements must be preserved, re-engineered, or replaced.

1. Free Markets and the "Invisible Hand"

Smith's concept of free markets rests on a structural claim: Individuals pursuing their own self-interest in voluntary exchange can generate broad prosperity without central planning. Prices emerge from supply and demand, competition disciplines inefficiency, and decentralized decision-making coordinates economic activity. In this vision:

- Individuals and firms voluntarily exchange goods and services.
- Prices reflect supply and demand rather than decree.

- Competition rewards efficiency and innovation.
- Government focuses on property rights, contracts, and public goods.

Smith's "invisible hand" was not a moral defense of greed but a coordination mechanism: When incentives are properly aligned, individual self-interest can unintentionally advance collective welfare. Historical experience confirms that market systems broadly consistent with this logic outperform centralized planning.[30] It also shows that the mechanism breaks down under conditions of extreme scale, financial complexity, and concentrated power. Inclusive Capitalism begins with Smith's insight about decentralized coordination and redesigns the surrounding incentive architecture so that market forces remain generative rather than extractive at scale.

2. Private Property

Smith viewed private property as foundational to a functioning market economy. Ownership incentivizes work, investment, and stewardship; absence of ownership breeds neglect and underinvestment. He extended property rights not only to land and capital but to one's own labor, calling it "the most sacred and inviolable" form of property.[31]

In Smith's framework:

- Property rights support capital formation and long-term planning.
- Owners have incentives to manage resources productively.
- Secure ownership limits arbitrary state power.

History validates these claims. Societies that protect property rights have consistently outperformed those with pervasive state control.[32] However, Smith underestimated the consequences of extreme concentration. When ownership becomes highly concentrated, coercive power can shift from public to private hands. Exclusion is intrinsic to property rights; at modest levels it is functional, at extreme levels it undermines opportunity, legitimacy, and social cohesion.[33] Inclusive Capitalism treats this not as a moral problem but as a design challenge: how to preserve strong ownership incentives while preventing pathological concentration that destabilizes the system itself.

3. Competition

For Smith, competition was capitalism's primary disciplinary force. It constrains pricing power, encourages innovation, and protects consumers. He warned explicitly that monopoly and collusion would corrupt markets and undermine social benefit.

In competitive markets:

- Firms must innovate or lose share.
- Prices tend toward cost-reflective levels.
- Consumers gain choice and affordability.

Empirically, competition works best in early phases of market formation, when entry barriers are low and scale is limited. Over time, however, competition tends to generate its opposite: scale. Successful firms acquire the ability to set terms, raise barriers, and shape regulation.[34] Inclusive Capitalism starts from Smith's insight that competition is socially beneficial and asks a modern question he could not fully answer: How do we preserve real competition when firms operate at global scale with network effects and institutional capture?

Smith's second claim regarding competitive markets—that prices tend toward cost-reflective levels—is central to understanding why the 1776 formulation of capitalism no longer maps cleanly onto the economic realities of 2026. Large and growing segments of the modern economy now exhibit marginal costs that are effectively zero or near zero.[35] In such domains—software, digital media, data services, and certain knowledge goods—Smith's own logic implies that competitive prices should converge toward zero.

This outcome is not theoretical. It is explicitly embraced by the designers of open-source software, whose objective is to drive prices to zero in order to maximize diffusion, innovation, and collective benefit. The challenge is not that Smith's principle fails but that its implications now collide with institutional structures designed for scarcity-based production. A system that assumes positive marginal costs struggles to reward innovation when competitive prices collapse by design.[36]

Inclusive Capitalism accepts Smith's objective—that competition should push prices toward their true economic cost—but rejects the conclusion that innovators must therefore go unrewarded. The task is not to preserve artificial scarcity but to redesign the incentive mechanisms, ownership structures, and institutional pathways through which innovation is compensated. When value creation no longer depends on pricing exclusion, rewards must be decoupled from unit scarcity and reattached to contribution, adoption, and societal impact.

What appears counterintuitive within the classical capitalist frame becomes tractable once the architecture is updated. Inclusive Capitalism provides the framework for doing so, a framework developed in detail in Book Two, where innovation is rewarded not by restricting access but by expanding it.

4. Division of Labor

Smith identified division of labor as the principal driver of productivity growth. Specialization increases skill, speed, and output, generating surplus that can be reinvested and traded.[37] At the same time, he acknowledged its human cost: repetitive work could degrade individual capability and dignity.[38]

Division of labor, in his account:

- Increases skill and speed.
- Reduces waste and lowers cost.
- Encourages process innovation and mechanization.
- Generates surplus output that can be traded and reinvested.

Subsequent history confirms that division of labor drove explosive productivity growth and, particularly in early stage capitalism, degraded individual capability and dignity.[39] Specialization and process optimization delivered extraordinary gains but also provoked resistance, displacement, and alienation. For Inclusive Capitalism, the challenge is not whether to automate or specialize but how to design systems so that productivity gains translate into shared prosperity rather than social dislocation.

The most far-reaching implication of Smith's analysis of the division of labor lies in his first observation: that specialization increases skill, speed, and productivity. Inclusive Capitalism extends this insight to its logical—and existential—limit. What happens when gains in productivity become so extreme that a small fraction of the population can produce all the goods and services a society requires?

This is no longer a speculative question. In contemporary advanced economies, particularly the United States, productivity growth is increasingly concentrated among a relatively small cohort of highly skilled workers, capital-intensive firms, and automated systems.[40] It is no longer implausible to imagine a scenario in which ten million Americans—augmented by advanced technologies—can supply the material needs of the entire nation. The corresponding question is unavoidable: What becomes of the remaining population when labor is no longer economically required at scale?

Current trends point in this direction. Output per worker continues to rise rapidly in leading sectors, while labor-force participation, job creation, and wage growth stagnate outside the top decile.[41] The traditional capitalist response—absorbing displaced labor into new industries—becomes progressively less reliable as automation, AI, and capital deepening compress the demand for human labor faster than new scarcity-based roles can emerge.

Inclusive Capitalism offers a clear and structurally distinct answer. Rather than treating the displacement of labor as a failure to be remedied through temporary redistribution or perpetual job creation, it reframes the role of human contribution itself. When material production no longer requires universal labor participation, economic purpose must shift from producing goods to improving societal well-being.

Under this framework, the majority of the population is not rendered redundant but reoriented toward domains where human contribution remains both valuable and intrinsically non-automatable: childcare, healthcare, education, elder care, community-building, creative expression, scientific exploration, cultural production, innovation, environmental stewardship, and other activities aligned with collectively defined social priorities and individual purpose. In this respect, Inclusive Capitalism converges—without ideological inheritance—on an insight often associated with Marx: that human flourishing need not be tethered exclusively to commodity production.[42]

Crucially, this outcome does not arise from moral exhortation but from institutional design. The incentive systems, monetary structures, and governance mechanisms of Inclusive Capitalism are constructed to reward contributions to societal well-being directly, rather than indirectly through artificial labor scarcity. In doing so, the system addresses not only the economics of non-scarce goods and services but the most consequential non-scarce resource of the coming era: human potential itself.

5. The Role of Government
Smith advocated limited but essential government. He opposed both micromanagement and capture.

Government, in his view, should:

- Protect property rights and enforce contracts.
- Provide basic public goods (defense, justice, infrastructure, some education).
- Avoid micromanaging the allocation of capital and labor.

Historically, capitalism has repeatedly required regulation to correct abuses, stabilize crises, and address backlash.[43] Inclusive Capitalism treats this pattern not as a failure of leaders but as a failure of system design. When an economic system requires continuous emergency intervention to remain tolerable, its incentive structure is misaligned. The objective is to design institutions where socially beneficial behavior is the default outcome, reducing the need for reactive regulation.

6. Free Trade
Smith rejected mercantilist protectionism, arguing that trade allows nations to specialize and mutually benefit. He also believed trade could reduce conflict by aligning interests.[44]

His argument parallels his case for division of labor:

- Nations should specialize in what they produce relatively well.
- Trade allows all parties to benefit from specialization.
- Protectionism diverts resources into less productive uses.

History shows both the power and fragility of this vision.[45] Trade expansion drives growth; trade shocks provoke backlash. Inclusive Capitalism does not resolve the free-trade debate directly. Instead, it argues that a system that distributes gains more broadly and cushions disruption will sustain political support for openness more reliably than one that concentrates benefits narrowly.

7. Capital and Investment
Smith emphasized productive capital—tools, machinery, infrastructure, and skills—as the true source of wealth. Accumulation and reinvestment fuel growth. Yet accumulation also generates capitalism's most destabilizing dynamic: capital begetting capital, opportunity clustering around existing wealth, and exclusion hardening over time.

In his framework:

- Investment in machinery and infrastructure raises productivity.
- Profits should be reinvested, not merely consumed.
- Financial institutions channel savings into productive uses.

Inclusive Capitalism accepts capital accumulation as essential while treating concentration as a mathematical and institutional problem. The objective is not to punish success but to design financial and investment structures that expand opportunity, resilience, and participation rather than reinforcing self-perpetuating advantage.

This concludes the architectural review of Smith's seven building blocks, along with a high-level view of how these building blocks are leveraged in Inclusive Capitalism. The principles explain both capitalism's dynamism and its fragility. In the sections that follow, we widen the lens—examining how later thinkers, legislators, and industrial leaders translated these principles into law, practice, and culture, and how the resulting early capitalist system produced both unprecedented progress and predictable failures.[46]

David Ricardo, in *Principles of Political Economy and Taxation* (1817), formalized two ideas that proved especially influential: comparative advantage and economic rent.[47] His argument for free trade—that "under a system of perfectly free commerce, each country naturally devotes its capital and labor to such employments as are most beneficial to each"—reframed international exchange from a mercantilist zero-sum contest into a potential positive-sum game. In doing so, Ricardo gave early-stage capitalism a powerful intellectual justification for dismantling protectionist barriers and reorienting national policy around global efficiency rather than bullion hoarding.

Charles Babbage, in *On the Economy of Machinery and Manufactures* (1832), focused on production itself.[48] He analyzed how division of labor, machine design, and process engineering could increase output and lower cost. His observation that "the economy of machinery depends on the effective arrangement of the work" captured a new industrial logic: Productivity arose not only from individual effort but from systematic organization. In modern terms, Babbage gave capitalism an early "operations research" mindset—one that treated the factory as an optimization problem rather than simply a place where labor met capital.

At the same time, critics such as Karl Marx and Friedrich Engels challenged capitalism at its foundations. In *The Communist Manifesto* (1848), they argued that "the history of all hitherto existing society is the history of class struggles," portraying capitalism as a system in which owners systematically expropriate surplus value from workers.[49] For them, the very same features that Smith and Ricardo saw as productive—private ownership of capital, wage labor, and market competition—generated alienation, exploitation, and periodic crises. Their critique ensured that capitalism was never simply celebrated; from its earliest decades, its gains were weighed against its harms.

This doctrinal diversity is crucial. It shows that early-stage capitalism was never underpinned by a unified "economic science." Rather, it was shaped by competing theories that often reflected ideological priors as much as empirical validation.[50] Inclusive Capitalism takes this history seriously: When core policy swings back and forth between opposing doctrines, decade after decade, it is evidence of deep prima-facie validity problems in the underlying models. One of our central claims is that economics must be rebuilt on a more stable foundation—anchored in societal well-being and mathematically coherent incentive design—if it is to function as a genuine decision science rather than an arena for recurring doctrinal pendulum swings.

If doctrine supplied the intellectual frame, legislation translated early-stage capitalism into lived reality. Law and policy in the late eighteenth and early nineteenth centuries reveal an emerging system that promised freedom and prosperity, yet repeatedly required corrective intervention to manage its own excesses. This dialectic—unfettered markets followed by regulatory response—recurs throughout the history traced in this book.

In Britain, the Combination Acts of 1799 and 1800 prohibited labor unions and collective bargaining, explicitly protecting the interests of industrial employers.[51] These Acts presumed that unfettered contract between individual worker and employer would yield fair outcomes—a doctrinal extension of laissez-faire thinking into labor markets. Their eventual repeal recognized something different: that, in practice, power was so asymmetric tilted toward industrialist that unregulated labor markets did not deliver legitimate or sustainable outcomes. From the start, capitalism required institutional counterweights to its own internal logic.

The Factory Acts of 1833–1847 marked an even more explicit departure from pure laissez-faire.[52] By limiting child labor, reducing hours, and imposing minimum safety standards, Parliament acknowledged that the unregulated factory system was producing outcomes so harsh that political and moral backlash became unavoidable. Early industrialists could have recognized that relentless cost-cutting at the expense of human dignity would trigger state intervention and entrench demands for oversight. Instead, they behaved rationally within the prevailing incentive structure—prioritizing short-term profit and competitive survival—forcing government to step in. This pattern, visible here in embryonic form, repeats in every subsequent phase of capitalism.

Trade policy followed a similar arc. The Corn Laws, which imposed tariffs on imported grain, epitomized mercantilist protectionism in an industrializing society.[53] Their repeal in 1846, along with the later repeal of the Navigation Acts in 1849, marked a decisive shift toward liberal trade policies. These reforms lowered food prices, broadened access to basic goods, and signaled that national prosperity would now be pursued through open markets rather than tightly managed trade monopolies. Yet even these landmark victories for free trade did not end the underlying tension: Domestic constituencies hurt by exposure to global competition continually pushed back, a dynamic that continues today in debates over tariffs, supply chains, and industrial policy.

Financial legislation and institutional design were equally transformative.[54] Revisions to the Bank of England's charter in the early nineteenth century, culminating in the Bank Charter Act of 1844, formalized the Bank as a central institution with authority over note issuance and monetary stability. This centralization enabled more reliable currency management and facilitated industrial expansion. It also introduced a new form of technocratic power—an institutional layer between markets and politics that would become central to modern capitalism. Subsequent debates between monetarists such as Milton Friedman,[55] discretionary American central bankers like Ben Bernanke and Jay Powell, and fiscal activists in the Keynesian tradition highlight a deeper problem: our monetary and fiscal regimes remain complex, fragile, and only partially understood, with each crisis revealing how little consensus there is on "what works."[56]

From the perspective of Inclusive Capitalism, the lesson is not that regulation or central banking are inherently good or bad, given the circumstances driving the need for those regulations, but that a system that repeatedly oscillates between extremes—tight control, then deregulation; austerity, then stimulus; aggressive oversight, then rollback—is signaling design failure. When incentives are misaligned at the core, regulation becomes a patch, not a solution. It is reactive, polarizing, and ultimately unstable. A core tenet of Inclusive Capitalism is that by removing, or at least substantially mitigating, the conditions that give rise to regulation, all stakeholders benefit—particularly industrial leadership. The task, therefore, is not to regulate behavior after the fact but to re-engineer the system so that desirable behavior emerges by design.

Culturally, early-stage capitalism normalized several patterns that still shape behavior today.[57] Industrial leaders learned that short-term profit maximization, aggressive cost reduction, and relentless pursuit of market share were rewarded—even when these strategies provoked public outrage and regulatory response. Workers and communities learned that improvements in productivity often arrived as threats: job loss, wage pressure, and erosion of bargaining power. Political actors learned that they could mobilize either side—capital or labor—by promising to push the pendulum in their direction. The result is an implicit culture of "ping-pong economics," with policy and rhetoric alternately privileging capital or labor, state intervention or market primacy, without resolving the underlying design flaws.

Amid these doctrinal clashes and legislative experiments, one document stands out as especially relevant to Inclusive Capitalism: The Constitution of the United States.

The preamble—"We the People . . . to form a more perfect Union . . . promote the general Welfare, and secure the Blessings of Liberty to ourselves and our Posterity"—explicitly grounds governmental authority in the people, not in monarchs or corporate charters.[58] Its core commitments map closely onto Adam Smith's moral vision: a framework in which institutions exist to serve broad human flourishing, not to extract from it. Checks and balances, periodic elections, judicial review, and a bill of rights were all mechanisms to ensure that no actor—individual, faction, or branch—could convert political power into unchecked self-enrichment.

From the standpoint of this book, the Constitution is instructive because it instantiated, at the level of political design, what has never been fully achieved at the economic level. Government was explicitly chartered to serve the people; large enterprises never were. As a result, American capitalism today both reflects and violates the constitutional spirit. It has generated extraordinary innovation, wealth creation, and global influence, and by many conventional metrics—GDP, GDP per capita, currency status—the United States remains the most successful large-scale capitalist society in history. Yet the system also produces persistent inequality, recurring crises, and deep political polarization. In that sense, capitalism as currently instantiated falls short of the constitutional aspiration to "promote the General Welfare" in a way that is durable, inclusive, and broadly legitimate.[59]

Seen through this lens, Inclusive Capitalism embraces capitalism and the American constitutional order. It is an attempt to extend the constitutional principle—institutions exist to serve the people—into the economic domain. In practical terms, that means rechartering our largest enterprises so that, like the branches of government, they operate within a set of rules, metrics, and accountability structures explicitly oriented toward societal well-being. It also means designing incentives so that industrial leadership can pursue its own self-interest while advancing rather than undermining that broader goal.

Industrial Leader Incentives and Behaviors During Early Capitalism

From doctrine, we now turn to industrial leadership behavior. Industrial leaders in the early decades of capitalism operated under a set of forces that made extraordinary innovation and extraordinary exploitation two sides of the same coin. This period reveals how the system behaves in its purest form—before regulatory frameworks, labor protections, or mature financial institutions emerged—and therefore offers a uniquely clear view into the incentives that shaped behavior. These incentives, more than personal morality or individual temperament, drove both the transformative achievements of the era and the practices that would be condemned today. With respect to personal morality of the industrial leadership, the innovative side of the coin and the resultant benefits of the innovations outweighed the exploitative side of the same coin, and still does today.[60]

Early industrialists lived and worked within an environment defined by first-mover advantage, technological uncertainty, and unforgiving competition. The Industrial Revolution unfolded rapidly, with breakthroughs in steam power, mechanized spinning, and iron production arriving in quick succession.[61] Those who adopted new machinery early earned extraordinary returns; those who hesitated risked near immediate ruin. Richard Arkwright reinvested nearly all profits into new mills and constant mechanical improvement; James Watt and Matthew Boulton pursued patents, defended them aggressively, and commercialized steam power with relentless intensity.[62] These were rational strategies, not outliers. In a system where technological obsolescence could occur within a single season, industrialists survived by expanding rapidly, lowering costs, and defending their advantage with vigor. Sound familiar?[63]

The labor environment reinforced this dynamic. With no statutory limits on working hours, ages, or conditions, labor costs represented the most flexible lever available to industrialists trying to maintain competitive footing.[64] Managers rationally resorted to fourteen-hour shifts, child labor, and strict disciplinary regimes because the system rewarded these choices. Many owners saw such harshness not as cruelty but as the unavoidable cost of progress, consistent with the prevailing cultural ethos that valorized discipline, sacrifice, and the accumulation of capital through frugality.[65] Even comparatively humane leaders such as Josiah Wedgwood relied on exacting oversight and low wages for unskilled workers.[66] The incentives favored extraction at the margin, and extraction became the norm.

Daily life for industrialists reflected the immense pressures of the era. They rose before dawn to inspect machinery, negotiate with suppliers, discipline workers, plan expansions, and manage complex supply chains. Evenings were spent in ledgers, correspondence, or seeking loans. Arkwright routinely worked sixteen-hour days; Watt wrote often of exhaustion and fear that rivals would overtake him; Matthew Boulton—despite famously declaring that he sold "what the world desires to have—power"—lived in a state of constant vigilance.[67] Their wealth was real but fragile. Factories burned down, banks failed, and recessions struck without warning.[68] The Panic of 1837 wiped out many who had borrowed heavily for expansion, and with no bankruptcy protection or social safety nets, failure meant destitution. In such an environment, long-term thinking was difficult, and practices that harmed workers were often rationalized as necessary for firm survival.

The industrialists' social worlds reflected their new status as a class between the old aristocracy and the laboring population.[69] Their social circles formed around merchant associations, scientific societies, and business clubs where they debated machinery, trade policy, and political reform. The Lunar Society in Birmingham—whose members included Watt, Boulton, and Wedgwood—illustrates this environment of restless experimentation and pragmatic ambition.[70] Yet their success also made them targets. The Luddite uprisings of 1811–1816, during which textile workers smashed machinery that displaced their labor, often resulted in owners calling in private militias or military troops. Mill owner William Cartwright's request for armed protection in 1812, which resulted in worker deaths, shows the combustible mixture of fear, economic pressure, and social upheaval that defined the age.[71]

A few leaders recognized that better working conditions could yield higher productivity and long-term stability. Robert Owen's New Lanark stands as the most notable counterexample to the prevailing belief that competitiveness required relentless labor extraction, illustrating that alternative incentive structures could produce both economic and social gains.[72] But Owen's model remained an exception. The wider system punished humane practices: They raised costs immediately, while their benefits accrued slowly. Firms that emulated Owen risked being undercut by competitors operating under leaner, harsher regimes. Without incentives and institutions that rewarded inclusive behavior—and without customer, investor, or regulatory pressures—

there was little reason to behave differently. The mathematical logic of capital accumulation overwhelmed moral instincts: More hours meant more output, more profits, more reinvestment, and more scale.[73]

The combination of pressures—technological uncertainty, capital scarcity, weak financial institutions, and absence of labor protections—created an environment where narrow self-interest often diverged from broader social well-being. Industrialists did not set out to create systems of exploitation; rather, they responded rationally to the incentives they faced.[74] But the predictable result was an escalating cycle of overwork, danger, and unrest, which eventually prompted popular backlash and the first serious wave of government intervention.[75] The Factory Acts, repeal of the Combination Acts, and other early legislation were not arbitrary impositions—they were societal reactions to structural incentives that had produced increasingly untenable conditions.

This period thus provides one of the clearest lessons for understanding both the strength and instability of capitalism: Self-interest unaligned with societal well-being can generate unprecedented prosperity, but—particularly at scale—it produces exclusion, conflict, and pressure for external correction.[76] Every major intervention over the two centuries that followed can be understood as an attempt to repair this misalignment reactively rather than by design. The broader argument of Inclusive Capitalism is that correction must occur in advance, through design, so that innovation and inclusion reinforce rather than undermine one another.

Lived Experience of the Workforce and Population During Early Capitalism

Having examined leadership incentives, we now turn to the lived experience of the workforce. The lived experience of workers in the early decades of capitalism reveals the other half of the system's dual nature. Just as industrialists operated under powerful incentives that drove innovation, workers operated under incentives—and constraints—that made their lives harsh, precarious, and often brutally short.[77] Yet their experience was not only misery; early capitalism offered real gains over feudal and mercantile life: greater mobility, more varied forms of work, rising consumption possibilities, and early signs of social advancement. The task here is to hold both realities in view while continually asking a central question: Could the extraordinary economic gains of this era have been achieved without imposing such severe human costs?

For many workers, the transition from rural life to factory employment offered some promise.[78] Agricultural labor under feudal and post-feudal arrangements could be seasonal, unstable, and highly dependent on landlords and harvest cycles. Factory work, by contrast, provided steady wages—even if meager—and a chance, however slim, for upward mobility. Urban centers like Manchester, Birmingham, and Leeds offered the possibility of dense commercial life, access to markets, and, eventually, incremental improvements in living standards that provided more varied diets, greater availability of goods, and the early stirrings of mass literacy.[79] These gains were real, and they help explain why millions voluntarily moved from countryside to city.

But these gains came wrapped in conditions that were often harsh and dangerous. Factory labor routinely demanded twelve to sixteen hours a day under strict supervision, in poorly ventilated spaces filled with smoke, dust, and noise. Machinery lacked basic safety protections, making serious injury common rather than exceptional. The 1833 mill fire in Leeds—where locked exits trapped workers inside—was not an anomaly but a revealing example of how efficiency routinely took precedence over human safety.[80]

Wages were barely sufficient for survival. A male worker's earnings—roughly twenty shillings per week—translated to subsistence-level income in modern terms, and women and children earned far less.[81] Housing consumed half or more of a family's earnings. Diets were dominated by bread, porridge, and potatoes. Malnutrition was chronic. During downturns such as the Cotton Famine of the 1840s, the collapse of U.S. cotton exports triggered mass layoffs and widespread starvation in northern England.[82] There were no safety nets, no state assistance, and no guarantee that a family could endure even a brief downturn in global supply chains.[83]

Living conditions in industrial cities intensified these hardships. Most workers lived in narrow, back-to-back tenements with no sanitation, no drainage, and little ventilation. Waste filled the streets; water was often contaminated; and epidemics of cholera, typhoid, and tuberculosis were frequent.[84] In mid-nineteenth-century Manchester, life expectancy for working-class residents hovered around twenty-six years—half that of wealthier citizens. Child mortality was catastrophic: in some neighborhoods, more than half of all children died before age five.[85] The physical residential environment of early capitalism was, in many respects, even more dangerous than the factory floor itself.

Child labor was not incidental but central to the factory system. Children as young as five worked long hours in textile mills, mines, and match factories, often performing dangerous tasks that exposed them to injury, chronic illness, and premature death.[86] Contemporary investigations such as the Sadler Report of 1832 documented beatings, exhaustion, and working conditions so severe that child labor became a visible moral crisis rather than a hidden abuse.[87]

Given these conditions, resistance was inevitable. Workers attempted to unionize but met force at nearly every turn. Early strikes were crushed by hired militias or by troops. During the Luddite uprisings, machinery was destroyed, not out of irrational technophobia but in response to rapid displacement of skilled artisans with no compensation or alternative employment. Events like the Peterloo Massacre of 1819—where cavalry charged peaceful demonstrators demanding parliamentary reform—exposed the deep social fracture emerging within liberal capitalism's first century.[88]

Subsequent movements such as Chartism, which demanded voting rights and representation, were responses not to ideological abstractions but to lived hardships.[89]

Legislative reforms slowly followed. The Factory Act of 1833 limited child labor and required rudimentary schooling; the Mines Act of 1842 barred women and children from underground work; and the Ten Hours Act of 1847 capped daily work for women and children.[90] These reforms were moral victories, but they were also economic interventions—society's effort to counteract structural incentives that favored extraction over dignity. In a sense, every one of these laws is empirical evidence that early capitalism, left to its own devices, did not reliably produce the outcomes Smith imagined when he described his "system of natural liberty."[91]

The central evaluative question is unavoidable: were the gains worth the costs? Early capitalism delivered unprecedented increases in output, productivity, and technological progress.[92] It enabled urbanization, expanded access to goods, and set the stage for the remarkable growth trajectories of the nineteenth and twentieth centuries.[93] Yet it did so by imposing burdens on workers that were, by any humane standard, indefensible—and by creating social tensions that triggered cycles of protest, repression, and later governmental oversight.

The deeper lesson, consistent across two and a half centuries, is that the architecture of incentives matters more than the character of individuals. Industrialists and workers alike behaved rationally under the systems they confronted. If societies continue to rely on systems that reward extraction, scarcity, and short-term advantage—even inadvertently—we should expect the same outcomes, adjusted only by degree and technology.[94] The challenge for Inclusive Capitalism is to design a system in which the extraordinary benefits witnessed in this period—innovation, productivity growth, rising living standards—can be realized without the corrosive costs. The historical record suggests that this is not only desirable but necessary if the next century of progress is to avoid repeating the worst dynamics of the first.[95]

Early Stage Capitalism – What Worked and What Did Not Work

Evaluating early-stage capitalism requires holding two truths simultaneously: this period generated the single greatest economic inflection point in human history and it imposed staggering social, environmental, and human costs that neither Adam Smith nor the early industrialists anticipated.[96] The challenge is to disentangle these forces, understand why they arose, and ask whether the benefits could have been achieved without the devastation—an inquiry that lies at the heart of Inclusive Capitalism.[97]

One of the most significant achievements of early capitalism was its extraordinary acceleration of economic growth. The transition from agrarian production to mechanized industry unleashed productivity gains without historical precedent. As Smith observed, "The greatest improvements in the productive powers of labour . . . have been the effects of the division of labour."[98] Mechanization in textiles, metallurgy, and transport multiplied output while lowering costs, expanding access to goods, and ultimately raising material standards of living. Just as important was the role of the industrialists themselves.[99] Their willingness to risk everything—to borrow heavily, reinvest profits, experiment with untested machinery, and endure grueling work schedules—was central to this surge. Given the stagnation that preceded industrialization, the magnitude of the gains appears unambiguous: society had more goods, more services, more opportunity, and more dynamism than ever before.[100]

Second, early capitalism also ignited a sustained wave of technological innovation. The competitive pressures of the factory system created powerful incentives to discover better methods, improve machinery, and scale production. Joseph Schumpeter famously characterized capitalism as "a method of economic change" propelled by "creative destruction."[101] Steam power, rotary motion, iron smelting, mechanical looms, and precision engineering did not merely increase output; they created entirely new industries and reshaped the global economy.[102] In this era, innovation was not an episodic event but a structural feature of the system itself.

A third achievement was the emergence of a new middle class with increasing economic and political influence. Entrepreneurs, merchants, engineers, and skilled workers found pathways to upward mobility that had been structurally unavailable under feudal or mercantilist arrangements.[103] Their rising incomes fueled new markets for manufactured goods and provided the political pressure that ultimately dismantled protectionist mercantilist policies in favor of freer trade and more liberal property rights. This middle class became both the symbol and the beneficiary of early capitalism's promise.[104]

Yet these gains were tightly coupled to severe and pervasive costs. Industrial workers endured brutal conditions: twelve to sixteen hour shifts, dangerous machinery, polluted air, contaminated water, crowded tenements, malnutrition, and child labor on a scale difficult to fathom today. Women and children were exploited systematically because their labor was cheaper.[105] Engels' account of Manchester is painful to read but accurate: factory owners maximized profit by minimizing every expenditure related to worker safety or well-being.[106] The "invisible hand" did not check these abuses; instead, it amplified the incentives that produced them.

Two additional consequences—environmental degradation and rapid, unplanned urbanization—were both predictable and largely ignored. Industrial cities became polluted, disease-ridden, and overwhelmed.[107] Karl Polanyi later argued that industrial capitalism created a "dis-embedded economy" that detached production from natural limits.[108] This critique applies as much to early industrial Manchester as to global climate and environmental consequences today.[109]

The core question is why these costs emerged so consistently across industries and regions. The answer lies in the incentives inherent to early capitalism: extreme competition, fragile financing, volatile markets, and a constant threat of failure.[110] Industrialists were rewarded for minimizing labor costs, maximizing output, and reinvesting aggressively.[111] They were punished—often irreversibly and disastrously—for hesitation, excess generosity, or misjudged innovation.[112] Under those incentives, and without countervailing institutions, the system naturally produced unequal gains, harsh working conditions, and the beginnings of the regulatory edifice that would follow.[113]

Robert Owen stands as a counterfactual that illuminates what might have been possible.[114] His reforms at New Lanark—shorter hours, child education, clean housing, fair pricing, and early health and welfare programs—demonstrated that industry could be both profitable and humane.[115] Owen was not a socialist in the modern sense; he was a capitalist industrialist who believed that enlightened management and improved working conditions were not only morally necessary but economically advantageous. His mills returned healthy profits, attracted global attention, and offered a living example of an alternative trajectory for industrial capitalism.

Yet Owen's model was not broadly adopted. He succeeded because of his unusual personal convictions, his control over a single integrated industrial community, and his willingness to sacrifice short-term profit for long-term productivity and social benefit—traits that were dramatically at odds with prevailing incentives.[116] Most industrialists lacked the freedom, the temperament, or the financial margins to emulate him. His approach required institutional support that did not exist. His ideas influenced later cooperative movements and social reforms, but the mainstream of industrial capitalism continued along a path shaped by competitive pressure rather than ethics or foresight. In that sense, Owen's example reinforces rather than refutes the need for structural change: because if humane capitalism requires extraordinary moral leadership alone, it cannot scale.[117]

The final inescapable insight from this period is that the incentives that generated extraordinary progress also generated extraordinary harm.[118] Industrialists behaved as rational actors responding to the rules of the system. They drove innovation and growth but also exploitation and degradation. Workers gained wages and access to manufactured goods but lost safety, health, and autonomy. The system delivered unprecedented prosperity but at the cost of division, protest, and sustained political backlash—patterns that echo loudly today.[119]

Early-stage capitalism worked spectacularly on its own terms but only because those terms excluded the well-being of much of the population and ignored the long-term consequences for social cohesion and the environment.[120] The lesson is not that capitalism failed, nor that its successes justify its costs, but that the system's core design—its incentives and its institutional scaffolding—determines whether progress emerges with or without devastation. And that is why cosmetic reforms or episodic regulation cannot resolve the structural tensions embedded from the start.[121] It is also why a modern redesign aimed at aligning self-interest with societal well-being is not merely desirable but necessary if we hope to preserve the dynamism capitalism unleashed while avoiding the consequences it repeatedly produces.

If Robert Owen demonstrated that better outcomes were possible, early-stage capitalism demonstrated that they would not emerge organically. That tension sets the stage for what follows—and frames the mandate for Inclusive Capitalism.

Conclusions and Insights From Early Capitalism That Inform Inclusive Capitalism's Design

The core diagnostic emerging from early-stage capitalism is that extraordinary progress can coexist with extraordinary harm when incentives push leaders toward short-term survival rather than long-term value creation.[122] Industrialists behaved rationally under the rules they were given. The problem was not their intentions but the architecture of the system itself. If survival depends on relentless cost-cutting, sixteen-hour days, and a willingness to sacrifice worker welfare, environmental quality, and community stability,[123] then even capable and well-intentioned leaders will rationally feel compelled—and frequently act—to choose ruthlessness over restraint. The lesson is not that industrialists were uniquely immoral, though moral failures certainly existed, but that they operated within systems where decency carried existential cost.

This dynamic remains fully intact today. Leaders in technology, healthcare, pharmaceuticals, logistics, and energy routinely confront life-or-death decisions—not for themselves alone but for their companies and careers. Modern analysts from Friedman to Taleb have noted the fragility of systems in which competitive pressure creates extreme downside risk for even small missteps.[124] Miss a product cycle, lose a regulatory race, or slip behind a competitor, and a decade of work can evaporate. Under those conditions, even good leaders make decisions that create collateral damage for society. It is no surprise that the very individuals most responsible for technological progress are often among the most distrusted. A system that demands superhuman resilience, encourages secrecy over shared knowledge, and ties survival to maximizing short-term margins will reliably produce both innovation and resentment.[125]

The task is to design a system where the incentives that generate innovation no longer require these destructive tradeoffs—where leaders can pursue breakthrough advances without placing their firms, their employees, or themselves in existential jeopardy. This is not a utopian aspiration. It is a design problem. Early-stage capitalism demonstrated that people will work extraordinarily hard, take extraordinary risks, and push technological boundaries when the incentives are aligned.[126] What must change is the structure around those incentives:

- Innovation should be rewarded but not in a way that makes failure catastrophic.[127]
- Knowledge should flow more freely, so that breakthroughs diffuse quickly—much as steam power, textile machinery, and metallurgical techniques spread in

the early industrial era but without the secrecy and zero-sum behavior that slowed adoption and amplified inequality.[128]

- Entrepreneurs should still emerge with immense wealth and influence aligned with their efforts and risks taken but through systems that broaden opportunity rather than concentrate it.[129]
- Long-term horizons must replace short-term survival pressures, allowing companies to invest in environmental stewardship, human dignity, and workforce development without being punished by markets for doing so.[130]
- The pace of innovation should accelerate, not slowly, under a system that reduces duplication, shortens development cycles, and leverages shared knowledge while preserving competitive differentiation.[131]

None of this is incompatible with capitalism. On the contrary, Adam Smith envisioned a system that served the people, elevated the general welfare, and generated widespread prosperity—not a system that oscillates between unrestrained exploitation and heavy-handed intervention.[132] The evidence across economic history shows that the system's most destructive episodes emerge not from too much liberty or too much regulation but from misaligned incentives that make exploitation the rational choice.

Addressing that misalignment must occur at the core, not at the margins. Early-stage capitalism established the foundations—private property, markets, competition, investment—but it also embedded the unintended consequences that would recur throughout the Gilded Age, the Progressive Era, the New Deal, and contemporary capitalism. For more than two centuries, societies have tried to patch the system through regulation, redistribution, or alternating ideological swings. None of these have resolved the underlying design flaw.

Inclusive Capitalism aims to do what has not yet been attempted: re-engineer the incentive architecture itself, so that the same creative energies that powered early industrialization—risk-taking, ingenuity, perseverance, and ambition—are channeled toward outcomes that expand societal well-being rather than erode it. In a system designed correctly, curing cancer becomes more profitable than treating it; preventing disease becomes more valuable than billing for it; reducing scarcity becomes a source of competitive advantage rather than a threat to revenue.

That is the ambition of what follows. We treat early capitalism as the baseline architecture against which all later interventions (regulation, welfare state, neoliberalism, alternative systems) should be evaluated. The next chapters will continue the diagnostic—through the Gilded Age, the rise of regulation, the mid-century stabilization, and modern capitalism's fractures—always asking the same question: What drove the behavior of economic leaders, what consequences followed, and how could things have been designed differently from the start? We will see in the subsequent chapters an examination of attempted fixes, not new systems. By the time the diagnosis is complete, the necessary architecture for Inclusive Capitalism will be unambiguous. The solutions are not easy, but they are far from impossible—once the problem is properly understood.

Notes

1 Gates, Bill. *Source Code: My Beginnings*. New York: Knopf, 2025, 92–107; Isaacson, Walter. *The Innovators: How a Group of Hackers, Geniuses, and Geeks Created the Digital Revolution*. New York: Simon & Schuster, 2014, 303–311.

2 Landes, David S. *The Unbound Prometheus: Technological Change and Industrial Development in Western Europe from 1750 to the Present*. Cambridge: Cambridge University Press, 2003, 41–92.

3 Adam Smith, *An Inquiry into the Nature and Causes of the Wealth of Nations*, ed. Edwin Cannan (Chicago: University of Chicago Press, 1976), I.ii.2–3, 14–15.

4 Hobsbawm, Eric. *Industry and Empire: The Birth of the Industrial Revolution*. New York: The New Press, 1999, 13–52.

5 North, Douglass C. *Institutions, Institutional Change and Economic Performance*. Cambridge: Cambridge University Press, 1990, 3–14.

6 Adam Smith, *An Inquiry into the Nature and Causes of the Wealth of Nations*,, I.i.1–3.

7 Joseph A. Schumpeter, *Capitalism, Socialism, and Democracy* (New York: Harper & Brothers, 1942), 81–86.

8 Adam Smith, *An Inquiry into the Nature and Causes of the Wealth of Nations*,, I.ii.2–3, 14–15.

9 David Ricardo, *Principles of Political Economy and Taxation* (London: John Murray, 1817), 85–93.

10 Keynes, John Maynard. "The Scope and Method of Political Economy." In *The Collected Writings of John Maynard Keynes*, Vol. XIII: *The General Theory and After: Part I*, edited by Donald Moggridge, 289–315. London: Macmillan, 1973.

11 Hobsbawm, Eric. *The Age of Revolution: Europe 1789–1848*. New York: Vintage Books, 1996, 31–78; Polanyi, Karl. *The Great Transformation*. Boston: Beacon Press, 1944, 35–76.

12 Adam Smith, *An Inquiry into the Nature and Causes of the Wealth of Nations*,, I.ii.2–3, 14–15.

13 Karl Marx and Friedrich Engels, *The Communist Manifesto* (London: Penguin Classics, 2011), 73–82.

14 Williams, Raymond. *Keywords: A Vocabulary of Culture and Society*. Rev. ed. New York: Oxford University Press, 1983, 51–54.

15 Hall, Peter A., and David Soskice, eds. *Varieties of Capitalism: The Institutional Foundations of Comparative Advantage*. Oxford: Oxford University Press, 2001.

16 Adam Smith, *Wealth of Nations*, IV.ii.9–11, 452–456.

17 Varian, Hal R., Carl Shapiro, and Joseph Farrell. *Information Rules: A Strategic Guide to the Network Economy*. Boston: Harvard Business School Press, 1999, 3–24.

18 Adam Smith, *Wealth of Nations*, IV.iii.2.

19 Charles Babbage, *On the Economy of Machinery and Manufactures* (London: Charles Knight, 1832), 55–63.

20 Robert C. Allen, *The British Industrial Revolution in Global Perspective* (Cambridge: Cambridge University Press, 2009), 60–75.

21 Larry Neal, *The Rise of Financial Capitalism* (Cambridge: Cambridge University Press, 1990), 121–132.

22 Locke, John. *Two Treatises of Government*. Edited by Peter Laslett. Cambridge: Cambridge University Press, 1988 [orig. 1689], II, §§4–15, 287–305; Smith, Adam. *An Inquiry into the Nature and Causes of the Wealth of Nations*. Indianapolis: Liberty Fund, 1981 [orig. 1776], Book I, chs. 1–3.

23 Adam Smith, *Wealth of Nations*, IV.iii.2.

24 Mokyr, Joel. *The Lever of Riches: Technological Creativity and Economic Progress*. New York: Oxford University Press, 1990, 1–28.
25 Smith, Adam. *An Inquiry into the Nature and Causes of the Wealth of Nations*. Indianapolis: Liberty Fund, 1981 [orig. 1776], Book IV, ch. 9.
26 Adam Smith, *An Inquiry into the Nature and Causes of the Wealth of Nations*,, I.ii.2–3, 14–15.
27 Adam Smith, *Wealth of Nations*, V.i.f.50–61, 781–782.
28 Adam Smith, *Wealth of Nations*, IV.ii.9–11, 452–456.
29 Adam Smith, *Wealth of Nations*, I.i.1–3.
30 Friedrich Hayek, *The Use of Knowledge in Society, American Economic Review 35, no. 4* (1945): 519–530.
31 Adam Smith, *Wealth of Nations*, I.x.c.12, 145–147.
32 Friedrich Hayek, *The Use of Knowledge in Society*, 519–530.
33 Adam Smith, *Wealth of Nations*, V.i.f.50–61, 781–782.
34 Karl Polanyi, *The Great Transformation* (Boston: Beacon Press, 1944), 35–43.
35 Varian, Hal R., Carl Shapiro, and Joseph Farrell. *Information Rules: A Strategic Guide to the Network Economy*. Boston: Harvard Business School Press, 1999, 3–24.
36 Karl Polanyi, *The Great Transformation*, 35–43.
37 Adam Smith, *Wealth of Nations*, I.i.1–3.
38 Adam Smith, *Wealth of Nations*, V.i.f.50–51.
39 E. P. Thompson, *The Making of the English Working Class* (New York: Vintage, 1966), 191–223.
40 Joseph A. Schumpeter, *Capitalism, Socialism, and Democracy*, 81–86.
41 Autor, David H., David Dorn, Lawrence F. Katz, Christina Patterson, and John Van Reenen. "The Fall of the Labor Share and the Rise of Superstar Firms." *Quarterly Journal of Economics* 135, no. 2 (2020): 645–709.
42 Karl Marx and Friedrich Engels, *The Communist Manifesto*, 73–82.
43 Karl Polanyi, *The Great Transformation*, 35–43.
44 Adam Smith, *Wealth of Nations*, IV.iii.2.
45 David Ricardo, *Principles of Political Economy and Taxation*, 85–93.
46 E. P. Thompson, *The Making of the English Working Class*, 191–223.
47 David Ricardo, *Principles of Political Economy and Taxation*, 85–93.
48 Charles Babbage, *On the Economy of Machinery and Manufactures*, 55–63.
49 Karl Marx and Friedrich Engels, *The Communist Manifesto*, 73–82.
50 Schumpeter, Joseph A. *History of Economic Analysis*. New York: Oxford University Press, 1954, 3–43, 473–521.
51 Thompson, E. P. *The Making of the English Working Class*. New York: Vintage Books, 1966, 549–558.
52 *Parliamentary Debates, Factory Act of 1833, Hansard 3rd ser., vol. 19* (1833), 722–732.
53 Irwin, Douglas A. *Against the Tide: An Intellectual History of Free Trade*. Princeton, NJ: Princeton University Press, 1996, 89–120.
54 Larry Neal, *The Rise of Financial Capitalism* (Cambridge: Cambridge University Press, 1990), 121–132.
55 Milton Friedman, *Capitalism and Freedom* (Chicago: University of Chicago Press, 1962), 8–11.
56 Paul Krugman, *The Return of Depression Economics* (New York: Norton, 2009), 21–28.
57 Thompson, E. P. "Time, Work-Discipline, and Industrial Capitalism." *Past & Present* 38 (1967): 56–97.
58 U.S. Const. pmbl.; Bailyn, Bernard. *The Ideological Origins of the American Revolution*. Cambridge, MA: Harvard University Press, 1967, 198–229.
59 U.S. Const. pmbl.; Stiglitz, Joseph E. *The Price of Inequality*. New York: W. W. Norton, 2012, 1–39; Sen, Amartya. *Development as Freedom*. New York: Alfred A. Knopf, 1999, 3–36.

60 Mokyr, Joel. *The Lever of Riches: Technological Creativity and Economic Progress*. 1–28, 81–120.
61 Robert C. Allen, *The British Industrial Revolution in Global Perspective*, 60–75.
62 Christine MacLeod, *Heroes of Invention* (Cambridge: Cambridge University Press, 2007), 178–192.
63 Chandler, Alfred D. *The Visible Hand: The Managerial Revolution in American Business*. Cambridge, MA: Harvard University Press, 1977, 79–121, 285–336.
64 E. P. Thompson, *The Making of the English Working Class*, 268–276.
65 E. P. Thompson, *The Making of the English Working Class*, 191–223.
66 Maxine Berg, *The Age of Manufactures*, 1700–1820 (London: Routledge, 1994), 201–210.
67 Jenny Uglow, *The Lunar Men* (New York: Farrar, Straus & Giroux, 2002), 214–251.
68 Kindleberger, Charles P., and Robert Aliber. *Manias, Panics, and Crashes: A History of Financial Crises*. 6th ed. New York: Palgrave Macmillan, 2011, 33–72.
69 E. P. Thompson, *The Making of the English Working Class*, 191–223.
70 Jenny Uglow, *The Lunar Men* (New York: Farrar, Straus & Giroux, 2002), 214–251.
71 Patrick O'Brien, *The British Industrial Revolution in Global Perspective*, Economic History Review 64, no. 1 (2011): 1–22.
72 Robert Owen, *A New View of Society* (London: Longman, 1813), 55–73.
73 Charles Kindleberger, *Manias, Panics, and Crashes* (New York: Wiley, 1978), 45–53.
74 E. P. Thompson, *The Making of the English Working Class*, 268–276.
75 *Parliamentary Debates, Factory Act of 1833, Hansard 3rd ser., vol. 19* (1833), 722–732.
76 Ibid.
77 E. P. Thompson, *The Making of the English Working Class*, 268–276.
78 Ibid.
79 Judith Flanders, *The Victorian City: Everyday Life in Dickens' London* (New York: Thomas Dunne Books, 2012), 54–67.
80 Hobsbawm, Eric. *Industry and Empire: The Birth of the Industrial Revolution*. 52–59.
81 E. P. Thompson, *The Making of the English Working Class*, 268–276.
82 Leon Faucher, *Manchester in 1844: Its Present Condition and Future Prospects* (London: Simpkin, Marshall & Co., 1844), 76–84.
83 Polanyi, Karl. *The Great Transformation: The Political and Economic Origins of Our Time*. 71–80.
84 Peter Brimblecombe, *The Big Smoke: A History of Air Pollution in London since Medieval Times* (London: Methuen, 1987), 97–110.
85 Leon Faucher, *Manchester in 1844: Its Present Condition and Future Prospects* (London: Simpkin, Marshall & Co., 1844), 76–84.
86 Humphries, Jane. *Childhood and Child Labour in the British Industrial Revolution*. Cambridge: Cambridge University Press, 2010, 83–128.
87 Great Britain. Parliament. *Report of the Select Committee on the Bill for the Regulation of Factories (Sadler Report)*. London: House of Commons, 1832.
88 Patrick O'Brien, *The British Industrial Revolution in Global Perspective*, Economic History Review 64, no. 1 (2011): 1–22.
89 E. P. Thompson, *The Making of the English Working Class*, 268–276.
90 *Parliamentary Debates, Mines and Collieries Act of 1842, Hansard 3rd ser., vol. 64* (1842), 1190–1198.
91 Smith, Adam. *An Inquiry into the Nature and Causes of the Wealth of Nations*. Indianapolis: Liberty Fund, 1981 [orig. 1776], Book IV, ch. 9.
92 Charles Babbage, *On the Economy of Machinery and Manufactures*, 55–63.
93 Robert C. Allen, *The British Industrial Revolution in Global Perspective*, 60–75.
94 Karl Polanyi, *The Great Transformation*, 35–43.
95 Acemoglu, Daron, and James A. Robinson. *Why Nations Fail: The Origins of Power, Prosperity, and Poverty*. New York: Crown Business, 2012, 74–91.

96 Robert C. Allen, *The British Industrial Revolution in Global Perspective*, 60–75.
97 Maxine Berg, *The Age of Manufactures*, 1700–1820 (London: Routledge, 1994), 201–210.
98 Adam Smith, *Wealth of Nations*, I.i.1–3.
99 Chandler, Alfred D. *The Visible Hand: The Managerial Revolution in American Business*. 1–12, 79–121.
100 Patrick O'Brien, *The British Industrial Revolution in Global Perspective*, Economic History Review 64, no. 1 (2011): 1–22.
101 Joseph A. Schumpeter, *Capitalism, Socialism, and Democracy*, 81–86.
102 Charles Babbage, *On the Economy of Machinery and Manufactures*, 55–63.
103 Judith Flanders, *The Victorian City: Everyday Life in Dickens' London*, 54–67.
104 Patrick O'Brien, *The British Industrial Revolution in Global Perspective*, Economic History Review 64, no. 1 (2011): 1–22.
105 *Parliamentary Committee on Factories, The Sadler Report* (1832), 12–19.
106 Friedrich Engels, *The Condition of the Working Class in England*, ed. Victor Kiernan (London: Penguin Classics, 1987), 87–108.
107 Stephen Mosley, *The Chimney of the World: A History of Smoke Pollution in Victorian and Edwardian Manchester* (London: Routledge, 2001), 63–79.
108 Karl Polanyi, *The Great Transformation*, 35–43.
109 *Climate Change 2022: Mitigation of Climate Change*. Cambridge: Cambridge University Press, 2022, Summary for Policymakers, 1–28.
110 Christine MacLeod, *Heroes of Invention* (Cambridge: Cambridge University Press, 2007), 178–192.
111 Chandler, Alfred D. *The Visible Hand: The Managerial Revolution in American Business*. 79–121, 285–336.
112 Roy Porter, *London: A Social History* (Cambridge: Harvard University Press, 1995), 212–221.
113 Hobsbawm, Eric. *The Age of Revolution: Europe 1789–1848*. New York: Vintage Books, 1996, 31–78.
114 Robert Owen, *A New View of Society* (London: Longman, 1813), 55–73.
115 Ian Donnachie, Robert Owen: *Owen of New Lanark and New Harmony* (East Linton: Tuckwell Press, 2000), 67–81.
116 Gregory Claeys, *Citizens and Saints*: Politics and Anti-Politics in Early British Socialism (Cambridge: Cambridge University Press, 1989), 101–112.
117 Ian Donnachie, Robert Owen: *Owen of New Lanark and New Harmony* (East Linton: Tuckwell Press, 2000), 67–81.
118 Polanyi, Karl. *The Great Transformation: The Political and Economic Origins of Our Time*. 71–80, 136–170.
119 Hobsbawm, Eric. *The Age of Revolution: Europe 1789–1848*. New York: Vintage Books, 1996, 31–78, 289–307.
120 Peter Brimblecombe, *The Big Smoke: A History of Air Pollution in London since Medieval Times*, 97–110.
121 North, Douglass C. *Institutions, Institutional Change and Economic Performance*. 3–14.
122 Robert C. Allen, *The British Industrial Revolution in Global Perspective*, 60–75.
123 E. P. Thompson, *The Making of the English Working Class*, 268–276.
124 Friedman, Milton. *Capitalism and Freedom*. Chicago: University of Chicago Press, 1962, 7–21; Taleb, Nassim Nicholas. *Antifragile: Things That Gain from Disorder*. New York: Random House, 2012, 3–32.
125 Joseph A. Schumpeter, *Capitalism, Socialism, and Democracy*, 81–86.
126 Charles Babbage, *On the Economy of Machinery and Manufactures*, 55–63.
127 Adam Smith, *Wealth of Nations*, I.x.c.12, 145–147.
128 Mokyr, Joel. *The Enlightened Economy: An Economic History of Britain 1700–1850*. New Haven, CT.

129 Schumpeter, Joseph A. *Capitalism, Socialism and Democracy*. New York: Harper & Brothers, 1942, 81–106.
130 Mazzucato, Mariana. *Mission Economy: A Moonshot Guide to Changing Capitalism*. London: Allen Lane, 2021, 33–61.
131 von Hippel, Eric. *Democratizing Innovation*. Cambridge, MA: MIT Press, 2005, 1–38.
132 Adam Smith, *Wealth of Nations*, V.i.f.50–51.

4 The Gilded Age: Smithian Capitalism on Steroids

The Gilded Age is the clearest historical x-ray of capitalism's extraordinary power—and its equally extraordinary vulnerabilities.[1] Spanning the late nineteenth and early twentieth centuries, it was a period in which industrial scale, technological acceleration, and financial innovation combined to produce unprecedented national prosperity while simultaneously amplifying the system's deepest structural flaws. The core takeaway of this chapter is that the very forces that propelled the United States into global leadership—massive productivity gains, entrepreneurial boldness, and the rapid scaling of new technologies—also generated the unintended consequences that now define the logic of modern capitalism: extreme wealth concentration, political capture, systemic fragility, speculative excess, and the erosion of dignity among those excluded from the boom.[2] The Gilded Age demonstrates that prosperity and pathology are not competing narratives of American capitalism; they are two manifestations of the same underlying system.[3] Understanding this duality is essential to understanding why redesign at the core is now necessary.

A critical transition during the Gilded Age is the shift of industrial leadership from the United Kingdom to the United States.[4] This shift is often attributed to cultural differences, national character, or frontier values, but such explanations are incomplete. The two societies were—and remain—deeply similar in language, legal tradition, commercial norms, and industrial know-how. A more compelling explanation lies in institutional dynamics. By the mid-nineteenth century, Britain had begun layering regulatory constraints onto its industrial system in response to the excesses documented in the previous chapter. Factory Acts, labor restrictions, and social reforms addressed genuine harms, but they also narrowed the operating envelope for rapid experimentation, cost compression, and scale expansion.[5] The result was not humane capitalism by design but a gradual dampening of industrial dynamism. The United States, by contrast, inherited British technology and expertise while operating under a far looser regulatory regime, abundant capital, vast internal markets, and weak labor protections.[6] Predictably, industrial leadership migrated toward the environment where innovation and scale were least constrained. The lesson is not that regulation caused British decline but that patches applied after the fact displaced leadership without resolving the underlying incentive problem.[7]

What emerged in the United States was not simply a continuation of early-stage capitalism but its amplification under conditions of unprecedented scale, speed, and institutional permissiveness.[8] Freed from the regulatory constraints that had begun to temper British industrial expansion, American capitalism became the most concentrated expression of the system's core incentives—innovation, accumulation, and competitive survival—operating at continental scale.[9] The Gilded Age thus represents capitalism under maximum load: a historical moment in which its productive potential and its structural vulnerabilities were both pushed to their limits.[10]

 | https://doi.org/10.1515/9783112235485-005

The lesson is not to reject economic dynamism but to redesign it. A new prescription is required—one that preserves capitalism's capacity for innovation and growth without reproducing the destructive patterns that followed unchecked expansion.[11]

What Was the "Gilded Age"?

The term "Gilded Age" derives from Mark Twain and Charles Dudley Warner's 1873 novel *The Gilded Age: A Tale of Today*, a satire of post–Civil War America that exposed the linkages between greed, political corruption, and social pretension.[12] "Gilded" described an era glittering on the surface but decayed beneath it. Characters pursued wealth through land speculation, political bribery, and influence-peddling; one exclaimed, "Beautiful credit! The foundation of modern society." The financial foundation that had emerged during the mercantile period became, by this time, a fertile substrate for speculative excess and asset bubbles, including those that would culminate in the panic of 1893 and ultimately the crash of 1929.[13] Such bubbles tend to accompany periods of strong economic growth—Tulip Mania in the Dutch Golden Age, the dot-com boom of 2000, and perhaps the present enthusiasm surrounding digital assets and AI. Twain's narrative captures the manipulation of officials, pervasive bribery in Washington, and the fragile optimism of a society enthralled by wealth yet unprepared for the consequences when its illusions collapsed. Those illusions did collapse on a global scale early in the next century—a topic addressed in the following chapter.

Speculative excess, political corruption, and disillusionment did not arise spontaneously during the Gilded Age; they emerged from the very architecture of the American growth model. In *Capitalism in America: A History* (2018), Alan Greenspan and Adrian Wooldridge argue that capitalism propelled the United States to global primacy through its embrace of "creative destruction," Joseph Schumpeter's term for the relentless cycle of innovation that replaces the old with the new.[14] This dynamism produced rapid economic growth, technological breakthroughs, and astonishing opportunities for those positioned to capitalize on them. Herman Melville captured the national ethos: "We are the pioneers of the world . . . sent on through the wilderness of untried things."[15] Entrepreneurs like John Jacob Astor, who built fortunes through fur trading and early Manhattan real estate, symbolize the era's promise—individual ambition advancing the nation's economic trajectory.

But this same dynamism explains why Twain's darker themes—corruption, excess, instability—were so pervasive. When innovation accelerates faster than institutions can adapt, when scale outruns governance, and when financial engineering outpaces real productive capacity, the system becomes vulnerable to precisely the pathologies observed during the Gilded Age.[16] The lesson is not that capitalism fails but that capitalism without a modern architecture cannot manage the consequences of its own success.

Factors that Ignited the Gilded Age

Several forces conspired to ignite the Gilded Age. First were technological breakthroughs that revolutionized production. Railroads, advanced steelmaking, telegraph networks, mechanized manufacturing, and the spread of electricity transformed the U.S. economy from a predominantly agrarian system into an industrial powerhouse.[17] This transition replicated, at larger scale, the one Britain had undergone roughly half a century earlier. It enabled large-scale production, broader market integration, and astonishing gains in productivity—particularly for those who controlled the pivotal technologies. As Greenspan and Wooldridge note in *Capitalism in America*, "Railroads created the world's first great business empires . . . enabling unprecedented scale and efficiency."[18] They linked raw materials in the West to factories in the East and brought finished goods to national markets, making possible the rise of industrial giants such as Andrew Carnegie in steel and John D. Rockefeller in oil.

A second enabling force—arguably the most decisive—was the prevailing commitment to laissez-faire governance. The Federal government largely refrained from intervening in business practices, embracing a belief that minimal regulation would accelerate prosperity.[19] Smith's model of a lightly governed, decentralized market was taken as a guiding principle but applied in an environment Smith never anticipated: one dominated not by small producers but by massive and rapidly scaling industrial enterprises with the ability to influence prices, control supply chains, and shape entire markets. As Greenspan observes, this hands-off policy regime allowed entrepreneurs to accumulate wealth "in ways previously unimaginable," often at the direct expense of laborers, farmers, and smaller competitors.[20]

Another critical factor that enabled the explosive rise of the Gilded Age was the near-total absence of worker pushback mechanisms. Industrial expansion proceeded in an environment where labor had virtually no institutional power and few legal protections.[21] Factories, mines, and railroads demanded long hours under dangerous conditions, while wages lagged far behind the wealth flowing to industrial leaders. For years, the imbalance went largely unchecked, allowing rapid capital accumulation, cost compression, and reinvestment that further accelerated economic growth. But as conditions worsened, the accumulated frustration eventually boiled over. Major confrontations such as the Homestead Strike of 1892 and the Pullman Strike of 1894 revealed both the extent of worker grievances and the structural weakness of laissez-faire capitalism at industrial scale. The federal government repeatedly sided with business, deploying troops to break strikes and preserve output. As Greenspan observed, "While the industrialists amassed unprecedented fortunes, workers found themselves on the losing end of an unbalanced economic system."[22] The lack of early worker voice helped fuel the dynamism of the age but also laid the groundwork for the backlash that ultimately ended it.

Political corruption deepened these vulnerabilities. As Mark Twain suggested in naming the era, the glitter of prosperity masked a system in which business and politics were deeply entwined. Political machines such as Tammany Hall exchanged favors, contracts, and protection for votes, ensuring that economic and political power reinforced one another.[23] Corporate influence shaped tariffs, infrastructure decisions, banking rules, and regulatory forbearance. Scandals such as Crédit Mobilier—where railroad executives used bribery to secure favorable federal contracts—exposed the extent of collusion between public officials and private monopolies. Adam Smith had warned explicitly against allowing "merchants and manufacturers" to shape public policy, noting that their interests rarely align with those of society as a whole.[24] Yet during the Gilded Age, it was precisely this alignment of concentrated wealth and political influence that took hold. The absence of campaign finance limits and meaningful conflict-of-interest rules ensured that industrialists could shape the legal environment in which they operated, entrenching their power and accelerating the inequality that defined the era.

The consequences of this unrestrained era are well known. The absence of meaningful guardrails enabled the emergence of monopolies, trusts, and cartels—entities whose scale was orders of magnitude beyond anything Smith imagined. The 1890 Sherman Antitrust Act attempted to rein in such behaviors, but weak enforcement rendered it largely ineffective in its early decades.[25] Consolidation therefore proceeded largely unchecked: Standard Oil controlled nearly the entire U.S. refining capacity; J.P. Morgan stitched together vast railroad trusts; Carnegie Steel set industry prices and wages with little meaningful competition. In a span of just decades, the "invisible hand" inverted, as competitive markets hardened into concentrated power and exclusionary systems that eroded the very societal well-being they were meant to advance.

What the Gilded Age ultimately reveals is not that capitalism fails under pressure but that capitalism without an architecture appropriate to its scale becomes something fundamentally different from what Smith envisioned.[26] The forces that made the United States an economic powerhouse also created the conditions for instability, disillusionment, and political backlash. This duality—prosperity entwined with peril—remains at the heart of today's economic challenges.

Inclusive Capitalism's project is, in part, a response to this history. It asks whether we can retain the dynamism that fueled the Gilded Age without reproducing its pathologies. The first step is understanding the forces that made the Gilded Age both extraordinary and unsustainable. The next chapters build on this understanding, showing why an architectural redesign is essential if we are to foster growth without allowing scale and incentive structures to generate dramatic concentration, instability, and excessive systemic exclusion once again.[27]

Economic Doctrines, Legal Framework, and Cultural Norms During the Gilded Age

Economic doctrines, legal frameworks, and cultural norms played decisive roles in shaping the Gilded Age, and together they help explain why the United States eventually surpassed the United Kingdom as the world's dominant economic power. Although the two countries shared a common intellectual inheritance in Adam Smith, their institutional trajectories diverged sharply. Britain entered the late nineteenth century as the mature industrial leader, increasingly constrained by entrenched class structures, older legal institutions, imperial commitments that pulled capital outward rather than reinvesting it domestically, and an expanding regulatory framework developed in response to earlier industrial excesses. The United States, by contrast, blended Smithian ideas with frontier fluidity, weak aristocratic constraints, and a national culture that celebrated risk, mobility, and reinvention.[28] This unique combination created a more permissive and often more volatile environment in which entrepreneurship could scale initiatives with unprecedented speed.

The United Kingdom's industrial leadership had been built on early mechanization, disciplined capital markets, and a legal system that protected contracts and creditors with formidable rigor. But by the Gilded Age, those same institutions were becoming sources of rigidity and constraint.[29] Britain's banking system remained conservative, oriented toward trade finance rather than entrepreneurial risk, and was dominated by institutions wary of industrial speculation after earlier crises.[30] Cultural norms emphasized continuity, incremental improvement, and the preservation of established firms. Even the class system shaped economic dynamics: social mobility was limited, and leadership in finance and industry often originated from inherited positions rather than meritocratic ascent. These constraints did not eliminate growth, but they did reduce the dynamism and appetite for large-scale industrial reinvention. By the late 1800s, Britain's growth slowed, not because it lacked talent or ideas but because its institutional and cultural architecture channeled them conservatively.

The United States, meanwhile, developed a very different economic temperament. Its banking system was fragmented and unstable, but it was far more willing to fund industrial speculation and frontier ventures.[31] Legal frameworks were more permissive, allowing rapid firm formation, looser corporate governance, and more aggressive consolidation. American contract and property law was shaped by a culture of land speculation and westward expansion, and privileged entrepreneurial freedom over creditor protection. Social norms reinforced these tendencies. The absence of a formal aristocracy, combined with strong narratives of self-made success, made society more accepting of vast wealth disparities as long as they were associated with visible innovation and output. This alignment of doctrine, law, and culture allowed entrepreneurs like Carnegie, Rockefeller, and Vanderbilt to build organizations that simply could not have scaled under Britain's more established constraints.[32]

Political norms also played a role. American governance in the Gilded Age often blurred the line between public authority and private influence. Weak regulatory oversight, combined with a political culture tolerant of patronage and lobbying, allowed industrialists to shape legislation, acquire land grants, and secure privileged access to infrastructure.[33] Although this contributed to corruption and exploitation, it also accelerated industrial consolidation and national-scale integration of markets. Britain, with stronger parliamentary oversight and a more mature civil service, limited such excesses, but also lacked mechanisms to mobilize capital and political will on the scale required for the new age of railroads, steel, and electrification.

Taken together, these contrasts explain much of the divergent economic trajectory between the two nations. The United Kingdom entered the Gilded Age with superior institutions for stability but inferior institutions for industrial acceleration. The United States had inferior institutions for stability but superior institutions for explosive growth. American legal permissiveness, cultural dynamism, and speculative finance combined into a system that rewarded expansion above all else—even when that expansion generated social harm.[34] In the long arc of history, it was this architecture that enabled the United States to eclipse Britain as the world's economic leader.

A contemporary parallel can be drawn with China today. China's rapid ascent reflects a different configuration of doctrines, legal structures, and cultural norms—combining centralized coordination, large-scale investment, and an ambitious national mission. As Ray Dalio and others have noted, China's economic model has demonstrated exceptional capacity for mobilizing resources, executing long-horizon industrial plans, and scaling infrastructure and technology at unprecedented speed.[35] But it also operates with constraints familiar from earlier hegemonic transitions: capital controls, demographic pressures, overleveraged property sectors, and political interventions that can undermine private initiative.[36] Whether China displaces the United States or enters a prolonged stagnation will depend not only on geopolitics but on whether its institutional design can evolve from a mobilization economy to an innovation-led one—without incurring unsustainable social or fiscal costs. Daron Acemoglu argues that China's limited inclusiveness is a structural constraint on long-run growth, while Dalio interprets many of these same characteristics as indicators of a broader transition in global economic leadership.[37]

These historical comparisons underscore a core lesson for Inclusive Capitalism. Economic outcomes are inseparable from cultural norms and institutional architecture. Britain's emphasis on stability and hierarchy limited its flexibility; America's celebration of entrepreneurial dominance enabled growth but also magnified inequality and volatility; China's centralized ambition fuels speed but risks brittle overreach. Inclusive Capitalism seeks to offer a bridge between these extremes—a design that preserves dynamism and scale without sacrificing dignity or stability; that respects culture while structuring incentives that can operate across cultures; and that aligns economic power with broad societal well-being rather than narrow extraction.

History shows that economic leadership shifts when a nation's institutions no longer match the demands of the technological and social environment.[38] The Gilded Age reveals what can happen when growth outpaces governance; Britain's experience reveals what happens when governance outpaces adaptation; China's trajectory shows the potential and limits of coordinated ambition.[39] The architecture envisioned in this book is designed to help societies—regardless of culture—capture the benefits of rapid growth while mitigating its costs. In this sense, Inclusive Capitalism aims to provide the institutional flexibility that historical systems lacked, offering a path toward prosperity that does not depend on repeating the crises and inequalities of the past.

The Incentives That Created the "Robber Barrons" and Drove Their Behaviors

The Gilded Age marked the rise of a new class of industrial leaders who harnessed emerging technologies, expanding capital markets, and a permissive legal environment to build enterprises of unprecedented scale. These figures were alternately celebrated as "captains of industry" for their role in driving growth and castigated as "robber barons" for the methods by which that growth was achieved.[40] Both labels capture part of the truth. Together, they reflect the central tension of the era: extraordinary economic dynamism coupled with equally extraordinary concentration of power.

The industrial leaders of the Gilded Age were not merely entrepreneurs but system builders—founders, consolidators, and financiers who reshaped entire sectors. By standardizing production, slashing costs, and exploiting economies of scale, they drove prices down, expanded access to essential goods, and propelled the United States to industrial preeminence. At the same time, they exploited gaps in law and governance, engaged in exclusionary consolidation, suppressed labor, and influenced policy in ways that entrenched their dominance.[41] In doing so, they operated within—and actively shaped—the operational rules of their industries. Understanding both the public benefits and the private costs of these strategies is essential to the task of institutional design: preserving the upside of scale, innovation, and coordination without reproducing the exclusion, capture, and fragility that accompanied them.

This chapter examines a representative set of these figures—John D. Rockefeller, Andrew Carnegie, J. P. Morgan, Cornelius Vanderbilt, Jay Gould, James J. Hill, and Henry Clay Frick. Some of these names are widely familiar; others less so. All, however, exerted outsized influence on the structure of American capitalism and, through it, on the global economy. Their careers illustrate not merely individual ambition but how rational behavior under a particular incentive architecture can generate both transformative progress and enduring systemic risk.[42]

John D. Rockefeller was the founder of Standard Oil and is often regarded as the wealthiest American of all time.[43] He revolutionized the oil industry, using both horizontal and vertical integration practices to consolidate and monopolize control over oil refining and virtually every other activity associated with the oil business in the United States. Through Standard Oil operations, Rockefeller significantly reduced the price of kerosene in the late nineteenth century, making it more affordable for the average American. In 1865, kerosene was priced at approximately 58 cents per gallon. By 1870, this had decreased to 26 cents, and by 1885, it had further dropped to around 8 cents per gallon.[44] This substantial price reduction was achieved through several strategic initiatives and enhancing operational efficiencies within Standard Oil. He invested in advanced refining technologies and optimized processes to increase yield and reduce waste. He hired chemists to help improve the kerosene yield per barrel of oil and to utilize by-products more effectively. By controlling every aspect of production, from extraction to distribution, Standard Oil minimized costs, improved processes, throughput, and margins. This approach allowed the company to produce barrels internally at a lower cost than purchasing from external suppliers, further reducing expenses. Rockefeller secured the most favorable shipping rates by promising railroads consistent and substantial shipments. These agreements enabled Standard Oil to lower transportation costs, which further contributed to the overall reduction in kerosene prices. The decrease in kerosene prices had a profound societal impact. Before these reductions, only the wealthy could afford oil for lighting, primarily using expensive whale oil. The affordability of kerosene allowed middle- and working-class families to illuminate their homes, providing the additional benefit of extending productive hours well into the evenings. As noted by historian Burton Folsom Jr., “By the 1870s, with the drop in the price of kerosene, middle- and working-class people all over the nation could afford the one cent an hour that it cost to light their homes at night.”[45]

Rockefeller’s methods of achieving dominance in the oil industry led to accusations of unethical practices. He engaged in price-cutting to drive competitors out of business, made secret deals with railroads to undercut competition, and formed the Standard Oil Trust, which controlled over 90% of the oil market at its peak. Critics claimed that he stifled competition and manipulated markets to amass his vast fortune. In *Capitalism in America: A History*, Alan Greenspan writes, “Rockefeller ruthlessly absorbed or crushed his competition, but he also drove down the price of oil products, benefiting consumers while consolidating his control over the industry.”[46]

Rockefeller was among the first major American philanthropists, donating over $540 million during his lifetime—an extraordinary figure that translates to approximately $17 billion in 2026 dollars and underscores the unprecedented scale of wealth accumulation in the Gilded Age.[47] By comparison, Bill Gates has donated more than $50 billion—nearly three times Rockefeller’s lifetime giving in real terms—illustrating both the vastly larger scale of modern wealth creation and the changing institutional role of philanthropy in capitalism.

Rockefeller established several foundations, including the Rockefeller Foundation in 1913, which focused on public health, medical training, and the arts. His contributions led to significant advancements, such as the development of vaccines for diseases like meningitis and yellow fever.[48] Rockefeller's commitment to education was profound. He provided substantial funding to institutions such as the University of Chicago, transforming it into a world-class university. He also supported the establishment of Central Philippine University in 1905, the first Baptist university and the second American university in Asia. Additionally, his General Education Board, founded in 1903, promoted education at all levels across the United States, with a particular focus on supporting Black schools in the South. Rockefeller's philanthropic efforts extended to public health. He founded the Rockefeller Institute for Medical Research in 1901, which later became Rockefeller University, which has seen numerous Nobel laureates. He also established the Rockefeller Sanitary Commission in 1909, which played a crucial role in eradicating hookworm disease in the American South.

Rockefeller's Standard Oil demonstrates how cost-reducing efficiency, when paired with preferential access to capital and transportation, can evolve into durable market exclusion. By reinvesting scale advantages into railroad rebates, vertical integration, and aggressive acquisition, Standard Oil transformed lower prices into structural dominance—ultimately provoking antitrust intervention.[49] The pattern is instructive: Once efficiency advantages compound faster than competitive entry, markets cease to self-correct.

Rockefeller and his peers delivered extraordinary economic gains through scale, consolidation, and process optimization, dramatically lowering the cost of essential inputs and accelerating American industrial growth. Yet these efficiencies were inseparable from exclusionary practices—predatory pricing, restrictive contracts, and market domination—that ultimately undermined competitive legitimacy.[50] The same system that rewarded transformative efficiency also made coercive consolidation a rational strategy, producing both unprecedented prosperity and inevitable backlash. Philanthropy emerged only after the fact as a partial corrective, repairing social harms that the economic architecture itself had generated.[51] Inclusive Capitalism addresses this contradiction at the level of system design, preserving the incentives for ambition, innovation, and scale while eliminating the structural conditions that make exclusion and extraction the price of success.

Andrew Carnegie, a Scottish-American industrialist, built the most dominant steel enterprise of the Gilded Age, making Carnegie Steel the largest and most profitable steel producer of its time.[52]

His impact on economic development rivaled—and in some respects exceeded—that of Rockefeller. By relentlessly driving down the cost of steel, Carnegie made a foundational industrial input dramatically more abundant and affordable, enabling the rapid expansion of railroads, bridges, factories, and urban construction that defined late-nineteenth-century American growth. He achieved this through aggressive adoption of new production technologies, first implementing the Bessemer process and later transitioning to open-hearth steelmaking, which allowed greater control, higher yields, and lower unit costs.[53] Like Rockefeller in oil, Carnegie pursued vertical integration—controlling raw materials, transportation, and manufacturing—to minimize costs, stabilize supply, and outcompete rivals. Economies of scale and continuous process optimization allowed Carnegie Steel to undercut competitors while improving quality, making inexpensive, high-grade steel a backbone of American industrialization and a central driver of the nation's rise as a global economic power.

Carnegie was also characterized as a "robber baron" for his harsh labor practices, particularly during the 1892 Homestead Strike, when his company violently suppressed a workers' strike over wages and working conditions.[54] Similar to other "captains of industry" of the era, Carnegie was criticized for accumulating immense wealth at the expense of his workers, who labored under dangerous and grueling physical and environmental conditions. Greenspan notes, "Carnegie's steel empire was built on innovation and efficiency, but his reputation was marred by the brutal realities of industrial labor in his mills."

Yet Carnegie himself was acutely aware of this tension. In *The Gospel of Wealth* (1889), he argued that the accumulation of vast private fortunes imposed a moral obligation on the wealthy to redistribute their wealth in ways that advanced the welfare and happiness of the common man.[55] He famously stated, "The man who dies thus rich dies disgraced." Carnegie believed in the power of knowledge and education. He funded the establishment of 2,509 libraries worldwide, with 1,679 in the United States alone.[56] These institutions provided free access to books and learning resources, empowering countless individuals to educate themselves. He founded and supported numerous educational establishments, including Carnegie Mellon University in Pittsburgh and the Carnegie Institution for Science in Washington, D.C. These institutions have evolved and are both historical and contemporary leaders in research and higher education.

Carnegie was also a committed advocate of international peace. In 1910, he established the Carnegie Endowment for International Peace with the explicit aim of reducing conflict among nations through diplomacy, research, and education.[57] His philanthropy extended broadly into the arts and sciences, including the creation of institutions such as Carnegie Hall and the Carnegie Museums of Pittsburgh, which continue to shape cultural and scientific life. These initiatives reflected Carnegie's belief that private wealth carried a responsibility to advance human progress beyond material production alone.

The parallels between Andrew Carnegie's legacy and that of John D. Rockefeller are striking and instructive. Both dramatically reduced the cost of foundational industrial inputs—steel and oil—making them more abundant and affordable, thereby accelerating economic growth and enabling downstream industries critical to modern society. Yet both achieved these gains through strategies that concentrated power, suppressed competition, and intensified social division—patterns whose consequences persist across subsequent eras.[58]

Both also turned to large-scale philanthropy as a corrective mechanism. These similarities were not coincidental, nor primarily a function of individual character;

they were artifacts of an unconstrained, liberal, Smithian capitalist system operating at scale. The recurring combination of extraordinary societal benefit and equally extraordinary social cost reflects a systemic design problem. The question this chapter returns to is whether the gains achieved by figures like Carnegie and Rockefeller could have been realized without the accompanying damage—and what kind of economic architecture would make that possible.

John Pierpont Morgan (1837–1913) was a powerful financier and banker who played a central role in reorganizing and consolidating industries such as railroads, steel, and electricity, which were vital to the U.S. economy.[59] He founded the banking house J.P. Morgan & Co., which became a financial empire that remains a global industry behemoth to this day. In 1892, Morgan facilitated the merger of Edison General Electric and Thomson-Houston Electric Company, resulting in the creation of General Electric, a company that became a leader in electrical innovations. In 1901, he orchestrated the consolidation of several steel companies to form U.S. Steel, the world's first billion-dollar corporation, which played a significant role in the nation's industrial growth. During the Panic of 1907, Morgan led efforts to stabilize the financial system by organizing a coalition of bankers to provide liquidity to endangered banks and trust companies, effectively acting as a lender of last resort and restoring public confidence in the banking sector during periods of financial crisis.[60] Morgan was a key enabler of many of the industrial leaders of the Gilded Age and a personification of the value of Smithian capitalism but also, similar to Rockefeller and Carnegie, surfaced the downside.

J. P. Morgan came to be labeled a "robber baron" because of the extraordinary degree of economic power he accumulated and exercised. Through aggressive consolidation, he reorganized and stabilized entire industries—most notably railroads—often creating monopolies or near-monopolies that sharply curtailed competition.[61] His control over capital markets and access to liquidity allowed him to influence prices, corporate governance, and even government policy during moments of crisis. Critics argued that this concentration of power enriched a narrow financial elite while marginalizing consumers, workers, and smaller firms. As historian H. W. Brands observed, Morgan became "the living embodiment of capitalist power," a figure capable of stabilizing the economy in moments of panic but whose influence simultaneously raised fears of unchecked private authority over public life.[62]

Alongside this concentration of economic power, Morgan became a major patron of cultural and educational institutions. He supported the American Museum of Natural History, the Metropolitan Museum of Art, and the Lying-In Hospital of the City of New York.[63] He also founded the Morgan Library, assembling one of the world's most important collections of manuscripts, rare books, and artworks. These contributions significantly enriched the cultural and intellectual infrastructure of the United States and remain publicly accessible to this day.

Morgan's dual legacy mirrors that of his contemporaries. He operated rationally within the prevailing rules of early American capitalism, contributing to rapid economic growth, industrial coordination, and increased access to capital. His methods were exclusionary, highly centralized, and socially divisive, concentrating economic power at a scale that provoked public unease and political response.[64] His later-life philanthropy functioned, as it did for many Gilded Age leaders, as a partial corrective to the very inequalities and power imbalances the system had rewarded. Once again, the pattern is not best explained by individual virtue or vice but by an economic architecture that simultaneously incentivized extraordinary progress and extraordinary concentration of power.

Cornelius Vanderbilt (1794–1877), also known as "The Commodore," was both a shipping and railroad tycoon who played a key role in expanding the nation's transportation infrastructure.[65] He started in the steamboat industry and later shifted his focus to railroads, consolidating several major railroads and creating an efficient network. He gained control of the New York and Harlem Railroad, the Hudson River Railroad, and the New York Central Railroad, eventually merging them to form a cohesive system. This integration improved efficiency and reduced travel times between major cities, notably offering the first rail service from New York City to Chicago. Vanderbilt commissioned the construction of Grand Central Depot in New York City, which opened in 1871. This major transportation hub streamlined rail services and facilitated commerce. The project also provided employment opportunities during the economic downturn of 1873.[66]

Cornelius Vanderbilt likewise earned the label of "robber baron" through aggressive consolidation and cutthroat competition, using his financial power to dominate shipping and railroad networks and eliminate rivals.[67] A statement often attributed to him—"What do I care about the law? Hain't I got the power?"—is widely regarded as misattributed, yet its endurance is telling: Whether or not Vanderbilt uttered it, the sentiment captures the prevailing ethos of the Gilded Age, in which economic power routinely outpaced legal and institutional constraint.[68] What is striking is how closely Vanderbilt's legacy mirrors those of Rockefeller and Morgan. Their stories are nearly interchangeable: dramatic efficiency gains, falling prices, and national growth on one side; exclusionary consolidation, political influence, and social backlash on the other. This similarity is not coincidental, nor simply the product of individual character. It reflects a shared incentive environment—a loosely constrained, laissez-faire variant of Smithian capitalism in which scale was rewarded, enforcement was weak, and consolidation was rational strategy rather than aberration. These industrialists were not independently improvising identical approaches; they were responding to the same underlying system design.

Unlike many of his contemporaries, Vanderbilt was not deeply engaged in philanthropy for most of his life. His most significant charitable act came late, at age eighty, when in 1873 he donated $1 million to establish Vanderbilt University in Nashville, Tennessee—then the largest single philanthropic gift in American history.[69] Contemporary accounts suggest the gift was strongly encouraged by his second wife, who was born in Alabama, and reflected an interest in strengthening educational opportunity in the post–Civil War South. Vanderbilt University remains one of the nation's leading institutions, and this late-life gift stands in contrast to the limited role philanthropy otherwise played in Vanderbilt's career.

Jay Gould and Henry Clay Frick could both be considered archetypes of the "robber barons."[70] Gould was an infamous financier and railroad magnate known for his speculative schemes and manipulation of financial markets. He played a key role in the development and consolidation of several railroads, but his reputation was tarnished by numerous scandals. He was involved in stock manipulation, insider trading, and bribery. One of his most notorious actions was his attempt, along with James Fisk, to corner the gold market in 1869, which led to the financial panic known as "Black Friday."[71] His ruthless pursuit of personal gain, often at the expense of the broader economy, made him one of the most despised figures of the Gilded Age. As Greenspan observes in *Capitalism in America*, "Gould's actions showed the dangers of unchecked capitalism, where speculators could manipulate markets and cause economic chaos.

Henry Clay Frick was a steel and coal magnate and partner of Andrew Carnegie known for his harsh treatment of laborers.[72] Frick's reputation as a "robber baron" was solidified during the Homestead Strike of 1892, when he locked out striking workers and hired Pinkerton detectives to break the strike, resulting in violent clashes that left several dead. His anti-union stance and ruthless approach to labor disputes made him a symbol of the brutal conditions and exploitations faced by workers during the Gilded Age.

James J. Hill was a counterpoint to Gould and Frick, known for his solid business ethics.[73] He was the "Empire Builder," a railroad tycoon who built and expanded the Great Northern Railway, connecting the American Midwest to the Pacific Northwest. Unlike other railroad magnates, Hill focused on building his railroads without government subsidies, and his lines were known for their efficiency and profitability. Hill is often contrasted with other Gilded Age figures because he built his empire through careful planning and efficient management rather than monopolistic practices. He focused on providing quality service to customers and maintaining fair competition, which led some to regard him tilted more toward a "captain of industry" than a "robber baron."[74] As Greenspan writes, "Hill was the rare businessman of the Gilded Age whose reputation was built not on crushing competition but on building a sustainable business that contributed to national growth."[75]

The day-to-day lives of these "captains of industry" varied considerably from their predecessor industrialists in the United Kingdom in the first half of the nineteenth century. The early industrialists lived close to their factories and were hands-on involved with their business to the point of micromanagement.[76] The Gilded Age industrialists led lives marked by immense wealth and influence. Their daily routines were characterized by a combination of rigorous work schedules and strategic decision-making, along with opulent leisure activities.

Industrialists like Andrew Carnegie and John D. Rockefeller were deeply involved in the management of their enterprises at an executive rather than operational level.[77] They often began their days early, reviewing reports, making strategic decisions, and meeting with key associates to discuss business expansions and innovations. They were not involved with day-to-day operations. Evenings frequently were consumed with attending or hosting lavish social events. Andrew Carnegie's mansion in New York City was a hub for gatherings with politicians, intellectuals, and other influential figures.[78] These events served both social and networking purposes, reinforcing their status and facilitating business alliances. Membership in exclusive clubs was common among these industrialists. The Ardsley Country Club, founded in 1895, catered to industrialists such as J. P. Morgan and the Rockefeller brothers, and while offering further opportunities for high level business networking they also provided amenities like golf, tennis, and yachting.[79]

These social gatherings of the Gilded Age industrialists bring to mind Adam Smith's observation that even informal meetings among individuals of the same trade could lead to collusion against the public interest. "People of the same trade seldom meet together, even for merriment and diversion, but the conversation ends in a conspiracy against the public, or in some contrivance to raise prices."[80] This insight highlights Smith's concern that such gatherings, though seemingly innocent, often result in agreements that harm consumers by manipulating market conditions. The gatherings by the Gilded Age industrialists seemed anything but innocent. In fact, it is an example of the champions of laissez-faire, Smithian capitalism, violating one of the core ground rules associated with competition and the public interest. It is illustrative of how the practice of Smithian capitalism in the Gilded Age varied considerably from the theoretical intent of the chief architect. This is the gap that Inclusive Capitalism is designed to solve, by eliminating the conditions that lead to this type of collusive behavior counter to the best interest of the public but without excessive, conflict-based, poorly executed government intervention.

This profile of the Gilded Age's industrial leaders makes one conclusion unavoidable: Our system reliably produces far more Rockefellers, Carnegies, Morgans, Vanderbilts, Goulds, and Fricks than the likes of a James J. Hills just profiled.[81] This is not a matter of ethics, personality, or individual virtue. It is a matter of design. The rules of the system reward certain behaviors—rapid consolidation, suppression of rivals, aggressive cost extraction, political influence, and the pursuit of scale at, seemingly, any social cost—and those who master this rulebook rise to the top.[82] The question is therefore not why so many "robber barons" emerged but why the system made that archetype the most adaptive strategy. The recurrence of these patterns across sectors, decades, and geographies shows that the outcomes were predictable, not accidental. And it shows why simply changing individual leaders cannot fix what is structural.

What drove these behaviors was the logic of profit maximization under the constraints—and freedoms—of the era. Pursuing wealth through efficiency, innovation, and integration created extraordinary public benefits: falling prices for necessities such as kerosene and steel; massive expansions of infrastructure; and technological breakthroughs that transformed daily life. But the same profit motive, operating without countervailing incentives and institutions, produced the darker side of the Gilded Age: monopolistic consolidation, brutal working conditions, systematic exclusion, and political corruption. Industrialists formed trusts to eliminate competition, exerted downward pressure on wages, and used lobbying, bribery, and insider influence to shape legislation in their favor.[83] These were not aberrations. They were the predictable expression of rational actors optimizing within a system that valued scale, concentration, and control above all else.

Adam Smith, John Maynard Keynes, and Milton Friedman each help illuminate this duality.[84] Smith saw self-interest as the engine of prosperity. Yet Smith also insisted that competitive markets depend on dispersed power, fair play, and moral constraints—conditions that did not hold at industrial scale. Keynes admired the entrepreneur's capacity to drive progress but warned that capitalism without guardrails permits "the nastiest of men, for the nastiest of motives," to shape outcomes for everyone else.[85] Friedman, echoing Smith, argued that businesses should pursue profits "within the rules of the game," but the Gilded Age demonstrated what happens when the rules themselves are incomplete, permissive, or easily captured.[86] All three were correct within their frames. All three reveal why outcomes diverged so sharply from intent.

Unchecked capitalism in the Gilded Age did not fail because its leaders were uniquely ruthless; it failed because its incentives, institutions, and societal norms made ruthlessness adaptive. Government eventually intervened through antitrust actions, labor protections, and regulatory expansion, but these measures were reactive, conflict-driven, and often blunt. In some cases—particularly in the rise of heavy regulation and the ideological swing toward Marxian alternatives—the cure became more distortionary than the disease.[87] The enduring question is whether governments can establish a rule set that preserves capitalism's productive dynamism while preventing the systemic pathologies that emerge at scale.

Inclusive Capitalism answers that question by redesigning the incentive structure rather than relying on perpetual regulation or heroic leadership. The goal is not to suppress profit but to change what profit signals. Under a restructured architecture, the most profitable path becomes the one that measurably expands societal well-being, broadens access, accelerates innovation, and avoids exclusionary consolidation. Instead of prominence in rewarding short-term extraction, the system rewards long-term, outcome-based value creation across society. This requires redefining success metrics, reshaping corporate obligations, modernizing the monetary structure, and realigning incentives so that the James Hills of the world are not exceptions but the norm: a tall order but one that, as we will illustrate, is doable and necessary within a capitalist framework.

The power of this shift is that it preserves the sources of the Gilded Age's extraordinary achievements—ambition, ingenuity, entrepreneurship, scale—while neutralizing the incentives that produced its injustices. The chapter's core argument is therefore simple: We do not need better people; we need better rules. And when we change the rules with clear, scientific, empirically grounded design, the system can produce the same level of dynamism without the collateral damage. Inclusive Capitalism is the architecture that makes this possible.

Lived Experience of the Population During the Gilded Age

The lived experience of the working class during the Gilded Age makes clear why eliminating capitalism's downside is not a luxury or moral abstraction but a practical necessity.[88] On the surface, the United States was booming—GDP soared, new industries emerged, infrastructure spread across the continent, and the financial markets of New York became the envy of the world. But beneath that surface was a world defined by danger, deprivation, volatility, and a near-total absence of worker protections. The question of why reform was necessary—even when headline metrics look strong—finds its answer in the human cost embedded in the system. Economic growth, under the rules of the Gilded Age, was purchased with the lives, bodies, and security of millions of workers.[89]

Industrial capitalism in the late nineteenth century was new, raw, and often brutal.[90] Between 1881 and 1900, roughly 35,000 American workers died each year in industrial and related workplace accidents—a figure published in the *Journal of Economic History* that, even if overstated, was alarming at any plausible scale.[91] To place this in perspective: 35,000 annual deaths is nearly ten times the number of deaths from mass shootings in 2024 and nearly double the number of total gun deaths in the United States today.[92] Even if the true number was 10% of that estimate, the shock to modern sensibilities would be enormous. Today's society would not tolerate any workplace deaths; the Gilded Age "tolerated" ten to a hundred per day, depending on the industry and year, as the routine collateral damage of progress.

A comparison of railroad workers in Britain and America makes the point vividly (Table 4.1). In 1889, fatality rates per thousand trainmen were 4.26 in Britain and 8.52 in the United States.[93] By 1901, Britain had reduced this to 2.21, while the United States still recorded 7.35.[94] Whether coupling rail cars, braking, or performing maintenance, American workers faced risks that were three to four times higher than their British counterparts.

Table 4.1: Comparative Safety of British and American Railroad Workers, 1889–1901.

(Fatality Rates per Thousand Workers per Year)			
	1889	**1895**	**1901**
British railroad workers	1.14	0.95	0.89
All causes			
British trainmen	4.26	3.22	2.21
All causes			
Coupling	0.94	0.83	0.74
American Railroad workers	2.67	2.31	2.5
All causes			
American trainmen	8.52	6.45	7.35
All causes			
Coupling	1.73c	1.2	0.78
Braking	3.25c	2.44	2.03

Source: Aldrich, *Safety First*, Table 1 and Great Britain Board of Trade, General Report.

The gap was not technological; Both nations had access to similar equipment. The gap was institutional and cultural: Britain had begun implementing safety norms, labor rights, and regulatory oversight. The United States had not.

Against this backdrop, it is no surprise that worker anger boiled over. No fewer than 100,000 workers went on strike every year during the 1880s and 1890s.[95] In 1892 alone, there were 1,298 strikes involving 164,000 workers.[96] While industrial leaders spent evenings in the dining rooms of the Ardsley Country Club, their labor force faced a daily reality of twelve-hour shifts, dangerous machinery, cramped tenements, and the constant threat of unemployment.[97] Unions expanded rapidly because they were the only available counterweight to the power of industrial capital. And when owners responded with strikebreakers, injunctions, or violence, conflict escalated.

The Homestead Strike of 1892 remains one of the era's most visceral demonstrations of this dynamic (Figure 4.1). Henry Clay Frick, managing the Homestead Steelworks for Andrew Carnegie, sought to break the skilled-worker union that controlled workflow on the shop floor.[98] When negotiations collapsed, he locked workers out and hired three hundred Pinkerton agents, armed and instructed to force their way into the plant.[99]

Gunfire broke out as the barges carrying the Pinkertons approached the mill along the Monongahela River. After a bloody standoff, the agents surrendered—only for six thousand state militiamen to arrive five days later, march through town, and reopen the plant by force. The state did not serve as a neutral actor; it aligned unequivocally with the owners. The union was crushed.

The Pullman Strike of 1894, though triggered by different circumstances, repeated the pattern.[100] George Pullman reduced wages during a national downturn but refused to reduce the rents or prices imposed on workers living in his company town.

Figure 4.1: Harper's Weekly illustration of the Pennsylvania state militia marching on the Homestead.

The result was a strike that spread nationwide under the leadership of Eugene Debs and the American Railway Union.[101] Railroad owners responded strategically, loading U.S. Mail onto trains so that any strike interference could be framed as a federal offense. President Grover Cleveland dispatched federal troops to suppress the strike, and when Debs refused to comply with a federal injunction, he was jailed. Again the message was clear: In a contest between labor and capital, the government would not be an impartial arbiter.

Pullman's actions were driven by economic pressure; Frick's by union confrontation; but from the vantage point of the workers, the catalyst hardly mattered. What mattered was the systemic dynamic: downward pressure on wages, hazardous conditions, and the consistent alignment of state power with industrial leadership.[102] Workers had none of the upside of the system—no ownership share, no participation in decision-making, no insulation from downturns—and bore nearly all the risk. Predictably, resentment escalated into violence.

This is the core analytical lesson for Inclusive Capitalism. The extreme outcomes of the Gilded Age were typically not attributed to unusually cruel individuals or isolated abuses. They were more the product of incentives embedded in the architecture of the system. When the rules reward cost extraction and punish restraint, firms will cut wages, defer safety, suppress organization, and externalize harms. When downturns strike, firms will protect margins by shifting risk to workers. When political influence becomes a competitive advantage, firms will purchase it. And when labor has no meaningful stake in the upside, conflict becomes the only leverage available.

Inclusive Capitalism seeks to break this dynamic by altering the incentive structure itself. Broader participation in the upside—through levels of shared ownership, sectoral value credits, and outcome-based rewards—aligns worker and firm interests.

Broader participation in the downside—through risk-sharing mechanisms—reduces the need for violent or political confrontation when shocks occur. And the refactoring of currency into sector-specific micro-systems acts like "containerization" in engineering: it isolates failures, preventing macroeconomic volatility from cascading into basic-needs markets.[103]

In short, the experience of the working class in the Gilded Age shows both the human cost of capitalism's architectural flaws and the necessity of redesign. A system cannot be stable when gains are privatized and risks are socialized downward. It cannot remain legitimate when prosperity for some requires precarity for many. And it cannot achieve its full productive potential when the workforce is treated as expendable. By reengineering incentives at the core, Inclusive Capitalism aims to preserve the extraordinary strengths of market dynamism while eliminating the unnecessary suffering that once fueled the violent turning points of American industrial history.

What Worked and What Did Not During the Guild Age

The Gilded Age delivered both extraordinary progress and extraordinary harm. When we step back from the individual stories of industrial leadership and the lived experiences of workers, the larger pattern becomes unmistakable: The very same forces that generated unprecedented prosperity also generated deep instability, inequality, and civic corrosion.[104] Understanding this duality—how the same incentives produced both the gold and the rot—is essential for designing a system that amplifies the former without repeating the latter.

Economically, the Gilded Age was one of the most transformative periods in American history. From the 1870s to the early twentieth century, the United States vaulted from an agrarian republic to the world's preeminent industrial power.[105] The Bessemer and open-hearth processes slashed the cost of steel; Rockefeller's refining advances made kerosene and later gasoline widely affordable; electrification, the telegraph, and the telephone changed daily life; and railroads—nearly 190,000 miles of track by 1900—integrated what had been a continental patchwork of regional markets into a unified economic system. As Alan Greenspan observed, industrialization "was not just about making more things faster; it was a series of transformative technologies that fundamentally changed the way people lived and worked."[106] These innovations lowered the price of basic goods, expanded consumer access, and catalyzed the rise of a new managerial middle class. America became, in Robert Wiebe's phrase, "the workshop of the world."[107]

The era also produced enduring civic assets through large-scale philanthropy. Carnegie's libraries, universities, and scientific institutions, Rockefeller's global public-health advances, and Vanderbilt's support for higher education created public goods that still shape educational and scientific life today. Carnegie's dictum that "the man who dies thus rich dies disgraced" became an early articulation of philanthropy as a civic obligation, and these institutions remain among the most significant positive legacies of the age.[108]

But these achievements came at staggering cost. Economic inequality reached historic extremes. A small number of industrialists accumulated unprecedented fortunes while millions of workers lived in squalor, a divide vividly documented by Jacob Riis in *How the Other Half Lives*.[109] Long hours, unsafe mills, and starvation wages were common, and children worked alongside adults in some of the country's most dangerous industries. Labor exploitation was not an aberration—it was an equilibrium outcome of a system that rewarded cost extraction and offered workers no bargaining power or institutional protections.

The era's downside was exacerbated by governance vacuums. Political corruption was pervasive, from municipal machines like Tammany Hall to national scandals such as Crédit Mobilier.[110] As Malcolm Harris notes, "corporate interests were so deeply intertwined with political power that it became hard to tell where government ended and business began."[111] With no modern campaign finance limits and minimal regulatory oversight, industrialists shaped legislation, secured subsidies, and protected their empires through influence rather than competition.

Monopoly power was another defining pathology. With little antitrust enforcement, giants like Standard Oil and U.S. Steel grew into trusts that controlled prices, restricted entry, and stifled competition. Greenspan observed that such unchecked consolidation "allowed business leaders to amass unprecedented control over markets," generating resentment and eventually provoking the trust-busting reforms of the Progressive Era.[112]

Environmental destruction compounded these issues. Mining, logging, and rapid urbanization degraded landscapes and polluted waterways with virtually no restraints. As Harris emphasizes, the Gilded Age appetite for raw materials "left a legacy of environmental degradation," a phenomenon intensified in mining towns and resource-extraction regions left behind once deposits were exhausted.[113]

Mass immigration deepened social complexity and dislocation. Millions of new arrivals provided essential labor yet endured discrimination, harsh factory conditions, overcrowded tenements, and political scapegoating. Xenophobia culminated in the Chinese Exclusion Act of 1882—the first major federal immigration restriction—reflecting fractures within a society grappling with rapid demographic and economic upheaval.[114]

Taken together, the Gilded Age demonstrates a fundamental truth: The forces that generated America's industrial miracle were inseparable from the forces that generated its worst social harms. The incentives of laissez-faire capitalism delivered innovation, efficiency, and massive increases in productive capacity—but they also rewarded monopoly formation, labor exploitation, political capture, and environmental ruin. The system produced dazzling progress precisely because it had no guardrails, but the absence of guardrails ensured that much of that progress was accompanied by avoidable suffering.

This dual legacy is the foundation for the design problem that Inclusive Capitalism seeks to solve. The challenge is not to choose between innovation and equity, growth and stability, or markets and social well-being. The challenge is to redesign incentives so that the behaviors that were socially destructive in the Gilded Age become unprofitable, and the behaviors that produced genuine progress become even more rewarding. The Gilded Age shows us what markets can accomplish under strong incentives—and what they inevitably destroy when those incentives misalign. The task now is to build a system that captures the gold without recreating the rot.

Forces That Brought the Gilded Age to an End

The Gilded Age did not end because its economic engine failed. It ended because the social, political, and institutional stresses generated by its own success became unsustainable.[115] The same incentives that had fueled unprecedented innovation and industrial expansion also produced widening inequality, labor unrest, political corruption, and public mistrust. By the early twentieth century, these pressures converged into a broad movement—social, legal, democratic, and intellectual—that reshaped the American economic order.[116] The end of the Gilded Age was not a sudden collapse but a gradual political and institutional recalibration: an acknowledgment that laissez-faire capitalism, left entirely to its own devices, generated both tremendous prosperity and destabilizing social costs.

One of the most powerful forces pushing the Gilded Age toward its conclusion was the rising wave of labor conflict. By the 1890s, the social contract had frayed to the breaking point. Workers endured long hours, low pay, unsafe conditions, and no institutional recourse.[117] As early as 1886, the Haymarket Affair in Chicago signaled the rising militancy of the labor movement and the willingness of governments to use force on behalf of employers. The Homestead Strike of 1892 and the Pullman Strike of 1894 crystallized the deeper structural tension: the industrial economy had scaled far faster than the institutional mechanisms needed to mediate conflict. Workers did not merely strike out of dissatisfaction—they struck because they had no other path to redress. Each confrontation revealed the same structural pattern: private power dominated public authority, and when the two came into conflict, government sided with capital.[118] The cumulative effect of these clashes was not only widespread hardship but growing public recognition that an unregulated industrial order was incompatible with social stability. Eric Foner notes that the labor battles of the 1890s "highlighted the imbalance of power in American society and fueled demands for reform."[119] The industrial boom had created a working class large enough and organized enough to demand political and legal protection, and this demand increasingly shaped national discourse.[120]

Political corruption was another decisive catalyst. The Gilded Age was marked by powerful political machines, corporate influence on legislation, and scandals that eroded public trust. The Crédit Mobilier scandal and the pervasive influence of railroad barons exposed the degree to which business interests had captured the state. As Malcolm Harris observes, Gilded Age capitalism blurred public and private power so thoroughly "that it became hard to tell where government ended and business began."[121] Such corruption was not merely a moral problem; it was a governance problem that undermined market legitimacy. A functioning capitalist system depends on public faith in the fairness of the rules, and by the 1890s that faith was eroding. Reform movements—civil service reform, merit-based hiring, campaign finance scrutiny—began gaining traction, culminating in the Pendleton Act and early Progressive Era political reforms.[122] The public demanded institutions that would temper private influence and restore democratic accountability, and politicians increasingly understood that unchecked corporate power was destabilizing the system that had enabled it.

A third force driving the end of the Gilded Age was the rise of a new intellectual and political consensus about the role of government. Classical laissez-faire had lost credibility as a universal doctrine. The dramatic boom-and-bust cycles of the late nineteenth century—panics in 1873, 1884, 1890, and 1893—exposed the vulnerability of a financial system dependent on trusts, lightly regulated banks, and highly leveraged railroads. Each crisis imposed immense costs not only on industrialists but on the broader public, who absorbed the brunt of unemployment, wage cuts, and lost savings. These recurrent collapses demonstrated that markets were not self-equilibrating in the way classical economists had imagined. As Louis Brandeis, Henry Carter Adams, and eventually John Maynard Keynes would argue, unregulated financial markets create collective risks that private actors cannot manage alone.[123] The emergence of the Progressive movement at the turn of the century reflected a broader intellectual shift: the recognition that government had a constructive role to play not in replacing markets but in setting the boundaries within which markets could function safely. The creation of the Interstate Commerce Commission (1887), the Sherman Antitrust Act (1890), and the establishment of the Federal Reserve (1913) were milestones in this rebalancing.[124] Each represented an attempt to correct structural deficiencies of the Gilded Age—monopolization, predatory pricing, financial instability—while preserving the dynamism of the underlying economic system.

A fourth force was the demographic and political pressure generated by mass immigration and urbanization. The influx of millions of immigrants transformed the social fabric of American cities, overwhelming existing infrastructure and intensifying competition for low-wage jobs. Urban poverty, overcrowded tenements, and public health crises became highly visible reminders that the gains of industrialization were not evenly shared. Journalists such as Jacob Riis exposed these conditions to a national audience, puncturing the myth that laissez-faire prosperity was broadly beneficial.[125] Urban political reformers—many of them middle-class professionals—advocated for sanitation systems, building codes, child labor restrictions, and compulsory education laws. These reforms were not anti-growth; they were intended to preserve social cohesion by ensuring that industrialization did not turn cities into what Riis called "hot-beds of epidemics."[126] The combination of immigrant labor, urban concentration, and visible poverty created the political will for interventions that improved public health and living conditions, thereby tempering some of the most destructive consequences of unregulated capitalism.

The growth of antitrust sentiment was perhaps the clearest institutional marker of the Gilded Age's end. Popular resentment toward monopolies reached a crescendo after decades of consolidation across railroads, oil, steel, and finance. Standard Oil became the symbol of market power used against the public interest. As Alan Greenspan notes, Rockefeller's ability to eliminate competition and dictate market prices demonstrated "the dangers of unchecked private power."[127] Public pressure demanded action, and the Supreme Court's 1911 decision to break up Standard Oil marked the symbolic conclusion of the Gilded Age era of unbounded consolidation. Antitrust enforcement, though uneven, signaled a new principle: The state would act to preserve competition rather than assume market actors would police themselves.

Finally, the First World War accelerated the transition. The war demanded national mobilization, regulatory coordination, and federal oversight of industries ranging from railroads to food production. This experience demonstrated that coordinated government action could accelerate outcomes and levels of efficiencies that markets alone could not. It also expanded the electorate's expectations of what government could and should do to stabilize economic life.[128] By the time the 1920s began, the institutional architecture of the Gilded Age—pure laissez-faire, permissive consolidation, minimal labor law, weak financial oversight—was no longer politically tenable. The Progressive Era reforms had already reshaped antitrust law, labor protections, food safety standards, and administrative governance. The Gilded Age had not collapsed; it had been outgrown.

In sum, the forces that brought the Gilded Age to an end were not ideological but structural. Labor unrest revealed the need for bargaining mechanisms and basic protections.[129] Political corruption provoked demands for institutional accountability. Repeated financial crises demonstrated the necessity of regulatory frameworks. Urban dislocation created political pressure for public health and welfare reforms. And the rise of monopoly power forced the state to reassert the conditions for fair competition. These forces did not reject capitalism; they rejected a version of capitalism whose incentives produced instability, inequality, and civic decay alongside innovation and growth. The lesson is not that markets failed but that markets alone could not sustain their own legitimacy.

This is the core insight for the design of Inclusive Capitalism. A well-functioning system must reward innovation and enterprise, but it must also ensure that the pursuit of self-interest does not impose intolerable costs on the broader public. The end of the Gilded Age was the first major American attempt to reconcile these competing demands. It succeeded in some areas and failed in others—but it provides the historical template for how incentive redesign, not ideology, determines whether capitalism strengthens or destabilizes society.

Conclusions and Insights from the Gilded Age for the Design of Inclusive Capitalism

The Gilded Age demonstrates that capitalism at its most dynamic level is capable of extraordinary achievement. No alternative system—mercantilism, communism, or the various forms of twentieth-century command-and-control—has ever produced a comparable burst of innovation, productivity, or transformative infrastructure. The United States vaulted into global leadership because industrialists harnessed scale, technology, and entrepreneurial ambition in ways the world had never seen. Those forces remain powerful today. AI, cloud computing, and synthetic biology now play the role once held by oil, steel, and railroads. Space programs, private rockets, and megayachts mirror the palatial mansions of an earlier elite. And, once again, the nation is experiencing rising inequality, strained affordability, political polarization, a migration crisis, and deep concern over social cohesion.

That parallel is a warning.[130] When history repeats itself across centuries—as the patterns of the Gilded Age repeat one hundred years later—it is almost never because "the people" have failed. It is because the system has reproduced the same incentives. Both sides of today's ideological divide see echoes of the Gilded Age in the present—and both are correct. Neo-classical advocates look back at the late nineteenth century and see a golden age of innovation, scale, and national ascendance. Their case is strong: industrialists did lower prices, expand opportunity, and build the infrastructure that made modern America possible. Likewise, progressives look back and see exploitation, premature death, dangerous work, monopoly power, political corruption, and mass suffering. Their case is just as strong. The Gilded Age was both remarkable and intolerable. Our own era, like the Gilded Age, is generating extremes on both ends of the spectrum—large breakthroughs accompanied by profound instability.

The core insight is that unchecked capitalism naturally produces these extremes because the incentive structure rewards the extraction of private gains regardless of public cost.[131] At scale, Adam Smith's invisible hand becomes an "extractive claw." And as long as incentives push industrialists toward behaviors that maximize profit regardless of social consequence, economic history will continue to oscillate between neo-classical booms and progressive backlashes. The "ping-pong" between laissez-faire and heavy intervention is itself proof that neither approach produces a stable equilibrium.

The lesson from James J. Hill is telling. Hill demonstrated that long-term, ethical, efficiency-driven entrepreneurship is possible within capitalism—and that it can produce extraordinary benefits. But Hill was exceptional. His behavior stands out because the system did not reward it. Rockefeller, Carnegie, and Vanderbilt became symbols of the age not because they were more talented than Hill but because their strategies best matched the incentives. When the system rewards extraction and consolidation, the most skilled competitors will extract and consolidate. When the system rewards stewardship, long-term thinking, shared benefit, and broad-based growth, leaders will behave accordingly. It is the system, not the moral fiber of individuals, that determines the slope and direction of economic behavior at scale.

The patterns of the Gilded Age point to a simple but consequential conclusion: capitalism does not require a new ideology, nor a rejection of Smith's core insights about self-interest, specialization, or voluntary exchange. What it requires is correction of institutional design flaws that first became visible at scale during the Gilded Age—and that have reasserted themselves in the twenty-first century.[132]

When efficiency advantages compound faster than competitive entry, markets cease to self-correct. When scale converts innovation into durable exclusion, prosperity and backlash become structurally linked. And when the accumulation of wealth and power diverges from the creation of societal well-being, corrective intervention becomes inevitable. These are not moral failures or historical accidents; they are design failures.

The implication is clear. The task is not to suppress ambition, innovation, or scale but to realign the incentive structures and institutional constraints within which they operate—so that value creation expands opportunity rather than forecloses it, and so that economic dynamism no longer depends on exclusion, fragility, or extraction. This is the central premise of Inclusive Capitalism: to restore the competitive, open, and generative market system Smith envisioned by repairing the structural conditions under which it breaks down at scale.

The Gilded Age did not collapse under failure but under success taken too far. Its contradictions—concentration, exclusion, and systemic fragility—accumulated faster than its institutions could adapt. What followed was Smithian capitalism's first great reckoning: a period defined by backlash, reform, and the attempt to contain a system whose productive power had outpaced its governance.[133] Understanding this reckoning is essential, because it established the pattern that would repeat throughout the twentieth century—progress followed by correction, innovation followed by instability—without ever resolving the underlying design tension.

Notes

1 H. W. Brands, *American Colossus: The Triumph of Capitalism, 1865–1900* (New York: Doubleday, 2010).

2 Thomas Piketty, *Capital in the Twenty-First Century* (Cambridge: Harvard University Press, 2014), historical inequality comparisons.

3 Alan Greenspan and Adrian Wooldridge, *Capitalism in America: A History* (New York: Penguin Press, 2018), esp. chapters 2–5.

4 Robert H. Wiebe, *The Search for Order, 1877–1920* (New York: Hill and Wang, 1967).
5 Mark Aldrich, *Safety First: Technology, Labor, and Business in the Building of American Work Safety, 1870–1939* (Baltimore: Johns Hopkins University Press, 1997), table 1.
6 Frederick Jackson Turner, "The Significance of the Frontier in American History," Annual Report of the American Historical Association (1893).
7 North, Douglass C. *Institutions, Institutional Change and Economic Performance.* Cambridge: Cambridge University Press, 1990, 3–14.
8 H. W. Brands, *American Colossus: The Triumph of Capitalism, 1865–1900.*
9 Alan Greenspan and Adrian Wooldridge, *Capitalism in America: A History*, esp. chapters 2–5.
10 Chandler, Alfred D. *The Visible Hand: The Managerial Revolution in American Business.* Cambridge, MA: Harvard University Press, 1977, 285–336.
11 Robert H. Wiebe, *The Search for Order, 1877–1920.*
12 Mark Twain and Charles Dudley Warner, *The Gilded Age: A Tale of Today* (Hartford: American Publishing Company, 1873).
13 Alan Greenspan and Adrian Wooldridge, *Capitalism in America: A History*, esp. chapters 2–5.
14 Ibid.
15 Herman Melville, *White-Jacket; or, The World in a Man-of-War* (New York: Harper & Brothers, 1850), 167.
16 Chandler, Alfred D. *The Visible Hand: The Managerial Revolution in American Business.* 285–336.
17 H. W. Brands, *American Colossus: The Triumph of Capitalism, 1865–1900.*
18 Alan Greenspan and Adrian Wooldridge, *Capitalism in America: A History*, esp. chapters 2–5.
19 Sklar, Martin J. *The Corporate Reconstruction of American Capitalism, 1890–1916.* 1988, 3–32.
20 Alan Greenspan and Adrian Wooldridge, *Capitalism in America: A History*, esp. chapters 2–5.
21 Montgomery, David. *The Fall of the House of Labor: The Workplace, the State, and American Labor Activism, 1865–1925.* 1987, 13–52.
22 Alan Greenspan and Adrian Wooldridge, *Capitalism in America: A History*, esp. chapters 2–5.
23 Twain, Mark, and Charles Dudley Warner. *The Gilded Age: A Tale of Today.* Hartford, CT: American Publishing Company, 1873.
24 Adam Smith, *The Wealth of Nations* (London: W. Strahan and T. Cadell, 1776), Book I, Chapter II; Book IV, Chapter II.
25 U.S. Congress, *An Act to Protect Trade and Commerce against Unlawful Restraints and Monopolies* (Sherman Antitrust Act), 1890.
26 North, Douglass C. *Institutions, Institutional Change and Economic Performance.* 1990, 3–14.
27 Ibid.
28 Frederick Jackson Turner, "The Significance of the Frontier in American History," Annual Report of the American Historical Association (1893).
29 Robert H. Wiebe, *The Search for Order, 1877–1920.*
30 Cameron, Rondo. *Banking in the Early Stages of Industrialization: A Study in Comparative Economic History.* New York: Oxford University Press, 1967, 92–123.
31 U.S. Department of the Treasury, *Annual Report of the Secretary of the Treasury on the State of the Finances* (various years, 1870–1900).
32 Lamoreaux, Naomi R. *The Great Merger Movement in American Business, 1895–1904.* 1985, 1–26.
33 Richard White, *Railroaded: The Transcontinentals and the Making of Modern America* (New York: W. W. Norton, 2011).
34 Kolko, Gabriel. *The Triumph of Conservatism: A Reinterpretation of American History, 1900–1916.* New York: Free Press, 1963, 1–28.
35 Ray Dalio, *Principles for Dealing with the Changing World Order* (New York: Simon & Schuster, 2021).

36 Naughton, Barry. *The Chinese Economy: Adaptation and Growth*. 2nd ed. Cambridge, MA: MIT Press, 18, 381–434.
37 Ray Dalio, *Principles for Dealing with the Changing World Order*.
38 North, Douglass C. *Institutions, Institutional Change and Economic Performance*. 1990, 3–14.
39 Ray Dalio, *Principles for Dealing with the Changing World Order*.
40 Burton W. Folsom Jr., "The Myth of the Robber Barons," *The Freeman* 35, no. 12 (December 1985).
41 Lamoreaux, Naomi R. *The Great Merger Movement in American Business, 1895–1904*. 1985, 1–26.
42 Schumpeter, Joseph A. *Capitalism, Socialism and Democracy*. New York: Harper & Brothers, 1942, 81–106.
43 Ron Chernow, *Titan: The Life of John D. Rockefeller, Sr.* (New York: Random House, 1998).
44 Ibid.
45 Burton W. Folsom Jr., "The Myth of the Robber Barons," *The Freeman* 35, no. 12 (December 1985).
46 Alan Greenspan and Adrian Wooldridge, *Capitalism in America: A History*, esp. chapters 2–5.
47 Ron Chernow, *Titan: The Life of John D. Rockefeller, Sr.* (New York: Random House, 1998).
48 Ibid.
49 U.S. Congress, *An Act to Protect Trade and Commerce against Unlawful Restraints and Monopolies* (Sherman Antitrust Act), 1890.
50 Ibid.
51 Ibid.
52 David Nasaw, *Andrew Carnegie* (New York: Penguin Press, 2006).
53 Livesay, Harold C. *Andrew Carnegie and the Rise of Big Business*. 2nd ed. New York: Pearson, 1999, 78–110.
54 U.S. Strike Commission Report, "Report on the Chicago Strike of June–July 1894," U.S. Government Printing Office, 1895.
55 Andrew Carnegie, "Wealth," *North American Review* 148 (1889): 653–64.
56 David Nasaw, *Andrew Carnegie* (New York: Penguin Press, 2006).
57 Ibid.
58 Matthew Josephson, *The Robber Barons: The Great American Capitalists, 1861–1901* (New York: Harcourt, Brace, 1934).
59 Jean Strouse, *Morgan: American Financier* (New York: Random House, 1999).
60 Chernow, Ron. *Titan: The Life of John D. Rockefeller, Sr.* New York: Random House, 1998, 557–562; Rockefeller Foundation. "John D. Rockefeller Biography." Rockefeller Foundation Historical Archive.
61 Richard White, *Railroaded: The Transcontinentals and the Making of Modern America*.
62 H. W. Brands, *American Colossus: The Triumph of Capitalism, 1865–1900*.
63 Jean Strouse, *Morgan: American Financier* (New York: Random House, 1999).
64 Tarbell, Ida M. *The History of the Standard Oil Company*. New York: McClure, Phillips & Co., 1904, vol. 1, 1–40, 140–178.
65 T. J. Stiles, *The First Tycoon: The Epic Life of Cornelius Vanderbilt* (New York: Alfred A. Knopf, 2009).
66 White, Richard. *Railroaded: The Transcontinentals and the Making of Modern America*, 208–246.
67 Matthew Josephson, *The Robber Barons: The Great American Capitalists, 1861–1901*.
68 T. J. Stiles, *The First Tycoon: The Epic Life of Cornelius Vanderbilt* (New York: Alfred A. Knopf, 2009).
69 Ibid.
70 Matthew Josephson, *The Robber Barons: The Great American Capitalists, 1861–1901*.
71 Brands, H. W. *The Money Men: Capitalism, Democracy, and the Hundred Years' War over the American Dollar*. New York: W. W. Norton, 2006, 83–101.
72 David Nasaw, *Andrew Carnegie* (New York: Penguin Press, 2006).
73 Great Northern Railway Company Records, James J. Hill Papers, Minnesota Historical Society.

74 H. W. Brands, *American Colossus: The Triumph of Capitalism, 1865–1900.*
75 Alan Greenspan and Adrian Wooldridge, *Capitalism in America: A History*, esp. chapters 2–5.
76 Chandler, Alfred D. *The Visible Hand: The Managerial Revolution in American Business.* 1–12, 79–121.
77 Ron Chernow, *Titan: The Life of John D. Rockefeller, Sr.*
78 David Nasaw, *Andrew Carnegie* (New York: Penguin Press, 2006).
79 Carver, Grant. *Ardsley Country Club: A Centennial History.* Ardsley-on-Hudson, NY: Ardsley Country Club, 1995, 1–25.
80 Adam Smith, *The Wealth of Nations*, Book I, Chapter II; Book IV, Chapter II.
81 Matthew Josephson, *The Robber Barons: The Great American Capitalists, 1861–1901.*
82 Louis D. Brandeis, *Other People's Money and How the Bankers Use It* (New York: Frederick A. Stokes, 1914).
83 Lamoreaux, Naomi R. *The Great Merger Movement in American Business, 1895–1904.* 1985, 1–26.
84 Smith, Adam. *An Inquiry into the Nature and Causes of the Wealth of Nations.* Indianapolis: Liberty Fund, 1981 [orig. 1776], Book I, chs. 1–3.
85 Keynes, John Maynard. *The General Theory of Employment, Interest, and Money.* London: Macmillan, 1936, chs. 12, 24.
86 Friedman, Milton. *Capitalism and Freedom.* Chicago: University of Chicago Press, 1962, 7–21.
87 Polanyi, Karl. *The Great Transformation: The Political and Economic Origins of Our Time.* Boston: Beacon Press, 1944, 136–170.
88 Robert H. Wiebe, *The Search for Order, 1877–1920.*
89 Mark Aldrich, *Safety First: Technology, Labor, and Business in the Building of American Work Safety, 1870–1939.*
90 Engels, Friedrich. *The Condition of the Working Class in England.* Oxford: Oxford University Press, 2009 [orig. 1845], 1–64.
91 Aldrich, Mark. "Accidents and Safety: The Railroad Problem." *Journal of Economic History* 36, no. 4 (1976): 887–917.
92 Centers for Disease Control and Prevention (CDC). *Fatal Injury Reports: National, Regional, and State, 2018–2023.* WISQARS (Web-based Injury Statistics Query and Reporting System), U.S. Department of Health and Human Services; Gun Violence Archive. *2024 Mass Shootings and Fatalities Database.*
93 Great Britain Board of Trade, *General Report upon Railway Accidents* (London: HMSO, 1902).
94 Nelson W. Aldrich, "Report on Railroad Safety," Senate Committee on Interstate Commerce, 1902.
95 U.S. Strike Commission Report, "Report on the Chicago Strike of June–July 1894," U.S. Government Printing Office, 1895.
96 Ibid.
97 Jacob A. Riis, *How the Other Half Lives: Studies among the Tenements of New York* (New York: Charles Scribner's Sons, 1890).
98 David Nasaw, *Andrew Carnegie* (New York: Penguin Press, 2006).
99 U.S. Strike Commission Report, "Report on the Chicago Strike of June–July 1894," U.S. Government Printing Office, 1895.
100 Ibid.
101 Eugene V. Debs, testimony in *In re Debs*, 158 U.S. 564 (1895).
102 Robert H. Wiebe, *The Search for Order, 1877–1920.*
103 Baldwin, Carliss Y., and Kim B. Clark. *The Power of Modularity: Design Rules, Volume 1.* Cambridge, MA: MIT Press, 2000, 1–35.
104 Robert H. Wiebe, *The Search for Order, 1877–1920.*
105 Alan Greenspan and Adrian Wooldridge, *Capitalism in America: A History*, esp. chapters 2–5.
106 Ibid.
107 Robert H. Wiebe, *The Search for Order, 1877–1920.*

108 Carnegie, Andrew. "Wealth." *North American Review* 148, no. 391 (1889): 653–664.
109 Jacob A. Riis, *How the Other Half Lives: Studies among the Tenements of New York* (New York: Charles Scribner's Sons, 1890).
110 H. W. Brands, *American Colossus: The Triumph of Capitalism, 1865–1900.*
111 Malcolm Harris, *Palo Alto: A History of California, Capitalism, and the World* (New York: Little, Brown, 2023).
112 Alan Greenspan and Adrian Wooldridge, *Capitalism in America: A History*, esp. chapters 2–5.
113 Malcolm Harris, *Palo Alto: A History of California, Capitalism, and the World* (New York: Little, Brown, 2023).
114 Eric Foner, *Reconstruction: America's Unfinished Revolution, 1863–1877* (New York: Harper & Row, 1988).
115 Robert H. Wiebe, *The Search for Order, 1877–1920.*
116 Ibid.
117 Mark Aldrich, *Safety First: Technology, Labor, and Business in the Building of American Work Safety, 1870–1939.*
118 Grover Cleveland, "Proclamation 369—Regarding Obstruction of the U.S. Mail," July 8, 1894.
119 Eric Foner, *Reconstruction: America's Unfinished Revolution, 1863–1877* (New York: Harper & Row, 1988).
120 Robert H. Wiebe, *The Search for Order, 1877–1920.*
121 Malcolm Harris, *Palo Alto: A History of California, Capitalism, and the World* (New York: Little, Brown, 2023).
122 Robert H. Wiebe, *The Search for Order, 1877–1920.*
123 Louis D. Brandeis, *Other People's Money and How the Bankers Use It* (New York: Frederick A. Stokes, 1914).
124 Sklar, Martin J. *The Corporate Reconstruction of American Capitalism, 1890–1916*. 1988, 3–32, 129–168.
125 Jacob A. Riis, *How the Other Half Lives: Studies among the Tenements of New York* (New York: Charles Scribner's Sons, 1890).
126 Ibid.
127 Alan Greenspan and Adrian Wooldridge, *Capitalism in America: A History*, esp. chapters 2–5.
128 Skocpol, Theda. *Protecting Soldiers and Mothers: The Political Origins of Social Policy in the United States*. Cambridge, MA: Harvard University Press, 1992, 1–32.
129 U.S. Strike Commission Report, "Report on the Chicago Strike of June–July 1894," U.S. Government Printing Office, 1895.
130 Ray Dalio, *Principles for Dealing with the Changing World Order.*
131 Friedrich Hayek, *The Constitution of Liberty* (Chicago: University of Chicago Press, 1960), chapters on spontaneous order and institutional limits.
132 Alan Greenspan and Adrian Wooldridge, *Capitalism in America: A History*, esp. chapters 2–5.
133 Ibid.

5 Laissez-Faire Capitalism's Great Reckoning

The early twentieth century was the Great Reckoning with the Gilded Age.[1] In the span of just three decades, economies that had seemed invincible were shaken to the core, and the intellectual foundations of laissez-faire capitalism underwent their most profound transformation since Adam Smith. Between 1914 and 1945, the world lurched through a sequence of catastrophes so severe that they shattered the political, economic, and social structures that had defined the nineteenth century.[2] Two world wars, the Russian Revolution, the Great Depression, hyperinflation across Europe, the Dust Bowl, genocide in Armenia and Ukraine, the rise of totalitarian ideologies, and the detonation of nuclear weapons in Japan all unfolded within the lifetime of a single generation. The great promises of the Gilded Age collided with their consequences, and when the dust settled, the old version of capitalism had been irreversibly altered.[3]

This period was not merely a collection of tragic historical events; it was a structural crisis of the economic order itself.[4] The same forces that had propelled the United States and parts of Europe into unprecedented prosperity—rapid industrialization, dramatic productivity gains, corporate scale, and financial innovation—had also generated a level of inequality, political instability, labor conflict, and market volatility that societies could no longer absorb. The Great Reckoning of laissez-faire capitalism was not caused by any single failure but by the systemic brittleness that emerged when the Gilded Age's upside and downside were both pushed to extremes.

By the early 1900s, both the limitations of laissez-faire capitalism and the inadequacy of government responses to the Gilded Age's social crises had become impossible to ignore.[5] The Progressive Era (1890s–1920s) emerged as a direct reaction to the excesses of the prior epoch: a reform movement that sought to rein in monopoly power, protect workers, reduce corruption, and modernize governance.[6] It was, in effect, society's attempt to retrofit moral, legal, and institutional safeguards onto a system that had strayed from its original moral foundation.[7] Antitrust enforcement, food and drug regulations, child labor laws, public health investments, campaign finance reforms, conservation efforts, and the professionalization of public administration all traced their roots to this period of great reckoning. These reforms were not a rejection of capitalism; instead, it can be said that they saved capitalism from itself.

Yet reform alone was not enough to prevent the systemic breakdown that followed. The First World War upended global trade and finance. The chaotic reopening of markets in the early 1920s combined with unsustainable credit expansion, fragile banking networks, and speculative bubbles to create the conditions that triggered the Great Depression. Unemployment soared, asset prices collapsed, and faith in capitalism evaporated across much of the democratic world.[8] Extremist ideologies—fascism, communism, militarism—rose on the promise of ending the instability that capitalism seemed unable to control.[9] As John Maynard Keynes wrote in 1933, the "outstanding

 | https://doi.org/10.1515/9783112235485-006

faults of the economic society in which we live" were its inability to safeguard employment and its tendency to concentrate wealth in the hands of the few.[10] Both were legacies of the Gilded Age, and both fueled the political upheavals of the 1920s and 1930s.

By mid-century, the international order that had supported classical liberal capitalism—free trade, the gold standard, minimal regulation, and private capital dominance—had collapsed.[11] In its place emerged a new hybrid model: an interventionist, state-guided capitalism shaped by Keynesian macroeconomic management, social insurance, industrial policy, and global institutions designed to mitigate the volatility that had destroyed the pre-1914 system. The United States and United Kingdom reinvented capitalism through the New Deal, the welfare state, and the Bretton Woods system.[12] Western Europe rebuilt its economies through coordinated reconstruction programs and social democratic compacts. Even the architects of the old laissez-faire order, such as Friedrich Hayek, conceded that some institutional guardrails were necessary to preserve freedom under modern conditions.[13]

The first half of the twentieth century thus marks capitalism's pivotal transition—a period in which the system proved both its extraordinary potential and its structural fragility. The Gilded Age demonstrated what capitalism could create. The Progressive Era and the crises that followed revealed what capitalism, left unmodified, could destroy. This tension—between capitalism's capacity to generate immense prosperity and its tendency to generate instability, inequality, and social fracture—defines the central challenge of modern economic design.

A striking feature of this period—one that complicates any simple narrative of decline—is that the pace of technological innovation did not slow during the Great Reckoning.[14] Even as the economic and political foundations of laissez-faire capitalism fractured, transformative breakthroughs continued to reshape daily life and extend the productive frontier. Automobiles redefined mobility, and within that sector Henry Ford pioneered large-scale industrial manufacturing through the assembly line, reorganizing labor markets and giving rise to increasingly complex and interdependent supply chains.[15] Aviation advanced rapidly from fragile experimentation to military capability and, soon thereafter, commercial transport. Electrification spread into homes, factories, and cities, enabling lighting, appliances, refrigeration, radio, and the early infrastructure of modern communications. Advances in chemistry and materials science produced synthetic fertilizers, industrial compounds, and pharmaceuticals, while mass media—from broadcast radio to motion pictures—created national cultures and integrated consumer markets.[16]

Taken together, these developments demonstrate that innovation did not collapse with the erosion of laissez-faire capitalism; it persisted and, in many domains, accelerated even as the institutional order that had governed the Gilded Age was being dismantled.[17] The question, therefore, is not whether capitalism remained innovative under stress but why its innovative capacity proved so resilient amid social upheaval and economic instability. Initial explanations point to cumulative learning from the

Gilded Age, the rise of dedicated industrial research laboratories, the diffusion of scientific and engineering education, wartime demand, and the early emergence of coordinated public–private investment.[18] This chapter examines how these forces sustained technological progress even as the economic system that first unleashed it entered its most consequential period of redesign.

Inclusive Capitalism treats the Great Reckoning of laissez-faire capitalism as a foundational source of insight: It is the period when capitalism's extraordinary productive power collided with its own social, political, and institutional limits, forcing correction rather than denial. The Great Reckoning was the period in which capitalism first became institutionally self-correcting rather than socially self-destructive. It also serves as an empirical guide for deriving the design principles needed to preserve capitalism's innovative engine while eliminating its systemic harms. The goal is not to abandon the mechanisms that produced the Gilded Age's extraordinary innovations, nor to repeat the heavy-handed corrective cycles that characterized the Progressive Era, the Depression, and the postwar settlement. Rather, it is to revise the incentive structures and institutional architecture so that capitalism's benefits can be sustained without requiring violent periodic resets. The lessons of 1870–1945 reveal that when incentives diverge from societal well-being, when scale is allowed to morph into monopoly, when currency systems amplify rather than buffer economic cycles, and when innovation rewards a narrow elite, the system becomes unstable—and with time often catastrophically so.[19] The challenge ahead is to preserve what worked, eliminate what failed, and design a durable framework in which prosperity and social stability reinforce one another rather than collide.

This chapter explores how the crises of the early twentieth century emerged from the structural flaws of Gilded Age capitalism, how reform movements attempted to address those flaws, and what insights these historical patterns provide for constructing an economic system that can meet twenty-first-century challenges without repeating the upheavals of the past.

What Was the Great Reckoning?

The Great Reckoning—often termed the Progressive Era in the United States but more accurately understood as a global, early-twentieth-century rebalancing of industrial capitalism—was the period during which laissez-faire capitalism confronted its own structural contradictions and was compelled to evolve. Spanning roughly the 1890s through the late 1930s, it marked the transition from nineteenth-century classical liberalism, grounded in minimal state intervention, to a new political-economic settlement in which the state assumed an active role in shaping market conditions, social protections, and macroeconomic stability. John Gerard Ruggie's paper, "International Regimes, Transactions, and Change: Embedded Liberalism in the Postwar Economic Order," argued that the post-World War II period sought economic order through compromises between liberalization of trade and social protections through state intervention.[20] It was not a repudiation of capitalism but a refactoring of its operating system.

At its core, the Great Reckoning reflected a growing recognition that industrial-scale capitalism had outgrown the institutional framework inherited from the agrarian and early industrial eras. The emergent corporate economy—characterized by national and international markets, continent-spanning firms, increasingly complex supply chains, rapidly advancing technologies, and powerful financial institutions—exposed the limits of the laissez-faire toolkit. Governments, courts, and electorates responded by revising the "rules of the game," seeking to manage industrial concentration, labor relations, urbanization, and technological disruption without destabilizing society or eroding democratic legitimacy.[21]

Several defining characteristics distinguish this period:

1. It was an era of institutional construction. Antitrust statutes, food and drug regulation, central banking, securities oversight, workers' compensation, and early social insurance programs emerged as durable pillars of modern capitalist governance.[22]
2. It introduced a more explicit conception of market fairness, grounded in the view that competition requires enforceable rules to prevent coercion, fraud, and abuses of power by dominant firms, rather than assuming such outcomes would self-correct.[23]
3. It marked the birth of modern regulatory capitalism. Specialized agencies—such as the Interstate Commerce Commission, the Federal Trade Commission, and later the Securities and Exchange Commission—began shaping market behavior through standards, monitoring, and enforcement rather than episodic legislative intervention alone.[24]
4. It established the foundations of countercyclical macroeconomic management, culminating in the Keynesian insight that governments must stabilize aggregate demand, intervene during downturns, and coordinate fiscal and monetary policy at scale to prevent systemic collapse.[25]
5. Finally, It transformed public expectations of the state. The Great Reckoning normalized the idea that government should protect consumers, preserve competitive markets, safeguard the safety of food, water, and workplaces, and provide a basic social safety net—expectations that would define the political economy of the twentieth century.[26]

The decline of laissez-faire capitalism was not confined to the United States; it unfolded across the industrialized world as nations confronted the same structural failures—periodic mass unemployment, volatile capital flows, concentrated economic power, and the social unrest that accompanied them.[27] In Europe, the devastation of World War I, the hyperinflation of the early 1920s, and the Depression of the 1930s exposed the limitations of the 19th-century liberal model. After World War II, a new institutional framework emerged that embedded economic management not only within national governments but also within a growing set of international bodies. The Bretton Woods system, established in 1944, created the IMF and the World Bank to stabilize exchange rates, coordinate reconstruction, and prevent the destabilizing spirals in capital and trade that had characterized the interwar period.[28] Wartime economic planning—rationing, industrial coordination, centralized resource allocation—had demonstrated that state-managed systems could mobilize productive capacity on a scale markets alone had never achieved. These lessons carried directly into the post-war settlement, shaping an international order that blended markets, planning, and institutional oversight.

By the mid-20th century, laissez-faire capitalism had been replaced almost everywhere by mixed economies that combined private enterprise with sustained government involvement.[29] Across the United States, Western Europe, and parts of East Asia, governments adopted Keynesian doctrines aimed at maintaining full employment, smoothing economic cycles, and preventing the type of collapses that had threatened democratic stability in the 1930s. As Eric Hobsbawm observed in *The Age of Extremes* (1994,) "The epoch of the laissez-faire economy and minimal state intervention . . . was now over."[30] In practice this meant welfare states, automatic stabilizers, labor protections, financial regulation, industrial policy, and large public investments in infrastructure, education, and scientific research. What looked like a "mid-life crisis" of laissez-faire capitalism in the United States was in fact a global transition toward an operating model that sought to retain the dynamism of markets while taming their most destructive tendencies.

Yet even this global mixed-economy framework left the core structural incentives of industrial leadership largely intact, which is why many of the unintended consequences—concentration, cycles, instability, exclusion—reemerged late in the twentieth century and again in the 21st.[31] This underscores the central argument of Inclusive Capitalism: when technology advances faster than institutional design, economic systems lose their capacity to allocate resources legitimately and sustainably. Just as mercantilist structures collapsed under industrialization, today's capitalist incentives have fallen out of alignment with modern productive realities. Reform must therefore be architectural rather than reactive—built into institutions, not layered atop their failures.

Importantly, the Great Reckoning was not uniform across nations.[32] The United States emphasized antitrust, consumer protection, and regulatory oversight; Western Europe leaned more heavily into social insurance and the welfare state; and other nations experimented with varying degrees of state planning or mixed economies.[33] Yet, across these diverse paths, the underlying pattern was the same: Industrial capitalism required new guardrails to remain legitimate, productive, and socially sustainable.[34]

The Great Reckoning is best understood as the era that capitalism became externally corrected at the institutional level.[35] Markets still generated innovation, growth, and competition—but now operated within structures designed to curb the excesses that had made the Gilded Age both brilliant and brittle. In this sense, it was a foundational recalibration: a recognition that capitalism's extraordinary strengths could only be preserved if its worst pathologies were contained exogenously. Yet as technology, scale, and finance evolved, these institutions failed to adapt at the same pace, gradually eroding their effectiveness and enabling a renewed drift toward laissez-faire conditions.[36]

This chapter reframes that era not as an anomaly or historical detour but as an indispensable case study in how systems evolve when their internal incentives no longer align with societal well-being—precisely the design problem Inclusive Capitalism seeks to solve for the twenty-first century.

What Triggered the Great Reckoning of Laissez-Faire Capitalism?

Long before the Great Depression, New Deal, world wars, and progressive reforms forced a break with the Gilded Age model, a set of simmering structural conditions had accumulated beneath the surface of the industrial economy.[37] These background forces produced mounting pressure that laissez-faire institutions were not designed to absorb.

First, extreme concentration of wealth and corporate power created vast asymmetries between industrial leadership and the workforce; the share of national income going to labor stagnated while the share going to capital expanded rapidly, producing visible social fractures.[38]

Second, labor markets lacked institutional mechanisms for worker voice, bargaining, or protection, leaving wage earners exposed to exploitation, unsafe conditions, and sudden economic shocks.

Third, urbanization, immigration, and rapid technological change created demographic and cultural stresses that overwhelmed existing social infrastructure; cities lacked capacity for sanitation, housing, and public services, accelerating disease, poverty, and public frustration.

Fourth, the rise of national industrial monopolies produced distortions in pricing, output, and market access, while political corruption—through party machines, patronage networks, and corporate influence—eroded trust in institutions.

Finally, the gold standard tightly constrained monetary policy, leaving governments unable to stabilize business cycles, mitigate deflation, or respond to panics.[39] These conditions created a fragile economic and social equilibrium: spectacular productivity and innovation coexisted with deep insecurity, political distrust, and an increasingly combustible social contract.

The Great Reckoning was not merely a slow erosion of laissez-faire principles—it was catalyzed by discrete shocks that exposed systemic vulnerabilities. The Panic of 1893 revealed the fragility of a financial system dependent on gold reserves, railroad overexpansion, and speculative leverage.[40] The successive labor conflicts of the 1890s—the Homestead Strike, Pullman Strike, and dozens of mass walkouts—demonstrated the explosive consequences of unmediated conflict between capital and labor.[41] The 1907 banking panic further weakened confidence in self-regulating markets and led directly to the creation of the Federal Reserve.[42] World War I showed that governments could coordinate production, labor, and capital at scale far more effectively than laissez-faire doctrine allowed, normalizing state economic planning. The Russian Revolution of 1917 terrified Western elites and emboldened reformers, showing that failure to address inequality could open space for revolutionary alternatives. The 1918 influenza pandemic revealed the absence of national public-health capacity in rapidly urbanized societies. The stock market crash of 1929 and the ensuing Great Depression were the defining rupture: Unemployment soared above 20 percent, banking systems collapsed, international trade unraveled, and deflation spiraled.[43] The Depression delegitimized the classical claim that markets would self-correct, creating political space for Roosevelt's New Deal, Keynesian fiscal theory, the regulation of financial markets, social insurance programs, and the acceptance of government responsibility for macroeconomic stabilization. World War II completed the transition by embedding large-scale public-private coordination, national planning, and international economic architecture (Bretton Woods) as the normative model.[44]

The structural and political environment of 2025 bears striking resemblance to the pre-reckoning landscape, suggesting that many of the same forces are again converging.[45] Wealth concentration has returned to Gilded Age levels, with a very small number of firms dominating critical sectors such as technology, logistics, healthcare, and finance. Labor markets show widening divides between high-skill and low-skill workers, with limited mobility and growing precarity.[46] Technological accelerants—AI, automation, data platforms—are transforming production and employment as fundamentally as electrification and mechanization did more than a century ago, while public institutions lag in adapting to the speed and scale of change. The monetary and financial system once again exhibit excess: high leverage, growing fiscal deficits, asset-price inflation, and highly speculative tendencies. The fragility of global supply chains have exposed interdependencies analogous to the gold-standard constraints of the early twentieth century.[47] Political polarization and declining institutional trust mirror the fractures of the earlier era, while rising geopolitical competition and concerns about global realignments evoke the pre-WWI environment. Climate stress, immigration pressures, and demographic shifts add additional layers of systemic risk. As in the Gilded Age, public frustration is rising in parallel with record levels of innovation, creating a combustible mix of admiration, fear, and resentment toward dominant firms and economic elites.[48] Without the structural redesign proposed by Inclusive Capitalism, the probability of a twenty-first-century "second Great Reckoning"—whether economic, political, or geopolitical—rises significantly.

Legal Framework, Economic Doctrines, and Cultural Norms the Define the Great Reckoning

The Great Reckoning unfolded within a far more elaborate institutional environment than any prior phase of capitalism, marked by a rapidly expanding body of law, a contested but increasingly interventionist economic doctrine, and cultural norms undergoing swift transformation under the pressures of industrialization, urbanization, migration, and politics. The legal architecture of the period—from antitrust statutes to labor law, banking reform, and administrative agencies—redefined the boundaries between private enterprise and public authority.[49] Economic thought fractured into competing schools that challenged classical orthodoxy and introduced new models for managing cycles, crises, and social risk.[50] And cultural norms shifted as mass consumer culture, new conceptions of individual rights, rising class consciousness, and evolving attitudes toward the state reshaped expectations about fairness, responsibility, and the role of institutions in daily life. Together, these forces formed the legal, economic, and cultural framework that both responded to the excesses of the Gilded Age and established the operating conditions of twentieth-century capitalism.[51]

The legal framework of the Great Reckoning emerged from a growing recognition that the laissez-faire architecture of the Gilded Age had produced outcomes so extreme—and so visibly inconsistent with the promises of liberal capitalism—that government intervention was no longer viewed as an ideological choice but a practical necessity. In the United States, this shift began in earnest under Theodore Roosevelt, accelerated significantly under Woodrow Wilson, and culminated in the transformative and unprecedented legal reforms of Franklin D. Roosevelt.[52] Their collective efforts constructed the scaffolding of modern regulatory capitalism: antitrust enforcement, financial system redesign, consumer protection, labor rights, and the administrative state. Each of these initiatives reflected an attempt—imperfect, often contradictory—to rein in the excesses of industrial power while preserving the dynamism that laissez-faire capitalism had unleashed. Over time, however, these efforts proved incomplete, stabilizing capitalism temporarily without resolving the underlying incentive tensions—tensions that would later re-emerge in recurring cycles of deregulation, concentration, and corrective intervention.[53]

Theodore Roosevelt's presidency marked the first large-scale federal attempt to confront the structural distortions of late nineteenth-century capitalism.[54] Roosevelt viewed concentrated corporate power as fundamentally incompatible with competitive markets and the moral legitimacy of the system itself. His administration made aggressive use of the Sherman Antitrust Act of 1890, which had existed largely as symbolic legislation until Roosevelt attempted to turn it into a genuine economic instrument. His actions against the Northern Securities Company (1902) and later Standard Oil signaled a belief that no private entity—regardless of efficiency or success—should possess more power than the republic that chartered it. Roosevelt's consumer-protection agenda, embodied in the Pure Food and Drug Act (1906) and the Meat Inspection Act (1906), reflected a broader Progressive conviction that information asymmetry and unregulated production were producing intolerable risks for the public. His "Square Deal" articulated the era's emerging legal philosophy: not hostility toward wealth but hostility toward the abuses enabled by the legal vacuum of laissez-faire.[55] Roosevelt's reforms were not ideological departures from capitalism but pragmatic correctives—necessary stabilizers for a system whose incentives had veered far from the Smithian ideal.

Woodrow Wilson deepened and institutionalized these reforms, embedding them into a more comprehensive legal and administrative architecture. The Clayton Antitrust Act (1914) refined the Sherman Act by explicitly prohibiting price discrimination, exclusive dealing, and interlocking directorates—practices that the Gilded Age titans had perfected as tools of market domination.[56] The same year, Wilson created the Federal Trade Commission, introducing a permanent regulatory body empowered not merely to punish unfair competition but to police it proactively. His most enduring structural reform—the Federal Reserve Act (1913)—reconfigured the nation's monetary system.[57] The Federal Reserve introduced a lender of last resort, centralized monetary authority, and mechanisms to prevent bank panics—conditions unachievable under nineteenth-century decentralized banking. Wilson saw these reforms as consistent with liberty itself: a government acting not to dominate markets but to ensure their functioning and fairness. Yet the Fed's creation also represented a profound shift in the legal structure of capitalism: the state assumed responsibility for macroeconomic stability, and monetary policy became a central tool of economic governance.[58]

Franklin D. Roosevelt's New Deal constituted an even larger departure from laissez-faire principles, expanding legal intervention into nearly every domain of economic life.[59] Confronted with the systemic collapse of the Great Depression—bank failures, deflation, unemployment, shattered demand—FDR believed that only direct federal action could restore functionality to the economic system.[60] The Banking Act of 1933 (Glass-Steagall) separated commercial and investment banking to prevent speculative excesses from threatening depositors and the real economy.[61] The Securities Act of 1933 and the Securities Exchange Act of 1934 created disclosure requirements, outlawed fraud, and established the Securities and Exchange Commission—imposing transparency on capital markets that had previously thrived on opacity.[62] The Wagner Act (1935) institutionalized collective bargaining and protected the right to unionize, permanently altering the legal power balance between labor and capital. The Social Security Act (1935) created a federal safety net that fundamentally changed the social contract.[63] Roosevelt described his legal philosophy as "bold, persistent experimentation," but the legal results were far more than experimental: They became the foundation of the modern managed economy.[64]

The cumulative effect of these reforms was the construction of a legal order that replaced laissez-faire capitalism with what some scholars describe as regulatory capitalism, a hybrid system in which the state functioned as referee, stabilizer, and at times direct participant in economic life. This architecture's broad contours still shape the modern-day neo-classical policy consensus, even as the modern variant operates with far greater financialization and weaker social compacts than its mid-century predecessor. Regulatory capitalism addressed many of the most acute failures of the Gilded Age—bank runs, financial manipulation, cartelization, unsafe working conditions, and catastrophic swings in the economic cycle. But it also introduced a new set of long-term challenges: expansive bureaucracy, persistent fiscal imbalance, regulatory overreach, and a slow, decades-long drift away from entrepreneurial dynamism.[65] These pathologies would eventually fuel the late-twentieth-century revival of laissez-faire doctrines, confirming that neither extreme—unregulated capitalism nor hyper-interventionist capitalism—can produce a stable equilibrium.

From the vantage point of Inclusive Capitalism, the legal framework of the Great Reckoning is instructive not because government intervention succeeded or failed in isolation but because it reveals that both laissez-faire excess and regulatory excess stem from the same design failure: incentives and institutions that no longer coordinate economic activity at technological scale or align industrial leadership with long-term societal well-being. The legal reaction of the Great Reckoning was necessary, perhaps unavoidable, given the incentives and institutions of the Gilded Age. But it was also fundamentally reactive—symptom-level regulation layered atop a system whose underlying incentive structure remained unchanged. The lesson for twenty-first-century reform is therefore not to choose between the poles of laissez-faire and interventionism but to design a framework where the most powerful actors in the economy find it in their own interest to create broad-based prosperity, competitive markets, and long-term stability. The legal history of the Great Reckoning provides ample evidence not only of what governments can do but of what economic systems must be designed to prevent.

The legal and regulatory architecture of the Great Reckoning fundamentally altered the operating environment of capitalism, but statutes alone did not supply the intellectual framework for steering a modern industrial economy. Once antitrust enforcement, consumer protections, labor guarantees, and financial oversight had constrained the most visible excesses of the Gilded Age, policymakers faced a deeper question: What economic doctrine could guide this newly empowered state apparatus—and justify when, how, and to what extent the government should intervene?[66] The Progressive Era created the legal tools, but it was the economic upheavals of the 1930s that demanded a coherent theory of how to use them. Into this vacuum stepped John Maynard Keynes, whose critique of classical laissez-faire provided both the rationale for abandoning the old orthodoxy and the blueprint for a managed, demand-stabilized capitalist system. The next stage of this chapter therefore turns from the institutional hardware of the Progressive reforms to the intellectual software—Keynesian economics—that would animate, legitimize, and ultimately define economic governance for the remainder of the twentieth century.[67]

Keynesianism

The era of Keynesian economics began as a diagnosis of a system that stalled and stayed stalled.[68] During the Great Depression, output and employment collapsed while prices did not fall enough to clear markets. John Maynard Keynes argued that modern, money-using economies are demand-constrained: When private spending falters, the economy can settle into a state with idle resources and involuntary unemployment.[69] Because expectations, liquidity preference, and uncertainty suppress private investment, the state must step in as spender and stabilizer. The mechanism is straightforward: countercyclical fiscal policy (deficits in slumps, surpluses in booms), complemented by monetary policy that keeps interest rates low when confidence is weak.[70] The ambition was not to replace markets but to smooth their cycles so that markets could function.

Originally developed as a response to crisis, the economic doctrine that emerged from the Great Reckoning did not remain as a temporary manual. Within a decade, it evolved into a full operating system for modern capitalism—one capable of coordinating governments, central banks, and private industry in peacetime.[71] Several thinkers contributed key components, each adding a conceptual building block to what became known as the Keynesian Consensus.

Paul Samuelson, whose *Foundations of Economic Analysis* (1947) trained two generations of economists, translated Keynes's arguments into a systematic macroeconomic toolkit that policymakers could actually use.[72] Samuelson's great accomplishment was not originality but clarity: He took Keynes's insights about demand failures and formalized them into a coherent set of equations, diagrams, and comparative-statics tools. His framework made the new doctrine teachable, testable, and administrable.

John Hicks played the complementary role of providing the map.[73] His IS–LM diagram, introduced in 1937 (Figure 5.1), distilled the economy into two interacting markets: the "IS" curve representing the real economy of investment and saving, and the "LM" curve representing the monetary economy of liquidity and money supply.

Where these curves intersect, Hicks showed, the economy can settle into a stable position even with idle factories and unemployed workers—a graphical demonstration of Keynes's underemployment equilibrium. IS–LM gave central banks and treasuries a shared language: fiscal policy shifts the IS curve; monetary policy shifts the LM curve. With one picture, Hicks turned Keynesian ideas into a practical control panel.

Richard Kahn contributed the mechanism that made the doctrine scalable: the multiplier.[74] Kahn demonstrated mathematically how an initial dollar of spending—private or public—does not stop with the first transaction but sets off a chain of secondary income and consumption effects. This explained why recessions could be severe and why targeted spending could have an outsized impact on employment. For policymakers, the multiplier justified well-calibrated intervention rather than passive observation.

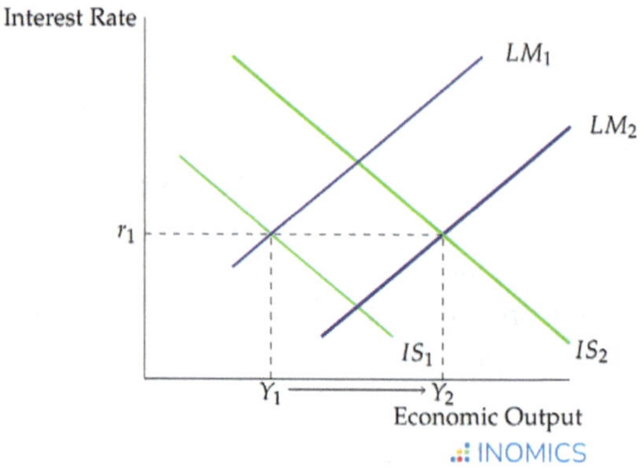

Figure 5.1: IS-LM Diagram.

Franco Modigliani and later Robert Solow extended Keynesianism beyond crisis management into long-run planning.[75] Modigliani's life-cycle hypothesis explained how households smooth consumption over time and why saving responds predictably to demographics and interest rates. Solow built the first robust model of growth, showing how capital accumulation, labor-force expansion, and—crucially—technological progress jointly determine long-run living standards. With these additions, Keynesianism gained a growth architecture rather than remaining a short-run stabilization tool. The doctrine could now support national budgeting, investment planning, and industrial strategy.

James Tobin added the financial dimension.[76] His portfolio-balance approach made clear that monetary policy works partly by shifting the composition of private portfolios—safe assets versus risky assets, cash versus bonds—affecting not only interest rates but also risk premia, credit flows, and financial stability. Tobin's work anticipated, by decades, the modern understanding that macroeconomic policy must account for financial frictions, asset-price swings, and balance-sheet vulnerabilities.

By the late 1940s this collection of ideas solidified and was embodied into the postwar Keynesian Consensus.[77] The new doctrine treated macroeconomic stability not as an emergent property of markets but as a public good requiring institutional support. Three operational habits followed:

1. Insure households and firms against shocks: Progressive taxation, unemployment insurance, Social Security, deposit insurance, and farm-price supports acted as automatic stabilizers—dampening recessions without requiring new legislation each time.[78]
2. Lean against recessions using public demand: When private demand faltered, governments were expected to spend: on infrastructure, research, national defense, or direct employment programs.[79] The goal was to prevent the economy from spiraling downward due to pessimistic expectations or liquidity traps.

3. Build institutions to prevent destabilizing cascades: Bretton Woods, the IMF, the World Bank, national central banks with lender-of-last-resort powers, and financial-market regulation all emerged from the recognition that panic, contagion, and deflation are systemic risks—not moral failings of individuals or firms.[80]

The result was a mixed economy in which markets remained the primary allocators of resources but governments stood ready to dampen volatility, protect households, and coordinate responses to systemic threats. In practice, Keynesianism operated less like an ideology than like a set of pragmatic engineering principles: when demand is collapsing, add demand; when financial markets freeze, thaw them; when shocks threaten households, buffer them.

Within this Keynesian institutional architecture—and, more importantly, under the extraordinary and fundamentally non-repeatable post-war conditions that uniquely favored the United States—the economy delivered three decades of full employment, rapid productivity gains, rising median incomes, and remarkable macroeconomic stability.[81] A central issue, however, is whether these outcomes were achieved because of Keynesian policy or despite it. The evidence strongly suggests that the primary drivers were the conditions themselves: unmatched industrial dominance after European and Japanese devastation, pent-up consumer demand from wartime rationing, an unprecedented demographic boom, cheap domestic energy, and an international monetary order designed around American supremacy.[82] When these structural advantages faded in the 1970s—foreign competition intensified, demographics shifted, oil prices spiked, and the Bretton Woods system collapsed—the Keynesian model ceased to deliver its textbook results. The apparent success of the "Keynesian era," in other words, was more a testament to unique postwar advantages than the efficacy of the Keynesian doctrine itself. As later sections argue, once the conditions evaporated, the ideal outcomes evaporated with them. This motivates the search for system-level solutions capable of producing durable prosperity without relying on historical accidents or oscillation between Keynesian intervention and laissez-faire retrenchment.

The critics of Keynesian economics were varied and important. Monetarists led by Milton Friedman accepted stabilization as an aim but argued that money, not fiscal deficits, was the clean instrument; they blamed policy mistakes for both the Depression's depth and later inflations.[83] The New Classical school emphasized rational expectations, policy credibility, and "rules over discretion," arguing that ad-hoc stimulus is blunted by behavior and can invite time inconsistency and inflation bias.[84] Public Choice economists warned that politicians would use deficit tools for permanent transfer rather than temporary stabilization. Austrians attacked the project more fundamentally, arguing that state steering distorts signals, misallocates capital, and erodes liberty.

What aspects of Keynesian economics worked? Post-war stabilization was real. Automatic stabilizers and occasional discretionary programs shortened recessions, cushioned unemployment, and underwrote broad middle-class formation. The institutionalization of countercyclical policy helped avoid Depression-scale collapses. In acute crises, aggressive fiscal and monetary response prevented deeper slumps, financial runs, and deflationary spirals.[85] Keynesianism also normalized the insight that macro risk is systemic and requires system-level tools.

What did not work became equally clear over time. The stagflation of the 1970s exposed limits: Governments could fuel demand but not guarantee real growth when supply was constrained.[86] Over time, stabilization bled into secular deficit finance, while financialization increasingly diverted stimulus into asset inflation rather than productive capacity. The doctrine proved reactive rather than preventive, treating symptoms more effectively than causes.

Proponents today include New Keynesians, who refine Keynes's ideas with price stickiness, forward-looking expectations, and rules-based policy tools, while preserving the argument that government must act as an economic insurer during deep recessions.[87] Thoughtful critics accept the emergency toolkit but insist on guardrails: fiscal anchors, monetary independence, and tighter links between support and real supply capacity.[88]

These refinements help at the macro level but do not offset a critical limitation of Keynesian economics: Macroeconomic policy operates at an abstraction far removed from the decision-making reality of industrial leaders.[89] It can stabilize demand after collapse, but it does not prevent the micro-level behaviors that create instability in the first place. Monetary and fiscal levers are pulled after damage has occurred rather than shaping incentives that guide pricing, risk-taking, and investment.[90]

The evidence now points to a single structural conclusion: Capitalism's modern failures arise when industrial leadership incentives no longer match technological realities or societal needs.[91] In such systems, exogenous correction becomes routine, politics becomes reactive, and stability depends on perpetual intervention. Keynes taught us how to stop the bleeding. The task now is to redesign the system so the wounds are less frequent and less severe.

The Great Reckoning reshaped not only law and economics but the moral vocabulary of capitalism itself. It redefined fairness, authority, responsibility, and acceptable behavior in an industrial society. The Progressive Era inverted the Gilded Age's norms of heroic individualism and deference to concentrated power.[92] A new moral center of gravity emerged that demanded accountability, broadened ethical expectations, and expanded the social contract.

Public attitudes toward large corporations shifted dramatically. Size moved from a symbol of efficiency to a marker of democratic risk. Muckraking journalism altered expectations of corporate conduct and reframed concentrated power as a threat to republican self-government.[93] Roosevelt's trust-busting both reflected and reinforced this cultural transformation.

Norms surrounding labor and welfare evolved in parallel. Workplace danger and poverty came to be viewed as social failures rather than natural by-products of progress. The Triangle Shirtwaist Factory fire crystallized this shift and cemented the belief that worker safety was a collective responsibility.[94] These norms laid the cultural groundwork for New Deal social insurance.

Perhaps the most enduring shift was the normalization of the belief that the state bore responsibility for macroeconomic outcomes. Recessions ceased to be viewed as inevitable acts of nature and became policy failures to be prevented. These expectations proved durable and reshaped the legitimacy of public institutions.

In sum, the Great Reckoning redefined the moral backbone of modern capitalism.[95] It reshaped norms around power, risk, responsibility, and inclusion, forming the cultural substratum upon which Keynesian economics and regulatory capitalism were built. And it establishes a central insight for Inclusive Capitalism: durable economic reform requires aligning incentives, institutions, and norms—not merely alternating between crisis intervention and retrenchment.

Same Incentives with New Constraints Evoke Old Behaviors by Industrial Leaders

The industrial leadership did not fundamentally change its objectives or playbook in response to the Progressive legal order, Keynesian doctrine, or shifting social norms.[96] The reforms constrained tactics—raising compliance costs, narrowing certain forms of collusion or consolidation, and empowering labor at the margin—but they left the core incentive structure intact: pursue growth, market power, and shareholder returns within whatever rules prevail. The predictable result was a more adversarial, compliance-heavy equilibrium rather than a values-level realignment. Business leaders adapted, contested, and occasionally pre-empted regulation; they did not reorient strategy around public-interest metrics because the system never paid them to do so.

Henry Ford (1863–1947) is often perceived as one of the fiercest opponents of the reform movements of the early twentieth century, though his record is far more complex.[97] He genuinely believed in the social intent behind many Progressive Era objectives, yet vehemently rejected the mechanisms—unions, collective bargaining, regulatory oversight, and state intervention—that reformers relied upon. Inside Ford Motor Company, he moved faster and further than his peers on wages, hours, and working conditions. His decision in 1914 to introduce the five-dollar day, effectively doubling prevailing factory wages and cutting the workday from nine to eight hours, stunned the business world and demonstrated in practice that higher compensation and higher productivity could reinforce one another. Turnover collapsed, production soared, and workers could afford to buy the very cars they built. Ford was proud of this alignment of worker welfare and industrial efficiency, often insisting that "the only prosperity the people can afford to be satisfied with is the kind that lasts," and he saw his policies as a way to lift ordinary workers into the middle class and create a mass-consumption society.[98]

At the same time, Ford remained deeply and aggressively anti-union. He argued that unions undermined a worker's independence and opposed them with the same forceful conviction that earlier industrialists brought to anti-labor campaigns. "Labor union organizations are the worst thing that ever struck the earth," he wrote in *My Life and Work* (1922).[99] To Ford, benevolent management—so long as that management was his own—was the superior alternative to state-mandated protections or collective bargaining. This conviction drove him to tolerate, and sometimes directly authorize, the violent suppression of labor organizers by Ford Service Department enforcers and local police. The contrast between his wage reforms and his coercive anti-union stance reveals the essential dynamic: Ford embraced improvements that preserved managerial control and rejected reforms that redistributed power.

Philosophically, Ford was an uncompromising laissez-faire capitalist. He distrusted government intervention in nearly all forms, preferred voluntary employer action to statutory mandates, and believed economic independence would flourish if "people are left alone" and government simply "serves" rather than "dominates." He criticized New Deal policies as both economically misguided and morally corrosive, arguing that "burdening people with debt is an old deal, not a new deal."[100] Yet Ford simultaneously insisted that the moral purpose of business was service rather than profit alone—a claim that coexisted, somewhat uneasily, with his hostility toward the mechanisms that would have institutionalized protections for workers beyond Ford Motor Company.

Ford's stance during the mid-twentieth century captures the broader pattern among industrial leaders: selective adoption of Progressive goals where they complemented corporate strategy, paired with fierce resistance whenever reform threatened autonomy, authority, or the firm's internal power structure. His wage revolution, shorter hours, and productivity breakthroughs aligned with elements of Inclusive Capitalism—but his motives were grounded in the long term competitiveness and stability of Ford Motor Company, not in a systemic commitment to societal well-being. His invasive surveillance of employees, his reliance on intimidation, and his rejection of worker representation all point to the same underlying incentive structure: The firm optimizes for itself, and benevolence survives only where it reinforces the corporate objective function.

The Ford story also underscores why Progressive legislation, Keynesian stabilization, and cultural pressure failed to change the deeper dynamics of leadership behavior. Ford responded to constraints, anticipated reforms, and occasionally pre-empted them, but nothing altered the core incentives that drove elite decision-making. Just as with the industrial leaders of the Gilded Age, modern entrepreneurs, despite being far more attuned to societal expectations, remain subject to an incentive matrix that rewards control, scale, and return on capital above all else.[101] The persistent recurrence of concentration, social division, exclusion, and recurring conflict between government and industry signals that the root cause lies not in individual leaders but in the architecture of the system itself. Inclusive Capitalism consistently argues that only a structural redesign of incentives—not regulatory after-the-fact correction—can break the cycle of reactive, "ping-pong" economics and align industrial leadership with societal well-being by default rather than exception.

Another takeaway from Henry Ford's response to the Great Reckoning is especially instructive for the design and social logic of Inclusive Capitalism. Ford broadly accepted the objectives of reform—higher wages, mass affordability, and social stability—but resisted the methods through which those objectives were imposed, particularly external regulation and adversarial oversight.[102] Inclusive Capitalism is built on the premise that this tension can be resolved at the level of incentives rather than authority: When industrial leaders are properly incentivized and evaluated, they can pursue societal well-being more effectively than under misaligned incentives corrected only through exogenous constraint. One of the model's most compelling advantages is that it converts industrial leaders from compliance targets into active agents of social progress. Under clear, outcome-based metrics and real accountability tied to those metrics, leaders are empowered to implement policies and operational tactics that advance societal well-being as a core function of value creation—rather than as a concession extracted after the fact.[103]

Alfred P. Sloan, long-serving president and CEO of General Motors, represented a different archetype of early twentieth-century industrial leadership—less paternalistic than Ford, more technocratic and managerial, and deeply committed to the autonomy of the corporation. Sloan revolutionized corporate structure through decentralized divisions, professional management, and a marketing ethos tuned to consumer preference. These innovations helped transform GM into the dominant automotive company of the century.[104] But they also reflected Sloan's core belief that markets, not governments, were the legitimate regulators of industrial conduct.

Sloan advocated fiercely for free enterprise and minimal state intrusion, and he regarded the New Deal as a dangerous enlargement of federal authority. He argued repeatedly that political actors, bureaucrats, and organized labor lacked the experience and discipline to guide industrial activity. "It is my firm conviction," he wrote, "that any form of government regulation of business is bound to result in an ever-increasing interference with the exercise of initiative."[105] His participation in the American Liberty League—founded explicitly to oppose Roosevelt's policies—demonstrated the intensity of his conviction that government-led reform threatened the profit system and the flexibility corporations required to respond to markets.

Yet Sloan also argued that industrial leaders had responsibilities beyond narrow shareholder return. He urged business to develop what he called "industrial statesmanship," a broader outlook that considered the community and the long-term health of the enterprise together.[106] This philosophy partly reflected self-interest: A stable consumer base, predictable economic environment, and high public regard were good for business. But it also reflected his view that voluntary corporate leadership, not government mandates, should manage the social consequences of industrial capitalism. Inclusive Capitalism embeds Sloan's vision in institutional architecture by aligning incentives so that voluntary corporate leadership and societal well-being reinforce one another—an alignment the historical record makes clear cannot be sustained under existing capitalist institutions.

Much like Ford, Sloan modernized management and scaled worker opportunity in ways that looked progressive—but he did so selectively, only where it reinforced GM's competitive strategy. When labor demands or New Deal policies threatened managerial autonomy, Sloan resisted fiercely. He opposed collective bargaining, fought back against union organizing, and viewed regulation as a slippery slope toward bureaucratic control. The pattern matches the broader dynamic of the period: Industrialists adapted around the new constraints, but nothing fundamentally altered the incentive architecture that governed their decisions. The resulting environment—higher wages and safer factories alongside bitter labor conflicts and political hostility—became a case study in how constraints shape behavior without changing the underlying motivations.[107]

Thomas Edison stands apart from Ford and Sloan not only in temperament but in vocation. As an inventor and founder of General Electric, Edison was less directly engaged in labor relations or regulatory politics. Yet his views and business conduct reveal another facet of early twentieth-century industrial incentives: a belief in private initiative, limited government, and the natural legitimacy of market dominance when achieved through innovation.[108]

Edison's business practices—most notably his attempts to secure exclusive control over key technologies such as electrical distribution and recorded sound—make clear his preference for minimal regulatory oversight. He built vertically integrated structures that, in effect, functioned as monopolies. He was not hostile to scale; he saw it as the natural reward for technological superiority. Yet Edison also consistently criticized certain features of the existing financial system, particularly the gold standard and interest-bearing debt. His remark that "gold is a relic of Julius Caesar, and interest is an invention of Satan" reflected a suspicion that the monetary system penalized productive labor and innovation.[109] His 1922 proposal for a commodity-backed, interest-free credit facility for farmers was an early version of what Inclusive Capitalism would call a domain-specific currency—money issued to match productive capacity rather than constrained by legacy financial conventions.

Edison's personal ethics differed markedly from Ford's. He refused to contribute to offensive weaponry, proudly noting that he had "never invented an instrument of war."[110] His advocacy for nonviolence extended to his treatment of animals and influenced his adoption of vegetarianism. Morally, Edison embodied a gentler posture than many of his contemporaries. But ethically elevated behavior did not translate into systemic independence from the incentive structure. Edison still operated within a competitive environment where monopoly advantage, intellectual property accumulation, and close alignment with capital markets determined success.

Edison therefore illustrates a core thesis of this chapter: Ethical character alone cannot counteract systemic incentives. His nonviolent principles and humanistic instincts did not prevent him from constructing corporate structures that concentrated power and discouraged competition. In this sense, he underscores that the outcomes of capitalism are shaped less by leaders' moral preferences than by the architecture of the system in which they operate.[111]

Vannevar Bush, engineer, founder of Raytheon, and architect of America's wartime research mobilization, provides perhaps the clearest example of how incentives, context, and national imperatives interact. Bush was politically conservative and openly skeptical of the New Deal's economic reforms. He distrusted bureaucratic expansion and believed government economic planning risked entangling enterprise in political currents rather than productive logic.

Yet Bush also became one of the strongest advocates for federal support of science, especially during and after World War II. His 1945 report, *Science—The Endless Frontier*, argued that national prosperity, public welfare, and long-term economic growth required sustained government investment in basic research.[112] He recommended establishing the National Research Foundation (later the National Science Foundation) because private markets, as then structured, could not reliably fund foundational science. Inclusive Capitalism addresses this limitation by realigning incentives so that private-sector, open, collaborative innovation is structurally rewarded. As Jon Gruber observes, the public-sector substitute has increasingly struggled to sustain this function on its own.[113]

Superficially, Bush's positions look contradictory: skepticism of government intervention on the one hand, enthusiastic support for government-funded research on the other. But in incentive terms, the positions are perfectly consistent. Government spending that empowered scientists and engineers—particularly in ways that allowed industry to build new sectors and defense applications—was aligned with Bush's institutional interests and his vision for national capability. Regulation that constrained corporate autonomy or redistributed bargaining power toward labor was not.[114]

Bush's career reveals how industrial leaders supported state intervention when it complemented their strategic goals and opposed it if it constrained them. The selective logic is not hypocrisy; it can be seen as quite the opposite, an incentive-driven rationality. Modern analogues abound today, where entrepreneurs who denounce government intrusion simultaneously depend on large federal contracts for aerospace, defense, or infrastructure. Bush's role thus clarifies this key conclusion: Constraints produce resistance, support flows toward aligned incentives, and the underlying behavioral architecture persists unchanged until the system itself is redesigned.[115]

Pierre S. du Pont, chairman of the DuPont Company, exemplifies the conservative reaction to the Progressive Era and the New Deal.[116] He strongly opposed Roosevelt's reforms, viewing them as threats to free enterprise and the autonomy of large corporations. In 1934 he co-founded the American Liberty League—one of the most well-funded anti–New Deal organizations—to oppose federal intervention, expand legal challenges against Roosevelt's policies, and promote a revival of classical liberal economic principles.

Du Pont's positions on labor law were equally revealing. Serving on the National Labor Board, he rejected the principle that a union chosen by a majority of workers should serve as the exclusive bargaining agent. Instead, he argued for proportional representation that would allow separate negotiations with company unions or individual workers—a structure that would have diluted collective bargaining power and preserved managerial discretion. His stance was not merely philosophical; it reflected the direct incentives of large industrial firms that sought to avoid the wage rigidities, conflict, and perceived political intrusion associated with national labor law.[117]

Du Pont's business practices also attracted scrutiny under the antitrust laws that he and his peers criticized. His company's large share acquisition of General Motors gave it pervasive influence over supply contracts and ultimately led to the landmark U.S. Supreme Court case *United States v. E. I. du Pont de Nemours & Co.* (1957), where the Court ruled that the stock position violated Section 7 of the Clayton Act because it substantially reduced competition.[118] The case shows, again, that industrial leaders rarely changed behavior voluntarily; external legal pressure forced compliance when incentives pushed strongly toward consolidation.

In many ways, du Pont embodied the high-modernist industrialist: strategic, disciplined, confident in corporate rationality, and deeply skeptical of democratic intervention in economic life. He also illustrates how even the most sophisticated leaders remained governed by an incentive structure that rewarded concentration, scale, and control. Regulatory reforms constrained his actions, but they did not alter the underlying system logic that generated them.[119]

A deeper reading of Ford, Sloan, Edison, Bush, and du Pont reveals a pattern that is far more compelling than a simple story of self-interest or reactionary resistance. Each, in his own way, and in a departure from the previous generation of industrial leaders, demonstrated a genuine impulse toward responsibility, stewardship, and long-term thinking. Ford doubled wages and shortened hours not because a regulator forced him to but because he believed it was good business and—at least partly—the right thing to do. Sloan advocated for "industrial statesmanship," urging business leaders to consider community welfare. Edison rejected violence and argued for reforms in the monetary system to help farmers. Bush championed public investment in scientific research for national well-being. Even du Pont, the least sympathetic to reform, acknowledged that business had obligations that extended beyond shareholders.[120]

Across this diverse set of personalities, the common thread is not hostility to progress; it is hostility to external control. These leaders wanted to shape solutions themselves. They resisted reforms not because they rejected fairness, safety, or shared prosperity but because they believed that:

1. legislators and regulators lacked understanding of the operational and competitive realities of industrial production,[121]
2. government solutions tended to be blunt, reactive, and often harmful,[122]

3. top-down mandates removed the autonomy they saw as essential to innovation and long-term success.[123]

In other words, they wanted to do the right thing—but on their own terms, within an incentive framework that supported, rather than constrained, their judgment.[124]

This is the critical design insight that emerges from the Great Reckoning: regulation constrained the symptoms of capitalism's failures without addressing their root cause, and without enlisting the people whose decisions shape the system. The result was a century of conflict—an adversarial posture between government and industry, each believing the other to be fundamentally misguided.

This dynamic persists. Today's industrial leaders—especially in technology—often express a genuine desire to contribute to societal well-being. Yet they remain deeply skeptical of external actors who prescribe solutions without grasping the complexities of scaling global platforms, supply chains, scientific research, or frontier technologies.[125] They see the flaws of the system vividly, but they are trapped inside incentive structures that make reform risky, costly, or irrational.

The cumulative evidence of the Gilded Age and its reckoning makes one point difficult to contest: Industrial leaders acted largely in accordance with the incentives they were given, and it was those incentives—not personal virtue or vice—that shaped the era's defining outcomes.[126] Increasing oversight is not the remedy; what is needed is a framework that makes doing the right thing the winning strategy. And crucially, industrial leaders need to be treated not as adversaries or subjects of reform but as co-architects of a system designed for long-term societal well-being.

The historical record overwhelmingly supports this conclusion. When industrial leaders had the agency to experiment—Ford's wage reform, Sloan's organizational innovation, Bush's scientific mobilization—the results were transformative.[127] When solutions were imposed unilaterally from outside, the result was conflict, circumvention, and unintended consequences.

This is the basis for engaging the industrial leadership of today in the project of Inclusive Capitalism. Not through mandates. Not through moral pressure. But through system redesign that aligns self-interest with societal interest, restores agency to those who build and operate the economy, and eliminates the structural incentives that generate conflict and crisis.[128]

This insight—that many leaders genuinely want to do the right thing but lack a system in which doing so is rational—is the bridge between the failures of the Great Reckoning and the promise of the Inclusive Capitalism framework.

How Reform Affected the Lived Experience of the Population

For ordinary Americans, the lived reality of the early twentieth century was defined by conditions that were often brutal, precarious, and dangerous.[129] Despite a handful of forward-looking industrialists, daily life for the nation's workers—factory hands, miners, garment workers, agricultural laborers, and service employees—was harsh enough to spark outrage, activism, and ultimately the wave of reforms that characterized the Great Reckoning. The era opened with a workforce laboring ten to twelve hours a day, six days a week, for wages barely sufficient to keep a family out of poverty.[130] Industrial accidents were shockingly common: around 1913 it is estimated that 25,000 workers died on the job in a single year, and another 700,000 were injured seriously enough to miss weeks or months of work.[131] These conditions coexisted with the celebrated achievements of industrial titans, revealing how laissez-faire capitalism, as then instantiated, could simultaneously produce breathtaking innovation and appalling human hardship.

The cruelty of those conditions was not abstract. Upton Sinclair's *The Jungle* (1905) offered a vivid portrayal of Chicago's meat-packing plants, and contemporary investigative reporting across industries documented unpaid hours, arbitrary wage deductions, and dangerous shop-floor practices that stripped workers of autonomy and security.[132] The adoption of Frederick Taylor's scientific management in factories further intensified these pressures, turning workers into interchangeable components within tightly optimized production systems.[133] Tragedies such as the 1911 Triangle Shirtwaist fire—where 146 young immigrant women died because locked doors prevented escape—illustrated how profit-driven management practices, absent regulation, translated directly into preventable loss of life.

Conditions in heavy industry were often worse. Steel workers endured twelve-hour shifts, seven days a week, while coal miners labored in some of the deadliest workplaces in the nation, facing explosions, cave-ins, lethal dust, and pervasive corporate control over housing, stores, and wages.[134] Between 1880 and 1923, more than 70,000 miners are believed to have died from on-the-job accidents, with countless others suffering chronic disease.[135] Violent confrontations such as the 1914 Ludlow Massacre underscored how labor conflict, private policing, and state power often aligned against workers in the absence of institutional protections.[136]

It was precisely these conditions that progressive reforms sought to correct. Public outrage, investigative journalism, rising worker activism, and the visibility of industrial tragedy pushed state and federal governments to intervene through safety regulations, factory inspections, mine-safety laws, and early workers' compensation systems. The Great Depression then transformed reform from a moral crusade into a national emergency. With unemployment reaching 25 percent and mass displacement spreading across the country, the New Deal introduced a federal safety net—Social Security, unemployment insurance, public works, wage and hour standards, and restrictions on child labor—and empowered collective bargaining through the Wagner Act.[137] For the first time in American history, the federal government accepted responsibility for basic economic security.

And these reforms worked—materially. Workplace fatalities fell sharply, the standard workweek shortened, child labor largely disappeared from industrial settings, and union contracts raised wages while stabilizing employment. The pace of improvement varied, but by mid-century the country had moved decisively away from the most extreme abuses of early twentieth-century industrial capitalism.

Yet, for all the genuine progress, core structural flaws persisted. Reform constrained behavior without transforming the underlying incentive structure, allowing inequality, uneven labor standards, and periodic crises to re-emerge over time.[138] The lived experience of ordinary people thus shows both the necessity and the limits of the Great Reckoning's reforms. They alleviated suffering and corrected the most visible failures, but they did not resolve the deeper design problem that allowed radically different worker realities to coexist within the same economy. This unresolved tension is precisely where Inclusive Capitalism begins.[139]

Summary of What Worked and What Did Not During the Great Reckoning

The Great Reckoning succeeded on one critical front: It stopped a system that was visibly in jeopardy from coming apart. It addressed the most egregious wounds created by laissez-faire capitalism's first century—dangerous workplaces, unchecked monopolies, financial panics, and a widespread collapse in public trust. But while the reforms of the era saved the system from self-destruction, they did not re-architect it. They treated acute symptoms without altering the underlying incentive structures that produced those symptoms in the first place. As a result, much of what the era accomplished was both necessary and yet insufficient—enough to avert catastrophe but not enough to prevent the cycles that would repeat and dominate the next hundred years.

The Great Reckoning stopped the bleeding. Reforms dramatically mitigated the worst abuses of the industrial age. Workplace safety standards, child-labor laws, shorter hours, minimum wages, and union rights reduced the brutalities workers had long endured.[140] The reforms did not eliminate hardship—but compared to the early 1900s, the improvement was unmistakable.

A basic social floor was constructed in the United States. The creation of Social Security, unemployment insurance, and public assistance programs stabilized millions of families and reduced the desperation that had fueled unrest.[141] For the first time, the United States established a baseline of economic security—modest by modern standards but transformative for the era.

Keynesian macro-tools smoothed crises. Countercyclical fiscal spending, an expanded monetary toolkit, and new institutions (FDIC, SEC, FHA, Bretton Woods, the IMF/World Bank) provided mechanisms to prevent the self-reinforcing spirals of collapse that had characterized the 1873, 1893, and 1929 depressions.[142] These tools never eliminated recessions—but they dramatically reduced their depth and duration. They also worked again in 2008 and 2020, confirming that stabilization policy can dampen panic even when it cannot prevent the conditions that create panic.[143]

Industrial capacity and innovation accelerated. Ironically, even as capitalism was being reined in, its innovative engine intensified. Automobiles, aviation, electrification, mass communications, chemicals, plastics, and wartime technologies reshaped society. Productivity surged. Living standards rose. The U.S. emerged from World War II as the world's industrial and technological epicenter.[144] These achievements demonstrate that capitalism's innovative core remained powerful even under growing regulation.

The middle class expanded. Unionization, wage floors, and the wartime/postwar boom elevated millions into stable, asset-building livelihoods. For roughly three decades after World War II, the United States experienced rising median incomes, broad homeownership, and unusually equal distribution of gains compared to the Gilded Age before it or the neoliberal period after it.[145] It was a unique period, one that has not been repeated since.

Taken together, these accomplishments gave the impression that the system had been "fixed." But the durability of that impression depended on an exceptional, non-repeatable post-war environment—global destruction elsewhere, U.S. industrial dominance, a unique demographic profile, and geopolitical conditions that likely will never occur again.

Despite the real gains, the Great Reckoning did not—and could not—solve the underlying design flaws of capitalism as then instantiated. The incentive structure never changed.

Industrial leaders gained new constraints but not new motivations. Regulation limited excesses, but it did not create positive incentives for inclusive behavior. The system still rewarded cost-cutting over long-term worker welfare, scale over competition, and short-term gains over societal resilience.[146] The result was a permanent, conflict-based environment: unions vs. management, regulators vs. industry, courts vs. corporations. The rules changed; the game did not.

The underlying causes of crises remained. Speculative excesses, credit bubbles, asset booms, and panics persisted. The Great Depression was not the last of its kind—only the largest. Subsequent crises (1973, 1980–82, 1987, 2000, 2008, 2020) reveal that macro-policy can mitigate damage but cannot prevent its recurrence.[147] Every generation solves the last crisis and inadvertently lays the groundwork for the next.

The administrative state grew without solving root problems. Regulations multiplied. Agencies expanded. Oversight ballooned. But these layers of supervision were compensatory—responses to failures—rather than well-architected solutions. As critics from Hayek to Friedman argued, once intervention begins, it rarely recedes; each distortion invites another correction.[148] The alternative—removing the guardrails—simply recreates the conditions that led to the Great Depression. Both paths miss the deeper issue: neither rewires incentives.

Social conflict was suppressed, not resolved. The class tensions of early capitalism did not disappear—they were merely contained. The postwar middle-class boom eased conflict temporarily, but inequality resurged when economic conditions changed.[149] By the 1970s, stagflation reignited debates about the limits of government intervention; by the 1980s, deregulation and neoliberal policy took center stage; by the 2000s, globalization and technology reintroduced extreme disparities. The system oscillated—Keynesian to laissez-faire and back again—without ever converging.

Reform created dependency on government backstopping. The shift to Keynesian management made the economy reliant on federal intervention to stabilize markets. But this reliance masked, rather than eliminated, the underlying forces that drive instability. The government became the insurer of last resort for industrial leaders and financial markets, reinforcing moral hazard and expectations of perpetual rescue.[150]

The Great Reckoning was a historic necessity. It prevented collapse, alleviated suffering, and modernized the social contract. It demonstrated that unregulated capitalism produces unacceptable social costs and that democratic societies will not tolerate those costs indefinitely.

But its solutions were compensatory rather than structural. They cured symptoms, not causes. By overlaying a regulatory and welfare apparatus onto the old incentive system without redesigning that system, the Great Reckoning created a century-long dynamic defined by recurring economic cycles, persistent inequality, regulatory–industrial conflict, political polarization, and a widening gap between technological possibility and social reality.[151]

In short: the Great Reckoning healed the wounds of the early twentieth century but left the disease untreated. It protected workers and stabilized markets, but it did not redesign capitalism so that inclusive, long-term, socially aligned behavior becomes the natural equilibrium rather than the exception. This unresolved tension is the central reason why the twenty-first century now confronts a renewed reckoning —and why a systems-level redesign, such as Inclusive Capitalism, is needed to break the century-long pattern rather than repeating it with sharper amplitudes and higher stakes.

The Transition to the Golden Age of Capitalism in the USA

The Great Reckoning did not end so much as lose its urgency when the world changed around it. The legal, economic, and cultural architecture built between 1900 and 1945 remained intact after the war, but its meaning shifted because the environment shifted.[152] The United States emerged uniquely advantaged after World War II: Its industrial base was untouched, its rivals were in ruins, global demand surged for American goods, and demographic forces produced an unprecedented expansion of the labor force and consumer base. Under these conditions—high global demand, constrained foreign competition, rapid capital deepening, rising productivity, and a cohesive social fabric—the regulatory and Keynesian frameworks designed during the crisis years suddenly looked visionary.[153] They appeared to produce prosperity, stability, and inclusion, even though their success now rested on circumstances no economic doctrine could reliably reproduce.

As long as those extraordinary conditions persisted, the postwar order seemed to validate the Great Reckoning's reforms. But when the external supports eroded—when Europe and Japan recovered, global competition intensified, demographics shifted, geopolitical costs mounted, and inflationary pressures returned—the limitations of the earlier framework became starkly visible. The same institutional architecture that once appeared stabilizing began to reveal tensions: rigidities in labor markets, conflicts between regulation and innovation, and structural incentives that still pointed industrial leaders toward short-termism. In this sense, the Great Reckoning never truly concluded; its unfinished business simply went dormant during a rare historical window. When that window closed, the old contradictions resurfaced, setting in motion the oscillations and policy pendulum swings that defined the late twentieth century and set the stage for today's renewed search for fundamental redesign.[154]

Conclusions and Insights for Inclusive Capitalism

The Great Reckoning demonstrated that regulation can stop the bleeding, but it cannot heal the underlying wound. What the first half of the twentieth century revealed—again and again—is that industrial leaders were not, in the main, villains. Many wanted to do the right things for their firms, their employees, and society. Ford raised wages voluntarily. Sloan spoke of industrial statesmanship. Edison pushed for humane conditions and ethical finance. Bush built the foundations of modern scientific progress. Even Du Pont, though fiercely anti-New Deal, believed he was defending a system essential to prosperity. Their instinct was not to exploit but to retain agency: to solve problems internally, to innovate, and to lead without having solutions imposed on them by political actors who did not understand the operational realities of running complex enterprises. This is precisely why reform "worked" only partially—it constrained behavior but did not engage the productive institutions at the level of their incentives, decision rules, and chartering logic.

The Great Reckoning addressed symptoms with admirable determination, yet it never solved the root causes that produced those symptoms. Regulation stabilized markets but also created bureaucratic sprawl and distortions. Keynesian demand management softened recessions but did nothing to prevent the formation of the bubbles that caused them. And businesses, understandably, resisted rules imposed from afar rather than embracing a coherent framework that aligned their incentives with societal well-being.

Inclusive Capitalism begins from this historical lesson: the productive core of the economy—firms, supply chains, industrial laboratories, and the leaders who guide them—must not be treated as the objects of reform but as its authors. Industrial leaders generally want to build enduring enterprises, advance technology, expand markets, and maintain the legitimacy of the system that enables their work. They are natural partners in redesign; what they resist is being commanded by institutions that neither bear the operational consequences of their directives nor understand the dynamics of innovation, capital allocation, or risk. A rearchitected system must therefore embed the goals of the Great Reckoning—fairness, safety, stability, inclusion—into the core economic institutions themselves: into how large enterprises are chartered, how value is measured, how currencies function, and how incentives reward long-term societal contribution rather than short-term extraction.

This is why regulation alone cannot prevent the reemergence of Gilded Age conditions. The United States and other advanced economies already see many of the same warning lights flashing: rising wealth concentration, declining worker bargaining power, winner-take-most market structures, speculative bubbles, and public frustration with institutions and government agencies perceived as unresponsive or captured. History teaches that when these pressures build, a reckoning eventually follows—through crisis, backlash, or political reaction. The positive outcome is not guaranteed; it depends on whether the system is redesigned before the pressures become unmanageable. A century ago, reforms were reactive, uneven, and externally imposed. A sustainable path forward requires something different: industrial leadership and public institutions co-designing the rules of the game such that doing the right thing—for workers, for communities, for innovation, for stability—is also the rational, self-reinforcing choice for the firm.

That is the central insight of Inclusive Capitalism. The lessons of the Great Reckoning must be built into the architecture of the productive economy, not grafted onto it after the fact. Only by reengineering the incentive structures, aligning value with societal well-being, and updating the core design of capitalism to the realities of the twenty-first century can we avoid the recurring pendulum swings that have defined economic history—and instead build a system that is durable, inclusive, innovative, and stable by construction rather than by emergency intervention.

Notes

1 Karl Polanyi, *The Great Transformation: The Political and Economic Origins of Our Time* (Boston: Beacon Press, 1944), 3–29, 71–80, 130–163.

2 Eric Hobsbawm, *The Age of Extremes: The Short Twentieth Century, 1914–1991* (New York: Vintage Books, 1996).

3 Ibid.

4 Ibid.

5 Richard Hofstadter, *The Age of Reform: From Bryan to F.D.R.* (New York: Vintage Books, 1955).

6 Ibid.

7 Karl Polanyi, *The Great Transformation: The Political and Economic Origins of Our Time.*

8 Barry J. Eichengreen, *Golden Fetters: The Gold Standard and the Great Depression, 1919–1939* (New York: Oxford University Press, 1992), pp. 2–6, 122–125.

9 Eric Hobsbawm, *The Age of Extremes: The Short Twentieth Century, 1914–1991*, pp. 93–115.

10 John Maynard Keynes, "*Economic Possibilities for Our Grandchildren,*" in Essays in Persuasion (London: Macmillan, 1931), 358–373.

11 Barry J. Eichengreen, *Globalizing Capital: A History of the International Monetary System*, 2nd ed. (Princeton, NJ: Princeton University Press, 2008), pp. 3–14, 56–62.

12 John Gerard Ruggie, "International Regimes, Transactions, and Change: Embedded Liberalism in the Postwar Economic Order," International Organization 36, no. 2 (1982): 393–399.

13 Friedrich A. Hayek, *The Constitution of Liberty* (Chicago: University of Chicago Press, 1960), pp. 257–265, 285–291.

14 Alexander J. Field, *A Great Leap Forward: 1930s Depression and U.S. Economic Growth* (New Haven, CT: Yale University Press, 2011), pp. 1–9, 67–92.

15 David A. Hounshell, *From the American System to Mass Production, 1800–1932* (Baltimore: Johns Hopkins University Press, 1984), pp. 217–245.

16 Joel Mokyr, *The Lever of Riches: Technological Creativity and Economic Progress* (New York: Oxford University Press, 1990), pp. 199–214, 229–236.

17 Alexander J. Field, *A Great Leap Forward: 1930s Depression and U.S. Economic Growth*, pp. 1–12, 67–92, 201–205.

18 David A. Hounshell, *From the American System to Mass Production, 1800–1932*, pp. 355–382, 396–402.

19 Karl Polanyi, *The Great Transformation: The Political and Economic Origins of Our Time*, pp. 71–80, 136–140, 257–268.

20 John Gerard Ruggie, "International Regimes, Transactions, and Change: Embedded Liberalism in the Postwar Economic Order," *International Organization* 36, no. 2 (1982): 382–387, 393–399.

21 Robert H. Wiebe, *The Search for Order, 1877–1920* (New York: Hill and Wang, 1967), pp. 3–20, 164–189.

22 Ibid.

23 Friedrich A. Hayek, *The Constitution of Liberty*, pp. 112–123, 257–265.

24 Alfred D. Chandler Jr., *The Visible Hand: The Managerial Revolution in American Business* (Cambridge, MA: Harvard University Press, 1977), pp. 284–305, 336–352.

25 John Maynard Keynes, *The General Theory of Employment, Interest and Money* (London: Macmillan, 1936), pp. 3–12, 246–264, 378–384.

26 John Gerard Ruggie, "International Regimes, Transactions, and Change: Embedded Liberalism in the Postwar Economic Order," *International Organization* 36, no. 2 (1982): 382–387, 393–399.

27 Barry J. Eichengreen, *Globalizing Capital: A History of the International Monetary System*, 2nd ed., pp. 3–14, 56–62, 91–109.

28 *United Nations Monetary and Financial Conference (Bretton Woods), Final Act and Related Documents* (Washington, DC: U.S. Department of State, 1944), pp. 1–10, 47–63.
29 John Gerard Ruggie, "International Regimes, Transactions, and Change: Embedded Liberalism in the Postwar Economic Order," *International Organization* 36, no. 2 (1982): 382–387, 393–399.
30 Eric Hobsbawm, *The Age of Extremes: The Short Twentieth Century, 1914–1991* (London: Michael Joseph, 1994), 1–51, 87–141.
31 Thomas Piketty, *Capital in the Twenty-First Century* (Cambridge, MA: Harvard University Press, 2014), 257–335.
32 Robert H. Wiebe, *The Search for Order, 1877–1920*, 3–35, 165–196.
33 Peter Baldwin, *The Politics of Social Solidarity: Class Bases of the European Welfare State, 1875–1975* (Cambridge: Cambridge University Press, 1990), pp. 161–178, 231–252.
34 Karl Polanyi, *The Great Transformation: The Political and Economic Origins of Our Time*, 3–29, 71–80, 130–163.
35 Ibid.
36 Barry J. Eichengreen, *Globalizing Capital: A History of the International Monetary System*, 2nd ed., pp. 181–205, 215–227.
37 Karl Polanyi, *The Great Transformation: The Political and Economic Origins of Our Time*, 3–29, 71–80, 130–163.
38 Thomas Piketty, *Capital in the Twenty-First Century*, 257–335.
39 Barry Eichengreen, *Golden Fetters: The Gold Standard and the Great Depression, 1919–1939*, 3–44, 188–242.
40 Niall Ferguson, *The Ascent of Money: A Financial History of the World* (New York: Penguin Press, 2008), 160–206, 267–310.
41 David Montgomery, *The Fall of the House of Labor: The Workplace, the State, and American Labor Activism, 1865–1925* (Cambridge: Cambridge University Press, 1987), pp. 83–110, 130–146.
42 Milton Friedman and Anna J. Schwartz, *A Monetary History of the United States, 1867–1960* (Princeton, NJ: Princeton University Press, 1963), pp. 150–168, 172–176.
43 Milton Friedman and Anna J. Schwartz, *A Monetary History of the United States, 1867–1960*, pp. 299–305, 312–319.
44 Adam Tooze, *The Deluge: The Great War, America and the Remaking of the Global Order*, 1916–1931 (New York: Viking, 2014), 1–42, 370–415.
45 Thomas Piketty, *Capital in the Twenty-First Century*, 257–335.
46 David H. Autor, "Skills, Education, and the Rise of Earnings Inequality among the 'Other 99 Percent,'" *Science* 344, no. 6186 (2014): 843–851.
47 Barry J. Eichengreen, *Golden Fetters: The Gold Standard and the Great Depression, 1919–1939*, pp. 2–6, 56–62.
48 Richard Hofstadter, *The Age of Reform: From Bryan to F.D.R.*, pp. 32–56, 141–173.
49 Robert H. Wiebe, *The Search for Order, 1877–1920*, 3–35, 165–196.
50 John Maynard Keynes, *The General Theory of Employment, Interest and Money*, –26, 247–259.
51 Alan Greenspan and Adrian Wooldridge, *Capitalism in America: A History* (New York: Penguin Press, 2018), 159–294 (chs. 6–9).
52 Robert H. Wiebe, *The Search for Order, 1877–1920*, 3–35, 165–196.
53 Barry J. Eichengreen, *Globalizing Capital: A History of the International Monetary System*, 2nd ed., pp. 181–205, 215–227.
54 Richard Hofstadter, *The Age of Reform: From Bryan to F.D.R.*, pp. 172–195.
55 Robert H. Wiebe, *The Search for Order, 1877–1920*, 3–35, 165–196.
56 Herbert Hovenkamp, *Enterprise and American Law, 1836–1937* (Cambridge, MA: Harvard University Press, 1991), pp. 250–262.
57 U.S. Congress, *Federal Reserve Act*, 38 Stat. 251 (1913).

58 John Maynard Keynes, *The General Theory of Employment, Interest and Money*, 3–26, 247–259.
59 Richard Hofstadter, *The Age of Reform: From Bryan to F.D.R.*, pp. 231–258.
60 Alan Greenspan and Adrian Wooldridge, *Capitalism in America: A History* (New York: Penguin Press, 2018), 159–294 (chs. 6–9).
61 U.S. Congress, *Banking Act of 1933 (Glass-Steagall Act)*, 48 Stat. 162 (1933).
62 Louis D. Brandeis, *Other People's Money and How the Bankers Use It* (New York: Frederick A. Stokes, 1914), 1–41, 92–121.
63 Ibid.
64 Ibid.
65 Friedrich Hayek, *The Constitution of Liberty*, 220–245.
66 John Maynard Keynes, *The General Theory of Employment, Interest and Money*, 3–26, 247–259.
67 Paul A. Samuelson, *Foundations of Economic Analysis* (Cambridge, MA: Harvard University Press, 1947), 253–294.
68 John Maynard Keynes, *The General Theory of Employment, Interest and Money*, 3–26, 247–259.
69 Ibid.
70 John Hicks, "*Mr. Keynes and the 'Classics': A Suggested Interpretation,*" Econometrica 5, no. 2 (1937): 147–159.
71 Paul A. Samuelson, *Foundations of Economic Analysis*, 253–294.
72 Ibid.
73 John Hicks, "*Mr. Keynes and the 'Classics': A Suggested Interpretation,*" 147–159.
74 Richard Kahn, "*The Relation of Home Investment to Unemployment,*" Economic Journal 41, no. 162 (1931): 173–198.
75 Paul A. Samuelson, *Foundations of Economic Analysis*, 253–294.
76 Niall Ferguson, *The Ascent of Money: A Financial History of the World*, 160–206, 267–310.
77 Paul A. Samuelson, *Foundations of Economic Analysis*, 253–294.
78 John Maynard Keynes, *The General Theory of Employment, Interest and Money*, 3–26, 247–259.
79 Ibid.
80 Barry Eichengreen, *Golden Fetters: The Gold Standard and the Great Depression, 1919–1939*, 3–44, 188–242.
81 Alan Greenspan and Adrian Wooldridge, *Capitalism in America: A History* (New York: Penguin Press, 2018), 159–294 (chs. 6–9).
82 Adam Tooze, *The Deluge: The Great War, America and the Remaking of the Global Order*, 1916–1931 (New York: Viking, 2014), 1–42, 370–415.
83 Milton Friedman, *Capitalism and Freedom* (Chicago: University of Chicago Press, 1962), 7–21, 85–107.
84 Robert E. Lucas Jr., "Econometric Policy Evaluation: A Critique," *Carnegie-Rochester Conference Series on Public Policy* 1 (1976): 19–46.
85 Niall Ferguson, *The Ascent of Money: A Financial History of the World*, 160–206, 267–310.
86 Barry Eichengreen, *Golden Fetters: The Gold Standard and the Great Depression, 1919–1939*, 3–44, 188–242.
87 John Hicks, "*Mr. Keynes and the 'Classics': A Suggested Interpretation,*" 147–159.
88 Friedrich Hayek, *The Constitution of Liberty*, 220–245.
89 James M. Buchanan, *The Limits of Liberty* (Chicago: University of Chicago Press, 1975), 37–58.
90 Jon Gruber, *Public Finance and Public Policy*, 6th ed. (New York: Worth Publishers, 2019), 33–36.
91 Thomas Piketty, *Capital in the Twenty-First Century*, 257–335.
92 Robert H. Wiebe, *The Search for Order, 1877–1920*, 3–35, 165–196.
93 Hofstadter, Richard. *The Age of Reform: From Bryan to F.D.R.* New York: Vintage Books, 1955, 185–227.

94 *New York Factory Investigating Commission, Preliminary Report* (Albany: J. B. Lyon Company, 1912), 9–34.
95 Karl Polanyi, "*Our Obsolete Market Mentality*," Commentary 3, no. 2 (1947): 109–117.
96 Chandler, Alfred D. *The Visible Hand: The Managerial Revolution in American Business*. Cambridge, MA: Harvard University Press, 1977, 285–336.
97 Nevins, Allan, and Frank Ernest Hill. *Ford: The Times, the Man, the Company*. New York: Charles Scribner's Sons, 1954, vol. 2, 343–390.
98 Ford, Henry, and Samuel Crowther. *My Life and Work*. Garden City, NY: Doubleday, Page & Company, 1922, 116–124, 181–192.
99 Ford, Henry, and Samuel Crowther. *My Life and Work*. Garden City, NY: Doubleday, Page & Company, 1922, 202–203.
100 Ford, Henry. *Today and Tomorrow*. Garden City, NY: Doubleday, Doran & Company, 1926, 57–61.
101 Fligstein, Neil. *The Transformation of Corporate Control*. Cambridge, MA: Harvard University Press, 1990, 1–33, 145–176.
102 Ford, Henry, and Samuel Crowther. *My Life and Work*. Garden City, NY: Doubleday, Page & Company, 1922, 116–124, 181–205.
103 Kaplan, Robert S., and David P. Norton. *The Balanced Scorecard: Translating Strategy into Action*. Boston: Harvard Business School Press, 1996, 1–23, 149–176; Porter, Michael E., and Mark R. Kramer. "Creating Shared Value." *Harvard Business Review* 89, no. 1–2 (2011): 62–77.
104 Chandler, Alfred D. *Strategy and Structure: Chapters in the History of the Industrial Enterprise*. Cambridge, MA: MIT Press, 1962, 17–49; Sloan, Alfred P., Jr. *My Years with General Motors*. New York: Doubleday, 1963, 63–112.
105 Sloan, Alfred P., Jr. *My Years with General Motors*. New York: Doubleday, 1963, 410–412.
106 Sloan, Alfred P., Jr. *My Years with General Motors*. New York: Doubleday, 1963, 415–420.
107 Montgomery, David. *The Fall of the House of Labor: The Workplace, the State, and American Labor Activism, 1865–1925*. Cambridge: Cambridge University Press, 1987, 219–267.
108 *Thomas A. Edison Papers*, Library of Congress, Series 3, Notebooks and Correspondence, 1910–1925.
109 Ibid.
110 Ibid.
111 Chandler, Alfred D. *The Visible Hand: The Managerial Revolution in American Business*. Cambridge, MA: Harvard University Press, 1977, 285–336.
112 Vannevar Bush, *Science—The Endless Frontier* (Washington, DC: U.S. Government Printing Office, 1945), 1–32.
113 Jon Gruber, *Public Finance and Public Policy, 6th ed.* (New York: Worth Publishers, 2019), 33–36.
114 Bush, Vannevar. *Science, the Endless Frontier*. Washington, DC: U.S. Government Printing Office, 1945.
115 North, Douglass C. *Institutions, Institutional Change and Economic Performance*. Cambridge: Cambridge University Press, 1990, 3–14.
116 Chandler, Alfred D., Jr., and Stephen Salsbury. *Pierre S. du Pont and the Making of the Modern Corporation*. New York: Harper & Row, 1971, 471–515.
117 Montgomery, David. *The Fall of the House of Labor: The Workplace, the State, and American Labor Activism, 1865–1925*. Cambridge: Cambridge University Press, 1987, 359–412.
118 Chandler, Alfred D., Jr., and Stephen Salsbury. *Pierre S. du Pont and the Making of the Modern Corporation*. New York: Harper & Row, 1971, 583–610.
119 Fligstein, Neil. *The Transformation of Corporate Control*. Cambridge, MA: Harvard University Press, 1990, 1–33, 145–176.
120 Chandler, Alfred D., Jr., and Stephen Salsbury. *Pierre S. du Pont and the Making of the Modern Corporation*. New York: Harper & Row, 1971, 408–435.

121 Chandler, Alfred D. *The Visible Hand: The Managerial Revolution in American Business*. Cambridge, MA: Harvard University Press, 1977, 287–336.
122 Polanyi, Karl. *The Great Transformation: The Political and Economic Origins of Our Time*. Boston: Beacon Press, 1944, 136–170.
123 Hayek, Friedrich A. "The Use of Knowledge in Society." American Economic Review 35, no. 4 (1945): 519–530.
124 Alfred P. Sloan Jr., *My Years with General Motors* (New York: Doubleday, 1963), 3–38, 423–456.
125 Chandler, Alfred D. *The Visible Hand: The Managerial Revolution in American Business*. Cambridge, MA: Harvard University Press, 1977, 287–336.
126 Karl Polanyi, "*Our Obsolete Market Mentality*," Commentary 3, no. 2 (1947): 109–117.
127 Ford, Henry, and Samuel Crowther. My Life and Work. Garden City, NY: Doubleday, Page & Company, 1922, 116–124; Sloan, Alfred P., Jr. My Years with General Motors. New York: Doubleday, 1963, 63–112; Bush, Vannevar. Science, the Endless Frontier. Washington, DC: U.S. Government Printing Office, 1945.
128 North, Douglass C. *Institutions, Institutional Change and Economic Performance*. Cambridge: Cambridge University Press, 1990, 3–14.
129 Riis, Jacob A. *How the Other Half Lives: Studies among the Tenements of New York*. New York: Charles Scribner's Sons, 1890.
130 Montgomery, David. *The Fall of the House of Labor: The Workplace, the State, and American Labor Activism, 1865–1925*. Cambridge: Cambridge University Press, 1987, 219–267.
131 U.S. Bureau of Labor Statistics. *Historical Statistics of the United States, Colonial Times to 1970*. Washington, DC: U.S. Government Printing Office, Series D 740–755.
132 Sinclair, Upton. *The Jungle*. New York: Doubleday, Page & Company, 1906.
133 Taylor, Frederick Winslow. *The Principles of Scientific Management*. New York: Harper & Brothers, 1911, 36–52, 85–110.
134 Brody, David. *Steelworkers in America: The Nonunion Era*. Cambridge, MA: Harvard University Press, 1960, 3–38.
135 U.S. Bureau of Mines. *Historical Statistics on Fatalities in the Mining Industry, 1870–1970*. Washington, DC: U.S. Government Printing Office, 1975.
136 Andrews, Thomas G. Killing for Coal: America's Deadliest Labor War. Cambridge, MA: Harvard University Press, 2008, 237–285.
137 Kennedy, David M. *Freedom from Fear: The American People in Depression and War, 1929–1945*. New York: Oxford University Press.
138 Karl Polanyi, *The Great Transformation: The Political and Economic Origins of Our Time*, 3–29, 71–80, 130–163.
139 Acemoglu, Daron, and James A. Robinson. *Why Nations Fail: The Origins of Power, Prosperity, and Poverty*. New York: Crown Business, 2012, 74–91.
140 Eric Hobsbawm, *The Age of Extremes: The Short Twentieth Century, 1914–1991*, 1–51, 87–141.
141 Kennedy, David M. *Freedom from Fear: The American People in Depression and War, 1929–1945*.
142 John Maynard Keynes, *The General Theory of Employment, Interest and Money*, 3–26, 247–259.
143 Blinder, Alan S., and Mark Zandi. *The Financial Crisis: Lessons for the Next One*. New York: Century Foundation Press, 2015, 1–34, 99–138.
144 Milward, Alan S. *War, Economy and Society, 1939–1945*. Berkeley: University of California Press, 1977, 63–95.
145 Goldin, Claudia, and Lawrence F. Katz. The Race between Education and Technology. Cambridge, MA: Harvard University Press, 2008, 153–192.
146 Lazonick, William. *Sustainable Prosperity in the New Economy? Business Organization and High-Tech Employment in the United States*. Kalamazoo, MI: W.E. Upjohn Institute for Employment Research, 2009, 33–72.

147 Niall Ferguson, *The Ascent of Money: A Financial History of the World*, 160–206, 267–310.
148 Friedrich Hayek, *The Constitution of Liberty*, 220–245.
149 Hobsbawm, Eric. The Age of Extremes: The Short Twentieth Century, 1914–1991. New York: Vintage Books, 1994, 257–286.
150 Robert E. Lucas Jr., *"Econometric Policy Evaluation: A Critique,"* Carnegie-Rochester Conference Series on Public Policy 1 (1976): 19–46.
151 Karl Polanyi, *"Our Obsolete Market Mentality,"* Commentary 3, no. 2 (1947): 109–117.
152 Hobsbawm, Eric. The Age of Extremes: The Short Twentieth Century, 1914–1991. New York: Vintage Books, 1994, 257–286.
153 Ibid.
154 Harvey, David. *A Brief History of Neoliberalism*. New York: Oxford University Press, 2005, 1–38, 152–182.

6 The Golden Age of American Capitalism

The post-war decades are often described as the golden age of American capitalism not because the underlying economic architecture was flawless but because the United States entered a historically rare alignment of structural advantages that positively, but temporarily, magnified the performance of the system.[1] Between 1945 and the early 1970s, the nation enjoyed a confluence of factors that are unlikely to recur for generations, if ever: unmatched industrial capacity after the devastation of Europe and Asia, a young and rapidly expanding workforce, abundant natural resources, cheap land, high social cohesion, and an international monetary and trade order constructed to American specifications.[2] In Ray Dalio's framing, this was a moment deep in the "rising power" phase of the long-term cycle, when institutional strength, demographic momentum, technological leadership, and geopolitical dominance reinforce each other.[3] Thomas Sowell's work on the interplay between demographics and cultural norms also helps explain the era's exceptional productivity and stability: A workforce with relatively homogeneous expectations about work, family, and education, combined with high levels of civic participation and future-oriented saving behavior, created behavioral conditions that magnified economic outcomes.[4]

In such an environment it was difficult to get things wrong. Even policies or institutional designs that would ordinarily have slowed investment or constrained business decisions appeared tolerable because the underlying economic advantages were so overwhelming. Public investment, military spending, and industrial policy all produced high returns because the United States sat at the center of global demand, capital accumulation, and technological diffusion.[5] Industrial leaders continued to expand, hire, and innovate because the opportunity frontier was vast and global competitors were incapacitated. The system performed well despite these policies, not because of them.

Society-wide well-being rose in ways that seemed to validate the Keynesian-operational model of the mixed economy. Rising median wages, high labor-force participation, broad homeownership, expanding education access, low inequality relative to the Gilded Age, and sustained productivity growth created the impression that a stable formula had been found.[6] But this prosperity insulated many citizens from recognizing that the engine's performance depended heavily on temporal conditions that included rebuilding demand abroad, demographic expansion at home, a world trading system anchored in American hegemony, and a geopolitical order that funneled capital and talent toward the United States.[7] These temporal conditions would eventually dissipate by the mid-1970s.

These structural conditions also created expectations—implicit entitlements—about what American capitalism should deliver. A generation came to assume rising real wages, abundant middle-class jobs, stable energy and commodity prices, and predictable economic cycles. Yet none of these expectations were inherent properties of

 | https://doi.org/10.1515/9783112235485-007

the economic system itself. They were artifacts of a particular historical window. As the underlying conditions changed, the apparent stability and self-correcting nature of the era vanished. Productivity slowed, global competition intensified, the youth-weighted demographic pyramid inverted as the population aged, and U.S. geopolitical dominance narrowed.[8] The resulting stagflationary crisis of the 1970s reflected the exhaustion of the post-war equilibrium, not the failure of any single economic doctrine.[9] It marked the return of structural scarcity, exposed the limits of Keynesian demand management, and reopened the debate between state-led and market-led frameworks.

An additional insight is that industrial leadership itself evolved materially during this period. Compared with the harsh excesses of the Gilded Age, the behavior of large-scale industrial leaders in the first half of the twentieth century reflects a meaningful—though incomplete—shift. Beginning with the Great Reckoning, executives increasingly experimented with more balanced approaches to labor, compensation, and workplace organization. Henry Ford's wage reforms are the most visible example, but they were part of a broader pattern.[10] Violent labor confrontations became less common, the most brutal working conditions gradually receded, and even leaders hostile to regulation began to treat workers as long-term assets rather than disposable inputs. This change did not arise from moral conversion alone. It emerged from a confluence of forces—new legal constraints, national mobilization imperatives, tighter labor markets, advances in management science, organizational learning at scale, and shifting cultural norms amplified by mass media that made public reputation, consumer sentiment, and legitimacy economically salient.[11] The result was clear improvement in leadership practice, demonstrating that industrial leaders are not immutable or inherently ruthless, but responsive to context. Yet this responsiveness also underscores the deeper problem: while norms and institutions improved behavior at the margin, the underlying incentive structure remained misaligned with societal well-being. As a result, progress coexisted with persistent volatility, inequality, and systemic risk—a pattern that continues today in the form of affordability crises, social polarization, and concentrated power.[12] The lesson for Inclusive Capitalism is therefore not that leadership must be restrained but that incentives must be redesigned so that the improved stewardship already demonstrated becomes the dominant, self-reinforcing equilibrium rather than a conditional or fragile outcome.[13]

The central insight for Inclusive Capitalism is that system performance cannot be evaluated in isolation from its temporal environment. Economic doctrines can appear successful when they operate in the slipstream of favorable conditions, and ineffective when those conditions deteriorate. The task is not to replicate the policies of the Golden Age, which were themselves contingent, but to understand the structural conditions that enabled such broad-based gains—and then design a modern architecture that can deliver similar outcomes without relying on historical accidents or once-in-a-century advantages.

Definition of the Golden Age of American Capitalism

The Golden Age of American capitalism refers to the roughly three decades following World War II, when the United States experienced patterns of economic performance and social mobility unmatched before or since. Between 1945 and the mid-1970s, the economy expanded at unprecedented rates: GDP rose from approximately $228 billion to nearly $1.7 trillion, unemployment remained low, real wages rose consistently across the income distribution, and the median American family experienced a steady, tangible improvement in living standards.[14] Homeownership surged, educational attainment expanded, life expectancy rose, and of considerable importance, a broad middle class took shape. It was the only period in American history when virtually every social class saw material gains at the same time and in roughly the same proportion. Unlike the Gilded Age, this era delivered high growth with far fewer social costs, fewer labor abuses, and much greater economic stability. It was a system that still bore the institutional imprint of the Great Reckoning policies—strong labor protections, financial regulation, antitrust oversight, and Keynesian macro management—but operated inside a uniquely favorable environment that magnified the benefits while it muted the drawbacks of those policies.

This era was characterized by several reinforcing features. The United States enjoyed a large, growing, and industrious workforce supported by both high birthrates and sustained immigration; a considerably large and rapidly expanding domestic market that enabled economies of scale; abundant natural resources that were still in the process of early-stage exploitation; and an entrepreneurial culture willing to take risks, move across the country in search of opportunities, and start new ventures when employment options were limited or unsatisfactory. The political and institutional environment was unusually stable. The rule of law, property rights, and competition norms prevailed and appeared secure. The country was united around a shared national purpose forged through the war effort and sustained by a broad belief in upward mobility.[15]

These conditions translated directly into exceptional productivity growth. Data from the U.S. Bureau of Labor Statistics shows that labor productivity in the nonfarm business sector rose sharply throughout the mid-twentieth century, with especially strong gains from the late 1940s through the early 1970s.[16] Indexed to 100 in 1900, U.S. productivity rose gradually in the early decades of industrialization, accelerated during wartime mobilization, and then entered a sustained postwar three-decade-long climb that far outpaced later periods.[17] This was not a brief spike but a pronounced multi-decade trend: Productivity growth averaged 2.8 percent or more annually between 1947 and 1973, a rate that has not been matched since.[18] Crucially, these gains were broadly shared. Unlike later productivity surges, wages generally tracked output, reinforcing the perception that the system was fair, durable, and self-correcting. For a generation of Americans, rising productivity meant rising incomes, shorter workweeks, and expanding opportunity rather than displacement or insecurity.

As a result, the system appeared not only stable but virtuous. Growth generated opportunity; opportunity reinforced confidence; confidence encouraged investment, mobility, and risk-taking. Capital, labor, and institutions were aligned in a way that allowed the economy to compound advantages rather than amplify conflicts. That apparent harmony—high productivity, shared gains, social mobility, and macro stability—is the essence of what later generations labeled the Golden Age.

What is often missed in retrospective praise, however, is how contingent this performance was on conditions that no longer exist. The open land that once absorbed population growth and enabled affordable housing has given way to chronic housing shortages in major metropolitan areas.[19] The industrial leadership that once dominated global manufacturing—steel, automobiles, heavy equipment—has eroded to the point where icons such as U.S. Steel became acquisition targets rather than global leaders.[20] The resource abundance that once lowered input costs and supported industrial expansion has been replaced by geopolitical supply-chain risk and environmental constraint. The workforce that once combined pride and upward aspiration has aged, slowed in growth, and, in many cases, shifted toward expectations of entitlement rather than opportunity-driven sacrifice.[21] Immigration has become more constrained, labor mobility is lower, and demographic tailwinds have become headwinds.

Most importantly, the global environment has normalized. Europe and Japan rebuilt. Emerging economics industrialized. Competitive advantage diffused. The United States no longer sat alone at the center of global production, capital formation, and demand.[22] The Golden Age conditions that made it difficult to get economic policy wrong—abundant land, cheap energy, favorable demographics, uncontested global industrial leadership, and postwar dominance—have largely evaporated. What remains is the institutional architecture of that era, operating in a fundamentally different world. Inclusive Capitalism begins from this recognition: The performance of an economic system cannot be evaluated apart from the conditions in which it operates, and systems designed for one historical era cannot be assumed to function indefinitely when those conditions change.

How the Golden Age Emerged

The Golden Age did not emerge simply because Keynesian economics was in fashion or because policymakers designed particularly effective institutions. As we have presented, it emerged from the convergence of an extraordinary set of non-repeatable conditions that placed the United States in a position of unparalleled global advantage. Many of these conditions were exogenous to economic doctrine—demographic, geopolitical, cultural, and resource-based drivers that existed at a precise period in history and then gradually dissipated.[23] Isolating these factors is essential for understanding why post-war prosperity was so dramatic, why Keynesian policies appeared so effective, and why the same policies produced very different outcomes once the underlying conditions changed.

The demographic foundation was unusually strong. High birthrates during the first half of the century and sustained immigration produced a large, youthful labor force. Between 1850 and 1950, the U.S. population expanded from 23 million to 151 million, and then to 203 million by 1970.[24] This created a vast pool of low-cost labor while also expanding the domestic consumer base—an unusually powerful dual engine for industrial expansion. The American ethos of hard work, sacrifice, and upward mobility intensified this dynamic, reflecting what Thomas Sowell describes as the cultural capital of immigrant groups and the self-reliant traditions of frontier society.[25] A population willing to work long hours, relocate frequently, and pursue entrepreneurial opportunity amplified the productivity gains of industrialization.

Natural resources also magnified this demographic advantage. The United States possessed abundant reserves of coal, iron, and timber; fertile plains conducive to mechanized agriculture; and enormous oil discoveries in Pennsylvania, Texas, and California.[26] Accessible land and the Homestead Act opened pathways to economic mobility unavailable in most of Europe.[27] Resource wealth enabled the construction of physical infrastructure on a scale no other nation matched during this period. While many of these resource-driven advantages faded by the late twentieth century, in the Golden Age they were still producing substantial growth dividends.

Geopolitics delivered another decisive boost. The United States emerged from both world wars physically intact, with its industrial base strengthened rather than destroyed.[28] Europe and Japan lay in ruin, ensuring that American manufacturers faced little global competition while simultaneously benefiting from extraordinary export demand. The Bretton Woods system established the dollar as the world's reserve currency, and the U.S. became both the world's central banker and its primary industrial supplier. As Ray Dalio emphasizes, this placed the United States at the high point of a long-term power cycle: creditor nation, reserve-currency issuer, technological leader, and geopolitical hegemon.[29] In such a position, even imperfect policy structures could produce strong results.

Institutional design amplified these advantages. As Daron Acemoglu notes, inclusive institutions—secure property rights, rule of law, democratic accountability—encouraged investment and innovation.[30] The United States possessed these institutional features at precisely the time they were needed and during a period when the nation's resource base, demographics, and geopolitical standing were strongest. The result was a virtuous cycle in which economic policy appeared unusually potent, even though much of the performance was driven by conditions external to policy itself. The fact that the country thrived despite extremely high statutory tax rates illustrates the scale of the underlying advantages.[31] Industrial leaders simply adapted around the policy constraints—finding reinvestment channels, deferrals, and other ways to reduce effective tax burdens—because the opportunity frontier was unquestionably vast and profitable.

By the late 1960s and early 1970s, many of the non-economic drivers that had powered the postwar Golden Age were diminishing or reversing. Population growth slowed, immigration patterns shifted, natural resources matured or began to show signs of scarcity, Europe and Japan completed their reconstruction, and geopolitical competition intensified. At the same time, rising public debt, expanding regulatory layers, and global commodity shocks increasingly strained the Keynesian policy apparatus.[32] The Golden Age was a time-bounded phase within a longer economic cycle, not a permanent equilibrium. Once its enabling conditions faded, the same institutional and policy framework proved far less resilient.[33]

Keynesian tools and postwar regulatory frameworks functioned as operational overlays rather than as structural solutions. They smoothed volatility, reduced downside risk, and stabilized expectations, but they did not generate the underlying surplus that made broad-based prosperity possible. In effect, doctrine rode a powerful historical wave; it did not create it. When that wave receded, the apparent effectiveness of the doctrine receded with it—revealing that the core incentive architecture of capitalism remained largely unchanged. This distinction matters, because it explains why repeated efforts to replicate Golden Age policies in a fundamentally different economic environment have failed to reproduce Golden Age outcomes.

Economic Doctrines, Legal Framework, and Cultural Norms During the Golden Age

Having established the extraordinary non-economic conditions that defined the postwar American landscape, we turn now to the economic doctrines that governed the second half of the twentieth century, commonly described as the Keynesian Era. From the end of World War II through the early 1970s, American prosperity unfolded under what was widely regarded as a Keynesian Consensus—a belief that active fiscal and monetary policy could stabilize capitalism, smooth economic cycles, and sustain near-full employment. For a generation of policymakers, economists, and industrial leaders, Keynesianism did not merely appear useful; it appeared scientific, humane, and empirically validated.[34]

The appeal of Keynesian economics must be understood in its historical context. Classical laissez-faire capitalism had suffered a catastrophic loss of legitimacy during the Great Depression.[35] The prolonged collapse of output, employment, and confidence shattered the core Smithian assumption that markets reliably self-correct within a socially tolerable timeframe. In this environment, laissez-faire capitalism was no longer merely questioned; it was widely perceived as failing. Keynes therefore emerged not as a marginal critic of the system but as a theorist offering a way to preserve it. The General Theory provided an explanation for mass unemployment that did not rest on moral failure, worker indiscipline, or temporary shocks.[36] Instead, Keynes argued that capitalist economies could become trapped in persistent demand shortfalls—macroeconomic states characterized by idle resources and involuntary unemployment. The implication was decisive: Waiting for markets to self-heal was not only inefficient but socially and politically destabilizing, and therefore unacceptable.[37]

Keynesian economics gained further credibility because it appeared to work in practice. The New Deal's deficit-financed public works, employment programs, and social insurance mechanisms did not end the Great Depression outright, but they materially reduced suffering and helped restore confidence in economic governance. World War II then provided an unintended but decisive empirical validation. Massive deficit spending—on a scale previously unimaginable—mobilized idle labor and capital with extraordinary speed.[38] Industrial output surged, unemployment collapsed, and factory utilization reached levels unseen in the prewar economy. For many observers, the lesson appeared unmistakable: When private demand falters, government spending can activate production and employment where markets alone fail to do so.[39]

By the late 1940s and 1950s, Keynesianism had crystallized into what became known as the neoclassical synthesis. This framework blended Keynesian demand management with neoclassical microeconomics and was formalized, taught, and disseminated through Paul Samuelson's enormously influential 1948 textbook *Economics*.[40] Within universities, policy institutions, and central banks, Keynesianism became orthodoxy. Alternative schools—monetarism, Austrian economics, and early supply-side arguments—were not merely debated; they were sidelined.[41] To challenge Keynesian doctrine during this period was to challenge what appeared to be an absolute—a settled science of sorts.

The intellectual confidence of the Keynesian era was reinforced by its apparent operational clarity. Keynesian theory translated cleanly into policy tools: deficit spending during downturns, fiscal restraint during expansions, countercyclical taxation, and monetary accommodation to support employment. The Phillips Curve, interpreted at the time as a stable trade off between inflation and unemployment, further strengthened the belief that macroeconomic outcomes could be managed through expert calibration (Figure 6.1).[42]

As later noted by critics such as Thomas Sowell, policymakers were aware of inflationary risks but judged them manageable—especially when weighed against the trauma of Depression-level unemployment.[43]

At the same time, economics itself was undergoing a transformation. The discipline aspired to greater mathematical rigor, formal modeling, and predictive authority. Keynesianism aligned naturally with this ambition. Aggregate demand equations, multipliers, consumption functions, and investment schedules gave economists—and by extension policymakers—a sense that macroeconomic outcomes could be engineered. This intellectual shift elevated economists into positions of unprecedented influence. Councils of Economic Advisers, central banks, treasury departments, and international institutions increasingly relied on Keynesian frameworks to guide decision-making.[44] Economics, at least in appearance, had become sufficiently technical to govern capitalism itself.

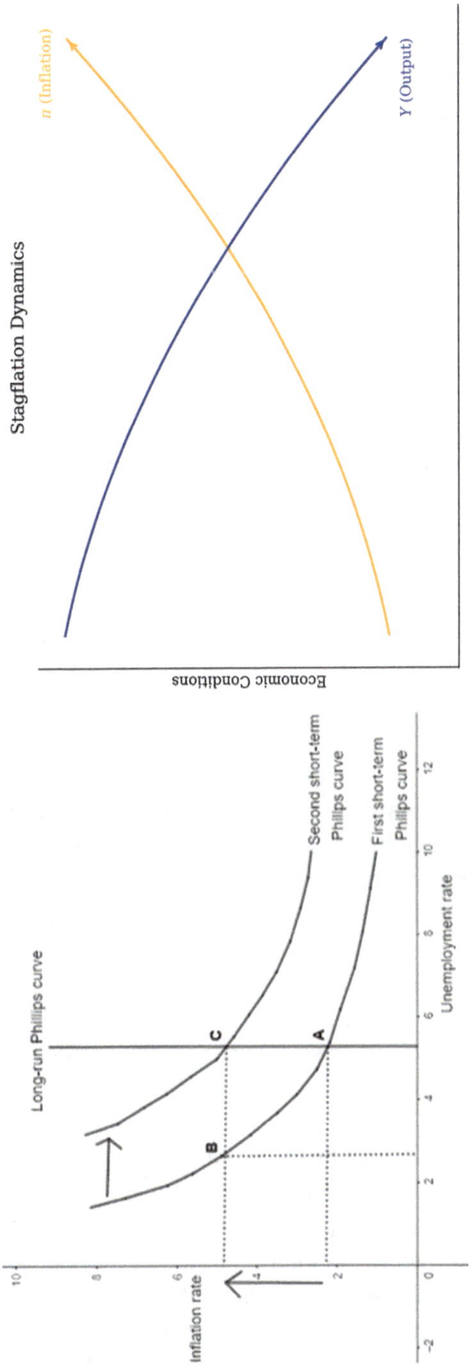

Figure 6.1: Effect of Stagflation on Philips Curve.

The early postwar policy record further entrenched this confidence. Fears of a return to Depression following demobilization proved unfounded. Pent-up consumer demand, accumulated wartime savings, and supportive fiscal policy fueled rapid expansion. One of the most consequential Keynesian-inspired interventions was the Servicemen's Readjustment Act of 1944—the GI Bill—which provided education benefits, unemployment compensation, and home-loan guarantees to returning veterans.[45] The program dramatically expanded college enrollment, accelerated homeownership, and helped create a skilled, consumption-oriented middle class. Its success, however, depended critically on the surrounding conditions: abundant land, low construction costs, favorable demographics, and enormous unmet demand for housing and education.

From the perspective of Inclusive Capitalism, the GI Bill illustrates a crucial point. By securing foundational needs—education, housing, and income continuity—the policy enabled individuals to invest in their own human capital.[46] Productivity gains followed not because incentives were coerced but because opportunity, effort, and ambition were allowed to reinforce one another. This dynamic is visible in Bureau of Labor Statistics data, which shows that U.S. labor productivity grew at historically high and sustained rates throughout the postwar decades, particularly from the late 1940s through the early 1970s. Output per hour rose steadily as industrial capacity, education, infrastructure, and technological diffusion combined to lift both wages and living standards in tandem.[47]

The Keynesian commitment to macroeconomic management was codified institutionally with the Employment Act of 1946, which declared it federal policy to promote maximum employment, production, and purchasing power.[48] The Act established the Council of Economic Advisers, embedding Keynesian reasoning directly into executive governance. This marked a dramatic and decisive departure from Smithian capitalism. Economic outcomes were no longer treated as emergent properties of decentralized exchange alone but as variables subject to active management by the state.

Keynesian influence also reshaped America's global posture. The Bretton Woods system institutionalized managed capitalism at an international scale that marked a decisive shift from America's earlier isolationism toward global economic leadership.[49] Fixed exchange rates, dollar-gold convertibility, and multilateral oversight through the IMF and World Bank created a stable financial environment that supported postwar trade and investment.[50] For nearly three decades, this system reinforced American industrial leadership and global stability. Yet it also carried latent fragilities. Persistent U.S. deficits, overseas military spending, and the growing international supply of dollars eventually strained the system beyond its capacity. The Nixon Shock of 1971—ending gold convertibility and severing the dollar's formal anchor—was not the result of a carefully designed institutional evolution but a forced inflection driven by mounting structural pressures: persistent balance-of-payments deficits, rising inflation, declining gold reserves, and the growing incompatibility between domestic policy objectives and the constraints of the Bretton Woods system.

Keynesianism also manifested in politically unexpected ways, producing policy outcomes that defied conventional partisan expectations and remained familiar to contemporary readers. Republican President Eisenhower preserved New Deal programs and launched the Interstate Highway System—one of the largest public works projects in history—and under marginal tax rates exceeding 90 percent. Democratic President Kennedy, by contrast, pursued a major tax cut to stimulate demand.[51] These were not ideological contradictions. They reflected the methodological neutrality of Keynesianism, which prioritized demand stabilization over ideological commitments. Since the framework specified the macroeconomic objective (sufficient demand) but remained largely agnostic about the institutional means, it could be invoked to justify expansive public spending, steep progressive taxation, or tax cuts alike—contributing to its unusually broad political appeal.

However, the persistence of extraordinarily high statutory tax rates during the Golden Age should not be misinterpreted as evidence that punitive taxation was benign. In practice, industrial leaders and high earners systematically adapted through depreciation allowances, reinvestment vehicles, deferred compensation, and legal shelters.[52] Moreover, effective tax rates were in practice far lower than headline figures suggested. This reinforces a core insight for Inclusive Capitalism: incentives matter, and when systems rely on constraint rather than alignment, sophisticated actors respond with avoidance, complexity, and rent-seeking rather than withdrawal.

A further, and increasingly consequential, shortcoming of Keynesian economics is that it is structurally grounded in a scarcity-based conception of value and production, and therefore fails to account for domains where marginal cost collapses toward zero.[53] Keynesian models presume that output, employment, and income are constrained by scarce capital, labor, and physical resources, and that failures in economic coordination then manifest primarily as insufficient aggregate demand. This framework becomes increasingly incomplete when viewed through the lens of our current economy where some of the most economically and socially valuable goods—open-source software, digital knowledge, data, media, algorithms, and increasingly AI-generated outputs—are non-rival, reproducible at near-zero cost, and expand through broad participation and contribution rather than bounded by narrow participation in transactional commercial exchanges. In such domains, demand stimulation does little to improve welfare, because scarcity is no longer the binding constraint. The problem is not underconsumption but mismeasurement, mis-incentivization, and institutional misalignment.[54]

Keynesianism, however, can mitigate the damage when a scarcity-based capitalist system breaks down—arguably making it the most effective economic Band-Aid ever devised—but it does not redesign the system to function coherently in an economy whose expanding productive base and emerging conditions of partial non-scarcity fundamentally alter how value is created and distributed.[55] As a result, it treats symptoms rather than causes, stabilizing an architecture that was never designed to optimize value creation, distribution, or incentives under contemporary technological conditions. In this sense, Keynesian economics solved a historic crisis of capitalism when it came off the rails, but it did not—and could not—offer a general solution for a post-industrial, digitally mediated economy where the nature of value itself has changed.

The neoclassical consensus that emerged from Keynesian economics—often framed as rules-based macroeconomic management combining discretionary fiscal policy, independent central banking, and inflation targeting—has delivered periods of stability, but it remains an inherently fragile equilibrium. It functions less as a durable system than as a carefully balanced teeter-totter, oscillating between stimulus and restraint, credibility and discretion, market discipline and state intervention. When conditions are benign, the balance holds; when shocks accumulate, as they often do, it can tip abruptly, as it did in 2008 and again in 2020.[56] The fact that the last systemic failure occurred less than two decades ago underscores that the problem has not been solved, merely deferred.

By the late 1960s, the Keynesian framework began to strain under conditions that no longer resembled those of the immediate postwar period. Great Society programs layered atop escalating Vietnam War expenditures pushed the economy toward overheating.[57] Inflation accelerated, deficits widened, and the assumption that policymakers could reliably fine-tune demand without destabilizing side effects proved overly optimistic. The stagflation of the 1970s would ultimately expose the limits of Keynesian management and reopen the door to Smithian ideas—setting the stage for the next chapter in capitalism's evolution.

Industrial Leadership Incentives and Behaviors

Having established the defining Keynesian economic and legal frameworks of the Golden Age of Capitalism, we turn our lens toward the industrial leaders who operated within that environment and examine how their behavior differed from that of their Gilded Age predecessors. While power and scale remained concentrated, the norms of leadership shifted meaningfully. Overt violence toward labor largely disappeared, professional management replaced founder dominance, and long-term corporate viability became an explicit concern alongside profitability.[58] These changes reflected not a moral awakening but altered incentives created by scale, regulation, organized labor, and global competition. Henry Ford II provides a useful case study at this transition point.

Henry Ford II (1917–1987) assumed control of Ford Motor Company in 1945, inheriting a firm weakened by mismanagement, both under his father Edsel Ford and under the return of his grandfather Henry Ford who assumed control after the death of Edsel.[59] His primary motivation was not ideological but existential: Ford had to modernize or risk decline in a maturing, increasingly competitive industry. Unlike his grandfather, whose success rested on technological disruption and personal authority,

Henry Ford II operated in a system where survival depended on managerial discipline, financial control, and coordination at scale. He responded by professionalizing the company, recruiting experienced executives, and assembling the "Whiz Kids," a group of analytically trained managers who introduced modern budgeting, planning, and performance controls.[60] These changes allowed Ford to compete more effectively with General Motors and signaled a broader shift from founder-led enterprise to institution-led capitalism.

Ford II worked long hours at headquarters in Dearborn but delegated authority far more than his grandfather, reflecting the realities of scale. He cultivated relationships with politicians, regulators, and foreign leaders, recognizing that global expansion required alignment with state power.[61] Under his leadership, Ford expanded aggressively into Europe and South America, embedding the company within the postwar global economy.[62] At the same time, his personal life—marked by conspicuous wealth, elite social circles, and turbulent relationships—illustrated a growing distance between industrial leadership and the workforce, even as wages and conditions improved relative to earlier eras.

Politically, Ford II was a moderate Republican rather than an ideologue. He opposed excessive regulation and was deeply skeptical of unions, particularly the United Auto Workers.[63] While the violent labor conflicts of earlier capitalism had largely disappeared, Ford II argued that union wage demands and benefit structures rendered American automobiles structurally uncompetitive. His position reflected a genuine concern about costs but also a persistent incentive bias: Labor was treated as a variable to be constrained, while long-term innovation investment remained secondary to protecting margins and market share.

Ford II's economic nationalism became more pronounced as Japanese automakers entered the U.S. market in force during the 1960s and 1970s. Toyota, Honda, and Nissan produced smaller, cheaper, more fuel-efficient, and increasingly more reliable vehicles—an advantage magnified by the oil shocks of the 1970s.[64] Detroit's business model, optimized for large vehicles and stable domestic demand, proved brittle under these conditions. Ford II became a vocal critic of Japan's government-industry coordination, which included subsidies, protectionist policies, and long-term investment strategies.

Although philosophically opposed to government intervention, Ford II lobbied aggressively for it when competitive pressure mounted. He supported import quotas on Japanese automobiles, contributing to the voluntary export restraints that limited Japanese car shipments to the United States. He argued for government investment in automotive research and development and criticized U.S. safety and environmental regulations, claiming they imposed disproportionate costs on American manufacturers.[65] This apparent contradiction is best understood through incentives rather than ideology: Ford defended laissez-faire principles when they favored his firm and sought protection when they did not. This pattern is consistent across industrial history and central to the case for Inclusive Capitalism.[66]

David Packard (1912–1996) and William Hewlett (1913–2001) represent a distinct break from both Gilded Age industrialists and the managerial titans of heavy manufacturing. They were early founders of what became the American technology industry, but more importantly, they embodied a new leadership archetype shaped by knowledge work, engineering complexity, and rapid innovation cycles. Their success was not built on scale economies in labor or raw materials but on human capital, experimentation, and continuous learning.[67] This difference in production function fundamentally altered incentives—and, in turn, leadership behavior.

Hewlett and Packard founded Hewlett-Packard in 1939 in a Palo Alto garage, famously seeding what would become Silicon Valley.[68] William Hewlett was the technical visionary, deeply immersed in engineering and product design, while David Packard focused on business strategy, organizational design, and long-term institutional health. Together they developed what became known as the "HP Way," a management philosophy that emphasized trust in employees, decentralization of decision-making, open communication, and respect for individual dignity.[69] Unlike the hierarchical, command-and-control structures common in mid-century American industry, HP operated on the premise that innovation emerged from empowered engineers rather than imposed directives.

Both founders were notably accessible. They spent time in laboratories, spoke directly with engineers and technicians, and cultivated a culture in which ideas could flow upward rather than being filtered through layers of management. Work-life balance, flexible schedules, and respect for personal autonomy were not peripheral benefits but core components of the company's operating model. This was not altruism; it was incentive-aligned design. HP's primary productive asset was cognitive labor. Retaining talent, sustaining curiosity, and avoiding burnout were essential to maintaining competitive advantage.[70] In contrast to industries reliant on repetitive manual labor, coercive discipline would have destroyed value rather than extracted it.

This highlights a central theme for Inclusive Capitalism: leadership behavior is heavily conditioned by the nature of the work and the incentive structure surrounding it. The same capitalist system that produced brutal conditions in slaughterhouses and mines also produced humane, collaborative cultures in research-driven enterprises. The difference was not morality; it was system design. Where productivity depends on creativity rather than compliance, inclusive leadership becomes economically rational.

Politically, Hewlett and Packard were firm believers in free enterprise but not in the manner of laissez-faire indifference. David Packard, a Republican, served as Deputy Secretary of Defense under President Nixon from 1969 to 1971, where he worked on procurement reform and efficiency within the Department of Defense.[71] Both founders strongly supported government investment in basic research, national defense technology, and STEM education.[72] They understood that innovation ecosystems—particularly in electronics and computing—depend on long-horizon public goods that markets alone underprovide. This placed them closer to Vannevar Bush than to Chicago-school purists:

skeptical of bureaucratic overreach, but supportive of targeted state involvement when incentives aligned with long-term innovation.

Hewlett and Packard thus resemble the most forward-thinking industrialists of early capitalism—more like James Hill—than the dominant industrial leaders of the mid-twentieth century. Yet even HP was not immune to the structural forces that eventually undermine innovative firms at scale.[73] As the company grew larger, more diversified, and more financially complex, the incentive structure shifted. Performance metrics increasingly emphasized quarterly earnings, cost control, and asset optimization rather than exploratory innovation. Over time, the very culture that made HP exceptional eroded—not because leadership forgot its values or altered their cultural core but because the institutional charter and measurement system no longer rewarded them.

The decline of Hewlett-Packard as an inspirational innovator mirrors the fate of other once-great technology firms such as Digital Equipment Corporation and, to a lesser extent, IBM.[74] In each case, the organization became better at exploiting past successes than at creating future ones. Scarcity re-entered the system—not scarcity of ideas but scarcity of incentive to pursue them. Capital was allocated defensively, talent became risk-averse, and innovation slowed.[75] Creative destruction from within eventually followed, benefiting competitors but imposing high social costs on employees, communities, and their long-term innovative and technological progress.

This outcome is often treated as inevitable, even desirable. Inclusive Capitalism rejects that assumption. The repeated failure of innovative firms to sustain leadership is not a law of nature; it is a design flaw. Charters and performance metrics at scale reward extraction rather than exploration, efficiency rather than adaptability, and short-term financial returns rather than long-term societal value creation. As a result, mature firms rationally shift from abundance-creating innovation to scarcity-preserving optimization.

Hewlett and Packard demonstrate what becomes possible when incentives favor creation rather than control. Their leadership style was not merely enlightened; it was economically coherent within the context of knowledge-based production. Inclusive Capitalism builds on this lesson. The solution is not nostalgia for the "HP Way," nor reliance on heroic founders, but institutional redesign—charters, metrics, and incentives that systematically reward ongoing innovation, human capital development, and non-scarcity outcomes. When those incentives are embedded, leadership behavior follows naturally. When they are not, even the best cultures tend towards decay.

Juan Trippe (1899–1981) was among the most consequential industrialists of the mid-twentieth century, not because he refined an existing industry but because he effectively created a new one at global scale.[76] As the founder and long-time leader of Pan American World Airways, Trippe transformed aviation from an elite novelty into a central infrastructure of modern capitalism. Where railroads had once unified continents, Trippe envisioned airlines unifying the world.

Trippe's ambition was expansive and explicit. He believed that air travel should be accessible, reliable, and global, not confined to wealthy travelers or short domestic routes. From the beginning, Pan Am was conceived not as a regional carrier but as an international system.[77] Trippe pursued routes across Latin America, the Atlantic, and the Pacific long before competitors recognized their strategic or commercial value. His daily life reflected this global orientation: constant travel, negotiations with foreign governments, meetings with heads of state, and relentless lobbying for landing rights and international aviation agreements. Pan Am's success depended as much on diplomacy as on engineering.[78]

Trippe's leadership style was demanding and authoritarian. He ran Pan Am with iron discipline, pushing pilots, engineers, and executives to meet exacting standards.[79] Unlike Hewlett and Packard's collaborative culture, Pan Am under Trippe was hierarchical and centralized. Safety, precision, and brand prestige were paramount, and Trippe tolerated little dissent. Yet this style was not gratuitous. Commercial aviation in its early decades was unforgiving; failure could be fatal and reputational damage irreversible. In this environment, Trippe believed that centralized control and relentless pursuit of compliance with standards were necessary to build public trust in flying itself.

Innovation was Trippe's defining obsession. He worked closely with aircraft manufacturers, most notably Boeing, to push technological boundaries that airlines typically accepted as fixed. Trippe was instrumental in the development and commercial adoption of the Boeing 707, ushering in the Jet Age and collapsing travel times across oceans. This decision was bold and risky. Jet aircraft required massive capital investment, new maintenance infrastructure, retraining of crews, and uncertain consumer demand. Trippe nonetheless forced the transition, convinced that scale, speed, and efficiency would redefine global commerce. In doing so, he demonstrated a recurring trait of transformative industrial leaders across eras: a willingness to absorb near-term risk in pursuit of long-term systemic advantage.[80]

Trippe was also a pro-business nationalist. He viewed Pan Am not merely as a company but as an extension of American economic and geopolitical influence.[81] During the Cold War, he saw international aviation as a strategic asset and worked closely with U.S. government officials to ensure American dominance in global air travel. Trippe maintained close relationships with administrations from Roosevelt through Kennedy, positioning Pan Am as the de facto flag carrier of the United States—even though it was privately owned. He was a staunch anti-communist and believed that expanding American commercial presence abroad was both good business and good foreign policy.

This alignment with government power was central to Pan Am's rise—and ultimately to its vulnerability. Pan Am benefited enormously from U.S. diplomatic support, preferential access to international routes, and regulatory frameworks that limited competition.[82] At the same time, Trippe publicly embraced free enterprise and opposed excessive government interference. As with Henry Ford II and Thomas Watson Jr., this created an inherent tension. Pan Am thrived in a system where government action shaped markets in its favor, even as its leadership articulated Smithian commitments to competition and private enterprise.

From an incentive perspective, Trippe's success was enabled by a unique postwar environment. The United States dominated global aviation technology, fuel costs were low, demand for international travel was expanding rapidly, and regulatory regimes favored large incumbents. Scale worked in Pan Am's favor. However, as conditions changed—fuel shocks, deregulation, rising competition, and shifting consumer preferences—the same scale became a liability.[83] Pan Am's cost structure, global footprint, and reliance on political privilege proved difficult to unwind. Trippe's centralized, visionary leadership, so effective in building the system, was less suited to adapt and pivot the company once the environment he relied on turned hostile.

Trippe's story illustrates a broader lesson about capitalism at scale. Visionary leadership can create entire industries, but when incentives are tied to protected access, national privilege, or regulatory advantage, resilience erodes.[84] Pan Am did not fail because Trippe lacked imagination or discipline; it faltered because the system in which it operated changed faster than its institutional architecture could adapt.

Inclusive Capitalism interprets Trippe's legacy not as a caution against ambition but as a warning about dependency. When success is contingent on government-mediated advantages rather than continuously renewed productive efficiency and innovation, long-term sustainability is compromised. The solution is not less scale, nor less leadership, but better system design—enterprise charters and performance metrics that reward ongoing societal value creation rather than positional and situational dominance.[85]

Juan Trippe remains a towering figure in industrial history: tireless, visionary, and unafraid of risk. He helped compress the world, accelerate globalization, and redefine how people and goods move across the planet. Yet his career also underscores a central theme of this book: Even the greatest industrial leaders cannot outrun misaligned incentives forever. If capitalism is to remain innovative without repeating cycles of rise and collapse, it must evolve beyond reliance on extraordinary individuals and toward structures that make the right outcomes more inevitable rather than heroic.[86]

Thomas J. Watson Jr. (1914–1993) presided over one of the most consequential corporate transformations of the twentieth century. When he assumed leadership of IBM in the 1950s, the company was still rooted in mechanical tabulators and electromechanical accounting machines.[87] Watson Jr. recognized earlier than most that the future belonged to electronic computing and made the decisive—and extraordinarily risky—bet to reposition IBM as the dominant force in the emerging mainframe computer era. This transition required not incremental improvement but wholesale reinvention: new technologies, new organizational capabilities, and unprecedented capital investment.

Watson Jr. was a demanding and exacting leader. He was deeply involved in major product decisions, personally reviewed system architectures, and maintained close oversight of the company's largest customers—many of them government and military agencies.[88] He expected long hours, precision, and unwavering commitment from IBM employees. Loyalty was not optional; it was cultural doctrine. IBM under Watson Jr. was disciplined, hierarchical, and highly structured, in sharp contrast to the more decentralized and collegial cultures emerging simultaneously in firms like Hewlett-Packard. Yet this rigor was not arbitrary. IBM's core products—large, mission-critical computing systems—required reliability, standardization, and flawless execution. Failure was not merely costly; it could be catastrophic for customers whose operations depended on IBM systems.

Politically, Watson Jr. leaned liberal by the standards of his time. He was an early and outspoken supporter of civil rights, enforcing non-segregation policies within IBM well before federal mandates required it.[89] This stance was not without internal and external resistance, particularly in the American South, yet Watson viewed it as both morally necessary and strategically sound. A national technology leader, in his view, could not afford internal practices that undermined social legitimacy or talent acquisition. In this respect, Watson's leadership aligned closely with Inclusive Capitalism's core insight: Social inclusion and long-term enterprise value are not in conflict when incentives are properly aligned.

IBM's rise under Watson Jr. was inseparable from its deep integration with the U.S. government. The company became a cornerstone of defense computing, census operations, space exploration, and Cold War logistics. Government contracts provided IBM with scale, funding, and early demand for advanced systems that would have been difficult—perhaps impossible—to finance solely through private markets at the time.[90] Watson Jr. actively cultivated relationships with political and military leaders, positioning IBM as a strategic national asset in the technological rivalry with the Soviet Union.

This relationship exposes a recurring pattern in capitalist history. Many industrial leaders, including Watson Jr., publicly embraced Smithian principles—limited government, market competition, and private enterprise—while simultaneously benefiting from large-scale government spending.[91] This was not hypocrisy so much as structural inevitability. When the state becomes the dominant early customer for a new technology—railroads, aviation, semiconductors, computing, or aerospace—the boundary between public and private interests blurs. The incentives push firms toward cooperation with government, even as their ideological commitments remain formally pro-market.

Inclusive Capitalism treats this pattern as a design flaw rather than a moral failing. When firms must rely on government demand, protection, or oversight to remain competitive, incentives distort behavior on both sides. Corporations lobby for favorable treatment; governments expand regulatory reach to manage dependency. The result is an unstable equilibrium characterized by rent-seeking, politicization of markets, and recurring legitimacy crises.[92]

Watson Jr.'s IBM demonstrates both the power and the limits of this model. The company achieved technological dominance and operational excellence, yet over time became constrained by its own scale, bureaucracy, and dependence on large institutional customers. Innovation slowed as systems grew more complex and risk tolerance declined. Like Hewlett-Packard and Digital Equipment Corporation, IBM struggled to sustain its early creative momentum once the incentive structure shifted from invention to preservation.[93]

The lesson is not that Watson Jr. led poorly—by historical standards, he led exceptionally well. The lesson again is that even disciplined, forward-thinking leadership cannot overcome misaligned system incentives indefinitely.[94] When success depends on navigating government relationships rather than continuously expanding productive capacity and innovation, long-term dynamism erodes.

Inclusive Capitalism proposes a different path: re-chartered enterprises with incentive structures that reduce reliance on government intervention by aligning private success directly with societal value creation. By redesigning charters, metrics, and rewards, the system can preserve the benefits of scale without reproducing the conflicts that defined IBM's later decades.[95] Watson Jr.'s legacy, viewed through this lens, is not a cautionary tale about leadership—but a powerful case study in why leadership alone is not enough.

Howard Hughes (1905–1976) stands apart from nearly every other industrial leader of the Golden Age. Where many captains of industry balanced innovation with organization, Hughes embodied obsession.[96] He was not merely an executive directing engineers; he was an engineer, pilot, and experimenter himself. His life and career illustrate both the extraordinary upside and the profound fragility of innovation-driven capitalism when it becomes concentrated in a single individual operating without durable institutional constraints.

Hughes was driven by a relentless pursuit of technical perfection. In aviation and defense, he consistently pushed beyond what was considered practical or economical.[97] He personally designed aircraft, oversaw engineering decisions, and frequently piloted experimental planes himself—placing his own life at risk to test the limits of new technologies. Hughes Aircraft Company grew into a major defense contractor, developing advanced radar systems, missiles, and aerospace technologies that played critical roles during World War II and the Cold War. Many of these innovations would later underpin the modern aerospace and defense industries.

Unlike industrialists such as Henry Ford II or Alfred Sloan of General Motors, Hughes had little interest in managerial systems, delegation, or organizational stability. He distrusted bureaucracy, avoided formal governance, and resisted institutional discipline. Decision-making was centralized and exceptionally concentrated to him. This approach occasionally produced breakthroughs precisely because it ignored conventional constraints. Hughes could fund projects others deemed impossible or irrational, absorbing losses in pursuit of long-term technological advantage. In this sense, he exemplified a recurring pattern in capitalist history: Radical innovation often emerges where incentives reward vision over efficiency.[98]

Yet Hughes also demonstrated the limits of this model. Over time, his perfectionism mutated into paralysis. Projects were delayed indefinitely as designs were revised again and again in pursuit of unattainable ideals. The most famous example, the H-4 Hercules ("the Spruce Goose"), became a symbol of both audacity and excess—an engineering marvel that flew once, briefly, and never fulfilled its intended purpose.[99] Hughes's inability to accept "good enough" increasingly conflicted with the operational realities of large-scale production and national defense requirements.

Hughes's personal life further complicated his leadership. He became profoundly reclusive, paranoid, and obsessed with secrecy and control. He locked himself in hotel rooms for months at a time, issuing instructions through intermediaries, refusing physical contact, and imposing elaborate security protocols. While some degree of eccentricity has always accompanied great innovators, Hughes illustrates how fragile innovation becomes when it depends too heavily on a single individual's psychological stability rather than institutionalized processes.

Despite his distrust of government, Hughes relied heavily on military contracts. Like many Smithian capitalists before and after him, he opposed regulation, taxation, and political interference—yet benefited enormously from state spending.[100] Hughes Aircraft thrived on defense funding, and his aviation projects were often justified on national security grounds. This contradiction mirrors patterns seen repeatedly in capitalism at scale: Industrial leaders decry government involvement in principle while depending on it in practice when it aligns with their interests. Contemporary parallels are obvious in today's aerospace, defense, cyber security, AI infrastructure buildouts and space-launch sectors.

The nature of Hughes's work helps explain both his leadership style and his contradictions. Building experimental aircraft, radar systems, and advanced aerospace technologies required a workforce radically different from the labor forces of earlier capitalist epochs. These were not interchangeable factory hands or miners but elite engineers, physicists, and machinists. Such work tolerated—and sometimes rewarded—idiosyncratic leadership. Innovation at the frontier often thrives under looser social norms, unconventional hierarchies, and intense individual focus. Hughes's environment allowed for a wider range of leadership behavior than would have been possible in steel mills or textile factories.

From the perspective of Inclusive Capitalism, Hughes represents both promise and warning. His career demonstrates how innovation can flourish when incentives prioritize technological advancement over short-term profitability.[101] At the same time, it shows the danger of systems that rely on exceptional individuals rather than resilient institutions. Hughes Aircraft succeeded despite weak governance, not because of it. When Hughes himself deteriorated, the system had no internal corrective mechanisms.

This is a recurring structural problem. Capitalism, as traditionally instantiated, often rewards innovation without ensuring continuity. When incentives focus on heroic individual achievement rather than distributed capability, systems become brittle. Hughes's brilliance produced extraordinary advances, but the lack of institutional alignment meant those advances were vulnerable to delay, misallocation, and eventual stagnation.

Inclusive Capitalism addresses this failure mode directly. Innovation should not—and historically does not—depend on benefits sustained through reliance on idiosyncratic genius operating outside robust institutional frameworks.[102] Instead, enterprises must be chartered and incentivized to sustain innovation systematically—rewarding long-term societal value creation, technological progress, and human capital development, rather than the prominence of short-term financial extraction or personal dominance. Properly designed systems allow innovators to thrive without requiring them to carry the entire enterprise on their shoulders.

Howard Hughes leaves a complex legacy. His technological ambitions produced substantial benefits—advances in radar, aerospace engineering, and defense technologies that accelerated progress across modern industry.[103] Yet his life also reveals a deeper lesson: Innovation is most durable when it is embedded in institutions rather than concentrated in individuals. Capitalism must evolve from reliance on singular mavericks toward systems that make innovation continuous, distributed, and resilient by design.

In that sense, Hughes was not merely a maverick industrialist—he was a stress test. He revealed both the extraordinary heights capitalism can reach and the structural weaknesses that emerge when incentives, governance, and human limits are misaligned.

Walt Disney (1901–1966) represents a fundamentally different archetype of industrial leadership from the titans of heavy industry, finance, or defense. Where steel, oil, and aviation leaders organized capital around physical production and national power, Disney organized creativity itself.[104] He transformed storytelling, animation, and entertainment into scalable industrial systems—creating one of the most influential cultural enterprises of the twentieth century and demonstrating that capitalism could produce not only material abundance but shared meaning, imagination, and joy.

Disney's defining trait was an almost obsessive commitment to quality, immersion, and emotional resonance. He believed that entertainment should aspire to excellence rather than toward mere profitability.[105] This conviction repeatedly put him at odds with financiers and even his own managers. Early in his career, Disney risked bankruptcy to produce Snow White and the Seven Dwarfs (1937), the first full-length animated feature film. Industry experts widely predicted failure. Instead, the film became a massive success and validated animation as a serious art form and commercial medium. Disney consistently reinvested profits into new creative technologies—

color, sound synchronization, multiplane cameras—long before returns were guaranteed.

Unlike many industrial leaders of the Golden Age, Disney understood that innovation required aligning incentives around creativity rather than extraction. He built environments where artists, animators, and engineers could collaborate across disciplines. At the same time, Disney was a demanding leader. He expected relentless dedication, imposed exacting standards, and did not hesitate to replace employees who failed to meet his expectations. He was not a gentle manager, nor was he a pure idealist. His 1941 labor strike, triggered by pay disparities and credit allocation among animators, exposed tensions between creative ideals and hierarchical control.[106] Disney's response—deep resentment toward unions—mirrored a broader pattern among industrial leaders who embraced internal benevolence but resisted external constraints.

Disney's most profound innovation came not in film but in systems design. Disneyland, which opened in 1955, was not merely an amusement park; it was a new form of institution. Disney designed it as a fully integrated environment where narrative, engineering, operations, and customer experience reinforced one another. Cleanliness, safety, predictability, and wonder were engineered deliberately. Employees were "cast members," guests were participants, and every detail—from trash can spacing to sightlines—was optimized for human experience.[107] This was capitalism organized around lived experience rather than throughput or scale alone.

Disney's approach to incentives was subtle but powerful. Creative talent was rewarded not only with compensation but with identity, pride, and participation in something larger than themselves. Unlike extractive systems that motivate through fear or scarcity, Disney motivated through belonging and purpose. Yet even here, structural limits remained. Control stayed centralized. Creative risk ultimately depended on Disney himself. After his death, the company struggled to sustain innovation until governance structures evolved to institutionalize what had previously lived in a single mind.

From an economic perspective, Disney's work is notable for operating largely outside traditional Keynesian or industrial frameworks. His products were non-scarce in the economic sense: stories, characters, and experiences that could be replicated at near-zero marginal cost once created.[108] In this way, Disney prefigured today's digital economy. Yet the economic system of his time lacked the tools to properly value such contributions. Disney succeeded by building proprietary ecosystems but the broader system still rewarded financial extraction over creative abundance.

Disney's relationship with government further illustrates the recurring contradictions of capitalism at scale. He was personally conservative, anti-communist, and skeptical of unions, yet relied on public infrastructure, favorable zoning, and state cooperation—particularly in Florida—to realize his most ambitious projects.[109] The creation of Walt Disney World involved quasi-governmental arrangements granting the company extraordinary autonomy. As with other industrial leaders of the era, Disney resisted regulation in principle while benefiting from institutional privilege in practice.

From the perspective of Inclusive Capitalism, Walt Disney stands as one of the most compelling proofs that capitalism can be aligned with societal well-being when incentives reward creation rather than extraction. His enterprises generated employment, cultural cohesion, and shared experience at a national—and eventually global—scale. Yet his career also exposes the fragility of systems built around exceptional individuals rather than durable institutional design.

Disney showed what is possible when creativity is treated as a primary economic input and when organizations are designed around human experience. He also revealed the limits of such systems when governance, incentives, and succession are insufficiently formalized. Inclusive Capitalism builds on this lesson: the future of economic progress lies not in regulating creativity after the fact, nor in idolizing visionary founders, but in designing institutions that systematically reward innovation, cultural value, and long-term societal well-being—at scale, and can evolve independent of any single individual, in a sustainable manner.[110]

In that sense, Walt Disney was not merely an entertainer or entrepreneur. He helped pioneer an economic domain where value scaled through abundance rather than scarcity—one that capitalism has yet to fully understand, measure, properly value, or optimize.[111]

Lived Experience of the Population

The Golden Age of capitalism was also the Golden Age for the American workforce, standing in stark contrast to every period reviewed thus far.[112] The postwar decades marked a historic expansion of prosperity for working Americans. For the first time, wages rose steadily alongside productivity, job security was widespread, and homeownership became attainable for large segments of the blue-collar workforce.[113] This era diverged sharply from the Great Depression, the Gilded Age, and early industrial capitalism, when low wages, dangerous conditions, and economic precarity defined daily life for most workers.[114]

From roughly 1945 to 1970, manufacturing employment in the United States was abundant and relatively stable. The automotive, steel, electrical equipment, and consumer goods industries expanded rapidly. Many workers remained with a single employer for decades and retired with company pensions. Unionization played a central role in securing higher wages, health benefits, and safer working environments. For the first time in American history, a typical factory worker could realistically support a middle-class lifestyle on a single income—an outcome that would have been inconceivable in prior eras and is again increasingly proving difficult in the current era.[115] Overtime pay, paid vacations, employer-sponsored health insurance, and regulated working hours became standard. The forty-hour workweek replaced the sixty to eighty-hour weeks that had characterized earlier phases of capitalism.[116]

Working conditions during the Golden Age differed dramatically from those of early capitalism and the Gilded Age. Previously, workers could be hired and dismissed at will, endured dangerous and physically punishing labor, faced shifts lasting twelve to sixteen hours, and had no legal protections regarding wages, safety, or age of employment. Child labor was common, unions were weak or violently suppressed, and benefits were virtually nonexistent. During the Great Depression, conditions deteriorated further, with unemployment peaking near 25 percent and even employed workers facing wage cuts and sharply reduced hours.[117]

Government policy in the Golden Age reinforced the gains in the lived experience of the workforce. The GI Bill of 1944 provided returning veterans with access to affordable mortgages, education, and unemployment benefits, catalyzing the largest expansion of middle-class homeownership in American history.[118] Combined with the postwar baby boom, this fueled suburban development on a massive scale. Developments such as Levittown symbolized a new standard of living: modest homes with modern appliances, garages, and private yards. Mass production and expanding consumer credit made refrigerators, washing machines, televisions, and automobiles affordable to working families. The diffusion of modern appliances and household services sharply reduced the time required for domestic labor, freeing households to allocate more time to leisure, family life, and participation outside the home.

This reality stands in sharp contrast to earlier capitalist eras, when workers lived in overcrowded tenements or company-owned housing with poor sanitation, unreliable heat, and limited access to electricity or plumbing. Homeownership was rare. During the Great Depression, millions lost even rented housing and were forced into shantytowns—Hoovervilles—on the margins of cities. Food insecurity was widespread, and families relied heavily on soup kitchens and emergency relief. Leisure was virtually nonexistent.

Between 1945 and 1975, automobile ownership became commonplace due to continued gains in productivity and scale. The Interstate Highway System enabled suburban commuting and reshaped daily life. Paid vacations became common, and workers increasingly participated in leisure activities that had previously been the domain of the affluent. Family road trips, amusement parks, drive-in theaters, bowling alleys, and public recreation facilities flourished. Television replaced radio as the dominant form of home entertainment. Civic and social engagement expanded through PTAs, sports leagues, community organizations, and social clubs. A broad, confident middle class emerged and actively participated in civic life.[119]

By contrast, earlier generations of workers typically lived near factories in polluted urban centers. Transportation options were limited and unreliable. Long walks to work were common. During the Great Depression, car ownership was out of reach for most families, public transportation was often unaffordable for the unemployed, and leisure activities were severely curtailed. Weekends and vacations were luxuries few could imagine. Children frequently worked instead of attending school. Entertainment, when affordable at all, was limited to saloons, inexpensive theaters, or radio programming.

Healthcare and education also improved materially during the Golden Age. Employer-sponsored health insurance expanded rapidly. Medical advances, including the polio vaccine in 1955, significantly improved public health outcomes. Life expectancy increased, and healthcare access was broader and more affordable than in prior eras. The GI Bill enabled millions of Americans to attend college, dramatically expanding access to higher education.[120] Public universities grew rapidly at the state and local levels, creating new pathways for upward mobility across regions and social classes.

Again, this stands in stark contrast to earlier capitalist periods. Workplace injuries once resulted in immediate dismissal rather than treatment. Education was largely reserved for elites. During economic downturns, children routinely left school to support their families. Malnutrition, untreated illness, and preventable disease were common among working populations.

The contrast could not be more striking. Under the Golden Age of capitalism, the basic necessities of food, shelter, clothing, education, and healthcare became broadly accessible to the majority of the workforce, while leisure and cultural participation expanded dramatically. Life for working Americans shifted from near-subsistence toward what became known as the American Dream. Although access remained uneven due to persistent social and cultural barriers, the American Dream was attainable for a far larger share of the population than at any prior point in history—and arguably more so than in many periods that followed.[121]

The critical question is how the same economic system—operating with the same population and resource base—produced such radically different outcomes across eras. The answer lies not in capitalism alone but in a confluence of non-economic circumstances, technological maturity, the nature of work enabled by those technologies, and the economic doctrines and institutional frameworks governing production and distribution. The Golden Age did not represent a permanent equilibrium. Beginning in the 1970s, many of these favorable conditions eroded. Societal divides widened, economic volatility increased, and the foundations of middle-class security began to weaken.[122]

Both laissez-faire, unchecked Smithian capitalism and Keynesian economics produced unintended consequences. The Golden Age masked—but did not eliminate—those underlying structural flaws. Neither Keynesianism nor the neoclassical synthesis ultimately resolves them, because neither addresses the root causes that determine how incentives, scale, and institutional design shape outcomes for the workforce over time.

What Worked and What Did Not During the Golden Age of Capitalism

During the Golden Age of American capitalism, nearly everything appeared to work. Economic growth was strong, broadly shared, and sustained for decades. Productivity gains translated into rising wages. Employment was stable. Social mobility expanded. The American Dream was not aspirational rhetoric but a lived reality for much of the workforce.[123] This extraordinary alignment forces three deeper questions that matter directly for the design of Inclusive Capitalism: why such conditions failed to emerge earlier; what made shared prosperity possible during the Golden Age; and why that prosperity proved so short-lived once the Golden Age ended.

The answer to the first question is uncomfortable but clear: Earlier phases of capitalism did not produce workforce-empowering outcomes because the system did not reward them. Early English industrialists and later the robber barons of the Gilded Age could have raised wages, improved conditions, and invested in human capital—but under conditions of labor surplus, weak institutions, and intense competitive pressure, doing so was irrational within the prevailing incentive structure. Growth, scale, and cost minimization were rewarded even when achieved at the direct expense of worker well-being.[124] Adam Smith's assumption that self-interest would reliably align with the social good failed at scale, because the "invisible hand," absent inclusive incentives and institutions, became extractive rather than generative.

When improvement did occur prior to the Golden Age, it emerged reactively rather than by design. Capitalism's mid-life crisis produced reforms only after exploitation generated social instability, political backlash, and systemic risk. Workforce protections were imposed externally through legislation and crisis response, not adopted organically by industrial leadership. The American Dream did not arrive earlier because the system generally punished those who attempted to deliver it and rewarded those who extracted the most value in the shortest time. Exploitative equilibria persisted not because industrial leaders were uniquely immoral but because the system's incentives made inclusion an economic liability.[125]

The second question—what enabled the Golden Age's shared prosperity—goes to the heart of Inclusive Capitalism and centers on a defining feature of the era: non-scarcity. For roughly three decades, the United States operated in an environment where scarcity was unusually muted across multiple dimensions. Labor was abundant and increasingly skilled; land and housing were widely available; energy was cheap; capital was plentiful; and global competition was limited by the postwar destruction of peer economies. Demand was vast and unmet, both domestically and internationally. Under these conditions, economic growth did not require zero-sum tradeoffs. Rising productivity could lift wages without compressing margins.

This non-scarcity environment was reinforced by complementary institutional choices. Workforce-empowering legislation reduced downside risk and stabilized expectations. That said, it is critical to note that Keynesian demand management worked at a time when productive capacity, population growth, and technological progress were all expanding simultaneously—but did not when those conditions changed.[126]

Technological innovation shifted large segments of work toward higher-skill, more creative, and more rewarding activities, further easing distributional conflict. In this context, shared prosperity became not only politically feasible but economically natural. The system appeared harmonious because abundance dampened conflict and masked unresolved structural tensions.

The question of why these conditions faded—and why the system proved unable to sustain shared prosperity once non-scarcity receded—is the subject of the next chapter and, in many ways, the remainder of this book. What matters here is the central takeaway. The Golden Age demonstrated that non-scarcity can enable broad-based prosperity even within imperfect institutional systems. But it also showed that prosperity built on favorable external conditions is inherently fragile and time-bounded—even when that window spans decades, as it did in the Golden Age. When abundance gives way to constraint, incentives reassert themselves. Without structural alignment, inclusion becomes optional, then uneconomic, and ultimately unsustainable.[127]

For Inclusive Capitalism, the lesson is decisive. The postwar era reveals what is possible—but also what must change. Shared prosperity cannot depend on rare historical conditions or continual crisis response. It must be engineered into the system itself. That requires rearchitecting incentives, metrics, and institutional charters so that workforce empowerment, long-term investment, and societal well-being remain rational outcomes even when scarcity returns.[128]

Why the Golden Age of Capitalism Came to an End

The Golden Age of American capitalism did not so much end as it unraveled once the extraordinary non-economic conditions that sustained it dissipated. The most important of these was the erosion of U.S. industrial and geopolitical primacy. By the late 1960s and early 1970s, Europe and Japan had fully rebuilt from wartime devastation and re-entered global markets as formidable competitors.[129] Industries in which the United States had enjoyed near-monopoly conditions—steel, automobiles, consumer electronics, shipbuilding—became globally competitive seemingly overnight. At the same time, the demographic tailwinds that had fueled growth began to weaken. The baby boom matured, labor-force growth slowed, immigration became more restrictive, and productivity gains from postwar industrialization began to plateau.[130] Abundant land gave way to urban congestion and housing constraints, while easily and cheaply exploitable natural resources were increasingly depleting or politically constrained. The forgiving environment that had allowed inefficiencies to be absorbed quietly were gone.[131]

These shifts occurred with surprising speed. The oil shocks of the 1970s exposed new forms of scarcity just as global competition intensified, revealing that the post-war system had been operating under assumptions of cheap energy, expanding capacity, and uncontested demand.[132] Cultural norms also evolved. A generation that had known sacrifice, scarcity, and existential threat gave way to one raised in abundance, stability, and expectation. Work ethic, risk tolerance, and attitudes toward entitlement subtly but meaningfully changed, altering labor dynamics and political pressures. None of these changes were inherently negative, but together they marked the end of the conditions under which the Golden Age had functioned. What followed was not the sudden failure of capitalism but the re-exposure of its unresolved structural tensions—setting the stage for the reassertion of Smithian ideas and the pendulum swing explored in the next chapter.[133]

Conclusions and Insights for Inclusive Capitalism from The Golden Age of Capitalism

The first and most important insight the Golden Age offers Inclusive Capitalism is that it functions as a genuine proof of concept. For roughly three decades, the United States demonstrated that a large, complex capitalist economy could deliver broad-based prosperity rather than concentrated gain. This outcome was not perfect, nor was it permanent, but it was real. Abundance—driven by favorable temporal conditions—and institutional support—though incomplete and often reactive—combined to produce rising wages, stable employment, social mobility, and a shared sense of progress. The lesson is not that the Golden Age provides a template to be replicated wholesale; its enabling conditions were historically unique and fleeting. The lesson is that inclusive outcomes are not utopian. When scarcity is reduced and institutions partially align incentives toward stability and participation, capitalism can generate shared prosperity at scale. Inclusive Capitalism begins from this empirical reality: inclusion is achievable, even under non-ideal economic architectures, when the system's dynamics favor abundance over extraction.

The second insight is more structural and more enduring: Shared prosperity cannot be sustained without well-architected corporate governance. The industrial leadership profiles of the Golden Age reveal a recurring pattern that persists today—heroic individuals bearing disproportionate authority, risk, and reward. These leaders were often brilliant, visionary, and intensely driven. They built extraordinary enterprises. Yet the system relied too heavily on personal virtue, restraint, or luck rather than durable institutional design. The United States was founded on a profound rejection of kingship in government, embedding checks, balances, term limits, and accountability into its constitutional architecture. Yet in the economic sphere, we have long tolerated—and at times celebrated—de facto kings of industry. This admiration is understandable but dangerous. Hero-centric capitalism scales innovation, but it also scales fragility, succession risk, and the externalization of harm when individual incentives drift out of alignment with societal needs.

Inclusive Capitalism therefore requires a governance model that preserves the creative power of exceptional leaders while constraining their most destructive failure modes. We want industrial leaders to retain the authority necessary to build boldly, innovate decisively, and take meaningful risk—but within systems that temper idiosyncrasy, distribute accountability, and ensure orderly transfer of power. Leadership should be service-oriented rather than sovereign, accountable not only to capital but to workers and society at large. The U.S. constitutional tradition offers a powerful analogy: Liberty is preserved not by eliminating authority but by structuring it. Inclusive Capitalism extends this logic to the firm itself, replacing hero dependence with institutionalized stewardship, shared upside, and embedded responsibility. Only through such governance can abundance be sustained once favorable external conditions fade—and only then can shared prosperity become a feature of the system rather than a historical accident.

Notes

1 Hobsbawm, Eric. *The Age of Extremes: The Short Twentieth Century, 1914–1991*. New York: Vintage Books, 1994, 257–286.
2 Milward, Alan S. *War, Economy and Society, 1939–1945*. Berkeley: University of California Press, 1977, 63–95; Eichengreen, Barry. *Globalizing Capital: A History of the International Monetary System*. 2nd ed. Princeton, NJ: Princeton University Press, 2008, 91–132.
3 Dalio, Ray. *Principles for Dealing with the Changing World Order*. New York: Avid Reader Press, 2021, pp. 1–75, 147–204.
4 Sowell, Thomas. *Basic Economics*. New York: Basic Books, 2000, pp. 19–54, 233–276.
5 Ruggie, John Gerard. "International Regimes, Transactions, and Change." *International Organization* 36, no. 2 (1982): 379–415.
6 Goldin, Claudia, and Lawrence F. Katz. *The Race between Education and Technology*. Cambridge, MA: Harvard University Press, 2008, 153–210.
7 Hobsbawm, Eric. *The Age of Extremes: The Short Twentieth Century, 1914–1991*, 257–286.
8 Gordon, Robert J. *The Rise and Fall of American Growth*. Princeton, NJ: Princeton University Press, 2016, pp. 13–71, 245–289.
9 Hobsbawm, Eric. *The Age of Extremes: The Short Twentieth Century, 1914–1991*, 285–322.
10 Ford, Henry. *My Life and Work*. Garden City, NY: Doubleday, Page & Co., 1922, pp. 82–112, 181–208.
11 Bordo, Michael D., and Barry Eichengreen, eds. *A Retrospective on the Bretton Woods System*. Chicago: University of Chicago Press, 1993, pp. 1–28, 461–514.
12 Piketty, Thomas. *Capital in the Twenty-First Century*. Cambridge, MA: Harvard University Press, 2014, pp. 211–264, 297–343.
13 North, Douglass C. *Institutions, Institutional Change and Economic Performance*. Cambridge: Cambridge University Press, 1990, 3–14.
14 Bureau of Economic Analysis. *National Income and Product Accounts (NIPA), Postwar Historical Series*. Washington, DC: U.S. Department of Commerce, tables on GDP, compensation of employees, and personal income.

15 Hobsbawm, Eric. *The Age of Extremes: The Short Twentieth Century, 1914–1991.* New York: Vintage, 1996, pp. 252–315, 404–461.

16 U.S. Bureau of Labor Statistics. *Productivity and Costs: Historical Time Series, 1947–1973.* Washington, DC: U.S. Department of Labor, tables on nonfarm business productivity and unit labor costs.

17 Gordon, Robert J. *The Rise and Fall of American Growth.* Princeton, pp. 13–71, 245–289.

18 U.S. Bureau of Labor Statistics. *Productivity and Costs: Historical Time Series, 1947–1973.* Washington, DC: U.S. Department of Labor, tables on nonfarm business productivity and unit labor costs.

19 Jackson, Kenneth T. *Crabgrass Frontier: The Suburbanization of the United States.* New York: Oxford University Press, 1985, 11–42, 283–309.

20 Gordon, Robert J. *The Rise and Fall of American Growth.* 541–579.

21 Goldin, Claudia, and Lawrence F. Katz. *The Race Between Education and Technology.* pp. 1–29, 67–124.

22 Ruggie, John Gerard. *"International Regimes, Transactions, and Change."* 379–415.

23 Hobsbawm, Eric. *The Age of Extremes: The Short Twentieth Century, 1914–1991.* pp. 252–315, 404–461.

24 Maddison, Angus. *The World Economy: A Millennial Perspective.* Paris: OECD, 2001, pp. 23–60, 95–140.

25 Sowell, Thomas. *Basic Economics.*, pp. 19–54, 233–276.

26 Wright, Gavin. *The Origins of American Industrial Success, 1879–1940.* New York: American Economic Association, 1990, 7–33.

27 Crafts, Nicholas, and Gianni Toniolo, eds. *Economic Growth in Europe Since 1945.* Cambridge: Cambridge University Press, 1996, pp. 1–38, 71–118.

28 Hobsbawm, Eric. *The Age of Extremes: The Short Twentieth Century, 1914–1991.* pp. 252–315, 404–461.

29 Dalio, Ray. *Principles for Dealing with the Changing World Order.*, pp. 1–75, 147–204.

30 Acemoglu, Daron, and James A. Robinson. *Why Nations Fail.* New York: Crown Business, 2012, pp. 74–81, 102–104, 301–335.

31 Friedman, Milton. *Capitalism and Freedom.* Chicago: University of Chicago Press, 1962, pp. 7–34, 85–126.

32 Ibid.

33 Harvey, David. *A Brief History of Neoliberalism.* New York: Oxford University Press, 2005, 1–38.

34 Samuelson, Paul A. *Economics.* New York: McGraw-Hill, 1948, pp. 253–321.

35 Kindleberger, Charles P. *The World in Depression, 1929–1939.* Berkeley: University of California Press, 1973, pp. 291–336.

36 Keynes, John Maynard. *The General Theory of Employment, Interest and Money.* London: Macmillan, 1936, pp. 3–51, 245–284.

37 Ibid.

38 Kindleberger, Charles P. *The World in Depression, 1929–1939.* 291–336.

39 Keynes, John Maynard. *The General Theory of Employment, Interest and Money.* 3–51, 245–284.

40 Samuelson, Paul A. *Economics.* 253–321.

41 Friedman, Milton. *Capitalism and Freedom.* 7–34, 85–126.

42 Samuelson, Paul A. *Economics.* 253–321.

43 Sowell, Thomas. *Basic Economics.*, pp. 19–54, 233–276.

44 Skidelsky, Robert. *John Maynard Keynes: Fighting for Freedom, 1937–1946.* New York: Viking, 2000, 379–428.

45 Mettler, Suzanne. *Soldiers to Citizens: The G.I. Bill and the Making of the Greatest Generation.* New York: Oxford University Press, 2005, 1–38; U.S. Congress. *Servicemen's Readjustment Act of 1944,* Pub. L. No. 78–346, 58 Stat. 284.

46 Goldin, Claudia, and Lawrence F. Katz. *The Race Between Education and Technology.* pp. 1–29, 67–124.
47 Gordon, Robert J. *The Rise and Fall of American Growth.* Princeton, pp. 13–71, 245–289.
48 Employment Act of 1946. Pub. L. No. 79–304, 60 Stat. 23.
49 Ruggie, John Gerard. “International Regimes, Transactions, and Change.” 379–415.
50 Bordo, Michael D., and Barry Eichengreen, eds. *A Retrospective on the Bretton Woods System,* pp. 1–28, 461–514.
51 Kennedy, John F. *Special Message to the Congress on Tax Reduction and Reform.* January 24, 1963.
52 Brownlee, W. Elliot. *Federal Taxation in America: A Short History.* 3rd ed. New York: Cambridge University Press, 2016, 149–178.
53 Romer, Paul M. “Endogenous Technological Change.” *Journal of Political Economy* 98, no. 5 (1990): S71–S102.
54 Mazzucato, Mariana. *The Entrepreneurial State.* London: Anthem Press, 2013, pp. 19–58, 89–122.
55 Keynes, John Maynard. *The General Theory of Employment, Interest, and Money.* London: Macmillan, 1936, chs. 12, 24; North, Douglass C. *Institutions, Institutional Change and Economic Performance.* 3–14.
56 Minsky, Hyman P. *Stabilizing an Unstable Economy.* New Haven, CT: Yale University Press, 1986, 13–45.
57 Stein, Herbert. *The Fiscal Revolution in America.* Chicago: University of Chicago Press, 1969, 287–316.
58 Chandler, Alfred D. *The Visible Hand: The Managerial Revolution in American Business.* Cambridge, MA: Harvard University Press, 1977, 79–121, 285–336.
59 Nevins, Allan. *Ford: The Times, the Man, the Company.* New York: Scribner, 1954, pp. 528–602.
60 Sloan, Alfred P., Jr. *My Years with General Motors.* New York: Doubleday, 1963, 290–312; Nevins, Allan, and Frank Ernest Hill. *Ford: Decline and Rebirth, 1933–1962.* New York: Charles Scribner's Sons, 1963, 351–402.
61 Ruggie, John Gerard. “International Regimes, Transactions, and Change.” 379–415.
62 McCraw, Thomas K. *American Business, 1920–2000.* Chicago: University of Chicago Press, 2000, pp. 1–42, 87–132.
63 Ibid.
64 Gordon, Robert J. *The Rise and Fall of American Growth.* 13–71, 245–289.
65 Iacocca, Lee, with William Novak. *Iacocca: An Autobiography.* New York: Bantam Books, 1984, 221–248, 287–305; Halberstam, David. *The Reckoning.* New York: William Morrow, 1986, 513–548.
66 Chandler, Alfred D., Jr. *The Visible Hand.* pp. 1–58, 285–338.
67 Romer, Paul M. “Endogenous Technological Change.” *Journal of Political Economy* 98, no. 5 (1990): S71–S102.
68 Packard, David. *The HP Way.* New York: HarperBusiness, 1995, pp. 3–48, 111–156.
69 Ibid.
70 Amabile, Teresa M., and Steven J. Kramer. *The Progress Principle: Using Small Wins to Ignite Joy, Engagement, and Creativity at Work.* Boston: Harvard Business Review Press, 2011, 1–38; Pfeffer, Jeffrey. *Competitive Advantage through People: Unleashing the Power of the Work Force.* Boston: Harvard Business School Press, 1994, 3–29.
71 Packard, David. *The HP Way.* New York: 3–48, 111–156.
72 Bush, Vannevar. *Science, the Endless Frontier.* Washington, DC: U.S. Government Printing Office, 1945, pp. 5–33.
73 Malone, Michael S. *Bill & Dave: How Hewlett and Packard Built the World's Greatest Company.* New York: Portfolio/Penguin, 2007, 1–52, 379–420; Christensen, Clayton M. *The Innovator's Dilemma: When New Technologies Cause Great Firms to Fail.* Boston: Harvard Business School Press, 1997, 1–30, 177–199.

74 Christensen, Clayton M. *The Innovator's Dilemma: When New Technologies Cause Great Firms to Fail.* Boston: Harvard Business School Press, 1997, 15–28, 103–131; Schein, Edgar H. *DEC Is Dead, Long Live DEC: The Lasting Legacy of Digital Equipment Corporation.* San Francisco: Berrett-Koehler, 2003, 1–36.
75 Christensen, Clayton M. *The Innovator's Dilemma: When New Technologies Cause Great Firms to Fail.* 15–30, 177–199.
76 Daley, Robert. *An American Saga: Juan Trippe and His Pan Am Empire.* New York: Random House, 1980, pp. 3–52, 187–244.
77 Ibid.
78 Ibid.
79 Ibid.
80 Schumpeter, Joseph A. *Capitalism, Socialism and Democracy.* New York: Harper & Brothers, 1942, 81–106.
81 Ruggie, John Gerard. "International Regimes, Transactions, and Change." 379–415.
82 Ibid.
83 Stiglitz, Joseph E. *Globalization and Its Discontents.* New York: W. W. Norton, 2002, pp. 3–22, 89–132.
84 Acemoglu, Daron, and James A. Robinson. *Why Nations Fail: The Origins of Power, Prosperity, and Poverty.* 74–91.
85 Mazzucato, Mariana. *The Entrepreneurial State.* 19–58, 89–122.
86 Ibid.
87 Watson, Thomas J., Jr. *Father, Son & Co.* New York: Bantam, 1990, pp. 65–118, 219–266.
88 Ibid.
89 Ibid.
90 Mazzucato, Mariana. *The Entrepreneurial State.* 19–58, 89–122.
91 Mazzucato, Mariana. *The Entrepreneurial State: Debunking Public vs. Private Sector Myths.* New York: PublicAffairs, 2013, 69–118.
92 Stiglitz, Joseph E. *Globalization and Its Discontents.* 3–22, 89–132.
93 McCraw, Thomas K. *American Business, 1920–2000.* 1–42, 87–132.
94 Stiglitz, Joseph E. *Globalization and Its Discontents.* 3–22, 89–132.
95 Chandler, Alfred D., Jr. *The Visible Hand.* pp. 1–58, 285–338.
96 Bartlett, Donald L., and James B. Steele. *Howard Hughes: His Life and Madness.* New York: W. W. Norton, 1979, pp. 215–268, 371–424.
97 Ibid.
98 Romer, Paul M. "Endogenous Technological Change." *Journal of Political Economy* 98, no. 5 (1990): S71–S102.
99 Bartlett, Donald L., and James B. Steele. *Howard Hughes: His Life and Madness.* 215–268, 371–424.
100 Mazzucato, Mariana. *The Entrepreneurial State.* 19–58, 89–122.
101 Romer, Paul M. "Endogenous Technological Change." *Journal of Political Economy* 98, no. 5 (1990): S71–S102.
102 Ibid.
103 Bartlett, Donald L., and James B. Steele. *Howard Hughes: His Life and Madness.* 215–268, 371–424.
104 Watts, Steven. *The Magic Kingdom: Walt Disney and the American Way of Life.* Columbia, MO: University of Missouri Press, 1997, pp. 1–41, 217–284.
105 Ibid.
106 Ibid.
107 Ibid.
108 Romer, Paul M. "Endogenous Technological Change." *Journal of Political Economy* 98, no. 5 (1990): S71–S102.

109 Watts, Steven. *The Magic Kingdom: Walt Disney and the American Way of Life.* Columbia, MO: University of Missouri Press, 1997, pp. 1–41, 217–284.
110 Mazzucato, Mariana. *The Entrepreneurial State.* 19–58, 89–122.
111 Romer, Paul M. "Endogenous Technological Change." *Journal of Political Economy* 98, no. 5 (1990): S71–S102.
112 Gordon, Robert J. *The Rise and Fall of American Growth.* 13–71, 245–289.
113 U.S. Bureau of Labor Statistics. *Productivity and Costs: Historical Time Series, 1947–1973.* Washington, DC: U.S. Department of Labor, tables on nonfarm business productivity and unit labor costs.
114 Sinclair, Upton. *The Jungle.* New York: Doubleday, 1906, pp. 1–87.
115 Cohen, Lizabeth. *A Consumers' Republic: The Politics of Mass Consumption in Postwar America.* New York: Alfred A. Knopf, 2003, 25–61.
116 U.S. Department of Commerce. *Historical Statistics of the United States: Colonial Times to 1970.* Washington, DC: U.S. Government Printing Office, 1975, Series D and E (labor, wages, hours).
117 Kindleberger, Charles P. *The World in Depression, 1929–1939.* 291–336.
118 Cohen, Lizabeth. *A Consumers' Republic.* New York: Knopf, 2003, pp. 11–52, 194–247.
119 Ibid.
120 Goldin, Claudia, and Lawrence F. Katz. *The Race Between Education and Technology.* pp. 1–29, 67–124.
121 Cohen, Lizabeth. *A Consumers' Republic: The Politics of Mass Consumption in Postwar America.* New York: Alfred A. Knopf, 2003, 25–61.
122 Cowie, Jefferson. *Stayin' Alive: The 1970s and the Last Days of the Working Class.* New York: The New Press, 2010, 1–34, 143–172.
123 Gordon, Robert J. *The Rise and Fall of American Growth.* 13–71, 245–289.
124 Ibid.
125 North, Douglass C. *Institutions, Institutional Change and Economic Performance.* Cambridge: Cambridge University Press, 1990.
126 Eichengreen, Barry. *Hall of Mirrors: The Great Depression, the Great Recession, and the Uses—and Misuses—of History.* New York: Oxford University Press, 2015, 203–233.
127 North, Douglass C. *Institutions, Institutional Change and Economic Performance.* 3–14.
128 Acemoglu, Daron, and James A. Robinson. *Why Nations Fail.* pp. 74–81, 102–104, 301–335.
129 Crafts, Nicholas, and Gianni Toniolo, eds. *Economic Growth in Europe Since 1945.* pp. 1–38, 71–118.
130 Gordon, Robert J. *The Rise and Fall of American Growth.* 13–71, 245–289.
131 Maddison, Angus. *The World Economy: A Millennial Perspective.* pp. 23–60, 95–140.
132 Dalio, Ray. *Principles for Dealing with the Changing World Order.*, pp. 1–75, 147–204.
133 Friedman, Milton. *Capitalism and Freedom.* 7–34, 85–126.

7 Adam Smith Strikes Back

The revival of Smithian capitalism did not begin as an intellectual counterrevolution. It began as a loss of confidence. By the late 1960s and early 1970s, the foundations that had sustained the Golden Age were eroding rapidly, and the Keynesian framework that had once seemed both humane and technically competent appeared increasingly unable to explain, much less manage, the new reality.[1] What followed was not a clean theoretical transition but a disorderly unraveling of assumptions—about growth, inflation, labor, energy, geopolitics, and the capacity of the state to intervene and fine-tune a complex economy.

The first shock came from the exhaustion of the postwar non-economic conditions. The demographic tailwinds that had fueled expansion slowed as the baby boom generation matured and labor-force growth decelerated. Europe and Japan—fully rebuilt and reindustrialized—began competing aggressively with U.S. firms, eroding America's postwar industrial dominance. The United States shifted from creditor to debtor, from major exporter to net importer, and from industrial leadership to contested position within the global economy. Resource abundance gave way to constraint and disruption, most visibly through the oil shocks of 1973 and 1979, which exposed the fragility of an energy-intensive growth model. Scarcity re-entered the system abruptly, and policy instruments designed for abundance proved poorly suited to the transition.

At the same time, the Keynesian policy apparatus began to fail on its own terms. Fiscal expansion layered atop the Vietnam War and Great Society programs pushed aggregate demand beyond the economy's productive capacity. Supply-side growth slowed, productivity gains weakened, and inflation accelerated even as unemployment rose—producing stagflation, a phenomenon Keynesian theory had treated as unlikely, if not impossible. The presumed stable trade-off between inflation and employment collapsed, undermining confidence in discretionary macroeconomic management.

Monetary institutions fared no better. The Bretton Woods system, which had anchored global stability through fixed exchange rates and dollar–gold convertibility, became untenable under persistent U.S. fiscal deficits, rapid monetary expansion, and the accumulation of dollars abroad.[2] The 1971 suspension of gold convertibility marked a structural break in the international monetary order. Money was severed from any external anchor, and monetary policy became explicitly discretionary. The ensuing decade of experimentation culminated in the disinflation engineered by Federal Reserve Chair Paul Volcker between 1979 and 1982.[3] While effective in restoring price stability, the strategy induced a deep recession and drove unemployment above 10 percent, producing lasting labor-market dislocation.

Intellectually, this failure reopened questions that had been suppressed rather than resolved during the Keynesian era. Milton Friedman argued that inflation was

 | https://doi.org/10.1515/9783112235485-008

fundamentally a monetary phenomenon and that discretionary stabilization policy amplified, rather than smoothed, economic volatility.[4] Austrian and classical economists renewed warnings about distorted price signals, moral hazard, and the unintended consequences of intervention at scale. These critiques gained influence not because they were novel but because events rendered them unavoidable.

The Smithian revival that followed was therefore less a nostalgic return than a corrective swing. Markets were re-centered as information systems for coordinating economic behavior through prices, profits, and losses, rather than as moral mechanisms expected to align automatically with social outcomes.[5] Analytical emphasis returned to incentives and price signals, while concerns about distribution, dignity, and long-term institutional health receded from the core of economic analysis. Government shifted, at least in theory, from manager to referee. Yet this revival carried its own blind spots. It restored confidence in markets without adequately confronting the scale, concentration, and institutional pathologies that had accumulated during the Golden Age and its aftermath.

The Smithian revival was neither a mistake nor a betrayal of capitalism's promise. It was a necessary corrective to a system that had lost credibility, discipline, and legitimacy under late-stage Keynesian management. By restoring the primacy of prices, incentives, competition, and monetary credibility, it reestablished capitalism's capacity for innovation and growth. But it did not—and could not—resolve the deeper structural problem that emerges once capitalism operates at scale. The revival assumed that removing constraints would restore market discipline, yet it largely ignored how scale, financialization, and global integration transform incentives themselves.

This distinction matters because it explains both the revival's success and its eventual failure. Markets did not stop working; they worked exactly as designed under the prevailing incentive structure. Innovation accelerated, capital became more mobile, and efficiency increased—but gains concentrated, volatility intensified, and legitimacy eroded. The failure was not Smith's insight but the assumption that it could scale indefinitely without institutional adaptation.

This chapter examines the Smithian revival not as triumph or failure but as a necessary reaction to a system that had drifted out of balance. Keynesianism did not falter because it was ineffective in crisis—its role during the Depression and wartime mobilization is indisputable—but because it offered no coherent framework for managing economic maturity, renewed scarcity, and scale. Smithian capitalism returned because the prevailing alternative had lost credibility. Importantly, it returned into a world fundamentally different from the one Adam Smith described two centuries earlier. Understanding that mismatch is essential to explaining both the revival's achievements and its limits.

The Smithian Revival: Definition and Core Characteristics

The Smithian revival refers to the reemergence, beginning in the late 1970s and consolidating through the 1980s and 1990s, of classical liberal, laissez-faire, economic principles centered on markets, prices, competition, and private enterprise as the primary engines of economic coordination. While often labeled "neoliberalism," the revival is more accurately understood as a modernized form of Smithian capitalism—adapted to a global, financialized, post-industrial world but rooted in much older ideas about self-interest, price signals, market self-regulation, and limited government.[6]

At its intellectual core, the Smithian revival re-centered the market as an information system rather than as a moral abstraction. Prices were treated not merely as allocative tools but as compressed signals reflecting dispersed knowledge, relative scarcity, and opportunity cost. In this view, economic coordination could not be reliably engineered by centralized authorities without distorting those signals and degrading system performance. This perspective drew heavily from the Austrian School of economics—most notably the work of Friedrich Hayek—who argued that economic order emerges spontaneously from voluntary exchange rather than from top-down design and that no planner can aggregate or process the knowledge embedded in millions of individual decisions.[7]

In the American context, this revival was articulated most forcefully by Milton Friedman, whose work reframed macroeconomic instability as a failure of monetary governance rather than as a structural flaw of capitalism itself. Friedman challenged Keynesian demand management by asserting that inflation was "always and everywhere a monetary phenomenon," and that discretionary fiscal policy often introduced more volatility than it resolved. He advocated rules-based monetary policy, floating exchange rates, and market-determined prices, repositioning the state as the steward of a stable monetary framework rather than as an active manager of economic outcomes.[8]

Politically, the Smithian revival crystallized through the parallel leadership of President Ronald Reagan in the United States and Prime Minister Margaret Thatcher in the United Kingdom. While operating in different national and institutional contexts, both advanced a shared agenda: deregulation of product and financial markets, reductions in marginal tax rates, privatization of state-owned enterprises, and a deliberate weakening of organized labor's bargaining power. In the United Kingdom, Thatcherism pursued similar objectives within a more statist legacy, emphasizing privatization, labor market reform, and the dismantling of corporatist arrangements that had insulated entire industries from competition.

At the global level, the Smithian revival was institutionalized through what became known as the Washington Consensus—a term used to describe a broadly shared policy framework promoted by international financial institutions headquartered in Washington, most notably the International Monetary Fund and the World Bank. The

Consensus articulated a set of reform principles that emphasized fiscal discipline, trade liberalization, capital account openness, privatization of state-owned enterprises, deregulation, and the protection of property rights.

A defining characteristic of this period was the elevation of efficiency as the dominant evaluative metric. Firms were increasingly assessed by return on capital, shareholder value, and cost minimization, while financial markets—empowered by deregulation and technological change—became central arbiters of corporate performance. Capital allocation accelerated, innovation in financial instruments expanded, and competitive pressures intensified, while issues of scale, concentration, and systemic risk were generally treated as secondary concerns rather than as central design challenges.

This assumption would later be questioned. In testimony following the 2008 financial crisis, Alan Greenspan acknowledged that the expectation of effective self-discipline in financial markets had proven incomplete, underscoring a broader limitation of the Smithian revival as it had been operationalized.[9]

In sum, the Smithian revival was a reassertion of capitalism's classical operating logic under modern conditions: decentralized markets, price-mediated coordination, profit-driven investment, and constrained government. It succeeded in restoring growth and unleashing innovation, but it also reintroduced vulnerabilities associated with scale, wealth concentration, and misaligned incentives—vulnerabilities that were embedded from the start and would take time to surface.

Drivers of the Smithian Revival

The Smithian revival of the 1980s was not ideological nostalgia; it was a reaction to the rapid unravelling of the postwar economic order in the 1970s. What is striking is not that the Golden Age ended but how quickly confidence collapsed. Within a decade, the United States moved from the exuberance of postwar industrial dominance—symbolized by oversized Cadillacs and unconstrained consumption—to an era defined by downsizing, energy anxiety, and economic insecurity, embodied by the underpowered and unreliable Chevy Vega and Ford Pinto. This abrupt reversal suggests not a slow structural decay but the sudden exhaustion of a set of conditions that had masked deeper and persistent weaknesses in the system for decades.[10]

The most visible manifestation of this breakdown was stagflation—the simultaneous presence of high inflation, rising unemployment, and weak growth. This outcome directly contradicted a central Keynesian assumption: that inflation and unemployment move along a stable trade-off.[11] Keynesian tools had been designed for economies characterized by slack demand and idle resources. By the early 1970s, the U.S. economy no longer fit that profile. Demand stimulus, once growth-enhancing, became inflationary, revealing the limits of discretionary macroeconomic management under mature conditions.

By the late 1960s, the U.S. economy had become capacity-constrained across multiple dimensions. Unemployment was already low, industrial plant utilization was high, and the postwar capital-deepening phase had largely run its course.[12] Cheap energy—long a silent enabler of expansion—became a binding input as oil prices rose sharply.[13]

As established earlier, the oil shocks of the 1970s exposed the fragility of an energy-intensive growth model operating at capacity, turning Keynesian demand management from a stabilizer into an accelerant of inflation. The OPEC embargo and the Iranian Revolution sharply constrained global petroleum supplies, driving energy prices dramatically higher and transmitting cost shocks throughout the economy. Because energy was a foundational input—fuel, transportation, manufacturing, and chemicals—these shocks produced persistent cost-push inflation. Growth slowed even as prices surged, and gasoline shortages, production cutbacks, and declining real incomes became everyday realities.[14] Keynesian stimulus, applied reflexively to counter rising unemployment, intensified inflation without addressing the underlying supply constraint.

The oil shocks alone do not explain the depth or persistence of stagflation. They struck an economy already primed for instability by years of expansionary fiscal policy. The Vietnam War and Great Society programs had been financed largely through deficits rather than taxation.[15] In the early 1960s this approach was sustainable because excess capacity remained and debt growth aligned with economic expansion. By the late 1960s, the economy was operating at near full employment. Additional demand no longer produced more output; it produced higher prices. Political reluctance to align spending with taxation allowed inflationary pressures to accumulate. Temporary measures such as wage and price controls suppressed symptoms briefly but worsened distortions, allowing inflation to reemerge with greater force once controls were lifted.

Monetary policy compounded these dynamics. The Federal Reserve accommodated inflation rather than confronting it, influenced both by political pressure and by a prevailing bias toward preserving employment. Inflation expectations became entrenched. The suspension of gold convertibility in 1971 removed the last external constraint on monetary expansion.[16] Money creation became more discretionary, and inflation shifted from episodic to systemic.

Equally important were structural changes that would have challenged the postwar order regardless of policy choices. The advantages that had underpinned the Golden Age were inherently time-bounded. By the 1970s, Europe and Japan had rebuilt with modern factories, disciplined cost structures, and, in many cases, superior manufacturing practices. Industries that had enjoyed decades of protected dominance—steel, automobiles, consumer appliances—suddenly faced intense competition. Many American firms, insulated during the postwar boom, had underinvested in innovation, efficiency, and quality. When global competition returned, they were unprepared.[17]

Taken together, these forces exposed the limits of the postwar framework. The Golden Age did not fail because Keynesianism was useless in crisis but because the system had matured into conditions—scarcity, competition, and constraint—for which it was never designed. The Smithian revival that followed was therefore less a rejection of the postwar order than an attempt to restore market discipline in a world where abundance could no longer be taken for granted.[18]

This loss of industrial dominance interacted destructively with domestic labor arrangements. Strong unions, automatic cost-of-living adjustments, and rigid employment contracts limited firms' ability to adapt. Inflation fed wage increases, wage increases raised costs, and higher costs fed further inflation. At the same time, productivity growth slowed sharply after 1973, producing a structural squeeze of rising costs, stagnant output, and declining competitiveness.[19]

Regulatory rigidity further reduced resilience. Extensive controls in energy, transportation, and finance limited adaptive responses to shocks. The economic system that emerged in the 1970s was far less flexible than the one that had powered the postwar expansion. Keynesian tools, effective in a world of abundance, proved blunt and destabilizing in a world defined by scarcity, competition, and constraint.[20]

The speed with which Keynesian economics fell out of favor is itself diagnostic. Within a single decade, the dominant policy framework unraveled. If Keynesianism had been the true engine of postwar prosperity, it would not have collapsed so quickly when conditions changed. Its failure under stress reveals its true nature: a powerful but temporary corrective economic model, and not a durable foundation.[21] It addressed the most visible failure mode of capitalism—mass unemployment during demand collapse—but without correcting deeper incentive structures, institutional design flaws, or the dynamics introduced by scale.[22]

This realization opened the door to the Smithian revival. Monetarism, Austrian economics, supply-side theory, and ultimately neoliberal policy frameworks gained traction not because they were flawless but because Keynesianism had proven incapable of managing a mature, inflation-prone economy.[23] Reaganomics, Thatcherism, and the Washington Consensus reflected a search for discipline, flexibility, and growth in a world no longer defined by postwar abundance.

The deeper conclusion for Inclusive Capitalism is decisive. The Golden Age was not produced by Keynesian economics. It was produced by an era of extraordinary non-economic conditions—demographics, resources, global industrial dominance, and technological catch-up—that temporarily aligned with Keynesian tools.[24] When those conditions faded, the tools failed. Keynesian economics was essential in crisis, effective in triage, but incapable of sustaining long-term health.

That Keynesianism went out of fashion so rapidly is not an indictment of its usefulness in emergencies; it is an indictment of mistaking it for a sustainable system. The challenge ahead is not to oscillate endlessly between Keynesian intervention and laissez-faire retrenchment but to redesign capitalism itself so that shared prosperity does not depend on fleeting historical events.[25]

Economic Doctrines, Legal Framework, and Cultural Norms of the Smithian Revival

It is often said that a well-designed system operating within defined control limits produces predictable behavior and diagnosable failures. In engineering contexts, tolerance boundaries can be specified, deviations measured, and corrective action taken. Our economic system does not meet this standard. The transition from the Golden Age of American capitalism to the stagflation of the 1970s occurred with startling speed, despite continuity in population, culture, and resources. Within a decade, the United States moved from global industrial leadership to defensive retrenchment. As an illustration, the U.S. automotive industry, shaped by decades of domestic dominance and short-term financial incentives, proved ill-prepared to adapt to intensifying international competition, lacking the organizational capacity to pivot toward smaller, more fuel-efficient, and lower-cost vehicles. This was not an anomaly. The Great Depression less than fifty years earlier represented an equally abrupt collapse following the Roaring Twenties. Decades later, sophisticated financial engineering again drove the system off a cliff. These repeated discontinuities reveal an economy that is not in control. We have accumulated better emergency responses but not a system capable of preventing recurrent failure modes.

This instability has not gone unnoticed by economists. Dani Rodrik has been particularly influential in critiquing large-scale macroeconomic models that claim general validity. He argues that equilibrium-based frameworks—most notably Dynamic Stochastic General Equilibrium (DSGE) models—rest on unrealistic assumptions about rationality, efficiency, and institutional neutrality. As a result, these models tend to perform worst precisely where predictive power matters most: during periods of structural change, crisis, or institutional breakdown. The inability of such models to anticipate the 2008 financial crisis is a prominent example. Rodrik advocates a pluralist approach: a toolbox of context-specific models rather than a single universal framework.[26]

This critique reinforces a deeper point. If no coherent macro model can reliably diagnose or predict system-level behavior, the problem may not be the models alone but the system they attempt to represent. An economy governed by unstable incentives, misaligned metrics, and scale-amplified feedback loops cannot be rendered predictable through better mathematics alone. Unlike physical systems, where first principles are fixed, economic systems embed human incentives that can be redesigned. From the perspective of Inclusive Capitalism, this makes the problem solvable—but only by rethinking foundations rather than oscillating between doctrinal extremes.

The Smithian revival of the late twentieth century must be understood against this backdrop. The collapse of Keynesian confidence during the 1970s created an intellectual vacuum. Stagflation—simultaneous inflation and unemployment—directly contradicted the core Keynesian assumption of a stable tradeoff between the two.[27] Demand management no longer appeared either reliable or appropriate as a foundational tool of the system. At the same time, the Soviet Union's economic stagnation further weakened the credibility of state planning. Together, these failures set the stage for a dramatic shift in economic doctrine.

Neoclassical economics, often labeled neoliberalism, reasserted itself as the dominant framework in the 1980s and 1990s. It emphasized deregulation, privatization, free trade, capital mobility, and monetary discipline. This revival drew heavily on the intellectual foundations laid by Milton Friedman and the Austrian School, particularly Friedrich Hayek. Their arguments resonated not merely because they were elegant but because they spoke directly to the lived experience of policymakers and citizens confronting inflation, bureaucratic expansion, and perceived policy failure.[28]

Friedman argued that markets allocate resources more efficiently than political processes, and that government intervention often produces unintended consequences that outweigh its intended benefits. His monetarist framework reframed inflation as primarily a monetary phenomenon rather than a structural or distributive one, yielding a clear and actionable prescription: constrain money supply growth and limit discretionary fiscal activism.[29] For a public experiencing mortgage rates above 18 percent and a federal funds rate approaching 20 percent in the early 1980s, this message carried immediate resonance. His insistence that government act as referee rather than player appealed to a society fatigued by perceived policy overreach.

Hayek provided a deeper philosophical foundation for this revival. He argued that economic knowledge is inherently decentralized and that prices serve as information carriers that no central authority can fully aggregate or process. Even well-intentioned attempts to centrally manage complex economies would, in his view, distort these signals and erode individual freedom.[30] These warnings resonated strongly during the Cold War, as the limitations of centrally planned economies—most visibly in the Soviet Union—became increasingly apparent.

Together, Friedman and Hayek rearticulated Adam Smith's core insight: that economic coordination emerges from decentralized decision-making operating within appropriate rules.[31] Yet the neoliberal revival of this vision differed materially from the environment Smith had described. Early capitalism functioned in a world of smaller firms, localized markets, limited financialization, and modest scale effects. Neoliberal capitalism emerged under very different conditions—characterized by multinational corporations, global capital mobility, deep financial markets, and increasingly winner-take-most dynamics.

Neoliberalism assumed that removing constraints would restore market discipline but often underestimated how scale alters incentives. In early capitalism, the combination of proximity, reputation, and limited market power constrained behavior. In globalized markets, those disciplining forces weaken or disappear. Deregulation under such conditions does not simply free markets; it can amplify concentration, short-termism, and rent extraction unless offset by new forms of institutional design.[32]

The policy implementation of the Smithian revival reflected this tension. Reagan and Thatcher championed tax cuts, deregulation, and labor market flexibility. The Washington Consensus extended these principles globally through trade liberalization, privatization, and capital market openness. While these reforms succeeded in restoring growth and taming inflation in many contexts, they did not resolve the system's underlying instability. Financial crises, rising inequality, and renewed boom-bust cycles followed.

Even leading proponents acknowledged important limits. Thomas Sowell emphasized the informational role of prices and warned consistently against substituting political judgment for market signals, while stressing that incentives—not intentions—govern outcomes. Paul Samuelson, though associated with the Keynesian synthesis, ultimately acknowledged that unregulated markets tend toward instability and concentration rather than self-correcting equilibrium.

The Cold War amplified the appeal of the Smithian revival by framing economic organization as a lived contrast between freedom and control rather than an abstract policy debate. The division between East and West Germany offered a stark illustration of how institutional design shapes daily life. Centrally planned systems produced scarcity and constraint; market systems produced higher living standards and broader opportunity. The conclusion—that capitalism is the superior foundation—remains valid.

Yet the neoliberal variant that emerged in the late twentieth century did not resolve capitalism's underlying structural weaknesses; it displaced them. The Smithian revival restored confidence in markets as coordinating mechanisms, but it did not repair the incentive failures that emerge at scale. In effect, one stabilizing framework was replaced with another, rather than redesigning the system's core architecture.[33]

The task ahead is therefore not to abandon Smith, Friedman, or Hayek but to complete their project under modern conditions. That requires redesigning incentives, governance, and measurement so that markets generate sustained abundance without recurring crisis, concentration, or legitimacy loss.[34]

Industrial Leadership Incentives and Behaviors

As the United States entered the Smithian revival of the late twentieth century, industrial leadership effectively split into two broad classes. The first consisted of leaders presiding over traditional, capital-intensive industries—autos, steel, energy, consumer electronics, and heavy manufacturing—that had once been the backbone of American industrial dominance. The second was a new breed of entrepreneurs emerging from software, semiconductors, computing, and later the internet—industries where scale, capital structure, and labor dynamics were fundamentally different. This divergence in leadership behavior, incentives, and outcomes would prove decisive for America's economic trajectory.[35]

The first class—leaders of legacy industries—largely failed soon after global competition intensified. American automakers, steel producers, and consumer-electronics firms entered the 1970s and 1980s burdened by high cost structures, complacent product strategies, and incentive systems optimized for short-term financial performance rather than long-term competitiveness. Japanese and later South Korean manufacturers demonstrated superior quality, efficiency, and process innovation, yet U.S. incumbents responded slowly, defensively, and often politically rather than strategically. Rather than reinvesting aggressively in manufacturing innovation, supply-chain modernization, and workforce capability, many firms focused on financial engineering, share protection, and regulatory lobbying.[36]

In the automotive sector, leadership failures were especially visible. By the time fuel-efficient, high-quality imports gained traction, Detroit had already locked itself into a cycle of adversarial labor relations, bloated model lines, and incremental product updates. Executives frequently blamed unions, regulation, and foreign trade practices while underinvesting in quality systems and platform redesign. Later figures such as Bill Ford Jr. openly acknowledged that American automakers had been slow to adapt, yet meaningful transformation often came only after existential crisis—bankruptcy threats, government bailouts, or forced restructurings. Similar patterns played out in steel, consumer electronics, and energy-equipment manufacturing. In many cases, leadership behavior reflected a deeper incentive failure: compensation, promotion, and prestige were tied to market share defense and near-term financial metrics rather than technological reinvention.[37]

Public policymakers were, at best, passive enablers of this stagnation and, at worst, complicit. Trade protections, subsidies, and regulatory accommodations were frequently used to delay adjustment rather than accelerate renewal. Instead of forcing competitive reinvestment, policy often insulated incumbents from consequences, reinforcing managerial complacency. The result was not merely industrial decline but a slow erosion of national capability in sectors once considered strategically vital.

In sharp contrast, the second class of industrial leaders—those driving the emerging technology economy—responded to the same Smithian revival with radically different behavior. Entrepreneurs in software, computing, and later networking and internet services operated in environments where legacy assets were minimal, capital requirements were lower, and global reach was immediate. These leaders were not defending incumbents; they were creating entirely new markets. Figures such as Bill Gates exemplified this new model. Rather than lobbying for protection, Gates and his peers competed relentlessly on innovation, scale, and platform dominance. Their incentives rewarded speed, ecosystem control, and reinvestment in technical talent.

This second group effectively rescued American global leadership—not through traditional manufacturing strength but through control of the digital stack. Software, operating systems, semiconductors, and later cloud infrastructure became the new levers of power. Productivity gains shifted from factory floors to codebases. Value creation moved from physical throughput to intellectual property and network effects.

These leaders embraced globalization rather than fearing it, leveraging global supply chains while anchoring strategic control domestically.[38]

Yet even here, the seeds of future problems were planted. While the new technology leaders were far more innovative and globally competitive, they too operated under incentive systems that concentrated power, rewarded winner-take-most outcomes, and often elevated individual "hero" founders rather than durable institutional governance. The system celebrated kings of industry even as it nominally rejected kings in government.[39]

Taken together, these two leadership classes illustrate a central thesis for Inclusive Capitalism. The failure of traditional industrial leaders was not inevitable; it was the predictable outcome of incentive structures that rewarded preservation over reinvention. The success of technology leaders was not purely meritocratic; it was enabled by structural conditions that allowed innovation to scale rapidly with limited friction. In both cases, outcomes were shaped less by ideology than by incentives and governance design. Understanding this split is essential before examining individual profiles—because it clarifies that leadership behavior is not a matter of character alone but of the systems that reward or punish specific choices.[40]

Roger Smith (1925–2007) stands as a defining figure of the first class of industrial leaders during the Smithian revival: executives who inherited vast, mature enterprises built for a different era and struggled to adapt them to global competition, technological change, and shifting incentive structures. Smith served as Chairman and CEO of General Motors from 1981 to 1990, precisely when the American automotive industry began losing its long-held dominance.[41]

Smith understood that General Motors faced profound structural challenges. Japanese automakers had surpassed GM on quality, cost efficiency, and reliability. Fuel shocks had exposed the firm's dependence on large, inefficient vehicles. Labor costs were high, product cycles were slow, and coordination across GM's sprawling divisions was weak. Smith did not deny these realities; he diagnosed them clearly. His response was ambitious: to remake GM into a technologically sophisticated, globally competitive manufacturer through automation, financial discipline, and structural reform.[42]

The centerpiece of Smith's strategy was automation. He believed robotics and computer-integrated manufacturing would restore competitiveness by reducing labor dependence and improving consistency. Under his leadership, GM invested tens of billions of dollars in factory automation—often before the technology was mature enough to deliver promised gains. The acquisition of Electronic Data Systems (EDS) and Hughes Aircraft symbolized Smith's conviction that information systems and advanced engineering would define manufacturing's future. In practice, however, GM attempted to graft advanced technology onto an organizational culture and incentive system that remained misaligned with product quality and long-term innovation.[43]

Smith also pursued financial restructuring, emphasizing capital allocation discipline and investment return metrics more than product excellence or customer experience. This shift reflected a broader transformation in American corporate governance during the 1980s, as shareholder value and financial performance displaced long-term industrial craftsmanship as dominant objectives.[44] GM became more adept at managing balance sheets than producing world-class vehicles, and innovation was discussed more often than it was structurally rewarded.

Labor relations under Smith further illustrate the incentive failure. While not overtly hostile to unions, management continued to treat labor primarily as a cost center rather than a strategic asset. The adversarial relationship with the United Auto Workers persisted even as Japanese competitors demonstrated the productivity benefits of cooperative labor-management models. GM's incentive structure rewarded short-term cost containment over workforce capability development, reinforcing stagnation rather than renewal.[45]

Perhaps most telling is that Smith's failures were not rooted in ignorance or bad faith. He was widely regarded as one of the most intelligent executives of his generation. Yet he operated within a governance framework that concentrated authority without sufficient feedback, rewarded financial engineering over industrial excellence, and limited strategic adaptability. GM's board structure, internal silos, and legacy obligations constrained reform. Smith possessed authority but lacked institutional mechanisms to realign incentives at scale.

By the end of his tenure, General Motors was weaker, not stronger. Market share eroded, product quality lagged, and automation investments failed to deliver anticipated productivity gains. The firm survived only to require government intervention decades later. The conditions that made future bailouts necessary were established during this period.[46]

From the perspective of Inclusive Capitalism, Roger Smith is a cautionary figure rather than a villain. He exemplifies what happens when leadership is evaluated primarily through financial metrics within institutions designed for a different era. He had intelligence, authority, and resources—but lacked a system that aligned long-term innovation, workforce engagement, and societal value creation. His tenure illustrates why hero-centric leadership in legacy institutions is fragile and why scale without properly designed incentives magnifies failure rather than success.[47]

James McNerney represents a later, more financially sophisticated incarnation of this same leadership class. Serving as Chairman and CEO of Boeing from 2005 to 2015, after senior roles at General Electric and 3M, McNerney embodied the managerial orthodoxy that emerged from the Smithian revival: operational discipline, financial rigor, and shareholder primacy.[48]

McNerney brought GE's metrics-driven management culture to one of the most technologically complex and safety-critical industries in the world. His mandate was to improve margins, stabilize cash flows, and restore investor confidence. In the short run, these objectives were met. Boeing's share price rose, costs were constrained, and financial performance improved.[49]

Beneath the surface, however, Boeing's incentive structure shifted away from engineering excellence and long-term system integrity toward near-term financial performance. Design authority fragmented, production schedules increasingly overrode engineering judgment, and risk was pushed outward to suppliers. These changes did not immediately cause failure, but they altered the organization's internal balance in ways that would later prove costly.[50]

The aggressive outsourcing strategy behind the 787 Dreamliner illustrates the pattern. Large portions of design and manufacturing were delegated to global partners to reduce costs and accelerate development. Instead, coordination failures, delays, and cost overruns followed, weakening Boeing's internal engineering capability and institutional coherence.[51]

As with Roger Smith, McNerney's leadership was rational within the incentive framework he inherited. Boards rewarded financial performance; markets rewarded margin expansion. Under those conditions, prioritizing short-term metrics over institutional resilience was predictable. The deeper lesson is not individual failure but systemic design failure—one that Inclusive Capitalism seeks to address directly.[52]

From the perspective of Inclusive Capitalism, McNerney illustrates why scale fundamentally changes the rules. In earlier eras, managerial mistakes were constrained by proximity, transparency, and feedback. In global, capital-intensive systems, the lag between decision and consequence can span years, allowing misaligned incentives to persist long after damage is locked in. Leadership accountability becomes opaque and diluted, while risk accumulates silently.[53]

McNerney's tenure did not cause Boeing's later crises outright, but it laid critical groundwork. By prioritizing shareholder returns, outsourcing core competencies, and subordinating engineering culture to financial logic, Boeing became vulnerable. When shocks eventually arrived, the organization lacked the internal coherence, talent, and trust required to respond effectively.[54]

As with Roger Smith, the lesson is not that a different hero would have saved the enterprise. It is that hero-centric leadership operating within misaligned governance structures is insufficient at scale. Inclusive Capitalism argues that institutions like Boeing must be re-chartered so that long-term system integrity, workforce capability, and societal responsibility are rewarded structurally—not habitually left to the discretion or virtue of individual executives.

With this pattern established, the chapter can now pivot to a contrasting class of leaders—those who built new institutions around emerging technologies. Figures like Bill Gates, John Chambers, and Ken Olsen operated in environments where incentive alignment, innovation velocity, and institutional design initially reinforced one another. Their stories illuminate not only what went right—but why it proved so difficult to sustain under the prevailing economic architecture.

Bill Gates represents the archetype of the second class of industrial leaders that emerged during the Smithian revival: founders operating in fundamentally new technological domains, unconstrained by legacy capital structures, and driven by platform-level ambition rather than incremental optimization. Gates co-founded Microsoft in 1975 with a singular vision—to make software the central organizing layer of the emerging personal computing ecosystem.[55] His strategic insight was that value would migrate away from hardware and toward operating systems and applications that could scale across machines, users, and industries. This vision materialized most clearly in Microsoft Windows and the Office Suite, which became the de facto standards for personal and enterprise computing and, in doing so, helped define the information age.[56]

Gates' primary contribution was not inventing software per se but industrializing it. He recognized that software, unlike physical goods, could be replicated at near-zero marginal cost once developed, creating extraordinary scale advantages for first movers who controlled standards. Microsoft's licensing model—selling software to Original Equipment Manufacturers (OEMs) rather than end users—allowed it to embed itself deeply into the global Personal Computer supply chains. This was Smithian capitalism at its most powerful: competition, scale, intellectual property, and network effects reinforcing one another to create unprecedented value creation. Under Gates' leadership, Microsoft became one of the most valuable companies in the world and a central pillar of U.S. technological dominance at a moment when traditional manufacturing industries were losing ground.[57]

Gates himself embodied the incentive structure of this era. He was famously intense, intellectually dominant, and relentlessly competitive. He worked extraordinary hours, absorbed vast quantities of technical and strategic information, and expected the same from those around him. Microsoft's internal culture was widely described as high-pressure and unforgiving, particularly for engineers. Performance mattered more than harmony, and dissent—especially when it challenged Gates' technical judgment—often carried career consequences. Yet this culture was not accidental; it was well aligned with the task at hand. Building platform software in a fast-moving, winner-take-most environment rewarded speed, decisiveness, and intellectual rigor far more than consensus or compassion. Many employees became extraordinarily wealthy through stock options, reinforcing the performance-driven ethos and tying individual incentives tightly to company success.[58]

At the same time, Microsoft's dominance exposed the darker side of scale-driven capitalism. By the late 1990s, the company's control over operating systems attracted intense antitrust scrutiny. The U.S. government argued that Microsoft had abused its market power—most notably by bundling Internet Explorer with Windows—to suppress competition.[59] These legal battles forced Microsoft to modify its business practices and marked a rare moment when the state directly confronted a technology platform at global scale. Importantly, the antitrust case did not arise from malicious intent but from a system that rewarded platform control without built-in constraints. Gates played the game as it was designed; the system simply lacked guardrails for its own success.[60]

Strategically, Gates also experienced the limits of dominance. The rise of the internet initially caught Microsoft off guard, allowing competitors such as Netscape—and later Google and AWS—to establish new centers of gravity in search, advertising, and cloud services.[61] This episode illustrates a recurring pattern in capitalist systems: Even the most formidable incumbents can misread inflection points when incentives favor defending existing rents over embracing disruptive shifts. Microsoft adapted eventually, but the episode underscores how incentive structures shape attention and risk tolerance at the top.

Gates' later transition into full-time philanthropy adds an important dimension to his profile. Through the Bill & Melinda Gates Foundation, he redirected his analytical rigor and capital toward global health, education, and poverty reduction. In many ways, this phase of his life represents a second attempt at systems design—applying metrics, incentives, and scale to problems markets do not naturally solve. Yet it also highlights a structural failure: Societal well-being remained something to be addressed after wealth creation, rather than embedded within the productive economic system itself.

From the perspective of Inclusive Capitalism, Gates is neither hero nor villain. He is a proof point. His success demonstrates what happens when incentives are tightly aligned with innovation, scale, and long-term platform thinking. His excesses—market dominance, cultural harshness, and post hoc philanthropy—demonstrate what happens when those same incentives lack balancing mechanisms. Inclusive Capitalism seeks not to blunt figures like Gates but to design institutional frameworks that preserve their capacity to build transformative systems while embedding accountability, succession, and societal alignment directly into corporate governance—so that extraordinary talent serves not only markets but society by design rather than correction.

John Chambers embodies the second class of industrial leadership that emerged during the Smithian revival: technology-driven builders who constructed entirely new economic infrastructure as opposed to those trying to defend legacy industries. As CEO of Cisco Systems from 1995 to 2015, Chambers pursued a singular and historically consequential mission—to build the backbone of the internet age. Under his leadership, Cisco became the dominant provider of networking hardware and software enabling high-speed data transmission across enterprises, governments, and institutions worldwide. Few individual executives have shaped the physical and logical interconnected communications architecture of the modern digital economy as directly as Chambers.[62]

Chambers' core insight was that networking—not computing alone—would define the next phase of economic growth. While much of the technology sector focused on personal computers and software applications, Chambers recognized that scalable, standardized connectivity would be the true multiplier. Cisco's routers and switches, built around open standards such as TCP/IP, became the ubiquitous digital plumbing of the global economy. This infrastructure allowed data, capital, ideas, and services to move at unprecedented speed, fundamentally reshaping commerce, communication, and organizational design. In this sense, Chambers did not merely ride the internet boom—he helped make it operational.[63]

Cisco's rise was fueled by an aggressive and unusually disciplined acquisition strategy. Under Chambers, Cisco completed more than 170 acquisitions, often purchasing small, innovative firms and rapidly integrating their technologies into Cisco's platform or expand a product line.[64] This approach allowed Cisco to stay at the technological frontier while avoiding the internal inertia that often afflicts large enterprises. Acquisitions were not singularly speculative; they were tightly aligned with Cisco's strategic roadmap. The result was sustained dominance across multiple networking layers, from core wide area infrastructure to localized enterprise level networks.

The dot-com boom of the late 1990s elevated Chambers to near-mythic status. At its peak in 2000, Cisco briefly became the most valuable company in the world. When the bubble burst, Cisco market capitalization went into a freefall within months. Chambers' response to the crash revealed a defining feature of his leadership. Rather than denying reality or doubling down on failed assumptions, he executed rapid restructuring, absorbed losses, and reset expectations. While painful—including large layoffs—the response preserved Cisco's sector dominance and long-term viability. Unlike many dot-com era firms, Cisco survived and remains central to global networking.

Culturally, Chambers stood in sharp contrast to many leaders of the first industrial class reviewed earlier in this chapter. He placed unusual emphasis on employee engagement, communication, and trust. Chambers was known for regularly meeting with teams at all levels, listening to concerns, and fostering a sense of shared mission. Cisco consistently ranked as one of the best places to work during his tenure. This was not incidental. Chambers understood that in a knowledge-intensive, fast-moving industry, human capital was the primary scarce resource. Treating employees as disposable inputs would have undermined the very innovation engine on which Cisco depended.

At the same time, Chambers was unapologetically competitive. Cisco defended its market position aggressively, and took on hundreds of formidable competitors including equally aggressive technology innovators such as Juniper Networks and Huawei. As the industry evolved toward cloud computing and software-defined networking, Cisco struggled at times to pivot away from its hardware-centric model. These challenges highlight a recurring theme of this book: Even exemplary leadership operating within successful incentive structures can be constrained by institutional momentum and legacy architectures. Cisco adapted but not without friction.

From the perspective of Inclusive Capitalism, Chambers' tenure offers several critical insights. First, new industries provide a temporary window in which incentives naturally align with innovation, workforce investment, and long-term value creation. During periods of technological expansion and exponential commercial growth, abundance masks structural weaknesses. Second, even highly capable leaders remain subject to the incentive frameworks of capital markets. Cisco's acquisition-driven growth and market dominance were rewarded handsomely by investors, reinforcing scale and concentration dynamics that later became sources of vulnerability.[65]

Most importantly, Chambers illustrates that leadership quality alone is insufficient to guarantee durable societal benefit. While Cisco's technologies enabled extraordinary productivity gains and global connectivity, the broader system failed to ensure that those gains translated inclusively across society. The same networks that empowered innovation also facilitated labor arbitrage, capital concentration, and winner-take-all dynamics in adjacent sectors. These outcomes were not the result of malicious intent but of system design that rewarded scale without embedding countervailing obligations.

John Chambers' legacy is therefore twofold. He stands as one of the most effective builders of modern economic infrastructure, a central figure in making the internet commercially and institutionally viable. At the same time, his career underscores the limits of even enlightened industrial leadership within an economic architecture that prioritizes growth, dominance, and shareholder value over long-term societal alignment.

As this chapter progresses from profiles of Bill Gates to that of Ken Olsen, the contrast will sharpen further. Together, these leaders reveal both the extraordinary creative power of Smithian capitalism during periods of technological expansion and the necessity of re-architecting governance and incentives if that power is to remain inclusive, resilient, and socially constructive over time.[66]

Ken Olsen (1926–2011) occupies a uniquely instructive position in the history of American capitalism. He was both a builder of one of the most innovative technology companies of the twentieth century and, ultimately, a principal architect of its collapse. As founder and long-time CEO of Digital Equipment Corporation (DEC), Olsen helped democratize computing decades before the personal computer revolution—yet his decisions later accelerated DEC's decline with remarkable speed. Olsen therefore represents a hybrid of the two leadership classes introduced earlier: visionary infrastructure builder and, later, incumbent leader unable to adapt when scale and technology shifted beneath him.

Olsen founded DEC in 1957 with a mission that was genuinely transformational for its time: to make computing affordable, interactive, and accessible to engineers, scientists, and businesses that could not afford IBM mainframes. DEC's PDP and VAX minicomputers reshaped how organizations used computing. Instead of submitting batch jobs to centralized IT departments, engineers could interact directly with machines in real time. This shift empowered innovation across science, manufacturing, and academia. By the late 1970s and 1980s, DEC was second only to IBM in computing, employing over 120,000 people and generating tens of billions in revenue.

DEC was not merely a hardware company. It pioneered technologies that underpin modern computing: clustering, distributed systems, advanced operating systems (VMS), Ethernet, and peer-to-peer networking architectures. Engineers revered Olsen, and DEC cultivated a collaborative, engineering-driven culture with high compensation, generous benefits, and intellectual autonomy. Olsen himself lived modestly, avoided ostentation, and was guided by a strong moral and religious framework. He believed deeply that technology should serve human progress rather than personal enrichment.

Yet the same conviction that made Olsen a great builder also made him dangerously inflexible. As computing shifted from centralized and departmental systems to personal computers and workstations, Olsen dismissed the PC as a "toy" and framed it as a threat to serious computing rather than its next evolutionary step in computing. Rather than embracing decentralization, he attempted to reassert architectural control. One example was "VAXmate," which repositioned the PC as an intelligent terminal dependent on centralized VAX systems. Customers rejected the concept almost viscerally. What users wanted was autonomy, not managed dependence.

More consequential were Olsen's strategic technology decisions. DEC ceded key software—DEC's MICA platform, now known as Windows Server—to Microsoft, enabling a competitor to dominate enterprise software. Instead, DEC committed enormous capital to wafer-scale integration, a technically ambitious but commercially disastrous bet. At the networking layer, Olsen championed the CLNP protocol rather than TCP/IP, placing DEC on the wrong side of the internet's eventual standardization. Each of these choices reflected technical sophistication divorced from market reality.[67]

Crucially, DEC's governance structure amplified Olsen's blind spots. His authority was effectively unchecked. There were no institutional mechanisms to force strategic correction when evidence mounted that the industry had moved on. Engineers knew the internet mattered. Customers made their preferences clear. Yet the company remained captive to its founder's mental model. Within less than a decade, DEC went from industry icon to acquisition target, sold to Compaq in 1998 for less than its cash reserves on hand.

From the perspective of Inclusive Capitalism, the lesson is not that Olsen lacked intelligence, integrity, or work ethic—he possessed all three in abundance. The failure was structural. DEC depended too heavily on heroic leadership without adequate counterweights. The system allowed one individual's outdated assumptions to override distributed intelligence across the organization. Risk and reward were not sufficiently shared. Power did not rotate. Feedback loops were weak.

Olsen's story highlights a core design challenge for modern capitalism: how to preserve visionary leadership while preventing catastrophic entrenchment. We want leaders with Olsen's technical depth and moral seriousness. We do not want systems in which a single leader's misalignment can destroy decades of accumulated human capital, technological progress, and public value. This is not a question of personality; it is a question of architecture.

The broader context reinforces this point. By the late twentieth century, management science had matured. Best practices were widely documented. Executive education proliferated. The most egregious abuses of earlier capitalism—industrial violence, lethal working conditions, total disregard for labor—had largely disappeared. Basic management hygiene was in place. And yet the same incentive structures persisted: winner-take-all outcomes, capital concentration, and vulnerability to leadership failure at scale.

Ken Olsen's rise and fall therefore stands as one of the clearest case studies in why Inclusive Capitalism must move beyond hero-centric governance. The solution lies not in weakening leadership but in redesigning corporate charters, incentive systems, and accountability structures so that innovation survives leadership error, adapts to technological discontinuity, and continues to serve both enterprise and society long after any single founder's vision has run its course.

Lived Experience of the Workforce during the Smithian Revival

The lived experience of the workforce during the Smithian revival diverged sharply along two paths, mirroring the bifurcation in industrial leadership examined earlier. On one side were workers who benefited enormously from the technological revolution—software engineers, financiers, senior managers, and globally mobile professionals whose skills scaled with capital and networks. On the other side were workers in traditional industries and mid-skill roles who faced job losses, wage stagnation, declining security, and an erosion of dignity. This was not a temporary dislocation but a structural shift. As the economy liberalized, globalized, and digitized, the postwar middle class—once the backbone of shared prosperity—began to thin and fragment.[68] Economist Dani Rodrik has emphasized that a broad, stable middle class is not merely a social outcome but a prerequisite for durable economic and political stability.[69] During the Smithian revival, however, the economy increasingly took on a "K-shaped" trajectory: where those at the top of the skills, capital, and network distribution saw accelerating gains, while those below experienced stagnation or decline. The result was not mass immiseration of the Gilded Age variety but something just as insidious. Material deprivation increasingly manifested as unaffordability—of housing, education, healthcare—and as a loss of status, agency, and dignity rather than outright physical hardship. The brutality of early capitalism was replaced by insecurity and exclusion.[70]

The technological leaders of this era created an entirely new class of work—highly paid, intellectually engaging, and scalable. For these workers, the Smithian revival delivered extraordinary opportunity. Stock options, rapid career mobility, and global demand for technical expertise transformed a minority of the workforce into participants in unprecedented wealth creation. At the same time, globalization and deregulation exposed large segments of the labor force to international competition and automation, as the conditions of the Golden Age rapidly dissipated.

From roughly 1970 to 2010, this transformation reshaped not only wages and job security but the meaning of work itself. Under the postwar model, work conferred identity, stability, and social standing. Under the neoclassical model, work increasingly became transactional and precarious for those outside the technological elite. Productivity continued to rise, yet median wages stagnated. Benefits shifted from those provided by employers to the responsibility of individuals. Risk migrated downward. The decline of unions removed a key institutional buffer, while the retreat of government from labor market stabilization and financial market governance compounded exposure to shocks—most visibly in 2008.

Critically, this outcome was not the result of malice or neglect by technological leaders. On the contrary, many genuinely believed they were building tools that liberated humans from drudgery—and they were right. The tragedy lies in the system's inability to translate technological abundance into shared prosperity. The liberation of workers from low-value, repetitive labor should have been a societal gift. Instead, under existing rules, it often became a pathway to underemployment, downward mobility, or permanent exclusion. The parallels to earlier capitalist transitions—such as the displacement of skilled artisans during industrial mechanization—are unmistakable, even if the surface conditions differ.[71]

This tension becomes more acute as artificial intelligence accelerates these trends. Tasks once considered safely "middle skill"—software development, analysis, management—are increasingly automatable. Under current incentive structures, AI threatens to further concentrate opportunity among a narrow elite while expanding the ranks of those whose labor is undervalued or unnecessary. The challenge is not technological; it is institutional. The core question is not whether society can produce abundance but whether it can distribute dignity in a world of labor non-scarcity.

Inclusive Capitalism begins precisely here. If work is no longer scarce, dignity must not depend exclusively on employment. The Smithian revival demonstrated that markets excel at innovation but are indifferent to distribution and status. Without redesigned incentives and institutions, the same dynamics that once produced slums and factory abuse now produce unaffordability, anxiety, and social fragmentation. The task ahead is not to resist technology, nor to retreat into nostalgia for mid-century labor markets, but to re-architect the economic system so that the gains from abundance—whether generated by globalization, software, or AI—are shared in ways that preserve agency, purpose, and human dignity.[72]

Where we go next depends on whether we treat this bifurcation as an unavoidable feature of modern capitalism or as a design failure that can be corrected. That question—and the answer proposed by Inclusive Capitalism—becomes unavoidable as we move deeper into an economy defined not by scarcity of production but by scarcity of inclusion.

What Worked and What Did Not During the Smithian Revival

The Smithian revival delivered a powerful demonstration of capitalism's strengths when constraints are lifted and incentives are sharply aligned toward efficiency, innovation, and capital formation. From the late 1970s through the early 2000s, market-oriented reforms unleashed an extraordinary wave of technological progress, particularly in computing, networking, biotechnology, and finance. Deregulation, privatization, and tax reform lowered barriers to entry and rewarded entrepreneurial risk-taking. Capital flowed more freely, markets integrated globally, and firms scaled at unprecedented rates. Few periods in history produced comparable advances in productivity-enhancing technologies or created so many entirely new industries in such a short span of time.

The rise of Silicon Valley exemplified what worked best under the Smithian revival. Firms such as Microsoft, Intel, Cisco, and later Google and Amazon thrived in an environment that rewarded speed, experimentation, and aggressive competition. High-skilled workers captured enormous gains, both financially and professionally, as technology-intensive jobs proliferated. Global trade expanded rapidly, lowering consumer prices and increasing product variety. Financial markets deepened and broadened, enabling households to participate indirectly in wealth creation through pensions, equity-linked savings, and investment vehicles tied to capital markets. For those positioned on the right side of the technological frontier, the system worked extraordinarily well.[73]

At the same time, the revival exposed—and amplified—capitalism's long-standing structural weaknesses. The same forces that accelerated innovation also intensified inequality, volatility, and geographic divergence. While productivity rose sharply, wage growth for the median worker stagnated. Manufacturing employment collapsed as firms optimized globally, hollowing out industrial regions and eroding the economic foundation of the middle class. Labor institutions weakened, job security declined, and risk shifted decisively from firms to individuals. The economy became more efficient in aggregate but far less inclusive in distribution.

This bifurcation was not incidental; it was systemic. Capital and high-skill labor benefited from scale, mobility, and compounding returns, while routine labor faced substitution, offshoring, and declining bargaining power. As Dani Rodrik and others have noted, the erosion of the middle class undermines both social cohesion and long-term political stability.[74] Human dignity suffered not through overt exploitation, as in earlier eras, but through unaffordability, precarity, and the quiet loss of economic agency. The economy increasingly resembled a K-shaped distribution of outcomes, even as headline growth metrics remained strong.

The revival also revealed the limits of deregulation in finance. Confidence in market self-regulation, reinforced by sophisticated quantitative models, led to the systematic removal of post-Depression safeguards. Financial innovation outpaced institutional understanding and oversight. Leverage increased, opacity deepened, and short-term profit incentives dominated risk management. When the housing bubble burst, losses cascaded across a tightly coupled global system. The crisis of 2008 did not end the Smithian revival, but it revealed a core vulnerability—a system engineered for speed and returns but structurally fragile when operating at scale.

Importantly, the response to 2008 demonstrated that the policy toolkit had evolved since the 1930s. Aggressive monetary intervention and emergency fiscal measures prevented a possible full-scale depression. However, these responses were largely improvised, symptom-focused, and politically destabilizing. They treated collapse, not cause. The underlying incentive structures—short-termism, financialization, and the primacy of money as the sole metric of success—remained intact.

In sum, the Smithian revival revealed both the power and the limits of unrestrained capitalism. It reaffirmed that markets are unparalleled engines of innovation, coordination, and value creation. At the same time, it demonstrated that without redesigned institutions, those gains tend to concentrate, generate instability, and ultimately erode the system's legitimacy. The period did not falter because markets were allowed to function but because scale fundamentally transformed their effects—and the incentive structures governing behavior were never recalibrated to operate coherently at that scale.

The central lesson for Inclusive Capitalism is therefore not to reject the Smithian revival but to complete it. Innovation, competition, and entrepreneurship must be preserved. What must change are the governing architectures that determine how success is measured, how risk is shared, and how gains are distributed. The crisis of 2008 was not an endpoint but a warning. Without system-level redesign, the same dynamics will recur—likely faster, larger, and with higher stakes.

Forces That Result in the Decline and Transition from the Smithian Revival

The reemergence of laissez-faire, Smithian capitalism in the late twentieth century was neither irrational nor accidental. It arose as a reaction to the visible failures of Keynesian demand management in the 1970s and restored dynamism to economies that had become sclerotic, overregulated, and inflation-prone. For a time, it appeared to work. Growth resumed, innovation accelerated, and capital markets expanded rapidly. Yet by 2008, it had become clear that the second great experiment in unconstrained Smithian capitalism was reaching its own breaking point. As with earlier epochs, the boom carried within it the seeds of its collapse.

The Great Recession of 2008 stands as the unmistakable endpoint of the Smithian revival. Like the Great Depression, it followed a prolonged period of excess—this time characterized not by industrial overcapacity but by financial leverage, regulatory arbitrage, and speculative asset inflation. Highly leveraged financial institutions, opaque derivatives, and interconnected global markets created a system that appeared robust in normal times but proved catastrophically fragile under stress. When the U.S. housing bubble burst, securities built on increasingly fragile subprime residential mortgages collapsed in value. Because risk had been widely distributed but poorly understood, losses cascaded rapidly across institutions and borders.

What began as a U.S. subprime mortgage crisis quickly became a global financial panic. The failure of Lehman Brothers in September 2008 exposed the illusion that market discipline alone could ensure systemic stability. It became evident that the largest financial institutions had not managed risk as free-market theory assumed they would. In testimony before Congress, former Federal Reserve Chairman Alan Greenspan acknowledged a fundamental error in his worldview. He conceded that he had "found a flaw in the model" that assumed firms, acting in their own self-interest, would reliably protect shareholders and maintain adequate safeguards. Instead, competitive pressure and short-term-oriented returns had driven a race to the bottom in lending standards and risk management. Self-interest, at scale, had not produced prudence—it had produced fragility.[75]

The response to the crisis further underscored the limits of the Smithian revival. Governments and central banks intervened on an unprecedented scale, deploying tools that had not existed—or had not been politically acceptable—during earlier crises. Massive liquidity injections, emergency lending facilities, bank recapitalizations, and quantitative easing stabilized the system and prevented a second Great Depression. Yet much of this response was improvised. Policies were developed under extreme uncertainty, often justified ex post rather than grounded in settled theory. The crisis revealed not only the failure of market self-regulation but also the absence of a coherent framework for governing a financial system that had grown vastly more complex, interconnected, and leveraged than its nineteenth-century antecedent.

The decline of the Smithian revival was not confined to advanced economies. The failure of the Washington Consensus played a parallel role on the global stage.[76] While market liberalization, privatization, and fiscal discipline delivered benefits in some contexts, their application as a near-universal prescription proved deeply destabilizing in others. In Russia, rapid privatization without institutional foundations produced oligarchic concentration rather than competitive markets. In much of Latin America, liberalization was accompanied by volatility, inequality, and social backlash.[77] Venezuela represents an extreme case, where the collapse of market credibility paved the way for authoritarian populism and economic disintegration. These outcomes undermined the legitimacy of the Smithian revival not only as an economic doctrine but as a credible long-term development model capable of delivering stability and broad-based prosperity.

In the aftermath of 2008, advanced economies did not return fully to Keynesianism, nor did they double down on laissez-faire orthodoxy. Instead, they settled into a renewed version of the neoclassical consensus—a pragmatic, technocratic balancing act that relies on ongoing corrective intervention to offset known defects in the system. Monetary policy became the primary stabilizing tool, with fiscal policy playing a secondary and often politically constrained role. The result has been a form of managed instability: economic cycles appear somewhat dampened but at the cost of ever-greater intervention, complexity, expanding balance sheets, and reliance on expert discretion.[78]

While economic volatility may have been partially contained, other forms of instability have intensified. Societal divides have widened. Wealth and opportunity have become increasingly concentrated. Political extremism has risen across many advanced democracies. Trust in institutions has eroded, and a pervasive sense of systemic risk has taken hold. The neoclassical consensus now rests on a tenuous foundation—a system that acknowledges its own structural flaws but addresses them through continuous patching rather than redesign.

This is the central lesson of the Smithian revival's decline. The problem was not simply excessive deregulation, flawed models, or insufficient oversight. It was the assumption that a system designed for smaller-scale, slower-moving economies could be indefinitely extended to a global, financialized, and technologically accelerated world without fundamental redesign. The neoclassical consensus, like Keynesianism before it, functions as a stabilizing overlay atop a system with known defects. It mitigates symptoms, but it does not resolve root causes or eliminate recurring risks.

The result is a prolonged state of economic and social imbalance—less dramatic than the collapses of the past but potentially more corrosive in its long-term effects. Correcting this condition requires more than oscillating between policy regimes. It requires rethinking the architecture of the system itself: how incentives are structured, how risk and reward are shared, how institutions scale, and how societal well-being is embedded into the core logic and metrics of economic production. That is the task Inclusive Capitalism takes up next.[79]

Conclusions and Insights for Inclusive Capitalism

Our review of capitalism is now complete. From its early industrial origins through the Great Recession of 2008, the historical record reveals a system of extraordinary power coupled with equally extraordinary fragility. No other economic system has matched capitalism's capacity to accelerate innovation, generate wealth, extend life expectancy, and raise material living standards across large populations. Yet no other system has so consistently produced recurring instability, widening inequality, and periodic social fracture when allowed to operate at scale without structural correction.[80]

Capitalism's achievements are not in dispute. Since the Industrial Revolution, market-based systems have multiplied global output, lifted billions from extreme poverty, and enabled technological advances that reshaped human life. The market mechanism, secure property rights, competition, and entrepreneurial dynamism remain the most effective tools ever developed for coordinating scarce resources and harnessing human creativity. As economists from Adam Smith to Paul Samuelson and Friedrich Hayek observed, no centralized authority can replicate the information-processing capacity of markets operating through incentives and voluntary exchange.[81]

But the historical record also makes clear that capitalism does not naturally produce fairness, stability, or shared prosperity. Left unchecked, Smithian dynamics tend toward concentration, extraction, and boom–bust cycles—especially as institutions scale beyond local markets into national and global systems. The invisible hand that Adam Smith envisioned as a moderating force functions well in small, competitive environments; at scale, however, it often mutates into an extractive claw. This outcome is not primarily a moral failure of industrial leaders but a predictable consequence of misaligned incentives operating within large, complex systems.

The great divide in capitalist economic thought over the past century—between laissez-faire Smithian capitalism and Keynesian interventionism—reflects competing attempts to manage these unintended consequences. The laissez-faire camp placed its faith in long-run self-correction, often underestimating the human cost of waiting. The Keynesian camp sought to smooth cycles and stabilize employment through fiscal and monetary intervention, achieving success at correcting major market failures, while failing to address the conditions that manifested in the 1970s. Both approaches ultimately treated symptoms rather than root causes; one relied too heavily on markets correcting themselves, the other relied too heavily on governments reacting after failures had already manifested.

The Golden Age of American capitalism stands as a critical proof point. It demonstrated that when abundance—driven by favorable non-economic conditions—coincides with institutional support, societies can achieve broad-based prosperity. Rising productivity translated into rising wages; growth was broadly shared; dignity at work became the norm rather than the exception. Yet that success was contingent, not structural. It depended on time-bounded and unique conditions—demographics, geopolitical dominance, resource abundance, and technological tailwinds—that could not and did not persist. When those conditions faded, the underlying design flaws of the system reasserted themselves.

The Smithian revival of the late twentieth century restored many of capitalism's dynamic strengths but also reintroduced its familiar pathologies. Deregulation, globalization, and financialization reignited innovation and growth, particularly in technology-driven sectors. At the same time, they hastened the hollowing out of the middle class, weakened labor's bargaining position, and re-concentrated economic power. The Great Recession of 2008 exposed the limits of faith in self-regulating markets once again. Even the most ardent defenders of market efficiency, including senior policymakers, conceded that prevailing models had failed to account for systemic risk and incentive-driven excess.

The central insight for Inclusive Capitalism is therefore not that capitalism failed—but that it succeeded exactly as designed, and that its design is no longer fit for scale, technological non-scarcity, or modern societal expectations. The task is not to abandon capitalism but to complete it.[82]

Three conclusions follow. First, capitalism's dynamism and moral foundation must be preserved. Incentives matter. Competition matters. Innovation matters. Any alternative that suppresses these forces—most notably communism, and to a lesser extent state-heavy forms of socialism—has consistently produced worse outcomes in innovation, growth, freedom, and human welfare. The historical record on this point is decisive.

Second, governance must be fundamentally rethought, particularly within large enterprises. The past century reveals a recurring "hero" or "king" model of industrial leadership—brilliant, driven individuals exercising enormous power with limited internal accountability. Sometimes this produces transformative progress; sometimes it produces catastrophic failure. Democracies rejected kings in government centuries ago, yet continue to tolerate—and often celebrate—their equivalents in the economic sphere. Inclusive Capitalism requires governance architectures that preserve visionary leadership while constraining its most destructive tendencies, ensuring accountability, succession, and alignment with societal outcomes. The U.S. constitutional system offers instructive analogies: separation of powers, checks and balances, and rule-based authority rather than personality-driven control.

Third, metrics, incentives, and institutions must be modernized. GDP, profit maximization, and short-term shareholder returns are inadequate proxies for societal well-being in an economy increasingly characterized by non-scarcity—particularly in software, information, media, education, and, soon, aspects of healthcare and energy. When success is measured narrowly, behavior follows narrowly. Inclusive Capitalism demands metrics that reward long-term value creation, innovation that expands abundance, workforce empowerment, and improvements in societal well-being. Incentives must be re-engineered so that doing the right thing for society is also the rational thing for firms and leaders.

What ultimately undermined the Smithian revival was not markets but scale. The doctrines revived in the late twentieth century were forged in an era of small firms, localized markets, limited financial leverage, and weak network effects. They were redeployed into an economy dominated by multinational corporations, global capital flows, complex financial instruments, and winner-take-most dynamics. The theory remained Smithian; the operating environment did not. Incentives that once disciplined behavior now amplified concentration. Competition that once diffused power now entrenched it. Efficiency gains that once broadened prosperity increasingly externalized risk.[83]

Seen through this lens, the revival's limitations were structural rather than ideological. Removing constraints restored growth, but it also accelerated the very forces—short-termism, extraction, systemic fragility—that earlier constraints had tried, imperfectly, to contain. The problem was not that markets were trusted too much but that institutions were not redesigned to reflect how markets behave once they reach global scale. Inclusive Capitalism begins precisely here: not by rejecting Smithian logic but by updating its institutional expression so that incentives remain generative rather than extractive as scale increases.[84]

These insights frame what Inclusive Capitalism is—and is not. It is not a rejection of markets. It is not a call for heavier-handed central planning. It is not an attempt to revive mid-century Keynesianism or to resurrect nineteenth-century laissez-faire. It is an effort to redesign the operating system of capitalism itself so that its extraordinary productive power serves inclusive ends by design rather than by accident.

Before turning to that redesign, however, intellectual honesty requires us to examine the most prominent historical alternatives. Socialism and communism arose as responses to capitalism's failures, not from ignorance of them. They addressed real problems—but did so in ways that ultimately produced outcomes worse than the conditions they sought to remedy, particularly in the case of communism. The next two chapters examine these systems not as strawmen but as serious attempts to solve the same underlying challenges. Understanding why they falter is essential to ensuring that Inclusive Capitalism, by design, proposes a system that addresses known challenges and mitigates the risk of recurring mistakes.

Notes

1 Maddison, Angus. *The World Economy: A Millennial Perspective.* OECD, 2001, pp. 125–143.
2 Bordo, Michael, and Barry Eichengreen. *A Retrospective on the Bretton Woods System.* University of Chicago Press, 1993, pp. 3–98.
3 Volcker, Paul, and Toyoo Gyohten. *Changing Fortunes.* Times Books, 1992, pp. 167–214.
4 Friedman, Milton. *A Monetary History of the United States.* Princeton University Press, 1963, pp. 186–213.
5 Smith, Adam. *The Wealth of Nations.* 1776. Modern Library ed., pp. 26–31, 456–459.
6 Smith, Adam. *The Wealth of Nations.* pp. 26–31, 456–459.
7 Hayek, Friedrich A. *The Use of Knowledge in Society.* American Economic Review 35, no. 4 (1945): 519–530.
8 Friedman, Milton. *The Role of Monetary Policy.* American Economic Review 58, no. 1 (1968): 1–17.
9 Greenspan, Alan. *Testimony before U.S. Congress,* October 23, 2008.
10 Maddison, Angus. *The World Economy: A Millennial Perspective.* pp. 125–143.
11 Blanchard, Olivier. *The Phillips Curve: Back to the '60s?* American Economic Review 106, no. 5 (2016): 31–34.
12 Gordon, Robert J. *The Rise and Fall of American Growth.* Princeton University Press, 2016, pp. 589–642.
13 Yergin, Daniel. *The Prize.* Free Press, 1991, pp. 585–621.
14 Ibid.
15 Maddison, Angus. *The World Economy: A Millennial Perspective.* pp. 125–143.
16 Nixon, Richard. *Address to the Nation on the Economic Policy.* August 15, 1971.
17 Gordon, Robert J. *The Rise and Fall of American Growth.* pp. 589–642.
18 Smith, Adam. *The Wealth of Nations.* pp. 26–31, 456–459.
19 Gordon, Robert J. *The Rise and Fall of American Growth.* pp. 589–642.

20 Krugman, Paul. *How Did Economists Get It So Wrong?* New York Times, September 6, 2009.
21 Rodrik, Dani. *Economics Rules*. Oxford University Press, 2015, pp. 1–38.
22 Sowell, Thomas. *Knowledge and Decisions*. Basic Books, 1980, pp. 41–72.
23 Friedman, Milton. *A Monetary History of the United States*. pp. 186–213.
24 Maddison, Angus. *The World Economy: A Millennial Perspective*. pp. 125–143.
25 Smith, Adam. *The Theory of Moral Sentiments*. 1759. Liberty Fund ed., pp. 82–94.
26 Rodrik, Dani. *Economics Rules*. pp. 1–38.
27 Friedman, Milton. *The Role of Monetary Policy*. American Economic Review 58, no. 1 (1968): 1–17.
28 Hayek, Friedrich A. *The Use of Knowledge in Society*. 519–530.
29 Friedman, Milton. *The Role of Monetary Policy*: 1–17.
30 Hayek, Friedrich A. *The Use of Knowledge in Society*. 519–530.
31 Smith, Adam. *The Wealth of Nations*. pp. 26–31, 456–459.
32 Jensen, Michael. *Agency Costs of Free Cash Flow*. American Economic Review 76, no. 2 (1986): 323–329.
33 Rodrik, Dani. *Economics Rules*. pp. 1–38.
34 Smith, Adam. *The Theory of Moral Sentiments*. 1759. Liberty Fund ed., p. 82–94.
35 Hobsbawm, Eric. *Age of Extremes*. Vintage, 1996, pp. 393–403.
36 Gordon, Robert J. *The Rise and Fall of American Growth*. pp. 589–642.
37 Ibid.
38 Rodrik, Dani. *The Globalization Paradox*. Oxford University Press, 2011, pp. 1–42.
39 Piketty, Thomas. *Capital in the Twenty-First Century*. Harvard University Press, 2014, pp. 297–335.
40 Samuelson, Paul. *The Collected Scientific Papers, Vol. 5*, MIT Press, 1986, pp. 878–901.
41 Gordon, Robert J. *The Rise and Fall of American Growth*. pp. 589–642.
42 Ibid.
43 Ibid.
44 Jensen, Michael. *Agency Costs of Free Cash Flow*: 323–329.
45 Gordon, Robert J. *The Rise and Fall of American Growth*. pp. 589–642.
46 Ibid.
47 Samuelson, Paul. *The Collected Scientific Papers, Vol. 5*, pp. 878–901.
48 Jensen, Michael. *Agency Costs of Free Cash Flow*: 323–329.
49 Ibid.
50 Colander et al. *The Financial Crisis and the Systemic Failure of Economics*. Critical Review 21, no. 2–3 (2009): 249–267.
51 Ibid.
52 Samuelson, Paul. *The Collected Scientific Papers, Vol. 5*, pp. 878–901.
53 Rodrik, Dani. *Economics Rules*. pp. 1–38.
54 Colander et al. *The Financial Crisis and the Systemic Failure of Economics*: 249–267.
55 Walter Isaacson. *The Innovators*. New York: Simon & Schuster, 2014, pp. 332–402.
56 Hobsbawm, Eric. *Age of Extremes*. 393–403.
57 Jensen, Michael. *Agency Costs of Free Cash Flow*: 323–329.
58 Ibid.
59 Walter Isaacson. *The Innovators*. pp. 332–402.
60 Rodrik, Dani. *Economics Rules*. pp. 1–38.
61 Michael A. Cusumano and David B. Yoffie. *Competing on Internet Time*. New York: Free Press, 1998, pp. 1–58, 199–230.
62 Gawer, Annabelle, and Michael A. Cusumano. *Platform Leadership: How Intel, Microsoft, and Cisco Drive Industry Innovation*. Boston: Harvard Business School Press, 2002, esp. chapters 4–5.
63 Ibid.

64 Cusumano, Michael A., and David B. Yoffie. *Competing on Internet Time: Lessons from Netscape and Its Battle with Microsoft*. New York: Free Press, 1998, pp. 1–58, 199–230.
65 Piketty, Thomas. *Capital in the Twenty-First Century*. pp. 297–335.
66 Smith, Adam. *The Theory of Moral Sentiments*. pp. 82–94.
67 Walter Isaacson. *The Innovators*. pp. 332–402.
68 Piketty, Thomas. *Capital in the Twenty-First Century*. pp. 297–335.
69 Rodrik, Dani. *Economics Rules*. pp. 1–38.
70 Ibid.
71 Hobsbawm, Eric. *Industry and Empire: From 1750 to the Present Day*. London: Penguin, 1999, chapters 2–4.
72 Smith, Adam. *The Theory of Moral Sentiments*. pp. 82–94.
73 Rodrik, Dani. *The Globalization Paradox*. pp. 1–42.
74 Ibid.
75 Greenspan, Alan. *Testimony before U.S. Congress*, October 23, 2008.
76 Williamson, John. *What Washington Means by Policy Reform*. Latin American Adjustment, Institute for International Economics, 1990, pp. 7–20.
77 Rodrik, Dani. *The Globalization Paradox*. pp. 1–42.
78 Rodrik, Dani. *Economics Rules*. pp. 1–38.
79 Smith, Adam. *The Theory of Moral Sentiments*. pp. 82–94.
80 Hobsbawm, Eric. *Age of Extremes*., pp. 393–403.
81 Hayek, Friedrich A. *The Use of Knowledge in Society*: 519–530.
82 Smith, Adam. *The Theory of Moral Sentiments*. pp. 82–94.
83 Piketty, Thomas. *Capital in the Twenty-First Century*. pp. 297–335.
84 Smith, Adam. *The Theory of Moral Sentiments*. pp. 82–94.

8 Communism: A Reaction to Early Capitalism's Failures

One of the most consequential unintended consequences of Adam Smith's original formulation of capitalism was communism. Communism emerged not as an abstract philosophical exercise but as a direct reaction to the lived experience of workers under early capitalism, particularly in the United Kingdom, where unsafe working conditions, extreme inequality, poverty-level wages, and the absence of political or economic recourse created fertile ground for radical alternatives. In this context, Karl Marx framed communism as both a diagnosis of capitalism's structural failures and a proposed evolutionary path toward a "just" and classless society grounded in historical materialism.[1]

The original communist vision was clearly utopian in intent. It imagined a future in which private ownership of the means of production would give way to collective ownership, exploitation would disappear, and abundance would be shared equitably. History, however, unfolded in the opposite direction. As implemented in the twentieth century, communist systems rapidly concentrated political authority, producing totalitarian governance structures rather than worker emancipation. Rather than abundance, centrally planned economies generated chronic shortages and recurrent famine, particularly under forced collectivization campaigns.[2] Rather than dignity of work, communist regimes imposed coercion, surveillance, and repression, with labor camps and internal purges becoming structural features of governance rather than temporary deviations.[3]

From the perspective of Inclusive Capitalism, the most instructive failure of communism lies in its concentration of political power and its breakdown of incentive formation for both leadership and labor. Communist systems systematically severed the link between effort, innovation, and reward, a problem identified early by critics of central planning who argued that rational allocation was impossible without price signals.[4] Industrial and political leaders were rewarded for ideological conformity and loyalty rather than efficiency or societal outcomes, while workers received guaranteed employment and wages largely independent of productivity. This incentive structure predictably produced widespread shirking and minimal effort, patterns documented in factory-level studies of socialist labor systems.

The economic consequences followed naturally. Output quality deteriorated as firms focused on meeting quotas rather than satisfying real demand, while shortages became chronic and innovation slowed dramatically. As János Kornai demonstrated, these outcomes were not transitional failures but stable features of mature socialist systems operating under soft budget constraints.[5] This stagnation did not arise because individuals lacked intelligence or capability, but because deviation, experimentation, and risk-taking were penalized rather than rewarded. Where capitalism at

 | https://doi.org/10.1515/9783112235485-009

scale can over-reward self-interest, communism attempted to extinguish self-interest altogether, eliminating a central driver of creativity and continuous improvement.

Modern capitalism has since addressed many of the most egregious abuses that originally spirited Marxist critique, particularly through labor protections, safety standards, and social insurance. Yet the conditions that allowed communism to gain legitimacy have not disappeared. Concentration of power, economic insecurity, and distrust of elites persist in new forms, even as material deprivation increasingly manifests as unaffordability rather than starvation. Hannah Arendt's analysis of totalizing political systems remains relevant here, particularly as modern technology expands the capacity for surveillance and centralized control.[6] Digital monitoring, algorithmic governance, and artificial intelligence make the prospect of a technologically enforced authoritarian state far more plausible today than in the twentieth century, and potentially far more durable once established.

Any discussion of communism also requires reference to socialism, which occupies an intermediate position between laissez-faire capitalism and restrictive communism. Socialist systems generally preserve more market mechanisms and maintain better incentive alignment than full central planning, but still weaken the link between value creation and reward as scale increases. Comparative evidence from Eastern Europe shows that while socialist systems avoided the most catastrophic outcomes of communism, they nonetheless experienced slower innovation, fiscal strain, and declining economic dynamism as they matured.

This chapter examines communism not as a caricature but as a serious historical attempt to solve real problems created by early capitalism—and as a profound failure in systems design. The central lesson is not that inequality and exploitation should be tolerated but that removing incentives is not a solution to misaligned incentives. As Karl Popper warned, ideological systems that suppress feedback and adaptation ultimately undermine both freedom and learning.[7] By understanding precisely where and why communism failed, we can identify the mistakes that must be avoided when correcting capitalism's remaining flaws. Only with that clarity can Inclusive Capitalism be constructed as a system that preserves human motivation, rewards contribution, and delivers shared prosperity without coercion.[8]

What Exactly is Communism?

Communism, as a formal economic and social doctrine, was articulated most clearly by Karl Marx and Friedrich Engels, in much the same way that Adam Smith articulated the foundations of capitalism. Marx and Engels did not invent their ideas in isolation. Rather, they synthesized and radicalized a body of thought that had been developing for more than a century in response to inequality, property relations, and the social consequences of early industrial capitalism.[9]

One of the earliest intellectual precursors to communism was Jean-Jacques Rousseau. While Rousseau was not a communist, his critique of private property and social inequality profoundly influenced later socialist and communist thinkers. In his analysis of the origins of inequality, Rousseau argued that social hierarchy emerged not from nature but from institutionalized property relations, framing private ownership as a contingent social construct rather than a natural right—a line of reasoning that later anti-capitalist theories would radicalize.[10]

A more explicitly communist vision emerged during the French Revolution with François-Noël Babeuf, whose Conspiracy of the Equals, a 1796 insurrectionary plot, represented one of the first attempts to translate egalitarian theory into revolutionary political action. Babeuf rejected the limited political equality of the Revolution, arguing that formal rights were meaningless without material equality and communal ownership. His insistence that economic equality must be enforced rather than merely proclaimed marks one of the earliest fully articulated communist programs.

Industrial reformers also contributed to the intellectual foundations of communism and socialism, most notably Robert Owen. Owen was a successful industrialist who became deeply critical of competition and private ownership as organizing principles, arguing that capitalism's incentive structure produced inequality, social conflict, and moral degradation. His cooperative experiments were not revolutionary in intent, but they reinforced the belief that collective ownership and planned social organization could outperform competitive markets in delivering human well-being. Engels later classified Owen as a foundational "utopian socialist," whose moral critique was powerful but structurally incomplete.[11]

Another influential figure in this lineage was Charles Fourier, who proposed reorganizing society into cooperative communities designed to harmonize human passions with social order. Fourier viewed capitalism as inherently alienating, fragmenting labor, social life, and identity. His emphasis on comprehensive social reorganization rather than incremental market reform became a defining feature of later communist thought. Like Owen and Babeuf, Fourier was ultimately incorporated by Marx and Engels into a broader historical narrative of socialism's development.

Marx and Engels synthesized these intellectual currents into a comprehensive critique of capitalism and a revolutionary alternative. In their framework, private ownership of the means of production enabled systematic exploitation of labor, while market competition produced recurring crises, inequality, and class conflict. Communism, in its theoretical form, proposed abolishing private ownership of productive assets, eliminating class distinctions, and organizing production collectively for social use rather than profit.[12] History would show, however, that while communism diagnosed real failures of early capitalism, its own incentive structure proved deeply flawed—a problem explored in the sections that follow.

How Communism as an Ideology Emerged

Communism, as a formal system of thought and political ambition, emerged in the nineteenth century, articulated most explicitly by Karl Marx and Friedrich Engels. Their works—most notably *The Communist Manifesto* (1848) and *Capital, Volume I* (1867)—represented the first systematic attempt to explain communism not as a moral aspiration or utopian experiment but as a historically determined outcome of economic development driven by material conditions and class relations.[13] Although earlier collectivist ideas existed in Plato's *Republic*, early Christian communities, and the writings of Jean-Jacques Rousseau, Marx and Engels reframed these impulses into a rigorously materialist theory grounded in production, ownership, and historical process.

Marx did not view communism as a normative choice that societies might freely adopt but as the necessary resolution of contradictions embedded within capitalism itself. In his framework, capitalism is dynamic and innovative, yet structurally unstable. Its failures are not accidental deviations from an otherwise sound system but logical consequences of its incentive structure and internal dynamics.[14]

First, Marx argued that capitalists extract profit by paying workers less than the value they produce, generating what he termed surplus value. This mechanism drives accumulation and growth but also suppresses wages relative to productivity over time. As purchasing power weakens, aggregate demand becomes insufficient to absorb output, producing recurring crises of overproduction.[15]

Second, Marx contended that competitive pressure compels capitalists to invest in productivity-enhancing technologies that displace labor. Because labor is the source of surplus value in his framework, this substitution produces a tendency toward a falling rate of profit, intensifying systemic instability and accelerating concentration of capital.[16]

Third, capital accumulation leads to increasing concentration of ownership, while workers become progressively alienated from both the products of their labor and the production process itself. Inequality widens, class antagonisms sharpen, and the social relations generated by capitalism come into conflict with its economic base. Marx viewed this divergence as unsustainable over time.[17]

Marx summarized this dynamic starkly in *The Communist Manifesto*: "What the bourgeoisie therefore produces, above all, is its own gravediggers."[18] Capitalism, in his view, was historically progressive relative to feudalism but incapable of sustaining itself indefinitely. Its internal contradictions would intensify until the system gave way to socialism and, ultimately, communism, driven by class struggle rather than reform.

Marx's analytical framework rested on dialectics, a method of understanding historical change through contradiction, conflict, and resolution. Adapting Hegelian dialectics to material conditions, Marx argued that economic structures shape social relations and consciousness, not the reverse. As he wrote in the Preface to *A Contribution to the Critique of Political Economy* (1859), "It is not the consciousness of men that determines their being, but their social being that determines their consciousness."[19]

Within this schema, every historical system contains internal contradictions. Feudalism collapsed as its social relations constrained productive forces. Capitalism, Marx argued, would likewise be superseded as private appropriation clashed with the increasingly social character of production. Class conflict between bourgeoisie and proletariat was, in his view, irreconcilable within capitalism, necessitating a revolutionary transition to socialism as a precursor to stateless, classless communism.[20]

Inclusive Capitalism acknowledges that many of the structural tensions identified by Marx are real. Productivity-enhancing technologies can suppress labor demand, concentrate capital, and create conditions of non-scarcity that existing institutions struggle to manage. Efficiency gains can weaken purchasing power and generate political resentment. These dynamics have recurred repeatedly in capitalist history. However, Marxism failed catastrophically in practice because it destroyed the very incentive structures that sustain innovation, coordination, and adaptive learning.[21]

As implemented by Lenin, Stalin, Mao, and their successors, communism replaced flawed market incentives with far more destructive political ones. Industrial leaders were rewarded for ideological conformity rather than performance, while workers faced weak links between effort and reward. The result was systematic misreporting, stagnation, repression, and chronic underperformance rather than liberation.[22]

The tragedy of communism was therefore not merely inefficiency but incentive inversion. Initiative was punished, conformity rewarded, and feedback suppressed. Class struggle did not yield emancipation but a Pyrrhic victory in which societies destroyed much of their productive and organizational capacity. Inclusive Capitalism seeks to address the genuine contradictions of Smithian capitalism without repeating Marxism's fatal errors, by redesigning institutions, metrics, and incentives so that innovation, growth, and societal well-being reinforce rather than undermine one another.[23]

Marx himself acknowledged, late in life, that historical transitions need not always be violent. He conceded that in certain institutional contexts—particularly England, America, and possibly Holland—workers might pursue their objectives through peaceful, democratic means.[24] Inclusive Capitalism takes this opening seriously, arguing that by correcting capitalism's unintended consequences at the system level, societies need not pass through socialism or communism at all to achieve stability, dignity, and shared prosperity.[25]

Communist Economic Doctrines, Legal Framework, and Cultural Norms

Let us explore communism in more detail. Just as capitalism has manifested in multiple forms, from Smithian to Keynesian and many points in between, communism as well as socialism have also taken different institutional and cultural forms. Communism itself, however, is more narrowly defined when grounded in Marxist theory.[26] It is not merely a preference for redistribution or state involvement but a comprehensive rejection of private ownership of the means of production and of market coordination as the organizing principle of society.[27]

A central tenet of communism is the abolition of private ownership of productive assets, including factories, land, and capital. This position is often misunderstood. Marx and Engels did not object to personal possessions or goods for individual use. Their critique was directed at private ownership of productive property, which they believed enabled class domination and alienation under capitalism. In *Das Kapital*, Marx wrote that the capitalist mode of production produces capitalist private property, which in turn generates its own negation through proletarian revolution.[28]

This book is not an exercise in Marxist exegesis. An extensive scholarly literature is devoted to interpreting what Marx and Engels intended by their writings, which leave substantial room for ambiguity. For example, there is persistent uncertainty about where Marxism draws the line between personal and productive property, or how small-scale enterprise should be treated. What is clear is that large-scale private enterprise is incompatible with a communist society, whereas socialist systems have historically allowed greater flexibility. In practice, this ambiguity enabled later leaders to interpret Marxism in ways that diverged sharply from any plausible reading of his original vision.[29]

The stated goal of communism is a classless society without exploitation or state coercion. In its idealized form, communism envisions a social order based on common ownership, voluntary association, and human freedom, where distribution follows the principle "from each according to his ability, to each according to his needs." Marx articulated this vision in *Critique of the Gotha Program*, assuming a post-scarcity world in which industrial productivity had eliminated material want and individuals could freely develop their capacities without economic compulsion.[30]

This maxim functions within communism much as the "invisible hand" functions rhetorically within capitalism: as a simplifying slogan that gestures toward moral intent while obscuring deeper structural limitations. It also exposes the central weakness of Marx's proposed remedy. While Marx correctly identified many unintended consequences of early Smithian capitalism, his solution rested on assumptions about human motivation that do not withstand examination through history, psychology, or institutional experience.[31] Inclusive Capitalism shares Marx's concern with exploitation, alienation, and the concentration of capital, and it likewise recognizes that technological progress can generate domains of non-scarcity. Where it departs decisively is in rejecting the premise that classlessness, need-based distribution, or the severance of reward from contribution can sustain durable prosperity or human dignity. Inclusive Capitalism instead advances a different organizing principle—"from each according to ability and chosen effort, to each according to contribution"—on the grounds that dignity, innovation, and abundance depend on a persistent alignment between effort, reward, and social value.[32]

History demonstrates that incentives matter for both leadership and labor.[33] In communist systems, industrial leadership was not rewarded for innovation, long-term value creation, or service to society. Instead, subordinated to party loyalty was both a primary incentive and subjected to coercive control. At the same time, workers were systematically disincentivized from effort, initiative, and responsibility, due to the massive gap between Marx's vision of behavior drivers in theory and what actually happened on the factory floor. When contribution is decoupled from reward, the rational response is minimal compliance. This dynamic was visible across communist systems, where labor norms converged toward doing as little as possible without punishment, while informal economies and corruption became the true engines of survival. Note that these same constructs also apply to socialist systems in which redistribution dis-incentivizes worker ambition as well as the desire to accumulate capital.

The experience of the Soviet Union illustrates this clearly. Lenin argued in *The State and Revolution* that all citizens would become employees of a single national syndicate, working for the common good.[34] In practice, this required a transitional dictatorship of the proletariat, which centralized coercion and eliminated dissent. The gulag system, forced collectivization, and suppression of independent thought were not aberrations but structural responses to incentive failure. Maoist China followed a similar trajectory. The Great Leap Forward (Chinese Communist Party campaign 1958–1962) attempted to impose immediate collectivized labor under the assumption that ideological commitment would substitute for incentives. The result was catastrophic famine, economic collapse, and tens of millions of deaths.[35] These outcomes were not accidents. Friedrich Hayek warned in *The Road to Serfdom* that attempts to override individual incentives through central planning would inevitably lead to authoritarianism.[36] By eliminating price signals and profit as feedback mechanisms, planners assume knowledge and coordination capacities that no society possesses.

Communism's failure is therefore not merely economic or political but anthropological.[37] It rests on an idealized view of human behavior that consistently fails when scaled. While the moral aspiration of meeting human needs is compelling, the institutional means chosen by communism reliably destroy the very abundance and dignity they promise to deliver. By contrast, capitalism's invisible hand aligns with observable human behavior but fails at scale without institutional correction. Inclusive Capitalism seeks to resolve this tension by preserving self-interest, property, and competition, while redesigning incentives and metrics so that contribution to societal well-being, rather than extraction or scarcity, is rewarded.

The gap between theory and practice under communism is far larger than the gap between Adam Smith's vision and early capitalism.[38] Marx offered few concrete prescriptions for governance, leaving later leaders to improvise. Lenin, Mao, and others transformed Marxism into rigid, centralized systems that bore little resemblance to voluntary association or democratic control. States that labeled themselves communist were, in Marxist terms, socialist states in permanent transition, characterized by central planning, single-party rule, and forced collectivization.

Understanding why communism took hold nonetheless is essential. It gained traction because it offered a coherent diagnosis of suffering, a moral framework for resistance, and a promise of historical redemption. In the context of industrial exploitation, urban slums, child labor, and repeated economic crises, communism functioned as a secular religion of the oppressed. It appealed not only to workers but also to intellectuals, students, and anti-imperialist movements who saw capitalism as inseparable from domination.

Many of the conditions that fueled the rise of communism still exist today in modified form. Wealth concentration, labor insecurity, inability to afford basic necessities, resentment toward elites, and speculative excesses are again prominent, even in advanced capitalist societies. While material conditions are vastly improved in absolute terms, relative deprivation and loss of economic agency remain potent destabilizing forces.[39] The resurgence of socialist sentiment in the United States is evidence that contemporary capitalism, as currently structured, fails to meet the needs of a large share of the population.

The lesson is not that communism offers a viable alternative. History has rendered its verdict decisively.[40] The lesson is that capitalism must be redesigned so that its power to generate abundance does not again produce the grievances that make destructive ideologies attractive. Inclusive Capitalism addresses this by aligning incentives with societal well-being, replacing GDP as the primary metric, and ensuring that both industrial leadership and the workforce are rewarded in proportion to their contribution. Only then can capitalism remain both effective and morally defensible in a world of scale, technology, and emerging non-scarcity.[41]

Industrial Leadership Incentives and Behaviors Under Soviet and Maoist Communism

Lenin and Mao translated Marxian theory into practice in the first half of the twentieth century but in doing so fundamentally altered its incentive structure. Marx envisioned communism as the natural evolution of capitalism, emerging after industrial abundance had been achieved and class contradictions had resolved themselves.[42] Vladimir Lenin reinterpreted Marxism to fit a semi-feudal Russia, arguing that a disciplined revolutionary vanguard could accelerate history itself, skipping capitalism altogether. In *What Is to Be Done?* (1902), Lenin asserted that "without revolutionary theory there can be no revolutionary movement," reframing communism from a descriptive theory into a prescriptive, centralized program.[43] This reinterpretation placed enormous power in the hands of political leadership while severing performance from market feedback.

For the Russian peasantry and working class, communism promised land, bread, and peace after centuries of czarist repression and war mobilization. In practice, the working class received no land, experienced repeated waves of famine, and lived under permanent militarization. The incentives facing both leaders and workers were fatally misaligned. Political loyalty replaced competence. Ideological conformity replaced problem-solving. Risk-taking, experimentation, and dissent—critical inputs to progress—were punished rather than rewarded.[44]

Mao Zedong applied a similar transformation in China, adapting communism to a society without a large industrial proletariat. Mao elevated the peasantry as the revolutionary class and fused Marxism with nationalism, positioning the communist party as the embodiment of the nation itself. In *On Practice* (1937), Mao argued that "correct ideas do not fall from the sky. They come from social practice."[45] Unfortunately, so did incorrect ones—and under Maoist communism there was no reliable mechanism to distinguish between the two. Policy failures were interpreted as ideological failures, requiring political purification rather than course correction. The result was catastrophic, most notably during the Great Leap Forward, where production quotas divorced from physical reality led directly to mass famine.

To ensure a parallel analysis with capitalism, mercantilism, and feudalism, it is instructive to examine the role of industrial leadership under communism. In capitalist systems, industrial leaders derive authority from ownership, innovation, and market success. Under communism, industrial leaders were state-appointed managers, technocrats, or military-industrial bureaucrats. Their power flowed from political loyalty and ideological reliability, not entrepreneurial acumen. Soviet and Chinese enterprise directors operated within centrally planned systems governed by five-year plans, production quotas, and ministerial oversight. "Success" was defined as meeting targets, regardless of waste, inefficiency, or human cost.

Figures such as Alexei Kosygin in the Soviet Union or Li Fuchun in China managed enormous industrial systems with virtually no autonomy. Profit was irrelevant. Customer demand was irrelevant. Innovation that deviated from the plan was dangerous. Friedrich Hayek warned that centralized planning systematically elevates those most willing to suppress dissent and distort information: "the worst get on top."[46] The incentive system selected for compliance, not excellence. This was not an accident; it was a structural outcome.

Although communist ideology denounced class privilege, it quickly produced a new bureaucratic elite—the nomenklatura. Party-approved officials enjoyed privileged access to housing, healthcare, education, and scarce consumer goods unavailable to ordinary citizens. Yet even these elites lived under constant threat. Political favor was reversible. Industrial leaders who missed targets, spoke candidly, or aligned with the wrong faction were purged, imprisoned, or executed.[47] In Stalin's USSR, factory heads and economic ministers were routinely liquidated. In Mao's China, the Cultural Revolution destroyed careers and lives indiscriminately. There was no stable concept of success or failure grounded in performance. Both were subject to political reinterpretation.

Mao's slogan "to rebel is justified" epitomized the incentive pathology. Ostensibly a call to resist privilege, it became a mechanism for encouraging mass rebellion against competence, expertise, and authority itself. Red Guards were mobilized against teachers, engineers, managers, and even parents. Excellence became a liability. Standing out invited suspicion. Innovation became existentially dangerous.

And yet, even under communism, isolated exceptions emerged—almost exclusively in sectors aligned with national survival, particularly defense. Andrei Tupolev was one of the most consequential aircraft designers of the twentieth century and a paradoxical figure in the history of industrial leadership. He stands as a rare example of sustained technological excellence produced not because of the Soviet system but in spite of it.[48] Tupolev designed or oversaw the development of more than one hundred aircraft, including bombers, transports, and passenger jets that shaped both Soviet military power and global aviation. His career illustrates how extreme political control distorts incentives, how technical talent can survive under repression, and how much innovation was lost due to systemic fear.

Tupolev's technical foundation was exceptional. He trained as an engineer at the Imperial Moscow Technical School, where he studied under Nikolai Zhukovsky, the father of modern aerodynamics.[49] This placed Tupolev at the intellectual center of early aviation science. He was deeply grounded in first principles: materials science, structural mechanics, and aerodynamics. Unlike many later bureaucratic managers, Tupolev was an engineer first and always. He believed strongly in rigorous testing, incremental improvement, and engineering discipline over ideological enthusiasm.

Early in his career, Tupolev became a pioneer of all-metal aircraft construction, moving beyond wood and fabric designs at a time when such a shift was risky and controversial.[50] His insistence on aluminum alloys and stressed-skin construction laid the groundwork for modern aircraft design. This technical judgment, initially resisted by political overseers, ultimately proved decisive. Tupolev's success was rooted in competence, not ideology.

Politically, Tupolev was not a communist ideologue. He was pragmatic, cautious, and deeply aware of the dangers of visibility. Unlike some contemporaries who attempted to align themselves enthusiastically with party rhetoric, Tupolev avoided political theory almost entirely. His worldview appears to have been shaped less by Marxism than by engineering realism. He believed systems should work, structures should not fail, and designs should be validated by physics rather than slogans. This quiet pragmatism likely contributed to his survival.

That survival was far from guaranteed. In 1937, during Stalin's Great Purge, Tupolev was arrested on fabricated charges of espionage and sabotage.[51] He was imprisoned in the Lubyanka and later transferred to a Sharashka—a secret prison laboratory where incarcerated scientists were forced to work for the state. This episode is critical for understanding incentive failure under communism. Tupolev, one of the most valuable engineers in the country, was treated as disposable. Fear replaced trust. Coercion replaced motivation.

Yet even under imprisonment, Tupolev continued to design aircraft, including bombers that would later play key roles in World War II. His release came not from justice but from necessity. The state needed his expertise. This transactional relationship—talent exploited under threat—was characteristic of the system. Tupolev's eventual rehabilitation and restoration to prominence did not erase the underlying message: Excellence offered no protection.

As a manager, Tupolev ran design bureaus that were hierarchical, disciplined, and technically demanding but notably different from the surrounding political culture. Within his teams, engineering merit mattered. He recruited aggressively from universities and research institutes, promoted based on technical contribution, and shielded subordinates where possible from ideological interference.[52] This internal culture was one of the few spaces in the Soviet system where competence retained value.

However, even Tupolev could not escape systemic constraints. Innovation was bounded by five-year plans, political interference, and rigid production targets. Design choices were often influenced by military doctrine rather than market demand or passenger comfort. When the Soviets reverse-engineered the American B-29 bomber into the Tu-4, Tupolev executed the task flawlessly—but the project itself symbolized stagnation rather than leadership.

In the postwar period, Tupolev oversaw the development of civil aircraft such as the Tu-104, one of the world's first jet airliners. While technically impressive, these aircraft lagged Western counterparts in reliability, efficiency, and passenger experience. The reason was not Tupolev's capability but the absence of feedback loops. Airlines could not reject designs. Passengers had no choice. Failure carried no market penalty—only political risk.[53]

From the perspective of Inclusive Capitalism, Tupolev is not an argument for authoritarian efficiency. He is evidence of extraordinary human potential constrained by catastrophic incentive design. The Soviet system extracted value from Tupolev while suppressing the conditions that would have allowed ten Tupolevs to flourish. His success was singular where it should have been systemic.

The deeper lesson lies in governance. Tupolev held immense technical authority but little institutional autonomy. He could build aircraft but not shape the system that governed their use, improvement, or succession. When he aged, power did not transition smoothly; it remained centralized and politicized. The system depended on individuals rather than institutions—precisely the failure mode Inclusive Capitalism seeks to avoid.

Tupolev's life underscores a central theme of this book: Genius alone is insufficient. Without incentives aligned to societal well-being, even the greatest minds are underutilized, misdirected, or destroyed. Inclusive Capitalism seeks to preserve the creative power embodied by figures like Tupolev while eliminating the fear-based coercion that defined their context. The goal is not to produce heroes who survive bad systems but systems that consistently produce excellence.

Andrei Tupolev and William Boeing both shaped modern aviation, yet their careers illuminate opposite failures—and strengths—of their respective systems. Tupolev operated inside a centralized, coercive political economy where innovation was demanded by the state but autonomy was conditional and revocable. His imprisonment during the Stalinist purges makes clear that even exceptional technical talent was subordinate to political control.[54] Incentives were blunt: deliver results aligned with state priorities or face ruin. Remarkably, Tupolev still produced enduring designs but at enormous personal and systemic cost, with fear substituting for governance and feedback suppressed until failure became unavoidable.

Boeing, by contrast, worked within a market-based system that tolerated—and even celebrated—private industrial power but only up to a point. He voluntarily retired after the U.S. government enforced antitrust action under the 1938 Civil Aeronautics Act, which required the breakup of United Aircraft and Transport Corporation. This intervention curtailed Boeing's vertical integration and personal control, not because he failed technically or ethically but because the system recognized the long-term risks of concentrated power, even in benevolent hands. The American system was imperfect and disruptive, but it imposed institutional guardrails rather than personal punishment. Boeing lost control; Tupolev lost freedom.

The contrast is instructive. The Soviet model subordinated innovators to political authority, destroying human capital through fear. The American model constrained innovators through law, sometimes bluntly, but preserved individual dignity and systemic adaptability. Inclusive Capitalism draws lessons from both: Genius must be empowered to build yet constrained by institutions that prevent concentration of unchecked power. The goal is neither repression nor idolization of industrial leaders but governance that aligns innovation with societal well-being while ensuring leadership succession, accountability, and resilience over time.[55]

Anatoly Alexandrov was one of the most influential scientists in the soviet nuclear program and a central figure in the development of nuclear power and naval propulsion.[56] His career illustrates a different but equally instructive failure mode of communist systems: not the suppression of innovation through terror alone but the gradual erosion of responsibility, feedback, and accountability at scale. Alexandrov was not imprisoned like Tupolev, nor marginalized like many dissidents. Instead, he rose to the highest scientific and institutional ranks—yet the system he helped lead ultimately produced one of the most catastrophic technological failures in modern history.

Alexandrov's technical background was formidable. Trained as a physicist, he made early contributions to polymer physics and electrical insulation before being drawn into defense research during World War II. His wartime work on demagnetization of ships—protecting Soviet vessels from magnetic mines—earned him Stalin's trust and accelerated his entry into the nuclear establishment. From that point forward, Alexandrov became deeply embedded in the state's most sensitive scientific programs.

His primary technical legacy lies in nuclear reactor design and nuclear propulsion. Alexandrov was a key architect of the Soviet nuclear navy and played a central role in developing pressurized water reactors for submarines and icebreakers. These efforts were genuine engineering achievements. Nuclear icebreakers transformed Arctic navigation, and nuclear submarines reshaped global military balance. Alexandrov believed deeply in nuclear energy as a civilizational force—clean, powerful, and essential for national progress.

Politically, Alexandrov was a loyalist, though not an ideologue in the Marxist sense. Unlike Tupolev, who kept distance from political doctrine, Alexandrov embraced the role of the technocratic servant of the state. He believed that science, properly organized, could substitute for markets. He trusted centralized planning, expert committees, and hierarchical control. In this respect, Alexandrov exemplifies the "high modernist" confidence that technical expertise alone can manage complex systems without distributed feedback.[57]

This belief shaped his managerial worldview. As president of the Academy of Sciences of the Soviet Union from 1975 to 1986, Alexandrov presided over one of the most powerful scientific institutions in the world. He emphasized discipline, secrecy, and compliance with state objectives. Decision-making authority was concentrated. Dissenting technical opinions were discouraged, not through overt violence but through career pressure and reputational risk. The system rewarded alignment and punished friction.

Nowhere were these incentive failures more consequential than in reactor safety culture. Alexandrov strongly defended the RBMK (Reaktor Bolshoy Moshchnosti Kanalnyy) reactor design implemented at Chernobyl, even after early warning signs emerged. The RBMK was attractive to planners because it was cheaper, used domestically produced fuel, and could be refueled while operating. These advantages aligned with production metrics and political targets—but came at the cost of intrinsic safety. Rather than treating safety as a primary design constraint, it became an operational concern subordinated to output and schedule.

The Chernobyl disaster in 1986 exposed the full cost of this incentive structure. Engineers followed procedures without understanding system-level risk. Operators lacked authority to halt unsafe experiments. Designers had normalized design flaws. Leadership suppressed negative information. Alexandrov initially defended the reactor design and resisted acknowledgment of systemic failure. Only later did he concede deeper flaws. By then, the damage—human, environmental, and institutional—was irreversible.[58]

Could such a sequence of events occur in the United States? In fact, a closely related episode did occur in the late 1990s, not long after the Chernobyl disaster. The Millstone Nuclear Power Plant, located on the Connecticut River delta, was shut down by the Nuclear Regulatory Commission following one of the earliest and most consequential whistleblower cases in U.S. nuclear history.[59] At Millstone, financial and production incentives had gradually distorted operational behavior, leading engineers to raise concerns through the Hartford Courant about safety practices that bore troubling parallels to the organizational failures observed at Chernobyl. These disclosures revealed that compliance documentation and operational shortcuts had, over time, displaced a genuinely robust safety culture. As a result, plant leadership was required to demonstrate that the facility operated within a formally defined "Safety-Conscious Work Environment," a process in which the authors were heavily involved.[60] The Millstone case remains one of the most salient U.S. examples of how misaligned incentives—when left unchecked—can erode institutional safeguards even within highly regulated, technically sophisticated systems.

From the perspective of Inclusive Capitalism, Alexandrov's career demonstrates a critical distinction between intelligence and wisdom. He was unquestionably brilliant. But brilliance operating inside a system that suppresses feedback, penalizes dissent, and optimizes for political metrics rather than societal well-being becomes dangerous at scale. The failure was not nuclear physics; it was governance.[61]

Alexandrov's incentives were misaligned in a subtle but profound way. Success was measured by deployment, not resilience. Authority increased with compliance, not with demonstrated caution. Responsibility was diffuse, while power was centralized. The workforce beneath him learned to optimize for approval rather than truth. In such a system, catastrophic risk accumulates silently.

The contrast with Inclusive Capitalism is instructive. Inclusive Capitalism does not reject expertise or centralized coordination where appropriate. But it insists on institutional designs that reward truth-telling, surface risk early, and distribute accountability. Systems that produce energy, food, medicine, or knowledge at scale must be designed to fail safely, learn continuously, and correct themselves without requiring disaster as the trigger.[62]

Alexandrov's legacy is therefore not a condemnation of scientists, nor of ambition, nor of nuclear energy itself. It is a warning about systems that elevate technical elites without embedding them in structures of accountability to society. His life shows that even well-intentioned, highly competent leaders can preside over disaster when incentives reward conformity over correctness.

In the end, Anatoly Alexandrov did what the system asked of him—and that is precisely the problem. Inclusive Capitalism is built on the opposite premise: that systems must be designed so that doing the right thing for society is the easiest, most rewarded path for leaders, engineers, and workers alike.

Viktor Chernomyrdin represents the archetype of the late-Soviet industrial technocrat who successfully migrated into post-Soviet political power. Trained as an engineer, Chernomyrdin spent most of his early career inside the Soviet gas industry, rising through managerial ranks during an era when technical competence, party loyalty, and administrative discipline mattered more than entrepreneurship or innovation. He joined the Communist Party in 1961 and embodied its pragmatic, managerial wing rather than its ideological extremes.[63]

His defining role came as Minister of the Gas Industry in the late Soviet period and then, critically, as the founding chairman of Gazprom in 1989–1992.[64] Gazprom was conceived as a state-controlled yet commercially oriented energy giant, and Chernomyrdin played a central role in preserving its coherence during the chaotic collapse of the Soviet Union. Unlike many contemporaries, he resisted fragmenting Gazprom during privatization, arguing that energy infrastructure required centralized coordination. This decision helped Russia retain leverage over its most important strategic asset—but also laid the groundwork for future rent extraction.[65]

As Prime Minister from 1992 to 1998, Chernomyrdin oversaw Russia's transition toward market economics while attempting to stabilize collapsing institutions. His leadership style was cautious, incremental, and consensus-driven. He was not a reformist visionary but a stabilizer. Yet the incentive environment he operated in was deeply flawed: Political survival depended on balancing oligarchs, regional power brokers, and state monopolies rather than optimizing productivity or societal well-being. As a result, state capture intensified rather than receded.

Chernomyrdin illustrates a core failure mode of post-Soviet capitalism: technocratic continuity without institutional redesign. Competent managers inherited vast assets but lacked incentive structures aligned with transparency, competition, or long-term public benefit. The outcome was neither socialism nor competitive capitalism but a hybrid system that drifted toward kleptocracy (a government run by those who systemically steal country's resources)—state power fused with monopolistic control rather than re-architected governance.[66]

Boris Berezovsky embodies the opposite pole of post-Soviet leadership: not the technocrat but the opportunistic power broker. Trained as a mathematician, Berezovsky entered business during perestroika and rose rapidly during the 1990s privatization wave. His ascent was not driven by industrial mastery or innovation but by exploiting institutional vacuum—weak property rights, politicized courts, and insider access to state assets.[67]

Berezovsky assembled holdings across automobiles, oil, and media, most notably gaining influence over ORT television.[68] His daily life revolved around deal-making, political alliances, and information control. He played a significant role in Boris Yeltsin's 1996 re-election campaign and later helped facilitate Vladimir Putin's rise, believing he could shape the new leader as he had others. This miscalculation proved fatal to his position.

His incentive structure was purely extractive. Value was not created through production or innovation but through arbitrage of power, media influence, and state access. In this sense, Berezovsky was not an aberration but a rational actor within a broken system. Privatization transferred ownership without governance, and markets were introduced without rule of law. Under such conditions, rent-seeking dominated productive output of enterprises.

When Putin consolidated power and moved to reassert state control over oligarchs, Berezovsky fled Russia and spent his final years in exile, stripped of influence and significant assets.[69] His death in 2013 marked the end of an era in which political manipulation substituted for institutional legitimacy.

Berezovsky's trajectory underscores a central lesson for Inclusive Capitalism: Ownership without accountability produces predators, not builders. When incentives reward proximity to power rather than contribution to society, the most aggressive actors win—and the system corrodes from within.

Taken together, Viktor Chernomyrdin and Boris Berezovsky illustrate two distinct but complementary failure modes that emerge when large-scale economic systems transition without redesigned incentives and governance. Chernomyrdin represents continuity without reform: technically competent, stabilizing, and pragmatic leadership operating inside monopolistic structures that preserved control but failed to align performance with societal outcomes.

Berezovsky represents disruption without discipline: opportunistic actors rationally exploiting institutional voids where ownership was separated from accountability and political access substituted for value creation. Both outcomes contrast sharply with the idealized western narrative of entrepreneurial capitalism, yet they reflect the same underlying flaw—systems that scale faster than their governance.[70]

Where incentives reward control, proximity to power, or short-term extraction rather than contribution and stewardship, leaders behave accordingly. Inclusive Capitalism draws its lesson precisely here: neither technocratic continuity nor unfettered privatization produces durable prosperity. Only well-architected institutions—embedding accountability, shared risk and reward, and clear obligations to society—can channel human ambition away from the primacy of capture and toward sustained societal well-being.

At its core, an economic system should motivate the maximum number of people to perform at their maximum level in service of societal well-being. Soviet and Maoist communism achieved the opposite. Leaders were incentivized to conform, conceal failure, and enforce ideology. Workers were incentivized to do the minimum required to avoid punishment. Effort, creativity, and initiative had no upside and, instead, a pronounced downside. As Thomas Sowell observed, "in the absence of a price system, economic failure cannot be reliably detected until catastrophe."[71]

Communism removed incentives at both the leadership and workforce levels to contribute uniquely and excellently. Instead, it rewarded ideological alignment divorced from practical reality. The result was least-common-denominator behavior, systemic stagnation, and eventual collapse. With the limited exception of military programs, there were no enduring industrial leaders, no sustained innovation, and no rising societal well-being. The lesson for Inclusive Capitalism is unambiguous: Removing incentives does not produce equality or justice—it produces fear, conformity, and decay.

Lived Experience of the Population Under Communism

The lived experience of the workforce under communism reveals perhaps the most severe misalignment between economic theory, human incentives, and practical outcomes in modern history. While Marxist theory promised the emancipation of labor and the end of exploitation, the burden of communism's contradictions fell overwhelmingly on workers themselves. Life for the workforce under communist regimes was shaped by a persistent gap between ideological aspiration and material reality. Understanding this lived experience requires examining how assumptions about motivation, productivity, and human behavior translated into economic, social, and political conditions on the factory floor and in everyday life.[72]

Karl Marx and Friedrich Engels famously asserted in *The Communist Manifesto* (1848) that "the proletarians have nothing to lose but their chains."[73] They envisioned a revolutionary transformation in which workers would no longer be alienated from their labor and where production would become voluntary, creative, and fulfilling. Marx described an ideal future in which "the free development of each is the condition for the free development of all."[74] Vladimir Lenin echoed this vision in State and Revolution (1917), imagining a society in which the state would eventually wither away and production would be coordinated by a self-directed proletariat.[75]

Ironically, this vision becomes increasingly plausible only with advanced technology—technology that removes drudgery and enables more autonomous, creative work. As history unfolded, capitalism proved capable of generating such technological progress, while communism largely shut it down.[76] In practice, communist systems locked workers into precisely the forms of monotonous, compulsory labor that Marx most despised.

Under communist regimes, labor was highly regimented and tightly controlled by the state. In the Soviet Union, particularly under Stalin, the workplace functioned as an extension of political authority. The Five-Year Plans imposed ambitious production targets that prioritized output over safety, autonomy, and human well-being. Workers were assigned jobs by central planners, movement between occupations was restricted, and strict disciplinary codes governed daily life.[77] Absenteeism, underperformance, or perceived dissent could result in severe punishment, including imprisonment or exile to labor camps in the Gulag system.

The reality bore an uncomfortable resemblance to the exploitation Marx and Engels had condemned—except that now it was enforced in the name of the workers themselves. As Thomas Sowell observed in Marxism: *Philosophy and Economics* (1985), "The coercion required to make collectivism work has been in inverse proportion to its promises of liberation."[78] Faced with coercion and the absence of meaningful rewards, workers responded rationally: They minimized effort, avoided visibility, and learned not to stand out.

Material conditions reinforced this dynamic. Despite claims of worker empowerment, daily labor under communism was often monotonous, inefficient, and poorly rewarded. Consumer goods were scarce, quality was low, and shortages were chronic because production was disconnected from demand and incentives. The sardonic saying attributed to Soviet workers—"we pretend to work, and they pretend to pay us"—captured the collapse of the ideological promise of fulfilling labor.[79]

Friedrich Hayek had warned in *The Road to Serfdom* (1944) that centralized planning would erode individual freedom and culminate in rule by an unaccountable minority rather than genuine equality.[80] The lived experience of workers under communism bore out this warning with remarkable consistency.

Social life under communism was equally shaped by state oversight and ideological conformity. Regimes typically guaranteed basic necessities—housing, healthcare, and education—but quality and availability varied widely. Urban workers might receive state housing and medical care, yet apartments were often overcrowded and poorly maintained, and services were underfunded.[81] In rural areas, especially under forced collectivization, living conditions were frequently catastrophic.

The Holodomor in Ukraine (1932–1933) and The Great Leap Forward in China (1958–1962) caused mass famine and tens of millions of deaths—events with no parallel in the history of capitalism, even at its worst.[82] These outcomes were not accidental but flowed directly from incentive structures that rewarded ideological compliance and output statistics rather than human survival.

Social mobility existed in theory but rarely in practice. Advancement was officially tied to merit and labor achievement, as in the Stakhanovite movement (a Soviet labor campaign promoting extreme productivity norms by glorifying model workers to pressure others to exceed output targets) of the Soviet Union. In reality it depended far more on political loyalty and party membership.

Under Mao Zedong, the Cultural Revolution (1966–1976) further destabilized social life by encouraging mass denunciations and the persecution of intellectuals, professionals, and even ordinary workers.[83] Mao's declaration that "revolution is not a dinner party" captured both the ideological fervor and the human cost of these campaigns.[84] The result was widespread fear, disruption of education and production, and the destruction of social trust.

Politically, the workforce existed in one-party states that allowed little dissent or participation. Although workers were nominally the ruling class, real power was monopolized by party elites. Trade unions functioned not as defenders of worker interests but as instruments of state control, enforcing production targets and ideological discipline. Elections, where they existed, were symbolic. Surveillance was pervasive, particularly in Eastern Bloc states such as East Germany, where the Stasi maintained extensive files on ordinary citizens. Dissent carried grave risks, shaping a workforce culture defined less by empowerment than by resignation and caution.[85]

Once again, the gap between theory and practice was stark. It would be incomplete, however, to portray all worker experiences under communism as uniformly negative. In certain periods and places—such as during the Khrushchev Thaw or the post-Mao reform era—workers enjoyed stability, employment security, and access to improving basic services that compared favorably with conditions in some capitalist societies.[86] The absence of unemployment provided psychological security, even if wages and living standards remained low.

Yet this security came at the cost of stagnation, inefficiency, and suppressed innovation. One of the most instructive lessons from this experience concerns the idea of guaranteed employment "even if economically inefficient." Capitalist systems, particularly those driven by technological change, generate displacement and insecurity, undermining psychological well-being and access to basic services through affordability constraints.[87] Communist systems eliminated unemployment but did so by suppressing incentives, innovation, and productivity.

Inclusive Capitalism draws a different conclusion: Efficiency must be defined at the societal level rather than exclusively at the firm or sector level. The objective is not to choose between insecurity and stagnation but to design systems in which technological progress, workforce dignity, and economic security reinforce one another.[88] How to operationalize societal efficiency—aligning incentives so that productivity gains translate into broad well-being rather than exclusion—is taken up explicitly in book two. The lived experience of the workforce under communism reveals perhaps the most severe misalignment between economic theory, human incentives, and practical outcomes in modern history. While Marxist theory promised the emancipation of labor and the end of exploitation, the burden of communism's contradictions fell overwhelmingly on workers themselves. Life for the workforce under communist regimes was shaped by a persistent gap between ideological aspiration and material reality. Understanding this lived experience requires examining how assumptions about motivation, productivity, and human behavior translated into economic, social, and political conditions on the factory floor and in everyday life.[89]

Karl Marx and Friedrich Engels famously asserted in *The Communist Manifesto* (1848) that "the proletarians have nothing to lose but their chains."[90] They envisioned a revolutionary transformation in which workers would no longer be alienated from their labor and where production would become voluntary, creative, and fulfilling. Marx described an ideal future in which "the free development of each is the condition for the free development of all."[91] Vladimir Lenin echoed this vision in *State and Revolution* (1917), imagining a society in which the state would eventually wither away and production would be coordinated by a self-directed proletariat.[92]

Ironically, this vision becomes increasingly plausible only with advanced technology—technology that removes drudgery and enables more autonomous, creative work. As history unfolded, capitalism proved capable of generating such technological progress, while communism largely shut it down. In practice, communist systems locked workers into precisely the forms of monotonous, compulsory labor that Marx most despised.

Under communist regimes, labor was highly regimented and tightly controlled by the state. In the Soviet Union, particularly under Stalin, the workplace functioned as an extension of political authority. The Five-Year Plans imposed ambitious production targets that prioritized output over safety, autonomy, and human well-being. Workers were assigned jobs by central planners, movement between occupations was restricted, and strict disciplinary codes governed daily life. Absenteeism, underperformance, or perceived dissent could result in severe punishment, including imprisonment or exile to labor camps in the Gulag system.[93]

What Worked and What Did Not Under Communism

We now turn to an overall evaluation of communism—examining what it identified correctly, what it accomplished in practice (while limited and often temporary), where it failed fundamentally, and why it ultimately collapsed. This assessment is not undertaken to relitigate ideology but to extract durable lessons from one of the most consequential economic experiments in human history. Those lessons are essential to the design of Inclusive Capitalism, particularly in understanding how misaligned incentives, unrealistic assumptions about human behavior, and brittle institutional architectures can transform moral ambition into systemic failure.[94]

Communism, often evaluated primarily through the lens of its twentieth-century failures, is less frequently examined for the positive insights it offered and the problems it correctly identified and confronted. Although its ultimate aspirations were not realized in practice, communism, both as a theory and as a set of policies, addressed real and pressing issues of its time. Its contributions to economic development, social equality, and the ideological critique of capitalism deserve rigorous analysis, particularly when contextualized within the historical and political conditions in which communist regimes arose. At the same time, any such evaluation must remain grounded in the fact that communism ultimately failed, and that in practice it resulted in more death and destruction than perhaps any other economic or societal idea in human history.[95]

Communism emerged as a response to what Marx described as the "contradictions" of industrial capitalism—more accurately understood as the contradictions inherent in capitalism's unintended consequences.[96] Marx, Engels, and their intellectual successors confronted an economic system that, in their view, was defined by exploitation, inequality, and alienation. Marx wrote in the *Economic and Philosophic Manuscripts* of 1844, "The worker becomes all the poorer the more wealth he produces . . . The devaluation of the human world increases in direct relation with the increase in value of the world of things."[97] Framing these outcomes as defining characteristics of capitalism, however, rather than as unintended consequences, proved to be a critical analytical error. These conditions were not Adam Smith's intent. He did not set out to design a system defined by exploitation, inequality, and alienation. Nonetheless, such outcomes manifested rapidly and visibly, which is why the communist critique resonated so strongly at a time where workers labored under inhumane conditions, lived in poverty despite creating massive wealth, and had little political recourse.[98]

Communism correctly diagnosed many of the social costs of unregulated capitalism, including labor exploitation, income disparity, and recurring cycles of economic crisis. Even critics of communism, such as Friedrich Hayek, acknowledged that early capitalism required social correction. Hayek wrote, "There is no reason why in a society which has reached the general level of wealth ours has attained, the first concern of the state should not be to secure a certain minimum of sustenance for everyone."[99] In this sense, communism functioned as a forcing mechanism that compelled capitalist societies to confront their own failures and excesses.

Where communism was implemented, it often produced rapid modernization and industrialization, particularly in agrarian societies burdened by feudal or colonial legacies. The Soviet Union, for example, transformed from a primarily agrarian economy into a global industrial power in just a few decades.[100] Under Lenin's New Economic Policy and later Stalin's Five-Year Plans, industrial output increased dramatically.[101] Although the human cost was immense, the Soviet model demonstrated an ability to mobilize resources for national development at scale, something many capitalist societies had failed to achieve under similar starting conditions.[102]

Mao Zedong's China, despite the catastrophic failures of the Great Leap Forward, also addressed some of capitalism's unintended consequences. By the 1970s, China had significantly expanded literacy, healthcare access, and basic infrastructure.[103] Mao famously wrote, "A revolution is not a dinner party . . . a revolution is an insurrection, an act of violence by which one class overthrows another."[104] This revolutionary ethos enabled the Communist Party to dismantle deeply entrenched systems of inequality, including landlordism and legally sanctioned patriarchy.[105] In both China and the Soviet Union, communism initially succeeded in providing universal education, formal gender equality under the law, and state-guaranteed employment. These achievements contrast with the capitalist world's more gradual and uneven expansion of such rights.[106]

Communism also contributed meaningfully to the intellectual critique of liberal democracy and market economics. Even critics such as Thomas Sowell have acknowledged that communist regimes succeeded in delivering certain basic social goods. Sowell observed that "communist nations have often excelled at producing some of the most basic things people need, like food and shelter, though usually at great cost in freedom and efficiency."[107] Communist movements across the Global South, particularly in Vietnam, Cuba, and parts of Africa, played important roles in anti-colonial liberation. For many nations, Marxist ideology provided a compelling narrative of resistance to imperialism and a framework for national sovereignty and self-determination.[108]

The intellectual critique of Smithian capitalism also had substantial indirect effects. Marxist and socialist theories were taken seriously by Western intellectuals throughout the late nineteenth and early twentieth centuries. In Britain, France, Germany, and later the United States, academics, trade unionists, and reformers engaged deeply with Marx's analysis of labor exploitation, alienation, and inequality. Even critics acknowledged the power of his critique. John Maynard Keynes famously described

Das Kapital as "an obsolete economic textbook . . . scientifically erroneous," yet conceded that Marx raised moral and political questions capitalism had not adequately resolved.[109]

The existence of communism also had an indirect but significant influence on the evolution of capitalist governance. It contributed to the rise of Keynesian economics and the broader trend toward state intervention and economic planning in Western capitalist economies during the twentieth century. While Keynesianism and communism differ fundamentally in ideology and objectives, their historical trajectories intersected, particularly during the interwar period, the Great Depression, and the early Cold War. Keynesian economics was not a response to communism per se, but communism helped shape the political and social environment in which Keynesian ideas gained urgency and legitimacy, especially as a moderate alternative to the revolutionary appeal of Marxism.[110]

One of the most enduring effects of communism's presence was the way Western capitalist societies adapted, incorporating many social welfare mechanisms that were, at least in part, responses to the appeal of communism and socialism. Following the Bolshevik Revolution of 1917, Western governments began to view social unrest and inequality not merely as economic issues but as potential threats to political stability. The New Deal in the United States during the 1930s, the rise of social democracy in Scandinavia, and postwar social contracts in Western Europe were all influenced, to varying degrees, by concern over communism's appeal to the working class. Franklin D. Roosevelt, in 1944, called for a "Second Bill of Rights," emphasizing economic security as a foundation for freedom.[111] While Roosevelt never embraced socialism, his policies reflected a clear awareness that unchecked capitalism risked breeding revolution rather than reform.

Similarly, Western European countries after World War II expanded healthcare, education, housing, and labor protections, often under social democratic or Christian democratic parties that sought a middle path between laissez-faire, Smithian capitalism and authoritarian communism. As Harry Truman reportedly remarked around 1947, "The only thing that will defeat communism is to make capitalism work,"[112] a concise articulation of what Inclusive Capitalism seeks to achieve.

Communism also emboldened labor movements in capitalist countries. Workers' rights to organize, strike, and bargain collectively were increasingly recognized, not purely out of ideological alignment with socialism but because these rights served as a release valve that helped integrate working-class grievances into democratic political systems. The result was a system of regulated capitalism in which states guaranteed certain social protections while retaining private ownership and market dynamics. This model, which flourished in postwar Western Europe and the United States, has often been described as "embedded liberalism."[113]

During the Cold War from 1945 to 1991, Western nations not only engaged with communist ideas but actively sought to contain their spread, both militarily and ideologically. Governments funded cultural programs, academic exchanges, and media initiatives designed to present capitalism as more humane and democratic than communism. The Marshall Plan of 1948, which rebuilt Western European economies, was motivated in part by the desire to prevent the spread of communism in war-torn regions vulnerable to radical ideologies. As George Marshall stated in 1947, "The seeds of totalitarian regimes are nurtured by misery and want."[114]

Communism ultimately failed to deliver on its utopian promise. It did, however, succeed in identifying and attempting to redress real systemic injustices. Its contributions to social equality, basic welfare, education, and national sovereignty are historically significant. Communism worked, if only partially and temporarily, when it aligned with goals such as mobilizing underdeveloped societies, correcting extreme inequality, and redefining the role of the state. The fundamental problem was that it did so at immense human and economic cost, and without the self-correcting mechanisms that pluralistic political systems and market economies typically provide.[115]

The history of twentieth-century communism is replete with promises of liberation, equality, and abundance, yet in practice it produced some of the most severe episodes of human suffering and economic stagnation in modern history. Central to this tragic outcome was the system's failure to construct effective incentives—moral, material, or institutional—that could motivate productive labor, innovation, or civic responsibility. While communism aimed to eliminate exploitation and alienation, it frequently replaced them with coercion, inefficiency, and the widespread demoralization of entire populations.[116]

The absence of personal, market-based incentives, combined with the extreme centralization of power, not only deprived individuals of economic agency but also fostered systemic stagnation, waste, and terror. These outcomes were not aberrations; they were logical consequences of a system fundamentally misaligned with human behavior and institutional accountability. Karl Marx envisioned a society in which people would "hunt in the morning, fish in the afternoon, rear cattle in the evening, and criticize after dinner," liberated from the constraints of specialized and alienated labor.[117] Labor, in this imagined future, would be an act of self-expression rather than a means of survival. By abolishing private property and the wage relationship, communism sought to remove all coercive economic incentives, leaving only moral and collective motivations.

The fatal flaw was that Marx dramatically underestimated the role of material incentives and personal responsibility in coordinating complex economic activity. Friedrich Engels echoed this optimism, insisting that once class exploitation ended, people would work "freely according to their abilities."[118] Yet the Marxist tradition never produced a workable framework for motivating effort, allocating labor, or rewarding innovation once the profit motive and private ownership were extracted from the equation. Notably, one of the most formidable challenges for the architects of Inclusive Capitalism will be to define incentives that motivate effort and reward innovation once GDP is superseded by societal well-being metrics, particularly for large enterprises. Advances in technology, economic doctrine, and systems design make this objective not only possible but necessary. The first chapter of book two will frame this solution. The communist experience offers powerful lessons about the cost of ignoring fundamental aspects of human behavior.

Marx's assumptions about human motivation proved to be a critical blind spot. This blind spot was so severe that utopian aspirations repeatedly devolved into forced labor. In a parallel irony, Adam Smith's vision of an economy serving society manifested, in early industrial England, as widespread misery in factories, as discussed in the chapter on early-stage capitalism. Capitalism, over time, was able to self-correct sufficiently to survive. Communism was not. It failed repeatedly and catastrophically.[119] Whether capitalism can continue to self-correct without the deeper reengineering proposed by Inclusive Capitalism remains an open question; one that we address by advocating that reengineering is required which explicitly leverages advances in the behavioral science and modern technology to reduce, and ideally eliminate, recurring unintended consequences.

The Soviet Union under Lenin, and especially under Stalin, institutionalized a system that replaced voluntary incentives with compulsion, propaganda, and terror—far removed from the utopia Marx and Engels envisioned. The New Economic Policy of the 1920s briefly reintroduced market incentives, but it was soon dismantled in favor of forced collectivization and comprehensive state planning.[120] The first Five-Year Plan (1928–1932) epitomized the Stalinist model, emphasizing frenzied industrialization enforced through quotas, arrests, and executions. The behavior of Soviet factory managers under quota-based incentives illustrates the predictable failures of such systems.

One widely cited example involved nail factories given quotas measured by weight. To meet targets, some factories produced massive, unusable nails—heavy enough to satisfy tonnage requirements but useless in practice. When the metric was changed to the number of units produced, the same factories shifted to manufacturing tiny, flimsy nails of no practical value. This became a classic illustration of perverse incentives.[121] As economist Charles Kindleberger observed, "The moment quantity is measured without regard to utility, absurdity follows."

Similar distortions appeared elsewhere. Shoe factories were sometimes given production targets based on the number of units rather than pairs. To meet quotas quickly and avoid penalties, some produced only left shoes, reasoning that manufacturing matched pairs took longer. Because output was delivered to central warehouses regardless of usability, there was little accountability for real-world value. Cosmetic factories faced similar problems when lipstick quotas were measured by weight. Some responded by producing enormous, impractical tubes that satisfied plan metrics while ignoring consumer use entirely. In each case, the goal was not usefulness or satisfaction but compliance with abstract numerical targets.

Steel plants were given quotas based on tonnage, so they produced extremely long steel girders to maximize weight quickly. The result was girders so long they could not be transported by rail or used in construction without being cut down, wasting both time and material. Yet from the planner's perspective, the target was met.

Glass factories were sometimes evaluated by the weight of glass produced. To meet quotas, they manufactured thick, heavy sheets that were often too brittle for practical use. When the metric shifted to square meters, factories responded by producing extremely thin glass that shattered during transport or installation.

In some regions, tractor factories were pushed to produce as many tractors as possible, regardless of parts availability. As a result, thousands of tractors were delivered without tires, batteries, or engines, and often sat unused. In other periods, tractors were built but no fuel was allocated, rendering them essentially scrap metal. Official records nonetheless showed target fulfillment, and medals were awarded to managers. When targets could not be met, managers frequently resorted to creative accounting: submitting diluted chemicals labeled as concentrated, mislabeling consumer goods as military-grade or industrial-use to meet value quotas, or producing parts incompatible with existing machinery simply to satisfy numerical obligations.

From these examples, it should be clear that inappropriate incentives produce inappropriate behavior, and at scale can become the death knell of an economy, as they were in the Soviet Union. As Robert F. Kennedy stated in his 1967 speech at the University of Kansas, when critiquing GDP as a measure of economic success: "The Gross National Product counts air pollution and cigarette advertising, and ambulances to clear our highways of carnage . . . It counts the destruction of the redwoods and the loss of our natural wonder in chaotic sprawl . . . Yet the Gross National Product does not allow for the health of our children, the quality of their education, or the joy of their play . . . It measures everything, in short, except that which makes life worthwhile."[122]

Kennedy was, in effect, arguing for replacing GDP with a measure of societal well-being. A cornerstone principle of the re-architecting of capitalism proposed in Inclusive Capitalism is precisely this claim: that GDP is an inappropriate incentive as well as a primary driver of capitalism's unintended consequences. These unintended consequences, in turn, were among the forces that unleashed the horrors of communism as envisioned by Marx and instantiated by Lenin and Mao. GDP must be augmented with societal well-being as the core metrics of capitalism going forward. Chapter Two of Book Two explores in depth why GDP is fundamentally misaligned with human flourishing; Kennedy's critique, prescient as it was, only scratched the surface. The misalignment is far more profound!

Agricultural collectivization produced widespread resistance among peasants, who slaughtered livestock and burned crops rather than surrender them to state collectives. The human cost was catastrophic. The Holodomor, the engineered famine in Soviet Ukraine from 1932 to 1933, killed between 3.5 and 5 million people.[123] Farmers were deprived of any incentive to produce surplus, knowing it would be confiscated by the state—an arrangement disturbingly similar to the feudal economy of Tsarist Russia that communism purported to replace.

Stalin's regime relied on fear—more accurately, terror—to drive productivity. The Gulag system of forced labor camps became the backbone of industrial projects such as the White Sea–Baltic Canal, constructed by prisoners under inhuman conditions with primitive tools and little food. Aleksandr Solzhenitsyn described the Gulag as a society "where the human spirit is trampled beneath the boots of command and quotas."[124] Again, not exactly Marx's utopia.

The Stakhanovite movement, intended to create incentives through moral exhortation and rewards, produced perverse outcomes. Once a worker exceeded quotas, targets were raised for all, transforming success into punishment. The system encouraged cheating, sabotage, and resentment. As Thomas Sowell later observed, "The motivation to work cannot be legislated into existence, nor can it be beaten into existence—not for long."[125]

Despite vast natural resources and early industrial gains, the Soviet economy began to stagnate by the 1970s, culminating in the so-called Era of Stagnation under Brezhnev. With no meaningful price signals, weak innovation, and a bloated bureaucracy, productivity flatlined. A 1983 CIA estimate placed Soviet per capita GDP at less than half that of Western Europe, despite the Soviet Union's massive scale.

In China, Mao Zedong's attempt to reshape society through revolutionary enthusiasm culminated in the Great Leap Forward from 1958 to 1962, a campaign that abandoned rational incentive structures in favor of mass mobilization. Communes were formed, private farming abolished, and labor redirected to large-scale, often absurd projects such as backyard steel furnaces. Local officials falsified production data to meet ideological targets, leading the state to requisition excessive grain and leaving peasants to starve. The result was one of the deadliest famines in human history, with between 30 and 45 million deaths.[126] This catastrophe explains much of the momentum behind anti-communist sentiment in the United States and elsewhere.

Mao famously insisted, "To rebel is justified." This slogan encouraged not only criticism of authority but the dismantling of economic and social stability, including expertise and hierarchy—both essential for functioning incentive systems. The Cultural Revolution from 1966 to 1976 further destroyed what little economic rationality remained. Professionals, scientists, and technicians were persecuted, labor assignments were arbitrary, and productivity collapsed. Incentives for skill, effort, and innovation were replaced with political loyalty and revolutionary fervor.[127]

In Eastern European countries such as East Germany, Czechoslovakia, and Poland, similar failures unfolded. Central planning produced uniform mediocrity and chronic shortages. Incentives were systematically misaligned. Factory managers prioritized meeting state quotas over quality or consumer demand. Superficial compliance and falsification of output became routine. The phrase "we pretend to work, and they pretend to pay us" emerged not as capitalist satire but from workers themselves, trapped in a system that rewarded neither effort nor excellence and penalized neither idleness nor incompetence. This economic sclerosis fed political dissent, culminating in movements such as Solidarity in Poland, which fused economic grievances with demands for democratic reform.

In Cambodia under Pol Pot from 1975 to 1979, the abolition of markets, currency, and private property reached its most extreme and lethal expression. The Khmer Rouge sought to eliminate all class distinctions by emptying cities, forcing populations into rural communes, and executing anyone displaying signs of education or status. With no incentives, no property, and no functioning institutions, the economy collapsed. Nearly a quarter of the population—an estimated two million people—died from starvation, execution, or forced labor.[128] Again, not exactly the utopia Karl Marx had in mind.

North Korea remains the most enduring contemporary example of communism's perverse incentive structures. A rigid, militarized economy prioritizes loyalty over productivity, with famine and systemic deprivation recurring despite substantial natural and human potential. The regime's "Juche" (self-reliance) ideology replaces economic rationality with nationalist self-reliance enforced through surveillance and fear. The result is one of the most impoverished societies over more than a half century in the modern world.[129]

Forces That Resulted in the Decline of Communism

Friedrich Hayek warned that any system relying on centralized direction would eventually require coercion to function.[130] Thomas Sowell noted that the ultimate test of a system is not its intention but its consequences. The consequences of communism's broken incentive model were not limited to lower GDP or inefficient factories. They manifested as mass suffering, cultural decay, and the erosion of the human spirit. Communism revealed that no amount of ideology can replace the need for systems that respect human dignity, reward effort, and harness the decentralized intelligence of society. The result was communism self-exterminating in a spectacular manner. It was communism, rather than capitalism, that became its own gravedigger.[131]

The collapse of communism in the Soviet Union and the transformation of the People's Republic of China were not the result of isolated miscalculations or external pressures alone but rather the inevitable unraveling of an economic and political model that was internally contradictory, historically rigid, and structurally unsustainable. While these two regimes diverged significantly in their final trajectories—the Soviet Union dissolving into political collapse, the People's Republic of China evolving into a hybrid authoritarian capitalist state with mercantilist tendencies—they shared core pathologies: fundamental misalignment of incentives, institutional brittleness, ideological obsolescence, and a persistent failure to reconcile centralized control with the demands of a complex, modern economy.

The failures of the Soviet Union and Maoist China were not merely theoretical. They were manifest in well-documented human suffering, systemic stagnation, and political repression. These outcomes accumulated over decades and eventually exceeded the regimes' capacity to manage or conceal. In both cases, the eventual "death" of orthodox communism stemmed from the incompatibility of Marxist-Leninist doctrine with empirical economic and political realities.[132]

The Soviet model, shaped by Lenin's theory of the vanguard party and Stalin's totalitarian central planning, achieved early industrial gains through sheer mobilization of labor and resources. However, this model lacked mechanisms for adaptation, innovation, or individual initiative. By the 1970s, under Leonid Brezhnev, the Soviet economy entered what became known as the "Era of Stagnation," marked by declining productivity, deteriorating infrastructure, and minimal technological progress. Concurrently, the American economy entered a period of stagflation, prompting a shift away from Keynesian economics toward a reemergence of laissez-faire, Smithian capitalism. American capitalism evolved and adapted; the rigid Soviet system did not, and this rigidity ultimately led to self-destruction.

Soviet factories produced to fulfill quotas rather than to meet consumer demand. As discussed earlier and illustrated by the often darkly humorous anecdotes of Soviet industrial life, this produced grotesque economic absurdities: nails too heavy to use, shoes without pairs, and chronic shortages so severe that black markets became de facto institutions. The incentive problem was systemic and endemic. Meanwhile, military expenditures soared, consuming vast portions of GDP. The Soviet invasion of Afghanistan in 1979 further drained state finances and exposed the limits of imperial reach. Corruption, alcoholism, and bureaucratic malaise permeated the party apparatus. The KGB's vast surveillance network, designed to enforce ideological conformity, could not prevent the deepening cynicism of the population. The system persisted only through inertia and repression.[133]

The arrival of Mikhail Gorbachev in the mid-1980s introduced the twin reforms of perestroika (economic restructuring) and glasnost (political openness).[134] These reforms inadvertently exposed the full extent of systemic dysfunction. Perestroika attempted to decentralize economic control without establishing genuine markets, creating an incoherent hybrid with neither plan nor price. Glasnost unleashed long-suppressed grievances regarding famine, purges, repression, and economic incompetence. Far from revitalizing communism, these reforms accelerated its delegitimization.

By 1991, the Soviet Union ceased to exist. An ideology that had once justified mass mobilization and political terror could no longer sustain public belief. As Thomas Sowell observed, "The fatal flaw of communism is not in its aspirations, but in its means. Abolishing prices, property, and profit destroys not only prosperity but truth" (*Marxism: Philosophy and Economics*, 1985).[135] The challenge for Inclusive Capitalism is to evolve pricing, property, and profit in ways rooted in actual human behavior—true to Adam Smith's vision and informed by what failed under communism and socialism.

In China, the Maoist variant of communism produced some of the most catastrophic policy failures in human history. The Great Leap Forward (1958–1962), intended to transform China rapidly into an industrial power, imposed collectivized agriculture and backyard steel production on a predominantly peasant society. Local cadres, pressured to meet ideological quotas, falsified output data, leading the state to over-extract grain. The result was the deadliest famine of the twentieth century, with estimated deaths ranging from 30 to 45 million.[136]

Mao Zedong's revolutionary voluntarism substituted ideological purity for economic logic. He believed, consistent with his assertion that "Revolution is not a dinner party," that human will could overcome material constraints. The outcome was devastating. The abolition of traditional incentives destroyed agricultural productivity. As in Stalin's Soviet Union, the absence of feedback loops and punishment for truth-telling transformed information into propaganda and data into fiction. The Cultural Revolution (1966–1976) further shattered China's social and economic fabric. Intellectuals were purged, schools closed, industries disrupted, and millions of lives destroyed in a campaign to eradicate "bourgeois" elements. Mao's attempt to perpetuate revolution by mobilizing youth against the Communist Party's own institutions produced political chaos and arrested economic development for an entire decade.

After Mao's death, Deng Xiaoping, a purged pragmatist once exiled to work in a tractor factory, returned to power and initiated radical economic reforms. He famously declared, "It doesn't matter whether a cat is black or white, so long as it catches mice."[137] This statement marked the ideological death of communism as the governing economic foundation in China, even though the People's Republic persists and the Communist Party continues Maoist China's repressive, anti-democratic political practices. Deng reintroduced private property, market pricing, and foreign investment while maintaining tight political control. The state retained ownership of the "commanding heights" but allowed profit-seeking behavior, competition, and entrepreneurship—elements fundamentally antithetical to Marxist economic theory. The result was explosive growth and poverty reduction but at the cost of ideological coherence. China's model thus represents not the success of communism but its abandonment in favor of state-led capitalism under the guise of "socialism with Chinese characteristics." Marx envisioned the "withering away of the state"; China instead witnessed the entrenchment of technocratic authoritarianism—economically liberal while politically repressive.

In the Soviet Union and Maoist China, communism collapsed because its foundational premises were incompatible with the requirements of a functioning modern society. Marx and Engels believed that private property was the root of alienation and exploitation. Yet in abolishing it, communist regimes removed the incentives that drive human creativity, responsibility, and accountability. The state became the sole arbiter of value, resulting in chronic misallocation and waste.[138] To manage what could not be managed, the state resorted to propaganda and terror. Innovation was stifled, initiative punished, and truth subordinated to ideological necessity. Even

Lenin, toward the end of his life, hinted at the fragility of the Soviet experiment, writing in 1923, "We have not achieved a Communist society, and we are still far from it."[139] Hayek's warnings about the dangers of central planning proved tragically accurate. The system's inability to learn, correct, or admit error ensured that mistakes compounded until the structure itself became unsustainable.

The collapse of Soviet communism and the ideological retreat of Chinese communism were outcomes of structural failures rooted in Marxist-Leninist theory and amplified by authoritarian practice. Both regimes attempted to reengineer society using doctrines that disregarded human complexity, economic interdependence, and the necessity of individual autonomy.[140] In doing so, they unleashed immense suffering and eventually encountered the hard limits of coercive planning. China survives as a state and rising power but not as a communist society; it persists as a post-communist regime that preserved political control while abandoning exclusive central planning. The Soviet Union, unable to reform or rebrand itself, disintegrated.[141] The death of communism in these two titanic cases offers a profound historical lesson: ideology cannot substitute for incentive, and utopian ends cannot justify totalitarian means without destroying both. The tragedy lies not only in communism's failure but in the vast human cost incurred in the attempt to make it succeed.

This review of communism, together with the in-depth review of capitalism, evokes a personal sense of urgency around the need for systems-level improvement in the world's approach to economics. The unintended consequences of unchecked Smithian capitalism were so profound that an alternative—communism—captured roughly one-third of the world's population at its peak in the 1970s.[142] The hatred directed at those who deviated from communist doctrine—a doctrine itself neither clearly defined nor aligned with fundamental human behavior—resulted in incomprehensible suffering, death, and destruction, particularly among the most capable and driven members of society.

In the Soviet Union, aggregate deaths attributable to communism are estimated at 13 to 20 million, comparable to World War II fatalities.[143] These include approximately 5.5 to 8 million deaths from famine and collectivization between 1932 and 1933 (including the Holodomor); 700,000 to 1.2 million deaths during the Great Purge of 1936–1938; 1.5 to 2 million deaths in the Gulag system of forced labor from 1929 to 1953; 500,000 to 1 million deaths due to deportations and forced population transfers from the 1930s through the 1950s; and an additional 1 to 1.5 million deaths from the famine of 1946–1947.[144]

Deaths attributable to communism in Maoist China may have reached as high as 50 million.[145] These include the execution of 1 to 2 million landlords during the Land Reform Campaign of the late 1940s through 1952; famine resulting from the Great Leap Forward, causing an estimated 15 to 45 million deaths between 1958 and 1962; and political purges, mob violence, and state-sanctioned chaos during the Cultural Revolution (1966–1976), resulting in an additional 1 to 2 million deaths.[146]

Pol Pot's radical agrarian communism in Cambodia led to genocide, executions, and starvation accounting for approximately 1.7 to 2 million deaths—roughly one quarter of the population.[147] In North Korea, political prison camps, purges, and recurring famine have resulted in an estimated 500,000 to 3 million deaths since 1948.[148]

Nothing in capitalist history comes close to the level of death and destruction inflicted under communism. The worst abuses under capitalism—including the early English factories and the conditions that manifested during the Gilded Age in the United States—while involving exploitation, inequality, and class conflict, did not result in more than a fractional percentage of the purposeful death and destruction carried out by the Soviet, Red Chinese, Cambodian, and North Korean communist regimes. The unintended consequences of capitalism did, however, trigger Karl Marx to develop an alternative theory for how the world economy should evolve. While Marx's writings were often ambiguous and lacked clear, implementable solutions, they powerfully evoked passion among his followers, passion that ultimately contributed to a nearly unfathomable scale of death and destruction.

Communism collapsed in the Soviet Union and Maoist China, but the unintended consequences of capitalism remain, along with the resentment those consequences continue to generate—the same resentment that originally fueled Karl Marx. Today, dissatisfaction with capitalism persists due to familiar grievances: wealth inequality; perceptions that the system is rigged and lacks opportunity; continued exploitation of the workforce through globalization and offshoring; environmental degradation, particularly climate change; the unaffordability of basic necessities such as housing, health care, and education; and the expanding role and dominance of large enterprises in society, including health care benefit providers and global technology platforms.

While society has come a long way since the early days of capitalism—when conditions in English factories helped fuel both legislative reform and alternative ideologies—and while communism has waned as an external existential threat, risks remain. These risks persist most visibly in countries such as North Korea. In addition, socialism, in its various modern forms, which will be examined in depth in the following chapter, represents a significant challenge to capitalism within the United States and across the developed world. Democratic socialism and neo-Marxist thought advocate wealth redistribution, expanded state ownership, and the curtailment of free markets in key sectors such as health care, housing, and education.

The overriding moral critique centers on inequality, the commodification of human needs, and systemic exploitation. Political figures such as Bernie Sanders in the United States, Jeremy Corbyn in the United Kingdom, and Jean-Luc Mélenchon in France have mobilized younger generations around themes of wealth redistribution, public ownership, and anti-corporate policy. Movements advocating universal basic income, green new deals, and de-commodified public services reflect broader socialist currents operating beneath contemporary political discourse.

At the same time, modern socialist critiques erode capitalism's moral high ground by framing it as an economic model that is incompatible with justice and human dignity. Authoritarian populism from the right also poses an additional threat to laissez-faire, Smithian capitalism. Right-wing populist regimes often adopt pro-business, anti-socialist rhetoric while simultaneously undermining core capitalist institutions such as free markets, the rule of law, independent judiciaries, global trade, and a free press. In these systems, capitalism is used instrumentally rather than ideologically. Examples include Viktor Orbán in Hungary, Recep Tayyip Erdoğan in Turkey, and Vladimir Putin's oligarchic model in Russia.[149] Common features include crony capitalism, suppression of dissent, economic nationalism, and anti-globalism. The danger is that state-aligned clientelism replaces competitive capitalism, distorting markets, suppressing innovation, and eroding trust in institutions such as central banks, independent regulators, and the press—the very pillars of capitalist stability.

These risks to capitalism have evolved since the time of Karl Marx, but they are no less pernicious.[150] If capitalism is to survive rather than collapse under its own "contradictions," it must regain the moral high ground and address the unintended consequences of exclusion, wealth disparity, disenfranchisement, and environmental de-prioritization that fuel threats from both socialism and autocracy. The viable path forward lies neither in Keynesian expansionism on the left nor in neo-classical Smithian retrenchment on the right. An inclusive instantiation of Smithian capitalism offers a principled and pragmatic alternative. We now turn to the lessons derived from the various "communisms," with the explicit goal of ensuring that the builders of Inclusive Capitalism fully absorb and act upon them.

Conclusions and Insights for Inclusive Capitalism Derived from Communism

Communism offers a wealth of insights for the builders of Inclusive Capitalism. Specifically, the communist experience of the twentieth century—including its aspirations, limited achievements, and profound failures—provides a powerful repository of lessons for redesigning capitalism to be more inclusive, humane, resilient, and more rational from a mathematical perspective. While communism as a political and economic system ultimately collapsed under the weight of its own contradictions, the critiques it levied against capitalism—including inequality, exploitation, and alienation—remain salient. A thoughtful engagement with the communist experience does not require its replication but rather invites a recalibration of capitalism along more ethical, moral, and socially sustainable lines.

First, there is a lesson in the moral imperative of economic justice. Communism's enduring appeal rested on its uncompromising demand for equality and social justice. Marx's critique of capitalism, particularly in *Das Kapital* and *The Communist Manifesto*, highlighted the alienation of labor and the concentration of wealth in the hands of a few. Although his proposed solution—the abolition of private property and markets—proved disastrous, the moral questions he posed remain unresolved. "The free development of each is the condition for the free development of all."[151] Capitalism redesigned for inclusiveness must address extremes of inequality by ensuring access to opportunity and to the essentials of a dignified life, including education, healthcare, meaningful work, and housing. These are not socialist luxuries; they are democratic necessities.

The second lesson from the history of communism is the absolute centrality of incentives and individual agency. Communist economies collapsed in part because they eliminated personal incentives, operating under the assumption that moral exhortation or collective ownership alone would motivate productivity. In reality, as Friedrich Hayek and Thomas Sowell emphasized, incentives are not corruptions of virtue but mechanisms of coordination and motivation. "Incentives are not just devices; they are information" (Thomas Sowell, *Knowledge and Decisions*, 1980).[152] Capitalism's enduring strength lies in its capacity to harness individual creativity and ambition. The challenge for Inclusive Capitalism is to extend these incentives more broadly, ensuring that gains from productivity and innovation are shared not merely through wages but through meaningful "stakeholdership." Sowell criticized communism for misunderstanding both incentives and the distributed nature of knowledge. In *Marxism: Philosophy and Economics* (1985), he argued that the Marxist vision collapses when confronted with scarcity and human behavior, observing that "the idea of a world where all people would labor altruistically to produce goods and services to be distributed according to needs rather than contribution is a vision not of mankind, but of angels."[153]

Perhaps the most difficult challenge for Inclusive Capitalism involves the setting and distribution of incentives. American capitalism has long operated on a superstar model with super-sized rewards. Top performers—technology entrepreneurs, healthcare executives, investment bankers, elite software and AI engineers, professional athletes, and entertainers—have enjoyed incentives that reach into the stratosphere. In many cases, these individuals genuinely drive exceptional outcomes for their firms or industries. Communism, by contrast, nearly eliminated incentives altogether, and the system collapsed. Socialism dampens incentives, which may preserve equity but can also suppress performance and innovation. The objective of Inclusive Capitalism is to preserve the high-powered incentives that fuel entrepreneurship and innovation—one of the defining strengths of the United States—while dramatically broadening the incentive base. Crucially, this must be accomplished within a capitalist framework, without reliance on post-hoc redistribution through extreme marginal tax rates, excessive regulation, or total dependence on government-provided services for healthcare, education, childcare, and pensions. These issues will be examined further in the next chapter on socialism, particularly European-style democratic socialism, and expanded in depth in book two.

A third lesson from the communist experience is that the state must act as steward, not master. Communist regimes conflated the public good with state control, producing repression, inefficiency, and institutional fragility. At the same time, history has shown that entirely unregulated markets under Smithian capitalism are not sufficient. Under Inclusive Capitalism, the state functions as a steward whose primary responsibilities include chartering large enterprises around societal well-being rather than GDP alone, and establishing incentive structures consistent with that objective. These charters embed responsibility for addressing capitalism's unintended consequences through private, not purely public, mechanisms, while ensuring appropriate oversight, accountability, and long-term investment.

A fourth insight concerns participation and voice. Communism promised democratic control of economic life but delivered centralized authoritarianism. Genuine empowerment requires pluralism, transparency, and institutional accountability. A reformed capitalism must strengthen democratic participation not only in political institutions but also within enterprises and communities. There is substantial, often untapped wisdom embedded in the workforce, and ignoring that wisdom leads to insular and brittle decision-making. As C. Wright Mills observed, "Freedom is not merely the opportunity to do as one pleases; neither is it merely the opportunity to choose between set alternatives. Freedom is, first of all, the chance to formulate the available choices."[154]

A fifth takeaway concerns dignity in work. One of communism's central insights—however poorly executed—was that work should uplift rather than degrade. Technological advancement has proven to be the most effective path to dignity in work. Automation eliminates many of the most degrading and physically punishing tasks, while creating opportunities for more creative, voluntary, and cognitively engaging labor. The transformation of work in the United States during the late twentieth century illustrates this clearly: Software engineering offers vastly greater dignity and agency than tending a loom or laying railroad tracks. The rapid proliferation of AI is likely to accelerate this trend. A core objective of Inclusive Capitalism is to democratize and accelerate innovation by removing incentives to maintain artificial scarcity, promoting open collaboration, and enabling the broad diffusion of technological progress.

The collapse of communism does not invalidate its critiques. Rather, it exposes the dangers of addressing complex social problems through ideologies that seek unifying, all-encompassing solutions. The central challenge for twenty-first-century capitalism is to absorb the ethical urgency of socialism without replicating its structural failures. A redesigned capitalism must reconcile dynamism with dignity, innovation with inclusion, and freedom with fairness.

Implications for the Design of Inclusive Capitalism Derived from Communism

The experience of communism provides some of the clearest guidance available on what not to do when redesigning an economic system. Its failures were not accidental, nor were they merely implementation errors. They stemmed from foundational design choices that were misaligned with human behavior, incentives, and institutional realities. These lessons are essential for Inclusive Capitalism, particularly because its ambition is similarly large in scope and moral intent.

First, the communist experience demonstrates the danger of building an economic vision that is utopian in aspiration but detached from how humans actually behave. Marx's vision assumed that once material scarcity and class conflict were eliminated, individuals would naturally contribute according to ability and inclination, without the need for differentiated rewards, ownership, or accountability. In practice, this assumption proved catastrophically wrong. Human beings respond to incentives, social recognition, advancement in responsibility, personal growth, autonomy, and meaningful feedback. Systems that deny this reality do not elevate human nature; they suppress it and eventually rely on coercion to function.[155] Inclusive Capitalism must therefore reject idealized assumptions about altruism or universal prosocial behavior. Its design must begin with behavioral realism, acknowledging ambition, fear, creativity, status-seeking, and the desire for agency as permanent features of human systems.

Second, Inclusive Capitalism must ensure that its core metrics align directly with the motivations and behaviors of industrial leaders. Communism failed in part because it attempted to motivate leaders and managers through ideological loyalty and coercive targets rather than through aligned incentives. A parallel risk exists today in the widespread reliance on ESG-style frameworks that operate orthogonally to the dominant incentive structure. As long as GDP, share price, and short-term financial performance remain the decisive measures of success, alternative metrics—no matter how well intentioned—will remain marginal. Societal well-being metrics must therefore have real teeth and real benefits. They must influence access to capital, executive compensation, corporate charters, and strategic degrees of freedom. Crucially, these metrics cannot be designed in abstraction. Primary research with industrial leaders is required to ensure that societal well-being measures resonate with their aspirations, competitive realities, and identity as builders, rather than being perceived as external constraints or moral impositions.

Third, while utopianism must be avoided in system design, a compelling vision remains essential for change. Communism spread not because its economic mechanics were sound but because it articulated a powerful narrative that spoke directly to lived pain: exploitation, indignity, inequality, and exclusion. A technically sound redesign of capitalism will fail politically and culturally unless it is paired with a narrative that addresses these pain points clearly and credibly. Strategic vision is vital, but it must be anchored in implementable mechanisms rather than abstract promises.

Fourth, the primary audience for systemic change is industrial leadership, working in concert with open-minded policymakers. This mirrors the historical reality of early capitalism, where economic transformation was driven not primarily by mass movements but by the decisions of those who controlled capital, technology, and organizational structures. Communism sought to eliminate this class entirely, with disastrous results. Inclusive Capitalism instead seeks to reorient it. Industrial leaders possess the capacity to deploy capital, scale innovation, and reshape institutions far more rapidly than governments alone. Policymakers play a critical enabling role, particularly in chartering, oversight, and boundary-setting, but the locus of execution must remain within the productive system itself. Designing for this reality is not ideological concession; it is institutional pragmatism.

Fifth, communism raises an unavoidable question about the future of work under conditions of true labor non-scarcity. Marx's assertion that labor could become an act of self-expression rather than a means of survival was premature in his time, but it becomes newly relevant in the context of automation and artificial intelligence. A more automated economy challenges traditional assumptions about wage labor as the primary source of dignity, identity, and contribution. Inclusive Capitalism must therefore anticipate a future in which self-expression, creativity, care, and voluntary contribution play a larger role in societal value creation. This does not imply the elimination of incentives or markets but rather their evolution. Systems must reward contribution in broader forms, recognize non-market value creation, and ensure that the decoupling of survival from labor does not result in loss of agency or purpose.

Taken together, the communist experience underscores a central principle of Inclusive Capitalism: Moral intent is insufficient without institutional design that respects human behavior, aligns incentives, and evolves with technology. Where communism attempted to overwrite reality with ideology, Inclusive Capitalism must engineer reality to produce ethical outcomes by design.[156]

Notes

1 Marx, Karl, and Friedrich Engels. *The Communist Manifesto.* 1848. Penguin Classics ed., pp. 34–68.

2 Applebaum, Anne. *Red Famine.* Doubleday, 2017, pp. 29–92.

3 Arendt, Hannah. *The Origins of Totalitarianism.* Harcourt, 1973, pp. 318–368.

4 Mises, Ludwig von. *Economic Calculation in the Socialist Commonwealth.* Auburn ed., pp. 1–33.

5 Kornai, János. *Economics of Shortage.* North-Holland, 1980, pp. 25–81.

6 Arendt, Hannah. *The Origins of Totalitarianism.* pp. 318–368.

7 Popper, Karl. *The Open Society and Its Enemies, Vol. II.* Princeton University Press, pp. 87–122.

8 North, Douglass. *Institutions, Institutional Change, and Economic Performance.* Cambridge University Press, pp. 3–32.

9 Hobsbawm, Eric. *How to Change the World.* Yale University Press, 2011, pp. 49–92.

10 Engels, Friedrich. *Socialism: Utopian and Scientific.* Progress Publishers ed., pp. 45–83.
11 Ibid.
12 Hayek, Friedrich A. *Individualism and Economic Order.* University of Chicago Press, 1948, pp. 77–91.
13 Ibid.
14 Marx, Karl. *Capital, Vol. I.* Penguin Classics ed., 1976, pp. 125–177, 873–940.
15 Ibid.
16 Ibid.
17 Marx, Karl, and Friedrich Engels. *The Communist Manifesto.* pp. 34–68.
18 Ibid.
19 Engels, Friedrich. *Socialism: Utopian and Scientific.* Progress Publishers ed., pp. 45–83.
20 Hayek, Friedrich A. *Individualism and Economic Order.* pp. 77–91.
21 Mises, Ludwig von. *Economic Calculation in the Socialist Commonwealth.* pp. 1–33.
22 Kornai, János. *Economics of Shortage.* North-Holland, 1980, pp. 25–81.
23 Popper, Karl. *The Open Society and Its Enemies, Vol. II.* pp. 87–122.
24 Hobsbawm, Eric. *How to Change the World.* pp. 49–92.
25 Smith, Adam. *The Theory of Moral Sentiments.* Liberty Fund ed., pp. 82–94.
26 Marx, Karl, and Friedrich Engels. *The Communist Manifesto.* pp. 34–6
27 Marx, Karl. *Capital, Vol. I.* Penguin Classics ed., 1976, pp. 125–177, 873–940.
28 Ibid.
29 Lenin, Vladimir. *State and Revolution.* Penguin Classics ed., pp. 15–58.
30 Marx, Karl, and Friedrich Engels. *The Communist Manifesto.* pp. 34–6.
31 Sowell, Thomas. *Marxism.* William Morrow, 1985, pp. 23–71.
32 Rodrik, Dani. *Economics Rules.* Oxford University Press, 2015, pp. 1–38.
33 Kornai, János. *The Socialist System.* Princeton University Press, 1992, pp. 19–45, 221–245.
34 Lenin, Vladimir. *State and Revolution.* pp. 15–58.
35 Applebaum, Anne. *Red Famine.* pp. 29–92.
36 Hayek, Friedrich A. *The Use of Knowledge in Society.* American Economic Review 35, no. 4 (1945): 519–530.
37 Popper, Karl. *The Open Society and Its Enemies, Vol. II.* pp. 87–122.
38 Smith, Adam. *The Theory of Moral Sentiments.* Liberty Fund ed., pp. 82–94.
39 North, Douglass. *Institutions, Institutional Change, and Economic Performance.* Cambridge University Press, pp. 3–32.
40 Fukuyama, Francis. *The End of History and the Last Man.* Free Press, 1992, pp. 45–88.
41 Rodrik, Dani. *Economics Rules.* pp. 1–38.
42 Marx, Karl, and Friedrich Engels. *The Communist Manifesto.* pp. 34–6.
43 Lenin, Vladimir. *State and Revolution.* pp. 15–58.
44 Kornai, János. *The Socialist System.* pp. 19–45, 221–245.
45 Brandt, Loren & Rawski, Thomas. *China's Great Economic Transformation.* Cambridge University Press, pp. 3–38.
46 Hayek, Friedrich A. *Individualism and Economic Order.* pp. 77–91.
47 Conquest, Robert. *The Great Terror.* Oxford University Press, 2008 ed., pp. 35–88.
48 Figes, Orlando. *Revolutionary Russia, 1891–1991.* Metropolitan Books, 2014, pp. 186–233.
49 Ibid.
50 Ibid.
51 Conquest, Robert. *The Great Terror.* Oxford University Press, 2008 ed., pp. 35–88.
52 Figes, Orlando. *Revolutionary Russia, 1891–1991.* pp. 186–233.
53 Kornai, János. *Economics of Shortage.* North-Holland, 1980, pp. 25–81.
54 Conquest, Robert. *The Great Terror.* pp. 35–88.
55 North, Douglass. *Institutions, Institutional Change, and Economic Performance.* pp. 3–32.

56 Arendt, Hannah. *The Origins of Totalitarianism.* pp. 318–368.
57 North, Douglass. *Institutions, Institutional Change, and Economic Performance.* pp. 3–32.
58 Arendt, Hannah. *The Origins of Totalitarianism.* pp. 318–368.
59 U.S. Nuclear Regulatory Commission, *Millstone Lessons Learned Report, late 1990s.*
60 *NRC guidance on Safety-Conscious Work Environment (SCWE),* post-Millstone reforms.
61 North, Douglass. *Institutions, Institutional Change, and Economic Performance.* pp. 3–32.
62 Rodrik, Dani. *Economics Rules.* pp. 1–38.
63 Sachs, Jeffrey. *Poland's Jump to the Market Economy.* MIT Press, pp. 3–42.
64 Fortescue, Stephen. *Russia's Oil Barons and Metal Magnates: Oligarchs and the State in Transition.* New York: Palgrave Macmillan, 2006, pp. 63–98.
65 Åslund, Anders. *How Capitalism Was Built.* Cambridge University Press, pp. 1–31.
66 Ibid.
67 Judt, Tony. *Postwar.* Penguin, 2005, pp. 215–243.
68 Ibid.
69 Ibid.
70 North, Douglass. *Institutions, Institutional Change, and Economic Performance.* pp. 3–32.
71 Sowell, Thomas. *Marxism.* William Morrow, 1985, pp. 23–71.
72 Kornai, János. *The Socialist System.* pp. 19–45, 221–245.
73 Marx, Karl, and Friedrich Engels. *The Communist Manifesto.* pp. 34–68.
74 Ibid.
75 Lenin, Vladimir. *State and Revolution.* pp. 15–58.
76 North, Douglass. *Institutions, Institutional Change, and Economic Performance.* pp. 3–32.
77 Berliner, Joseph. *Factory and Manager in the USSR.* Harvard University Press, pp. 112–158.
78 Sowell, Thomas. *Marxism.* William Morrow, 1985, pp. 23–71.
79 Kornai, János. *Economics of Shortage.* North-Holland, 1980, pp. 25–81.
80 Hayek, Friedrich A. *The Road to Serfdom.* University of Chicago Press, 1944 (50th Anniversary ed., 1994), pp. 67–96.
81 Berliner, Joseph. *Factory and Manager in the USSR.* pp. 112–158.
82 Applebaum, Anne. *Red Famine.* pp. 29–92.
83 Brandt, Loren & Rawski, Thomas. *China's Great Economic Transformation.* Cambridge University Press, pp. 3–38.
84 Ibid.
85 Arendt, Hannah. *The Origins of Totalitarianism.* pp. 318–368.
86 Kornai, János. *The Road to a Free Economy.* Norton, 1990, pp. 1–28.
87 North, Douglass. *Institutions, Institutional Change, and Economic Performance.* pp. 3–32.
88 Rodrik, Dani. *Economics Rules.* pp. 1–38.
89 Kornai, János. *The Socialist System.* pp. 19–45, 221–245.
90 Marx, Karl, and Friedrich Engels. *The Communist Manifesto.* pp. 34–68.
91 Ibid.
92 Lenin, Vladimir. *State and Revolution.* Penguin Classics ed., pp. 15–58.
93 Conquest, Robert. *The Great Terror.* Oxford University Press, 2008 ed., pp. 35–88.
94 Rodrik, Dani. *Economics Rules.* pp. 1–38.
95 Conquest, Robert. *The Great Terror.* pp. 35–88.
96 Marx, Karl, and Friedrich Engels. *The Communist Manifesto.* pp. 34–6.
97 Marx, Karl. *Capital, Vol. I.* pp. 125–177, 873–940.
98 Hobsbawm, Eric. *How to Change the World.* Yale University Press, 2011, pp. 49–92.
99 Hayek, Friedrich A. *The Use of Knowledge in Society.* 519–530.
100 Davies, R. W. *The Industrialisation of Soviet Russia, Vol. 1.* Harvard University Press, pp. 3–56.
101 Lenin, Vladimir. *The Tax in Kind.* Progress Publishers, pp. 1–34.

102 Nove, Alec. *An Economic History of the USSR*. Penguin, 1992, pp. 162–214.
103 Naughton, Barry. *The Chinese Economy*. MIT Press, 2007, pp. 55–96.
104 Deng Xiaoping. *Selected Works, Vol. III.*. 116–123.
105 Brandt, Loren & Rawski, Thomas. *China's Great Economic Transformation*. pp. 3–38.
106 Kornai, János. *The Road to a Free Economy*. Norton, 1990, pp. 1–28.
107 Sowell, Thomas. *Marxism*. pp. 23–71.
108 Kornai, János. *The Road to a Free Economy*. pp. 1–28.
109 Keynes, John Maynard. "A Short View of Russia." In *Essays in Persuasion*. London: Macmillan, 1931, pp. 297–309.
110 Hobsbawm, Eric. *How to Change the World*. pp. 49–92.
111 Roosevelt, Franklin D. "State of the Union Address." January 11, 1944. In *The Public Papers and Addresses of Franklin D. Roosevelt, 1944–45*. New York: Harper & Brothers, 1950, pp. 32–41.
112 Truman, Harry S. *Public Papers of the Presidents of the United States: Harry S. Truman, 1947*. Washington, DC: U.S. Government Printing Office, 1963, pp. 594–596.
113 Ruggie, John Gerard. "International Regimes, Transactions, and Change: Embedded Liberalism in the Postwar Economic Order." *International Organization* 36, no. 2 (1982): 379–415.
114 Marshall, George C. "Address at Harvard University." June 5, 1947. In *Department of State Bulletin*, vol. 16, no. 415 (June 15, 1947): 1159–1160.
115 Popper, Karl. *The Open Society and Its Enemies, Vol. II: The High Tide of Prophecy—Hegel, Marx, and the Aftermath*. Princeton University Press, 1966, pp. 87–122.
116 Arendt, Hannah. *The Origins of Totalitarianism*. pp. 318–368.
117 Marx, Karl, and Friedrich Engels. *The German Ideology*. Written 1845–1846. In *Collected Works of Karl Marx and Friedrich Engels*, Vol. 5. Moscow: Progress Publishers, 1976, pp. 47–48.
118 Friedrich Engels, *Anti-Dühring: Herr Eugen Dühring's Revolution in Science*, trans. Emile Burns (Moscow: Progress Publishers, 1978), Part III, chap. 2.
119 Kornai, János. *The Socialist System: The Political Economy of Communism*. Princeton University Press, 1992, pp. 3–6, 221–245.
120 Service, Robert. *A History of Modern Russia: From Tsarism to the Twenty-First Century*. 3rd ed. London: Penguin, 2009, pp. 142–168.
121 Berliner, Joseph. *Factory and Manager in the USSR*. pp. 112–158.
122 Kennedy, Robert F. "Remarks at the University of Kansas." March 18, 1968. In *Public Papers of Robert F. Kennedy*. New York: Random House, 1969, pp. 388–392.
123 Applebaum, Anne. *Red Famine: Stalin's War on Ukraine*. New York: Doubleday, 2017, pp. 29–92.
124 Solzhenitsyn, Aleksandr. *The Gulag Archipelago, 1918–1956: An Experiment in Literary Investigation*. Vol. 1. Translated by Thomas P. Whitney. New York: Harper & Row, 1973, pp. 3–40.
125 Sowell, Thomas. *Marxism*. pp. 23–71.
126 Applebaum, Anne. *Red Famine*. Doubleday, 2017, pp. 29–92.
127 Brandt, Loren & Rawski, Thomas. *China's Great Economic Transformation*. pp. 3–38.
128 Arendt, Hannah. *The Origins of Totalitarianism*. Harcourt, 1973, pp. 318–368.
129 Ibid.
130 Hayek, Friedrich A. *Individualism and Economic Order*. pp. 77–91.
131 Fukuyama, Francis. *The End of History and the Last Man*. Free Press, 1992, pp. 45–88.
132 Popper, Karl. *The Open Society and Its Enemies, Vol. II*. Princeton University Press, pp. 87–122.
133 Arendt, Hannah. *The Origins of Totalitarianism*. pp. 318–368.
134 Gorbachev, Mikhail. *Perestroika*. Harper & Row, 1987, pp. 15–44.
135 Sowell, Thomas. *Marxism: Philosophy and Economics*. William Morrow, 1985, pp. 23–71.
136 Applebaum, Anne. *Red Famine*pp. 29–92.
137 Deng Xiaoping. *Selected Works, Vol. III*. Foreign Languages Press, pp. 116–123.
138 Berliner, Joseph. *Factory and Manager in the USSR*. pp. 112–158.

139 Lenin, Vladimir. *State and Revolution.* pp. 15–58.
140 North, Douglass. *Institutions, Institutional Change, and Economic Performance.* pp. 3–32.
141 Fukuyama, Francis. *The End of History and the Last Man.* pp. 45–88.
142 Åslund, Anders. *How Capitalism Was Built.* pp. 1–31.
143 Figes, Orlando. *Revolutionary Russia, 1891–1991.* Metropolitan Books, 2014, pp. 186–233.
144 Ibid.
145 Applebaum, Anne. *Red Famine.* pp. 29–92.
146 Ibid.
147 Arendt, Hannah. *The Origins of Totalitarianism.* pp. 318–368.
148 Ibid.
149 Fukuyama, Francis. *The End of History and the Last Man.* pp. 45–88.
150 North, Douglass. *Institutions, Institutional Change, and Economic Performance.* pp. 3–32.
151 Marx, Karl, and Friedrich Engels. *The Communist Manifesto.* pp. 34–68.
152 Sowell, Thomas. *Knowledge and Decisions.* pp. 23–71.
153 Ibid.
154 Mills, C. Wright. *The Power Elite.* Oxford University Press, 1956.
155 Hayek, Friedrich A. *The Use of Knowledge in Society.* 519–530.
156 North, Douglass. *Institutions, Institutional Change, and Economic Performance.* pp. 3–32.

9 Socialism: Virtue Without Victory

While capitalism has produced extraordinary advances in productivity, innovation, and aggregate wealth over the past two and a half centuries, the growing appeal of democratic socialism across the United States, Europe, and other advanced capitalist societies signals mounting dissatisfaction with how contemporary capitalism functions and how its institutions perform.[1] This movement is not driven by enthusiasm for centralized planning or state ownership but by a widening perception that current capitalist arrangements are failing to deliver on several of their foundational promises: broad-based prosperity, upward mobility, economic security, and social cohesion.[2]

In this sense, the rise of democratic socialism functions less as an endorsement of socialist doctrine than as a referendum on capitalism's unresolved unintended consequences. As with communism in the prior chapter, the movement signals a demand for systemic correction rather than ideological conversion.

At the center of democratic socialism's appeal is the perceived and actual erosion of economic security for large segments of the middle and working classes. In the U.S., despite record setting equity valuations, rising corporate profits, and rapid technological progress, many households experience stagnant real wages, lack of affordable housing, high student debt burdens, fragile employment arrangements, and healthcare systems that are costly, increasingly exclusionary, and operationally stressed. Thomas Piketty characterizes these dynamics as the reemergence of patrimonial capitalism, in which inherited wealth increasingly determines life outcomes and economic mobility slows across generations. The result is not merely inequality but a growing sense that the economic game is no longer fair.

This perception directly undermines capitalism's meritocratic legitimacy. Joseph Stiglitz has argued that when markets cease to reward effort, skill, and productive contribution, and instead concentrate wealth through rents, monopolistic power, and regulatory capture, it follows that—rather than serving public interest—as it bends toward serving special interest at the expense of public good, confidence in capitalism itself erodes.[3] Democratic socialism emerges here as a corrective impulse, advocating policies such as universal healthcare, publicly supported education, and progressive taxation not primarily as ideological commitments but as mechanisms to restore fairness, opportunity, and social trust.

Democratic socialism also gains traction from the belief that capitalism has weakened democratic governance. The growing entanglement of economic power and political influence has produced widespread skepticism that public policy reflects the preferences of ordinary citizens. Empirical research by Gilens and Page suggests that policy outcomes in the United States disproportionately reflect the interests of economic elites and organized business groups, while the preferences of the median voter exert limited influence.[4] This perceived democratic deficit has fueled support

 | https://doi.org/10.1515/9783112235485-010

for proposals that seek to reassert public control over key economic decisions. As Dani Rodrik has argued, the crisis of liberal democracy is inseparable from the crisis of capitalism itself; if markets are to retain legitimacy, they must operate within institutions that command democratic consent and serve social purpose. Inclusive Capitalism begins precisely from this premise, starting with the diminishing of GDP as the dominant performance metric and adding measures of societal well-being.

There is also a functional critique embedded in democratic socialism's rise. Capitalism excels at allocating private goods but has repeatedly underperformed in domains requiring collective action, including climate change mitigation, public health resilience, and long-term infrastructure investment. Even Alan Greenspan, long a proponent of deregulated markets, acknowledged after the financial crisis that he had overestimated the capacity of institutional self-interest to generate system-level stability.[5] Democratic socialism responds by foregrounding public goods and long-term investment but often does so through expansive state control and redistribution, which introduces its own set of inefficiencies and constraints.

Beyond economics, democratic socialism articulates a moral critique of capitalism's treatment of human dignity. Michael Sandel contends that when market logic is allowed to govern domains such as education, healthcare, and justice, civic norms rooted in fairness, obligation, and the public good are replaced by transactional reasoning, reducing citizens to consumers and weakening the moral foundations required for a functioning democratic society.[6] Thomas Sowell, despite his critique of socialism, has similarly observed that political instability is driven less by inequality per se than by perceived injustice. Calls for universal access to healthcare, education, and housing are therefore rooted not only in redistribution but in a broader demand for dignity, fairness, and inclusion.

The generational dimension of democratic socialism's appeal is especially revealing. Polling consistently shows that younger cohorts view socialism more favorably than capitalism, not due to exposure to Marxist theory but because their lived experience of capitalism includes repeated financial crises, climate risk, rising debt, and declining economic security.[7] The popularity of democratic socialism reflects a cultural inflection point, a demand for an economic order that is more inclusive, accountable, and oriented toward long-term societal resilience.

It is important, however, to distinguish diagnosis from prescription. The rise of democratic socialism is not primarily a demand for central planning but for moral and institutional recalibration. It expresses dissatisfaction with exclusion, insecurity, and misaligned incentives rather than a rejection of markets themselves. In this sense, democratic socialism highlights real failures but offers solutions that often trade dynamism and innovation for stability and redistribution. As Keynes himself noted, capitalism must be intelligent, just, and effective if it is to endure.[8]

Inclusive Capitalism is proposed as a response that preserves capitalism's strengths while addressing its failures at the system level. It is not a revolution but a re-architecture grounded in Adam Smith's original vision of markets as servants of society.[9] It preserves private property, deepens market participation, reduces reliance on centralized government intervention, and eliminates incentives for manufactured scarcity. Most critically, it displaces GDP as the predominant measure with societal well-being as the primary metric of success, aligning incentives with outcomes that matter to people rather than abstractions.

A natural question follows: why not simply adopt democratic socialism, which already addresses many of these concerns and has a demonstrated track record? The answer developed in this chapter is that democratic socialism, as currently practiced, delivers virtue without victory. It improves distribution but constrains growth, innovation, and long-term adaptability. In a world facing rapid technological change and unprecedented global challenges, societies require an economic system capable of maximizing societal well-being and the pace of innovation simultaneously. Inclusive Capitalism argues that modern technology, empirical economic insight, and systems-level design make this outcome achievable.

A widely used heuristic for contrasting capitalism and socialism is the observation that capitalism excels at growing the economic pie, while socialism focuses on dividing it. Although the phrase itself is often paraphrased in popular commentary, the underlying idea has a long intellectual lineage. Winston Churchill captured it succinctly in 1945 when he observed, "The inherent vice of capitalism is the unequal sharing of blessings; the inherent virtue of socialism is the equal sharing of miseries."[10] The remark is not merely rhetorical; it points to a fundamental distinction in how economic systems generate and allocate value.

Thomas Sowell offered a sharper analytical formulation of the same tension when he wrote, "Socialism in general has a record of failure so blatant that only an intellectual could ignore or evade it. It is the idea that you can redistribute income without first creating it." The core critique is not moral but structural. Redistribution presupposes production, and production depends on incentives, information, and institutional arrangements that socialism has historically struggled to preserve. Joseph Schumpeter, who was more sympathetic to socialism in theory than many of his contemporaries, nonetheless recognized the functional asymmetry between the systems. In *Capitalism, Socialism and Democracy* (1942), he argued that capitalism is uniquely capable of generating wealth through innovation and entrepreneurship, while socialism concerns itself primarily with allocating output according to notions of need or fairness.[11]

This chapter's examination of democratic socialism builds on that distinction. The objective is not to dismiss democratic socialism as morally unserious or intellectually shallow but to understand why it has consistently underperformed capitalism in generating sustained growth and innovation and why its appeal nonetheless persists. This analysis is essential for the construction of Inclusive Capitalism, which explicitly seeks to preserve capitalism's unparalleled capacity for wealth creation and innovation while addressing the distributional and societal failures that give democratic socialism its moral force.

Democratic socialism is the final of the major economic "isms" examined in this historical review, following capitalism, communism, and Keynesianism. Before exploring its internal logic and policy prescriptions, it is useful to position democratic socialism within the broader ideological spectrum already developed in the book.

At one end of the spectrum lies communism, which envisions a fully planned economy characterized by total state ownership of the means of production and the abolition of markets. Price signals are replaced by centralized planning, and individual economic agency is subordinated to collective objectives defined by the state.[12] At the opposite end lies neoclassical, Smithian capitalism, which emphasizes minimal government intervention, decentralized markets, individual choice, and supply-side growth driven by competition and private ownership.[13]

	"Left" ←			→ "Right"
Ism:	Communism	Democratic Socialism	Keynesianism	Neoclassical Capitalism
Vision:	Planned Utopia	Ethical Equality	Stabilized Markets	Market Purism
Markets:	Full state control	Social-market democracy	Mixed economy	Free market

Between these poles sit Keynesianism and democratic socialism. Keynesianism retains capitalist markets and private ownership but assigns the state an active role in stabilizing the economy through fiscal and monetary policy, particularly during periods of recession or excessive inflation.[14] Democratic socialism, by contrast, accepts markets and private property in principle but advocates for a significantly expanded role for the state in redistributing income, providing universal social services, and exercising public or social ownership over what it defines as "essential" sectors of the economy.[15] While Keynesianism seeks primarily to stabilize capitalism, democratic socialism seeks to reshape its outcomes.

Each of these systems reflects a different approach to balancing efficiency and equity, liberty and equality, and the relative roles of markets and the state. Historically, societies have treated these dimensions as requiring unavoidable tradeoffs. Greater efficiency was assumed to come at the cost of equity; while greater equality was assumed to require constraints on liberty and growth. These assumptions have driven what might be called reactive or "ping-pong" economics, where policy oscillates between market liberalization and state intervention in response to crises, excesses, or political pressure.

A central claim of Inclusive Capitalism is that many of these tradeoffs are neither inevitable nor optimal. They persist largely because of inherited assumptions about metrics, incentives, and institutional design. In particular, the elevation of GDP as the singular core metric of economic success has distorted decision-making across enterprises, governments, and financial markets.[16] Once GDP growth becomes the dominant objective, outcomes such as inequality, environmental degradation, loss of dignity in work, and social fragmentation are treated as market externalities rather than system-level failures.

By replacing GDP with societal well-being as the top-level metric, and by aligning enterprise incentives accordingly, Inclusive Capitalism aims to escape the false dichotomy between growth and fairness that underlies the capitalism-versus-socialism debate. When success is defined not solely by aggregate output but by improvements in human well-being, opportunity, resilience, and participation, it becomes possible to design institutions that simultaneously foster innovation and distribute its benefits more broadly, without resorting to heavy-handed redistribution or centralized control.[17]

Democratic socialism, as it exists today, represents an understandable but ultimately incomplete response to capitalism's shortcomings. It correctly identifies many of the pain points experienced by modern societies, including economic insecurity, inequality, and the erosion of public goods. However, its solutions tend to weaken the very mechanisms that generate growth and innovation, relying instead on redistribution, regulation, and state provision at scales that become increasingly difficult to sustain.[18] Inclusive Capitalism seeks to absorb the ethical urgency of democratic socialism while rejecting its structural compromises, offering a path forward that preserves capitalism's strengths while addressing its most destabilizing failures.

The remainder of this chapter will examine democratic socialism's core claims, its empirical performance, and its limits as a scalable economic model. Our analysis is not meant to serve as an endpoint but as a necessary input into the design of a system that can grow the pie, share it more broadly, and do so in a manner consistent with human behavior, democratic values, and long-term societal well-being.

What Exactly is Democratic Socialism?

To begin a substantive evaluation of democratic socialism, it is essential to distinguish it clearly from communism. Just as Keynesian economics and laissez-faire, Smithian capitalism represent the bookends of the capitalist family of systems, communism and democratic socialism define the extremes of the socialist tradition. In contemporary political and economic discourse, democratic socialism is best understood not as the negation of capitalism but as a set of institutional arrangements intended to constrain market outcomes in the service of greater equality, solidarity, and democratic accountability, while preserving core market mechanisms.[19]

Modern democratic socialism advocates broad social ownership or, more precisely, public control and regulation of essential economic resources, alongside universal provisioning of key services such as healthcare, education, and income security. These objectives are pursued within liberal-democratic governance frameworks that preserve civil liberties, electoral competition, and the rule of law. Unlike communism, democratic socialism does not seek the abolition of markets nor the elimination of private property. Instead, it aims to subordinate economic power to democratic oversight.

Thomas Piketty characterizes democratic socialism as "a participatory system that combines private property with temporary ownership, shared governance, and democratic accountability," designed to limit excessive concentration of wealth and ensure a more equitable distribution of economic power.[20] In this framing, capitalism is not rejected outright but is viewed as structurally incomplete without institutional constraints that prevent excessive rent extraction, monopolization, and social exclusion.

The intellectual genealogy of socialism reflects a gradual evolution rather than a singular rupture. Early utopian thinkers such as Robert Owen and Saint-Simon emphasized cooperative production and moral reform, while Marx and Engels offered a structural critique rooted in historical materialism. In *The Communist Manifesto* (1848), Marx and Engels framed socialism as a transitional stage preceding communism, involving the abolition of bourgeois property relations and the establishment of a dictatorship of the proletariat.[21] This revolutionary vision entailed the eventual withering away of the state once class distinctions disappeared.[22]

Modern democratic socialism departs sharply from this revolutionary tradition. It is evolutionary rather than dialectical, pluralistic rather than totalizing, and reformist rather than insurrectionary. As Marshall Goldman observed, many late-twentieth-century socialist reformers no longer sought the wholesale replacement of capitalism but its modification to address inequality and institutional failure.[23]

The distinction between communism and democratic socialism rests on three core dimensions: property relations, institutional structure, and mechanisms of change. Under communism, private ownership of the means of production is abolished entirely, with productive assets held by the state in the name of the people. This model draws directly from Marx's formulation in *Critique of the Gotha Program* (1875): "From each according to his ability, to each according to his needs."[24] The objective is a classless society in which individual claims to capital are erased.

Democratic socialism, by contrast, permits private property, particularly personal property and small-scale enterprise, while advocating collective or public ownership in strategic sectors such as healthcare, energy, education, and infrastructure. Competitive markets are retained where they function effectively, with state ownership applied selectively to address market failures.[25] As scholars of the Nordic model have noted, democratic socialism does not subordinate all economic activity to the state but uses public institutions to shape outcomes without extinguishing market signals.

Inclusive Capitalism diverges further still. Under Inclusive Capitalism, all property remains private, but large enterprises, particularly those operating in strategic sectors, are rechartered to optimize societal well-being rather than GDP alone.[26] This approach seeks to resolve the capital-labor conflict structurally rather than through redistribution or state ownership.

A defining failure of communism was its suppression of political pluralism. In practice, communist systems replaced democratic deliberation with single-party rule, extinguishing civil liberties, free press, and institutional accountability. Hayek warned in *The Road to Serfdom* (1944) that such centralization inevitably produces coercion: "The more the state plans, the more difficult planning becomes for the individual."[27] Democratic socialism explicitly rejects this authoritarian logic, treating political democracy and civil liberties as non-negotiable prerequisites.

Democratic socialists argue that democracy must extend beyond elections to include workplace participation, unions, and public input into economic governance. Piketty captures this view succinctly: "There can be no socialism without democracy, and no democracy without equality." Inclusive Capitalism similarly recognizes the need for strong leadership within enterprises, while introducing governance mechanisms that mitigate the tendency toward managerial autocracy without undermining operational efficiency.

Another critical distinction lies in incentives. Communist systems collapsed in large part because they dismantled the incentive structures necessary to motivate effort, innovation, and responsibility. Wage compression and reward decoupling produced predictable outcomes: minimal effort, risk avoidance, and stagnation. As Thomas Sowell observed, "No one spends someone else's money as carefully as he spends his own . . . and no one produces as diligently when the reward is the same regardless of effort."[28]

Democratic socialism responds by preserving incentives within a framework of redistribution and regulation. The objective is not absolute equality of outcomes but equality of opportunity, economic dignity, and a social floor below which no citizen should fall. Nordic social democracies are frequently cited as evidence that high taxation and redistribution can coexist with innovation and competitiveness.

Inclusive Capitalism shares the goals of opportunity, dignity, and security but rejects redistribution and regulation as primary tools. Instead, it proposes designing incentive structures that generate these outcomes endogenously, through market mechanisms aligned with societal well-being. Post-hoc redistribution, by contrast, is inherently political, prone to regulatory capture, and disconnected from value creation.

Finally, the ethical orientation of democratic socialism differs markedly from that of communism. Communism subordinated individual dignity to historical necessity, justifying repression and sacrifice in the name of an imagined future. Democratic socialism, grounded in the liberal tradition, emphasizes consent, solidarity, and human dignity.[29] It does not seek to eliminate competition or difference but to ensure that market outcomes do not undermine social cohesion.

While the ethical aspirations of democratic socialism are far more defensible than those of communism, they remain constrained by heavy taxation, extensive regulation, and persistent state intervention, all of which introduce systemic inefficiencies, dampen economic advances, and can increase political conflict. Inclusive Capitalism argues that these ethical goals can be achieved more effectively through systemic redesign rather than perpetual redistribution, yielding a model that is not merely morally appealing but economically victorious.

How Did Democratic Socialism Emerge?

Democratic socialism—the pursuit of socialist objectives through democratic and parliamentary means—emerged during the twentieth century as a defining force in European political life, as societies sought to address the social and economic dislocations produced by industrial capitalism without resorting to revolutionary upheaval.[30] As positioned earlier in this work, democratic socialism occupies a space modestly left of center on the ideological spectrum: distinct from communism in its rejection of revolutionary expropriation and one-party rule yet also distinct from classical and Smithian capitalism in its willingness to subordinate market outcomes to distributive and social objectives.[31]

Across Europe, and particularly in the United Kingdom, Sweden, France, and Germany, socialist and social-democratic parties translated this ideology into concrete legislative programs. These governments expanded welfare states, broadened social insurance, nationalized selected industries, and strengthened labor protections, all within democratic constitutional frameworks.

These developments were accompanied by vigorous intellectual debate. Proponents of democratic socialism drew on thinkers such as Eduard Bernstein, who argued early on for evolutionary rather than revolutionary socialism. Critics, most notably Friedrich Hayek and Milton Friedman, warned that expanding state intervention risked undermining economic freedom and individual liberty.[32] More recently, scholars such as Thomas Piketty have evaluated the legacy of social-democratic policies in reducing inequality.[33] Observers of the Soviet system, including Marshall Goldman, highlighted the economic pathologies of more authoritarian socialist models.

Economic Doctrines, Legal Framework, and Cultural Norms in Democratic Socialist Countries

In this section, we examine the major legislative milestones that defined democratic socialism in the United Kingdom, Sweden, France, and Germany during the twentieth century, along with the intellectual currents that shaped and critiqued these trajectories.[34] While each country followed a distinct path, together they form a coherent European narrative of social reform tempered by democratic governance and sustained intellectual contestation.[35]

Before considering the specific country instantiations of democratic socialism, it is important to distinguish between democratic socialism and social democracy. Democratic socialism is normatively committed to some form of social ownership or democratic control of capital, even when pursued through electoral and parliamentary means. Social democracy, by contrast, is capitalist in structure but redistributive in outcome: it accepts private ownership of the means of production and market coordination as foundational, while seeking to mitigate inequality, insecurity, and exclusion through taxation, regulation, and expansive social welfare systems.

This distinction is not merely semantic. It determines whether reform efforts ultimately aim to transform the ownership and control of productive assets or instead to stabilize and humanize capitalism while preserving its core institutional architecture. As a result, democratic socialism and social democracy differ fundamentally in their implications for incentives, innovation, capital formation, and long-run economic dynamism—differences that become decisive under conditions of globalization, technological acceleration, and non-scarcity.

United Kingdom

In Britain, the twentieth century opened with the gradual rise of the Labour Party and a growing consensus that the state had a role to play in addressing social problems generated by industrial capitalism, a development that broadly paralleled contemporaneous reforms in the United States.[36] Britain's earliest steps toward a welfare state predated Labour's ascent to power and were initiated by Liberal governments. The National Insurance Act of 1911 introduced contributory health and unemployment insurance for working people, marking a pioneering intervention in social policy. This legislation established an enduring precedent: the state could provide a social safety net while preserving a capitalist economic structure.

It was not until the aftermath of World War II, however, that democratic socialism decisively reshaped British society. The Labour government led by Clement Attlee (1945–1951) enacted a sweeping program of social reform and public ownership.[37] Influenced by wartime planning and the egalitarian ethos forged through shared sacrifice, Attlee's government sought to "win the peace" by constructing a more equitable postwar society. Approximately 20 percent of the economy was nationalized, including coal, railways, road transport, the Bank of England, civil aviation, healthcare, electricity, gas, and steel. These nationalizations were not merely ideological; they were explicitly intended to modernize key sectors, accelerate reconstruction, and ensure that essential services prioritized public need over narrow private ownership. In this respect, Britain's postwar settlement represented a far more extensive embrace of public ownership than contemporaneous developments in the United States.

At the same time, the British welfare state was dramatically expanded. The National Insurance Act of 1946 established a comprehensive system of social security, providing unemployment benefits, sickness coverage, and old-age pensions as universal rights. The National Health Service Act of 1946 created the National Health Service

(NHS), which came into operation in 1948 and provided universal healthcare funded through general taxation. These reforms reflected the influence of the 1942 Beveridge Report, authored by William Beveridge, which identified five fundamental social evils —Want, Disease, Ignorance, Squalor, and Idleness—that could be overcome through coordinated public policy.[38] Together, the Attlee government's reforms established universal social insurance, public healthcare, and state ownership of core industries, effectively creating what historians have described as a new social contract that shaped British society for decades.

These policy developments were rooted in a long tradition of democratic socialist thought. The Fabian Society, which included figures such as Sidney and Beatrice Webb and George Bernard Shaw, had advocated gradualist social reform since the late nineteenth century and exerted substantial influence on Labour's early intellectual foundations.[39] By 1918, Labour's constitution formally committed the party to common ownership of the means of production, a declaration of socialist principle that later informed and led to mid-century nationalizations. British democratic socialism was, however, notably pragmatic. Thinkers such as R. H. Tawney, in works including *The Acquisitive Society* (1921) and *Equality* (1931), offered a moral critique of unconstrained capitalism and articulated an ethical case for equality and social fellowship, providing philosophical grounding for Labour's program of "ethical socialism."[40] Economic ideas associated with John Maynard Keynes also shaped the postwar consensus, reinforcing the belief that high employment and social welfare could be sustained through active but prudent government management of the economy.[41]

By the mid-twentieth century, even Conservative governments accepted much of this social-democratic settlement, reflecting a broad political consensus around welfare provision and mixed ownership. Yet democratic socialism in Britain was not without formidable critics. Among the most influential were Friedrich Hayek and Milton Friedman. Hayek, who taught at the London School of Economics during the interwar and wartime periods, warned in *The Road to Serfdom* (1944) that even well-intentioned economic planning risked a gradual descent into authoritarianism.[42] He argued that the informational complexity of modern economies rendered comprehensive planning fundamentally unworkable, as no central authority could ever possess the dispersed knowledge held by millions of individuals. Markets, he argued, operate as a spontaneous order, coordinating information and incentives far more effectively than state planning.

Alongside Hayek, Milton Friedman, a leading figure of the Chicago School of economics, emerged as a forceful critic of the Keynesian and social-democratic orthodoxy. In *Capitalism and Freedom* (1962) and subsequent works, Friedman argued that many forms of government intervention—from welfare programs to state-owned enterprises—were inefficient and often corrosive to personal freedom.[43] During the late 1970s and 1980s, Friedman's ideas gained political traction on both sides of the Atlantic. In Britain, the Thatcher government adopted monetarist policies to combat inflation and pursued widespread privatization of industries nationalized under the Attlee government decades earlier.[44] This agenda represented a deliberate rollback of key democratic socialist institutions and signaled that the postwar settlement was neither permanent nor uncontested, even in its country of origin.

Despite these challenges, the core legislative legacy of twentieth-century British democratic socialism—the National Health Service, the social insurance system, and the broad acceptance that the state bears responsibility for ensuring a basic level of welfare—proved remarkably durable. By the end of the century, the Labour Party under Prime Minister Tony Blair rebranded itself as "New Labour," explicitly distancing itself from traditional socialist language, including the formal abandonment of Clause IV in 1995, which removed the party's commitment to common ownership.[45] Yet this shift reflected evolution rather than repudiation. Blair's government modernized and reoriented the welfare state rather than dismantling it. The British case thus illustrates a recurring pattern: the construction of democratic socialist institutions in the mid-twentieth century, sustained by broad consensus; a subsequent neoliberal challenge; and eventual adaptation rather than disappearance.

The parallels between Britain's economic evolution and that of the United States are instructive. Capitalism first emerged in Britain, as did social democracy, and Britain also experienced the earliest and most severe unintended consequences of unchecked, laissez-faire, Smithian capitalism.[46] While similar dynamics appeared in the United States, their scale and intensity were nowhere near the severity of Britain's earlier experience. As explored in the chapter on Early-Stage Capitalism, these consequences—brutal working conditions, stark inequality, and visible class conflict—were particularly acute in the United Kingdom. The reaction was correspondingly stronger, producing a more pronounced shift toward social democracy than what occurred in the United States, where the response instead took the more moderate form of Keynesian capitalism.

Britain's deeper movement to the left reflected a confluence of historical trauma, entrenched class divisions, institutional pathways for socialist politics, and a longstanding tradition of ethical critique. These forces culminated in Labour's rise to power in the mid-twentieth century. The interwar years were especially destabilizing: mass unemployment, industrial decline, and events such as the General Strike of 1926 laid bare the fragility of Britain's social order.[47] These conditions radicalized portions of the working class and generated electoral support for Labour's transformative agenda.

Unlike Britain, the United States never developed a durable, mass-based labor or socialist party. In the UK, the Labour Party emerged directly from the trade union movement and achieved parliamentary legitimacy by the early twentieth century. In the United States, socialist movements—such as those associated with Eugene Debs and the Socialist Party of America—remained marginal, were often suppressed during wartime and Red Scare periods, and never translated into durable political institutions.[48] As Seymour Martin Lipset famously observed, "Socialism failed in America because the country was born free," capturing the extent to which American political culture emphasized individualism and liberalism rather than class-based politics.[49]

Having examined Britain's distinctive path, we now broaden the analysis to three additional cases—Sweden, France, and Germany—each of which developed its own variant of social democracy under different historical and institutional conditions.

Sweden

The Swedish twentieth-century experience is often presented as the archetypal case of democratic socialism in practice. Frequently described as a "middle way" between unbridled capitalism and Soviet-style socialism, the Swedish model combined a dynamic market economy with an expansive welfare state and strong labor institutions.[50] For much of the twentieth century—particularly from 1932 to 1976, when the Social Democratic Workers' Party governed almost continuously—Sweden functioned as a laboratory for social-democratic policy experimentation.

The foundations of Swedish social democracy were laid in the early twentieth century through the expansion of suffrage and the rise of a highly organized labor movement. By the 1920s and 1930s, Swedish social democrats, led most notably by Per Albin Hansson, articulated the concept of folkhemmet, or "the people's home."[51] This metaphor envisioned society as a shared household in which all citizens contributed and, in return, were guaranteed security and dignity. Taking office during the depths of the Great Depression, Hansson's government pursued policies aimed at stabilizing the economy and protecting social cohesion, while deliberately avoiding the authoritarian temptations that overtook several European nations during the same period.

One of the most consequential developments of the 1930s was the Saltsjöbaden Agreement of 1938, a landmark accord between labor unions and employer organizations. Although not enacted through legislation, the agreement proved foundational to Swedish labor relations. It established a cooperative framework for collective bargaining, minimized industrial conflict, and institutionalized a norm of negotiation without heavy state intervention.[52] This consensus-based approach to labor policy became a defining feature of Swedish social democracy. During the same decade, the state expanded public works programs, introduced housing initiatives, and adopted countercyclical measures to reduce unemployment, reflecting a pragmatic willingness to intervene in the economy while preserving market mechanisms.

Intellectually, Swedish social democracy was shaped by an effort to reconcile socialist ideals with empirical social science. Central to this effort were Gunnar and Alva Myrdal, whose work became deeply influential in the design of the welfare state. In *Crisis in the Population Question* (1934), the Myrdals argued that declining birthrates and social instability could be addressed through comprehensive family support policies.[53] Their analysis led directly to child allowances, housing subsidies, and policies aimed at improving household security. The Myrdals and their contemporaries believed that disciplined social engineering—grounded in economics, sociology, and demographic research—could achieve both equity and efficiency without abandoning democracy.

By the post–World War II period, Sweden had constructed one of the most comprehensive welfare systems in the world. Universal healthcare, subsidized education, generous pensions, and broad income-support programs were all delivered within a capitalist market economy. The folkhemmet reached its apex during the postwar decades, producing high living standards, low poverty, and a relatively egalitarian income distribution. Sweden's achievements attracted global attention. In 1936, American journalist Marquis Childs famously described Sweden as "the middle way," praising its ability to combine prosperity with social harmony.[54] This model—extensive social guarantees alongside competitive markets—came to symbolize democratic socialism in action.

A defining characteristic of the Swedish system was its emphasis on compromise and institutional balance. Unlike more doctrinaire socialist movements, Swedish social democrats frequently governed through coalition and adapted policies in response to economic conditions. Under Prime Minister Tage Erlander, who served from 1946 to 1969, the government maintained a careful equilibrium between powerful trade unions, organized under the Swedish Trade Union Confederation, and influential business interests, represented by the Swedish Employers' Confederation.[55] Out of this balance emerged the Rehn–Meidner model in the 1950s, an innovative policy framework designed to reconcile full employment, low inflation, and income equality.[56] Through active labor-market policies, solidarity wage structures, and disciplined macroeconomic management, the model sought to promote productivity while cushioning workers from disruption. It represented one of the most sophisticated attempts within democratic socialism to align growth with equity.

Despite its successes, Sweden's model was not without critics. Conservative and classical liberal voices warned that high taxes and an expansive public sector could eventually dampen entrepreneurship and innovation. International observers also debated the sources of Sweden's performance. Milton Friedman frequently cited Sweden as a case worthy of both admiration and caution, suggesting that its success might owe as much to cultural homogeneity and high social trust as to policy design.[57] A quip often attributed to Friedman—that Swedish-Americans exhibited similarly low poverty without Sweden's welfare state—captured this line of critique. Thomas Sowell similarly emphasized the role of culture and social norms in shaping economic outcomes.[58] While these arguments remain contested, they underscore an important point: Sweden's achievements cannot be attributed solely to policy instruments but also to institutional trust, social cohesion, and a shared willingness to compromise.

By the 1970s, challenges to the Swedish model mounted, just as they did in many other advanced economies, including the United States. International oil shocks and broader economic turmoil hit Sweden hard. The Social Democrats, led in the 1970s by Olof Palme, responded with further ambitious proposals, most notably the Wage

Earner Funds—an initiative designed to gradually transfer corporate ownership to worker-controlled collective funds through share levies, inspired by economist Rudolf Meidner. Introduced in the late 1970s, the proposal represented a bold attempt to deepen economic democracy by shifting ownership without outright nationalization. However, it proved highly controversial, mobilizing strong business opposition and contributing to the Social Democrats' temporary loss of power in 1976, their first electoral defeat since 1932.

When the Social Democrats returned to government in the 1980s, significantly watered-down versions of the wage earner funds were implemented, only to be dismantled in the 1990s as Sweden moved toward a more market-friendly orientation. Nevertheless, by the end of the twentieth century, Sweden had firmly established a durable legacy of Democratic Socialist legislation, including near-universal cradle-to-grave welfare provisioning, strong worker rights (including workplace co-determination, which establishes formal rules for worker participation in employment-related decision-making), and extensive public provision of services ranging from healthcare to education. Thomas Piketty's analysis of inequality highlights Sweden, along with other Western European nations, as having achieved historically unprecedented income equality in the postwar decades through high taxation and social spending.[59] By the 1980s, total tax revenue in Sweden had risen to nearly 50 percent of GDP—among the highest levels globally—reflecting the scale at which national income was directed toward public services.

While later decades saw partial retrenchment and market-oriented reforms, often under Social Democratic governments adapting pragmatically to globalization, the intellectual ethos of Swedish Social Democracy—that a prosperous capitalist economy can and should be regulated and taxed to benefit society as a whole—remained largely intact. If Hayek warned of a "road to serfdom," Sweden's experience appeared to many as evidence that extensive social policy need not extinguish individual freedom.[60] Indeed, Sweden consistently ranked high on measures of democracy, civil liberties, and institutional trust even at the peak of its welfare-state expansion, offering a powerful counterexample to the most absolutist libertarian critiques.

Yet this narrative raises an important question. If Sweden represents the strongest empirical case for Social Democracy, why has the country recently swung to the political right? Since 2022, Sweden has been governed by a center-right coalition led by Prime Minister Ulf Kristersson of the Moderate Party. The coalition includes the Christian Democrats and the Liberal Party and operates with parliamentary support from the Sweden Democrats, a right-wing populist and nationalist party. Their cooperation is formalized through the Tidö Agreement, which emphasizes stricter immigration controls, tougher law enforcement, reduced taxation, increased defense spending, national standards for school funding, and improved healthcare efficiency.[61] The inclusion of the Sweden Democrats marks a notable shift in Swedish politics and reflects a broader rightward turn across much of Europe.

Among the several factors driving Sweden's political shift, immigration appears to be the most prominent. Sweden accepted more refugees per capita than any other Western country during the 2015–2016 European migrant crisis.[62] The scale and speed of this influx strained housing, education, welfare, and integration systems, particularly in suburban areas surrounding major cities. These pressures fueled the rise of the Sweden Democrats, who entered parliament in 2010 and grew steadily in influence. As Andreas Johansson Heinö of the Timbro Institute observed, "Sweden has gone from being a homogeneous country to one that now grapples with how to integrate large migrant populations . . . The political effects are profound."[63]

A second factor has been growing resentment, particularly outside major urban centers, toward what many perceive as elite-driven progressivism, multiculturalism, and social liberalism. For segments of the population, these trends have been interpreted as eroding traditional Swedish cultural identity and social cohesion, prompting a reactionary response. Similar dynamics are evident across Europe and the United States, where populist-right movements have gained traction in response to cultural anxiety and perceived elite detachment from everyday concerns.

Third, despite Sweden's continued prosperity, rising housing costs, longer healthcare queues, and concerns about welfare dependency have contributed to a perception that the welfare state is increasingly overstretched. Some voters fear that benefits are being disproportionately consumed by groups perceived as contributing less, making law-and-order policies and welfare chauvinism—benefits prioritized for "natives first"—potent political tools for right-leaning parties.

A fourth contributing factor lies in Sweden's own liberalization trajectory since the 1990s. Pensions, education, telecommunications, and other sectors were privatized, deregulated, or opened to competition, often under Social Democratic governments themselves. While these reforms improved efficiency in some areas, rising wealth inequality and uneven regional outcomes left parts of the working and middle classes feeling excluded, particularly outside metropolitan hubs such as Stockholm and Gothenburg.[64]

Sweden's rightward shift reflects a confluence of pressures: social challenges not easily addressed by traditional welfare mechanisms; growing disconnection between political elites and voters; and an increasing search for narratives centered on identity, sovereignty, and order. Whether Sweden's core Social Democratic institutions will endure, adapt, or erode further under these conditions remains an open and consequential question.

One final observation concerns the so-called "Swedish paradox," defined as relatively low-income inequality, reflected in an income Gini coefficient of approximately 0.31 (where 0 represents perfect equality and 1 represents maximum inequality), coexisting alongside very high wealth inequality, with a wealth Gini estimated near 0.87.[65] This illustrates how a society can redistribute income effectively while leaving ownership of capital largely untouched. Sweden achieves egalitarian living standards through one of the world's most progressive income tax systems, with marginal rates reaching roughly 52 percent (still below the United States' 91 percent marginal rate in the 1950s), while simultaneously maintaining minimal taxation on wealth through the abolition of wealth, inheritance, and gift taxes and relatively low capital gains taxes.[66] As Gabriel Zucman notes, "Sweden taxes labor heavily but taxes wealth very lightly, if at all."[67] The result is significant asset concentration among elites, while the bottom half of the population relies primarily on generous public services, which may reduce incentives for private wealth accumulation.

Several critical lessons for Inclusive Capitalism emerge from Sweden's experience with Social Democracy, as it is perhaps the most compelling historical example of virtue without victory. First, the system worked well for decades, particularly relative to more extreme forms of Socialism. It effectively mitigated many unintended consequences of Capitalism, including poverty, access to basic needs, and perceptions of systemic fairness. Sweden demonstrates that a collaborative economy protecting dignity and opportunity is indeed possible.

A second lesson is that substantial wealth inequality can coexist with social stability so long as access to the basics is universal and the system is perceived as fair. For many, not accumulating wealth is acceptable provided healthcare, education, housing, and security are assured. This reinforces the importance of measuring societal wellbeing beyond income alone.

Third, Sweden's repeated turn toward privatization and competition, even during periods of Social Democratic success, reinforces the insight that centralized control and lack of market discipline are ultimately unsustainable. Properly chartered, market-driven private enterprises remain essential.

Fourth, the system deteriorates when segments of the population are perceived as not contributing. This perception becomes particularly corrosive when it aligns with group identity. The implicit social contract—contribution in exchange for security—was strained, contributing to political backlash.

Finally, welfare systems falter when aggregate contributions fail to keep pace with promised benefits. Healthcare queues lengthen, and perceived fairness erodes, particularly among high contributors. Inclusive Capitalism must therefore ensure that contribution is maximized across society and that social floors are set at levels that preserve motivation rather than undermine it.

France

French Democratic Socialism can be summarized in a single word: dirigisme. Dirigisme refers to a model of state-directed economic development in which government plays an active role in guiding, regulating, and planning the economy, rather than leaving outcomes entirely to free-market forces.[68] It does not imply universal state ownership, but it does involve strategic intervention in sectors such as finance, energy, transportation, and industrial policy to advance national objectives. The term is most closely associated with post-World War II France, particularly under Charles de Gaulle and subsequent governments, when the French state planned major investments, nurtured national champions, and regulated markets while preserving a largely private economy. As Peter Hall describes it, "Dirigisme involves the deliberate steering of economic outcomes by the state through planning, regulation, and investment, without completely displacing private ownership."[69] If Keynesianism, as instantiated through the neoclassical consensus, represents the left boundary of capitalism while remaining fundamentally capitalist, dirigisme clearly falls within the democratic socialist camp due to the scope and intensity of strategic state intervention.

Democratic Socialism in France followed a more episodic and uneven trajectory than in northern Europe, shaped by the nation's revolutionary republican tradition and recurring political upheaval. During the Third Republic (1870–1940), French socialism initially found expression in figures such as Jean Jaurès, who advocated a humanist, parliamentary path to socialism prior to World War I. The first major breakthrough in democratic socialist legislation came with the Popular Front government of 1936–1937, led by Léon Blum.[70] Blum's Socialist Party (SFIO) formed a left coalition with the Radicals and the Communists amid widespread social unrest and economic distress.

Although short-lived, the Blum government enacted sweeping reforms that transformed labor relations in France. The Matignon Agreements of June 1936, negotiated against the backdrop of mass strikes, granted workers the right to collective bargaining, the right to strike without repression, two weeks of paid annual leave (a first in French history), and a reduction of the standard workweek from 48 to 40 hours without reductions of pay. These measures fundamentally altered daily life for millions of workers and brought France closer to the social-democratic models emerging elsewhere in Europe. Blum also nationalized the arms industry and reorganized the Bank of France, which had previously been controlled by a small financial elite, bringing it under broader public oversight. The Popular Front's guiding principle was that political democracy must be accompanied by social and economic democracy, a core tenet of democratic socialism. Blum's thinking blended Marxist analysis with republican ideals of liberty, equality, and fraternity.

World War II and the Vichy period interrupted these reforms, but the Liberation of France in 1944 reopened the path for democratic socialist policy.[71] Under the Provisional Government of the French Republic (1944–1946), in which Socialists played key roles alongside Gaullists and Communists, France undertook an ambitious program of nationalization and welfare construction. Drawing on the unfinished agenda of the Popular Front and the Resistance's social vision articulated in the 1944 Conseil National de la Résistance program, the government moved swiftly. Major banks and insurance companies were nationalized in 1945, followed by coal, electricity, and gas utilities, leading to the creation of state monopolies such as Électricité de France and Gaz de France. Société Anonyme des Usines Renault was expropriated and transformed into a state-owned enterprise, Régie Nationale des Usines Renault, while Air

France was consolidated under super-majority public ownership. These actions were motivated both by the need to rebuild and modernize a devastated economy and by a democratic socialist conviction that vital sectors should serve the public interest.

Alongside industrial restructuring, France established a comprehensive social security system. In 1945, Sécurité Sociale was introduced, providing universal coverage for health insurance, pensions, workplace injuries, and family allowances.[72] Designed by Pierre Laroque and inspired in part by the Beveridge model in Britain, the system was built around the principle of solidarity: those who were working and healthy would support those who were not. Through the Fourth Republic (1946–1958), these policies endured despite political instability, as coalition governments across ideological lines maintained a mixed economy with strong social protections.

This period marked the consolidation of French dirigisme. The state assumed a central role in planning and development, most visibly through national economic plans associated with Jean Monnet.[73] Importantly, even centrist and Gaullist governments did not reverse the Liberation-era nationalizations. Instead, they used the state sector as an engine of modernization, particularly in infrastructure, energy, and heavy industry. By mid-century, France had arrived at a broad consensus around a state-guided form of capitalism with robust welfare provision, aligning closely with democratic socialist principles even when not explicitly labeled as such.

French socialism itself remained internally contested. The presence of a strong Communist Party (PCF) forced the Blum's SFIO, and later the Socialist Party (PS), to navigate between revolutionary pressures and centrist coalitions. Nevertheless, the commitment to achieving socialism through democratic means persisted and culminated in the most ambitious experiment of the postwar era with the election of François Mitterrand in 1981.[74] For the first time, the Socialist Party held unified control of the French state. Mitterrand's 110 Propositions platform included expansive workers' rights, higher minimum wages and benefits, reduced working hours, and sweeping nationalizations.

Between 1981 and 1983, the Mitterrand government nationalized roughly three dozen major banks and financial institutions, effectively bringing most of the banking sector under state control.[75] Leading industrial firms in steel, chemicals, electronics, and computing were also nationalized. Social reforms reduced the legal workweek from 40 to 39 hours (and later to 35), expanded paid leave to five weeks, and lowered the retirement age to 60 for many workers. Workplace participation was strengthened through enhanced committee structures. This period represented the high-water mark of democratic socialist ambition in France.

Economic reality soon imposed constraints. Rising deficits, inflation, and pressure from global financial markets culminated in the 1983 tournant de la rigueur, a decisive pivot toward fiscal restraint and market accommodation to preserve France's position within the European Monetary System.[76] While state ownership persisted for some years, momentum toward further socialist transformation stalled. By the late 1980s and 1990s, successive governments—both conservative and socialist—privatized many previously nationalized enterprises, mirroring developments in the United Kingdom and across Europe during the neoliberal turn.

France's experience thus illustrates both the promise and the limits of democratic socialism. The reforms of 1936 and the post-1945 welfare state produced durable improvements in workers' rights and social security that remain integral to French society. At the same time, the early 1980s demonstrated the difficulty of sustaining radical redistribution and state control within an increasingly globalized capitalist system. Critics seized on these episodes as evidence of inevitable failure. Yet scholars such as Thomas Piketty have re-evaluated the postwar decades more favorably, noting that they coincided with historic reductions in inequality and broad improvements in living standards, driven by progressive taxation and expansive public sectors.

Taken together, the French case underscores a recurring theme of this book: democratic socialism proved effective at correcting some of capitalism's most damaging unintended consequences but struggled to remain viable once non-scarcity conditions faded and global market constraints tightened. Its enduring legacy lies not in providing a stable alternative system but in demonstrating how far social outcomes can be improved through deliberate institutional design—an insight central to the project of Inclusive Capitalism.

Indeed, wealth and income inequality in France declined during the era of Democratic Socialism, primarily through reductions at the top of the distribution rather than through rapid gains at the bottom. Wealth inequality fell dramatically. The top 10 percent owned roughly 90 percent of wealth in 1910, but by 1980 owned approximately 60–65 percent. Income inequality (pre-tax) also narrowed significantly: the top 10 percent share of income declined from roughly 45–50 percent to 30–35 percent between 1914 and 1980. However, absolute living standards for the bottom 50 percent improved more slowly than the top contracted. Thus, while the overall pie grew during the postwar boom, the dominant redistributive mechanism was subtractive at the top rather than strongly additive at the bottom.

France also exhibits a "French Paradox," though it is less pronounced than the Swedish Paradox. As of 2023, France shows moderate income inequality alongside relatively high wealth inequality, as measured by Gini coefficients. The Gini coefficient for income inequality is approximately 29.7, while the Gini coefficient for wealth inequality is approximately 64.5. These figures highlight France's effectiveness at income redistribution through taxation and social welfare, while also underscoring the persistent concentration of asset ownership. As in other advanced economies, redistributing income has proven far easier than redistributing capital, revealing a structural challenge that social democratic systems have struggled to overcome.

Three takeaways from France's experience with social democracy are particularly relevant to the foundation of Inclusive Capitalism: first, sustained and credible critiques of capitalism represent a genuine threat to its long-term viability if its unintended consequences are not addressed; second, inclusive innovation is a far more sustainable path than subtractive equality; and third, it is ultimately in the self-interest of industrial leaders to embrace Inclusive Capitalism and inclusive innovation rather than resist reform.

France's twentieth-century embrace of social democracy illustrates how potent—and at times existential—critiques of capitalism can become when the system fails to deliver broadly shared prosperity. In response to economic dislocation, inequality, and a perception that profit was being prioritized over public welfare, French intellectuals and political leaders advanced social democratic reforms that directly challenged the legitimacy and structure of laissez-faire capitalism. From Léon Blum's Popular Front in the 1930s to the nationalizations under François Mitterrand in the early 1980s, these efforts were not merely rhetorical critiques but concrete attempts to reshape or partially replace the capitalist order. As Thomas Piketty has observed, when inequality becomes sufficiently extreme, the notion of meritocracy itself loses credibility. In this sense, social democracy in France functioned as both policy and corrective ideology, gaining momentum precisely because the prevailing economic system failed to serve large segments of society. The lesson is clear: if contemporary capitalism in the United States continues to generate exclusion, stagnant mobility, and systemic inequity, pressure for radical restructuring will intensify and may ultimately threaten the system's survival.

France's social democratic model relied heavily on what might be described as "equality through subtraction": high marginal tax rates, expansive redistribution, and bureaucratic controls designed to narrow disparities by constraining outcomes at the top. While these mechanisms delivered meaningful social protections, they also introduced rigidity, dampened entrepreneurial activity, and generated well-documented inefficiencies. As Friedrich Hayek warned, the more economic outcomes are centrally planned, the more difficult individual planning becomes.[77] By contrast, the Inclusive Capitalism framework is explicitly additive. It seeks to expand opportunity, participation, and value creation rather than redistribute value after the fact. Rather than relying on zero-sum redistribution, it focuses on designing incentive structures that broaden ownership, participation, and innovation. France's mixed experience with bureaucratic social equity reinforces the case for systemic inclusion driven by incentives rather than administrative redistribution.

Perhaps the most consequential insight from France's social democratic era lies in the strategic error made by industrial elites who resisted reform until state intervention became unavoidable. The sweeping measures of the Mitterrand period, including forced nationalizations and punitive taxation, were in many respects a political response to decades of unresolved inequality and exclusion. Had industrial leadership acted earlier to expand opportunity, strengthen workforce dignity, and ensure that the gains from growth were more broadly shared, the political demand for coercive redistribution may never have reached such intensity. From this perspective, Inclusive Capitalism is not a concession but a defensive and forward-looking strategy. Proactively designing inclusive, market-driven systems offers a far more favorable outcome for industrial leaders than reactive regulation, confiscatory policy, or externally imposed structural transformation.

Germany

Our final case study of Social Democracy in the twentieth century is Germany. Germany's path during this period traversed imperial rule, devastating wars, physical division, and eventual reunification. Within this turbulent history, the German Socialist movement was repeatedly forced to adapt, and did so in profound ways. German Democratic Socialism today is primarily associated with the Social Democratic Party of Germany (SPD), one of the world's oldest Socialist parties, founded in 1875. Although banned under Bismarck's Anti-Socialist Laws in the 1870s, the party's appeal continued to grow in practice through trade unions and electoral participation, and by the early twentieth century the SPD had become a mass political party.[78]

The SPD's theoretical outlook around 1900 was formally Marxist. The 1891 Erfurt Program emphasized class struggle and the eventual collectivization of production. In practice, however, the SPD contained a strong "revisionist" wing led by Eduard Bernstein.[79] Writing around the turn of the century, Bernstein argued that Marx's predictions of capitalist collapse were not being borne out empirically, and that Socialists should instead pursue incremental reform through democratic institutions.[80] This intellectual stance laid early groundwork for Democratic Socialism as a gradualist, parliamentary project rather than a revolutionary one. Bernstein's revisionism was controversial and strongly opposed by orthodox Marxists such as Karl Kautsky and Rosa Luxemburg, yet it foreshadowed the direction the SPD would ultimately take.

After World War I, the SPD decisively embraced the parliamentary path. In November 1918, SPD leader Friedrich Ebert became head of the provisional government following the Kaiser's abdication. The SPD-led government enacted progressive social legislation amid revolutionary instability. Most notably, the eight-hour workday was instituted in 1918 through an agreement between labor unions and industrialists, the Stinnes-Legien Agreement. The Weimar Constitution of 1919 further enshrined labor rights and worker participation, with Article 165 encouraging the formation of works councils.[81] During the Weimar era (1919–1933), the SPD alternated between government and opposition while social insurance programs expanded upon Bismarckian foundations. Health, accident, and pension insurance systems established in the 1880s were preserved and strengthened. This period represented Democratic Socialism under extraordinary strain, ultimately destroyed by the rise of Nazism in 1933. The Nazi regime outlawed the SPD and trade unions, violently suppressing all Socialist activity and ending Germany's democratic socialist experiment until 1945.

Following Germany's defeat and division after World War II, the two German states diverged sharply. East Germany, under Soviet domination, adopted a Communist system of state ownership and one-party rule. West Germany became a democracy with a mixed economy. In West Germany, the postwar era gave rise to the concept of the Sozialmarktwirtschaft, or Social Market Economy, principally articulated by economists such as Ludwig Erhard and Alfred Müller-Armack.[82] This framework sought to combine free-market Capitalism with a robust social safety net, effectively a Christian Democratic variant of Social Democracy. The Christian Democratic Union governed much of the postwar period under Chancellor Konrad Adenauer during which welfare institutions were retained and expanded. Social insurance programs grew, and generous unemployment benefits and pensions were introduced, including the 1957 pension reform that tied pensions to wage growth.

Meanwhile, the SPD rebuilt under leaders such as Kurt Schumacher and later Willy Brandt, confronting a decisive ideological turning point. In 1959, at Bad Godesberg, the SPD formally abandoned Marxist orthodoxy. The Bad Godesberg Program accepted the market economy and competition, committing the party to achieve social justice "as much as possible by competition and as much as necessary by planning." Demands for wholesale nationalization and class-struggle rhetoric were explicitly dropped.[83] The SPD repositioned itself as a center-left people's party committed to democracy and evolutionary reform. This marked a seminal moment in the intellectual history of Democratic Socialism. Germany's principal Socialist party aligned itself with Western liberal democracy, distancing itself from Soviet Communism and its own revolutionary past. By embracing the social market framework, the SPD helped cement a postwar consensus that paired Capitalist productivity with Social Democratic welfare guarantees.

When the SPD entered government in 1969 under Chancellor Willy Brandt, in coalition with the Free Democratic Party, Democratic Socialism arguably reached its governing apex in West Germany. Brandt's administration launched a series of social reforms expanding welfare, education, and civic participation. Measures included expanded access to higher education, pension reforms, new social programs such as rent subsidies and health coverage extensions, and liberalization of social and family law. A signature achievement was the 1972 Works Constitution Act, which strengthened the authority of works councils and reinforced industrial democracy.[84]

Brandt's successor, Helmut Schmidt (SPD, 1974–1982), continued a pragmatic Social Democratic course while navigating the economic turbulence of the 1970s.[85] Under Schmidt, the Co-Determination Act of 1976 required large firms to allocate nearly half of supervisory board seats to worker representatives. This law institutionalized one of the most extensive forms of worker participation in corporate governance in the Western world. While earlier precedents existed, the 1976 legislation generalized the principle across major industries. Co-determination was largely accepted by German business as part of the postwar settlement, reflecting a deeply embedded culture of social partnership between capital and labor.

By the late twentieth century, West Germany had become widely acknowledged as the canonical example of a successful social democracy. Although market-oriented critiques persisted, and modest welfare retrenchments occurred under conservative governments in the 1980s, the core institutions of the social market economy were never dismantled.[86] This underscores an important intellectual outcome. The social market economy represented a convergence of liberal and Socialist ideas, which was an implicit intellectual victory for Democratic Socialism in that even non-Socialist governments governed with an embedded social conscience.

This victory, however, was intellectual rather than absolute. Social Democracies proved more resilient than Communist systems, but they retained significant shortcomings, including insufficient incentives for enterprise leadership and labor, a tendency toward welfare overextension, and periodic insensitivity to market signals.[87] As an alternative, what is required is a system that preserves the virtues of Social Democracy while restoring the dynamism, innovation, and growth capacity of Capitalism. Such a system must be stable, sustainable, and predictable, avoiding the cyclical policy reversals that have characterized both capitalist and social democratic governance.

The fact that the Social Democratic Party's Bad Godesberg transformation centered on accepting the market, while the Christian Democratic Union's postwar success relied on accepting the welfare state, reflects a process of mutual ideological convergence. The experience of East Germany, the German Democratic Republic (GDR) further illuminates West Germany's Democratic Socialism by contrast. The GDR was a one-party state in which the Socialist Unity Party (SED) imposed Soviet-style central planning, state ownership of nearly all property, and an extensive but highly repressive welfare system. By the 1970s, East Germany provided guaranteed employment, subsidized housing, free healthcare, education, and social benefits not unlike those sought by Democratic Socialists in the West. Yet the absence of political freedom and economic adaptability meant that by the 1980s the GDR economy was stagnating, and public dissatisfaction was widespread.[88]

Marshall Goldman, an American economist who closely studied the Soviet bloc, documented the chronic inefficiencies and consumer shortages that plagued command economies.[89] The Soviet Union's own struggles with reform under perestroika were mirrored in East Germany's inability to innovate. In Goldman's analysis, the failure of these systems stemmed from the absence of market-based price signals and incentives necessary for effective resource allocation. This provided real-world confirmation of Hayek's earlier theoretical warnings.[90] When the two Germanys reunified in 1990, it became clear that the West German model, which preserved market mechanisms and political liberties, had dramatically outperformed the authoritarian Socialist model of the East in delivering prosperity. Reunification involved the rapid extension of West German laws and institutions across the former GDR, further validating the social market approach over Soviet-style Socialism.

West Germany invested vast financial resources to accelerate reunification, modernize infrastructure, align services, and raise living standards in the former East. The transition, however, was painful for many East Germans unfamiliar with a market-driven economy. Inefficient factories closed and unemployment surged, though the social safety net mitigated some of the shock. This episode illustrates that even well-intentioned Socialist guarantees, whether in East or West, are fragile when not supported by a sustainable economic base. By the end of the twentieth century, Germany had become one of the world's leading economies with a strong welfare state. Inequality was relatively contained compared to the United States, and manufacturing workers enjoyed high wages, substantial protections, and benefits. Thomas Piketty and others have emphasized that the period from roughly 1950 to 1980 in Western Europe was marked by historically high levels of taxation and social spending, which financed public health, education, and welfare and dramatically reduced poverty and inequality.[91] In Germany, this translated into the creation of a broad middle class and the near elimination of extreme deprivation.

Germany's intellectual landscape also produced a late-century counter-reaction to Social Democracy in the form of neoliberal thought. The Mont Pelerin Society, founded by Hayek in 1947, included German participants who later influenced policy toward privatization and deregulation in the 1980s and 1990s.[92] Yet even as Germany liberalized parts of its economy, including telecommunications and postal services, it never dismantled the core institutions of Social Democracy. The SPD returned to government in the late 1990s under Chancellor Gerhard Schröder and enacted controversial welfare and labor reforms, notably the Hartz IV reforms, aimed at reducing unemployment by tightening benefit eligibility. These reforms reflected adaptation under new constraints rather than abandonment of the Social Democratic model. Strong unions, co-determination, and a broad commitment to social insurance remained foundational features of German society, underscoring a durable consensus that Capitalism must be balanced by social responsibility.

If German Social Democracy represents one of the most successful historical syntheses of markets and social protection, the renewed polarization of German politics warrants close examination. Recent shifts include both a move to the right and the resurgence of extremism at both ends of the political spectrum. Historical memory is instructive here, as similar polarization a century earlier had catastrophic consequences.

Germany's recent rightward shift, marked by the resurgence of the Christian Democratic Union under Friedrich Merz and the electoral gains of the Alternative for Germany (AfD), has triggered a reconfiguration of welfare and fiscal priorities.[93] While governing coalitions still involve the Social Democrats, fiscal conservatism has regained prominence, raising the prospect of spending restraint in social programs. At the same time, parties on the left, particularly Die Linke, have experienced renewed support by emphasizing social protection as a counterweight to far-right populism. This reflects a broader pattern in which economic insecurity fuels political extremism on both ends of the spectrum.

As in Sweden, immigration has been the most salient driver of Germany's recent rightward shift. Germany's acceptance of over one million refugees during the 2015–2016 crisis profoundly altered its political landscape. Initial public support for

Chancellor Angela Merkel's humanitarian approach gave way to concerns about integration, public safety, cultural cohesion, and pressure on social systems. Parties such as the AfD capitalized on these anxieties with nationalist and anti-immigration messaging, significantly reshaping electoral dynamics.

Beyond cultural factors, immigration placed tangible strain on Germany's social infrastructure. Housing shortages intensified, healthcare and education systems faced increased demand, and labor-market integration progressed more slowly than anticipated. Bureaucratic barriers, language challenges, and insufficient childcare limited workforce participation among refugee populations. These pressures contributed to growing public perception that the state was failing to manage the economic implications of immigration effectively.

A key lesson for Inclusive Capitalism concerns immigration's economic dimension. Independent of cultural considerations, unmanaged immigration can strain social systems and fuel political backlash. Inclusive Capitalism must ensure that immigration is at least economically neutral, and ideally positive, so that economic pressures do not amplify social and political fragmentation, as has occurred in several European Social Democracies and in the United States.

A second major driver of polarization is cost-of-living pressure. Despite Germany's overall economic strength, many citizens face rising housing costs, stagnant real wages, and anxiety over industrial transformation related to energy transition and climate policy.[94] These dynamics mirror developments across Europe and the United States and lie largely beyond the capacity of traditional economic systems to address. Inclusive Capitalism proposes systemic reforms, including augmenting GDP with societal well-being metrics, refactoring currency, and re-chartering large enterprises, to address these pressures directly. Detailed mechanisms are developed in book two.

Hayek's warning that planning would inevitably erode freedom did not materialize in European Social Democracies, which remain vibrant democracies. However, recent trends suggest conditions that resemble those that originally motivated Hayek's concerns, namely polarization, institutional distrust, and susceptibility to authoritarian narratives. Hayek's warnings, along with those of Friedman, served as correctives, which in turn limited excesses and contributed to the late-twentieth-century market revival. The electoral success of reform-oriented leaders in Britain, France, and Germany during the 1980s demonstrates that Democratic Socialism must coexist with Capitalist dynamism to remain viable. The authors of *Inclusive Capitalism* contend that a more effective synthesis is possible, one that achieves sustained economic vitality while remaining genuinely inclusive.

Industrial Leadership Incentives and Behaviors Under Democratic Socialism

To deepen our understanding of how a maximally dynamic economy might be achieved within an inclusive framework, it is instructive to examine the lived experiences of industrial leaders, as we have done in previous chapters across the major phases of capitalism and communism.[95] Here we examine two representative industrial leaders from each of the Social Democracies reviewed thus far: the United Kingdom, Sweden, France, and Germany. The objective is to assess the virtues of their leadership styles, whether intrinsic or shaped by institutional constraints, as well as the opportunities forgone due to limits on dynamism. We conclude by examining how their leadership behaviors and outcomes might have differed under a more incentive-aligned and innovation-driven economic system.

Ingvar Kamprad, the founder of IKEA, was renowned for relentless personal frugality and an intense operational focus. He involved himself deeply in supply chain management, product design philosophy, and logistics innovation, most famously pioneering flat-pack shipping to reduce costs and expand global reach.[96] Kamprad emphasized direct engagement with employees and was known to visit IKEA stores anonymously to observe operations firsthand. He largely avoided overt political involvement, though it later emerged that he had brief youthful involvement with Swedish pro-fascist groups in the 1940s, a connection he publicly renounced and described as his greatest mistake.[97] In his mature years, Kamprad's worldview aligned with pragmatic capitalism operating within Sweden's Social Democratic framework, and he built IKEA successfully within a high-tax, high-service environment.

Kamprad embodied personal modesty, driving used Volvos, flying economy class, and living in modest homes despite becoming one of the world's wealthiest individuals. Through the IKEA Foundation, he supported global initiatives in education, healthcare, and refugee assistance, often anonymously, consistent with his preference for discretion. "Simplicity and humility characterize our way of life," Kamprad once stated.[98] This discretion is characteristic of European industrial leadership more broadly. Figures such as J.P. Morgan or Bill Gates are widely known in the United States, whereas Europe's industrial leaders often operate far from the spotlight.

Jacob and Marcus Wallenberg Sr. occupied a central position within Sweden's so-called bank–industrial complex, overseeing extensive crossholdings through Investor AB.[99] Their focus was less on operational entrepreneurship and more on corporate governance, strategic industrial stewardship, and long-term economic planning. The Wallenbergs worked quietly to preserve Sweden's industrial competitiveness as the country transitioned deeper into Social Democracy. They practiced what might be described as "silent diplomacy" with the Swedish state, supporting the welfare model in principle while actively advocating for business-friendly regulatory conditions.

During World War II, the Wallenbergs pursued controversial neutrality strategies aimed at safeguarding Swedish economic interests. Like Kamprad, they lived discreetly despite immense influence, adhering to a family code emphasizing responsibility, restraint, and institutional continuity. Public political commentary was rare. Instead, the Wallenberg Foundations became Sweden's largest private benefactors of research and education, donating billions of kronor to universities, hospitals, and cultural institutions.[100] Raoul Wallenberg, though not an industrial leader in the conventional sense, became globally renowned for his humanitarian actions in Budapest during the Holocaust, reflecting the family's broader ethos of service and obligation.

The Wallenbergs are best understood as a family dynasty rather than as a collection of individually prominent industrialists, with Raoul being the notable exception. Such dynastic structures are far more common within Europe's social democracies than in the United States. We will return to this observation after examining additional cases across other countries. For now, it is worth considering why durable family-controlled industrial leadership has proven more prevalent in social democratic systems than in the more fluid and celebrity-driven capitalist culture of the United States.

Marcel Dassault founded one of France's premier aerospace companies and was an engineer at heart, personally supervising military aviation development. His son, Serge Dassault, later expanded the enterprise into media ownership and advanced defense technologies, with a particular emphasis on national sovereignty. Both Marcel and Serge held conservative, pro-business views. Serge, in particular, was deeply involved in French conservative politics, serving as a senator and becoming a vocal defender of traditional values. Marcel Dassault, a survivor of the Buchenwald concentration camp, placed great emphasis on resilience, discipline, and national pride. Serge lived a more public life, engaging actively with political and media elites. The Dassault family supported veterans' causes, aerospace education, and right-leaning think tanks in France. Perhaps more than most industrial families in Europe, the Dassaults were resistant to a broad social democratic consensus, which may help explain why France's path to social democracy was more confrontational, uneven, and non-linear than that of countries such as Sweden.[101]

François and Édouard Michelin operated their family business according to a philosophy of industrial paternalism. They personally oversaw factory improvements, worker housing initiatives, and major technical innovations, including the development of the radial tire. Management emphasized not only profitability but also worker welfare and product excellence. The Michelin family supported France's social market economy, believing in a version of capitalism tempered by strong corporate responsibility. Unlike the Dassaults, the Michelins largely avoided direct political engagement, preferring to influence society through corporate behavior and long-term investment. They remained closely tied to Clermont-Ferrand, transforming the town into an industrial hub while maintaining a relatively private, family-centered lifestyle.[102] The Michelin Foundation funded housing, education, and healthcare for workers and their families well before such initiatives were mandated by the state. As with many European industrial leaders, the Michelin family operated as a discreet and enduring dynasty. While most readers recognize the Michelin brand, fewer are familiar with François and Édouard themselves, a contrast to figures such as Henry Ford. The Michelin family's values aligned far more closely with social democracy than those of the Dassault family.

The Wallenbergs, Dassaults, and Michelins were all family dynasties. Indeed, European social democracies have produced far more enduring family-based industrial dynasties than the United States. European firms historically relied more on private banks, family holdings, and state-supported credit than on open and liquid public capital markets. Long-term, patient capital was valued over rapid liquidity, and control mattered more than market exit. Preserving ownership within the family was seen as essential for stability, continuity, and social cohesion. As Peter Hall has observed, in Europe capital was stewarded across generations, whereas in America it was often maximized within a single generation or two.

In much of Europe, particularly Scandinavia, Germany, and France, family continuity was viewed as stabilizing rather than reactionary. Industrial dynasties symbolized responsibility, tradition, and social duty rather than overt greed. Leading families often cast themselves as national stewards rather than purely private profiteers. In contrast, American industrialists were more commonly perceived as temporary stewards of wealth, with dynastic accumulation becoming socially suspect under progressive and populist critiques in the early twentieth century, particularly through antitrust movements. While some European countries, such as postwar Britain, taxed estates aggressively, others, notably Sweden, Germany, and France, structured legal and financial frameworks to protect family industrial holdings. Sweden, for example, abolished inheritance taxes by 2005, and long before that, industrialists made extensive use of foundations and trusts—most notably the Wallenberg Foundations—to preserve dynastic control.[103]

European industrialists operated within explicit social democratic compromises. They accepted higher taxes and stronger labor protections in exchange for the ability to retain family control and long-term strategic autonomy. The state and industrial families often collaborated in nation-building projects, such as the German Mittelstand or French dirigisme. In the United States, entrepreneurs faced less direct political operational intervention but more frequent antitrust breakups, as seen with Standard Oil or AT&T. In Europe, business leadership was often viewed as a moral duty, almost a secular aristocracy with obligations to employees, communities, and national interests. In America, business was more commonly seen as an individual venture whose social value derived from innovation and growth. Personal wealth was tolerated, but dynastic dominance was culturally contentious.

These family dynasties, a form of modern aristocracy, suggest that Europe's elite successfully preserved power and wealth within the framework of Social Democracy.[104] Estimating their effective marginal tax rates is difficult, given their discretion and use of complex financial structures. For context, when U.S. marginal income tax rates reached 91 percent, effective rates were often closer to the mid-thirties. Sweden's headline marginal income tax rate stands at roughly 52 percent. A reasonable estimate for families such as the Wallenbergs might place effective marginal taxation between 15 and 25 percent on realized income, and potentially below 10 percent when accounting for total economic gains.[105] This dynamic is critical when evaluating the moral claims of social democracies and assessing the extent to which these systems truly enable inclusive opportunity.

In contrast to the low-profile European industrialists and family dynasties reviewed thus far, Sir Richard Branson, founder of the Virgin Group, cultivated a highly public entrepreneurial persona. He blended personal adventure, such as balloon flights and ocean crossings, with brand promotion and media visibility. Most readers are likely familiar with Branson. His leadership style was decentralized, empowering managers across Virgin's diverse portfolio of businesses. Ideologically, Branson leaned toward libertarian and pro-market positions, while also supporting environmental causes, drug policy reform, and select social initiatives. Unlike traditional European industrialists, he embraced celebrity culture as a strategic asset. Through the Virgin Unite foundation, Branson supports climate mitigation, healthcare initiatives, and humanitarian efforts. It is not coincidental that Branson's rise coincided with the neoliberal turn of the Thatcher era. One might reasonably infer a correlation between prevailing economic systems and the leadership styles they reward.

James Dyson, best known for the Dyson vacuum, represents yet another variant of industrial leadership. Dyson remained deeply involved in product engineering, holding hundreds of patents personally and maintaining tight control over research and development. He insisted on in-house technological supremacy and engineering excellence.[106] Dyson became a prominent advocate of Brexit, arguing that regulatory independence would enhance British innovation. He cultivated the image of the engineer-entrepreneur, emphasizing invention, professionalism, and restrained public presence, in the tradition of figures such as Thomas Edison, Bill Hewlett, and David Packard. Through the James Dyson Foundation, he has invested heavily in engineering education, scholarships, and STEM development.

Turning to Germany, the automotive industry provides particularly instructive examples. Ferdinand Porsche, founder of Porsche and an early architect of Volkswagen, was obsessively focused on automotive engineering excellence. His daily work centered on technical design and innovation, often involving long hours in factories and design rooms. Porsche, controversially, collaborated extensively with the Nazi regime during World War II, designing military vehicles, including the Tiger tank, and contributing early designs for the Volkswagen Beetle.[107] Forced labor was used in production, casting a lasting shadow over his legacy. While his technical achievements remain widely recognized, his political and ethical record remains deeply problematic. Porsche maintained a reserved, engineer's demeanor, focused on technical work rather than social display. In the postwar era, his descendants invested in automotive education and engineering research, although Ferdinand Porsche himself left a limited personal philanthropic footprint.

Carl Friedrich von Siemens expanded Siemens into one of the world's leading electrical engineering and industrial firms. His leadership style was technocratic and pragmatic, emphasizing technological modernization, organizational discipline, and global expansion. He navigated the instability of the Weimar Republic cautiously, supporting moderate industrial policies, and later maneuvered Siemens through the Nazi period, during which the company, like many major German firms, became implicated in wartime production and forced labor. Carl Friedrich von Siemens was markedly less flamboyant than many American industrial leaders, focusing instead on corporate internationalism and engineering excellence. The Siemens family later contributed extensively to scientific research, technical education, and cultural institutions in Germany through various foundations.

Throughout this history of economic systems, we have examined the behaviors of industrial leadership and how those behaviors were shaped, constrained, or amplified by the underlying economic systems in place. These empirical observations are critical to the design of Inclusive Capitalism. The objective is to preserve and enhance the dynamism and innovation associated with capitalism while systematically addressing its unintended consequences.

The behavior of industrial leaders across economic systems is not primarily a function of personality, culture, or national character. It is a function of incentives and institutional architecture. Different systems reward different forms of risk-taking, time horizons, capital deployment, and organizational design. Over time, leadership behavior converges toward what the system frames as rational.[108]

Three structural realities emerge.

First, democratic socialist systems embed an ongoing operational tradeoff between durability and dynamism. Industrial leaders operating within European social democracies have frequently built firms that match or exceed their American counterparts in engineering quality, operational discipline, and long-term resilience. Companies such as IKEA, Michelin, Siemens, and Dassault demonstrate that these systems can produce world-class industrial champions. The distinction is therefore not one of managerial talent or technical competence but of strategic ceiling.

European political–economic systems have historically emphasized patient capital, stakeholder governance, and financial stability. These features favor enterprises optimized for longevity, incremental innovation, and national or regional embeddedness.[109] Long-term bank financing, concentrated ownership, co-determination, and strong labor protections dampen volatility and encourage continuity, but they also discourage aggressive risk concentration, rapid equity dilution, and large-scale speculative expansion.[110]

As a result, European champions have tended to become globally competitive yet strategically conservative—optimized for durability and national stability rather than maximal innovation velocity or global dominance. This is not a critique of European leadership quality; it is an observation about how financial depth, risk tolerance, and capital mobility condition what even the most capable leaders can rationally attempt.

Second, the U.S. system structurally favors frontier innovation but also short-term financialization. U.S.-style capitalism—characterized by deep venture and public capital markets, high tolerance for prolonged losses, aggressive equity-based compensation, and permissive attitudes toward winner-take-most outcomes—has enabled a category of firm designed from inception to pursue extreme scale and rapid global enclosure. Companies such as Amazon, Google, Meta, Nvidia, and Tesla did not emerge merely because of individual genius; they emerged because the U.S. system permits prolonged loss-making investment, massive reinvestment of cash flows, and extreme risk concentration in pursuit of future dominance.[111]

These same incentives, however, also bias leadership toward short-term share-price maximization, financial engineering, and capital extraction when governance fails. Over recent decades, U.S. industrial leadership has increasingly prioritized stock buybacks, leveraged recapitalizations, and executive compensation tied to quarterly performance, often at the expense of long-term productive investment.[112] The erosion of long-horizon industrial stewardship is visible in sectors such as automotive manufacturing and commercial aerospace, where once-dominant American firms have struggled with quality control, supply-chain fragility, and declining engineering depth.

Thus, the U.S. system produces unmatched innovation at the frontier but also chronic instability and periodic hollowing-out of core industrial capacity.

Third, Inclusive Capitalism seeks to preserve dynamism while removing its destructive side effects. Inclusive Capitalism begins from the recognition that neither European social democracy nor U.S.-style capitalism offers a stable optimum. One system protects dignity but caps dynamism; the other unleashes innovation but tolerates exclusion and systemic fragility.

By redesigning incentives so that optimizing societal well-being becomes the dominant objective of enterprise leadership, Inclusive Capitalism aims to preserve capitalism's boundless innovation ceiling while eliminating its legitimacy floor. This requires replacing GDP as the singular top-level metric, re-chartering large enterprises around long-term value creation, and constructing capital markets that reward inclusive innovation rather than extractive financialization.

In short, systems define what leaders can rationally attempt. Inclusive Capitalism is proposed as an architecture in which leaders can rationally pursue extreme innovation, long-horizon investment, and broad participation simultaneously—without the tradeoffs that have historically forced societies to oscillate between stability and dynamism.

This distinction matters because it reveals the binding constraint in both systems. Democratic socialism has demonstrated an ability to humanize capitalism's outcomes but not to extend its innovation frontier at the pace required by modern technological change. The United States, conversely, has demonstrated unmatched capacity to generate transformative firms but at the cost of volatility, exclusion, and legitimacy erosion. The divergence is not cultural or moral; it is architectural.

The implication is not that one system produces better leaders than the other. It is that systems define the upper bound of what leaders can rationally attempt. Democratic socialist economies have historically limited downside risk and concentrated less upside, producing resilient but bounded industrial trajectories. U.S.-style capitalism has allowed extreme upside at the cost of extreme misalignment.[113] Inclusive Capitalism begins from the recognition that preserving capitalism's boundless innovation ceiling while eliminating its societal well-being downside and legitimacy floor is not achievable through counter-factual nostalgia but only through deliberate incentive and institutional redesign.

Economic structures and societal norms are deeply intertwined, shaping incentives, risk tolerance, visibility, and time horizons.[114] Each system involves tradeoffs across dimensions of dynamism, stability, stewardship, discretion, and inclusion. The challenge, and the opportunity, is to design a rational economic foundation that captures the innovative energy of capitalism and the social virtues of democratic socialism without inheriting their respective pathologies.[115] Advances in technology, data, and systems thinking make such an outcome achievable for the first time.

Lived Experience of the Population in Democratic Socialist Countries

The final empirical dimension to examine before drawing conclusions about democratic socialism—and its implications for Inclusive Capitalism—is the lived experience of the workforce. In broad terms, working life under European democratic socialism can be characterized as stable, protected, and highly unionized across most industrial and service-sector occupations.[116]

Under European social democracies, work life for both industrial and service workers was defined by security, predictability, and a steadily rising sense of dignity. Full employment was a shared political objective, particularly during the post–World War II period from roughly 1945 to 1975. Labor protections were extensive and enforceable, including strict rules governing termination, generous leave policies, mandated rest periods, and comprehensive workplace safety standards encompassing physical, environmental, and increasingly mental health considerations. Shorter workweeks became common by the 1970s. France later codified a 35-hour workweek in the 1990s, while Germany and Sweden achieved similar reductions of hours through sector-wide collective agreements. As Dick Geary observed, "The power of the trade union was not only in negotiations, but in the expectation of fairness in the workplace."[117] Union density was correspondingly high. Sweden and Denmark exceeded 70 percent union membership, while Germany remained above 50 percent through much of the mid-century. Collective bargaining was not merely tolerated but institutionalized through co-determination regimes, such as Germany's *Mitbestimmung* laws, and through national or sectoral labor accords.[118]

Social life for the workforce was communal, predictable, and modestly prosperous, standing in stark contrast to the lived experience under Soviet Communism. Rising wages combined with reduced working hours expanded leisure time, enabling summer holidays, weekend travel, and the rise of mass tourism, often supported by subsidized programs. Workers participated actively in community organizations, housing cooperatives, cultural clubs, and social movements, many of which were linked to labor unions or political parties. Public education systems expanded rapidly, offering free or nearly free access through secondary school and, in many countries, university education. For the first time, children of industrial workers entered professional and white-collar occupations in large numbers, marking the consolidation of a broad postwar middle class.[119]

Workers were not merely beneficiaries of Social Democracy; they were also among its principal architects. Socialist, Social Democratic, and Labour parties functioned as mass-membership organizations, funded, staffed, and energized largely by workers themselves. Political literacy among the working class was high, with debates over policy and party platforms taking place in union halls, workplaces, pubs, and labor-affiliated newspapers. As Gøsta Esping-Andersen noted, "The Nordic model did not deliver Social Democracy from above. It was the outcome of working-class organization and class compromise."[120] Labor activism remained largely peaceful. While strikes continued to serve as a pressure mechanism, they were increasingly embedded within formalized tripartite negotiations among labor, employers, and the state.[121] This institutionalization of conflict helped avoid the violent labor confrontations that characterized earlier phases of industrial capitalism.

Essential services—including healthcare, education, childcare, and transportation—were heavily subsidized or publicly provided, significantly reducing household expenses. Large-scale public housing initiatives, particularly in the United Kingdom and Sweden, ensured that low-income families had access to adequate housing. Although tax burdens were high, workers generally perceived life as affordable because post-tax, post-service living standards were strong. As Timothy Garton Ash summarized, "The Swedish worker pays more tax than the American, but takes home more healthcare, childcare, and peace of mind."[122] By the 1960s and 1970s, much of the working class had transitioned from subsistence to modest affluence. Ownership of consumer goods such as televisions and automobiles (notably the Volkswagen Beetle or Citroën 2CV) became commonplace, and foreign holidays became normalized experiences for large portions of the citizenry.

The principal downside of workforce empowerment under European Social Democracies lies in the institutional rigidities and economic frictions that often accompany it. While strong protections enhance worker dignity, security, and bargaining power, they can also constrain flexibility, competitiveness, and innovation when not paired with adaptive mechanisms. Stringent employment protection laws make workforce adjustments costly during downturns, discouraging hiring—particularly of younger and less-experienced workers—and contributing to dual labor markets divided between protected insiders and precarious outsiders. In countries such as France and Italy, strong job security for incumbents has reduced labor mobility and contributed to persistent structural unemployment. As the OECD observed, "Security for some becomes exclusion for others."[123]

Generous benefits—such as sick leave, parental leave, and pensions—are largely funded through payroll taxes, raising the cost of labor, especially for lower-skilled workers. This can render certain industries less viable domestically and accelerate automation or offshoring. Automation is often pursued not as a productivity frontier but as a necessity to remain cost-competitive with foreign producers. Employers may substitute capital for labor, dampening net job creation. Progressive taxation, wealth redistribution, and strong union norms can also compress income differentials, weaken incentives for entrepreneurial risk-taking or extraordinary individual effort. In highly egalitarian systems, ambition may be viewed as socially constrained, particularly when outsized rewards are perceived as illegitimate. Philippe Aghion cautions that "Equality can dull the edge of innovation when status competition and financial reward are heavily compressed."[124]

Where workforce empowerment includes co-determination, centralized wage bargaining, and strong sectoral unions, industries can be slow to restructure in response to global competition or technological disruption. Resistance to plant closures, layoffs, or major reorganizations can delay necessary adaptation, particularly in legacy sectors such as steel, automotive manufacturing, and energy. European automotive producers, for example, have been comparatively slow to adapt to electrification. Reduced flexibility in wage-setting, hiring, and work practices can impair firms' ability to respond rapidly to international cost pressures. In such environments, firms may ultimately resort to abrupt automation, outsourcing, or relocation, hollowing out domestic employment segments rather than facilitating gradual adjustment.

Finally, strong protections for incumbent workers can entrench an insider class with stable jobs and benefits, while new entrants—especially younger workers, immigrants, and those on temporary contracts—face significant barriers to secure employment. This can generate generational inequality and a two-tier labor market, undermining the egalitarian objectives of social democracy itself. As Assar Lindbeck observed, "The most protected workers are often the least productive, while the youngest and most adaptable are the least protected."[125]

What Works and What Does Not Under Democratic Socialism

The preceding account of life for the workforce under European social democracy—while perhaps somewhat rosier than lived reality—nonetheless presents a picture fundamentally different from that of early capitalism roughly a century earlier.[126] Much of this improvement is attributable to technological progress, capital accumulation, and productivity growth rather than to social democracy alone. Indeed, life for the American workforce during the postwar "Golden Age of Capitalism" was, by many measures, at least as rewarding as that experienced under European social democracy. Yet perception matters. In Europe, social democracy has become associated with dignified living conditions for the workforce, whereas capitalism—rightly or wrongly—has not. This association reflects the observed correlation between economic systems and worker outcomes, rather than a clean causal attribution.

A second crucial takeaway from the European experience is that social democracy emerged largely as a bottom-up response to capitalism's unintended consequences.[127] As in the United States and elsewhere, reform was driven by worker-led initiatives—unions, strikes, political mobilization, and social movements—rather than by voluntary transformation initiated by industrial leadership. In most cases, industrial elites resisted reform and developed mechanisms to preserve wealth and influence, whether through family dynasties, complex ownership structures, or enterprises whose economic power rivaled that of nation-states.[128] The net result has been the persistence of class divisions, durable wealth inequality, and recurring social conflict.

It is worth imagining an alternative trajectory: one in which industrial leadership proactively reshaped economic institutions with the explicit aim of optimizing societal well-being rather than defending incumbency. Such a system would allow both leadership and labor to prosper beyond what current models permit, not in opposition but through collaboration. This outcome is not utopian. It is a moral obligation—and the central objective of Inclusive Capitalism.

To conclude this review of social democracy, it is useful to distill the lessons from three perspectives: (i) the socialist, (ii) the laissez-faire Smithian capitalist, and (iii) the builders of Inclusive Capitalism.

From the socialist perspective, Thomas Piketty argues that democratic socialism represents the most morally defensible and economically stable framework for reconciling capitalism's productive power with social justice.[129] In his analysis, unfettered capitalism naturally concentrates wealth and power unless democratic institutions—progressive taxation, inheritance regulation, public education, and social investment—actively redistribute opportunity. Piketty supports universal access to public goods, meaningful worker voice in enterprise governance, and tax-based mechanisms to prevent the emergence of patrimonial capitalism. As he writes in *Capital and Ideology* (2002), "Every human society must justify its inequalities . . . Democratic Socialism offers a framework where power and property are not frozen, but circulatory."[130] Markets can generate wealth, but only democratic institutions, in his view, can allocate it justly and sustainably.

From the laissez-faire capitalist perspective, Milton Friedman reached a sharply different conclusion. Friedman believed that democratic socialism systematically underestimates the efficiency and adaptive capacity of free markets while overestimating the competence, neutrality, and restraint of the state.[131] Although he accepted the need for limited safety nets, he argued that competitive capitalism was vastly superior in generating long-term prosperity. In *Capitalism and Freedom* (1962), Friedman wrote that "Government should be a referee, not an active player . . . every intervention distorts incentives and invites special interests."[132]

Crucially, Friedman viewed economic freedom as inseparable from political freedom. "Economic freedom," he argued, "is . . . an indispensable means toward the achievement of political freedom."[133] Social democracy, by guaranteeing an expanding set of social rights through the state, risked concentrating decision-making authority and eroding individual autonomy. Even under democratic governance, Friedman warned, incremental expansions of state power carried latent coercive risks. He viewed welfare-state growth as a slippery slope toward bureaucratic dominance, in which distorted incentives and regulatory capture gradually undermine liberty.

More broadly, Friedman admired the United States' more individualistic and market-oriented model relative to Europe's corporatist systems. While acknowledging that postwar European social democracies delivered stability, he argued they did so at the cost of growth, innovation, and personal freedom. His oft-cited maxim captured this hierarchy of values: "A society that puts equality before freedom will get neither. A society that puts freedom before equality will get a high degree of both."[134]

The builders of Inclusive Capitalism see not a binary choice between Friedman and Piketty but a profound opportunity to synthesize the strongest insights of both—anchoring firmly in Friedman's emphasis on incentives and dynamism, while incorporating Piketty's insistence on fairness and legitimacy. Piketty argues that markets can create wealth but only democracy can allocate it justly. Inclusive Capitalism goes further: markets, when properly designed, are the most effective mechanism for optimizing societal well-being itself. A fair and transparent rule system that ensures equality of opportunity—not post-hoc redistribution—is the most durable path to moral and equitable outcomes, particularly as large portions of the economy move toward non-scarcity.[135]

Friedman was correct that democratic socialism underestimates the power of markets. But history also shows that markets, left entirely unchecked, are not reliably self-correcting. Evidence from the late nineteenth century, the Great Depression, and the early twenty-first century demonstrates that unbounded capitalism can produce neither broad-based freedom nor equality for the working majority.[136] Adam Smith's invisible hand, when scaled without constraint, has too often evolved into an extractive claw.

The solution is conceptually straightforward. The root cause is the incentive structure that governs industrial leadership and, by extension, society as a whole. To address this, incentives must be redesigned so that optimizing societal well-being becomes the dominant objective of enterprise leadership. This insight is no less obvious today than it was to Adam Smith when he proposed shifting the economic metric from the king's stock of gold to the productive output of goods and services.[137] That shift was revolutionary—and correct—but it has outlived its usefulness.

The next evolution of capitalism must reward the creation of non-scarcity rather than the exploitation of scarcity; maximize the pace of innovation; expand opportunity for all who are capable and motivated; ensure a robust but not demotivating social floor; and do so without relying primarily on heavy regulation. This is the foundation upon which Inclusive Capitalism is built.

Forces That Results in the Oscillation Away from Democratic Socialism

One of the most revealing empirical facts of modern economic history is not the success or failure of any single system but the persistent oscillation among them.[138] Over the past century—and with increasing frequency in the last several decades—nations have repeatedly swung between laissez-faire capitalism, Keynesian demand management, and social democracy. This pendulum motion is not confined to a particular geography, culture, or level of development. It appears in advanced European economies, in Latin America, and even within the same country across successive generations. This recurring oscillation is itself a powerful proof point: if any of these systems were structurally correct, stable, and abundance-creating, such reversals would be unnecessary.

Europe offers the clearest long-run illustration. After World War II, much of Western Europe adopted Keynesian and social-democratic frameworks to stabilize economies shattered by war and political extremism.[139] These models seemed appropriate at the time and did deliver genuine gains: full employment, rising living standards, and social cohesion during the postwar decades. Yet by the 1970s, inflation, fiscal imbalance, and declining productivity eroded confidence. The response was a sharp turn toward market liberalization in the 1980s—most visibly in the United Kingdom under Margaret Thatcher but echoed across continental Europe.[140]

By the 1990s and early 2000s, elements of social democracy were reintroduced under the banner of "Third Way" politics. More recently, Europe has once again begun drifting rightward, driven by fiscal stress, immigration pressures, demographic aging, and declining competitiveness. Sweden, Germany, the Netherlands, Italy, and France have all experienced renewed skepticism toward expansive welfare states and heavy regulation. This repeated cycling is not ideological caprice; it is a structural response to systems that temporarily solve one set of problems while sowing the seeds of the next crisis.[141]

If social democracy were a stable equilibrium—capable of sustaining innovation, fiscal balance, and social legitimacy indefinitely—Europe would not be re-testing market liberalism today. Likewise, if laissez-faire capitalism were self-correcting at scale, the postwar turn toward social protection would never have occurred. The oscillation reveals that each framework contains internal contradictions that eventually overwhelm its benefits.[142]

Latin America provides an even more striking example because the oscillations occur over shorter time horizons and with higher amplitude. Countries across the region have repeatedly alternated between market liberalization and state-led redistribution, often within a single generation.

Argentina is emblematic. Since the mid-twentieth century, Argentina has cycled through Peronist populism, military-backed market reforms, neoliberal liberalization in the 1990s, a return to expansive state spending in the 2000s, and once again to market-oriented austerity in the late 2010s and early 2020s. Each phase begins with moral and economic justification—and ends with inflation, debt crises, capital flight, or social unrest.[143]

Chile offers a complementary case. After decades as a poster child for market-oriented reform, Chile experienced widespread social protests in 2019, driven by inequality, cost-of-living pressures, and perceptions of exclusion. The political response was a sharp swing leftward, followed by voter rejection of expansive constitutional proposals and a subsequent re-centering. Again, oscillation—not equilibrium—defines the outcome.[144]

Similar patterns appear in Brazil, Peru, and Mexico. The lesson is not that these societies are uniquely unstable. Rather, they reveal in accelerated form what unfolds more slowly in Europe: systems that fail to foster broad-based abundance eventually lose legitimacy and are replaced, only for the replacement to fail in turn.[145]

Each of the three dominant frameworks fails for predictable structural reasons.

Laissez-faire capitalism excels at innovation and capital formation, but at scale it tends to produce exclusion, monopolization, and manufactured scarcity. Over time, wealth concentration erodes social mobility, weakens aggregate demand, and undermines political legitimacy. The system then invites corrective intervention.

Keynesian economics stabilizes downturns and smooths business cycles, but when applied persistently rather than cyclically, it becomes fiscally addictive. Deficit spending accumulates faster than productive capacity, debt servicing crowds out investment, and political incentives favor perpetual stimulus over structural reform. Eventually, inflation, currency instability, or debt crises force retrenchment.[146]

Social democracy addresses inequality and insecurity more directly, but it struggles with incentive alignment. As spending expands, regulation intensifies, and public ownership grows, marginal productivity declines. High effective tax rates on labor and enterprise reduce dynamism. Welfare systems, once generous, become fiscally fragile as demographics shift and participation ratios fall. When the least-productive segment of society becomes structurally disconnected from contribution, the system's moral legitimacy erodes from within.

Crucially, none of these systems reliably fosters non-scarcity. All three assume scarcity as a baseline condition—whether to be allocated by markets, smoothed by demand management, or redistributed by the state. As a result, they remain locked in zero-sum logic. Growth becomes episodic rather than structural, and innovation becomes defensive rather than expansive.

The continued global oscillation between these models is not a failure of political will or leadership. It is a failure of economic architecture. Societies are not irrational for abandoning systems that no longer deliver. They are rationally responding to frameworks that solve yesterday's problems while creating tomorrow's crises.[147]

If any of these paradigms were fundamentally correct—capable of sustaining abundance, legitimacy, and innovation simultaneously—we would observe convergence, not oscillation. Europe would not be drifting rightward again today. Latin America would not be perpetually rebooting its economic model. Advanced economies would not be trapped in cycles of stimulus, austerity, and backlash.[148]

The persistence of oscillation is therefore not a political phenomenon; it is an empirical indictment.

There is a better way—one that does not require swinging between extremes, sacrificing dynamism for equity or equity for growth. The missing ingredient is not ideology but incentive design. None of the prevailing systems aligns leadership incentives with the optimization of societal well-being under conditions of accelerating technological abundance.[149]

An economic system designed explicitly to foster non-scarcity—by rewarding inclusive innovation, maximizing contribution, and replacing extractive metrics with abundance-oriented ones—would not need to oscillate. It would be stable precisely because it removes the structural contradictions that force pendulum swings.

Inclusive Capitalism is proposed as that architecture: not a compromise between failed systems but a refactoring of their underlying incentive logic. Only by addressing this root cause can societies escape the cycle of oscillation and move toward a durable, abundance-based equilibrium.

Conclusions and Insights for Inclusive Capitalism

We have seen in this review of democratic socialism that it is a viable and, in many respects, good enough system—yet one that remains far from optimal. It delivers virtue without victory. Democratic socialism has demonstrated that societies can substantially mitigate many of capitalism's unintended consequences, particularly those related to worker security, access to basic services, and perceived fairness. At the same time, its structural limitations—especially around incentives, dynamism, and long-term sustainability—prevent it from serving as a durable endpoint. In the United States, democratic socialism is therefore best understood not as a destination, but as a likely default outcome should contemporary capitalism fail to address its most acute shortcomings within a reasonably short period of time.

The central takeaway from the European social democratic experience is that the contrast between European social democracy and American free-market capitalism reflects fundamentally different societal tradeoffs. In much of Europe—particularly in countries such as Sweden, Germany, and France—the postwar consensus prioritized worker protections, labor empowerment, and expansive social welfare systems, often embedded within corporatist frameworks that formally integrated unions and employers into economic governance. The United States, by contrast, emphasized market dynamism, limited regulation, and individual responsibility, operating under the belief that these conditions would maximize innovation, growth, and opportunity. Both systems largely delivered on their stated objectives: Europe achieved greater income equality and workforce stability, while the United States drove extraordinary technological progress, entrepreneurial dynamism, and aggregate wealth creation. Yet both models are now showing clear signs of strain.

European social democracies increasingly face challenges related to labor-market rigidity, insider–outsider dynamics, generational inequities, and the fiscal sustainability of expansive welfare commitments amid globalization, demographic aging, and slower productivity growth.[150] Meanwhile, the American model has produced historic levels of inequality, exclusion from opportunity, geographic and class polarization, affordability crises, and an erosion of social cohesion.[151] Neither system offers a complete or enduring answer to the demands of a twenty-first-century economy shaped by artificial intelligence, transnational capital, and rapidly evolving social contracts. Each clings to a partial vision—one prioritizing security over dynamism, the other dynamism over inclusion—that is increasingly inadequate when taken in isolation.

The conclusion is unavoidable: it is time to envision a new, more rational system that transcends this false dichotomy. Inclusive Capitalism is not an attempt to split the difference between Social Democracy and laissez-faire markets, nor a compromise between competing ideologies. It is a design advance. By removing the artificial tradeoff between innovation and dignity, competitiveness and fairness, Inclusive Capitalism seeks to build an economic platform in which empowered workers and dynamic enterprise are mutually reinforcing rather than adversarial.[152] Through the redesign of core metrics (replacing GDP as primary with societal well-being), the re-chartering of large enterprises, and the construction of innovation ecosystems that reward contribution rather than concentration, Inclusive Capitalism offers a coherent path beyond oscillation. It is not a return to the past, nor a reaction to failure, but a forward-looking architecture capable of sustaining abundance, legitimacy, and human flourishing at scale.

Notes

1 Karl Polanyi, *The Great Transformation* (Boston: Beacon Press, 2001), 130–160.

2 Thomas Piketty, *Capital and Ideology* (Cambridge, MA: Harvard University Press, 2020), 97–128.

3 Douglass C. North, *Institutions, Institutional Change and Economic Performance* (Cambridge: Cambridge University Press, 1990), 3–22.

4 Martin Gilens and Benjamin I. Page, *Testing Theories of American Politics: Elites, Interest Groups, and Average Citizens, American Political Science Review* 108, no. 3 (2014): 564–581.

5 Milton Friedman, *Capitalism and Freedom* (Chicago: University of Chicago Press, 2002), 7–21.

6 Albert O. Hirschman, *The Rhetoric of Reaction* (Cambridge, MA: Harvard University Press, 1991), 43–67.

7 Eric Hobsbawm, Age of Extremes: *The Short Twentieth Century* (New York: Vintage, 1996), 54–86.

8 John Maynard Keynes, *Essays in Biography* (New York: W. W. Norton, 1963), 287–290.
9 Adam Smith, *An Inquiry into the Nature and Causes of the Wealth of Nations* (Indianapolis: Liberty Fund, 1981), 456–468.
10 Churchill, Winston S. Speech at the Conservative Party Campaign Rally, Westminster, 22 October 1945. In *The Complete Speeches of Winston S. Churchill, 1897–1963*, vol. 7, edited by Robert Rhodes James, Chelsea House, 1974.
11 Schumpeter, Joseph A. *Capitalism, Socialism and Democracy*. New York: Harper & Brothers, 1942.
12 Vladimir I. Lenin, *The State and Revolution* (New York: International Publishers, 1932), 15–45.
13 Adam Smith, *An Inquiry into the Nature and Causes of the Wealth of Nations*, 456–468.
14 John Maynard Keynes, *Essays in Biography* (New York: W. W. Norton, 1963), 287–290.
15 Karl Polanyi, *The Great Transformation*, 130–160.
16 Robert F. Kennedy, *Remarks at the University of Kansas*, March 18, 1968, Public Papers of the Presidents.
17 Mancur Olson, *The Rise and Decline of Nations* (New Haven, CT: Yale University Press, 1982), 73–95.
18 Alec Nove, *The Economics of Feasible Socialism* (London: Routledge, 1983), 1–32.
19 Karl Polanyi, *The Great Transformation*, 130–160.
20 Thomas Piketty, *Capital and Ideology*, 97–128.
21 Karl Marx and Friedrich Engels, *The Communist Manifesto* (London: Penguin Classics, 2002), 219–240.
22 Karl Marx, *Critique of the Gotha Program* (New York: International Publishers, 1970), 10–21.
23 Goldman, Marshall I. *What Went Wrong with Perestroika*. New York: W. W. Norton, 1991.
24 Karl Marx, *Critique of the Gotha Program* (New York: International Publishers, 1970), 10–21.
25 Karl Polanyi, *The Great Transformation*, 130–160.
26 Douglass C. North, *Institutions, Institutional Change and Economic Performance*, 3–22.
27 Friedrich Hayek, *The Road to Serfdom* (Chicago: University of Chicago Press, 2007), 68–87.
28 Thomas Sowell, *Basic Economics* (New York: Basic Books, 2015), 49–67.
29 Václav Havel, *The Power of the Powerless* (Armonk, NY: M. E. Sharpe, 1985), 23–44.
30 Eric Hobsbawm, Age of Extremes: *The Short Twentieth Century*, 54–86.
31 Karl Polanyi, *The Great Transformation*, 130–160.
32 Friedrich Hayek, *The Road to Serfdom* (Chicago: University of Chicago Press, 2007), 68–87.
33 Thomas Piketty, *Capital and Ideology*, 97–128.
34 Eric Hobsbawm, Age of Extremes: *The Short Twentieth Century*, 54–86.
35 Karl Polanyi, *The Great Transformation*, 130–160.
36 Eric Hobsbawm, Age of Extremes: *The Short Twentieth Century*, 54–86.
37 Ibid.
38 William Beveridge, *Social Insurance and Allied Services*, London: HMSO, 1942.
39 McBriar, A. M. *Fabian Socialism and English Politics 1884–1918*.
40 Tawney, R. H. *The Acquisitive Society* (1921).
41 John Maynard Keynes, *Essays in Biography*, 287–290.
42 Friedrich Hayek, *The Road to Serfdom* (Chicago: University of Chicago Press, 2007), 68–87.
43 Milton Friedman, *Capitalism and Freedom*, 7–21.
44 Gamble, Andrew. *The Free Economy and the Strong State: The Politics of Thatcherism*.Durham, NC: Duke University Press, 1988, chapters 1–3.
45 Blair, Tony. *New Britain: My Vision of a Young Country*. Boulder, CO: Westview Press, 1996, pp. 39–55.
46 Polanyi, Karl. *The Great Transformation*. Beacon Press, 2001, pp. 35–75, 130–160.
47 Mowat, Charles. *Britain Between the Wars, 1918–1940*. University of Chicago Press, 1955.
48 Seymour Martin Lipset & Gary Marks, *It Didn't Happen Here: Why Socialism Failed in the United States*. W. W. Norton, 2000.

49 Seymour Martin Lipset, *American Exceptionalism: A Double-Edged Sword.*New York: W. W. Norton, 1996, esp. chs. 1–2.

50 Marquis Childs, *Sweden: The Middle Way*. New Haven: Yale University Press, 1936.

51 Francis Sejersted, *The Age of Social Democracy: Norway and Sweden in the Twentieth Century*. Princeton University Press, 2011.

52 János Kornai, *Economics of Shortage* (Amsterdam: North-Holland, 1980), 27–55.

53 Myrdal, Gunnar and Alva Myrdal. *Crisis in the Population Question*. London: P. S. King, 1934.

54 Childs, Marquis. *Sweden: The Middle Way*. New Haven: Yale University Press, 1936.

55 Esping-Andersen, Gøsta. *The Three Worlds of Welfare Capitalism*. Princeton University Press, 1990.

56 Jonas Pontusson, *The Limits of Social Democracy: Investment Politics in Sweden* (Ithaca, NY: Cornell University Press, 1992), 65–92.

57 Milton Friedman, *Capitalism and Freedom*, 7–21.

58 Thomas Sowell, *Marxism: Philosophy and Economics* (New York: HarperCollins, 1985), 41–59.

59 Thomas Piketty, *Capital and Ideology*, 97–128.

60 Friedrich Hayek, *The Road to Serfdom* (Chicago: University of Chicago Press, 2007), 68–87.

61 Government Offices of Sweden, *The Tidö Agreement: Agreement on Policy Cooperation between the Sweden Democrats, the Moderate Party, the Christian Democrats and the Liberal Party* (Stockholm: Government of Sweden, 2022).

62 OECD, *International Migration Outlook 2016* (Paris: OECD Publishing, 2016), 36–52.

63 Heinö, Andreas Johansson. *Integrationens politiska ekonomi* [The Political Economy of Integration]. Stockholm: Timbro, 2018, 9–18.

64 Piketty, Thomas. *Capital and Ideology*. Cambridge, MA: Harvard University Press, 2020, 402–430.

65 Ibid.

66 Ibid.

67 Zucman, Gabriel. *The Hidden Wealth of Nations: The Scourge of Tax Havens*. Chicago: University of Chicago Press, 2015, 45–78.

68 Hall, Peter A. *Governing the Economy: The Politics of State Intervention in Britain and France*. New York: Oxford University Press, 1986, 3–35.

69 Hall, Peter A., and David Soskice, eds. *Varieties of Capitalism: The Institutional Foundations of Comparative Advantage*. Oxford: Oxford University Press, 2001, 1–44.

70 Jackson, Julian. *The Popular Front in France: Defending Democracy, 1934–38*. Cambridge: Cambridge University Press, 1988, 1–25.

71 Paxton, Robert O. *Vichy France: Old Guard and New Order, 1940–1944*. New York: Columbia University Press, 1972, 285–320.

72 Laroque, Pierre. *La Sécurité sociale: Son histoire, ses problèmes*. Paris: Presses Universitaires de France, 1963, 23–61.

73 Monnet, Jean. *Mémoires*. Paris: Fayard, 1976, 315–352.

74 Lazare, Daniel. *The Frozen Republic: How the Constitution Is Paralyzing Democracy*. New York: Harcourt Brace, 1996, 178–196.

75 Hall, Peter A. *Governing the Economy: The Politics of State Intervention in Britain and France*. New York: Oxford University Press, 1986, 171–198.

76 Cohen, Stephen S. *The Making of United States International Economic Policy: Principles, Problems, and Proposals for Reform*. New York: Praeger, 1988, 143–165.

77 Friedrich Hayek, *The Road to Serfdom* (Chicago: University of Chicago Press, 2007), 68–87.

78 Eric Hobsbawm, *Age of Extremes: The Short Twentieth Century, 1914–1991* (New York: Vintage Books, 1996), 87–90.

79 Kautsky, Karl. *The Class Struggle (Erfurt Program)*. Translated by William E. Bohn. Chicago: Charles H. Kerr & Company, 1909, 29–52.

80 Bernstein, Eduard. *Evolutionary Socialism: A Criticism and Affirmation*. Translated by Edith C. Harvey. New York: Schocken Books, 1961 (orig. 1899), 1–48.

81 Kershaw, Ian. *To Hell and Back: Europe 1914–1949*. New York: Viking, 2015, 142–156.

82 Abelshauser, Werner. *The Dynamics of German Industry: Germany's Path toward the New Economy and the American Challenge*. New York: Berghahn Books, 2005, 235–262.

83 SPD (Social Democratic Party of Germany). *The Godesberg Program (1959)*. Bonn: Sozialdemokratische Partei Deutschlands, English translation in *Documents of German Politics*, Series IV, vol. 2, 1957–1961, edited by Werner Link, Oxford University Press, 1986, pp. 190–204.

84 Federal Republic of Germany. *Works Constitution Act (Betriebsverfassungsgesetz), 1972*, as amended. English translation in: Roger Blanpain and Michele Colucci (eds.), *International Encyclopaedia for Labour Law and Industrial Relations: Germany*, Kluwer Law International, pp. 1–45.

85 Schildt, Axel. *Helmut Schmidt: The Global Chancellor*. Oxford: Oxford University Press, 2018, 93–145.

86 Scharpf, Fritz W., and Vivien A. Schmidt, eds. *Welfare and Work in the Open Economy, Vol. 1: From Vulnerability to Competitiveness*. Oxford: Oxford University Press, 2000, 1–35, 137–170.

87 Kornai, János. *The Socialist System: The Political Economy of Communism*. Princeton University Press, 1992, 55–90.

88 Kornai, János. *The Socialist System: The Political Economy of Communism*. pp. 221–245.

89 Goldman, Marshall I. *What Went Wrong with Perestroika*. New York: W. W. Norton, 1991, pp. 1–45.

90 Friedrich Hayek, *The Road to Serfdom* (Chicago: University of Chicago Press, 2007), 68–87.

91 Thomas Piketty, *Capital and Ideology*, 97–128.

92 Mirowski, Philip, and Dieter Plehwe, eds. *The Road from Mont Pèlerin: The Making of the Neoliberal Thought Collective*. Cambridge, MA: Harvard University Press, 2009, 1–42, 161–198.

93 Bieber, Florian. "Germany after Merkel: The Rise of the AfD and the Reconfiguration of the Center-Right." *Journal of Democracy* 34, no. 1 (2023): 43–57.

94 OECD. *Economic Surveys: Germany 2023*. Paris: OECD Publishing, 2023, esp. sections on cost-of-living pressures, housing affordability, real wage stagnation, and energy-transition impacts.

95 Albert O. Hirschman, *Exit, Voice, and Loyalty* (Cambridge, MA: Harvard University Press, 1970), 15–34.

96 Kamprad, Ingvar. *The IKEA Testament: A Furniture Dealer's Testament*. IKEA internal document, 1976;Torekull, Bertil. *Leading by Design: The IKEA Story*. New York: HarperBusiness, 1998, esp. chapters on logistics innovation and flat-pack strategy.

97 Torekull, Bertil. *Leading by Design: The IKEA Story*. New York: HarperBusiness, 1998, pp. 45–47, 210–213.

98 Kamprad, Ingvar. *The IKEA Testament (A Furniture Dealer's Testament)*. Älmhult: IKEA Group, original internal publication, 1976; English edition excerpts reprinted in Torekull, Bertil. *Leading by Design: The IKEA Story*. New York: HarperBusiness, 1998, pp. 63–66.

99 Glete, Jan. *Networks and Organizations in the Swedish Industrialization*. Stockholm: Almqvist & Wiksell International, 1994, pp. 201–235.

100 Wallenberg Foundations. *Annual Report and Historical Overview of Grants to Research and Education*. Stockholm: Knut and Alice Wallenberg Foundation, various years; see also Henrekson, Magnus, and Ulf Jakobsson. "The Swedish Corporate Control Model: Convergence, Persistence, or Decline?" *Corporate Governance: An International Review* 20, no. 2 (2012): 212–227.

101 Hall, Peter A. *Governing the Economy: The Politics of State Intervention in Britain and France*. New York: Oxford University Press, 1986, 195–238.

102 Fridenson, Patrick. "Business, Paternalism, and Industrial Communities: The Michelin Case." In *Business History Review* 62, no. 1 (1988): 1–32.

103 Du Rietz, Gunnar, and Daniel Waldenström. "Swedish Wealth Taxation, 1911–2007." *Scandinavian Economic History Review* 66, no. 3 (2018): 201–225.

104 Piketty, Thomas. *Capital and Ideology*. Cambridge, MA: Harvard University Press, 2020, 237–276.

105 Du Rietz, Gunnar, and Daniel Waldenström. "Swedish Wealth Taxation, 1911–2007." *Scandinavian Economic History Review* 66, no. 3 (2018): 201–225.
106 Dyson, James. *Invention: A Life*. London: Hodder & Stoughton, 2021.
107 Lehmann, Richard von. *Ferdinand Porsche: Genesis of Genius*. Stuttgart: Motorbuch Verlag, 2000.
108 Douglass C. North, *Institutions, Institutional Change and Economic Performance*, 3–22.
109 Peter A. Hall and David Soskice, *Varieties of Capitalism* (Oxford: Oxford University Press, 2001).
110 Douglass C. North, *Institutions, Institutional Change and Economic Performance*, 3–22.
111 Joseph A. Schumpeter, *Capitalism, Socialism and Democracy* (New York: Harper & Brothers, 1942).
112 William Lazonick, "Profits Without Prosperity," *Harvard Business Review* (2014).
113 Hall, Peter A., and David Soskice, eds. *Varieties of Capitalism: The Institutional Foundations of Comparative Advantage*. Oxford: Oxford University Press, 2001.
114 North, Douglass C. *Institutions, Institutional Change and Economic Performance*. Cambridge: Cambridge University Press, 1990, 3–22.
115 Hall, Peter A., and David Soskice, eds. *Varieties of Capitalism: The Institutional Foundations of Comparative Advantage*. Oxford: Oxford University Press, 2001, 1–44.
116 Esping-Andersen, Gøsta. *The Three Worlds of Welfare Capitalism*. Princeton, NJ: Princeton University Press, 1990, 27–65.
117 Geary, Dick. *Labour and Socialist Movements in Europe Before 1914*. Oxford: Berg Publishers, 1989, 9–12.
118 Streeck, Wolfgang. *Re-Forming Capitalism: Institutional Change in the German Political Economy*. Oxford: Oxford University Press, 2009, 79–112.
119 Hobsbawm, Eric. *Age of Extremes: The Short Twentieth Century, 1914–1991*. New York: Vintage, 1996, 287–312.
120 Esping-Andersen, Gøsta. *The Three Worlds of Welfare Capitalism*. Princeton, NJ: Princeton University Press, 1990, pp. 18–34.
121 Katzenstein, Peter J. *Small States in World Markets: Industrial Policy in Europe*. Ithaca, NY: Cornell University Press, 1985, pp. 32–67.
122 Ash, Timothy Garton. *Free World: Why a Crisis of the West Reveals the Opportunity of Our Time*. New York: Random House, 2004, pp. 146–149.
123 OECD. *OECD Employment Outlook 2006: Boosting Jobs and Incomes*. Paris: OECD Publishing, 2006, pp. 64–69.
124 Philippe Aghion, Céline Antonin, and Simon Bunel, *The Power of Creative Destruction: Economic Upheaval and the Wealth of Nations* (Cambridge, MA: Harvard University Press, 2021), pp. 129–134.
125 Assar Lindbeck, *The Political Economy of the New Left: An Outsider's View* (New York: Harper & Row, 1971), 30–45.
126 Karl Polanyi, *The Great Transformation: The Political and Economic Origins of Our Time*, 130–160.
127 E. P. Thompson, *The Making of the English Working Class* (New York: Vintage Books, 1966), 9–14.
128 Thomas Piketty, *Capital and Ideology*, 409–452.
129 Thomas Piketty, *Capital and Ideology*, 97–128.
130 Ibid.
131 Milton Friedman, *Capitalism and Freedom*, 7–21.
132 Ibid.
133 Ibid.
134 Ibid.
135 Joseph E. Stiglitz, *The Price of Inequality* (New York: W. W. Norton, 2012), 155–180.
136 Karl Polanyi, *The Great Transformation*, 130–160.
137 Adam Smith, *An Inquiry into the Nature and Causes of the Wealth of Nations*, 456–468.
138 Eric Hobsbawm, *Age of Extremes: The Short Twentieth Century, 1914–1991*, 54–86.
139 Eric Hobsbawm, *Age of Extremes: The Short Twentieth Century, 1914–1991*, 87–130.

140 David Harvey, *A Brief History of Neoliberalism* (Oxford: Oxford University Press, 2005), 22–60.
141 Mancur Olson, *The Rise and Decline of Nations* (New Haven, CT: Yale University Press, 1982), 73–120.
142 Hirschman, Albert O. *The Rhetoric of Reaction: Perversity, Futility, Jeopardy.* Cambridge, MA: Harvard University Press, 1991, 43–67.
143 Dornbusch, Rudiger, and Sebastian Edwards, eds. *The Macroeconomics of Populism in Latin America.* Chicago: University of Chicago Press, 1991.
144 Piketty, Thomas. *Capital and Ideology.* Cambridge, MA: Harvard University Press, 2020, esp. chapters on Latin America and inequality.
145 Hobsbawm, Eric. *Age of Extremes: The Short Twentieth Century, 1914–1991.* New York: Vintage, 1996, chapters on postwar political economy and late-century neoliberal turn.
146 Reinhart, Carmen M., and Kenneth S. Rogoff. *This Time Is Different: Eight Centuries of Financial Folly.* Princeton, NJ: Princeton University Press, 2009.
147 Mancur Olson. *The Rise and Decline of Nations: Economic Growth, Stagflation, and Social Rigidities.* New Haven, CT: Yale University Press, 1982, chs. 1–4, 62–97.
148 Kenneth Rogoff and Carmen Reinhart. *This Time Is Different: Eight Centuries of Financial Folly.* Princeton: Princeton University Press, 2009.
149 Carl Benedikt Frey. *The Technology Trap: Capital, Labor, and Power in the Age of Automation.* Princeton: Princeton University Press, 2019.
150 OECD, *OECD Employment Outlook 2025: Setting the Scene — Demographic Change and the Labour Market* (Paris: OECD Publishing, 2025).
151 Thomas Piketty, *Capital and Ideology*, 97–128.
152 Adam Smith, *An Inquiry into the Nature and Causes of the Wealth of Nations*, 456–468.

10 The Unintended Consequences of Smithian Capitalism

Capitalism, as originally envisioned by Adam Smith more than two and a half centuries ago, has produced economic growth, productivity gains, and technological advancement unmatched by any alternative economic system.[1] Its capacity to mobilize human ingenuity, allocate resources, and scale innovation has reshaped civilization and lifted billions out of material deprivation. On this point, the historical record is unambiguous: no competing system has delivered comparable results.

Yet this success has come at a cost so substantial that it increasingly threatens the system's own legitimacy and durability. The same forces that made capitalism extraordinarily effective have also generated structural distortions severe enough to require extensive regulation, provoke recurring crises, and fuel growing support for alternative economic models.[2] Capitalism works—but it operates far from its attainable potential for broad prosperity, and at a social cost that places its long-term viability at risk.

Inclusive Capitalism begins from the premise that abandonment is neither necessary nor desirable. The objective is not to replace capitalism but to repair it—to retain what has worked exceptionally well while systematically addressing what is broken. The analysis in this book leads to a clear conclusion: for capitalism to persist and thrive, six systemic unintended consequences must be confronted and resolved.[3]

Our approach represents a deliberate departure from the historical pattern in which economic systems emerged largely as reactive responses to prevailing conditions, without a fully specified or consciously designed architecture. Adam Smith's original contribution was not a comprehensive system design but a decisive reframing of economic purpose—a reaction against mercantilism that redirected incentives toward production and exchange, even as it left much of the system's structure implicit and under-specified.[4] By redefining the objective of economic activity—from the accumulation of gold to the production and exchange of goods and services—Smith unlocked vast reserves of latent human potential and established the foundation for modern economic growth.

Today, an analogous redefinition is required. GDP is no longer an adequate proxy for success in an economy characterized by scale, complexity, and accelerating technological abundance.[5] The system's objective function must therefore evolve once again—from output maximization to the optimization of societal well-being.[6]

Such a redefinition is a prerequisite for meaningful architectural specification and coherent systems design. Durable systems are not improved through incremental fixes alone but through disciplined problem formulation—by identifying structural failures before prescribing solutions. This chapter therefore adopts a diagnostic stance. It synthesizes the six unintended consequences that emerge endogenously

 | https://doi.org/10.1515/9783112235485-011

from contemporary capitalism and that, if left unresolved, will predictably continue to generate instability, exclusion, and backlash.

The following chapter then turns to what must be preserved if a Smith-like realignment is to expand human flourishing once again.[7] Together, these chapters form the analytical foundation and visionary framework for Book Two of Inclusive Capitalism, where the system architecture required to move beyond oscillation and toward a stable, abundance-based equilibrium is developed in full.[8]

The Six Unintended Consequences of Capitalism

The six unintended consequences identified in this chapter are precisely that: unintended. Adam Smith did not design capitalism to incentivize scarcity, exclusion, instability, or moral indifference. On the contrary, his central objective was to expand abundance, opportunity, and prosperity through decentralized production and exchange. That these unintended consequences have emerged nonetheless is not a failure of intent but a failure of system evolution. The gap between Smith's aims and capitalism's present behavior is the central empirical fact this chapter confronts.[9]

Our historical analysis—from early industrial capitalism through the Gilded Age, Keynesian intervention, neoliberal resurgence, and the rise of democratic socialism—uncovers a consistent and revealing pattern. Each corrective movement arose in response to real and recurring failures of capitalism. Regulation emerged to counter exploitation and instability. Socialism and communism arose to address exclusion and inequality. Democratic socialism sought to reconcile growth with dignity and security.[10] Yet in every case, these responses treated symptoms rather than root causes. They mitigated specific harms while leaving the underlying incentive structure intact, producing cyclical oscillation rather than durable resolution.

When examined through a systems lens, the unintended consequences of contemporary capitalism are neither accidental nor ambiguous. They are emergent properties of a system optimized around a single-objective function, brilliant in its original context yet structurally incomplete—an objective that unlocked industrial growth but did not, and could not, anticipate the incentive misalignments that would emerge at scale.[11] The persistence of these consequences—and the persistence of reactive counter-movements they provoke—provides unusually strong empirical validation. Across geographies and political regimes, the same failures recur, generating regulation, redistribution, and ideological backlash with remarkable regularity. These dynamics now sit at the core of today's global affordability crisis, societal polarization, and loss of institutional trust.

What follows is therefore not a critique of capitalism's achievements, nor a catalog of grievances. It is a root-cause decomposition. The six unintended consequences identified here represent the minimal set of structural failures that repeatedly surface across historical epochs and economic variants. They explain why capitalism, despite its unmatched productive power, continually generates forces that constrain, dilute, or threaten its own legitimacy. If capitalism is to persist and thrive—rather than be indefinitely managed, constrained, or replaced—these consequences must be addressed directly at the level of incentives and system design.

We now turn to the specifics. The six unintended consequences of contemporary capitalism, in priority order, are:

1. Scarcity Incentive Trap: Capitalism incents scarcity rather than abundance.
2. Failure at Scale: Capitalism's invisible hand does not scale.
3. Structural Exclusion: Capitalism is exclusive with respect to opportunity.
4. Endogenous Instability: Capitalism is plagued by disruptive boom-bust cycles.
5. Short-Term Bias: Capitalism incents short-term gratification over societal well-being.
6. Amoral Optimization: Capitalism rewards efficiency at the expense of human dignity.

These six dynamics are deeply interrelated, mutually reinforcing, and self-amplifying at scale.[12] Together, they explain why repeated reform efforts—whether regulatory, redistributive, or ideological—have consistently failed to produce a stable, abundant, and broadly legitimate economic order.[13] Crucially, however, they are not immutable laws of human behavior or unavoidable features of market exchange. They are design failures.

Once correctly diagnosed, each of these consequences proves not only intelligible but tractable. Their persistence reflects neither moral deficiency nor political impossibility but the absence of a properly specified objective function and aligned incentive structure. That diagnosis—and the demonstration that these failures are systematically solvable without sacrificing capitalism's core strengths—is the central contribution of this book.

Let us now spend our Einsteinian "fifty-five minutes" examining the problem structure, causes, and context with the rigor such a redesign demands, so that the remaining time—perhaps a bit more—can be devoted to specifying an architecture worthy of the challenge. The architecture, systems engineering, and operational details of Inclusive Capitalism are developed in Book Two.

Unintended Consequence One: The Scarcity Incentive Trap

The most fundamental unintended consequence of contemporary capitalism is not inequality, volatility, or short-termism—important as those are—but something more basic: capitalism systematically rewards scarcity rather than abundance.[14] This design feature sits upstream of nearly every other failure examined in this book. When scarcity is profitable, abundance is discouraged. When value is extracted by limiting access, expanding access becomes economically irrational—even when it is technologically trivial, socially beneficial, or morally obvious.[15]

Across epochs and systems, our historical analysis has demonstrated a consistent pattern: industrial leaders are achievement-driven and respond overwhelmingly to incentives.[16] They do not act out of malice or benevolence but in accordance with the reward structures they face. Under capitalism, those structures reliably favor pricing power, control, along with exclusion as opposed to diffusion, access, and abundance.[17] The result is not accidental. It is systemic.

We observed a crude version of this dynamic under communism, where poorly designed incentives produced famously absurd outcomes: factories producing only left shoes to meet unit targets, nails made too large or too small to satisfy tonnage quotas, and output divorced entirely from usefulness.[18] These failures were not moral lapses; they were predictable responses to incentives. Capitalism, despite its far greater success, is not immune to the same pathology. Its incentive structure is simply more sophisticated—and therefore more pervasive.

In contemporary capitalism, scarcity-driven behavior is not anomalous; it is routine. Luxury brands destroy unsold inventory to preserve exclusivity. Governments pay to eliminate surplus agricultural output to stabilize prices. Retailers deliberately render goods unusable to prevent resale. Vast quantities of food are discarded to preserve margins even as food insecurity affects millions of households.[19] These are not edge cases. They are rational responses to a system in which price preservation matters more than human outcomes. When leaders are rewarded for margins rather than access, destruction becomes a feature, not a bug.

Scarcity is often disguised as "differentiation." In competitive markets, differentiation can indeed serve innovation by meeting diverse customer needs. But in practice, differentiation frequently becomes a proxy for artificial scarcity—particularly when monopoly, platform, or network power is present. Firms fragment solutions, restrict interoperability, delay standardization, or withhold open access not because doing so benefits society but because it preserves pricing power.[20] In sectors where marginal costs approach zero—software, data, digital services—this logic becomes especially perverse. Abundance is technologically feasible, yet institutionally suppressed.[21]

If capitalism were incented to optimize societal well-being rather than private extraction, abundance would be the rational outcome. Instead, the system systematically rewards leadership behaviors that preserve, manage, and monetize scarcity, even when abundance is technologically feasible and socially preferable.[22]

The reason is straightforward. Executive compensation, shareholder primacy, intellectual property regimes, and GDP-centric measurement converge on a common objective: maximize appropriable value rather than maximize access or social throughput. Under shareholder capitalism, executives are evaluated primarily on earnings per share, stock price appreciation, and return on equity. These metrics privilege margin protection, defensible positioning, and pricing power[23] —not the expansion of access or societal benefit.

This does not mean that every firm literally constrains physical output. Some business models—such as low-margin, high-volume retailers—compete by expanding supply and lowering prices. But even these firms operate inside a system whose ultimate scoreboard rewards profitability and equity valuation, not human outcomes. When supply expansion compresses margins or undermines pricing power, leaders are typically penalized by markets and boards—even if welfare improves.

The deeper point is therefore structural: the system does not reliably reward firms for maximizing societal throughput; it rewards them for maximizing monetizable capture. Scarcity need not be intentional to be systemic.

Stock-based compensation reinforces this logic. When the majority of executive pay is tied to equity performance, leaders rationally prioritize monopoly power, rent preservation, and control. Open diffusion, shared standards, and voluntary price compression undermine these goals, even when they accelerate innovation overall. GDP quietly reinforces the same bias. Selling one unit at a high price and selling many units at near-zero prices contribute similarly to aggregate GDP, even when the latter delivers vastly greater social value. GDP is indifferent to access, diffusion, and utilization. Combined with profit-maximizing incentives, it passively enables strategies that favor scarcity over abundance.

Modern intellectual property law entrenches this dynamic. Patents, copyrights, and trade secrets convert knowledge—non-rival and infinitely replicable—into exclusive assets. From an industrial leadership perspective, this is entirely rational. Intellectual property creates barriers to entry, pricing power, and leverage. Yet the social cost is substantial: slower diffusion, redundant R&D, inflated prices, and suppressed follow-on innovation.[24] Knowledge that could compound across society is instead fenced off.

Innovation persists despite these incentives, not because of them. The question is not whether capitalism innovates—it clearly does—but whether it innovates anywhere near its potential. When innovation is rewarded primarily through exclusion, entire classes of solutions never emerge. Pharmaceuticals illustrate the problem starkly. Research concentrates where returns are highest, not where human need is greatest.[25] Patent evergreening and exclusivity extensions preserve scarcity long after genuine innovation has ceased. The rare executive who pursues open-access cures is celebrated precisely because their behavior is exceptional.

Luxury retail, technology platforms, and data-driven businesses follow the same logic. Scarcity is not accidental; it is the product. Control, not diffusion, is rewarded. Across domains, the pattern is unmistakable: Capitalism rewards leaders who manage scarcity, not those who create abundance.[26]

This is not a moral failing of individuals. It is a design flaw in the system's objective function.[27]

The irony is that this incentive structure was once both brilliant and necessary. Adam Smith did not design a complete economic system. He reacted—correctly—to mercantilism by redefining economic success away from the accumulation of gold and toward production and exchange.[28] By doing so, he unlocked the Industrial Revolution and more than two centuries of growth. But Smith could not foresee an economy characterized by global scale, near-zero marginal costs, or technologies capable of producing non-scarcity across vast domains. The objective was not wrong; it was incomplete.[29]

Smithian capitalism has therefore evolved through a series of reactive corrections—communism, Keynesianism, socialism—each addressing real failures, yet each introducing new distortions.[30] None resolved the root cause. Scarcity persisted as the organizing principle, whether rewarded, regulated, or bureaucratically managed.[31]

Today, that principle is no longer merely incomplete; it is actively counterproductive. Technologies such as software, biotechnology, renewable energy, and artificial intelligence make abundance increasingly feasible.[32] Yet capitalism repeatedly pulls the reins just as abundance becomes possible. Firms idle capacity, delay diffusion, and throttle innovation to preserve margins. These behaviors will appear as absurd to future historians as Soviet production quotas do to us today.

Every other unintended consequence of contemporary capitalism flows downstream from this one. A system that must ration abundance will inevitably ration opportunity, resist diffusion, concentrate power, and erode dignity.[33] Exclusion, instability, short-termism, and social backlash are not separate failures; they are symptoms.

If Inclusive Capitalism is to succeed, it must begin here. Until the creation of abundance—rather than the management of scarcity—becomes the dominant source of reward, no amount of regulation, redistribution, or moral appeal will resolve the system's deeper contradictions.[34] The solution is not to abandon markets but to update their incentive structure—augmenting profit and GDP with explicit measures of societal well-being and rewarding leaders who expand access, diffusion, and contribution.[35]

This is the foundational problem. Everything else follows.

Unintended Consequence Two: Failure at Scale

After the scarcity incentive, the second unintended consequence of contemporary capitalism is the systematic pursuit of monopoly power by industrial leadership. Monopoly power is scarcity at scale—and the most visible, politically toxic, and destabilizing of capitalism's failures. Adam Smith's invisible hand functions tolerably well in fragmented markets, but it does not scale. Beyond a threshold of size, capital intensity, or network effects, coordination gives way to extraction. Capitalism then begins to contradict the very meritocratic and competitive ideals on which it rests.[36]

This conclusion is not ideological. It is one of the few points of near-universal agreement across economic thought. Adam Smith, Karl Marx, Friedrich Hayek, John Maynard Keynes, and Milton Friedman all condemned monopoly power, despite their deep disagreements elsewhere.[37] Yet none produced a durable solution that prevents monopoly formation while preserving capitalism's dynamism and the existential benefits of scale. The historical record is unambiguous: capitalism promotes competition in theory but repeatedly produces dominance in practice—particularly in markets characterized by scale economies, network effects, data accumulation, capital intensity, or regulatory complexity.[38]

The cost of addressing monopoly power after it emerges is extraordinary. Vast legal, legislative, compliance, and economic resources are consumed attempting to constrain dominance once markets are already tilted. By the time regulators intervene, monopoly power is entrenched, capital has been hoarded rather than risked, innovation has slowed, and emerging competitors have already been acquired or extinguished. Reactive regulation treats symptoms, not causes. It layers constraint atop a scarcity engine rather than redesigning the engine itself.[39]

To propose a credible alternative, we must first understand why monopoly power is a rational objective for industrial leaders operating under contemporary incentives. The canonical historical case remains Standard Oil.

By 1880, John D. Rockefeller's Standard Oil controlled roughly 90 percent of U. S. refining capacity. This dominance was not accidental. It was achieved through a coherent, profit-maximizing strategy: predatory pricing, secret railroad rebates that raised rivals' costs, trust structures that circumvented legal limits on corporate size, and aggressive vertical integration across the value chain.[40] These tactics were corrosive to competition and societal well-being—and largely illegal today—but they were rational responses to the incentive structure of the era.

Rockefeller justified Standard Oil's dominance as efficient and even socially beneficial, pointing to sharply lower kerosene prices that expanded access for working-class consumers. That claim was not entirely wrong. Scale delivered real efficiencies. Yet the broader experience for competitors, suppliers, and the public was one of coercion, exclusion, and market foreclosure. The Supreme Court ultimately ordered Standard Oil's breakup in 1911. Ironically, Rockefeller emerged even wealthier, as the successor firms' valuations surged. The episode illustrates a durable pattern: ex post regulation may curb behavior, but it rarely reverses concentration or its wealth effects.[41]

Standard Oil was not an anomaly. Similar dynamics recur across railroads, telecommunications (AT&T), finance, pharmaceuticals, and—most decisively—technology platforms. Geoffrey Moore's "gorilla" framework captures the lived reality of many operators: in certain market structures, dominance is not a deviation from capitalism's logic but its natural outcome. Once dominance emerges, it becomes self-reinforcing.[42]

Across sectors and eras, the same toolkit appears: predatory pricing, vertical integration, mergers and acquisitions, cartelization, regulatory capture, political influence, and the strategic use of intellectual property. Each tactic is rational under shareholder capitalism. Monopoly power stabilizes market share, protects margins, and reduces vulnerability to competitive undercutting. Used in combination, these tools can entrench dominance for decades. The long-term consequences for innovation, dynamism, and societal well-being are far less favorable.[43]

Monopoly power is not merely correlated with the scarcity objective; it is its most potent expression at scale. At small scale, scarcity incentives are disciplined by competition. In the world of the butcher, baker, and brewer, no actor can manufacture scarcity for long. The invisible hand still coordinates behavior tolerably well. At large scale, the situation changes qualitatively. When firms reach sufficient size—whether the British East India Company, Standard Oil, or the dominant platform firms of 2025—the capacity to manufacture scarcity becomes overwhelming.[44]

Scale itself is not the enemy. Scale is essential for productivity, efficiency, and technological progress. The problem is scale operating under a scarcity-maximizing objective. This distinction matters. Regulation, state ownership, and laissez-faire resignation have all been tried as responses to monopoly power, and all have proven unstable or insufficient. Inclusive Capitalism therefore treats monopoly as an architectural problem. Large-scale enterprises must be designed and chartered so that their objective is non-scarcity and societal well-being, not rent extraction. Without this shift, monopoly power remains both rational and inevitable.[45]

Joseph Schumpeter provides the most sophisticated classical defense of monopoly. In his theory of creative destruction, monopoly profits are the temporary reward for successful innovation. Dominance attracts challengers, challengers eventually succeed, and monopoly dissolves. Innovation, not regulation, is the disciplining force.[46] This logic holds under specific conditions: low barriers to entry, rapid diffusion of ideas, modest capital requirements, and weak network effects. Schumpeter himself acknowledged its limits. When monopolies become insulated from challenge, they ossify. His optimism assumed market conditions that increasingly fail to hold in modern economies.

Friedrich Hayek approached monopoly as a threat to markets' discovery function. Competition reveals information; monopoly suppresses it. Hayek believed most monopolies were unstable unless protected by government policy, and that open markets would erode dominance over time.[47] Yet this framework struggles to explain modern private monopolies rooted not in tariffs or licensing but in network effects, data accumulation, and ecosystem lock-in.

Geoffrey Moore's analysis resolves the tension. In technology markets, dominance often emerges not because a firm is best but because it becomes the standard. Once ecosystems coalesce around a platform, switching costs and coordination effects entrench power. Monopoly is not fragile; it is structural. There is always a gorilla.[48]

Milton Friedman shared Hayek's concern for freedom and competition, arguing that monopolies persist mainly due to government protection.[49] While this is sometimes true, it does not account for the durability of modern private monopolies. Nor does it explain why antitrust, despite more than a century of effort, has failed to prevent recurrent concentration. The historical record—from Standard Oil to the Great

Depression to modern platform markets—demonstrates that markets do not reliably self-correct monopoly power.[50]

The common thread across these analyses is not failure of enforcement, ideology, or leadership. It is the scarcity objective embedded in capitalism at scale. Monopoly power is not an accident; it is a rational strategy under incentives that reward exclusion, control, and rent extraction.[51] As long as large enterprises are rewarded for maximizing scarcity, monopoly power will remain the dominant strategy. Antitrust can slow or redirect behavior at the margins, but it cannot eliminate the underlying logic. Endless oscillation between deregulation and intervention is therefore inevitable.

Inclusive Capitalism proposes a different approach: redesign the objective function of large-scale enterprise. When success is defined by expanding access, accelerating diffusion, and optimizing societal well-being, monopoly extraction becomes economically irrational rather than merely illegal. This aligns with the stated aspirations of many industrial leaders, who have long argued that they would prefer to operate under clearer, purpose-aligned rules rather than face unpredictable regulatory backlash.[52]

Scarcity and monopoly power are not separate failures. They are mutually reinforcing outcomes of the same incentive structure. Together, they form a central engine driving exclusion, instability, and societal division. Changing that engine—rather than endlessly repairing its damage—is the only viable path forward.

Unintended Consequence Three: Structural Exclusion

Let us now turn to the third unintended consequence: exclusivity of opportunity. Capitalism cannot be meaningfully improved until its shortcomings are diagnosed with full candor, precision, and completeness. As argued throughout this chapter, these shortcomings are not incidental defects but six profound and interrelated unintended consequences that emerge when Smithian capitalism operates at scale.[53]

Adam Smith did not intend for capitalism to be exclusive—to serve a narrow elite while marginalizing the broader public. On the contrary, his vision was explicitly meritocratic: markets, when functioning properly, reward talent, effort, and productive contribution rather than inherited privilege or political favor. His observation about the butcher, the brewer, and the baker was not a romantic defense of commerce but a structural claim: in a competitive market, individuals advance primarily by creating value for others, not by extracting value through position.[54]

Smith also understood that this meritocratic dynamic was fragile. He warned that collusion, monopoly, and unequal privilege could subvert competition and redirect markets away from open opportunity and toward insider advantage. These were not rhetorical flourishes but structural warnings. Once economic actors coordinate to restrict entry, protect incumbency, or gatekeep access, markets cease to reward merit and begin to reward position. For this reason, capitalism's exclusivity is best understood as an unintended consequence rather than an intent: Smith articulated a vision grounded in openness and opportunity, while recognizing the conditions under which that vision could be corrupted. Our task is not to discard Smith's framework but to explain why—despite those warnings—capitalism repeatedly deviates from its meritocratic ideal, and how to counteract that deviation at the level of system design.[55]

Capitalism is often defended as meritocratic: the claim that free markets allocate opportunity to the most capable, regardless of background. In theory, competition disciplines favoritism, promotes mobility, and channels talent toward its highest-value uses. In practice, however, contemporary capitalism routinely rewards exclusivity rather than openness. Incumbents—whether individuals, firms, investors, or institutions—have strong incentives to protect their positions by narrowing access, raising barriers to entry, and concentrating opportunity within trusted networks. This is not merely unfair; it is economically inefficient. Vast pools of talent are excluded, innovation slows, and dynamism declines.[56]

Exclusion shows up everywhere: hiring, education, entrepreneurship, housing, and finance. Those who control scarce opportunities rationally behave as gatekeepers. In labor markets, hiring often favors insiders over merit. Even when explicit nepotism is absent, informal networks dominate selection for many high-paying and prestigious roles. Who one knows often matters more than what one can do. Referrals, insider signaling, and pedigree-based filters become dominant mechanisms for navigating hiring funnels—funnels increasingly mediated by automated tools that amplify credential heuristics. Those without access to elite networks, often due to socioeconomic background rather than lack of ability, are systematically excluded.[57]

Credentialism reinforces the pattern. Educational pedigree functions as a proxy for talent, even when job requirements do not justify it. Expensive degrees and elite affiliations become gatekeeping devices that filter applicants by socioeconomic background and social signaling rather than capability. The resulting pipeline is self-reinforcing: elite institutions feed elite labor markets, which feed elite capital markets, which then fund the next generation of elite institutions. The system produces the appearance of meritocracy while embedding inherited advantage into its operating logic.[58]

This is not a moral indictment of individuals. It is a predictable consequence of incentives. Firms and decision-makers use exclusivity as a form of risk minimization. Familiarity reduces perceived uncertainty. But that local optimization produces global inefficiency: talent misallocation, lost productivity, and a narrowing of opportunity that undermines capitalism's legitimacy.[59]

Exclusion is even more visible in capital allocation. In principle, capitalism should direct capital toward the best ideas, independent of the identity or background of the innovator. In practice, access to capital is among the most exclusive domains of the modern economy. Venture capital in particular is controlled by socially homogeneous networks that rely heavily on informal trust, pattern recognition, and referrals. Founders outside a narrow archetype—often defined by pedigree, geography, and existing connections—face substantial barriers to funding regardless of the intrinsic quality of their ideas.[60]

Geographic concentration intensifies the problem. Capital flows disproportionately to the places where capital already exists. Entrepreneurs in dominant hubs have vastly greater access to investors, mentors, and follow-on capital than equally capable founders outside those hubs. The result is not just unfairness; it is a structural misallocation of resources that reduces resilience, decentralization of innovation, and long-term growth. Talent is widely distributed; opportunity is not.[61]

This is the same pattern in a different domain: incumbents protecting incumbency. Capital tends to fund what looks familiar, where it is socially proximate, and where exit pathways are already established. Over time, the innovation economy becomes an insider economy. Opportunity becomes rationed rather than discovered. The meritocratic promise that underwrites capitalism's moral legitimacy is steadily eroded, replaced by the perception—often the reality—that success depends less on contribution than on access.[62]

The most consequential exclusionary dynamic is neither primarily moral nor ideological. It is mathematical and systemic. Wealth behaves like gravity. After a certain threshold, accumulation becomes self-reinforcing: capital attracts more capital simply by virtue of its position. This is the "black hole effect." Once wealth, market share, or positional leverage reaches sufficient scale, returns become nonlinear. The compounding of capital outpaces the compounding of labor income, and opportunity narrows for those outside the gravity well.[63]

The logic is simple. Wealth compounds exponentially; labor income grows linearly or modestly. When returns to capital persistently exceed growth in wages or productivity accessible to the median participant, inequality becomes structurally self-reinforcing. This divergence is not a cultural story or a partisan talking point. It is arithmetic. The system can remain formally "competitive" and still produce durable exclusion because compounding is cumulative and path-dependent.[64]

The black hole effect is amplified by human behavior and institution design. Those in power protect their power. Once incumbents accumulate wealth and influence, they can buy insulation: better education, better networks, better information, better legal protection, better lobbying power, and preferential access to deals. Economic power becomes political insulation, and political insulation becomes economic advantage. Opportunity does not merely become unequal; it becomes gated.[65]

This is why exclusion is not solvable in the sense of being eradicated permanently. It is rooted in human tendencies and mathematical feedback loops. But it can be countered. Systems can be designed to interrupt reinforcement and reopen access. That is the correct design stance: we cannot eliminate the human and mathematical tendencies, but we can build institutions that continuously counteract them.[66]

Most attempts to address exclusion have taken the form of post-hoc redistribution—taxing after the fact, regulating after failure, or intervening after concentration has already occurred. This approach is structurally weak for three reasons.

First, it is inherently political. Redistribution becomes a perpetual conflict over who owes what to whom, and both sides experience it as coercive: those paying experience it as confiscation; those receiving experience it as conditional and stigmatizing. Second, it is reactive and late. It intervenes after opportunity has already been denied—after networks have already selected insiders, after capital has already compounded, after winners have already entrenched themselves. Third, it fails to address the root cause: the incentive and governance structure that makes exclusion rational in the first place.[67]

If the system rewards scarcity, incumbency, and risk-minimized gatekeeping, exclusion will persist regardless of how much redistribution is layered on afterward. Post-hoc correction fights arithmetic with politics. It is not only inefficient; it is unstable.[68]

The solution must be anticipatory rather than reactive. The rules need to be fairer up front—creating a fairer, if never perfect, playing field—so that opportunity is broadened before outcomes harden into irreversible concentration. That means shifting from redistribution as the primary tool to institutional design as the primary tool.[69]

Inclusive Capitalism approaches exclusion as an incentive and architecture problem. If enterprises and financial institutions are rewarded for optimizing societal well-being—not merely local profit—then expanding participation becomes rational rather than charitable. Inclusion becomes strategy, not compliance. The question changes from "how much should we redistribute after inequality forms?" to "how do we design participation so inequality forms less rigidly in the first place?"[70]

Concretely, this means designing incentives and institutions that broaden access to the investment process and broaden participation in the upside: not by confiscating outcomes but by making the opportunity set less exclusive at the point where opportunity is created. It means enterprise charters and governance models that counteract the natural tendency of power to protect itself. It means structures that keep markets open to entrants, widen capital access, reduce gatekeeping, and reward diffusion of opportunity alongside diffusion of products.[71]

The goal is not utopia. It is counterforce. Capitalism at scale naturally generates exclusion through both human behavior and mathematical reinforcement. We cannot eliminate these tendencies. But we can design a system that continuously counters them—so that openness and mobility are not rare exceptions but durable features.[72]

Capitalism, as currently instantiated, is structurally exclusive with respect to opportunity. And until opportunity becomes endogenous—built into incentives and governance up front—no amount of post-hoc correction will prevent exclusion from reasserting itself.[73]

Unintended Consequence Four: Endogenous Instability

We have now examined three of the six unintended consequences of Smithian capitalism: the incentive toward scarcity, monopolization and the concentration of wealth, and the exclusion of opportunity. The fourth consequence is the recurrent pattern of vicious economic cycles and systemic instability that has characterized capitalism throughout its history, including within living memory. Capitalist economies have repeatedly oscillated between periods of rapid expansion and painful contraction. These boom-and-bust cycles are among the most visible and socially damaging outcomes of free-market capitalism as currently instantiated.[74]

At the heart of these cycles is a familiar pattern: when incentives reward short-term financial gain, capital flows toward speculation rather than durable value creation.[75] In periods of expansion, optimism, leverage, and risk-taking reinforce one another. Credit becomes abundant, asset prices rise, and investment accelerates. These dynamics fuel genuine growth, but they also allow imbalances to accumulate beneath the surface. Excessive leverage, speculative asset inflation, and fragile financial interdependencies gradually undermine stability. When confidence breaks—often triggered by a seemingly modest shock—the process reverses abruptly. Credit contracts, spending collapses, and layoffs cascade through the economy. What follows is not merely a correction of excess but a broad social disruption that imposes hardship on individuals who neither caused nor benefited from the preceding boom.[76]

This instability has repeated with remarkable regularity. The financial panics of the nineteenth century, the crash of 1929, the stagflation crises of the 1970s, the savings and loan collapse, the dot-com bust, and the 2008 global financial crisis all reflect variations of the same underlying dynamic.[77] Even Karl Marx, writing in the mid-nineteenth century, argued that capitalism's internal tensions would periodically erupt into destructive crises. While his prediction of capitalism's inevitable collapse has not materialized, his insight that unchecked market dynamics can generate destabilizing cycles has proven prescient.[78]

The Great Depression remains the most severe illustration. Between 1929 and 1933, industrial output collapsed, GDP contracted sharply, unemployment reached levels that shattered social order, and thousands of banks failed, wiping out household savings.[79] The policy response reshaped economic governance, giving rise to Keynesian countercyclical theory, deposit insurance, financial regulation, and a more active role for the state in stabilizing demand. These reforms moderated, but did not eliminate, volatility. Severe cycles continued, and the Great Recession of 2007–2009 demonstrated that even a technologically advanced economy remained vulnerable to systemic collapse. Jobs vanished, household wealth was destroyed, and communities experienced long-tail decline. Young entrants to the labor market suffered persistent earnings scarring long after markets recovered.[80]

A central insight emerges from this history: While booms generate enthusiasm and busts generate pain, neither outcome is distributed evenly. The upside of expansion is disproportionately captured by those closest to capital markets, while the downside of contraction is disproportionately borne by the working class and the public.[81] Those with diversified financial assets and institutional proximity recover faster; those dependent on wages and local labor markets experience deeper and longer hardship. Recessions leave structural scars: Inequality widens, social trust erodes, and political instability often follows. The global fallout from 2008 contributed to sovereign debt crises, extreme unemployment in parts of Europe, and rising populism. Economic instability translated into political fragility once again.[82]

This asymmetry is not accidental. It reflects the incentive structure embedded in contemporary capitalism. Speculation is rewarded during booms, while losses are socialized during busts through layoffs, austerity, and the need for emergency stabilization. The system does not merely cycle; it cycles in a way that repeatedly concentrates benefit and disperses pain. Inclusive Capitalism approaches this problem not by attempting to eliminate cycles entirely—an unrealistic objective—but by containing their human consequences and reducing their amplitude through a redesigned monetary and incentive architecture.[83]

Economists have long debated whether cycles are inherent to capitalism or primarily the result of policy failures. Milton Friedman offered one of the most influential defenses of the latter view. He argued that severe downturns, especially the Great Depression, were exacerbated—or even caused—by catastrophic monetary mismanagement.[84] Friedman's core remedy was rule-based monetary governance: stable and predictable expansion of the money supply to avoid destabilizing contractions. This framework influenced modern central banking and helped prevent outright monetary collapse during crises.[85]

Yet Friedman's approach runs into a practical wall: A single, economy-wide money supply is a blunt instrument trying to regulate an increasingly complex, heterogeneous system. Financial innovation, global capital flows, derivatives, and shadow banking make strict rules difficult to enforce. In crises, central banks abandon rule-based restraint and improvise, implicitly acknowledging that the system is not stable by construction. More fundamentally, even flawless monetary policy cannot fully resolve instability when incentives systematically reward leverage, short-term gains, and speculative asset inflation.[86]

Inclusive Capitalism therefore makes a different move. It treats cyclical instability as an architectural problem and decomposes it. Instead of relying solely on ex post stabilization—bailouts, emergency stimulus, and crisis improvisation—it seeks to decouple the population's access to essential goods and services from macroeconomic volatility ex ante. Essential commodities should not become scarce simply because financial markets misprice risk.[87]

This is where the micro-currency model becomes central. The objective is to isolate the basics—food, housing, energy, healthcare, and other essential goods and services—from the volatility of speculative capital markets. A currency tied explicitly to "the basics" acts as a stability layer: It anchors the purchasing power needed for human survival and dignity to the real capacity of society to deliver essentials, rather than to the oscillations of credit cycles and asset prices.[88] In practical terms, this creates a base existence floor for even the most challenged members of society, not as a discretionary welfare promise subject to political oscillation but as a systems-level guarantee built into monetary design.[89]

The micro-currency model has two additional advantages that directly reinforce Inclusive Capitalism's incentive thesis.

First, it aligns monetary discipline with real-domain dynamics rather than speculative arbitrage. In a system governed by a single, economy-wide money supply, all actors—regardless of sector—are forced to respond to the same blunt macro signal. This encourages financial engineering, leverage, and cross-sector speculation, because returns are often easier to extract by repositioning capital than by improving real-world production or access. Friedman's core intuition—that money should be governed by predictable rules—becomes far more behaviorally effective when applied at the sector level, where supply dynamics, marginal costs, and innovation curves are measurable and bounded. Sector-specific currencies tie monetary expansion directly to real output and availability, reducing incentives to exploit economy-wide liquidity conditions and rewarding contribution within each sector rather than financial arbitrage across sectors.[90]

Second, it changes incentives by insulating essential human outcomes from speculative risk. When the basics are stabilized, society is less vulnerable to the coercive politics of crisis. The working class is less exposed to collapse dynamics that destroy household stability through no fault of their own. At the same time, speculative actors face a different constraint: They can still pursue risk in capital markets, but the system no longer allows those risks to translate automatically into deprivation and scarcity for essentials.[91] The goal is not to abolish risk-taking or markets; it is to prevent speculative volatility from cascading into humanitarian volatility.[92]

This approach also clarifies a deeper point about why cycles persist. The problem is not that capitalism grows. It is that when it contracts, it does so indiscriminately, severing access to essentials and dignity from productive contribution. A well-engineered economy should not require emergency improvisation to protect basic human welfare. It should be stable by construction.[93]

Inclusive Capitalism therefore frames cyclical instability as a design failure of incentives and monetary architecture. By isolating the basics through micro-currencies, enabling sector-level monetarism rather than monolithic control, and guaranteeing a base level of existence, the system can preserve capitalism's dynamism while materially reducing the social destruction caused by its cycles. This is not a call for permanent stimulus, nor for centralized planning. It is a control-system correction: Constrain the harm, stabilize the essentials, and let innovation and competition operate above that floor without making human dignity collateral damage.[94]

Unintended Consequence Five: Short-Term Bias

The fifth unintended consequence of Smithian capitalism is its persistent tendency to privilege short-term gratification over long-term societal well-being. While often treated as a defect of modern corporate governance or financial markets, it is better understood as a systemic amplification of a deeply human bias: the preference for immediate rewards over delayed, uncertain benefits.[95] Capitalism did not invent this inclination. But in its contemporary form—particularly in the United States—it has evolved in ways that reward, normalize, and institutionalize short-termism across economic, political, and social domains.[96]

This is neither ideologically narrow nor politically partisan. Observers across the left, center, and right converge on the diagnosis that short-term thinking has become endemic, even if they disagree on its origins and remedies.[97] What distinguishes the current moment is not merely the presence of short-term incentives, which have always existed, but their dominance over nearly all major decision-making frameworks—from corporate strategy and capital allocation to public policy and household finance.[98]

The preference for short-term gratification is well documented in philosophy, history, and behavioral economics. Classical thinkers understood the danger clearly. In the direct democracy of ancient Athens, leaders who catered to popular appetites at the expense of long-term strategy were repeatedly elevated, often with disastrous results. Thucydides warned that demagoguery and short-term crowd pleasing undermined strategic judgment, contributing to catastrophic decisions during the Peloponnesian War. His lesson was structural: systems that reward immediate approval over long-term outcomes tend toward instability.

Modern behavioral economics formalizes this intuition through concepts such as hyperbolic discounting and present bias. Individuals systematically undervalue future benefits relative to immediate rewards, even when doing so is irrational over time.[99] A well-designed economic system would counterbalance this bias through institutions that reward patience, investment, and durability. Contemporary American capitalism, by contrast, often reinforces it.[100]

In today's economy, short-term metrics dominate corporate and financial decision-making. Publicly traded firms operate under intense pressure to meet quarterly earnings expectations and deliver immediate shareholder returns.[101] That pressure has measurable consequences. Rather than allocating capital toward long-horizon investment—research and development, workforce training, resilient infrastructure, or long-cycle innovation—many firms prioritize stock buybacks and dividend payouts that deliver immediate share-price support.[102] The system's scoreboard is tilted toward speed, and industrial leadership responds rationally.

The incentive structure facing corporate executives entrenches the dynamic. Compensation packages are frequently tied to near-term stock performance, encouraging strategies that maximize short-term valuation even when they compromise long-term resilience.[103] Executive tenures have shortened, reinforcing a "harvest now, exit early" mindset in which leaders capture upside while deferring costs to successors. On the investor side, ownership has become increasingly intermediated through institutional investors, hedge funds, and algorithmic strategies that operate on compressed time horizons.[104] Activist investors may threaten proxy battles or leadership changes if near-term targets are missed, even when management is pursuing sound long-term strategy. In this environment, patience is systematically penalized.

Short-term gratification is not confined to boardrooms. Modern consumer capitalism excels at satisfying immediate desires with remarkable efficiency. One-click purchasing, on-demand entertainment, and frictionless credit have transformed consumption into an almost instantaneous experience. These advances increase convenience and welfare in a narrow sense, but they also condition expectations toward immediacy and disposability, weakening norms of patience, maintenance, and long-term planning.[105]

The 2008 financial crisis illustrates the social cost of collective short-termism. Years of easy credit and speculative borrowing created a temporary illusion of prosperity, masking underlying fragility.[106] When the cycle reversed, the costs were socialized through a dramatic rise in unemployment, lost wealth, and long-term fiscal burdens. The crisis was not merely a failure of regulation or risk management; it was the logical culmination of incentives that rewarded immediate consumption and leverage while discounting long-term stability.[107] This pattern is repeated: gains are privatized during expansions, while losses are socialized during contractions. The working class and the public bear the brunt of volatility they did not design and often did not benefit from.[108]

A common objection arises: Does the surge in AI investment contradict the short-termism thesis? On the surface, it appears to. In practice, it largely confirms it. Much of the AI investment wave is not patient, society-level capital underwriting long-horizon diffusion and complementary investment. Rather, it is option-like capital chasing near-term platform dominance, winner-take-most dynamics, and short-cycle valuation expansion.[109] AI is unusually compatible with short-term financial signaling: Announcements and narratives move stock prices long before broad productivity gains materialize. Meanwhile, diffusion into the real economy—healthcare delivery, education outcomes, small-business productivity, public services—lags far behind the capital inflow. Historically, general-purpose technologies deliver their largest social returns only after complementary investments in skills, institutions, and organizational change. Those complementary investments are precisely what short-term capitalism underfunds.[110] In other words, AI survives in a short-term system not because the system has overcome short-termism but because AI can be capitalized and financialized quickly.

Viewed through this lens, the problem is the system repeatedly underinvests in the long-horizon goods that would increase resilience, broaden participation, and reduce fragility. Short-termism therefore has distributive and strategic consequences. It widens inequality by channeling value to capital holders while socializing long-term costs.[111] It weakens national competitiveness by discouraging sustained commitment to capabilities whose payoff arrives over decades rather than quarters. It also undermines legitimacy, as citizens see systems that reliably protect capital and institutions while exposing households to recurring instability.[112]

Across the ideological spectrum, diagnoses differ but converge on a common conclusion: current incentives systematically reward immediate gratification while underpricing long-term societal costs. From the left, the diagnosis is shareholder primacy and financial extraction; the remedies emphasize constraints—limits on buybacks, stakeholder representation, and stronger labor voice.[113] From the center, the diagnosis is misaligned incentives and governance; the remedies emphasize incremental extensions of time horizons—vesting reforms, improved disclosure, and long-term shareholding incentives.[114] From the right, the diagnosis emphasizes erosion of stewardship norms and institutional continuity; the remedies emphasize rebuilding durable ownership and stable institutional frameworks. Each perspective captures part of the truth. Yet all remain limited because they attempt to counterweight short-termism inside a system still optimized for short-term outputs.

Inclusive Capitalism treats short-termism as a design failure rather than a moral lapse, and responds with systems design rather than perpetual constraint. The core insight is simple: short-term gratification persists because it is rational under the current system. Firms, executives, and investors optimize for the metrics that define success. As long as GDP growth, quarterly earnings, and near-term financial returns dominate evaluation and reward structures, short-term behavior will remain the equilibrium outcome.[115]

The first element of the remedy is metric innovation. Inclusive Capitalism augments GDP with societal well-being as the top-level objective, explicitly incorporating long-horizon outcomes into how success is measured and rewarded.[116] Industrial leadership is not evaluated solely on near-term profitability but on progress toward longer-term societal objectives that underpin durable prosperity: affordability of essential goods and services, resilience of critical infrastructure, improved health outcomes, broad-based opportunity, and sustained innovation. The principle is straightforward: Leadership incentives must reflect long-term societal outcomes, not merely short-term financial extraction.

Crucially, this does not weaken ambition, risk-taking, or scale. It strengthens them by aligning private success with outcomes that compound over time rather than decay. Leaders who commit to difficult, capital-intensive, long-horizon projects are no longer penalized by a system that discounts the future. They are rewarded because their actions increase long-term societal well-being. This preserves decentralized decision-making, competitive markets, and entrepreneurial leadership while correcting the temporal bias embedded in current metrics.

The second element is institutional innovation: creating structures that can operate simultaneously across different time horizons without forcing all activity into a single quarterly cadence. Production-oriented activities must remain focused on short-term execution, efficiency, and marginal cost reduction. Innovation-oriented activities require insulation from short-term financial pressures so that learning, experimentation, and scale-up can occur over longer horizons. The failure of modern capitalism is not that production and innovation coexist but that both are governed by the same short-term scoreboard, forcing long-horizon investment to compete directly with quarterly earnings targets.[117]

At a deeper level, Inclusive Capitalism designs around human nature rather than against it. Humans exhibit present bias.[118] Systems that amplify this bias become unstable; systems that counterbalance it become resilient. Inclusive Capitalism does not assume better people. It assumes better systems. By redefining success and rebuilding incentives accordingly, it channels ambition, competition, and innovation toward outcomes that endure. Short-term responsiveness remains essential, but it no longer overwhelms long-term judgment.

Book Two develops the full architecture. Here, the conclusion is simple: short-termism is not inevitable. It is designed in. And what is designed in can be redesigned—by augmenting short-term output metrics with societal well-being, and by aligning incentives so that endurance, diffusion, and resilience become rational outcomes rather than heroic exceptions.[119]

Unintended Consequence Six: Amoral Optimization

The sixth and final unintended consequence of Smithian, laissez-faire capitalism is also the most corrosive to its legitimacy and long-term survival: its persistent tendency to prioritize efficiency over human dignity. Efficiency is indispensable—Adam Smith's division of labor remains one of the most powerful insights in economic thought[120]—but history shows that when efficiency becomes the dominant, unqualified objective, dignity is repeatedly treated as collateral damage.[121] This dynamic has been present from day one, from early English factory conditions to contemporary technocratic efficiency regimes that explicitly frame public and private institutions as machines to be optimized.[122]

Inclusive Capitalism is designed to learn from this record. Its aim is not to reject efficiency but to structure incentives and institutions such that efficiency and human dignity are jointly optimized rather than placed in opposition. There is nothing inevitable about their conflict. The persistence of the tradeoff is not a law of nature; it is a failure of system design.[123]

Concerns about the moral consequences of efficiency long predate modern capitalism. Aristotle distinguished between oikonomia—managing resources for a good life—and chrematistike—the pursuit of wealth for its own sake.[124] His point was not anti-commerce; it was that economic activity must remain subordinate to human ends. The Industrial Revolution converted this philosophical concern into concrete social crisis. Early industrial capitalism delivered extraordinary gains in output and productivity but often through conditions that violated basic standards of dignity: long hours, hazardous machinery, subsistence wages, and widespread child labor.[125] Factory owners did not do this because they were uniquely immoral. They did it because the incentive structure rewarded output and cost minimization, while dignity was either unmeasured or externalized.[126]

Crucially, these outcomes did not self-correct through market forces. If anything, they intensified when scale and concentration increased the rewards of ruthless efficiency.[127] Regulation emerged not as optional refinement but as society's blunt assertion that human beings could not be treated as disposable inputs. The historical cycle is clear: efficiency-driven harm becomes visible, public legitimacy collapses, and reactive governance follows—factory acts, safety standards, labor protections, and later welfare systems—each imposed after damage was already done.[128]

That pattern persists today. The technologies have changed, the abstractions have deepened, and the decisions have become more remote and more algorithmic—but the incentive logic remains strikingly similar.[129]

Efficiency disproportionately rewards capital holders and penalizes those displaced by the optimization process. This is not a moral claim; it is structural arithmetic. When efficiency gains raise profit margins, equity valuations rise and capital owners benefit immediately. When efficiency gains come from labor substitution or wage suppression, the displaced bear concentrated losses—often in the form of unemployment, income volatility, geographic immobility, health stress, and loss of dignity in work.[130] The pain is localized; the gains are generalized to owners.

This asymmetry has produced recurring backlash across capitalist history: the Luddite resistance was not opposition to technology per se but resistance to a system that used technology to strip agency and livelihood from workers without an internal mechanism for re-inclusion.[131] The modern equivalents are visible in populist and anti-elite movements, "1%" protests, and chronic distrust in institutions that repeatedly socialize costs while privatizing gains.[132] The recurring social response is itself a proof point: when a system systematically treats dignity as optional, it must be continuously defended through regulation, redistribution, or repression—and it will eventually lose legitimacy.[133]

The near-term concern is displacement and degradation of work. The longer-term concern is that AI could radically compress the labor required to produce essential goods and services. If a small fraction of the population can generate most of what society needs—through AI-augmented design, automated production, and near-zero marginal-cost services—then the old capitalist bargain breaks down: work for wages, consume through wages, and prove your economic worth through market employment.[134]

If "10% can produce what 100% needs," then what happens to the other 90%? Under the current incentive structure, the default trajectory is bleak: the 10% become increasingly central to production and capital formation, while the 90% are managed through a mix of low-wage service work, precarious gig labor, coercive means-testing, and reactive redistribution.[135] Worse, if economic dignity remains tethered to wage labor alone, then people will experience technological progress not as liberation but as exclusion—an acceleration of the very forces that already threaten capitalism's legitimacy.[136]

AI therefore turns the dignity problem into the defining systems challenge of the century. The question is not whether efficiency will increase. It will. The question is whether capitalism can be redesigned so that rising efficiency expands dignity and well-being rather than eroding them.

The standard responses—regulation and redistribution—are structurally downstream. They are reactive corrections applied after the system has already produced harm. They are also politically corrosive: Capital holders experience redistribution as confiscation; workers experience the means-testing apparatus as humiliation.[137] Both sides come to view the other as adversarial. The result is the familiar oscillation: efficiency-driven concentration, backlash, redistribution, retrenchment, repeat.

Inclusive Capitalism proposes a different approach: Make human dignity and societal well-being part of what the system optimizes up front, not what it compensates for afterward. The core move is to augment GDP and profit-centric metrics with a societal well-being objective that is real, measurable, and incentive-bearing—so that leaders are rewarded for expanding human outcomes, not merely compressing costs.[138]

This changes the dignity equation in two crucial ways. First, it changes what counts as "productive." If societal well-being is the top-level objective, then work that improves health, education, resilience, community stability, scientific progress, and environmental restoration becomes economically legible and rewardable—rather than treated as charity, volunteerism, or a cost center. Second, it creates a capitalist answer to the "90% problem." If automation reduces the labor required for essentials, then the released human capacity must be redirected toward unsolved problems—and rewarded in a market-consistent way.[139] The goal is not to pay people to be idle. The goal is to expand the frontier of socially valuable contribution, so that human ambition remains central even as basic production becomes less labor-intensive.

Under Inclusive Capitalism, the economy does not "discard" displaced labor; it rechannels contribution. As abundance expands in some sectors, the system shifts incentives so that value creation migrates toward domains where human creativity, care, judgment, and experimentation matter most: curing disease, rebuilding education, mental health, community resilience, climate adaptation, scientific discovery, institutional integrity, and the long tail of human needs that scarcity-based markets chronically under-serve.

This is where the Inclusive Capitalist thesis becomes decisive: industrial leaders are achievement-driven and respond to incentives. If the scoreboard rewards dignity-inclusive outcomes—affordability, access, resilience, and participation—then leadership ambition will reorganize around those aims, just as it has reorganized around profit maximization under GDP-dominant capitalism. The system does not require moral heroism. It requires correct design.[140]

Efficiency is not the enemy. Efficiency unmoored from dignity is the enemy. Smith's capitalism unleashed unprecedented productive power, but it left dignity as an assumption—something protected by proximity, sympathy, and modest governance.[141] Scale dissolved those safeguards. The result has been a repeating historical pattern: capitalism generates efficiency gains, those gains concentrate, displaced groups bear the costs, legitimacy collapses, and society responds reactively through regulation and redistribution.

AI makes this pattern untenable. If capitalism cannot internalize dignity—by rewarding societal well-being as a first-class objective—then rising efficiency will increasingly be experienced as exclusion rather than progress. Inclusive Capitalism therefore treats dignity not as a constraint on growth but as a design requirement for the next stage of growth. In an era of accelerating technological abundance, the legitimacy of capitalism will depend on whether it can convert efficiency into human flourishing at scale.

The Path Forward: An Inclusive Capitalist Architecture

This book has argued that capitalism's most serious failures are not accidental, episodic, or ideological. They are systemic. By identifying and rigorously defending the six unintended consequences that emerge when Smithian capitalism operates at modern scale, we have moved beyond surface-level critique and into the domain of diagnosis. That diagnosis makes a constructive conclusion possible. Systems that can be clearly understood can be deliberately redesigned. Capitalism's failures are not a reason to abandon it; they are a reason to complete it.

The central claim of Inclusive Capitalism is therefore neither radical nor nostalgic. It is architectural. Capitalism remains the most powerful engine of innovation, productivity, and human advancement ever created.[142] Yet it currently operates well below its achievable frontier. The same system that generated unprecedented wealth has also produced instability, exclusion, artificial scarcity, short-termism, and an erosion of dignity—outcomes that now threaten its legitimacy and durability. These consequences are not inevitable. They are the predictable result of incentives and objectives that were brilliant in 1776, transformative in the nineteenth and twentieth centuries, but incomplete for a world defined by scale, complexity, and technological abundance.[143]

History offers a powerful precedent for optimism. Adam Smith did not merely critique mercantilism; he reframed the purpose of economic activity itself. By redirecting incentives from hoarding toward production and exchange, he unlocked vast reserves of latent human potential and set civilization on a new trajectory. Inclusive Capitalism advances the claim that a comparable transformation is possible today. A principled redefinition of capitalism's objective—away from narrow output maximization and toward societal well-being—has the potential to generate gains in human flourishing on a scale analogous to Smith's original intervention.

What makes such a redesign feasible now is not moral aspiration alone but technological capability. For the first time in history, we possess the tools required to operationalize abundance and enforce incentives at scale. Technology enables near-zero marginal cost production in critical domains, real-time measurement of outcomes that GDP cannot capture, and incentive alignment that does not rely on ex post regulation or coercion. Equally important, technology allows systems to be modular, adaptive, and resilient—qualities that were unattainable in earlier eras of economic organization. Abundance is no longer theoretical. What has been missing is an architecture capable of harnessing it.[144]

Inclusive Capitalism proposes such an architecture. It does not seek to suppress markets, diminish ambition, or centralize control. On the contrary, it preserves and strengthens capitalism's defining virtues: competition, innovation, decentralized decision-making, and risk-taking. What changes is the scoreboard. When success is defined in terms of societal well-being rather than extraction, the same human energies that once optimized for scarcity, monopoly, and short-term gain can be redirected toward inclusion, resilience, and durable prosperity. Leaders respond to incentives. Capital flows toward opportunity. Systems evolve in the direction they reward.[145]

The result is a form of capitalism explicitly designed for today's technological landscape—one that addresses its unintended consequences at the level of system design rather than through perpetual correction. Scarcity is replaced with abundance where technology allows. Monopoly power is managed through incentive alignment rather than after-the-fact regulation.[146] Opportunity is broadened by design rather than rationed by networks. Cycles are dampened by insulating essentials from speculation. Short-termism is counterbalanced by metrics that reward endurance. Efficiency is preserved, but dignity is internalized.[147]

The final chapter of Book One frames this architecture at a high level, identifying the elements of capitalism that must be preserved and those that must be refactored. Book Two develops the full design in detail: the objectives, institutions, incentive structures, and operational mechanisms required to instantiate Inclusive Capitalism in practice. Together, they advance a simple but ambitious proposition: that capitalism can be made both more productive and more humane—not by abandoning its foundations but by completing them.[148]

The future of capitalism is not a choice between preservation and replacement. It is a choice between reactive decline and deliberate design. Inclusive Capitalism argues that the latter is not only possible but necessary—and that, done correctly, it can unlock a new era of shared prosperity worthy of the technological age we have entered.

Notes

1 Adam Smith, *An Inquiry into the Nature and Causes of the Wealth of Nations*, ed. Edwin Cannan (Chicago: University of Chicago Press, 1976), Book I, chs. 1–3.
2 Karl Polanyi, *The Great Transformation: The Political and Economic Origins of Our Time* (Boston: Beacon Press, 2001), 43–76.
3 Douglass C. North, *Institutions, Institutional Change and Economic Performance* (Cambridge: Cambridge University Press, 1990), 3–35.
4 Adam Smith, *An Inquiry into the Nature and Causes of the Wealth of Nations*, Book I, chs. 1–3.
5 Joseph E. Stiglitz, Amartya Sen, and Jean-Paul Fitoussi, *Mismeasuring Our Lives: Why GDP Doesn't Add Up* (New York: The New Press, 2010), 7–24.
6 Organisation for Economic Co-operation and Development (OECD), *How's Life? 2020: Measuring Well-being* (Paris: OECD Publishing, 2020), 25– 40.
7 Amartya Sen, "Capability and Well-Being," in *The Quality of Life*, ed. Martha Nussbaum and Amartya Sen (Oxford: Clarendon Press, 1993), 30–53.
8 W. Brian Arthur, *Complexity and the Economy* (Oxford: Oxford University Press, 2014), 1–24; and Donella H. Meadows, *Thinking in Systems: A Primer* (White River Junction, VT: Chelsea Green Publishing, 2008), 11–34.
9 Adam Smith, *An Inquiry into the Nature and Causes of the Wealth of Nations*, Book I, chs. 1–3.
10 Sheri Berman, *The Primacy of Politics: Social Democracy and the Making of Europe's Twentieth Century* (Cambridge: Cambridge University Press, 2006), 1–15, 167–214.
11 Joseph A. Schumpeter, *Capitalism, Socialism and Democracy* c, 81–86.
12 Karl Polanyi, *The Great Transformation: The Political and Economic Origins of Our Time* (Boston: Beacon Press, 1944), 136–140.
13 Karl Polanyi, *The Great Transformation: The Political and Economic Origins of Our Time*, 43–76.
14 Joseph E. Stiglitz, *The Price of Inequality: How Today's Divided Society Endangers Our Future* (New York: W. W. Norton & Company, 2012), 31–38; Elinor Ostrom, *Governing the Commons: The Evolution of Institutions for Collective Action*, 88–102.
15 Joseph E. Stiglitz, "Knowledge as a Global Public Good," *World Bank Research Observer* 14, no. 2 (1999): 308–325.
16 Douglass C. North, *Institutions, Institutional Change and Economic Performance*, 3–10; Milton Friedman, *Capitalism and Freedom* (Chicago: University of Chicago Press, 1962), 133–137.
17 Joseph A. Schumpeter, *Capitalism, Socialism and Democracy*, 3rd ed. (New York: Harper & Brothers, 1950), 81–86; Thomas Piketty, *Capital in the Twenty-First Century*, trans. Arthur Goldhammer (Cambridge, MA: Harvard University Press, 2014), 571–575.
18 János Kornai, *Economics of Shortage* (Amsterdam: North-Holland, 1980), 59–63.
19 John Kenneth Galbraith, *The Affluent Society* (Boston: Houghton Mifflin, 1998), 95–124.
20 Autor, David, David Dorn, Lawrence F. Katz, Christina Patterson, and John Van Reenen."The Fall of the Labor Share and the Rise of Superstar Firms." *Quarterly Journal of Economics* 135, no. 2 (2020): 645–709.
21 Michele Boldrin and David K. Levine, *Against Intellectual Monopoly* (Cambridge: Cambridge University Press, 2008), 27–78.
22 Joseph E. Stiglitz, "Knowledge as a Global Public Good,": 308–325.
23 Lynn A. Stout, *The Shareholder Value Myth* (San Francisco: Berrett-Koehler, 2012), 1–33.
24 Michele Boldrin and David K. Levine, *Against Intellectual Monopoly*, 27–78.
25 Joseph E. Stiglitz, "Knowledge as a Global Public Good,": 308–325.
26 Jean Tirole, *The Theory of Industrial Organization* (Cambridge, MA: MIT Press, 1988), 1–32.
27 Jerry Z. Muller, *The Mind and the Market: Capitalism in Western Thought* (New York: Alfred A. Knopf, 2002), 71–102.

28 Adam Smith, *An Inquiry into the Nature and Causes of the Wealth of Nations*, Book I, chs. 1–3.
29 Adam Smith, *The Theory of Moral Sentiments* (Indianapolis: Liberty Fund, 1982), Parts I and VI.
30 Karl Polanyi, *The Great Transformation: The Political and Economic Origins of Our Time*, 43–76.
31 Ibid.
32 Erik Brynjolfsson and Andrew McAfee, *The Second Machine Age* (New York: W. W. Norton, 2014), 13–54.
33 Karl Polanyi, *The Great Transformation: The Political and Economic Origins of Our Time*, 43–76.
34 Joseph E. Stiglitz, "Knowledge as a Global Public Good,": 308–325.
35 Joseph E. Stiglitz, Amartya Sen, and Jean-Paul Fitoussi, *Report by the Commission on the Measurement of Economic Performance and Social Progress* (Paris, 2009), 7–23.
36 Friedrich A. Hayek, "The Meaning of Competition," in *Individualism and Economic Order* (Chicago: University of Chicago Press, 1948), 92–106.
37 Ibid.
38 David Autor, David Dorn, Lawrence F. Katz, Christina Patterson, and John Van Reenen, "The Fall of the Labor Share and the Rise of Superstar Firms," *Quarterly Journal of Economics* 135, no. 2 (2020): 646.
39 Tim Wu, *The Curse of Bigness: Antitrust in the New Gilded Age* (New York: Columbia Global Reports, 2018), 1–34.
40 Supreme Court of the United States, *Standard Oil Co. of New Jersey v. United States*, 221 U.S. 1 (1911).
41 Ibid.
42 Geoffrey A. Moore, *Crossing the Chasm* (New York: HarperBusiness, 1991), 11–39.
43 Tim Wu, *The Curse of Bigness: Antitrust in the New Gilded Age*, 1–34.
44 Friedrich A. Hayek, "The Meaning of Competition," in *Individualism and Economic Order* (Chicago: University of Chicago Press, 1948), 92–106.
45 Jerry Z. Muller, *The Mind and the Market: Capitalism in Western Thought* (New York: Alfred A. Knopf, 2002), 71–102.
46 Joseph A. Schumpeter, *Capitalism, Socialism and Democracy* (New York: Harper & Brothers, 1942), 81–110.
47 Friedrich A. Hayek, "The Meaning of Competition," in *Individualism and Economic Order*, 92–106.
48 Geoffrey A. Moore, *Crossing the Chasm* (New York: HarperBusiness, 1991), 11–39.
49 Milton Friedman and Anna J. Schwartz, *A Monetary History of the United States, 1867–1960* (Princeton, NJ: Princeton University Press, 1963), 299–419.
50 Charles P. Kindleberger and Robert Z. Aliber, *Manias, Panics, and Crashes: A History of Financial Crises*, 6th ed. (New York: Palgrave Macmillan, 2011), 1–40.
51 Karl Polanyi, *The Great Transformation: The Political and Economic Origins of Our Time*, 43–76.
52 Joseph E. Stiglitz, Amartya Sen, and Jean-Paul Fitoussi, *Report by the Commission on the Measurement of Economic Performance and Social Progress*, 7–23.
53 Jerry Z. Muller, *The Mind and the Market: Capitalism in Western Thought* (New York: Alfred A. Knopf, 2002), 71–102.
54 Adam Smith, *An Inquiry into the Nature and Causes of the Wealth of Nations*, Book I, chs. 1–3.
55 Smith, Adam. *An Inquiry into the Nature and Causes of the Wealth of Nations*, esp. Book I, ch. 10; Book IV, ch. 2.
56 Thomas Piketty, *Capital in the Twenty-First Century*, trans. Arthur Goldhammer (Cambridge, MA: Harvard University Press, 2014), 1–92.
57 Mark S. Granovetter, "The Strength of Weak Ties," *American Journal of Sociology* 78, no. 6 (1973): 1360–1380.
58 Daniel Markovits, *The Meritocracy Trap* (New York: Penguin Press, 2019), 1–44.
59 William Julius Wilson, *The Truly Disadvantaged: The Inner City, the Underclass, and Public Policy* (Chicago: University of Chicago Press, 1987), 3–33.

60 Thomas Piketty, *Capital in the Twenty-First Century*, trans. Arthur Goldhammer (Cambridge, MA: Harvard University Press, 2014), 1–92.
61 Raj Chetty et al., "The Fading American Dream: Trends in Absolute Income Mobility since 1940," *Science* 356, no. 6336 (2017): 398–406.
62 Thomas Piketty, *Capital in the Twenty-First Century*, trans. Arthur Goldhammer (Cambridge, MA: Harvard University Press, 2014), 1–92.
63 Ibid.
64 Ibid.
65 Ibid.
66 Robert D. Putnam, *Our Kids: The American Dream in Crisis* (New York: Simon & Schuster, 2015), 1–54.
67 Thomas Piketty, *Capital in the Twenty-First Century*, trans. Arthur Goldhammer (Cambridge, MA: Harvard University Press, 2014), 1–92.
68 Herbert A. Simon, *The Sciences of the Artificial*, 3rd ed. (Cambridge, MA: MIT Press, 1996).
69 Acemoglu, Daron, and James A. Robinson. *Why Nations Fail: The Origins of Power, Prosperity, and Poverty*. New York: Crown Business, 2012, 74–91, 107–121, 399–430.
70 Ibid.
71 Ibid.
72 North, Douglass C. *Institutions, Institutional Change and Economic Performance*. Cambridge: Cambridge University Press, 1990, 3–14.
73 Thomas Piketty, *Capital in the Twenty-First Century*, trans. Arthur Goldhammer, 1–92.
74 Charles P. Kindleberger and Robert Z. Aliber, *Manias, Panics, and Crashes: A History of Financial Crises*, 6th ed. (New York: Palgrave Macmillan, 2011), 1–40.
75 Hyman P. Minsky, *Stabilizing an Unstable Economy* (New York: McGraw-Hill, 1986), 11–58.
76 Ibid.
77 Kindleberger, Charles P., and Robert Z. Aliber. *Manias, Panics, and Crashes: A History of Financial Crises*. 6th ed. New York: Palgrave Macmillan, 2011, 33–72, 193–252.
78 Karl Marx, *Economic and Philosophic Manuscripts of 1844*, in *Early Writings*, trans. Rodney Livingstone and Gregor Benton (London: Penguin, 1992), 279–346.
79 John Kenneth Galbraith, *The Great Crash 1929* (Boston: Houghton Mifflin, 1955), 1–34.
80 Milton Friedman and Anna J. Schwartz, *A Monetary History of the United States, 1867–1960*, 299–419.
81 Carmen M. Reinhart and Kenneth S. Rogoff, *This Time Is Different: Eight Centuries of Financial Folly* (Princeton, NJ: Princeton University Press, 2009), 1–44.
82 Barry Eichengreen, *Globalizing Capital: A History of the International Monetary System*, 3rd ed. (Princeton, NJ: Princeton University Press, 2019), 161–206.
83 Hyman P. Minsky, *Stabilizing an Unstable Economy* (New York: McGraw-Hill, 1986), 11–58.
84 Milton Friedman and Anna J. Schwartz, *A Monetary History of the United States, 1867–1960*, 299–419.
85 Ibid.
86 Hyman P. Minsky, *Stabilizing an Unstable Economy* (New York: McGraw-Hill, 1986), 11–58.
87 Amartya Sen, *Development as Freedom* (New York: Alfred A. Knopf, 1999), 3–36.
88 Minsky, Hyman P. *Stabilizing an Unstable Economy*. New Haven, CT: Yale University Press, 1986, 69–118.
89 Ibid.
90 Milton Friedman and Anna J. Schwartz, *A Monetary History of the United States, 1867–1960*, 299–419.
91 Amartya Sen, *Development as Freedom* (New York: Alfred A. Knopf, 1999), 3–36.
92 Ibid.

93 Simon, Herbert A. *The Sciences of the Artificial.* 3rd ed. Cambridge, MA: MIT Press, 1996, 111–137.
94 Minsky, Hyman P. *Stabilizing an Unstable Economy.* New Haven, CT: Yale University Press, 1986, 13–45, 69–118.
95 Laibson, David. "Golden Eggs and Hyperbolic Discounting." *Quarterly Journal of Economics* 112, no. 2 (1997): 443–477.
96 OECD, *Short-Termism and Capital Markets* (Paris: OECD Publishing, 2021), 17–52.
97 Ibid.
98 Gerald F. Davis, *Managed by the Markets: How Finance Re-Shaped America* (Oxford: Oxford University Press, 2009), 1–34.
99 O'Donoghue, Ted, and Matthew Rabin. "Doing It Now or Later." *American Economic Review* 89, no. 1 (1999): 103–124.
100 OECD, *Short-Termism and Capital Markets* (Paris: OECD Publishing, 2021), 17–52.
101 Alfred Rappaport, "Stock Market Signals to Managers," *Harvard Business Review* 63, no. 6 (1985): 57–62.
102 William Lazonick, "Profits Without Prosperity," *Harvard Business Review* 92, no. 9 (2014): 46–55.
103 Michael C. Jensen, "Agency Costs of Free Cash Flow, Corporate Finance, and Takeovers," *American Economic Review* 76, no. 2 (1986): 323–329.
104 Gerald F. Davis, *Managed by the Markets: How Finance Re-Shaped America* (Oxford: Oxford University Press, 2009), 1–34.
105 Daniel Kahneman, *Thinking, Fast and Slow* (New York: Farrar, Straus and Giroux, 2011), 31–58.
106 Carmen M. Reinhart and Kenneth S. Rogoff, *This Time Is Different: Eight Centuries of Financial Folly* (Princeton, NJ: Princeton University Press, 2009), 1–44.
107 Hyman P. Minsky, *Stabilizing an Unstable Economy* (New York: McGraw-Hill, 1986), 11–58.
108 Minsky, Hyman P. *Stabilizing an Unstable Economy.* New Haven, CT: Yale University Press, 1986, 13–45, 129–170.
109 Mazzucato, Mariana. *The Entrepreneurial State: Debunking Public vs. Private Sector Myths.* New York: PublicAffairs, 2013, 95–131.
110 Robert J. Gordon, *The Rise and Fall of American Growth* (Princeton, NJ: Princeton University Press, 2016), 1–38.
111 Piketty, Thomas. *Capital in the Twenty-First Century.* Cambridge, MA: Harvard University Press, 2014, 20–27, 296–305.
112 Stiglitz, Joseph E. *The Price of Inequality.* New York: W. W. Norton, 2012, 43–79, 243–260.
113 Lynn A. Stout, *The Shareholder Value Myth* (San Francisco: Berrett-Koehler, 2012), 1–33.
114 OECD, *Short-Termism and Capital Markets* (Paris: OECD Publishing, 2021), 17–52.
115 Ibid.
116 Joseph E. Stiglitz, Amartya Sen, and Jean-Paul Fitoussi, *Report by the Commission on the Measurement of Economic Performance and Social Progress*, 7–23.
117 Graham, John R., Campbell R. Harvey, and Shiva Rajgopal. "The Economic Implications of Corporate Financial Reporting." Journal of Accounting and Economics 40, no. 1–3 (2005): 3–73.
118 Daniel Kahneman, *Thinking, Fast and Slow* (New York: Farrar, Straus and Giroux, 2011), 31–58.
119 Mazzucato, Mariana. *Mission Economy: A Moonshot Guide to Changing Capitalism.* London: Allen Lane, 2021, 33–61.
120 Adam Smith, *An Inquiry into the Nature and Causes of the Wealth of Nations*, Book I, chs. 1–3.
121 Amartya Sen, *Development as Freedom* (New York: Alfred A. Knopf, 1999), 3–36.
122 E. P. Thompson, *The Making of the English Working Class* (New York: Vintage, 1966), 207–263.
123 Joseph E. Stiglitz, Amartya Sen, and Jean-Paul Fitoussi, *Report by the Commission on the Measurement of Economic Performance and Social Progress*, 7–23.
124 Aristotle, *Politics*, trans. C. D. C. Reeve (Indianapolis: Hackett, 1998), Book I.
125 E. P. Thompson, *The Making of the English Working Class* (New York: Vintage, 1966), 207–263.

126 Karl Polanyi, *The Great Transformation: The Political and Economic Origins of Our Time*, 43–76.
127 Chandler, Alfred D. Jr. *The Visible Hand: The Managerial Revolution in American Business*. Cambridge, MA: Harvard University Press, 1977, 1–11, 285–307.
128 Hobsbawm, Eric. *The Age of Revolution: 1789–1848*. New York: Vintage Books, 1962, 181–216.
129 Erik Brynjolfsson and Andrew McAfee, *The Second Machine Age*, 13–54.
130 Thomas Piketty, *Capital in the Twenty-First Century*, trans. Arthur Goldhammer, 1–92.
131 E. P. Thompson, *The Making of the English Working Class* (New York: Vintage, 1966), 207–263.
132 Thomas Piketty, *Capital in the Twenty-First Century*, trans. Arthur Goldhammer, 1–92.
133 Thomas Piketty, *Capital in the Twenty-First Century*, trans. Arthur Goldhammer, 1–92.
134 Erik Brynjolfsson and Andrew McAfee, *The Second Machine Age*, 13–54.
135 Amartya Sen, *Development as Freedom* (New York: Alfred A. Knopf, 1999), 3–36.
136 Thomas Piketty, *Capital in the Twenty-First Century*, trans. Arthur Goldhammer, 1–92.
137 Amartya Sen, *Development as Freedom* (New York: Alfred A. Knopf, 1999), 3–36.
138 Joseph E. Stiglitz, Amartya Sen, and Jean-Paul Fitoussi, *Report by the Commission on the Measurement of Economic Performance and Social Progress*, 7–23.
139 Amartya Sen, *Development as Freedom* (New York: Alfred A. Knopf, 1999), 3–36.
140 Joseph E. Stiglitz, Amartya Sen, and Jean-Paul Fitoussi, *Report by the Commission on the Measurement of Economic Performance and Social Progress*, 7–23.
141 Adam Smith, *The Theory of Moral Sentiments*, Parts I and VI.
142 Deirdre N. McCloskey, *Bourgeois Dignity: Why Economics Can't Explain the Modern World* (Chicago: University of Chicago Press, 2010), 3–38.
143 Albert O. Hirschman, *The Passions and the Interests: Political Arguments for Capitalism before Its Triumph* (Princeton, NJ: Princeton University Press, 1977), 9–32.
144 Mazzucato, Mariana. *Mission Economy: A Moonshot Guide to Changing Capitalism*. London: Allen Lane, 2021, 1–32.
145 Douglass C. North, *Institutions, Institutional Change and Economic Performance*, 3–35.
146 Tim Wu, *The Curse of Bigness: Antitrust in the New Gilded Age*, 1–34.
147 Amartya Sen, *Development as Freedom* (New York: Alfred A. Knopf, 1999), 3–36.
148 Adam Smith, *The Theory of Moral Sentiments*, Parts I and VI.

11 The Inclusive Capitalism Vision

This final chapter of Book One articulates the vision for Inclusive Capitalism that follows from the analysis developed thus far. Having identified and rigorously defended the six unintended consequences that emerge when Smithian capitalism operates at modern scale, the task now is not further diagnosis but synthesis.[1] The purpose of this chapter is to make explicit the vision for an Inclusive Capitalist system and to introduce design goals that pave the way to its architecture. The Inclusive capitalism architecture and characteristics of implementation, specified with considerable precision, is the domain of Book Two.

The central argument of this book has been that capitalism's most serious failures are not ideological, episodic, or accidental. They are systemic outcomes of incentives and objectives that were historically transformative but are no longer sufficient for an economy defined by scale, complexity, and accelerating technological abundance.[2] That diagnosis carries an important implication: if the failures are systemic, then they are also amenable to systemic redesign.[3] Capitalism does not need to be abandoned or constrained into stagnation. It needs to evolve—deliberately, coherently, and at the level of architecture.

This chapter therefore shifts from critique to construction. Its objective is not to propose specific policies or operational mechanisms but to define the Inclusive Capitalist vision that will guide the architecture construction and systems design. Vision, in this context, is not aspiration untethered from reality. It is a disciplined statement of purpose: what the system should optimize for, what it must preserve, and how its core incentives should behave once properly aligned.[4] Without such a vision, architecture degenerates into ad hoc reform. With it, design becomes tractable.

The chapter is organized into six sections.

First, it briefly summarizes why capitalism must evolve—and why it can. The argument is not that capitalism has failed but that it now operates well below its achievable frontier. The same system that once unlocked unprecedented human progress now systematically generates instability, exclusion, artificial scarcity, short-termism, and erosion of dignity.[5] These outcomes threaten legitimacy, but they also signal an opportunity: systems that can be clearly understood can be deliberately improved.[6]

Second, the chapter identifies what must be preserved. Inclusive Capitalism is not a rejection of capitalism's core strengths but their continuation under updated objectives. Decentralized decision-making, competition, innovation, risk-taking, and scale remain essential.[7] Any viable evolution must protect these features, not suppress them.

Third, the chapter establishes the Inclusive Capitalist vision itself. This section articulates what changes when the system's objective function expands from narrow output and extraction toward societal well-being. It describes how incentives reorganize when abundance, access, resilience, and participation become sources of reward rather than externalities to be regulated after the fact.[8]

 | https://doi.org/10.1515/9783112235485-012

Fourth, the chapter frames the role of technology as an enabler rather than a driver. Technological capability—near-zero marginal cost production, real-time measurement, modular control systems, and scalable incentive enforcement—makes Inclusive Capitalism feasible in ways that were impossible in earlier eras.[9] But technology does not substitute for design. It makes good design executable.[10]

Fifth, the chapter describes how the Inclusive Capitalist vision benefits the system's constituents: workers, entrepreneurs, investors, institutions, and society at large. The emphasis is not on redistribution or constraint but on expanding the opportunity set—so that participation, contribution, and dignity scale alongside productivity and innovation.[11]

Finally, the chapter transitions explicitly to Book Two. Having defined the vision and the objectives it implies, the remaining task is architectural: to specify the institutions, incentive structures, monetary mechanisms, and governance designs required to instantiate Inclusive Capitalism in practice. Book Two takes up that task in full.

This chapter is therefore the bridge between diagnosis and design. It closes Book One by making clear what an Inclusive Capitalist system is intended to achieve.

Why Capitalism Can and Must Evolve

Capitalism's achievements are extraordinary. No economic system has matched its capacity to mobilize human ingenuity, scale innovation, coordinate decentralized decision-making, or convert discovery into material abundance.[12] Over the past two and a half centuries, it has transformed living standards, extended life expectancy, reduced absolute poverty, and enabled scientific and technological progress at a pace unprecedented in human history.[13] These accomplishments are real, measurable, and historically incontestable.

Yet this success has come at a cost that is no longer defensible—and increasingly no longer survivable. The same system that generated unprecedented prosperity now systematically produces instability, exclusion, artificial scarcity, short-termism, and an erosion of dignity at a scale that threatens its own legitimacy.[14] Capitalism continues to function, but it does so in a state of chronic friction with the societies it serves.[15] The question is no longer whether capitalism works. It is whether capitalism, as currently instantiated, can endure.

The defining feature of contemporary capitalism is not failure but structural defects at the system level. It produces wealth while simultaneously generating social costs so large that vast institutional effort is devoted to mitigating its own side effects.[16] Regulation proliferates. Redistribution expands. Crisis management becomes permanent. Political polarization intensifies. Public trust erodes. The system increasingly resembles a powerful engine running without adequate control—capable of extraordinary output, yet prone to destructive oscillation.[17]

These costs are not marginal. They manifest in recurring financial crises that devastate households while preserving capital; in widening inequality that constrains opportunity and social mobility; in affordability crises that leave essential goods increasingly out of reach despite technological abundance; and a growing sense that the system is considerably out of balance given the extraordinary rewards related to extraction over contribution.[18] What was once tolerated as transitional friction is now experienced as structural injustice.

Critically, these costs are not borne evenly. The benefits of growth accrue disproportionately to those closest to capital, while the costs of instability, displacement, and adjustment fall disproportionately on the working and middle classes.[19] Over time, this asymmetry becomes politically and socially combustible.

Capitalism has always generated opposition. What is different today is the intensity, persistence, and breadth of that opposition.[20] The modern "third estate"—workers, households, and communities excluded from durable prosperity—are no longer merely dissatisfied. They are actionably angry.

This anger is visible across geographies and political systems. It fuels populism on both the left and the right. It erodes faith in institutions. It destabilizes democracies.[21] It expresses itself through protests, electoral revolts, rejection of expertise, and growing openness to non-capitalist alternatives—however historically discredited those alternatives may be.

Importantly, this anger is not primarily ideological. It is experiential. Large segments of the population experience a system that demands flexibility, risk, and sacrifice from them, while offering volatility instead of security and precarity instead of dignity.[22] When economic systems repeatedly socialize losses and privatize gains, legitimacy erodes regardless of aggregate performance.

No system—however productive—can survive indefinitely once a critical mass of participants no longer believes it is fair, responsive, or reformable.[23]

The response to capitalism's high costs has followed a predictable and historically consistent pattern: reactive correction. When excess becomes intolerable, societies intervene. Regulation expands. Redistribution increases. Markets are constrained. When those constraints dampen growth or innovation, backlash follows. Deregulation ensues. Capital is unleashed again. The cycle repeats.[24]

This oscillation—what might be called ping-pong economics—has not produced durable resolution. Regulation treats symptoms after harm has already occurred. Redistribution addresses outcomes rather than causes. Both approaches are politically fragile and economically inefficient.[25] Over time, they produce regulatory bloat, compliance industries, rent-seeking, and institutional fatigue without resolving the underlying dynamics that regenerate the same problems.

Alternative systems have not fared better. Communism and state socialism eliminated markets and incentives, producing stagnation, scarcity, and coercion rather than dignity and abundance.[26] Democratic socialism has achieved partial mitigation through redistribution and public provision but at the cost of dynamism, innovation velocity, and long-term fiscal sustainability.[27] None has solved the fundamental tension between productivity, inclusion, and legitimacy at scale.

The repeated failure of both regulation-heavy capitalism and market-suppressed alternatives suggests a deeper conclusion: the problem is not policy choice at the margin. It is system design at the core.[28]

Book One has argued that capitalism's failures are neither accidental nor mysterious. They arise from six unintended consequences that emerge predictably when Smithian capitalism operates at modern scale:[29]

1. Incentives that reward scarcity rather than abundance
2. The natural pursuit of monopoly power under scarcity-maximizing objectives
3. Structural exclusion of opportunity through compounding advantage
4. Endogenous instability driven by speculation and leverage
5. Systematic short-termism reinforced by dominant metrics
6. Optimization of efficiency at the expense of human dignity

These consequences are empirically robust, historically persistent, and mutually reinforcing. They appear across epochs, geographies, and institutional variants. Their recurrence is the strongest possible evidence that they are structural rather than contingent.

Crucially, they share a common root: incentives and institutional structures optimized around a narrow objective function that is misaligned with the realities of modern scale, complexity, and technological abundance.[30]

Capitalism does not fail because participants are immoral, irrational, or insufficiently regulated. It fails where it does because rational actors respond to the incentives they face.[31] Industrial leaders are achievement-driven. Capital flows toward rewarded behavior. Institutions evolve in the direction they are measured and compensated.[32]

For more than two centuries, capitalism has optimized for output, profit, and efficiency under conditions of scarcity. That objective was historically appropriate—and spectacularly successful. But when marginal costs collapse, when knowledge becomes non-rival, when scale amplifies power, and when technology decouples production from labor, the same objective produces pathological outcomes.[33]

Scarcity is preserved where abundance is possible. Monopoly becomes rational. Opportunity narrows. Cycles intensify. Time horizons compress. Dignity is externalized. These are not moral failures. They are design failures.[34]

If the problem is architectural, the solution must be architectural. Incremental reform layered atop a misaligned system cannot produce durable improvement,[35] nor can nostalgia for an earlier form of capitalism whose operating conditions no longer exist.

What is required is a redefinition of capitalism's objective function and the incentive structures that flow from it. Not the abandonment of markets, competition, or ambition—but their redirection toward outcomes compatible with technological abundance and social legitimacy.[36]

This is not unprecedented. Adam Smith himself did not "optimize" mercantilism; he replaced its organizing objective. By shifting the system's purpose from hoarding to production and exchange, he unlocked an entirely new growth regime. Inclusive Capitalism advances the claim that a comparable evolution is now both necessary and possible.

Unlike previous eras, we now possess the tools required to design economic systems deliberately. Technology enables real-time measurement of outcomes beyond GDP.[37] Modular architectures allow complexity to be decomposed rather than centrally controlled. Incentives can be enforced algorithmically rather than coercively. Abundance is increasingly feasible rather than theoretical.[38]

What has been missing is not capacity but intent.[39]

Capitalism must be redesigned because its current trajectory is unstable. It can be redesigned because its failures are now clearly diagnosed, its strengths remain unparalleled, and the technological means to align incentives with societal well-being finally exist.[40]

The question is no longer whether capitalism should change. It is whether that change will be reactive and destabilizing—or deliberate and designed.[41]

Inclusive Capitalism argues for the latter.

Preserving the Core Principles of Capitalism

Having demonstrated that the failures of contemporary capitalism arise from its underlying architecture rather than from isolated policy missteps, it is now essential to establish what must be preserved. Any credible redesign must begin with continuity, not rupture. Inclusive Capitalism is not a call for a new economic system, nor an attempt to rehabilitate alternative models that history has repeatedly shown to suppress dynamism, innovation, and individual freedom. It is an evolution of Smithian capitalism itself.

Adam Smith's framework remains the correct foundation. No other economic system has delivered comparable gains in productivity, innovation, and human advancement. The problem is not that capitalism failed; it is that it succeeded at a cost that has become too high to sustain.[42] When a system works extraordinarily well yet repeatedly generates instability, exclusion, and social backlash, the rational response is neither abandonment nor endless constraint but completion. We preserve what made capitalism powerful and redesign what causes it to fracture. That is not an ideological move. It is a pragmatic one.[43]

Any redesign that weakens capitalism's core mechanisms—markets, property, competition, risk-taking, scale, and rule-of-law governance—ultimately recreates the failures of central planning or technocratic control.[44] For that reason, Inclusive Capitalism begins by making explicit what cannot be abandoned. These are not historical artifacts or ideological preferences. They are the irreducible engines of prosperity and freedom. The question is not whether to preserve them but how to instantiate them in a world defined by scale, complexity, and technological abundance.[45]

Markets must remain the central coordinating mechanism of the economy. Their power lies in decentralized decision-making: the ability to aggregate dispersed knowledge, adapt dynamically to change, and align production with human preference without command or coercion. This epistemic advantage, recognized by Smith and later formalized by Hayek, has no substitute.[46] Every serious attempt to replace decentralized coordination with centralized planning has failed—not because planners lacked intelligence or good intentions but because no central authority can process the tacit, local, and evolving information embedded in millions of individual decisions.[47] The failure is epistemological, not moral.

At the same time, markets are only as effective as the signals they encode. When the dominant metric is GDP alone, markets optimize for transaction volume rather than societal value.[48] When exclusivity is over-rewarded, markets manufacture scarcity even where abundance is technologically feasible. When short-term financial returns dominate, markets drift toward volatility and away from durable value creation.[49] The task is therefore not to override markets but to improve what markets measure. Better metrics produce better markets. Inclusive Capitalism strengthens decentralized coordination by making market signals more accurate, not by replacing them.

Competition must also be preserved—not as an abstract ideal but as a discovery process. Competition reveals what works, disciplines incumbents, and prevents the ossification of power.[50] Across economic thought, there is near-universal agreement on this point. Smith, Marx, Hayek, Keynes, and Friedman all condemned monopoly power, despite disagreeing on almost everything else. Where reform efforts have consistently failed is their treatment of competition as something to be restored after concentration emerges, rather than something that must be structurally preserved by design.[51] Reactive antitrust and regulatory intervention arrive too late, after markets have already tilted. Inclusive Capitalism approaches competition architecturally, aligning incentives and restructuring institutions so that diffusion and entry remain rational outcomes rather than regulatory exceptions.

Entrepreneurial dynamism must likewise remain central. Capitalism's greatest strength is not efficiency but ambition. Entrepreneurs take risks, challenge incumbents, and pursue uncertain paths that no central planner would authorize. Failure is not a defect of capitalism; it is its cost of discovery.[52] Periods of extraordinary progress—from the Industrial Revolution to the digital age—were driven by leaders willing to risk capital, reputation, and career on uncertain outcomes.[53] Attempts to suppress failure in the name of stability inevitably produce stagnation, risk aversion, and bureaucratic inertia.[54]

History offers a clear warning about the alternative systems. Systems that attempt to neutralize or suppress entrepreneurial ambition in the name of equality or stability have consistently paid a far higher price.[55] Under Maoist collectivization, the most capable leaders were not merely constrained but physically eliminated or driven into ideological submission, with catastrophic human and economic consequences. In socialist systems more broadly, ambition was dulled rather than harnessed: innovation slowed, initiative was discouraged, and advancement became detached from contribution.[56] The result was not shared prosperity but stagnation—an economy incapable of mobilizing its most driven and creative individuals. These systems failed not because human ambition disappeared, but because it was misdirected, penalized, or stripped of agency.[57] Capitalism's historic advantage lies precisely in its ability to unleash the energies of exceptional leaders. The task, therefore, is not to weaken that dynamism but to channel it toward outcomes that expand societal well-being rather than merely private extraction.

What has gone wrong in contemporary capitalism is not that leaders became less capable or less ethical but that incentives increasingly reward short-term extraction over long-term contribution. Inclusive Capitalism preserves entrepreneurial ambition while realigning ambition, priorities and rewards. Risk-taking remains central, but success is defined in terms of contribution to societal well-being rather than the maximization of short-cycle financial returns. This does not weaken leadership incentives; it strengthens them by aligning private success with outcomes that compound over time.[58]

Scale must also be preserved. Large enterprises deliver efficiencies, infrastructure, and coordination that no collection of small actors could achieve.[59] Modern life—from energy systems and pharmaceuticals to global logistics and digital platforms—depends on scale. The problem is not size; it is purpose. Under scarcity-maximizing incentives, scale becomes a mechanism for entrenchment. Under abundance-aligned incentives, it becomes a diffusion engine.[60] Reform proposals that treat scale itself as pathological—advocating fragmentation, nationalization, or permanent constraint—sacrifice efficiency and innovation without resolving the underlying incentive problem. Inclusive Capitalism preserves scale while redesigning its charter, so that large enterprises remain engines of productivity without becoming engines of exclusion.

Finally, government must retain its proper role as referee rather than participant. Capitalism depends on government to enforce contracts, protect rights, maintain transparency, and uphold the rule of law.[61] When government functions in this capacity, markets flourish. When incentives are misaligned, however, governments are forced into ever-expanding intervention—regulating inputs, correcting outcomes, and managing crises.[62] This constant regulatory backfilling is not evidence of excessive government ambition; it is evidence of systemic design failure. Inclusive Capitalism seeks to restore government to its appropriate role by redesigning the incentives that currently necessitate heavy-handed intervention. When markets internalize societal well-being, government can once again focus on monitoring outcomes associated with societal well-being rather than continuous correction.

Taken together, these principles—decentralized markets, competition, entrepreneurial risk-taking, scale, and government as referee—define what must be preserved. They are the source of capitalism's unmatched success. Yet when left unrefined, they also contribute to the system's most damaging unintended consequences. The challenge, and the opportunity, is to preserve these mechanisms while redesigning the architecture that governs how they operate.

With this foundation clarified, the task shifts from diagnosis to vision. The next section articulates the inclusive capitalist vision: a coherent picture of how these preserved principles can be instantiated in a system explicitly designed for technological abundance, societal legitimacy, and durable prosperity. That vision, in turn, provides the blueprint for the architectural and institutional design developed in Book Two.

The Inclusive Capitalist Vision

The vision for Inclusive Capitalism is deliberately simple. It is not a rejection of capitalism, nor a hybridization with alternative systems that history has shown to suppress dynamism and initiative.[63] It is a continuation of the Smithian project: a capitalism that works for all by preserving what has always worked extraordinarily well, while deliberately addressing the unintended consequences that emerge when those same principles operate at modern scale.

Adam Smith envisioned an economic system that expanded abundance, widened opportunity, and aligned individual ambition with social benefit. That vision was partially realized—but incompletely instantiated. Capitalism delivered unprecedented productivity, innovation, and wealth creation, yet did so at costs that now threaten its own legitimacy. Inclusive Capitalism begins from the conviction that these costs are not inherent to markets or private enterprise but the result of an architecture that was never designed to manage scale, complexity, and technological abundance.

The central design objective is therefore not moderation or constraint but redirection. Inclusive Capitalism seeks to shift capitalism's organizing logic along six dimensions:[64]

1) From scarcity management toward abundance creation;
2) From monopoly extraction toward diffusion and access;
3) From exclusion toward broadened participation;
4) From exposure to volatility toward stability of essentials;
5) From short-term extraction toward long-horizon value creation; and
6) From efficiency alone toward productivity that explicitly incorporates human dignity.

These are not ideological preferences. They are system-level design goals derived directly from the six unintended consequences identified and defended throughout this book.

Achieving this shift requires an architectural reorientation rather than a single policy intervention. Inclusive Capitalism rests on four foundational pillars that together define the direction of redesign.[65]

First, incentives must be reengineered. Capitalism reliably produces the outcomes it rewards. As long as success is measured narrowly—through GDP growth, short-term profits, and financial extraction—leaders will rationally optimize for those outcomes.[66] Inclusive Capitalism therefore proposes a redefinition of success itself. Economic systems must measure and reward societal well-being alongside output, explicitly valuing affordability, access, resilience, health, opportunity, and long-term human flourishing.[67] This is not an appeal to altruism; it is a recalibration of the scoreboard that governs competitive behavior.

Second, institutions—particularly large enterprises—must be rechartered to reflect their true role in the modern economy. Today's dominant firms shape labor markets, innovation pathways, access to essentials, and even political outcomes. Treating them as purely private actors governed solely by shareholder returns is an institutional mismatch.[68] Inclusive Capitalism argues that Smith's principles of moral duty and fair play must be operationalized within enterprise governance itself.[69] This does not imply state control or bureaucratic planning. It implies aligning enterprise obligations with the societal systems they now effectively administer.

Third, monetary and capital structures must evolve to reflect economic heterogeneity. A single national currency tied to asset cycles cannot reliably stabilize a complex economy composed of radically different sectors with different cost structures, innovation curves, and social importance.[70] Inclusive Capitalism introduces the concept of currency and capital refactoring—sector-specific monetary mechanisms, micro-federal approaches, and new forms of value recognition—designed to stabilize essentials, reduce speculative spillovers, and align financial incentives with real-world production and access.

Fourth, the innovation process itself must become more inclusive. Capitalism's future cannot depend on a narrow pipeline of elite founders optimizing for short-cycle exits.[71] The rate of innovation that society requires—particularly in health, education, climate, and resilience—demands broader participation, more open collaboration, and faster diffusion of ideas.[72] Inclusive Capitalism seeks to maximize the rate of socially useful innovation, not merely its monetization, without reverting to blunt redistribution, heavy regulation, or centralized control.[73]

This chapter presents these pillars as a vision, not as a finished blueprint. There is no magic bullet embedded here, nor a claim that complexity can be eliminated through theory alone. What is offered is a coherent framework for system design—one capable of grounding legislation, corporate governance, measurement, and institutional control in a common objective function aligned with human well-being.[74]

The details will be debated, refined, tested, and revised for years. That is not a weakness of the approach; it is its defining strength. Inclusive Capitalism is conceived as an adaptive system, grounded in empirical evidence rather than ideology. Where Marx offered a theory, Keynes a policy regime, and neoliberalism a doctrine, this work aspires to provide something different: a complete architecture, capable of empirical validation, iteration, and long-term evolution.[75]

In this sense, Inclusive Capitalism is not a departure from Adam Smith but a continuation of his work. Smith provided the principles appropriate for the eighteenth century: decentralization, moral sentiments, competition, and fair play. He did not—and could not—design a global economic architecture capable of managing multinational enterprises, digital abundance, artificial intelligence, and planetary-scale interdependence. The absence of such an architecture is precisely what allowed capitalism to drift so far from his intent.[76]

The claim advanced here is ultimately optimistic. Capitalism can be rebuilt into a system that rewards innovation without exclusion, scale without concentration, efficiency without the erosion of dignity, and ambition without systemic fragility. The question is not whether capitalism will survive but whether it will adapt deliberately rather than reactively. Inclusive Capitalism offers a path for that adaptation—grounded in history, informed by empirical analysis, aligned with human well-being, and capable of evolving through scientific feedback.

Book Two develops this architecture in detail. This chapter closes Book One by framing the vision, clarifying the stakes, and preparing the reader for the design work that follows.

Technology as Enabler

Technology is not the solution to capitalism's failures. It is the enabler that makes a better solution possible. Inclusive Capitalism is fundamentally an architectural proposition—an incentive and institutional redesign—but that redesign becomes both feasible and urgent because technology changes two things at once: the boundary between scarcity and non-scarcity and the feasibility of rigorous measurement and enforcement at scale.[77]

The first role of technology is to create the catalyst for change: the emerging reality of non-scarcity across expanding domains of the economy. For most of human history, scarcity was an unavoidable fact of material life. An economic system that allocates scarce goods through markets and prices is therefore not only rational; it is historically unsurprising. The problem is that capitalism, as currently instantiated, still treats scarcity as its organizing principle even when technology makes abundance feasible. In domains where marginal costs approach zero—software, data, digital services, and increasingly knowledge-intensive processes—the natural economic outcome should be diffusion.[78] Yet the existing incentive structure frequently suppresses diffusion to preserve pricing power. This is not a moral failure of leadership. It is the predictable response to what the system rewards.[79]

That mismatch between technological possibility and incentive reality is one of the defining characteristics of the present era. It helps explain why capitalism appears increasingly illegitimate to many: the feasible frontier of abundance is plainly visible, yet the system continues to operate as if scarcity were an immutable constraint. As production becomes more automated and digital, the gap between what technology could deliver and what markets actually deliver widens. This gap is not merely frustrating; it becomes politically destabilizing. It fuels the perception that exclusion and scarcity are no longer natural conditions but manufactured outcomes.[80]

Inclusive Capitalism is designed explicitly to close that gap by shifting capitalism's incentive logic from scarcity management to abundance creation. The key is not to deny scarcity in domains where it remains real—land, certain minerals, location, some forms of energy storage, constrained physical infrastructure—but to refuse scarcity as the default operating assumption when technology makes non-scarcity possible. A system that continues to reward enclosure in non-scarce domains will systematically underperform relative to its achievable frontier. A system that instead rewards diffusion expands the pie—and expands the size of the pieces for all—because it unleashes compounding gains from reuse, recombination, and widespread participation.[81]

The second role of technology is to make rigorous societal well-being measurement and incentive enforcement viable at the scale a modern economy requires. One of the core weaknesses of twentieth-century economic frameworks—whether Keynesian management, neoliberal doctrine, or social-democratic redistribution—was that they treated economic governance as a coarse, macro-level control problem constrained by limited measurement and slow feedback. GDP served as the dominant scoreboard not because it captured human flourishing but because it was one of the few metrics that could be calculated with enough standardization to guide policy and markets. In the early industrial age, that was a brilliant and transformative proxy. It was also incomplete, because it elevated output above outcomes and monetized activity above lived experience.[82]

Technology changes that constraint. For the first time, it becomes possible to define, compute, audit, and reward a broader objective function without relying on vague moral claims or heavy-handed control. This is not because "data solves everything," but because measurement, feedback, and verification can now be structured in ways that earlier systems could not support. If capitalism is to be reoriented toward societal well-being, the metric must be concrete enough to guide incentives, and the incentive mechanisms must be enforceable enough to remain stable.[83]

This is where the definition stage becomes central. Societal well-being cannot be a slogan. It must be a measurable construct built from sector-specific components, governed by transparent rules, and anchored in causal logic rather than political preference. Conceptually, what we are doing is specifying a structured family of equations—more complex than classic Keynesian aggregates because the system we are managing is more complex—organized by sector and designed to capture three kinds of inputs.

The first class of measures is outcomes: observable results that directly reflect human welfare. These include health outcomes (e.g. preventable mortality, chronic disease burden); educational outcomes (learning proficiency, attainment); affordability and access outcomes (housing burden, energy shutoffs, essential service access); and resilience outcomes (infrastructure reliability, disaster recovery times).

The second class is enablement measures: the conditions that determine whether outcomes can improve, such as innovation pace, diffusion speed, capacity build-out, workforce readiness, and institutional capability.

The third class is externalities: the harms or spillovers that GDP ignores—pollution, safety risks, monopolistic lock-in, exclusion from opportunity, or the long-term fragility created by short-term extraction.[84]

The point is not to reduce human life to a spreadsheet. The point is to engineer a metric that is sufficiently rigorous to guide incentives. The system does not need perfect measurement; it needs measurement that is precise enough to be incentive-bearing, auditable, and resistant to gaming. That is why technology matters. It enables real-time sensing in critical infrastructure, standardized reporting in supply chains, verified outcome tracking in healthcare and education, and audit trails for claims that would otherwise be unprovable. It also enables modularity: the ability to run sector-level objective functions without forcing every domain into one macro instrument.[85]

This modularity is especially important for monetary design, where the failure of one-size-fits-all control has become increasingly obvious. A single, economy-wide money supply is a blunt instrument trying to govern a heterogeneous system with radically different elasticities, innovation curves, and marginal-cost dynamics. Monetary policy can stabilize some sectors while destabilizing others. Financial markets can amplify the effects of policy errors into the real economy—particularly into essentials. As the preceding chapter argued, this is one reason capitalism's cycles are so socially destructive: The population's access to the basics remains too tightly coupled to speculative cycles.[86]

Technology makes it feasible to decouple these domains through sector-specific monetary mechanisms—microcurrencies governed by transparent, rules-based logic tied to measurable supply dynamics in essential sectors. This is a way of applying monetarist discipline at a scope where it can actually work. Friedman's core intuition—that money should be governed predictably rather than discretionarily—becomes more tractable when the domain is bounded and the underlying supply capacity is measurable.[87] Food, housing, energy, healthcare, and other essentials have physical and service-capacity realities that can be tracked. A sector-specific monetary architecture can therefore stabilize essentials without forcing the entire economy into a single monetary posture, and without allowing speculative volatility to translate directly into humanitarian volatility.

The microcurrency model is not only a stabilization mechanism; it is an incentive mechanism. In a system governed by one national currency, there are often easier returns to be made by repositioning capital across sectors in response to macro liquidity conditions than by improving real capacity or access in any one domain. Sector-level monetary governance ties reward more tightly to contribution within a domain: expanding housing supply, increasing clinic capacity, improving grid reliability, accelerating diffusion of essential innovations. When the monetary architecture rewards capacity and access rather than financial positioning, the system becomes harder to game and easier to stabilize.[88]

All of this reinforces the most central finding of Book One: Capitalism's failures are not primarily the product of bad people but of misaligned incentives interacting with scale. Scale is essential. It delivers efficiency and diffusion that no exclusively small-firm driven economy could produce. But scale also concentrates authority, reduces competitive discipline, and amplifies externalities. When scale operates under incentives optimized narrowly for financial outcomes, the system predictably drifts toward concentration, enclosure, and instability. This is why reactive regulation becomes perpetual. It is why "ping-pong economics" emerges: deregulation until harm becomes intolerable, then heavy-handed correction until dynamism is suppressed, then retrenchment again. The oscillation is the symptom of an architecture that cannot reconcile scale with legitimacy.[89]

Technology does not eliminate that problem. It intensifies it unless the architecture changes. Artificial intelligence in particular accelerates both the potential for abundance and the risk of exclusion. It can reduce marginal costs, increase productivity, and expand access in domains where scarcity has long been accepted as unavoidable. But under today's incentive structure, it will also be deployed first for extraction: margin defense, labor substitution, and monopoly reinforcement. This is why the technology section must avoid techno-utopianism. The question is not whether technology can do good; it is whether the system rewards it for doing so.[90]

Inclusive Capitalism therefore treats technology as an enabler of two architectural moves that were previously out of reach. The first is designing for abundance: updating the incentive logic so that creating non-scarcity becomes the most rewarded form of value creation in domains where technology makes it feasible. The second is designing for measurable alignment: creating the rigorous mechanisms—definitions, equations, verification, reporting, and enforcement—required for societal well-being to function as a real objective function rather than an aspirational overlay.[91]

If technology makes this possible, architecture makes it work, and incentives make it stable. Technology provides the capability to produce abundance and to measure outcomes. Architecture provides the institutional structure that links those measures to market behavior. Incentives provide the equilibrium: the reason rational, achievement-driven leaders will build in the direction society actually wants.

This is the central point. We are not proposing that technology will save capitalism. We are proposing that technology has changed the feasible design space. It has made abundance possible in many domains, and it has made objective measurement and incentive enforcement possible at scales earlier eras could not support. Those capabilities create a narrow window of opportunity: capitalism can now be deliberately refactored to realize Smith's intent in a contemporary context, rather than continuing to evolve reactively and oscillate toward instability.

Book Two specifies the mechanisms: the sector-level formulations, the governance and audit systems, the incentive translation layers, and the monetary architecture that can preserve market dynamism while stabilizing essentials and rewarding inclusive outcomes. The purpose here is simply to establish why this is newly feasible and why it matters. Technology does not guarantee a better system—but it removes the excuse that a better system cannot be built.

What an Inclusive Capitalist Economy Feels Like

In systems thinking, the objective is not a slogan. It is the governing force that determines what the system selects for, what it rewards, what it tolerates, and what it suppresses. Deming's insight—that a system produces exactly what it is designed to produce—applies to economies as much as to factories or institutions.[92] Senge's point follows naturally: Once the objective function is explicit, the system becomes legible, and once it is legible, it becomes designable. Inclusive Capitalism begins with that discipline. It does not ask participants to become better people. It changes what the system makes rational.[93]

When the objective shifts from output and profit alone toward societal wellbeing, the economy begins to feel different because the incentives of its major constituents begin to align rather than collide. Today, capitalism often forces durable contradiction: Entrepreneurs seek scale but are rewarded for enclosure; workers seek stability but are exposed to cycles they did not create; investors seek returns but are pulled toward extraction because the scoreboard is narrow; leaders want to build but are pushed toward short-term signaling; institutions are tasked with protecting legitimacy but are forced into reactive regulation and redistributive conflict. Inclusive Capitalism reduces these contradictions not by wishful thinking but by changing the scoreboard so that private success is increasingly won through public benefit rather than through exclusion.[94]

The most immediate change is a shift in the system's emotional tone. Modern capitalism feels adversarial because its incentives make stakeholders opponents by default. Workers fear displacement; leaders fear missing quarterly expectations; policymakers fear backlash; households fear losing access to essentials in downturns; entrepreneurs fear being crushed by incumbents; incumbents fear disruption and respond by building moats. Under Inclusive Capitalism, the center of gravity moves from zero-sum defense to positive-sum creation, in the same sense that Smithian capitalism moved from mercantilism.[95] Competition remains fierce, but it becomes more consistently oriented toward expanding real value—access, diffusion, resilience, quality—rather than toward managing scarcity or extracting rents. The economy feels less like a contest over slices and more like a contest to enlarge the pie in measurable ways.[96]

For industrial leaders, this shift is not a moral burden; it is a liberation. In the current regime, many capable leaders are simultaneously powerful and constrained. They control vast enterprises, yet they are tethered to a narrow objective function that can make long-horizon, dignity-preserving decisions irrational. Inclusive Capitalism changes that. It expands the legitimate mandate of leadership by embedding societal well-being into the definition of success. That does two things at once: It increases leaders' capacity to act in ways they often privately judge to be "right," and it increases the rewards for doing so because the system now pays for outcomes that compound over time rather than for extraction that produces backlash.[97]

This is crucial: Inclusive Capitalism is not anti-leadership. It is pro-leadership but with better direction. The most achievement-driven leaders—those who today build empires by winning scarce advantage—now have a larger arena in which to win: They can build enduring advantage by creating abundance, by accelerating diffusion, by raising sector outcomes, and by producing resilience. Their power increases because their legitimacy increases. Their rewards increase because the system's objective is no longer structurally misaligned with the long-term conditions of a stable society. They are no longer forced to trade public trust for private performance.[98]

For entrepreneurs, the economy feels more open, more liquid in opportunity, and more genuinely meritocratic. Today's entrepreneurial path is often gated by geography, networks, and access to capital rather than by the intrinsic quality of ideas. And when entrepreneurs succeed, the system too often pushes them toward the same scarcity behaviors it claims to oppose: proprietary lock-in, closed ecosystems, and monopoly seeking as the rational endpoint. Inclusive Capitalism changes the reward structure so that a founder can win big by building diffusion and interoperability rather than enclosure, and so that the path to participation is wider.[99]

The result is not gentler entrepreneurship. It is more intense entrepreneurship—because the pool of participants expands and because the playing field becomes more contestable. The most capable and motivated builders gain the opportunity to innovate and advance at a pace rarely seen, because the system reduces friction where it is wasteful: redundant reinvention, closed interfaces, defensive legalism, and artificial barriers to adoption. When foundational building blocks are easier to access and recombine, when diffusion is rewarded rather than punished, the rate of experimentation and the rate of useful adoption both rise. The best entrepreneurs get a bigger game with more legitimate wins.[100]

Investors also experience a shift in what "good investing" means. Under a profit-only scoreboard, many forms of extraction are indistinguishable from value creation in the short run. Scarcity rents, monopoly tolls, and financial engineering can all look like performance. Inclusive Capitalism changes this by making long-horizon societal outcomes legible inputs into valuation and reward. Capital markets still allocate; risk is still priced; failure still happens. But the system increasingly favors strategies that build capacity and diffusion over strategies that simply harvest position.[101]

This matters because the investor class is not monolithic. Many sophisticated investors already understand that long-term stability is a prerequisite for durable returns. They worry about political backlash, institutional decay, and social fragmentation because those forces eventually destroy predictable compounding. Inclusive Capitalism makes that intuition investable. It provides a framework in which investing in resilience, affordability, broad participation, and long-horizon innovation is not "ESG charity" but a rational path to superior risk-adjusted returns because the system's objective and incentives now support it. The market remains a discovery mechanism—but it is discovering outcomes that better track the health of the society that sustains the market.[102]

For workers, the felt experience diverges by cohort, and Inclusive Capitalism is designed to address precisely those differences.

For the most capable and motivated workers—the people who want to build, learn, and advance—the economy becomes less brittle and less gated. Opportunity expands not by rhetoric but by design: more pathways into high-value work, more ability to re-skill without falling through the floor, and less dependence on insider networks as the primary currency of mobility. When essentials are stabilized and participation pathways broaden, workers can take productive risks: moving regions, changing careers, starting firms, retraining for harder roles. That flexibility is one of the most underappreciated forms of freedom, and it is often suppressed today by fragile household economics. Inclusive Capitalism restores it by making the baseline less punitive.[103]

For the broad middle of the workforce—those who are capable of contributing but are most exposed to exclusion—the economy feels less like a threat. The core improvement is not that life becomes frictionless; it is that the costs of systemic volatility and displacement stop falling disproportionately on the same people. When essentials are insulated and dignity is internalized, workers no longer bear the full downside of cycles they did not design. They can self-improve because the system gives them time, stability, and legible pathways, rather than forcing constant crisis management. Participation becomes more continuous. Dignity becomes less contingent.[104]

For those who are not capable of full participation—whether due to disability, severe limitation, age, or other constraints—the economy becomes morally legible again because it stops treating the floor as an afterthought. Inclusive Capitalism does not romanticize human nature or assume universal productivity. It assumes a society that remains stable only when the basics are secured as a systems feature rather than as a discretionary political concession. Housing, basic healthcare, and other essentials must not be periodically rationed as punishment for macro shocks or institutional failures. Under Inclusive Capitalism, the floor is embedded into the operating logic of the economy: not as a promise that can be withdrawn but as a designed property of the system. This changes the psychological experience of society for the least capable as well as for everyone else, because the system signals that dignity is not conditional on being economically "useful" in the narrowest sense.[105]

Institutions also behave differently, and this matters because institutional trust is the hidden substrate of functioning markets. Under today's capitalism, institutions are trapped in reactive mode: regulating after harm, redistributing after exclusion, bailing out after collapse, and arguing constantly about who deserves what. The result is politicization, distrust, and fatigue. Inclusive Capitalism reduces the need for perpetual backfilling by changing the system's default outputs. When enterprises are chartered against extraction incentives, when essentials are insulated, and when societal well-being is measured and rewarded, institutions can return to a more stable role: enforcing rules, auditing truth, maintaining fair competition, and preserving legitimacy—rather than trying to compensate continuously for predictable misalignment.[106]

This is why Inclusive Capitalism is not a magic bullet and is not a utopian claim about human nature. Humans will still compete, hoard, fear, form tribes, exploit loopholes, and rationalize selfishness. The difference is that the system no longer amplifies those tendencies as reliably. It introduces countervailing incentives—persistent, structural counterforce—that make the worst tendencies less rewarded and the most socially valuable behaviors more rewarded. It does not eliminate the gravity of compounding power, but it designs mechanisms that continuously counteract the black-hole effect by reopening participation and rewarding diffusion. It does not eliminate cycles, but it prevents cycles from automatically becoming humanitarian crises. It does not eliminate ambition, but it gives ambition a better target.[107]

The deepest way an Inclusive Capitalist economy "feels" different is that it restores legitimacy by making dignity and participation mutually reinforcing rather than mutually exclusive. People can compete without believing the system is rigged by design. Leaders can win without needing exclusion as the price of success. Workers can contribute without fearing that progress will discard them. Those who cannot contribute still retain a secure floor without stigma. And institutions can govern with fewer emergency interventions because the system is more stable by construction.[108]

That is the aim: not perfection but a rational basis for a modern economy—one that preserves capitalism's dynamism while removing the structural contradictions that have repeatedly forced societies into backlash, oscillation, and fracture.

From Vision to Architecture

With the vision for Inclusive Capitalism articulated, the task shifts decisively from diagnosis and alignment to design and construction. Book One has completed its work. It identified capitalism's six unintended consequences, traced them to their structural and incentive-based origins, and demonstrated that these failures are neither accidental nor inevitable. It then established a coherent vision for a form of capitalism capable of preserving its dynamism while internalizing societal well-being. This leaves a single remaining task: to translate that vision into an explicit, operational architecture. That translation is the purpose of Book Two.

This chapter aligned principles, incentives, and outcomes.[109] Book Two does not revisit the case for reform. It assumes it. Its objective is to define—precisely and unambiguously—the architecture required to instantiate Inclusive Capitalism in practice. This means moving from conceptual clarity to formal structure: from principles to mechanisms, from vision to equations, from aspiration to enforceable design.[110]

Each of the four pillars introduced in this chapter becomes the subject of a dedicated, in-depth treatment. These chapters do not argue why the pillars matter; they define how they function.

Specifically, Book Two will specify:

1. **Objective function and incentive structures**
   Explicit objective function formulations for societal well-being at the system and sector levels, including the mathematical structure of outcome measures, enabling conditions, externalities, weighting schemes, aggregation logic, and update mechanisms.[111] Concrete incentive mechanisms that reward societal well-being over financial extraction, including compensation design, capital allocation rules, prize systems, procurement standards, and performance-based obligations tied to measured outcomes.[112]
2. **Institutional forms and governance mechanisms**
   The legal and organizational structures required to support Inclusive Capitalism, including rechartered large enterprises, societal-well-being institutions, micro-fed monetary authorities, and innovation governance bodies.[113] Governance including charter enforcement, auditing regimes, transparency requirements, accountability structures, and escalation pathways that ensure integrity without reverting to centralized planning or regulatory micromanagement.[114]
3. **Monetary architecture**
   The design of sector-specific micro-currencies, issuance rules, convertibility constraints, governance mandates, and their interaction with the master currency—explicitly engineered to stabilize essentials and isolate households from speculative cycles.[115]
4. **Inclusive Innovation Process**
   An innovation process that fosters inclusive innovation, including innovation at scale, collaborative innovation, open source innovation, rapid diffusion of innovation, and merit-based proposal consideration.[116]

This architecture is not presented as a final or immutable blueprint. It is a starting framework—deliberately explicit, testable, and incomplete in the right way. Inclusive Capitalism is not a closed system; it is a system designed to evolve.[117] Its architecture must support transition paths from existing institutions, allow for sectoral variation, and incorporate continuous empirical feedback. Book Two therefore also addresses transitional strategies, pilot structures, phased adoption, and the mechanisms by which real-world data refines the design over time.[118]

That emphasis on feedback is not a concession; it is a feature. Economies are complex adaptive systems. Architectures that pretend otherwise fail.[119] Inclusive Capitalism is engineered to learn—to be stress-tested, iterated, and improved through evidence rather than defended as ideology. Its success depends not on theoretical elegance alone but on measurable performance and durable legitimacy.[120]

The confidence of this work rests on a simple fact: Every major failure diagnosed in Book One corresponds to a missing or misaligned architectural component. Scarcity persists because incentives reward it. Monopoly endures because scale lacks countervailing obligations. Exclusion hardens because opportunity is not designed in. Cycles devastate because essentials are coupled to speculation. Short-termism dominates because the scoreboard discounts the future. Dignity erodes because it is external to optimization.[121]

Book Two addresses each of these failures directly—not through policy patches but through system design.[122]

This is the handoff point. The moral case has been made. The historical record has been examined. The vision has been aligned with capitalism's enduring strengths. What follows is construction: the disciplined work of specifying an economic architecture capable of operating at modern scale, under modern technology, with modern institutions, and with human nature as it is rather than as we might wish it to be.[123]

Inclusive Capitalism does not ask whether capitalism can be saved. It assumes capitalism can be completed—and now turns to the work of building it.

Notes

1 Adam Smith, *An Inquiry into the Nature and Causes of the Wealth of Nations*, ed. R. H. Campbell and A. S. Skinner (Indianapolis: Liberty Fund, 1981), Vol. I, Book I, chs. 1–3, pp. 13–36; Book IV, ch. 2, pp. 450–471.

2 Joseph A. Schumpeter, *Capitalism, Socialism, and Democracy*, 3rd ed. (New York: Harper & Brothers, 1950), chs. 7–8, pp. 81–106.

3 North, Douglass C. *Institutions, Institutional Change and Economic Performance*. Cambridge: Cambridge University Press, 1990, 3–14.

4 W. Edwards Deming, *Out of the Crisis* (Cambridge, MA: MIT Press, 1986), chs. 1–3, pp. 23–67; Peter M. Senge, The Fifth Discipline (New York: Doubleday, 1990), chs. 1–2, pp. 3–42.

5 Joseph A. Schumpeter, *Capitalism, Socialism, and Democracy*, 3rd ed., chs. 7–8, pp. 81–106.

6 Douglass C. North, *Institutions, Institutional Change and Economic Performance (Cambridge*: Cambridge University Press, 1990), chs. 1–2, pp. 3–35.

7 Adam Smith, *The Theory of Moral Sentiments*, ed. D. D. Raphael and A. L. Macfie (Indianapolis: Liberty Fund, 1982), Part I, Section I, chs. 1–3, pp. 9–40.

8 Raghuram G. Rajan, *The Third Pillar: How Markets and the State Leave the Community Behind* (New York: Penguin Press, 2019), chs. 1–3, pp. 3–62.

9 Erik Brynjolfsson and Andrew McAfee, *The Second Machine Age* (New York: W. W. Norton, 2014), chs. 1–2, pp. 11–58.
10 Robert M. Solow, *Technical Change and the Aggregate Production Function, Review of Economics and Statistics 39, no. 3* (1957): 312–320.
11 Amartya Sen, *Development as Freedom* (New York: Alfred A. Knopf, 1999), chs. 1–2, pp. 3–53.
12 Adam Smith, *An Inquiry into the Nature and Causes of the Wealth of Nations*,, Vol. I, Book I, chs. 1–3, pp. 13–36; Book IV, ch. 2, pp. 450–471.
13 Maddison, Angus. *The World Economy: A Millennial Perspective*. Paris: OECD, 2001, 28–44.
14 Thomas Piketty, *Capital in the Twenty-First Century*, trans. Arthur Goldhammer (Cambridge, MA: Harvard University Press, 2014), Introduction and Part I, chs. 1–2, pp. 1–39.
15 Raghuram G. Rajan, *The Third Pillar: How Markets and the State Leave the Community Behind*, chs. 1–3, pp. 3–62.
16 Stiglitz, Joseph E. *The Price of Inequality*. New York: W. W. Norton, 2012, 1–39.
17 Minsky, Hyman P. *Stabilizing an Unstable Economy*. New Haven, CT: Yale University Press, 1986, 13–45.
18 Thomas Piketty, *Capital in the Twenty-First Century*, trans. Arthur, Introduction and Part I, chs. 1–2, pp. 1–39.
19 Raghuram G. Rajan, *The Third Pillar: How Markets and the State Leave the Community Behind*, chs. 1–3, pp. 3–62.
20 Ibid.
21 Ibid.
22 Amartya Sen, *Development as Freedom*, chs. 1–2, pp. 3–53.
23 W. Edwards Deming, *Out of the Crisis*, chs. 1–3, pp. 23–67; Peter M. Senge, The Fifth Discipline, chs. 1–2, pp. 3–42.
24 Hobsbawm, Eric. *The Age of Extremes: The Short Twentieth Century, 1914–1991*. New York: Pantheon Books, 1994, 257–286.
25 Polanyi, Karl. *The Great Transformation*. Boston: Beacon Press, 1944, 136–170; Streeck, Wolfgang. *Buying Time: The Delayed Crisis of Democratic Capitalism*. London: Verso, 2014, 73–105.
26 Ludwig von Mises, *Socialism: An Economic and Sociological Analysis*, trans. J. Kahane (Indianapolis: Liberty Fund, 1981), chs. 1–3, pp. 37–120.
27 János Kornai, *The Socialist System: The Political Economy of Communism* (Princeton: Princeton University Press, 1992), chs. 10–12, pp. 351–430.
28 Douglass C. North, *Institutions, Institutional Change and Economic Performance*, chs. 1–2, pp. 3–35.
29 Adam Smith, *The Theory of Moral Sentiments*, ed. D. D. Raphael and A. L. Macfie (Indianapolis: Liberty Fund, 1982), Part I, Section I, chs. 1–3, pp. 9–40.
30 Douglass C. North, *Institutions, Institutional Change and Economic Performance*, chs. 1–2, pp. 3–35.
31 Milton Friedman, *The Methodology of Positive Economics*, in *Essays in Positive Economics* (Chicago: University of Chicago Press, 1953), pp. 3–43.
32 Douglass C. North, *Institutions, Institutional Change and Economic Performance*, chs. 1–2, pp. 3–35.
33 Erik Brynjolfsson and Andrew McAfee, *The Second Machine Age*, chs. 1–2, pp. 11–58.
34 North, Douglass C. *Institutions, Institutional Change and Economic Performance*., 3–14.
35 Russell L. Ackoff, *Creating the Corporate Future* (Wiley, 1981), 15.
36 Douglass C. North, *Institutions, Institutional Change and Economic Performance*, chs. 1–2, pp. 3–35.
37 Simon, Herbert A. *The Sciences of the Artificial*. 3rd ed. MIT Press, 1996, 111–137.
38 Brynjolfsson, Erik, and Andrew McAfee. *The Second Machine Age: Work, Progress, and Prosperity in a Time of Brilliant Technologies*. New York: W. W. Norton, 2014, 7–13.
39 W. Edwards Deming, *Out of the Crisis*, chs. 1–3, pp. 23–67; Peter M. Senge, The Fifth Discipline, chs. 1–2, pp. 3–42.
40 Douglass C. North, *Institutions, Institutional Change and Economic Performance*, chs. 1–2, pp. 3–35.

41 Ray Dalio, *Principles for Dealing with the Changing World Order* (New York: Simon & Schuster, 2021), chs. 1–3, pp. 1–92.
42 Deaton, Angus. *The Great Escape: Health, Wealth, and the Origins of Inequality*. Princeton, NJ: Princeton University Press, 2013, 1–32.
43 Milton Friedman, *The Methodology of Positive Economics*, in *Essays in Positive Economics* (Chicago: University of Chicago Press, 1953), pp. 3–43.
44 Ludwig von Mises, *Socialism: An Economic and Sociological Analysis*, trans. J. Kahane, chs. 1–3, pp. 37–120.
45 Erik Brynjolfsson and Andrew McAfee, *The Second Machine Age*, chs. 1–2, pp. 11–58.
46 Friedrich A. Hayek, *The Use of Knowledge in Society*, American Economic Review 35, no. 4 (1945): 519–530.
47 Ludwig von Mises, *Socialism: An Economic and Sociological Analysis*, trans. J. Kahane, chs. 1–3, pp. 37–120.
48 Joseph E. Stiglitz, Amartya Sen, and Jean-Paul Fitoussi, *Report by the Commission on the Measurement of Economic Performance and Social Progress* (Paris: OECD, 2009), pp. 7–29, 41–92.
49 Ray Dalio, *Principles for Dealing with the Changing World Order* (New York: Simon & Schuster, 2021), chs. 1–3, pp. 1–92.
50 Joseph A. Schumpeter, *Capitalism, Socialism, and Democracy*, 3rd ed., chs. 7–8, pp. 81–106.
51 Ray Dalio, *Principles for Dealing with the Changing World Order* (New York: Simon & Schuster, 2021), chs. 1–3, pp. 1–92.
52 Frank H. Knight, *Risk, Uncertainty, and Profit* (Boston: Houghton Mifflin, 1921), chs. 7–9, pp. 233–312.
53 Schumpeter, Joseph A. *Capitalism, Socialism and Democracy*. New York: Harper & Brothers, 1942, 81–106.
54 Ibid.
55 János Kornai, *The Socialist System: The Political Economy of Communism*, chs. 10–12, pp. 351–430.
56 Ludwig von Mises, *Socialism: An Economic and Sociological Analysis*, trans. J. Kahane, chs. 1–3, pp. 37–120.
57 Ibid.
58 Mazzucato, Mariana. *Mission Economy: A Moonshot Guide to Changing Capitalism*. London: Allen Lane, 2021, 33–61.
59 Michael E. Porter, *The Competitive Advantage of Nations* (New York: Free Press, 1990), ch. 1, pp. 19–33.
60 Erik Brynjolfsson and Andrew McAfee, *The Second Machine Age*, chs. 1–2, pp. 11–58.
61 Amartya Sen, *Development as Freedom*, chs. 1–2, pp. 3–53.
62 Polanyi, Karl. *The Great Transformation*. Boston: Beacon Press, 1944, 136–170.
63 Ludwig von Mises, *Socialism: An Economic and Sociological Analysis*, trans. J. Kahane, chs. 1–3, pp. 37–120.
64 Ackoff, Russell L. *Redesigning the Future: A Systems Approach to Societal Problems*. New York: Wiley, 1974, 1–18.
65 Simon, Herbert A. *The Sciences of the Artificial*. 3rd ed. Cambridge, MA: MIT Press, 1996, 111–137.
66 Joseph E. Stiglitz, Amartya Sen, and Jean-Paul Fitoussi, *Report by the Commission on the Measurement of Economic Performance and Social Progress* (Paris: OECD, 2009), pp. 7–29, 41–92.
67 Stiglitz, Joseph E., Amartya Sen, and Jean-Paul Fitoussi. *Report by the Commission on the Measurement of Economic Performance and Social Progress*. Paris, 2009, 7–33.
68 Douglass C. North, *Institutions, Institutional Change and Economic Performance*, chs. 1–2, pp. 3–35.
69 Adam Smith, *The Theory of Moral Sentiments*, ed. D. D. Raphael and A. L. Macfie, Part I, Section I, chs. 1–3, pp. 9–40.

70 Minsky, Hyman P. *Stabilizing an Unstable Economy*. New Haven, CT: Yale University Press, 1986, 13–45.
71 Raghuram G. Rajan, *The Third Pillar: How Markets and the State Leave the Community Behind*, chs. 1–3, pp. 3–62.
72 Mazzucato, Mariana. *The Entrepreneurial State: Debunking Public vs. Private Sector Myths*. New York: PublicAffairs, 2013, 1–28, 183–214.
73 Amartya Sen, *Development as Freedom*, chs. 1–2, pp. 3–53.
74 W. Edwards Deming, *Out of the Crisis*, chs. 1–3, pp. 23–67; Peter M. Senge, The Fifth Discipline, chs. 1–2, pp. 3–42.
75 Ackoff, Russell L. *Redesigning the Future: A Systems Approach to Societal Problems*. New York: Wiley, 1974, 1–18.
76 Douglass C. North, *Institutions, Institutional Change and Economic Performance*, chs. 1–2, pp. 3–35.
77 Robert M. Solow, *Technical Change and the Aggregate Production Function, Review of Economics and Statistics 39, no. 3* (1957): 312–320.
78 Erik Brynjolfsson and Andrew McAfee, *The Second Machine Age*, chs. 1–2, pp. 11–58.
79 Milton Friedman, *The Methodology of Positive Economics*, in *Essays in Positive Economics* (Chicago: University of Chicago Press, 1953), pp. 3–43.
80 Thomas Piketty, *Capital in the Twenty-First Century*, trans. Arthur, Introduction and Part I, chs. 1–2, pp. 1–39.
81 Joseph A. Schumpeter, *Capitalism, Socialism, and Democracy*, 3rd ed., chs. 7–8, pp. 81–106.
82 Joseph E. Stiglitz, Amartya Sen, and Jean-Paul Fitoussi, *Report by the Commission on the Measurement of Economic Performance and Social Progress* (Paris: OECD, 2009), pp. 7–29, 41–92.
83 Stiglitz, Joseph E., Amartya Sen, and Jean-Paul Fitoussi. *Report by the Commission on the Measurement of Economic Performance and Social Progress*. Paris, 2009, 7–33.
84 Pigou, Arthur C. *The Economics of Welfare*. London: Macmillan, 1920, 183–214.
85 Baldwin, Carliss Y., and Kim B. Clark. *Design Rules, Vol. 1: The Power of Modularity*. Cambridge, MA: MIT Press, 2000, 1–35.
86 Ray Dalio, *Principles for Dealing with the Changing World Order* (New York: Simon & Schuster, 2021), chs. 1–3, pp. 1–92.
87 Friedman, Milton. *A Program for Monetary Stability*. Fordham University Press, 1960, 77–93; Goodhart, Charles. *The Evolution of Central Banks*. MIT Press, 1988, 1–38; Minsky, Hyman P. *Stabilizing an Unstable Economy*. Yale University Press, 1986, 13–45.
88 Minsky, Hyman P. *Stabilizing an Unstable Economy*. New Haven, CT: Yale University Press, 1986, 13–45.
89 Streeck, Wolfgang. *Buying Time: The Delayed Crisis of Democratic Capitalism*. London: Verso, 2014, 73–105.
90 Acemoglu, Daron, and Pascual Restrepo. "Artificial Intelligence, Automation, and Work." *Journal of Economic Perspectives* 33, no. 2 (2019): 3–30.
91 Kaplan, Robert S., and David P. Norton. *The Balanced Scorecard: Translating Strategy into Action*. Boston: Harvard Business School Press, 1996, 1–23, 149–176.
92 W. Edwards Deming, *Out of the Crisis*, chs. 1–3, pp. 23–67; Peter M. Senge, The Fifth Discipline, chs. 1–2, pp. 3–42.
93 Senge, Peter M. *The Fifth Discipline: The Art and Practice of the Learning Organization*. New York: Doubleday, 1990, 68–92.
94 Stiglitz, Joseph E., Amartya Sen, and Jean-Paul Fitoussi. *Report by the Commission on the Measurement of Economic Performance and Social Progress*. Paris, 2009, 7–33.
95 Adam Smith, *An Inquiry into the Nature and Causes of the Wealth of Nations*,, Vol. I, Book I, chs. 1–3, pp. 13–36; Book IV, ch. 2, pp. 450–471.
96 Joseph A. Schumpeter, *Capitalism, Socialism, and Democracy*, 3rd ed., chs. 7–8, pp. 81–106.

97 Adam Smith, *The Theory of Moral Sentiments*, ed. D. D. Raphael and A. L. Macfie, Part I, Section I, chs. 1–3, pp. 9–40.
98 Michael E. Porter, *The Competitive Advantage of Nations* (New York: Free Press, 1990), ch. 1, pp. 19–33.
99 Mazzucato, Mariana. *The Value of Everything: Making and Taking in the Global Economy.* New York: PublicAffairs, 2018, 157–190.
100 Mazzucato, Mariana. *Mission Economy: A Moonshot Guide to Changing Capitalism.* London: Allen Lane, 2021, 33–61.
101 Mazzucato, Mariana. *The Value of Everything: Making and Taking in the Global Economy.* New York: PublicAffairs, 2018, 157–190.
102 Raghuram G. Rajan, *The Third Pillar: How Markets and the State Leave the Community Behind,* chs. 1–3, pp. 3–62.
103 Amartya Sen, *Development as Freedom*, chs. 1–2, pp. 3–53.
104 Sen, Amartya. *Development as Freedom.* New York: Alfred A. Knopf, 1999, 3–36.
105 Rawls, John. *A Theory of Justice.* Cambridge, MA: Harvard University Press, 1971, 440–446.
106 Stiglitz, Joseph E., Amartya Sen, and Jean-Paul Fitoussi. *Report by the Commission on the Measurement of Economic Performance and Social Progress.* Paris, 2009, 7–33.
107 Minsky, Hyman P. *Stabilizing an Unstable Economy.* New Haven, CT: Yale University Press, 1986, 13–45.
108 Ostrom, Elinor. *Governing the Commons: The Evolution of Institutions for Collective Action.*, 25–56.
109 W. Edwards Deming, *Out of the Crisis*, chs. 1–3, pp. 23–67; Peter M. Senge, The Fifth Discipline, chs. 1–2, pp. 3–42.
110 Ackoff, Russell L. *Redesigning the Future: A Systems Approach to Societal Problems.* New York: Wiley, 1974, 1–18.
111 Simon, Herbert A. *The Sciences of the Artificial.* 3rd ed. Cambridge, MA: MIT Press, 1996, 111–137.
112 Mazzucato, Mariana. *Mission Economy: A Moonshot Guide to Changing Capitalism.* London: Allen Lane, 2021.
113 North, Douglass C. *Institutions, Institutional Change and Economic Performance.*, 3–14.
114 Ostrom, Elinor. *Governing the Commons: The Evolution of Institutions for Collective Action.*, 90–102.
115 Minsky, Hyman P. *Stabilizing an Unstable Economy.* New Haven, CT: Yale University Press, 1986, 13–45, 308–324.
116 Chesbrough, Henry W. *Open Innovation: The New Imperative for Creating and Profiting from Technology.* Boston: Harvard Business School Press, 2003, 1–26, 107–132.
117 Douglass C. North, *Institutions, Institutional Change and Economic Performance*, chs. 1–2, pp. 3–35.
118 Senge, Peter M. *The Fifth Discipline: The Art and Practice of the Learning Organization.* New York: Doubleday, 1990, 129–168.
119 Ibid.
120 Simon, Herbert A. *The Sciences of the Artificial.* 3rd ed. Cambridge, MA: MIT Press, 1996, 111–137.
121 Acemoglu, Daron, and James A. Robinson. *Why Nations Fail: The Origins of Power, Prosperity, and Poverty.* New York: Crown Business, 2012, 74–91.
122 Ackoff, Russell L. *Redesigning the Future: A Systems Approach to Societal Problems.* New York: Wiley, 1974, 1–18.
123 W. Edwards Deming, *Out of the Crisis*, chs. 1–3, pp. 23–67; Peter M. Senge, *The Fifth Discipline*, chs. 1–2, pp. 3–42.

Index

 | https://doi.org/10.1515/9783112235485-013